Project Management
Processes, Methodologies, and Economics

Avraham Shtub
Faculty of Industrial Engineering and Management
The Technion–Israel Institute of Technology

Jonathan F. Bard
Department of Mechanical Engineering
Graduate Program in Operations Research & Industrial Engineering
University of Texas at Austin

Shlomo Globerson
School of Business Administration
Tel Aviv University

PEARSON
Prentice
Hall

Upper Saddle River, NJ 07458

Library of Congress Cataloging-in-Publication Data

Shtub, Avraham
   Project management: Processes, methodologies, and economics / Avraham Shtub,
Jonathan F. Bard, Shlomo Globerson.--2nd ed.
     p. cm. -- (Prentice-Hall international series in industrial and systems engineering)
   Includes bibliographical references and index.
   ISBN 0-13-041331-3
    1. Engineering--Management. 2. Project management. I Bard, Jonathan F. II
Globerson, Shlomo, 1941- III. Title. IV. Series.

TA190.S59 2005
658.4'04--dc22

2004057264

Vice President and Editorial Director, ECS: *Marcia J. Horton*
Vice President and Director of Production and Manufacturing, ESM: *David W. Riccardi*
Acquisitions Editor: *Dorothy Marrero*
Editorial Assistant: *Richard Virginia*
Executive Managing Editor: *Vince O'Brien*
Managing Editor: *David A. George*
Production Editor: *Kevin Bradley*
Director of Creative Services: *Paul Belfanti*
Art Director: *Jayne Conte*
Cover Designer: *Bruce Kenselaar*
Art Editor: *Greg Dulles*
Manufacturing Manager: *Trudy Pisciotti*
Manufacturing Buyer: *Lynda Castillo*
Senior Marketing Manager: *Holly Stark*

© 2005 by Pearson Education, Inc.
Pearson Prentice Hall
Pearson Education, Inc.
Upper Saddle River, NJ 07458

Printed in the United States of America

10 9 8 7 6 5 4 3

ISBN 0-13-041331-3

Pearson Education Ltd., *London*
Pearson Education Australia Pty. Ltd., *Sydney*
Pearson Education Singapore, Pte. Ltd.
Pearson Education North Asia Ltd., *Hong Kong*
Pearson Education Canada, Inc., *Toronto*
Pearson Educación de Mexico, S.A. de C.V.
Pearson Education—Japan, *Tokyo*
Pearson Education Malaysia, Pte. Ltd.
Pearson Education, Inc., *Upper Saddle River, New Jersey*

This book is dedicated to Israel Shtub

Contents

Nomenclature

AC	annual cost		DOH	direct overhead costs
ACWP	actual cost of work performed		DSS	decision support system
AHP	analytic hierarchy process		EAC	estimate at completion
AOA	activity on arrow		ECO	engineering change order
AON	activity on node		ECR	engineering change request
AW	annual worth		EMV	expected monetary value
BAC	budget at completion		EOM	end of month
B/C	benefit/cost		EOY	end of year
BCWP	budgeted cost of work performed		ERP	enterprise resource planning
BCWS	budgeted cost of work scheduled		ETC	estimate to complete
CBS	cost breakdown structure		ETMS	early termination monitoring system
CCB	change control board			
CCBM	critical chain buffer management		EUAC	equivalent uniform annual cost
CDR	critical design review		EV	earned value
CE	certainty equivalent, concurrent engineering		EVPI	expected value of perfect information
C-E	cost-effectiveness		EVSI	expected value of sample information
CER	cost estimating relationship			
CI	cost index; consistency index; criticality index		FFP	firm fixed price
			FMS	flexible manufacturing system
CM	configuration management		FPIF	fixed price incentive fee
COO	chief operating officer		FW	future worth
CPIF	cost plus incentive fee		GAO	General Accounting Office
CPM	critical path method		GDSS	group decision support system
CR	capital recovery, consistency ratio		GERT	graphical evaluation and review technique
C/SCSC	cost/schedule control systems criteria			
			HR	human resources
CV	cost variance		IPT	integraded product team
DOD	Department of Defense		IRR	internal rate of return
DOE	Department of Energy		IRS	Internal Revenue Service

ISO	International Standards Organization		PDR	preliminary design review
IT	information technology		PERT	program evaluation and review technique
LCC	life-cycle cost		PMBOK	project management body of knowledge
LOB	line of balance			
LOE	level of effort		PMI	Project Management Institute
LP	linear program		PMP	project management professional
LRC	linear responsibility chart		PO	project office
MACRS	modified accelerated cost recovery system		PT	project team
			PV	planned value
MARR	minimum acceptable (attractive) rate of return		PW	present worth
			QA	quality assurance
MAUT	multiattribute utility theory		QFD	quality function deployment
MBO	management by objectives		RAM	reliability, availability, and maintainability; random access memory
MIS	management information system			
MIT	Massachusetts Institute of Technology			
			R&D	research and development
MPS	master production schedule		RDT&E	research, development, testing, and evaluation
MTBF	mean time between failures			
MTTR	mean time to repair		RFP	request for proposal
NAC	net annual cost		ROR	rate of return
NASA	National Aeronautics and Space Administration		SI	schedule index
			SOW	statement of work
NBC	nuclear, biological, chemical		SOYD	sum-of-the-years digits
NPV	net present value		SV	schedule variance
OBS	organizational breakdown structure		TQM	total quality management
			WBS	work breakdown structure
O&M	operations and maintenance		WP	work package
PDMS	product data management system		WR	work remaining

Preface

We all deal with projects in our daily lives. In most cases, organization and management simply amount to constructing a list of tasks and executing them in sequence, but when the information is limited or imprecise and when cause-and-effect relationships are uncertain, a more considered approach is called for. This is especially true when the stakes are high and time is pressing. Getting the job done right the first time is essential. This means doing the upfront work thoroughly, even at the cost of lengthening the initial phases of the project. Shaving expenses in the early stages with the intent of leaving time and money for revisions later might seem like a good idea but could have consequences of painful proportions. Seasoned managers will tell you that it is more cost-effective in the long run to add five extra engineers at the beginning of a project than to have to add 50 toward the end.

The quality revolution in manufacturing has brought this point home. Companies in all areas of technology have come to learn that quality cannot be inspected into a product; it must be built in. Recalling the 1980s, the global competitive battles of that time were won by companies that could achieve cost and quality advantages in existing, well-defined markets. In the 1990s, these battles were won by companies that could build and dominate new markets. Today, the emphasis is partnering and better coordination of the supply chain. Planning is a critical component of this process and is the foundation of project management.

Projects may involve dozens of firms and hundreds of people who need to be managed and coordinated. They need to know what has to be done, who is to do it, when it should be done, how it will be done, and what resources will be used. Proper planning is the first step in communicating these intentions. The problem is made difficult by what can be characterized as an atmosphere of uncertainty, chaos, and conflicting goals. To ensure teamwork, all major participants and stakeholders should be involved at each stage of the process.

How is this achieved efficiently, within budget, and on schedule? The primary objective in writing our first book was to answer this question from the perspective of the project manager. We did this by identifying the components of modern project management and showing how they relate to the basic phases of a project, starting with conceptual design and advanced development, and continuing through detailed design, production, and termination. Taking a practical approach, we drew on our collective experience in the electronics, information services, and aerospace industries. The purpose of this book is to update the developments in the field over the last 10 years and to expand on some of the concerns that are foremost in the minds of practitioners. In so doing, we have incorporated new material in many of the chapters specifically related to the *Project Management Body of Knowledge—PMBOK* published by the Project Management Institute. This material reflects the tools, techniques, and processes that have gained widespread acceptance by the profession because of their proven value and usefulness.

Over the years, numerous books have been written with similar objectives in mind. We acknowledge their contribution and have endeavored to build on their strengths. As such, we have focused on integrative concepts rather than isolated methodologies. We have relied on simple models to convey ideas and have intentionally avoided detailed mathematical formulations and solution algorithms—aspects of the field better left to other parts of the curriculum. Nevertheless, we do present some models of a more technical nature and provide references for readers who wish to gain a deeper understanding of their use. The availability of powerful, commercial codes brings model solutions within reach of the project team.

To ensure that project participants work toward the same end and hold the same expectations, short- and long-term goals must be identified and communicated continually. The project plan is the vehicle by which this is accomplished and, once approved, becomes the basis for monitoring, controlling, and evaluating progress at each phase of the project's life cycle. To help the project manager in this effort, various software packages have been developed; the most common run interactively on microcomputers and have full functional and report-generating capabilities. In our experience, even the most timid users are able to take advantage of their main features after only a few hours of hands-on instruction.

A second objective in writing this book has been to fill a void between texts aimed at low- to midlevel managers and those aimed at technical personnel with strong analytic skills but little training in or exposure to organizational issues. Those who teach engineering or business students at both the late undergraduate and early graduate levels should find it suitable. In addition, the book is intended to serve as a reference for the practitioner who is new to the field or who would like to gain a surer footing in project management concepts and techniques.

The core material, including most of the underlying theory, can be covered in a one-semester course. At the end of Chapter 1, we outline the book's contents. Chapter 3 deals with economic issues, such as cash flow, time value of money, and depreciation, as they relate to projects. With this material and some supplementary notes, coupled with the evaluation methods and multiple criteria decision-making techniques discussed in Chapters 5 and 6, respectively, it should be possible to teach a combined course in project management and engineering economy. This is the direction in which many undergraduate engineering programs are now headed after many years of industry prodding. Young engineers are often thrust into leadership roles without adequate preparation or training in project management skills.

Writing a textbook is a collaborative effort involving many people whose names do not always appear on the cover. In particular, we thank all those faculty who adopted the first edition of the book and provided us with their constructive and informative comments over the years. With regard to production, much appreciation goes to Lillian Bluestein for her thorough job in proofreading and editing the draft manuscript. We would also like to thank Chen Gretz-Shmueli for her contribution to the discussion in the human resources section. Finally, we are forever grateful to the phalanx of students who have studied project management at our universities and who have made the painstaking efforts of gathering and writing new material all worthwhile.

AVRAHAM SHTUB
JONATHAN F. BARD
SHLOMO GLOBERSON

About the Authors

Avraham Shtub is the Sharon and Stephen Seiden Professor of Project Management in the School of Industrial Engineering and Management at the Technion–Israel Institute of Technology. He received the Ph.D. degree in management science and industrial engineering from the University of Washington, the M.B.A. degree from Tel Aviv University, and the B.Sc. degree in electrical engineering from the Technion. He is a senior member of the Institute of Industrial Engineers and is certified as a Project Management Professional by the Project Management Institute. Professor Shtub's research focuses on the design and management of manufacturing systems, project management, and learning and forgetting. He is on the editorial boards of IIE Transactions and the International Journal of Production Research, and has previously served on the editorial boards of the Project Management Journal and the International Journal of Project Management.

Jonathan F. Bard is a professor of operations research and industrial engineering in the Mechanical Engineering Department at the University of Texas at Austin. He holds the Industrial Properties Corporation Endowed Faculty Fellowship, and serves as the Associate Director of the Center for the Management of Operations and Logistics. He received the D.Sc. degree in operations research from the George Washington University, the M.S. degree in aeronautics and astronautics from Stanford University, and the B.S. degree in aeronautical engineering from Rensselaer Polytechnic Institute. Professor Bard's research interests are in the design and analysis of manufacturing systems, personnel scheduling, R&D project management, and vehicle routing. Prior to beginning his academic career, he worked as a program manager for the Aerospace Corporation and as a systems engineer for Booz, Allen & Hamilton. He is currently the editor of IIE Transactions on Operations Engineering and serves on the editorial board of several other journals. He is a Fellow of IIE and a Senior Member of IEEE and INFORMS.

Shlomo Globerson is a professor in the School of Business Administration at Tel Aviv University. He received the Ph.D. degree in industrial engineering from the University of California, Berkeley, the M.S. degree in industrial engineering from the Faculty of Industrial Engineering and Management at the Technion–Israel Institute of Technology, and the B.Sc. degree in mechanical engineering from the Technion. His primary research and teaching activities center on project management and operations management. He has published seven books and over 80 articles. Professor Globerson is the former President of the Israeli chapter of the Project Management Institute and currently serves on the advisory board for the Industrial Engineering Handbook. He is also on the editorial boards of the Journal of Operations Management and the International Journal of Project Management.

Chapter 1

Introduction

1.1 NATURE OF PROJECT MANAGEMENT

Many of the most difficult engineering challenges of recent decades have been to design, develop, and implement new systems of a type and complexity never before attempted. Examples include the construction of oil drilling platforms in the North Sea off the coast of Great Britain, the development of the manned space program in both the United States and the former Soviet Union, and the worldwide installation of fiber optic lines for broadband telecommunications. The creation of these systems with performance capabilities not previously available and within acceptable schedules and budgets has required the development of new methods of planning, organizing, and controlling events. This is the essence of project management.

Succinctly, a project is an organized endeavor aimed at accomplishing a specific nonroutine or low-volume task. Although projects are not repetitive, they may take significant amounts of time and, for our purposes, are sufficiently large or complex to be recognized and managed as separate undertakings. Consequently, teams have emerged as the way of supplying the needed talents, but the use of teams complicates the flow of information and places additional burdens on management to communicate with and coordinate the activities of the participants.

The amount of time in which an individual or an organizational unit is involved in a project may vary considerably. Someone in operations may work only with other operations personnel on a project or may work with a team composed of specialists from various functional areas to study and solve a specific problem or to perform a secondary task.

Management of a project differs in several ways from management of a typical organization. The objective of a project team is to accomplish its prescribed mission and disband. Few firms are in business to perform just one job and then disappear. Because a project is intended to have a finite life, employees are seldom hired with the intent of building a career with the project. Instead, a team is pulled together on an ad hoc basis from among people who normally have assignments in other parts of the organization. They may be asked to work full time on the project until its completion; or they may be asked to work only part time, such as two days a week, on the project and spend the rest of the time at their usual assignments. A project may involve a short-term task that lasts only a matter of days, or it may run for years. After completion, the team normally disperses and its members return to their original jobs.

The need to manage large, complex projects constrained by tight schedules and budgets has motivated the development of methodologies different from those used to manage a typical enterprise. The Project Management Institute (PMI), a nonprofit organization, is in the forefront of developing such methodologies and of providing educational services in the form of workshops, training, and professional literature. One of its major publications is the Project Management Body of Knowledge (PMBOK). In addition, it offers a certification program, called the Project Management Professional, to experienced project managers who pass a written exam on the PMBOK.

1.2 RELATIONSHIP BETWEEN PROJECTS AND OTHER PRODUCTION SYSTEMS

Operations and production management contains three major classes of systems: (1) those designed for mass production, (2) those designed for batch (or lot) production, and (3) those designed for undertaking nonrepetitive projects common to construction and new product development. Each of these classes may be found in both the manufacturing and service sectors.

Mass production systems are typically designed around the specific processes used to assemble a product or perform a service. Their orientation is fixed, and their applications are limited. Resources and facilities are composed of special-purpose equipment designed to perform the operations required by the product or the service in an efficient way. By laying out the equipment to parallel the natural routings, material handling and information processing are greatly simplified. Frequently, material handling is automated and the use of conveyors and monorails is extensive. The resulting system is capital intensive and very efficient in the processing of large quantities of specific products or services for which relatively little management and control are necessary. However, these systems are very difficult to alter should a need arise to produce new or modified products or to provide new services. As a result, they are most appropriate for operations that experience a high rate of demand (e.g., several hundred thousand units annually) as well as high aggregate demand (e.g., several million units throughout the life cycle of the system).

Batch-oriented systems are used when several products or services are processed in the same facility. When the demand rate is not high enough or when long-run expectations do not justify the investment in special-purpose equipment, an effort is made to design a more flexible system on which a variety of products or services can be processed. Because the resources used in such systems have to be adjusted (set up) when production switches from one product to another, jobs are typically scheduled in batches to save setup time. Flexibility is achieved by using general-purpose resources that can be adjusted to handle different processes. The complexity of operations planning, scheduling, and control is greater than in mass production systems as each product has its own routing (sequence of operations). To simplify planning, resources are frequently grouped together on the basis of the type of processes that they perform. Thus, batch-oriented systems contain organizational units that specialize in a function or a process, as opposed to product lines that are found in mass production systems. Departments such as metal cutting, painting, testing, and packaging/shipping are typical examples from the batch-oriented manufacturing sector, whereas word processing centers and diagnostic laboratories are examples from the service sector.

In the batch-oriented system, it is particularly important to pay attention to material handling needs because each product has its specific set of operations and routings. Material handling equipment, such as forklifts, is used to move in-process inventory between departments and work centers. The flexibility of batch-oriented systems makes them attractive for many organizations.

In recent years, flexible manufacturing systems have been quick to gain acceptance in some industrial settings. With the help of microelectronics and computer technology, these systems are designed to achieve mass production efficiencies in low-demand environments. They work by reducing setup times and automating material handling operations but are extremely capital intensive. Hence, they cannot always be justified when product demand is low or when labor costs are minimal. Another approach is to take advantage of local economies of scale. Group technology cells, which are based on clustering similar products or components into families processed by dedicated resources of the facility, are one way to implement this approach. Higher utilization rates and greater throughput can be achieved by processing similar components on dedicated machines.

By way of contrast, systems that are subject to very low demand (no more than a few units) are substantially different from the first two mentioned. Because of the nonrepetitive nature of these systems, past experience may be of limited value, so little learning takes place. In this environment, extensive management effort is required to plan, monitor, and control the activities of the organization. Project management is a direct outgrowth of these efforts.

It is possible to classify organizations on the basis of their production orientation as a function of volume and batch size. This is illustrated in Fig. 1.1.

The borderlines between mass production, batch-oriented, and project-oriented systems are hard to define. In some organizations where the project approach has been adopted, several units of the same product (a batch) are produced, whereas other organizations use a batch-oriented system that produces small lots (the just-in-time approach) of very large volumes of products. To better understand the transition between the three types of systems, consider an electronics firm that assembles printed circuit boards in small batches in a job shop. As demand for the boards picks up, a decision is made to develop a flow line for assembly. The design and implementation of this new line is a project.

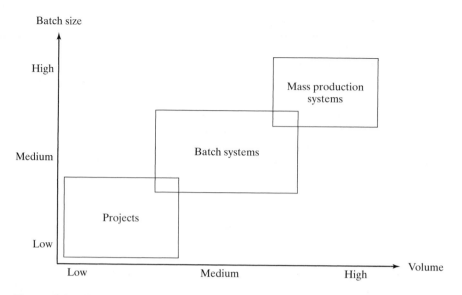

Figure 1.1   Classification of production systems.

1.3 CHARACTERISTICS OF PROJECTS

Although the Manhattan project—the development of the first atomic bomb—is considered by many to be the first instance when modern project management techniques were used, ancient history is replete with examples. Some of the better known ones include the construction of the Egyptian pyramids, the conquest of the Persian Empire by Alexander the Great, and the building of the Temple in Jerusalem. In the 1960s, formal project management methods received their greatest impetus with the Apollo program and a cluster of large, formidable construction projects.

Today, activities such as the transportation of American forces in Operation Iraqi Freedom, the pursuit of new treatments for AIDS, and the development of the joint U.S.–Russian space station are examples of three projects with which most of us are familiar. Additional examples of a more routine nature include

- Selecting a software package
- Developing a new office plan or layout
- Implementing a new decision support system
- Introducing a new product to the market
- Designing an airplane, a supercomputer, or a work center
- Opening a new store
- Constructing a bridge, dam, highway, or building
- Relocating an office or a factory
- Performing major maintenance or repair
- Starting up a new manufacturing or service facility
- Producing and directing a movie

1.3.1 Definitions and Issues

As the preceding list suggests, a project may be viewed or defined in several different ways: for example, as "the entire process required to produce a new product, new plant, new system, or other specified results" (Archibald 2003) or as "a narrowly defined activity which is planned for a finite duration with a specific goal to be achieved" (General Electric Corporation 1983). Generally speaking, project management occurs when emphasis and special attention are given to the conduct of nonrepetitive activities for the purpose of meeting a single set of goals.

By implication, project management deals with a one-time effort to achieve a focused objective. How progress and outcomes are measured, though, depends on a number of critical factors. Typical among these are technology (specifications, performance, quality), time (due dates, milestones), and cost (total investment, required cash flow), as well as profits, resource utilization, and market acceptance.

These factors and their relative importance are major issues in project management. With a well-defined set of goals, it is possible to develop appropriate performance measures and to select the organizational structure, required resources, and people who will team up to achieve these goals. Figure 1.2 summarizes the underlying

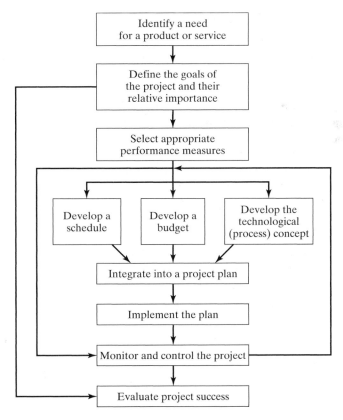

Figure 1.2 Major processes in project management.

processes. As illustrated, most projects are initiated by a need. A new need may be identified by a customer, the marketing department, or any member of the organization. When management is convinced that the need is genuine, goals may be defined and the first steps may be taken toward putting together a project team. Most projects have several goals covering such aspects as technical and operational requirements, delivery dates, and cost and should be ranked according to their relative importance.

On the basis of these rankings and a derived set of performance measures for each goal, the technological concept (or initial design) is developed along with a schedule and a budget for the project. The next step is to integrate the design, the schedule, and the budget into a project plan specifying what should be done, by whom, at what cost, and when. As the plan is implemented, the actual accomplishments are monitored and recorded. Adjustments, aimed at keeping the project on track, are made when deviations or overruns appear. When the project terminates, its success is evaluated on the basis of the predetermined goals and performance measures. Figure 1.3 compares two projects with these points in mind. In project 1, a "design to cost" approach is taken. Here, the budget is fixed and the technological goals are clearly specified. Cost, performance, and schedule all are given equal weight. In project 2, the technological goals are paramount and must be achieved, even if it means compromising the schedule and the budget in the process.

The first situation is typical of standard construction and manufacturing projects, whereby a contractor agrees to supply a system or a product in accordance with a given schedule and budget. The second situation is typical of "cost plus fixed fee" projects, whereby the technological uncertainties argue against a contractor's committing to a fixed cost and schedule. This arrangement is most common in a research and development (R&D) environment.

A well-designed organizational structure is required to handle projects as a result of their uniqueness, variety, and limited life span. In addition, special skills are required to manage them successfully. Taken together, these skills and organizational structures have been the catalyst for the development of the project management discipline. Many of the accompanying tools and techniques, though, are equally applicable in the manufacturing and service sectors.

Because projects are characterized by a "one time only" effort, learning is limited and most operations never become routine. This results in a need for extensive

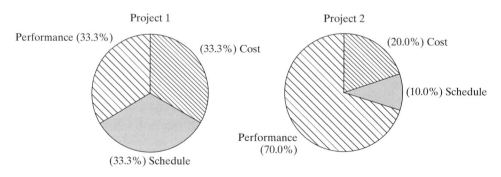

Figure 1.3   Relative importance of goals.

management involvement throughout the life cycle of the project. In addition, the lack of continuity leads to a high degree of uncertainty.

1.3.2 Risk and Uncertainty

In project management, it is common to refer to very high levels of uncertainty as sources of risk. Risk is present in most projects, especially in the R&D environment. Without trying to sound too pessimistic, it is prudent to assume that what can go wrong will go wrong. Principal sources of uncertainty include random variations in component and subsystem performance, inaccurate or inadequate data, and the inability to forecast satisfactorily as a result of lack of experience. Specifically, there may be

1. *Uncertainty in scheduling.* Changes in the environment that are impossible to forecast accurately at the outset of a project are likely to have a critical impact on the length of certain activities. For example, subcontractor performance or the time it takes to obtain a long-term loan are bound to influence the length of various subtasks. Methods are needed to deal with problematic or unstable time estimates. Probability theory and simulation both have been used successfully for this purpose, as discussed in Chapter 9.

2. *Uncertainty in cost.* Limited information on the duration of activities makes it difficult to predict the amount of resources needed to complete them on schedule. This translates directly into an uncertainty in cost. In addition, the expected hourly rate of resources and the cost of materials used to carry out project tasks may possess a high degree of variability.

3. *Technological uncertainty.* This form of uncertainty is typically present in R&D projects, in which new (not thoroughly tested and approved) technologies, methods, equipment, and systems are developed or used. Technological uncertainty may affect the schedule, the cost, and the ultimate success of the project. The integration of familiar technologies into one system or product may cause technological uncertainty as well. The same applies to the development of software and its integration with hardware.

There are other sources of uncertainty, including those of an organizational and political nature. New regulations might affect the market for a project, whereas the turnover of personnel and changes in the policies of one or more of the participating organizations may disrupt the flow of work.

To gain a better understanding of the effects of uncertainty, consider the three projects mentioned earlier. The transportation of American armed forces in Operation Iraqi Freedom faced extreme political and logistical uncertainties. In the initial stages, none of the planners had a clear idea of how many troops would be needed or how much time was available to put the troops in place. Also, it was unknown whether permission would be granted to use NATO air bases or even to fly over European and Middle Eastern countries, or how much tactical support would be forthcoming from U.S. allies.

The development of a treatment for AIDS is an ongoing project fraught with technological uncertainty. Hundreds of millions of dollars have already been spent with little progress toward a cure. As expected, researchers have taken many false steps, and many promising paths have turned out to be dead ends. Lengthy trial procedures and duplicative efforts have produced additional frustration. If success finally comes, it is unlikely that the original plans or schemes will have predicted its form.

The design of the U.S.–Russian space station is an example in which virtually every form of uncertainty is present. Politicians continue to play havoc with the budget, while special interest groups (both friendly and hostile) push their individual agendas; schedules get altered and rearranged; software fails to perform correctly; and the needed resources never seem to be available in adequate supply. Inflation, high turnover rates, and scaled-down expectations take their toll on the internal workforce, as well as on the legion of subcontractors.

Taking its cue from Parkinson, the American Production and Inventory Control Society has eloquently fashioned the following laws in an attempt to explain the consequences of uncertainty on project management.

Laws of Project Management

1. No major project is ever installed on time, within budget, or with the same staff that started it. Yours will not be the first.

2. Projects progress quickly until they become 90% complete, then they remain at 90% complete forever.

3. One advantage of fuzzy project objectives is that they let you avoid the embarrassment of estimating the corresponding costs.

4. When things are going well, something will go wrong.
   - When things just cannot get any worse, they will.
   - When things seem to be going better, you have overlooked something.

5. If project content is allowed to change freely, then the rate of change will exceed the rate of progress.

6. No system is ever completely debugged. Attempts to debug a system inevitably introduce new bugs that are even harder to find.

7. A carelessly planned project will take three times longer to complete than expected; a carefully planned project will take only twice as long.

8. Project teams detest progress reporting because it vividly manifests their lack of progress.

1.3.3 Phases of a Project

A project passes through a life cycle that may vary with size and complexity and with the style established by the organization. The names of the various phases may differ but typically include those shown in Fig. 1.4. To begin, there is a *conceptual design* phase during which the organization realizes that a project may be needed or receives a request from a customer to propose a plan to perform a project. Next there is an *advanced development or preliminary system design* phase in which the project manager (and perhaps a staff if the project is complex) plans the project to a level of detail sufficient for initial scheduling and budgeting. If the project is approved, then it will enter a more *detailed design* phase, a *production* phase, and a *termination* phase.

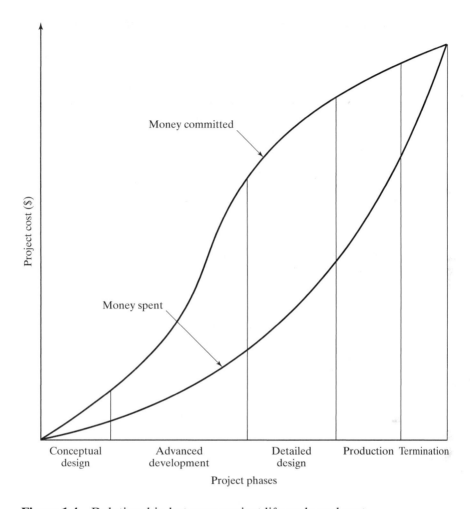

Figure 1.4   Relationship between project life cycle and cost.

In Fig. 1.4, the five phases in the life cycle of a project are presented as a function of time. The cost during each phase depends on the specifics, but usually the majority of the budget is spent during the production phase. However, most of this budget is committed during the advanced development phase and the detailed design phase before the actual work takes place. Management plays a vital role during the conceptual design phase, the advanced development phase, and the detailed design phase. The importance of this involvement in defining goals, selecting performance measures, and planning the project cannot be overemphasized. Pressures to start the "real work" on the project, that is, to begin the production (or execution) phase as early as possible, may lead to high cost and schedule risks as a result of the commitment of resources without adequate planning.

In most cases, a work breakdown structure (WBS) is developed during the conceptual design phase. The WBS is a document that divides the project into major hardware, software, data, and service elements. These elements are further divided and a list is produced identifying all tasks that must be accomplished to complete the project. The WBS helps to define the work to be performed and provides a framework for planning, budgeting, monitoring, and control. Therefore, as the project advances, schedule and cost performance can be compared with plans and budgets. Table 1.1 shows an abbreviated WBS for an orbital space laboratory vehicle.

The detailed project definition, as reflected in the WBS, is examined during the advanced development phase to determine the skills necessary to achieve the project's goals. Depending on the planning horizon, personnel from other parts of the organization may be used temporarily to accomplish the project. However, previous commitments may limit the availability of these resources. Other strategies might include hiring new personnel or subcontracting various work elements, as well as leasing equipment and facilities.

TABLE 1.1   Partial WBS for Space Laboratory

Index	Work element
1.0	Command module
2.0	Laboratory module
3.0	Main propulsion system
3.1	Fuel supply system
3.1.1	Fuel tank assembly
3.1.1.1	Fuel tank casing
3.1.1.2	Fuel tank insulation
4.0	Guidance system
5.0	Habitat module
6.0	Training system
7.0	Logistic support system

1.3.4 Organizing for a Project

A variety of structures are used by organizations to perform project work. The actual arrangement may depend on the proportion of the company's business that is project oriented, the scope and duration of the underlying tasks, the capabilities of the available personnel, preferences of the decision makers, and so on. The following five possibilities range from no special structure to a totally separate project organization.

1. *Functional organization.* Many companies are organized as a hierarchy with functional departments that specialize in a particular type of work, such as engineering and sales (see Fig. 1.5). These departments are often broken down into smaller units that focus on special areas within the function. Upper management may divide a project into work tasks and assign them to the appropriate functional units. The project is then budgeted and managed through the normal management hierarchy.

2. *Project coordinator.* A project may be handled through the organization as described above but with a special appointee to coordinate it. The project is still

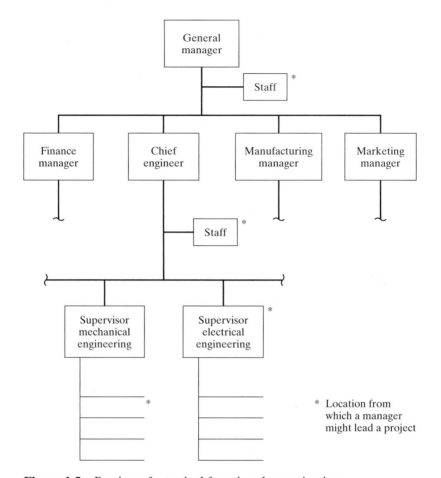

Figure 1.5   Portion of a typical functional organization.

funded through the normal channels, and the functional managers retain responsibility and authority for their portion of the work. The coordinator meets with the functional managers and provides direction and impetus for the project and may report its status to higher management.

3. *Matrix organization.* In a matrix organization, a project manager is responsible for completion of the project and is often assigned a budget. The project manager essentially contracts with the functional managers for completion of specific tasks and coordinates project efforts across the functional units. The functional managers assign work to employees and coordinate work within their areas. These arrangements are depicted schematically in Fig. 1.6.

4. *Project team.* A particularly significant project (development of a new product or business venture) that will have a long duration and require the full-time efforts of a group may be supervised by a project team. Full-time personnel are assigned to the project and are physically located with other team members. The project has its own management structure and budget as though it were a separate division of the company.

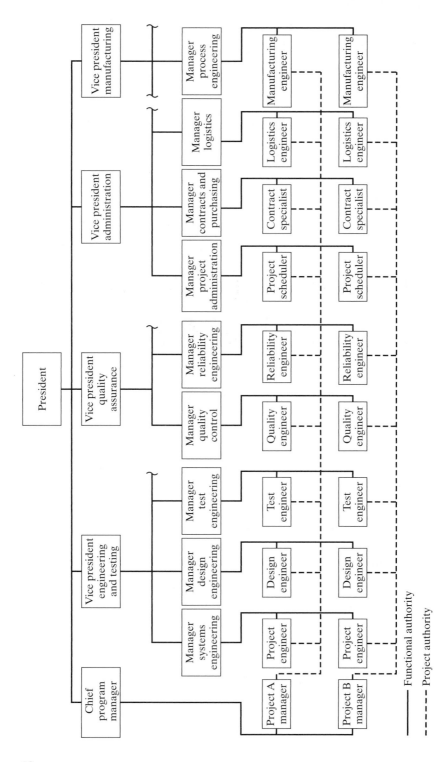

Figure 1.6 Typical matrix organization.

5. *Projectized organization.* When the project is extremely complex and of long duration, and involves a number of disparate organizations, it is advisable to give one person complete control of all the elements necessary to accomplish the stated goals. For example, when Rockwell International was awarded two multimillion-dollar contracts (the Apollo command and service modules, and the second stage of the Saturn launch vehicle) by NASA, two separate programs were set up in different locations of the organization. Each program was under a division vice president and had its own manufacturing plant and staff of specialists. Such an arrangement takes the idea of a self-sufficient project team to an extreme and is known as a *projectized* organization.

Table 1.2 enumerates some advantages and disadvantages of the functional and projectized organizations. Companies that are frequently involved in a series of projects and occasionally shift around personnel often elect to use a matrix organization. This type of organization provides the flexibility to assign employees to one or more projects. In this arrangement, project personnel maintain a permanent reporting relationship that connects vertically to the supervisor, who directs the scope of their work. At the same time, each person assigned to a project has a horizontal reporting relationship to the manager of a particular project, who coordinates his or her participation in that project. Pay and career advancement are developed within a particular discipline even though a person may be assigned to different projects. At times, this dual reporting relationship can give rise to a host of personnel problems.

TABLE 1.2   Advantages and Disadvantages of Two Organizational Structures

Functional organization	Projectized organization
Advantages	
Efficient use of technical personnel	Good project schedule and cost control
Career continuity and growth for technical personnel	Single point for customer contact
Good technology transfer between projects	Rapid reaction time possible
	Simpler project communication
Good stability, security, and morale	Training ground for general management
Disadvantages	
Weak customer interface	Uncertain technical direction
Weak project authority	Inefficient use of specialists
Poor horizontal communications	Insecurity regarding future job assignments
Discipline (technology) oriented rather than program oriented	Poor crossfeed of technical information between projects
Slower work flow	

Regardless of the structure, a project will usually draw on many of the organization's administrative support groups. It is unnecessary to duplicate existing services in procurement, legal, human resources, logistics, or most other support areas. In addition, the availability of microcomputers and project management software makes it possible to tie all of these functions together.

1.4 PROJECT MANAGER

The presence of uncertainty coupled with limited experience and hard-to-find data makes project management a combination of art, science, and, most of all, logical thinking. A good project manager must be familiar with a large number of disciplines and techniques. Breadth of knowledge is particularly important because most projects have technical, financial, marketing, and organizational aspects that inevitably conspire to derail the best of plans.

The role of the project manager may start at different points in the life cycle of a project. Some managers are involved from the beginning, helping to select the project, form the team, and negotiate the contracts. Others may begin at a later stage and be asked to execute plans that they did not have a hand in developing. At some point, though, most project managers deal with the basic issues: scheduling, budgeting, resource allocation, resource management, human relations, and negotiations.

It is an essential and perhaps the most difficult part of the project manager's job to pay close attention to the entire picture without losing sight of the critical details, no matter how slight. The project manager has to trade off different aspects of the project each time a decision is called for. Questions such as, "How important is the budget relative to the schedule?" and "Should more resources be acquired to avoid delays at the expense of a budget overrun, or should a slight deviation in performances be tolerated as long as the project is kept on schedule and on budget?" are common.

Some skills can be taught, whereas others come only with time and experience. We will not dwell on these but simply point them out as we define fundamental principles and procedures. Nevertheless, one of our basic aims is to highlight the practical aspects of project management and to show how modern organizations can function more effectively by adopting them. In so doing, we hope to provide all members of the project team with a comprehensive view of the field.

1.4.1 Basic Functions

The PMI identifies six basic functions that the discipline must address:

1. Manage the project's scope by defining the goals and work to be done in sufficient detail to facilitate understanding and corrective action, should the need arise.
2. Manage the human resources involved in the project.
3. Manage communications to ensure that the appropriate parties are informed and have sufficient information to keep the project on track.
4. Manage time by planning and meeting a schedule.
5. Manage quality so that the project's results are satisfactory.

6. Manage costs so that the project is performed in an efficient manner and within budget, if possible.

Managing a project is a complex and challenging assignment. Because projects are one-of-a-kind endeavors, there is little in the way of experience, normal working relationships, or established procedures to guide the participants. A project manager may have to coordinate many diverse efforts and activities to achieve the project goals. People from various disciplines and from various parts of the organization who have never worked together may be assigned to the project for different spans of time. Subcontractors who are unfamiliar with the organization may be brought in to carry out major tasks. The project may involve thousands of interrelated activities performed by people who are employed by any one of several different subcontractors or by the sponsoring organization.

For these and other reasons, it is important that the project leaders have an effective means of identifying and communicating the planned activities and their interrelationships. A computer-based scheduling and monitoring system is usually essential. Network techniques such as *critical path method* (CPM) and *program evaluation and review technique* (PERT) are likely to figure prominently in such systems. CPM was developed in 1957 by J.E. Kelly of Remington-Rand and M.R. Walker of Dupont to aid in scheduling maintenance shutdowns of chemical plants. PERT was developed in 1958 under the sponsorship of the U.S. Navy Special Projects Office, as a management tool for scheduling and controlling the Polaris missile program. Collectively, their value has been demonstrated time and again during both the planning and the execution phases of projects.

1.4.2 Characteristics of Effective Project Managers

The project manager is responsible for ensuring that tasks are completed on time and within budget but often has no formal authority over those who actually perform the work. He or she therefore must have a firm understanding of the overall job and rely on negotiation and persuasion skills to influence the array of contractors, functionaries, and specialists assigned to the project. The skills that a typical project manager needs are summarized in Fig. 1.7; the complexity of the situation is depicted in Fig. 1.8, which shows client, subcontractor, and top management interactions.

The project manager is a lightning rod, frequently under a storm of pressure and stress. He or she must deal effectively with the changing priorities of the client, the anxieties of his or her own management ever fearful of cost and schedule overruns, and the divided loyalties of the personnel assigned to the team. The ability to trade off conflicting goals and to find the optimal balance between conflicting pressures is probably the most important skill of the job.

In general, project managers need enthusiasm, stamina, and an appetite for hard work to withstand the onslaught of technical and political concerns. Where possible, they should have seniority and position in the organization commensurate with that of the functional managers with whom they must deal. Regardless of whether they are coordinators within a functional structure or managers in a matrix structure, they will frequently find their formal authority incomplete. Therefore, they must have the blend of technical, administrative, and interpersonal skills as illustrated in Fig. 1.7 to furnish effective leadership.

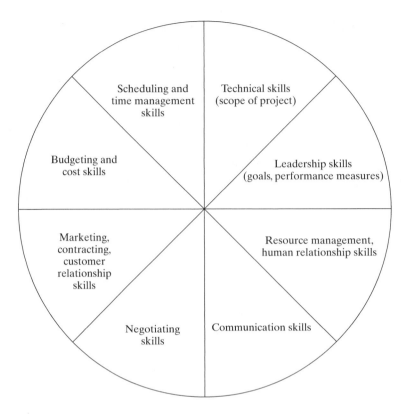

Figure 1.7   Important skills for the project manager.

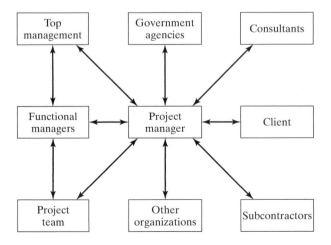

Figure 1.8   Major interactions of project
stakeholders.

1.5 COMPONENTS, CONCEPTS, AND TERMINOLOGY

The definition of a project fits a large variety of individual and organizational endeavors. Remodeling a house, writing a paper, building a new facility, introducing a new computer, and developing a training program are just a few examples. Although each project has a unique set of goals, there is enough commonality at a generic level to permit the development of a unified framework for planning and control. Project management techniques are designed to handle the common processes and problems that arise during a project's life cycle. This does not mean, however, that one versed in such techniques will be a successful manager. Experts are needed to collect and interpret data, negotiate contracts, arrange for resources, and deal with the welter of technical and organizational issues that impinge on both the cost and the schedule.

The following list contains the major components of a "typical" project.

- Project initiation, selection, and definition

  Identification of needs [e.g., by *quality function deployment* (QFD)]

  Development of (technological) alternatives

  Evaluation of alternatives

  Selection of the "most promising" alternatives

  Estimation of the *life-cycle cost* (LCC) of the promising alternatives

  Assessment of risk

  Development of a *configuration baseline*

  "Selling" the configuration and getting approval

- Project organization

  Selection of participating organizations

  Structuring the work content of the project into a WBS

  Development of the project organizational structure and associated communication and reporting facilities

  Allocation of WBS elements to participating organizations

- Analysis of activities

  Definition of the project's major tasks

  Development of a list of activities required to complete the project's tasks

  Development of precedence relations among activities

  Development of a network model

  Development of higher level network elements (hammock activities, subnetworks)

  Development of milestones

  Updating of the network and its elements

- Project scheduling

  Development of a calendar

  Estimation of activity durations

  Estimation of activity performance dates

Monitoring actual progress and milestones
Updating the schedule

- Resource management
  Definition of resource requirements
  Acquisition of resources
  Allocation of resources among projects/activities
  Monitoring resource use and cost

- Technological management
  Development of a configuration management plan
  Identification of technological risks
  Configuration control
  Risk management and control
  Total quality management (TQM)

- Project budgeting
  Estimation of direct and indirect costs
  Development of a cash flow forecast
  Development of a budget
  Monitoring actual cost

- Project execution and control
  Development of data collection systems
  Development of data analysis systems
  Execution of activities
  Data collection and analysis
  Detection of deviations in cost, configuration, schedule, and quality
  Development of corrective plans
  Implementation of corrective plans
  Forecasting of project cost at completion

- Project termination
  Evaluation of project success
  Recommendation for improvements in project management practices
  Analysis and storage of information on actual cost, actual duration, actual performance, and configuration

Each of these activities is discussed in detail in subsequent chapters. Here, we give an overview with the intention of introducing important concepts and the relationships among them. We also mention some of the tools developed to support the management of each activity.

1. *Project initiation, selection, and definition.* This process starts with identifying a need for a new service, product, or system. The trigger can come from any number of sources, including a current client, line personnel, or a proposed request from an outside organization. If the need is considered important and feasible solutions exist, then the need is translated into technical specifications through such techniques as QFD. Next, a study of an alternative approach may be initiated. Each alternative is evaluated on the basis of a predetermined set of performance measures, and the most promising are put on a candidate list. After this, an effort is made to estimate the costs and returns associated with the most suitable candidates. Cost estimates for development, production (or purchasing), maintenance, and operations form the basis of an LCC model that provides a framework for selecting the "optimal" alternative.

Because of uncertainty, most of the estimates are likely to be problematic. A risk assessment may be required if high levels of uncertainty are present. The risk associated with an unfavorable outcome is defined as the probability of that outcome multiplied by the cost associated with it. Major risk drivers should be identified early in the process, and contingency plans should be prepared to handle unfavorable events if and when they occur.

Once an alternative is chosen, design details are fleshed out during the concept formulation and definition phase of the project. Preliminary design efforts end with a configuration baseline. This configuration (the principal alternative) has to satisfy the customer's needs and be accepted and approved by management. A well-structured selection and evaluation process, in which all relevant parties are involved, increases the probability of management approval. A generic flow diagram for the processes of project initiation selection and definition is presented in Fig. 1.9.

2. *Project organization.* Many entities, ranging from private firms and research laboratories to public utilities and government agencies, may participate in a particular project. In the advanced development phase, it is common to define the work content [statement of work (SOW)] as a set of tasks and to array them hierarchically in a tree-like form known as the WBS. The relationship between participating organizations, known as the *organizational breakdown structure* (OBS), is similarly represented.

In the OBS, the lines of communication between and within organizations are defined, and procedures for work authorization and report preparation and distribution are established. Finally, lower-level WBS elements are assigned to lower-level OBS elements to form work packages and a responsibility matrix is constructed, indicating which organizational unit is responsible for which WBS element.

At the end of the advanced development phase, a more detailed cost estimate and a long-range budget proposal are prepared and submitted for management approval. A positive response signals the go-ahead for detailed planning and organizational design. This includes the next five functions.

3. *Analysis of activities.* To assess the need for resources and to prepare a detailed schedule, it is necessary to develop a detailed list of activities that are to be performed. These activities should be aimed at accomplishing the WBS tasks in a logical, economically sound, and technically feasible manner. Each task defined in the initial planning phase may consist of one or more activities. Feasibility is ensured by introducing precedence relations among activities. These relations can be represented graphically in the form of a network model.

The termination of important activities is defined as a milestone and is represented in the network model as a node. Milestones provide feedback in support of project control and form the basis for budgeting, scheduling, and resources management. As

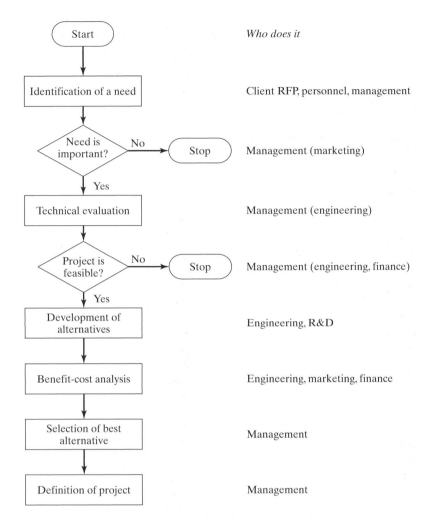

Figure 1.9   Major activities in the conceptual design phase.

progress is made, the model has to be updated to account for the inclusion of new activities in the WBS; the successful completion of tasks; and any changes in design, organization, and schedule as a result of uncertainty, new needs, or new technological and political developments.

4. *Project scheduling.* The expected execution dates of activities are important from both a financial (acquisition of the required funds) and an operational (acquisition of the required resources) point of view. Scheduling of project activities starts with the definition of a calendar specifying the working hours per day, working days per week, holidays, and so on. The expected duration of each activity is estimated and a project schedule is developed on the basis of the calendar, precedence relations among activities, and the expected duration of each activity. The schedule specifies the starting and ending dates of each activity and the accompanying slack or leeway. This information is used in budgeting and resource management. The schedule is used as a basis for work authorization and as a baseline against which actual progress is measured. It is updated throughout the life cycle of the project to reflect actual progress.

5. *Resource management.* Activities are performed by resources so that before any concrete steps can be taken, requirements have to be identified. This means defining one or more alternatives for meeting the estimated needs of each activity (the duration of an activity may be a function of the resources assigned to perform it). On the basis of the results and in light of the project schedule, total resource requirements are estimated. These requirements are the basis of resource management and resource acquisition planning.

When requirements exceed expected availability, schedule delays may occur unless the difference is made up by acquiring additional resources or by subcontracting. Alternatively, it may be possible to reschedule activities (especially those with slack) so as not to exceed expected resource availability. Other considerations, such as minimizing fluctuations in resource usage and maximizing resource utilization, may be applicable as well.

During the execution phase, resources are allocated periodically to projects and activities in accordance with a predetermined timetable. However, because actual and planned use may differ, it is important to monitor and compare progress to plans. Low utilization as well as higher-than-planned costs or consumption rates indicate problems and should be brought to the immediate attention of management. Large discrepancies may call for significant alterations in the schedule.

6. *Technological management.* Once the primary candidates are evaluated and a consensus forms, the approved configuration is adopted as a baseline. From the baseline, plans for project execution are developed, tests to validate operational and technical requirements are designed, and contingency plans for risky areas are formulated. Changes in needs or in the environment may trigger modifications to the configuration. Technological management deals with execution of the project to achieve the approved baseline. Principal functions include the evaluation of proposed changes, the introduction of approved changes into the configuration baseline, and the development of a total quality management program. The last involves the continuous effort to prevent defects, to improve the process, and to guarantee a final result that fits the specifications of the project and the expectations of the client.

7. *Project budgeting.* Money is the most common resource used in a project. Resources have to be acquired, and suppliers have to be paid. Overhead costs have to be assigned, and subcontractors have to be put on the payroll. The preparation of a budget is an important management activity that results in a time-phased plan summarizing expected expenditures, income, and milestones.

The budget is derived by estimating the cost of activities and resources. Because the schedule of the project relates activities and resource use to the calendar, the budget is also related to the same calendar. With this information, a cash flow analysis can be performed and the feasibility of the predicted outlays can be tested. If the resulting cash flow or the resulting budget is not acceptable, then the schedule should be modified. This is frequently done by delaying activities that have slack.

Once an acceptable budget is developed, it serves as the basic financial tool for the project. Credit lines and loans can be arranged and the cost of financing the project can be assessed. As work progresses, information on actual cost is accumulated and compared with the budget. This comparison forms the basis for controlling costs. The sequence of activities performed during the detailed design phase is summarized in Fig. 1.10.

8. *Project execution and control.* The activities described so far compose the first steps in initializing and preparing a project for execution. A feasible schedule that integrates task deadlines, budget considerations, resource availability, and technological requirements, while satisfying the precedence relations among activities, provides a good starting point for a project.

It is important, however, to remember that successful implementation of the initial schedule is subject to unexpected or random effects that are difficult (or impossible) to predict. In situations in which all resources are under the direct control of

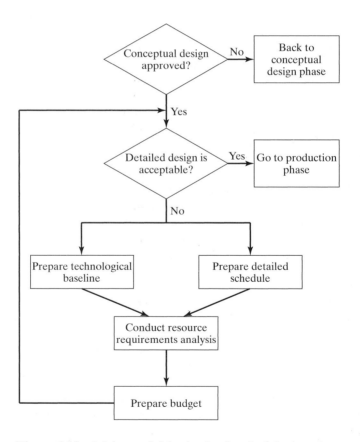

Figure 1.10   Major activities in the detailed design phase.

management and activated according to plan, unexpected circumstances or events may sharply divert progress from the original plan. For resources that are not under complete management control, much higher levels of uncertainty may exist. Sources of uncertainty such as a downturn in the economy, labor unrest, technology breakthroughs or failures, and new environmental regulations may always be a cause for alarm. These uncertainties should be monitored by keeping track of the effect they have on the project's progress.

Project control systems are designed with three purposes in mind: (1) to detect current deviations and to forecast future deviations between actual progress and the project plans, (2) to trace the source of these deviations, and (3) to support management decisions aimed at putting the project back on the desired course.

Project control is based on the collection and analysis of the most recent performance data. Thus, actual progress, cost, resource use, and technological achievements should be monitored continually. The information gleaned from this process is compared with the updated plans across all aspects of the project. Because deviations in one area (e.g., schedule overrun) may affect the performance and deviations in other areas (e.g., cost overrun), it is important to look at things from a systems point of view.

In general, all operational data collected by the control system are analyzed, and if deviations are detected, then a scheme is devised to put the project back on course. The existing plan is modified accordingly, and steps are taken to monitor its implementation.

During the life cycle of the project, a continuous effort is made to update original estimates of completion dates and costs. These updates are used by management to evaluate the success of the project and the efficiency of the participating organizations. These evaluations form the basis of management forecasts regarding the expected success of the project at each stage of its life cycle.

Special control systems are necessary when several projects are being conducted simultaneously. If the deviations in cost are positive for some projects and negative or zero for others, then the total budget might not be affected because the former cancels the latter. Nevertheless, if the deviations all are negative and actual cost tends to be higher than the expected cost, then the entire organization might find itself in a dilemma. These risks constitute the need for a control system so that the decision makers can be forewarned of any problems that could delay the project.

Schedule deviations might have a similar effect because payments are usually based on actual progress. If a schedule overrun occurs and payments are delayed, then cash flow difficulties might result. Schedule overruns might also cause excess load on resources as a result of the accumulation of work content. A well-designed control system in the hands of a well-trained project manager is the best way to counteract the negative effects of uncertainty that we can recommend.

9. *Project termination.* A project does not necessarily terminate as soon as its technical objectives are met. Management should strive to learn from past experience to improve the handling of future projects. A detailed analysis of the original plan, the modifications made over time, the actual progress, and the relative success of the project should be conducted. The underlying goal is to identify procedures and techniques that were not effective and to recommend ways to improve operations. An effort aimed at identifying missing or redundant managerial tools also should be initiated; new techniques for project management should be adopted when necessary, and obsolete procedures and tools should be discarded.

Information on the actual cost and duration of activities and the cost and utilization of resources should be stored in well-organized databases to support the planning effort in future projects. Only by striving for continuous improvement through programs based on past experience is competitiveness likely to persist in an organization. Policies, procedures, and tools must be updated on a regular basis.

1.6 MOVEMENT TO PROJECT-BASED WORK

Increased reliance on the use of project management techniques, especially for research and development, stems from the changing circumstances in which modern businesses must compete. Pinto (2002) pointed out that among the most important influences promoting a project orientation in recent years have been the following:

1. *Shortened product life cycles.* Products become obsolete at an increasingly rapid rate, requiring companies to invest ever-higher amounts in R&D and new product development.
2. *Narrow product launch windows.* When a delay of months or even weeks can cost a firm its competitive advantage, new products are often scheduled for launch within a narrow time band.
3. *Huge influx of global markets.* New global opportunities raise new global challenges, such as the increasing difficulty of being first to market with superior products.
4. *Increasingly complex and technical problems.* As technical advances are diffused into organizations and technical complexity grows, the challenge of R&D becomes increasingly difficult.
5. *Low inflation.* Corporate profits must now come less from raising prices year after year and more from streamlining internal operations to become ever more efficient.

The impact of these and other economic factors has created conditions under which companies that use project management are flourishing. Their success has encouraged more and more organizations to give the discipline a serious look as they contemplate how to become "project savvy." At the same time, they recognize that for all the interest in developing a project-based outlook, there is a severe shortage of trained project managers needed to convert market opportunities into profits. Historically, lack of training, poor career ladders, strong political resistance from line managers, unclear reward structures, and almost nonexistent documentation and operating protocols made the decision to become a project manager a risky move at best and downright career suicide at worst. Increasingly, however, management writers such as Tom Peters and insightful corporate executives such as Jack Welch have become strong advocates of the project management role. Between their sponsorship and the business pressures for enhancing the project management function, there is no doubt that we are witnessing a groundswell of support that is likely to continue into the foreseeable future.

Recent Trends in Project Management.   Like any robust field, project management is continuously growing and reorienting itself. Some of the more pronounced shifts and advances can be classified as follows:

1. *Risk management.* Developing more sophisticated up-front methodologies to better assess risk before significant commitment to the project.

2. *Scheduling.* New approaches to project scheduling, such as critical chain project management, that offer some visible improvements over traditional techniques.

3. *Structure.* Two important movements in organizational structure are the rise of the heavyweight project organization and the increasing use of project management offices.

4. *Project team coordination.* Two powerful advances in the area of project team development are the emphasis on cross-functional cooperation and the model of punctuated equilibrium as it pertains to intra-team dynamics. Punctuated equilibrium proposes that rather than evolution occurring gradually in small steps, real natural change comes about through long periods of stasis interrupted by some seismic event.

5. *Control.* Important new methods for tracking project costs relative to performance are best exemplified by earned value analysis. Although the technique has been around for some time, its wider diffusion and use are growing.

6. *Impact of new technologies.* Internet and web technologies have given rise to greater use of distributed and virtual project teams, groups that may never physically interact but must work in close collaboration for project success.

7. *Process-based project management.* The PMBOK (PMI Standards Committee 2000) views project management as a combination of the nine knowledge areas listed below. Each area is composed of a set of processes whose proper execution defines the essence of the field.

   - Integration management
   - Scope management
   - Time management
   - Cost management
   - Quality management
   - Human resource management
   - Communication management
   - Risk management
   - Procurement management

1.7 LIFE CYCLE OF A PROJECT: STRATEGIC AND TACTICAL ISSUES

Because of the degree to which projects differ in their principal attributes, such as length, cost, type of technology used, and sources of uncertainty, it is difficult to generalize the operational and technical issues they each face. It is possible, however, to discuss some strategic and tactical issues that are relevant to many types of projects. The framework for the discussion is the project life cycle, or the major phases through which a "typical" project progresses. An outline of these phases is depicted in Fig. 1.11 and elaborated

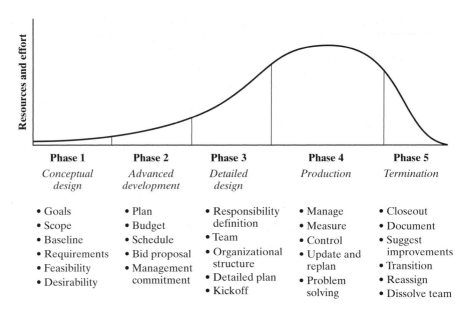

Figure 1.11   Project life cycle.

on by Cleland and Reland (2002), who identify the long-range (strategic) and medium-range (tactical) issues that management must consider. A synopsis follows.

1. *Conceptual design phase.* In this phase, an organization (client, contractor, subcontractor) initiates the project and evaluates potential alternatives. A client organization may start by identifying a need or a deficiency in existing operations and issuing a request for proposal (RFP). If the soliciting organization is a U.S. government agency, then the RFP will be published online at http://www.fedbizopps.gov, which replaced the *Commerce Business Daily* in 2002. Potential contractors can study the RFPs and develop a strategy for responding.

The selection of projects at the conceptual design phase is a strategic decision based on the established goals of the organization, needs, ongoing projects, and long-term commitments and objectives. In this phase, expected benefits from alternative projects, assessment of cost and risks, and estimates of required resources are some of the factors weighed. Important action items include the initial "make or buy" decisions for components and equipment, the development of contingency plans for high-risk areas, and the preliminary selection of subcontractors and other team members who will participate in the project.

In addition, upper management must consider the technological aspects, such as availability and maturity of the required technology and its performance and expected usage in subsequent projects. Environmental factors related to government regulations, potential markets, and competition also must be analyzed.

The selection of projects is based on a variety of goals and performance measures, including expected cost, profitability, risk, and potential for follow-on assignments. Once a project is selected and its conceptual design is approved, work begins on the second phase, when many of the details are ironed out.

2. *Advanced development phase.* In this phase, the organizational structure of the project is formed by weighing the tactical advantages and disadvantages of each possible arrangement mentioned in Section 1.3.4. Once a decision is made, lines of communication and procedures for work authorization and performance reporting are established. This leads to the framework in which the project is executed.

3. *Detailed design phase.* This is the phase in a project's life cycle in which comprehensive plans are prepared. These plans consist of

- Product and process design
- Final performance requirements
- Detailed breakdown of the work structure
- Scheduling information
- Blueprints for cost and resource management
- Detailed contingency plans for high-risk activities
- Budgets
- Expected cash flows

In addition—and most important—procedures and tools for executing, controlling, and correcting the project are developed. When this phase is completed, implementation can begin because the various plans should cover all aspects of the project in sufficient detail to support work authorization and execution.

The success of a project is highly correlated with the quality and the depth of the plans prepared during this phase. A detailed design review of each plan and each aspect of the project therefore is conducted before approval. A sensitivity analysis of environmental factors that contribute to uncertainty also may be needed. This analysis is typically performed as part of "what-if" studies using expert opinions and simulation as supporting mechanisms.

In most situations, the resources committed to the project are defined during the initial phases of its life cycle. Although these resources are used later, the strategic issues of how much to spend and at what rate are addressed here.

4. *Production phase.* The fourth life-cycle phase involves the execution of plans and in most projects dominates the others in effort and duration. The critical strategic issue here relates to maintaining top management support, while the critical tactical issues center on the flow of communications within and among the participating organizations. At this level, the focus is on actual performance and changes in the original plans. Modifications can take different forms—in the extreme case, a project may be canceled. More likely, though, the scope of work, schedule, and budget will be adjusted as the situation dictates. Throughout this phase, management's task is to assign work to the participating parties and to monitor actual progress and compare it with the baseline plans. The establishment and the operation of a well-designed communications and control system therefore are necessary.

Support of the product or system throughout its entire life (logistic support) requires management attention in most engineering projects for which an operational phase is scheduled to follow implementation. The preparation for logistic support includes documentation, personnel training, maintenance, and initial acquisition of spare parts.

Neglecting this activity or giving it only cursory attention can doom an otherwise successful venture.

   5. *Termination phase.* In this phase, management's goal is to consolidate what it has learned and translate this knowledge into ongoing improvements in the process. Current lessons and experience serve as the basis for improved practice. Although successful projects can provide valuable insights, failures can teach us even more. Unless we learn from our mistakes, we are bound to repeat them, making the task of continuous improvement little more than an empty exercise. Databases that store and support the retrieval of information on cost, schedules, resource utilization, and so on are assets of an organization. Readily available, accurate information is a key factor in the success of future projects.

   6. *Operational phase.* The operational phase is frequently outside the scope of a project and so may be carried out by organizations other than those involved in the earlier life-cycle stages. If, for example, the project is to design and build an assembly line for a new model of automobile, then the operation of the line (i.e., the production of the new cars) will not be part of the project because running a mass production system requires a different type of management approach. Alternatively, consider the design and testing of a prototype electric vehicle. Here, the operational phase, which involves operating and testing the prototype, will be part of the project because it is a one-time effort aimed at a very specific goal. In any case, from the project manager's point of view, the operational phase is the most crucial because it is here that a judgment is made as to whether the project has achieved its technical and operational goals.

   Strategic issues such as long-term relationships with customers, as well as customer service and satisfaction, have a strong influence on upper management's attitudes and decisions. Therefore, the project manager should be particularly aware of the need to open and maintain lines of communication between all parties, especially during this phase.

   In some projects, the transition from the production phase to the operational phase is gradual. This is the case when a project involves the production of a series of similar units. The first few units might be placed in operation while the remainder are still in various stages of completion. Special communications and control techniques (e.g., line of balance) have been developed for this type of situation to help the project manager carry out his or her duties throughout the life cycle of the project.

1.8 FACTORS THAT AFFECT THE SUCCESS OF A PROJECT

The project manager must handle a wide variety of tasks simultaneously. Decisions have to be made continuously at all levels regarding resource use, schedule adjustments, budgeting, organizational communications, technical problems, and human relations. There is a need to identify all of the basic issues, whether they be strategic, tactical, or operational, and to establish a priority scheme for helping the project manager focus on those that are critical. Of course, defining what is critical will vary from one phase of the project to another.

This issue was addressed in a study by Pinto and Slevin (1987), which aimed to find those factors that contribute most to a project's success and to measure their significance over the life cycle. They found the following 10 factors to be of primary importance. Additional insights are provided by Balachandra and Friar (1997) regarding new product development.

1. *Project mission and goals.* Well-defined and intelligible understanding of the project goals are the basis of planning and executing the project. Understanding the goals and performance measures used in the evaluation is important for good coordination of efforts and building organizational support. Therefore, starting at the conceptual design phase of the project life cycle, the overall mission should be defined and explained to team members, contractors, and other participants.

2. *Top management support.* The competition for resources, coupled with the high levels of uncertainty typically found in the project environment, often leads to conflict and crisis. The continuous involvement of top management throughout the life cycle of the project increases their understanding of its mission and importance. This awareness, if translated into support, may prove invaluable in resolving problems when crises and conflicts arise or when uncertainty strikes. Therefore, continued, solid communication between the project manager and top management is a catalyst for the project to be a success.

3. *Project planning.* The translation of the project mission, goals, and performance measures into a workable (feasible) plan is the link between the conceptual design phase and the production phase. A detailed plan that covers all aspects of the project—technical, financial, organizational, scheduling, communication, and control—is the basis of implementation. Planning does not end when execution starts, because deviations from the original plans during implementation may call for replanning and updating from one period to the next. Thus, planning is a dynamic and continuous process that links changing goals and performance to the final results.

4. *Client consultation.* The ultimate user of the project is the final judge of its success. A project that was completed on time according to the technical specifications and within budget but was never (or rarely) used can certainly be classified as a failure. In the conceptual design phase of the project life cycle, client input is the basis for setting the mission and establishing goals. In subsequent phases, continual consultation with the client can help in correcting errors previously made in translating goals into performance measures. However, as a result of changing needs and conditions, a mission statement that represented accurately the client's needs in the conceptual design phase may no longer be valid in the planning or implementation phases. As discussed in Chapter 6, the configuration management system provides the link between existing plans and change requests issued by the client, as well as the project team.

5. *Personnel issues.* Satisfactory achievement of technical goals without violating schedule and budgetary constraints does not necessarily constitute a complete success, even if the customer is satisfied. If relations among team members, between team members and the client, or between team members and other personnel in the organization are poor and morale problems are frequent, then project success is doubtful. Well-motivated teams with a sufficient level of commitment to the project and a good relationship with the client are the key determinants of project success.

6. *Technical issues.* Understanding the technical aspects of the project and ensuring that members of the project team possess the necessary skills are important responsibilities of the project manager. Inappropriate technologies or technical incompatibility may affect all aspects of the project, including cost, schedule, actual performances, and morale.

7. *Client acceptance.* Ongoing client consultation during the project life cycle increases the probability of success regarding user acceptance. In the final stages of implementation, the client has to judge the resulting project and decide whether it is acceptable. A project that is rejected at this point must be viewed as a failure.

8. *Project control.* The continuous flow of information regarding actual progress is a feedback mechanism that allows the project manager to cope with uncertainty. By comparing actual progress with current plans, the project manager can identify deviations, anticipate problems, and initiate corrective actions. Lower-than-planned achievements in technical areas as well as schedule and cost deviations detected early in the life cycle can help the project manager focus on the important issues. Plans can be updated or partially adjusted to keep the project on schedule, on budget, and on target with respect to its mission.

9. *Communication.* The successful transition between the phases of a project's life cycle and good coordination between participants during each phase requires a continuous exchange of information. In general, communication in the project team, with other parts of the organization, and between the project managers and the client is made easier when lines of authority are well defined. The organizational structure of the project should specify the communication channels and the information that should flow through each one. In addition, it should specify the frequency at which this information should be generated and transmitted. The formal communication lines and a positive working environment that enhances informal communication within the project team contribute to the success of a project.

10. *Troubleshooting.* The control system is designed to identify problem areas and, if possible, to trace their source through the organization. Because uncertainty is always a likely culprit, the development of contingency plans is a valuable preventive step. The availability of prepared plans and procedures for handling problems can reduce the effort required for dealing with them should they actually occur.

The foregoing list of factors that affect the success of a project is broad enough to provide a starting point for discussing the issues surrounding project management. Of course, the individual nature of projects gives rise to a unique set of factors that go beyond any attempts to generalize. Specific examples, usually in the form of case studies drawn from our collective experience, are given throughout the book to provide additional insights.

1.9 ABOUT THE BOOK: PURPOSE AND STRUCTURE

The book is designed to bridge the gap between theory and practice by presenting the tools and techniques most suited for modern project management. A principal goal is to give managers, engineers, and technology experts a larger appreciation of their roles by defining a common terminology and by explaining the interfaces between the underlying disciplines.

Theoretical aspects are covered at a level appropriate for a senior undergraduate course or a first-year graduate course in either an engineering or an MBA program. Special attention is paid to the use and evaluation of specific tools with respect to their real-world applicability. Whether the book is adopted for a course or is read by practitioners who want to learn the "tools of the trade," we have tried to present the subject matter in a concise and fully integrated manner.

The book is structured along functional lines and offers an in-depth treatment of basic processes; the economic aspects of project selection and evaluation; the technological aspects of configuration management; and the various issues related to budgeting, scheduling, and control. By examining these functions and their organizational links, a comprehensive picture emerges of the relationship that exists between project planning and implementation.

The end of each chapter contains a series of discussion questions and exercises designed to stimulate thought and to test the readers' grasp of the material. In some cases, the intent is to explore supplementary issues in a more open-ended manner. Also included at the end of each chapter is a team project centering on the design and construction of a solid waste disposal facility known as a thermal transfer plant. As the readers go from one chapter to the next, they are asked to address a particular aspect of project management as it relates to the planning of this facility.

Each of the remaining 14 chapters deals with a specific component of project management or a specific phase in the project life cycle. A short description of Chapters 2 through 15 follows.

Chapter 2 focuses on process-based project management; it begins with a discussion of life-cycle models and their importance in planning, coordination, and control. We then introduce the concept of a *process*, which is a group of activities designed to transform a set of inputs consisting of data, technology, and resources into the desired outputs. The remainder of the chapter is devoted to the processes underlying the nine project management knowledge areas contained in the PMBOK. As we explain, these processes, along with an appropriate information systems constitute the cornerstones of process-based project management.

In Chapter 3, we address the economic aspects of projects and the quantitative techniques developed for analyzing a specific alternative. The long-term perspective is presented first by focusing on the time value of money. Investment evaluation criteria based on net present value, internal rate of return, and the payback period are discussed. Next, the short-term perspective is given by considering the role that cash flow analysis plays in evaluating projects and comparing alternatives. Ideas surrounding risk and uncertainty are introduced, followed by some concepts common to decision making, such as expected monetary value, utility theory, breakeven analysis, and diminishing returns. Specific decisions such as buy, make, rent, or lease are also elaborated.

The integration of LCC analysis into the project management system is covered in Chapter 4. LCC concepts and the treatment of uncertainty in the analysis are discussed, as well as classification schemes for cost components. The steps required in building LCC models are outlined and explained to facilitate their implementation.

The idea that the cost of new product development is only a fraction of the total cost of ownership is a central theme of the chapter. The total LCC is determined largely in the early phases of a project, when decisions regarding product design and process selection are being made. Some of the issues discussed in this context include cost estimation and risk evaluation. The concept of the cost breakdown structure and how it is used in planning is also presented.

The selection of a project from a list of available candidates and the selection of a particular configuration for a specific project are two key management decisions. The purpose of Chapter 5 is to present basic techniques that can be used to support in this process. Checklists and scoring models are the simplest and first to be introduced. This is followed by a presentation of the formal aspects of benefit-cost and cost-effectiveness analysis. Issues related to risk and how to deal with it tie all of the material together. The chapter closes with a comprehensive treatment of decision trees. The strengths and weaknesses of each methodology are highlighted, and examples are given to demonstrate the computations.

It is rare that any decision is made on the basis of one criterion alone. To deal more thoroughly with situations in which many objectives, often incommensurate, must be juggled simultaneously, a value model that goes beyond simple checklists is needed. In Chapter 6, we introduce two of the most popular such models for combining incommensurate objectives into a single measure of performance. Multiattribute utility theory (MAUT) is the first presented. Basic theory is discussed along with the guiding axioms. Next, the concepts and assumptions behind the analytical hierarchy process (AHP) are detailed. A case study contained in the appendix documents the results of a project aimed at comparing the two approaches and points out the relative advantages of each.

The integrative notions of the OBS and the WBS are introduced in Chapter 7. The former combines several organizational units that reside in one or more organizations by defining communication channels for work authorization, performance reports, and assigning general responsibility for tasks. Questions related to the selection of the most appropriate organizational structure are addressed, and the advantages and disadvantages of each are presented.

Next, the WBS of projects is discussed. This structure combines into a hierarchical framework hardware, software, and services performed in a project. It further facilitates identification of the critical relationships that exist among various project components.

Subsequently, the combined OBS-WBS matrix is introduced, whereby each element in the lowest WBS level is assigned to an organizational unit at the lowest level of the OBS. This type of integration is the basis for detailed planning and control, as explained in subsequent chapters. We close with a discussion of human resources and the special needs that they engender for the project manager.

In Chapter 8, the process by which the technological configuration of projects is developed and maintained is discussed. The first topic relates to the importance of time-based competition, the use of teams, and the role of QFD in current engineering. We then show how tools such as benefit-cost analysis and MAUT can be used to select the best technological alternative from a set of potential candidates. Procedures used to handle engineering change requests via configuration management and configuration control are presented. Finally, the integration of quality management into the project and its relationship to configuration test and audit are highlighted.

Network analysis has played an important role in project scheduling over the past 40 years. In Chapter 9, we introduce the notions of activities, precedence relations, and task times and show how they can be combined in an analytic framework to provide a mechanism for planning and control. The idea of a calendar and the relationship between activities and time are presented, first by Gantt charts and then by network models of the activity-on-arrow/activity-on-node type. This is followed by a discussion of precedence relations; feasibility issues; and the concepts of milestones, hammock activities, and subnetworks. Finally, uncertainty is introduced along with the PERT approach to estimating the critical path and the use of Monte Carlo simulation to gain a deeper understanding of a project's dynamics.

Chapter 10 opens with a discussion of the type of resources used in projects. A classification scheme is developed according to resource availability, and performance measures are suggested for assessing efficiency and effectiveness. Some general guidelines are presented as to how resources should be used to achieve better performance levels. The relationship between resources and their cost and the project schedule is analyzed, and mathematical models for resources allocation and leveling are described.

In Chapter 11, we deal with the budget as a tool by which organizational goals, policies, and constraints are transformed into an executable plan that relates task completions and capital expenditures to time. Techniques commonly used for budget development, presentation, and execution are discussed. Issues also examined are the relationship between the duration and timing of activities and the budget of a project, cash flow constraints and liabilities, and the interrelationship among several projects performed by a single organizational unit.

The execution of a project is frequently subject to unforeseen difficulties that force deviation from the original plans. The focus of Chapter 12 is on project control—a function that depends heavily on the early detection of such deviations. The integration of OBS and WBS elements serves as a basis for the control system. Complementary components include a mechanism for tracing the source of each deviation and a forecasting procedure for assessing their implications if no corrective action is taken. Cost and schedule control techniques such as the earned value approach are presented, and the concept of cost/schedule control systems criteria is made clear.

Engineering projects in which new technologies are developed and implemented are subject to high levels of uncertainty. In Chapter 13, we define R&D projects and highlight their unique characteristics. The typical goals of such projects are discussed, and measures of success are suggested. Techniques for handling risk, including the idea of parallel funding, are presented. The need for rework or repetition of some activities is discussed, and techniques based on the Q-GERT approach to scheduling R&D projects are outlined. The idea of a portfolio is introduced, and tools used for portfolio management are discussed. A case study that involves screening criteria, project selection and termination criteria, and the allocation of limited resources is contained in the appendix.

A wide variety of software has been developed to assist the project manager perform his or her job. In Chapter 14, we discuss the basic functions and range of capabilities associated with these packages. A classification system is devised, and a process by which the most appropriate package can be selected for a project or an organization is outlined.

Most people find it difficult to give up a habit or to abandon an arrangement in which they feel comfortable or secure. Nevertheless, breaks must be made. Long-run goals should not be compromised for the sake of preserving the familiarity of the status quo. In Chapter 15, the need to terminate a project in a planned, orderly manner is discussed. The process by which information gathered in past projects can be stored, retrieved, and analyzed is presented. Postmortem analysis is suggested as a vehicle by which continuous improvement can be achieved in an organization. The goal is to show how projects can be terminated so that the collective experience and knowledge can be transferred to future endeavors.

It goes without saying that the huge body of knowledge in the area of project management cannot be condensed into a single book. Over the past 25 years alone, much has been written on the subject in technical journals, textbooks, company reports, and trade magazines. In an effort to cover some of this material, a bibliography of important works is provided at the end of each chapter. The interested reader can further his or her understanding of a particular topic by consulting these references.

TEAM PROJECT*

Thermal Transfer Plant

Introduction

To exercise the techniques used for project planning and control, the reader is encouraged to work out each aspect of the thermal transfer plant case study. At the end of each chapter, a short description of the relevant components of the thermal transfer plant is provided along with an assignment. If possible, the assignment should be done in groups of three or four to develop the interpersonal and organizational skills necessary for teamwork.

Not all of the information required for each assignment is given. Before proceeding, it may be necessary for the group to research a particular topic and to make some logical assumptions. Accordingly, there is no "correct solution" to compare recommendations and conclusions. Each assignment should be judged with respect to the availability of information and the force of the underlying assumptions.

Total Manufacturing Solutions, Inc.

Total Manufacturing Solutions, Inc. (TMS) designs and integrates manufacturing and assembly plants. Their line of products and services includes the selection of manufacturing and assembly processes for new or existing products, the design and selection of manufacturing equipment, facilities design and layout, the integration of manufacturing and assembly systems, and the training of personnel and startup management teams. The broad range of services that TMS provides to its customers makes it a unique and successful organization. Its headquarters are in Nashville, Tennessee, with branches in New York and Los Angeles.

*The authors wish to thank Warren Sharp and Ian St. Maurice for their help in writing this case study.

TMS began operations in 1980 as a consulting firm in the areas of industrial engineering and operations management. In the late 1990s, the company started its design and integration business. Recently, it began promoting just-in-time systems and group technology-based manufacturing facilities. The organization structure of TMS is depicted in Fig. 1.12; financial data are presented in Tables 1.3 and 1.4.

TMS employs approximately 500 people, 300 of whom are in the Nashville area, 100 in New York, and 100 in Los Angeles. Approximately 50% of these are industrial, mechanical, and electrical engineers, and approximately 10% also have MBA degrees, mostly with operations management concentrations. The other employees are technicians, support personnel, and managers. Some information on labor costs follows.

Engineers	$50,000/year
Technicians	$25/hour
Administrators	$35,000/year
Other	$10/hour

These rates do not include fringe benefits or overhead. Moreover, bear in mind that individual salaries are a function of experience, position, and seniority within the company.

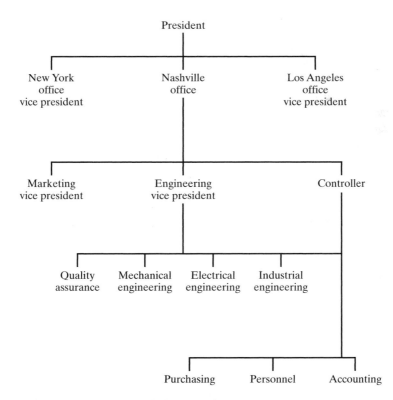

Figure 1.12   Simplified organization chart.

TABLE 1.3   TMS Financial Data: Income Statement

Income Statement ($1,000)
Year ending December 31, 2004

Net sales	$47,350
Cost of goods sold	
Direct labor	26,600
Overhead	6,000
	32,600
Gross profit	14,750
General and administrative	5,350
Marketing	4,900
	10,250
Profit before taxes	4,500
Income tax (32%)	1,440
Net profit	$3,060

TABLE 1.4   TMS Financial Data: Balance Sheet

Balance Sheet ($1,000)
Year ending December 31, 2004

Assets	
Current assets	
Cash	$1,100
Accounts receivables	1,500
Inventory	12
Other	3
Total current assets	2,615
Net fixed assets	325
Total assets	2,940
Liabilities	
Current liabilities	
Notes payable	35
Accounts payable	137
Accruals	90
Total current liabilities	262
Long-term debt	50
Capital stock and surplus	1,300
Earned surplus	1,328
Net worth	2,628
Total liabilities	$2,940

In the past 10 years, TMS averaged 20 major projects annually. Each project consisted of the design of a new manufacturing facility; the selection, installation, and integration of equipment; and the supervision of startup activities. In addition, TMS experts are consultants to more than 100 clients, many of whom own TMS-designed facilities.

The broad technical basis of TMS in the areas of mechanical, electrical, and industrial engineering and its wide-ranging experience are its most important assets. Management believes that the company is an industry leader in automatic assembly, material handling, industrial robots, command and control, and computer-integrated manufacturing. TMS is using subcontractors mainly in software development and, when necessary, for fabrication, because it does not have any shops or manufacturing facilities.

Recently, management has decided to expand its line of operations and services into the area of recycling and waste management. New regulations in many states are forcing the designers of manufacturing plants to analyze and solve problems related to waste generation and disposal.

Your team has been selected by TMS-Nashville to work on this new line of business. Your first assignment is to analyze the needs and opportunities in your geographical area. On the basis of a literature search and conversations with local manufacturers, environmentalists, and politicians, making whatever assumptions you believe are necessary, write a report and prepare a presentation that answers the following questions:

1. How well does this new line of business fit into TMS operations? What are the existing or potential opportunities?
2. How should a waste management project be integrated into TMS's current organizational structure?
3. What are the problems that TMS might encounter should it embark on this project? How might these problems affect the project? How might they affect TMS's other business activities?
4. If a project is approved in waste management, then what would its major life-cycle phases be?

Any assumptions regarding TMS's financial position and borrowing power, personnel, previous experience, and technological capabilities relating, for example, to computer-aided design, should be stated explicitly.

DISCUSSION QUESTIONS

1. Explain the difference between a project and a batch-oriented production system.
2. Describe three projects, one whose emphasis is on technology, one with emphasis on cost, and one with emphasis on scheduling.
3. Identify a project that is "risk free." Explain why this project is not subject to risk (low probability of undesired results, low cost of undesired results, or both).
4. In the text, it is stated that a project manager needs a blend of technical, administrative, and interpersonal skills. What attributes do you believe are desirable in an engineering specialist working on a project in a matrix organization?
5. Write a job description for a project manager.
6. Identify a project with which you are familiar, and describe its life-cycle phases and between 5 and 10 of the most important activities in each phase of its life cycle.
7. Find a recent news article on an ongoing project, evaluate the management's performance, and explain how the project could be better organized and managed.

8. Analyze the factors that affect the success of projects as a function of the project's life cycle. Explain in which phase of the life cycle each factor is most important, and why.

9. In a matrix management structure, the person responsible for a specific activity on a specific project has two bosses. What considerations in a well-run matrix organization reduce the resulting potential for conflict?

10. Outline a strategy for effective communication between project personnel and the customer (client).

11. Select a project and discuss what you think are the interfaces between the engineers and the managers assigned to the project.

12. The project plan is the basis for monitoring, controlling, and evaluating the project's success once it has started. List the principal components or contents of a project plan.

EXERCISES

1.1 What type of production system would be associated with the following processes?

a. A production line for window assemblies
b. A special order of 150 window assemblies
c. Supplying 1,000 window assemblies per month throughout the year

1.2 You decided to start a self-service restaurant. Identify the stages of this project and the type of production system involved in each stage, from startup until the restaurant is running well enough to sell.

1.3 Select two products and two services and describe the needs that generated them. Give examples of other products and services that could satisfy those needs equally well.

1.4 You have placed an emergency order for materials from a company that is located 2,000 miles away. You were told that it will be shipped by truck and will arrive within 48 hours, the time at which the materials are needed. Discuss the issues surrounding the probability that the shipment will reach you within the 48 hours. How would things change if shipment were by rail?

1.5 Your plumber recommends that you replace your cast iron pipes with copper pipes. He claims that although the price for the job is $7,000, he has to add $2,000 for unforeseen expenses. Discuss his proposal.

1.6 In statistical analysis, the coefficient of variation is considered to be a measure of uncertainty. It is defined as the ratio of the standard deviation to the mean. Select an activity, say, driving from your home to school, generate a frequency distribution for that activity, and calculate its mean and the standard deviation. Analyze the uncertainty.

1.7 Specify the type of uncertainties involved in completing each of the following activities successfully.

a. Writing a term paper on a subject that does not fall within your field of study
b. Undertaking an anthropological expedition in an unknown area
c. Driving to the airport to pick up a friend
d. Buying an item at an auction

1.8 Your professor told you that the different departments in the school of business are organized in a matrix structure. Functional areas include organizational behavior, mathematics (operations research and statistics), and computer science. Develop an organization chart that depicts these functions along with the management, marketing, accounting, and finance departments. What is the product of a business school? Who is the customer?

1.9 Provide an organizational structure for a school of business administration that reflects either a functional orientation or a product orientation.

1.10 Assume that a recreational park is to be built in your community and that the city council has given you the responsibility of selecting a project manager to lead the effort. Write a job description for the position. Generate a list of relevant criteria that can be used in the selection process, and evaluate three fictitious candidates (think about three of your friends).

1.11 Write an RFP soliciting proposals for preparing your master's thesis. The RFP should take into account the need for tables, figures, and multiple revisions. Make sure that it adequately describes the nature of the work and what you expect so that there will be no surprises once a contract is signed.

1.12 Explain how you would select the best proposal submitted in Exercise 1.11. That is, what measures would you use, and how would you evaluate and aggregate them with respect to each proposal?

1.13 The following list of activities is relevant to almost any project. Identify the phase in which each is typically performed, and order them in the correct sequence.

- Developing the network
- Selecting participating organizations
- Developing a calendar
- Developing corrective plans
- Executing activities
- Developing a budget
- Designing a project
- Recommending improvement steps
- Monitoring actual performance
- Managing the configuration
- Allocating resources to activities
- Developing the WBS
- Estimating the LCC
- Getting the customer's approval for the design
- Establishing milestones
- Estimating the activity duration

1.14 Drawing from your personal experience, give two examples for each of the following situations.

a. The original idea was attractive but not sufficiently important to invest in.
b. The idea was compelling but was not technically feasible.
c. The idea got passed the selection process but was too expensive to implement.
d. The idea was successfully transformed into a completed project.

1.15 List two projects with which either you or your organization is involved that are currently in each of the various life-cycle phases.

1.16 Select three national, state, or local projects (e.g., construction of a new airport) that were completed successfully and identify the factors that affected their success. Discuss the attending risks, uncertainty, schedule, cost, technology, and resources usage.

1.17 Identify three projects that have failed, and discuss the reasons for their failure.

BIBLIOGRAPHY

Elements of Project Management

Balachandra, R. and J. H. Friar, "Factors for Success in R&D Projects and New Product Development: A Contextual Framework," *IEEE Transactions on Engineering Management,* Vol. 44, No. 3, pp. 276–287, 1997.

Fleming, A. and J. Koppelman, "The Essence of Evolution of Earned Value," *Cost Engineering,* Vol. 36, No. 11, pp. 21–27, 1994.

General Electric Corporation, "Guidelines for Use of Program/Project Management in Major Appliance Business Group," in D. J. Cleland and W. R. King (Editors), *System Analysis and Project Management,* McGraw-Hill, New York, 1983.

Keller, R. T., "Cross-Functional Project Groups in Research and New Product Development: Diversity, Communications, Job Stress, and Outcomes," *Academy of Management Journal,* Vol. 44, pp. 547–555, 2001.

Pinto, J. K., "Project Management 2002," *Research Technology Management,* Vol. 45, No. 2, pp. 22–37, 2002.

Pinto, J. K. and D. P. Slevin, "Critical Factors in Successful Project Implementation," *IEEE Transactions on Engineering Management,* Vol. EM-34, No. 1, pp. 22–27, 1987.

Schmitt, T., T. D. Klastorin and A. Shtub, "Production Classification System: Concepts, Models and Strategies," *International Journal of Production Research,* Vol. 23, No. 3, pp. 563–578, 1985.

Books on Project Management

Archibald, R. D., *Managing High-Technology Programs and Projects,* Third Edition, John Wiley & Sons, New York, 2003.

Badiru, A. B., *Project Management in Manufacturing and High Technology Operations,* Second Edition, John Wiley & Sons, New York, 1996.

Cleland, D. I., *Guide to the Project Management Body of Knowledge* (*PMBOK Guide*), Project Management Institute, Newton Square, PA, 2002.

Cleland, D. I. and L. R. Reland, *Project Management: Strategic Design and Implementation,* Fourth Edition, McGraw-Hill, New York, 2002.

Kerzner, H., *Project Management: A Systems Approach to Planning, Scheduling and Control,* Seventh Edition, John Wiley & Sons, New York, 2000.

Kezsbom, D. S. and K. A. Edward, *The New Dynamic Project Management: Winning through the Competitive Advantage,* John Wiley & Sons, New York, 2001.

Meredith, J. R. and S. J. Mantel, Jr., *Project Management: A Managerial Approach,* Fourth Edition, John Wiley & Sons, New York, 1999.

PMI Standards Committee, *A Guide to the Project Management Body of Knowledge (PMBOK),* Project Management Institute, Newtown Square, PA, 2000 (http://www.PMI.org).

Randolph, W. A. and Z. B. Posner, *Checkered Flag Projects: Ten Rules for Creating and Managing Projects that Win!* Second Edition, Prentice Hall, Upper Saddle River, NJ, 2002.

Appendix 1A

Engineering Versus Management

1A.1 Nature of Management

Practically everyone has some conception of the meaning of the word *management* and to some extent understands that it requires talents that are distinct from those needed to perform the work being managed. Thus, a person may be a first-class engineer but unable to manage a high-tech company successfully. Similarly, a superior journeyman may make an inferior foreman. We all have read about cases in which an enterprise failed not because the owner did not know the field, but because he was a poor manager. To cite just one example, Thomas Edison was perhaps the foremost inventor of the last century, but he lost control of the many businesses that grew from his inventions because of his inability to plan and to direct and supervise others.

So what exactly is management, and what does a good manager have to know? Although there is no simple answer to this question, there is general agreement that, to a large extent, management is an art grounded in application, judgment, and common sense. To be more precise, it is the art of getting things done through other people. To work effectively through others, a manager must be able to perform competently the seven functions listed in Table 1A.1. Of those, planning, organizing, staffing, directing, and controlling are fundamental. If any of these five functions is lacking, then the management process will not be effective. Note that these are necessary but not sufficient functions for success. Getting things done through people requires the manager also to be effective at motivating and leading others.

The relative importance of the seven functions listed in Table 1A.1 may vary with the level of management. Top management success requires an emphasis on planning, organizing, and controlling. Middle-level management activities are more often concerned with staffing, directing, and leading. Lower-level managers must excel at motivating and leading others.

TABLE 1A.1   Functions of Management

Functions	Description
Planning	The manager first must decide what must be done. This means setting short- and long-term goals for the organization and determining how they will be met. Planning is a process of anticipating problems, analyzing them, estimating their likely impacts, and determining actions that will lead to the desired outcomes, objectives, or goals.
Organizing	Organizing means establishing interrelationships between people and things in such a way that human and material resources are effectively focused toward achieving the goals of the enterprise. Organizing involves grouping activities and people, defining jobs, delegating the appropriate authority to each job, specifying the reporting structure and interrelationships between these jobs, and providing the policies or other means for coordinating these jobs with each other.
Staffing	In organizing, the manager establishes positions and decides which duties and responsibilities properly belong to each. Staffing involves appraising and selecting candidates, setting the compensation and reward structure for each job, training personnel, conducting performance appraisals, and performing salary administration. Turnover in the workforce and changes in the organization make it in ongoing function.
Directing	Because no one can predict with certainty the problems or opportunities that will arise, duties must naturally be expressed in general terms. Managers must guide and direct subordinates and resources toward the goals of the enterprise. This involves explaining, providing instructions, pointing out proper directions for the future, clarifying assignments, orienting personnel in the most effective directions, and channeling resources.
Motivating	A principal function of lower management is to instill in the workforce a commitment and enthusiasm for pursuing the goals of the organization. Motivating refers to the interpersonal skills to encourage outstanding human performance in others and to instill in them an inner drive and a zeal to pursue the goals and objectives of the various tasks that may be assigned to them.
Leading	This means encouraging others to follow the example set for them, with great commitment and conviction. Leading involves setting examples for others, establishing a sense of group pride and spirit, and instilling allegiance.
Controlling	Actual performance will normally differ from the original plan, so checking for deviations and taking corrective actions is a continuing responsibility of management. Controlling involves monitoring achievements and progress against the plans, measuring the degree of compliance with the plans, deciding when a deviation is significant, and taking actions to realign operations with the plans.

1A.2 Differences between Engineering and Management

Many people start out as engineers and, over time, work their way up the management ladder. As Table 1A.2 shows, the skills required by a manager are very different from those normally associated with engineering (Badawy and Trystram 1995, Eisner 2002). Engineering involves hands-on contact with the work. Managers are always one or more steps removed from the shop floor and can influence output and performance only through others. An engineer can derive personal satisfaction and gratification in his or her own physical creations and from the work itself. Managers must learn to be fulfilled through the achievements of those whom they supervise. Engineering is a science.

TABLE 1A.2 Engineering versus Management

What Engineers Do	What Managers Do
Minimize risks, emphasize accuracy and mathematical precision	Take calculated risks, rely heavily on intuition, take educated guesses, and try to be "about right"
Exercise care in applying sound scientific methods, on the basis of reproducible data	Exercise leadership in making decisions under widely varying conditions, based on sketchy information
Solve technical problems on the basis of their own individual skills	Solve techno-people problems on the basis of skills in integrating the talents and behaviors of others
Work largely through their own abilities to get things done	Work through others to get things done

It is characterized by precision, reproducibility, proven theories, and experimentally verifiable results. Management is an art. It is characterized by intuition, studied judgments, unique events, and one-time occurrences. Engineering is a world of things; management is a world of people. People have feelings, sentiments, and motives that may cause them to behave in unpredictable or unanticipated ways. Engineering is based on physical laws, so most events occur in an orderly, predictable manner.

1A.3 Transition from Engineer to Manager

Engineers are often propelled into management out of economic considerations or a desire to take on more responsibility. Some organizations have a dual career ladder that permits good technical people to remain in the laboratory and receive the same financial rewards that attend supervisory promotions. This type of program has been most successful in research-intensive environments such as those found at the IBM Research Center in Yorktown Heights and the Department of Energy research laboratories around the United States.

Nevertheless, when an engineer enters management, new perspectives must be acquired and new motivations must be found. He or she must learn to enjoy leadership challenges, detailed planning, helping others, taking risks, making decisions, working through others, and using the organization. In contrast to the engineer, the manager achieves satisfaction from directing the work of others (not things), exercising authority (not technical knowledge), and conceptualizing new ways to do things (not doing them). Nevertheless, experience indicates that the following three critical skills are the ones that engineers find most troublesome to acquire: (1) learning to trust others, (2) learning how to work through others, and (3) learning how to take satisfaction in the work of others.

The step from engineering to management is a big one. To become successful managers, engineers usually must develop new talents, acquire new values, and broaden their point of view. This takes time, on-the-job and off-the-job training, and careful planning. In short, engineers can become good managers only through effective career planning.

REFERENCES

Badawy, M. K. and D. Trystram, *Developing Managerial Skills in Engineers and Scientists,* John Wiley & Sons, New York, 1995.

Eisner, H., *Essentials of Project and Systems Engineering Management,* Second Edition, John Wiley & Sons, New York, 2002.

Jones, G. R. and J. M. George, *Essentials of Contemporary Management,* McGraw-Hill, New York, 2003.

Moore, D. C. and D. S. Davies, "The Dual Ladder: Establishing and Operating It," *Research Management,* Vol. 20, No. 4, pp. 21–27, 1977.

Chapter 2

Process Approach to Project Management

2.1 INTRODUCTION

A project is an organized set of activities aimed at accomplishing a specific, nonroutine or low-volume task such as designing an e-commerce web site or building a hypersonic transport. Projects are aimed at meeting the objectives and expectations of their stakeholders. Because of the need for specialization, as well as the sheer number of man-hours usually required, most projects are undertaken by multidisciplinary teams. In some cases, the team members belong to the same organization, but often, at least a portion of the work is assigned to subcontracters, consultants, or partner firms. Leading the effort is the project manager, who is responsible for the successful completion of all activities.

Coordination between the individuals and organizations involved in a project is a complex task and thus a major component of the project manager's job. To ensure success, integration of deliverables produced at different geographical locations, at different times, by different people, in different organizations is required.

Projects are typically performed under time pressure, limited budgets, tight cash flows, and uncertainty using shared resources. The triple constraint of time, cost, and scope requires the project manager and his or her team constantly to make tradeoffs between these factors with the implicit goal of balancing risks and benefits. Moreover, disagreements among the stakeholders on the best course of action to follow can lead to conflicting direction and poor resource allocation decisions. Thus, a methodology is required to support the management of projects. Early efforts in developing such a methodology focused on specific tools for different aspects of the problem. Tools for project scheduling, such as the Gantt chart and the critical path method, were developed along with tools for resource allocation, project budgeting, and project control. Each is covered in considerable detail in the chapters that follow.

Nevertheless, although it is important to gain an appreciation of these tools, each is limited in the view that it provides the project manager. For example, tools for scheduling rarely address problems related to configuration management, and tools for budgeting typically do not address problems associated with quality. The integration of these tools in a way that supports decision making at each stage in a project's life cycle is essential for understanding the dynamics of the project environment. This chapter identifies the relevant management processes and outlines a framework for applying them to both single and multiple projects.

A project management process is a collection of tools and techniques that are used on a predefined set of inputs to produce a predefined set of outputs. The processes are interconnected and interdependent. Inputs to some are outputs of others. The full collection forms a methodology that supports all of the aspects of project management throughout a project's life cycle—from the initiation of a new project to its (successful) completion and termination.

The framework that we propose to organize and study the relevant processes is based on the nine knowledge areas identified by the Project Management Institute (PMI) and published as the Project Management Body of Knowledge (PMBOK). PMI also conducts a certification program based on the PMBOK. A Project Management Professional certificate can be earned by passing an exam and accumulating relevant experience in the project management discipline.

The benefit gained from implementing the full set of project management processes has been evident in many organizations. Despite that a project is defined as a unique, one-time effort, process-oriented management promotes learning and teamwork through the use of a common set of tools and techniques. A detailed description of their use is provided in the remainder of the book. Each chapter deals with a specific knowledge area and highlights the tools and techniques in the form of mathematical models, templates, charts, and checklists used in the processes developed for that area.

2.1.1 Life-Cycle Models

Because a project is a transitory effort designed to achieve a specific set of goals, it is convenient to identify the phases that accompany the transformation of an idea or a concept into a product or a system. The collection of such phases is defined as the *project life cycle.*

Analogous to a living being, a project is born (initiated), performed (lives), and at some point terminated (dies). This simple life-cycle model consisting of three phases is conceptually helpful in understanding project management processes because it is straightforward to associate each process with a project phase; however, it is not detailed enough for implementation, especially for projects in which each phase spans several months or years. As a consequence, more specific life-cycle models for families of similar projects have been developed. A specific life-cycle model is a set of stages or phases through which a family of projects goes, in which each phase may be performed sequentially or concurrently. The project life cycle defines the steps required to achieve the project goals as well as the contents of each step. The end of each phase often serves as a checkpoint or milestone for assessing progress. At this point, the current status of the project is compared with the original plan in an effort to identify deviations in cost, schedule, and performance so that any necessary corrective action can be taken.

For software projects, the spiral life-cycle model proposed by Boehm (1988) and further refined by Muench (1994) has gained widespread popularity, particularly within the U.S. Department of Defense (DOD). The model, shown in Fig. 2.1, is very useful for repetitive development in which a project goes through the same phases several times, each time becoming more complete; i.e., closer to the final product. It has two main distinguishing features. The first is a cyclic approach for incrementally expanding a system's definition and degree of implementation while decreasing its level of risk. The other is a set of anchor point milestones for ensuring stakeholder commitment to feasible and mutually satisfactory solutions. The general idea is to ensure that the riskier aspects of the project are completed first to avoid failures in an advanced phase.

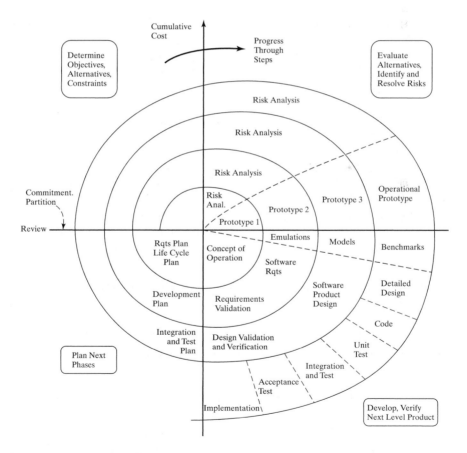

Figure 2.1   Spiral life-cycle model.

Construction projects also have their own set of life-cycle models, such as the one proposed by Morris (1988). In this model, a project is divided into four stages to be performed in sequence.

Stage I   (Feasibility) This stage terminates with a go/no go decision for the project. It includes a statement of goals and objectives, conceptual design, high-level feasibility studies, the formulation of strategy, and the approval of both the design and the strategy by upper management.

Stage II   (Planning and Design) This stage terminates with the awarding of major contracts. It includes detailed design, cost and schedule planning, contract definitions, and the development of the road map for execution.

Stage III   (Production) This stage terminates with the completion of the facility. It includes construction, installation of utilities, equipment acquisition and setup, landscaping, roadwork, interior appointments, and operational testing.

Stage IV   (Turnover and Startup) This stage terminates with full operation of the facility. It includes final testing and the development of a maintenance plan.

Clearly this model does not fit research and development (R&D) projects or software projects because of the sequential nature in which the work is performed. In R&D projects, for example, it is often necessary to undertake several activities in parallel with the hope that at least one will turn out to meet technological and cost objectives.

Several other life-cycle models follow:

- *Waterfall model.* Each phase is completed before the initiation of the following phase. This model is most relevant for information technology projects.
- *Incremental release model.* In the early phases, an imperfect version of the project is developed with the goal of maximizing market share. Toward the later phases, a final version of the product emerges. This is a special case of the spiral model.
- *Prototype model.* In the early phases, the rudimentary functions associated with the user interface are developed before the product itself is finalized. This model is most appropriate for information technology projects.

By integrating the ideas of project processes and the project life cycle, a methodology for project management emerges. The methodology is a collection of processes whereby each process is associated with a phase of the project life cycle. The project manager is responsible for identifying individuals who have the necessary skills and experience and for assigning them to the appropriate processes. His or her job is facilitated when the definition of inputs and outputs of each process is clear and when the team members are clear about the lines of authority, individual responsibilities, and overall project objectives. This will ensure a well-coordinated flow of information and good communications between project participants.

Life-cycle models are indispensable project management tools. They provide a simple yet effective means of monitoring and controlling a project at each stage of its development. As each phase comes to an end, the logic of the framework calls for all results to be documented and all deliverables to be certified with respect to quality and performance standards.

Figure 2.2   DOD life-cycle model.

2.1.2 Example of a Project Life Cycle

The DOD uses a simple life-cycle model for systems acquisition (US DOD 5000.2 1993). Its components are shown in Fig. 2.2. The project starts only after the determination of mission needs and approval is given. At the end of phase IV, the system is taken out of service. This is the end of the life cycle.

2.1.3 Application of the Waterfall Model for Software Development

The current standard guiding software development within DOD and the National Aeronautics and Space Administration is DOD-STD-2167A/498. As stated in the *Handbook for Parametric Cost Estimating* (DOD 1999) published by DOD on the web, the waterfall model captures the relevant phases of the development effort through a series of stages. There are specific objectives to be accomplished in each stage, and each activity must be deemed successful for work to proceed to the subsequent phase. The process is usually considered noniterative. Each phase requires the delivery of particular documentation (contract data requirements list). In addition, many of the phases require successful completion of a government review process. Critics of the waterfall model, in fact, find that the model is geared to recognize documents as a measure of progress rather than actual results.

The nine major activities described in DOD-STD-2167A/498 are as follows:

1. Systems concept/system requirements analysis
2. Software requirements analysis
3. Software parametric cost estimating
4. Preliminary design
5. Detailed design
6. Coding and computer software unit testing
7. Computer software component integration and testing
8. Computer software configuration item testing
9. System integration and operational testing

A schematic of the process, representing concurrent hardware and software development, is given in Fig. 2.3.

An alternative approach to software development involves the use of incremental builds. With this approach, software development begins with the design of certain core functions to meet critical requirements. Each successive software build (iteration on product development) provides additional functions or enhances performance. Once system requirements are defined and preliminary system design is complete,

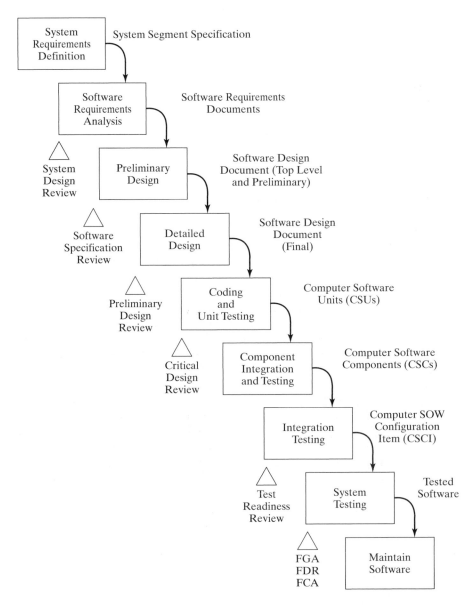

Figure 2.3   Waterfall model.

each build may follow the waterfall pattern for subsequent development phases. Each successive build will usually have to be integrated with previous builds.

2.2 PROJECT MANAGEMENT PROCESSES

A process is a group of activities designed to transform a set of inputs into the desired outputs. The transformation consists of the following three elements:

1. Data and information
2. Decision making
3. Implementation and action

A well-defined set of processes, supported by an appropriate information system (composed of a database and a model base) and implemented by a team trained in performing the processes, is a cornerstone in modern project management.

The following discussion is based on the work of Shtub (2001).

2.2.1 Process Design

The design of a process must address the following issues.

1. Data required to support decisions, including
   - data sources
   - how the data should be collected
   - how the data should be stored
   - how the data should be retrieved
   - how the data should be presented as information to decision makers

2. Models required to support decisions. A model is a simplified representation of reality that is used in part to transform data into useful information. When a real problem is too complicated to solve or some information is missing, simplifying assumptions are made and a model is developed. There are many types of models, including mathematical, physical, and statistical. The model—the simplified presentation of reality—is analyzed, and a solution is obtained. Sensitivity analysis is then used to evaluate the applicability of the solution found to the real problem and its sensitivity to the simplifying assumptions. Consider, for example, a simple way of estimating the time required to travel a given distance. Assuming a constant speed and movement in a straight line, one possibility would be time = distance/speed. This simple algebraic model is frequently used, although most vehicles do not travel at a constant speed or in a straight line. In a similar way, a variety of models are used in project management, including
   - models that support routine decisions
   - models that support ad hoc decisions
   - models used for project control

   Their value depends not on the fidelity with which they mimic reality but on how useful their estimates are in practice.

3. Data and models integration
- How data from the database are analyzed by the models
- How information generated by the models is transferred and presented to decision makers

2.2.2 PMBOK and Processes in the Project Life Cycle

A well-defined set of processes that apply to a large number of projects are discussed in the PMBOK. Although some of the PMBOK processes may not apply to all projects and others may need to be modified before they can be applied, the PMBOK is a widely accepted, widely known source of information. It suggests classifying processes in two ways.

1. By sequence:
- initiating processes
- planning processes
- executing processes
- controlling processes
- closing processes

2. By knowledge areas or management functions:
- processes in integration management
- processes in scope management
- processes in time management
- processes in cost management
- processes in quality management
- processes in human resource management
- processes in communication management
- processes in risk management
- processes in procurement management

The application of these processes in a specific organization requires customization, the development of supporting tools, and training.

2.3 PROJECT INTEGRATION MANAGEMENT

2.3.1 Accompanying Processes

Project integration management involves three processes:

1. Project plan development—gathering results of various planning processes
2. Project plan execution—implementation of the project plan
3. Integrated change control—change coordination for the entire project

The purpose of these processes is to ensure coordination among the various elements of the project. Coordination is achieved by retrieving inputs from the other processes, extracting the information from those inputs, and packaging the results in an integrated manner for use by the decision makers and other processes.

Integration management is concerned with the identification, monitoring, and control of all interfaces between the various components of a project, including

1. Human interface—the personnel associated with the various aspects of the project, such as subcontractors, consultants, stakeholders, and customers.
2. Scope interface—if the scope is not defined properly, then work may be performed twice or not at all.
3. Time interface—adequate resources must be provided to avoid delays and late deliverables. Timely information transfer is also a critical aspect.
4. Technological interface—if technology-related performance is not monitored closely, then integration problems can easily arise.

Proper integration management requires proper communication between members of the project's team; indeed, one of the nine areas of knowledge is communication management. The life-cycle model also plays an important role. The project plan is developed in the early phases of the project, whereas the execution of the plan and change control occur during the later phases. With a well-structured life-cycle model, it is straightforward to define the data, tools, supporting models for decision making, and activities required to achieve the project goals. It is also possible to implement an efficient training regimen for those responsible for performing the processes.

2.3.2 Description

The Project Plan.   The project plan and its execution are the major outputs of this process. The plan is based on inputs from other processes such as scope planning, schedule development, resource planning, and cost estimating, along with historical information and organizational policies. It is updated continuously on the basis of corrective actions triggered by approved change requests and analysis of performance measures. As a tool for coordination, the documents that define the plan must address

1. The time dimension—when is each stage performed
2. The scope dimension—what should be achieved
3. The human dimension—who does what
4. The resource and information dimension—the plan must deal with long lead items to ensure availability of resources and information

The primary purpose of the plan is to guide the execution of the project. It assists the project manager in leading the project team and in achieving the project's goals. Critical characteristics are fluidity and flexibility, allowing changes to be incorporated easily as they occur. The corresponding document typically consists of the following parts.

1. Preface, including a general review, goals, outputs, scope of work to be done, and technical specifications
2. Project organization description—interfaces, organizational structure, responsibilities
3. Management processes—for example, procurement, reporting, and monitoring
4. Technical processes—for example, design and verification
5. Execution—the way work will be done, scheduling and budget information, resource allocation, and information flow

The project plan should reflect the needs and expectations of the stakeholders. Therefore it could be extremely helpful for the project manager to perform an analysis to determine their principal concerns and perspectives. Information to be gathered might include

1. Stakeholder names and organizations with which they are associated
2. Their needs and expectations
3. Specific facts pertaining to each individual
4. Their influence level and their interest level

This information can be used to develop guidelines for managing the relationship between the project personnel and the stakeholders. The level of influence and the needs and expectations of any particular stakeholder may have a significant impact on the success or failure of the project. Moving in a direction that is at crossroads with an influential stakeholder can spell doom.

Execution of the Plan.   Execution of the project plan produces the deliverables. For integration management to be successful, the project manager must be skilled in the three areas listed below. Some of these skills are innate, whereas others can be learned:

1. The technology that is used by the project is referred to as the product scope. Often the project manager can delegate responsibilities for technological issues to a team member with detailed expertise. Most of the effort of the project manager, then, is related to integration—ensuring that the pieces come together properly.
2. The organizational factor—the project manager must understand the nature of the organization, the human interrelations, the common types of interactions, and so on. Organizational understanding can be expressed as follows:

   a. Human resources (HR) framework—the focus is on creating harmony among the organizational needs, needs of the project participants, and the project requirements.
   b. Cultural framework—the focus is on understanding the organizational culture, i.e., the cultural frame of reference.
   c. Symbolic framework—the focus is on positions and responsibilities, coordination, and monitoring. The organizational breakdown structure (OBS) and the work breakdown structure (WBS) aid in defining this framework. The project manager's authority is invested through the WBS but also through the political, HR, and cultural frameworks.
   d. Political framework—begins with the assumption that the project organization is a coalition of different stakeholders. Key points to bear in mind are internal struggle and governing power. Because of the transitory nature of a project, the project manager must use the stakeholders' power to advance his or her goals. Structurally speaking, the stakeholders can be divided into two groups:
      i. Stakeholders with an interest in the failure of the project
      ii. Stakeholders with an interest in the success of the project

The project manager must identify all of the stakeholders and their political influence, their objectives, and their ability to affect the project. Once again, he or she should spend some time to determine the significant needs and requirements of the chief stakeholders.

3. The business factor—the project manager must understand all aspects of the business associated with the project.

In terms of personal characteristics, the most successful project managers are

1. Efficient
2. Decisive
3. Supportive of team members' decisions
4. Confident
5. Articulate communicator
6. Highly motivated
7. Technologically oriented

Project execution involves the management and administration of the work described in the project plan. Usually most of the budget, time, and resources are spent during the execution phase. When the focus of the project is on new product development, success is often determined by the depth and details of the plan. As the saying goes, "measure twice, cut once." Vital tools and techniques for project implementation are as follows:

1. Authorization management system—enable the project manager to verify that an authorized team member is performing a specific task at the correct point of time.
2. Status review meetings—prescribed meetings for information exchange regarding the project.
3. Project management software—decision support software (including a database and a model base) to help the project manager plan, implement, and control all aspects of the project, including budgets, personnel, schedule, and other resources.
4. Monitoring system—software, spreadsheets, or other mechanisms for comparing budget outlays, work performed, and resources consumed over time with the original plan.

Integrated Change Control.   As the project activities proceed, changes are inevitable. A procedure must be put in place to identify, quantify, and manage the changes throughout the project life cycle. The main targets of change control are

1. Evaluation of the change requests to determine whether the benefits of the change will be sufficient to justify the corresponding disruption and expense
2. Determining that a change has occurred
3. Managing the actual changes when and as they occur

The original project scope and baseline must be maintained by continuously managing changes to the baseline. This is accomplished either by rejecting new changes or by approving changes and incorporating them into a revised project baseline. Change control makes use of the following modules in the configuration management system:

1. *Configuration identification.* Conceptually, each configuration element should be coded in a way that facilitates reference to its accompanying documents. Any changes approved in the configuration element should trigger a corresponding change in the documents, thus ensuring the correct description of the element.

2. *Change management.* A change is initiated via an engineering change request (ECR). The ECR contains the basis of the change along with a statement of the effect that it will have on activity times, schedules, and resource usage, as well as any new risks that may result.

To guarantee that each type of change is handled by the proper authority, a change classification system should be put in place. The most important changes are handled by the change control board (CCB) that represents all of the stakeholders. After a review, a change request can be accepted or rejected by the CCB. Once a request is accepted, it becomes an engineering change order (ECO). The ECO contains all relevant information, such as the nature of the change, the party responsible for its execution, its subcomponents, and the time when the change is to take place. In Chapter 8, we go into much greater detail on these issues.

2.4 PROJECT SCOPE MANAGEMENT

2.4.1 Accompanying Processes

Project scope management consists of the following five processes:

1. *Initiation.* This process is born of need or desire and involves some sort of cost-benefit analysis that leads to a go/no go decision. The project charter is created at the conclusion of this phase, and a project manager is selected. The charter defines the need that the project answers, the project time frame, and the budget.

2. *Scope planning.* The statement of work (SOW) identifies the project scope. It details the methods to achieve the work, the place where it is to be performed, and the mechanisms to be used to verify that it has been completed. It also specifies the initial schedule and the corresponding activities.

3. *Scope definition.* Division of the main project activities into smaller, manageable components. Two processes are joined at this point: (1) the WBS, which breaks down the overall scope of the project into work packages, and (2) the OBS, which specifies the responsible party for each work package identified. At the end of this process, all parts of the SOW (work packages) will have been assigned to individual managers.

4. *Scope verification.* For every deliverable, formal acceptance takes place only after satisfactorily comparing the work defined in the corresponding work packages with the work actually performed. Any discrepancies can lead to the rejection of the deliverable. Formal verification of the project scope is usually done at meetings with the help of summary progress reports. The formal verification of the product

scope usually takes place during acceptance testing of the final product. Each scope is verified with respect to the latest approved configuration.

5. *Scope change control.* Most of the changes are managed by the configuration management system. When a change affects the contract, it is likely to have an impact on the schedule and the budget.

The purpose of these processes is to ensure that the project includes all work (and only that work) required for its successful completion. In the following discussion, scope relates to

- the product scope—defined as the features and functions to be included in the product or service that translate into specific project and product
- the project scope—encompasses the project management processes defined as the work that must be done to deliver the product scope

The process management of projects deals mainly with the project scope because the product scope is context specific.

2.4.2 Description

Scope management encompasses the effort required to perform the work associated with a project, as well as the processes required to produce the intended products or services. The scope is defined in general terms rather than in terms of a specific product or service. Many alternatives may exist. On the basis of an appropriate set of evaluation criteria and a selection methodology, the best alternative is chosen, a project charter is issued, and a project manager is selected.

Projects are initiated in response to a need typically arising at a level in the organization that is responsible for setting strategic goals. Research has shown that the most important criterion guiding organizations in choosing projects is financial. Projects are selected for implementation when they support clear business goals and have an attractive rate of return or net present value. A second factor that is likely to trigger a new project is an advance in technology. In the home electronics industry, for example, the steady reduction in cost and increase in performance of integrated circuits and memory chips has forced firms to offer new products on a semiannual basis, just to remain competitive.

In summary, projects are initiated when

1. a defined need arises
2. there is strategic support and a willingness to undertake the project
3. the technology is compelling
4. there are available resources

Potential projects can be classified in several ways:

1. External versus internal projects; i.e., projects performed for customers outside the organization versus customers within the organization
2. Projects that are initiated to
   a. address a business opportunity

    b. solve a problem

    c. follow a directed order

3. Due date and completion time

4. Organizational priority

The first three scope management processes address the project charter, SOW, and WBS, respectively. An outline of what is included in each follows.

Project charter. A "go" document affirming that the project exists. It usually has the following components:

1. Project title

2. Project start date

3. Project manager

4. Project objectives

5. Project approach

SOW. The SOW gives information on

1. Scope of work—what work should be completed and how

2. Where the work will take place (at what physical location)

3. Duration of execution—initial schedule along with milestones for every product

4. Applicable standards

5. Product allocation

6. Acceptance criteria

7. Additional requirements—transportation needs, special documentation, insurance requirements, safety and security

WBS. The WBS decomposes the project into subprojects. Each subproject should be described with full detail of owner, schedule, activities, how each is to be performed and when, and so on. It is advisable to have a WBS template, especially for organizations with many similar projects. The template specifies how to divide the project into the work packages.

A disconcerting issue related to scope management is "scope creep," in which new features and performance requirements are added to the project without a proper change management process. By adhering to the management processes described in this chapter, scope creep can be minimized.

2.5 PROJECT TIME MANAGEMENT

2.5.1 Accompanying Processes

Time management establishes the schedule for tasks and activities defined in the work packages. The following five processes are included:

1. Activity definition

2. Activity sequencing

   3. Activity duration estimating
   4. Schedule development
   5. Schedule control

   The purpose of time management is to ensure the timely completion of the project. The accompanying schedule defines what is to be done, when it is to be done, and by whom. The schedule is used throughout the project to synchronize people, resources, and organizations involved and as a basis for control. When activities slip beyond their due dates, at least two major problems may arise:

   1. Time and money are often interchangeable. As projects are pushed beyond their due date, time-related costs are incurred.
   2. Most contracts specify rigid due dates with penalties for late deliveries. Alternatively, early deliveries may have incentives associated with them.

The time dimension is firm; whereas costs can be managed, time moves forward relentlessly. Scheduling issues create severe conflicts in some organizations, especially during the implementation phase and specifically in organizations that have a matrix structure. By implementing proper processes for project management, conflicts can be minimized.

2.5.2 Description

Tasks are defined in the SOW and then translated into the WBS. Each work package in the WBS is decomposed into a set of activities that reflect its predefined scope. Estimating the duration of each activity is a major issue in time management. Activity durations are rarely known with certainty and so are given as either point estimates or probability distributions. The work package manager is the best source of these estimates because he or she knows the technology. Sometimes an estimate can be derived from a database of similar activities. A problem is created when organizations do not maintain time-related records or do not associate parameters with an activity. The absence of parameterized data often precludes its use in deriving time estimates.

   In developing the schedule, precedence relations among activities are defined and a model such as a Gantt chart or network is constructed. Both technological and managerial precedence relations may be present. The former are drawn from the physical attributes of the product or system being developed. The latter emerge from procedures dictated by the organization; for example, issuing a purchase order usually requires that a low-ranking manager give his or her approval before the senior officer signs the final forms. Whereas managerial precedence relations can be sidestepped in some instances, say, if the project is late, technological precedence relations are invariant.

   An initial schedule is the basis for estimating costs and resource requirements. After a blueprint is developed, constraints imposed by due dates, cash flows, resource availability, and resource requirements of other projects can be added. Further tuning of the schedule may be possible by changing the combination of resources (modes) assigned to activities. In constructing a graph of cost versus duration, the modes correspond to the data points. Such graphs have two endpoints: (1) minimum cost (at maximum duration) and (2) maximum cost (at minimum duration). Implicit in this statement is the rule that the shorter the activity duration, the higher the cost.

As a first cut, the project manager normally uses the minimum cost–maximum duration point for each activity to determine the earliest finish time of the project. If the result is not satisfactory, then different modes for one or more activities may be examined. If the result still is not satisfactory, then more sophisticated methods can be applied to determine the optimal combination of costs and resources for each activity. One way to do this is to formulate the problem as an integer program and use either commercial software or specialized heuristics to find solutions.

Fast tracking some activities is also possible by repositioning them in parallel or overlapping them to a certain degree. In any case, the schedule is implemented by performing the activities in accordance with their precedence relations. Uncertainty, though, calls for a control mechanism to detect deviations and to decide how to react to change requests. The schedule control system is based on performance measures such as actual completion of deliverables (milestones), actual starting times of activities, and actual finishing times of activities. Changes to the baseline schedule are required whenever a change in the project scope is implemented.

2.6 PROJECT COST MANAGEMENT

2.6.1 Accompanying Processes

Project cost management involves four processes:

1. Resource planning
2. Cost estimating
3. Cost budgeting
4. Cost control

These processes are designed to provide an estimate of the cost required (1) to complete the project scope, (2) to develop a budget based on availability of funds, management policies, and strategy, and (3) to ensure that the project is completed within the approved budget.

2.6.2 Description

To complete the project activities, different resources are required depending on whether the work is to be done internally or by outside contractors. Labor, equipment, and information, for example, are required for in-house activities, whereas money is required for outsourcing. The work packages derived from the SOW contain plans for using resources and suggest different operational modes for each activity.

There are various methods of estimating activity costs, from detailed accounting procedures to guesswork. Formal accounting procedures can be tedious and time consuming and perhaps a waste of time in case the project is discarded. Thus, early in the project life cycle, rough order-of-magnitude estimates are best, although they are not likely to be accurate.

Estimates of the amount of resources required for each activity, as well as the timing of their use, are based on the activity list and the schedule. Resource allocation is performed at the lowest level of the WBS—the work package level—and requirements are rolled up to the project level and then to the organizational level. A comparison of resource requirements and resource availability along with corporate strategies and priorities forms the basis of the allocation decisions at the organizational level. Resource planning results in a detailed plan specifying which resources are required for each work package. By applying the resource cost rates to the resource plan and adding overhead and outsourcing expenses, a cost estimate of the project is developed. This provides a basis for budgeting. As determined by the schedule, cost estimates are time-phased to allow for cash flow analysis. Additional allocations may also be made in the form of, say, a management reserve, to buffer against uncertainty. The resulting budget is the baseline for project cost control.

Because of uncertainty, cost control is required to detect deviations and to decide how to react to get the project back on track and within budget. Change requests require a similar response. The cost control system is based on performance measures, such as actual cost of activities or deliverables (milestones), and actual cash flows. Changes to the baseline budget are required whenever a change in the project scope is implemented.

2.7 PROJECT QUALITY MANAGEMENT

2.7.1 Accompanying Processes

Project quality management consists of three processes:

1. Quality planning
2. Quality assurance
3. Quality control

The purpose of these processes is to ensure that the finished product satisfies the needs for which it was undertaken. Garvin (1987) suggested the following eight dimensions for measuring quality:

1. *Performance.* This dimension refers to the product or service's primary characteristics, such as the acceleration, cruising speed, and comfort of an automobile or the sound and the picture clarity of a TV set. The understanding of the customer's performance requirements and the design of the product or service to meet those requirements are key factors in quality-based competition.
2. *Features.* This is a secondary aspect of performance that supplements the basic functions of the product or service. Features could be considered "bells and whistles." The flexibility afforded a customer to select desired options from a long list of possibilities contributes to the quality of the product or service.
3. *Reliability.* This performance measure reflects the probability of a product's malfunctioning or failing within a specified period of time. It affects both the cost of maintenance and downtime of the product.
4. *Conformance.* This is the degree to which the design and operating characteristics of the product or service meet established standards.

5. *Durability.* This is a measure of the economic and technical service duration of a product. It relates to the amount of use that one can get from a product before it has to be replaced as a result of technical or economical considerations.

6. *Serviceability.* This measure reflects the competence and courtesy of the agent performing the repair work, as well as the speed and ease with which it is done. The reliability of a product and its serviceability complement each other. A product that rarely fails and—on those occasions when it does—can be repaired quickly and inexpensively, has a lower downtime and better serves its owner.

7. *Aesthetics.* This is a subjective performance measure related to how the product feels, tastes, looks, or smells and reflects individual preferences.

8. *Perceived quality.* This is another subjective measure related to the reputation of the product or a service. Reputation may be based on past experience and partial information, but in many cases, the customers' opinions are based on perceived quality as a result of the lack of accurate information on the other performance measures.

2.7.2 Description

Up to the mid-1980s, quality was defined as meeting or exceeding a specific set of performance measures. Since then, the need to understand user requirements and application requirements has been on the rise. Quality starts with the understanding of the stakeholders' requirements. Fitness of use is called for. The stakeholders require products that carry different grades at maximum achievable quality. Quality is the proper match for the desired requirements at the expected grade. The product should have specific characteristics.

Quality planning starts with the definition of standards or performance levels for each of the dimensions of quality. On the basis of the scope of the project, quality policy, standards, and regulations, a quality management plan is developed. The plan describes "the organizational structure, responsibilities, procedures, processes, and resources needed to implement quality management" (*ISO 9000 Revisions Progress to FDIS Status 2000*); i.e., how the project management team will implement its quality policy to achieve the required quality levels. Checklists and metrics or operational definitions are also developed for each performance measure so that actual results and performance can be evaluated against stated requirements.

To provide confidence that the project will achieve the required quality level, a quality assurance process is implemented. By continuously reviewing (or auditing) the actual implementation of the plan developed during quality planning, quality assurance systematically seeks to increase the effectiveness and efficiency of the project and its results. Actual results are monitored and controlled. The quality control process forms the basis of acceptance (or rejection) decisions at various stages of development.

2.8 PROJECT HUMAN RESOURCE MANAGEMENT

2.8.1 Accompanying Processes

HR management during the life cycle of a project is primarily concerned with the following three processes:

1. Organizational planning

2. Staff acquisition
3. Team development

Collectively, these processes are aimed at making the most effective use of people associated with the project. The temporary nature of the project structure and organization, the frequent use for multidisciplinary teams, and the participation of people from different organizations transform into a need for team building, motivation, and leadership if goals are to be met successfully.

2.8.2 Description

The work content of the project is allocated among the performing organizations by integrating the project's WBS with its OBS. As mentioned, work packages—specific work content assigned to specific organizational units—are defined at the lowest level of these two hierarchical structures. Each work package is a building block; i.e., an elementary project with a specific scope, schedule, budget, and quality objectives. Organizational planning activities are required to ensure that the total work content of the project is assigned and performed at the work package level and that the integration of the deliverables produced by the work packages into the final product is possible according to the project plan. The organizational plan defines roles and responsibilities, as well as staffing requirements and the OBS of the project.

On the basis of the organizational plan, manpower assessments are made along with staff assignments. The availability of staff is compared with the requirements, and gaps are identified. These gaps are filled by the project manager working in conjunction with the HR department of the firm or agency. The assignment of available staff to the project and the acquisition of new staff result in the creation of a project team that may be a combination of full-time employees assigned full time to the project, full-timers assigned part time, and part-timers. Subcontractors, consultants, and other outside HR may be part of the team as well.

The assignment of staff to the project is the first step in the team development process. To succeed in achieving the project goals, teamwork and a team spirit are essential ingredients. The transformation of a group of people who are assigned to a project into a high-performance team requires leadership, communication skills, and negotiation skills, as well as the ability to motivate people, to coach and to mentor them, and to deal with conflicts in a professional yet effective manner.

2.9 PROJECT COMMUNICATIONS MANAGEMENT

2.9.1 Accompanying Processes

The four processes associated with project communications management are:

1. Communications planning
2. Information distribution
3. Performance reporting
4. Administrative closure

These processes are required to ensure "timely and appropriate generation, collection, dissemination, storage, and ultimate disposition of project information" (PMBOK). Each is tightly linked with organizational planning. Communication between team members, with stakeholders, and with external parties and systems can take many forms. For example, it can be formal or informal, written or verbal, and planned or ad hoc. The decisions regarding communication channels, the information that should be distributed, and the best form of communication for each type of information are crucial in supporting teamwork and coordination.

2.9.2 Description

Communications planning is the process of selecting the communication channels, the modes of communication, and the contents of the communication between project participants, stakeholders, and the environment. Taking into account the information needs, the available technology, and constraints on the availability and distribution of information, the communications management plan specifies the frequency and the methods by which information is collected, stored, retrieved, transmitted, and presented to the parties involved in the project. On the basis of the plan, data collection as well as data storage and retrieval systems can be implemented and used throughout the project life cycle. The project communication system that supports the transmission and presentation of information should be designed and established early to facilitate the transfer of information.

Information distribution is based on the communication management plan and occurs throughout the project life cycle. As one can imagine, documentation of ongoing performance with respect to costs, schedule, and resource usage is important for several reasons. In general, performance reporting provides stakeholders with information on the actual status of the project, current accomplishments, and forecasts of future project status, and progress. It is also essential for project control because deviations between plans and actual progress trigger control actions. In addition to the timely distribution of information, historical records are kept to enable post-project analysis in support of organizational and individual learning.

To facilitate an orderly closure of each phase of the project, information on actual performance levels of all activities is collected and compared with the project plan. If a product is the end result, then performance information is similarly collected and compared with the product specifications at each phase of the project. This verification process ensures an ordered, formal acceptance of the project's deliverables by the stakeholders and provides a means for record keeping that supports organizational learning.

Communications planning should answer the following questions.

1. What information is to be provided?
2. Who will be the correspondent?
3. When and in what form is the information to be provided?
4. What templates are to be used?
5. What are the methods for gathering the information to be provided?

6. With what frequency will the information be passed?

7. What form will the communication take—formal, informal, handwritten, oral, hard copy, e-mail?

Information distribution is the implementation of the communication program. If the program is lacking appropriate definition, then it is possible to create a situation of information overload in which too much irrelevant information is passed to the various project participants at too great a frequency. When this happens, essential information may be overlooked, ignored, or lost. To be more precise regarding the appropriateness of various communication channels, we have:

- Informal communication. This is the result of an immediate need for information that was not answered by the communication plan.
- Verbal communication. This is vital in a project setting. The project manager must ensure that team meetings are held on a scheduled basis.

In summary, performance reporting at prescribed milestones and points in time (e.g., quarterly) enables the project manager to compare the actual status of each activity with the baseline. This provides the foundations for the change control process and allows for the collection and aggregation of knowledge. Finally, when the project is completed, the following steps are taken during administrative closure:

1. A project archive is created for future reference.

2. Official sign-off takes place, ensuring that the system developed fulfills the required criteria; if this is not the case, then some adjustments or waivers will be necessary.

3. Lessons learned are formalized with the intention of updating the organization's project management methodology. This is done by interviewing the team members, by analyzing the schedule and budget disruptions, by evaluating the original project plan to determine which assumptions were unrealistic, and by candidly assessing the performance of the participating organizations and personnel.

2.10 PROJECT RISK MANAGEMENT

2.10.1 Accompanying Processes

Risk is an unwelcome but inevitable part of any project or new undertaking. Risk management includes six processes:

1. Risk management planning

2. Risk identification

3. Qualitative risk analysis

4. Quantitative risk analysis

5. Risk response planning

6. Risk monitoring and control

These processes are designed to identify and evaluate possible events that could have a negative impact on the project. In light of the results, contingency measures must be developed to handle each type of disruption identified, as well as any uncertainty that could affect project planning, monitoring, and control.

2.10.2 Description

All projects have some inherent risk as a result of the uncertainty that accompanies any new endeavor. In many industries, the riskier the project, the higher the payoff. Thus, risk is at times beneficial because it has the potential to increase profits. Risk management is not risk avoidance but a method to control risks so that, in the long run, projects provide a net benefit to the organization; i.e., total profits exceed total losses at least. A guiding principle is to find the balance between risks and opportunities.

In trying to categorize a person's attitude toward risk, we have those who are risk averse, risk prone, or risk natural. For different circumstances and payoffs, the same person can fall into any of these categories. In Chapter 3, we discuss how to construct individual utility functions that capture risk attitudes in specific situations. In project management, these functions should reflect the inclination of the organization rather than a project manager. Risks can affect the scope, quality, schedule, cost, and other goals of the project such as client satisfaction. Major risks should be handled by performing a Pareto analysis to assess their magnitude. As a historical footnote, Villefredo Pareto studied the distribution of wealth in the 18th century in Milan and found that 20% of the city's families controlled approximately 80% of its wealth. His findings proved to be more general than the initial purpose of his study. In many populations, it turns out that a small percentage of the population (say, 15%–25%) accounts for a significant portion of a measured factor (say, 75%–85%). This phenomenon is known as the Pareto rule. Using this rule, it is possible to focus one's attention on the most important items in a population. Thus, in risk management, by focusing on the 10%–20% of the risks with the highest magnitude, it is possible to take care of approximately 80% of the total risk impact on the project.

In a Pareto analysis, events that might have the most severe effect on the project are identified first, for example, by examining the history of similar projects. A risk checklist is then created with the help of team members and outside experts. Next, the magnitude of each item on the list is assessed in terms of impact and probability. Multiplying these terms together gives the expected loss for that risk. When probability estimates are not readily available, methods such as simulations and expert judgments can be used.

A risk event is a discrete random occurrence that cannot be factored into the project plan explicitly. Risk events are identified on the basis of the potential difficulty that they impose on (1) achieving the project's objectives (the characteristics of the product or service), (2) meeting the schedule and budget, and (3) satisfying resource requirements. The environment in which the project is performed is also a potential source of risk. Historical information is an important input in the risk identification process. In high-tech projects, for example, knowledge gaps are a common source of risk. Efforts to develop, use, or integrate new technologies necessarily involve uncertainty and, hence, risk. External sources of risk include new laws, transportation delays, raw material shortages, and labor union problems. Internal difficulties or disagreements may also generate risks.

The probability of risk events and their magnitude and effect on project success are estimated during the risk quantification process. The goal of this process is to rank risks in order of the probability of occurrence and the level of impact on the project. Thus, a high risk is an event that is highly probable and may cause substantial damage. On the basis of the magnitude of risk associated with each risk event, a risk response is developed. Several responses are used in project management, including:

- Risk elimination—in some projects, it is possible to eliminate some risks altogether by using, for example, a different technology or a different supplier.
- Risk reduction—if risk elimination is too expensive or impossible, then it may be possible to reduce the probability of a risk event or its impact or both. A typical example is redundancy in R&D projects when two mutually exclusive technologies are developed in parallel to reduce the risk that a failure in development will harm the project. Although only one of the alternative technologies will be used, the parallel effort reduces the probability of a failure.
- Risk sharing—it is possible in some projects to share risks (and benefits) with some stakeholders such as suppliers, subcontractors, partners, or even the client. Buying insurance is another form of risk sharing.
- Risk absorption—if a decision is made to absorb the risk, then buffers in the form of management reserve or extra time in the schedule can be used. In addition, it may be appropriate to develop contingency plans to help cope with the consequences of any disruptions.

Because information is collected throughout the life cycle of a project, new information is used to update the risk management plan continuously. Risk response control implies the need for a continuous effort to identify new sources of risk, to update the estimates regarding probabilities and impacts of risk events, and to activate the risk management plan when needed. By constantly monitoring progress and updating the risk management plan, the impact of uncertainty can be reduced and the probability of project success can be increased. Being on the lookout for symptoms of risk is the first step in warding off trouble before it begins. One way to do this is to formulate a list of the most prominent risks to be checked periodically. Because risks change with time, the list must be updated continuously and new estimates of their impact and probability of occurrence must be derived.

2.11 PROJECT PROCUREMENT MANAGEMENT

2.11.1 Accompanying Processes

Procurement management for projects consists of the following six processes:

1. Procurement planning
2. Solicitation planning
3. Solicitation
4. Source selection

5. Contract administration
6. Contract closeout

These processes accompany the acquisition of goods and services from sources outside the performing organization, such as consultants, subcontractors, and suppliers. The decision to acquire such goods and services (the "make or buy" decision discussed in the next chapter) has a short-term or tactical-level (project-related) impact as well as a long-term or strategic-level (organization-related) impact. At the strategic level, core competencies should rarely be outsourced, even when such action can reduce the project cost, shorten its duration, reduce its risk, or improve quality. At the tactical level, outsourcing can alleviate resource shortages, help in closing knowledge gaps, and increase the probability of project success. Management of the outsourcing process from supplier selection to contract closeout is another important part of the project manager's job.

2.11.2 Description

The decision on which parts of a project to purchase from outside sources, and how and when to do it, is critical to the success of most projects. This is because significant parts of many projects are candidates for outsourcing and the level of uncertainty and consequent risk is different from the corresponding measures associated with activities performed in-house. To gain a competitive advantage from outsourcing, the planning, execution, and control of outsourcing procedures must be well defined and supported by data and models.

The first step in the process is to consider which parts of the project scope and product scope to outsource. This decision is related to capacity and know-how and can be crucial in achieving the project goals; however, a conflict may exist between the project goals and the goals of the stakeholders. For example, subcontracting may help a firm in a related industry develop the skills and capabilities that would give it a competitive advantage at some future time. This was the case with IBM, who outsourced the development of the disk operating system to Microsoft and the development of the central processing unit to Intel. The underlying analysis should take into account the cost, quality, speed, risk, and flexibility of in-house development versus the use of subcontractors or suppliers to deliver the same goods and services. The decisions should also take into account the long-term or strategic factors discussed earlier. Some additional considerations are

- the prospect of ultimately producing a less-expensive product with higher quality
- the lack of in-house skills or qualifications as defined by prevailing laws and regulations
- the ability to shift risks to the supplier

Once the decision to outsource is made, the following questions must be addressed:

- Should the purchase be made from a single supplier, or should a bid be issued?
- Should the purchase be for a single project or for a group of projects?
- Should finished products or parts be purchased or just the labor hours and have the work done in-house?

- How much should be purchased if, for example, quantity discounts are available?
- When should the purchase be made? There is a tradeoff between time at which a spending commitment is made and the risk associated with delaying the purchase.
- Should the idea of shared purchases be considered whereby joint orders are placed with (competing) organizations to receive quantity discounts or better contractual terms?

Once a decision is made to outsource, the solicitation process begins. This step requires an exact definition of the goods or services to be purchased, the development of due dates and cost estimates, and the preparation of a list of potential sources. Various types of models can be used to support the process by arraying the alternatives and their attributes against one another and allowing the decision maker to input his or her preferences for each attribute. The use of simple scoring models, such as those described in Chapter 5, or more sophisticated methods, such as those described in Chapter 6, can help the stakeholders reach a consensus by making the selection process more objective.

In conjunction with selecting a vendor, a contractual agreement is drawn up that is based on the following items:

1. Memorandum of understanding. This is a nonobligatory legal document that provides the foundations for the contract. It is preliminary to the contract.
2. SOW—description of required work to be purchased. The SOW offers the vendor a better understanding of the customer's expectations.
3. Product technical specifications.
4. Acceptance test procedure.
5. Terms and conditions—defines the contractual terms.

The contract is a legal binding document that should specify the following:

1. What—scope of work (deliverables)
2. Where—location of work
3. When—period of performance
4. Schedule for deliverables
5. Applicable standards
6. Acceptance criteria—the criteria that must be satisfied for the project to be accepted
7. Special requirements related to testing, documentation, standards, safety, and so on

Solicitation can take many forms. One extreme is a request for proposal (RFP) advertised and open to all potential sources; a direct approach to a single preferred (or only) source is another extreme. There are many options in between, such as requests for letters of inquiry, qualification statements, and pre-proposals. The main output of the solicitation process is one or more proposals for the goods or services required.

A well-planned solicitation planning process followed by a well-managed solicitation process is required for the next step—source selection—to be successful. Source selection is required whenever more than one acceptable vendor is available. If a proper selection model is developed during the solicitation planning process and all of the data required for the model are collected from the potential vendors during the solicitation process, then the rest is easy. On the basis of the evaluation criteria and organizational policies, proposals are evaluated and ranked to identify the top candidates. Negotiations with a handful of them follow to get their best and final offer. The process is terminated when a contract is signed. If, however, solicitation planning and the solicitation process do not yield a clear set of criteria and a manageable selection model, then source selection may become a difficult and time-consuming process; it may not end with the best vendor selected or the best possible contract signed. It is difficult to compare proposals that are not structured according to clear RFP requirements; in many cases, important information may be missing.

Throughout the life cycle of a project, contracts are managed as part of the execution and change control efforts. Deliverables in the form of test results, prototype models, subassemblies, documentation, and software, to name a few, are submitted and evaluated, payments are made; and, when necessary, change requests are issued. When these are approved, changes are made to the contract. Contract management is equivalent to the management of a work package performed in-house; therefore, similar tools are required during the contract administration process.

Contract closeout is the final process that signals formal acceptance and closure. On the basis of the original contract and all of the approved changes, the goods or services provided are evaluated and, if accepted, payment is made and the contract is closed. Information collected during this process is important for future projects and vendor selection. Effective management is based on such information.

2.12 THE LEARNING ORGANIZATION AND CONTINUOUS IMPROVEMENT

2.12.1 Individual and Organizational Learning

To excel as a project manager, an individual must have expertise in a number of arenas—planning, initiation, execution, supervision—and an ability to recognize when each phase of a project has been completed successfully and the next phase is ready to begin. If such an individual has facility with all aspects of the managerial process, then he or she will be in a prime position to educate, challenge, stimulate, direct, and inspire those whose work he or she is overseeing. In part by virtue of the authority with which he or she has been vested and in part by virtue of the expertise he or she will have accrued from years of experience along the way, a good project manager will be able to serve as a powerfully effective role model and as a source of knowledge and inspiration for those less experienced than he or she. In essence, organizational growth and development can be enhanced by way of this "trickle-down" effect from a project manager who enjoys his or her work and takes pride in doing it well; is him- or herself reliable, committed, and disciplined; can foster development of a strong work ethic and a sense of prideful accomplishment in those whom he or she is managing; and is a font of knowledge, a master strategist, and a visionary who never loses sight of the long-term goal.

The ability of groups to improve performance by learning parallels the same abilities found in individuals. Katzenbach and Smith (1993) explained how to combine individual learning with team building, a key component of any collective endeavor. Just as it is important for each person to learn and master his or her assignment in a project, it is equally important for the group to learn how to work as a team. By establishing clear processes with well-defined inputs and outputs and by ensuring that those responsible for each process master the tools and techniques necessary to produce the desired output, excellence in project management can be achieved.

2.12.2 Workflow and Process Design as the Basis of Learning

The one-time, nonrepetitive nature of projects means that uncertainty is a major factor that affects a project's success. In addition, the ability to learn by repetition is limited because of the uniqueness of most projects. A key to project management success is the exploitation of the repetitive parts of the project scope. By identifying repetitive processes (both within and between projects) and by building an environment that supports learning and data collection, limited resources can be more effectively allocated. Reuse of products and procedures is also a key to project success. For example, in software projects, the reuse of modules and subroutines reduces development time and cost.

A valuable step in the creation of an environment that supports learning is the design and implementation of a workflow management system—a system that embodies the decision-making processes associated with each aspect of the project. Beginning with the processes discussed in this chapter, each should be studied, defined, and implemented within a workflow management system. Definitional elements include the trigger or initiation mechanism of the process, inputs and outputs, skills and resource requirements, activities performed, data required, models used, relative order of execution, termination conditions, and, finally, an enumeration of results or deliverables. The workflow management system uses a workflow enactment system or workflow process engine that can create, manage, and execute multiple process instances.

By identifying processes that are common to more than one project within an organization, it is possible to implement a workflow system that supports and even automates those processes. Automation means that the routing of each process is defined along with the input information, processing tools and techniques, and output information. Although the product scope may vary substantially from project to project, when the execution of the project scope is supported by an automatic workflow system, the benefits are twofold: (1) the level of uncertainty is reduced because processes are clearly defined and the flow of information required to support those processes is automatic, and (2) learning is enabled. In general, a well-structured process can be taught easily to new employees or learned by repetition. For the organization that deals with many similar projects, efficiency is greatly enhanced when the same processes are repeated, the same formats are used to present information, and the same models are used to support decision making. The workflow management system provides the structure for realizing this efficiency.

2.13 ORGANIZATIONAL PROJECT MANAGEMENT MATURITY MODEL

Recently, PMI developed a new standard called the Organizational Project Management Maturity Model (OPM3; PMI 2003) aimed at evaluating an organization's ability to effectively support projects, programs, and portfolios. Its major contribution is that it expands the scope of the PMBOK much beyond the management of single projects.

The evaluation process is based on a four-dimensional matrix. The first dimension includes the following three domains: individual projects; programs, in which each consists of a few related projects; and the full project portfolio. Whereas individual projects are managed locally for the most part, programs and portfolios are managed at a higher level in an organization because of their strategic importance.

The second dimension relates to maturity issues and consists of the following four stages: standardization, measurement, control, and improvement. The third dimension relates to the sequential classification of processes identified in Section 2.2.2: initiation, planning, execution, control, and closeout. All five can be found in the three domains mentioned above (projects, programs, and portfolio). The fourth dimension focuses on best practices. There are a finite number of best practices that may be used for managing both the four maturity stages and the various aspects of the five processes.

One of the primary purposes of OPM3 is to identify which best practices are being used by the organization. To claim that a best practice is part of the business culture, tangible evidence should exist concerning the relevant capabilities. If a certain best practice, say, "establish an internal project management community," is absent and the organization wishes to realize it, then a specific plan for achieving the desired capabilities should be developed. For this example, the following four capabilities, arranged hierarchically, provide a plan outline.

> Level 1: Facilitate project management activities
> Level 2: Develop awareness of project management activities
> Level 3: Sponsor project management activities
> Level 4: Coordinate project management activities

The general understanding is that each capability is achieved only after all those below it are achieved; that is, a best practice exists only when the highest level of capability is realized in the organization.

TEAM PROJECT

Thermal Transfer Plant

Develop two project life-cycle models for the plant. Focus on the phases in the model and answer the following questions.

1. What should be done in each phase?
2. What are the deliverables?
3. How should the output of each phase be verified?

Discuss the pros and cons of each life-cycle model, and select the one that you believe is best. Explain your choice.

DISCUSSION QUESTIONS

1. Explain what a project life cycle is.
2. Draw a diagram showing the spiral life-cycle model for a particular project.
3. Draw a diagram showing the waterfall life-cycle model for a particular project.
4. Discuss the pros and cons of the spiral project life-cycle model and the waterfall project life-cycle model.
5. How are the processes in the PMBOK related to each other? Give a specific example.
6. How are the processes in the PMBOK related to the project life cycle? Give a specific example.
7. If time to market is the most important competitive advantage for an organization, then which life-cycle model should it use for its projects? Explain.
8. What are the main deliverables of project integration?
9. What are the relationships between a learning organization and the project management processes?
10. What are the characteristics of a good project manager?

EXERCISES

2.1 Find an article describing a national project in detail. On the basis of the article and of your understanding of the project, answer the questions below. State any assumptions that you believe are necessary to provide answers.
   a. Who were the stakeholders?
   b. Was it an internal or external project?
   c. What were the most important resources used in the project? Explain.
   d. What were the needs and expectations of each stakeholder?
   e. What were the alternative approaches for this project?
   f. Was the approach selected for the project the best in your opinion? Explain.
   g. What were the risks in the project?
   h. Rank the risks according to severity.
   i. What was done or could have been done to mitigate those risks?
   j. Was the project a success? Why?
   k. Was there enough outsourcing in the project? Explain.
   l. What lessons can be learned from this project?

2.2 Find an article that discusses workflow management systems (e.g., Stohr and Zhao 2001) and explain the following:
   a. What are the advantages of workflow systems?
   b. Under what conditions is a workflow system useful in a project environment?
   c. Which of the processes described in the PMBOK are most suitable for workflow systems?
   d. What are the disadvantages of using a workflow system in a project environment?

2.3 On the basis of the material in this chapter and any outside sources you can find, answer the following.
   a. Define what is meant by a "learning organization."
   b. What are the building blocks of a learning organization?
   c. What are the advantages of a learning organization?
   d. What should be done to promote a learning organization in the project environment?

BIBLIOGRAPHY

Adler, P. S., A. Mandelbaum, V. Nguyen and E. Schwerer, "From Project to Process Management: An Empirically-Based Framework for Analyzing Product Development Time," *Management Science,* Vol. 41, No. 3, pp. 458–484, 1995.

Boehm, B., "A Spiral Model of Software Development and Enhancement," *IEEE Computer,* Vol. 21, No. 5, pp. 61–72, 1988.

Franco, C. A., "Learning Organizations: A Key for Innovation and Competitiveness," *1997 Portland International Conference on Management of Engineering and Technology,* pp. 345–348, July 27–31, 1997.

Fricke, S. E. and A. J. Shenhar, "Managing Multiple Engineering Projects in a Manufacturing Support Environment," *IEEE Transactions on Engineering Management,* Vol. 47, No. 2, pp. 258–268, 2000.

Garvin, D. A., "Competing on the Eight Dimensions of Quality," *Harvard Business Review,* Vol. 65, No. 6, pp. 101–110, November–December 1987.

ISO 9000 Revisions Progress to FDIS Status, press release ref. 779, International Organization for Standardization, Geneva, Switzerland, 2000.

Katzenbach, R. J. and K. D. Smith, *The Wisdom of Teams,* Harvard Business School Press, Boston, MA, 1993.

Keil, M., A. Rai, J. E. C. Mann and G. P. Zhang, "Why Software Projects Escalate: The Importance of Project Management Constructs," *IEEE Transactions on Engineering Management,* Vol. 50, No. 3, pp. 251–261, 2003.

Morris, P. W. G., "Managing Project Interfaces: Key Points for Project Success," in D. I. Cleland and W. R. King (Editors), *Project Management Handbook,* Second Edition, Prentice Hall, Englewood Cliffs, NJ, 1988.

Muench, D., *The Sybase Development Framework,* Sybase, Oakland, CA, 1994.

PMI Standards Committee, *A Guide to the Project Management Body of Knowledge (PMBOK),* Project Management Institute, Newton Square, PA, 2000 (http://www.PMI.org).

PMI, *Organizational Project Management Maturity Model,* Project Management Institute, Newton Square, PA, 2003.

Shtub, A., "Project Management Cycle—Process Used to Manage Projects (Steps to go Through)," in G. Salvendy (Editor), *Handbook of Industrial Engineering: Technology and Operations Management,* Third Edition, pp. 1246–1251, John Wiley & Sons, New York, 2001.

Shtub, A., J. F. Bard and S. Globerson, *Project Management Engineering, Technology, and Implementation,* Prentice Hall, Englewood Cliffs, NJ, 1994.

Stevenson, T. H. and F. C. Barnes, "Fourteen Years of ISO 9000: Impact, Criticisms, Costs and Benefits," *Business Horizons,* Vol. 44, No. 3, pp. 45–51, 2001.

Stohr, E. A. and J. L. Zhao, "Workflow Automation: Overview and Research Issues," *Information Systems Frontiers,* Vol. 3, No. 3, p. 281, 2001.

U.S. Department of Defense Directive 5000.2, 1993.

U.S. Department of Defense, "Parametric Software Cost Estimating," in *Parametric Estimating Handbook,* Second Edition, International Society of Parametric Analysts (ISPA), 1999 (http://www.jsc.nasa.gov/bu2/PCEHHTML/pceh.htm).

Wyrick, D. A., "Understanding Learning Styles to Be a More Effective Team Leader and Engineering Manager," *Engineering Management Journal,* Vol. 15, No. 1, pp. 27–33, 2003.

Chapter 3

Engineering Economic Analysis

3.1 INTRODUCTION

The design of a system represents a decision about how resources will be transformed to achieve a given set of objectives. The final design is a choice of a particular combination of resources and a blueprint for using them; it is selected from among other combinations that would accomplish the same objectives but perhaps with different cost and performance consequences. For example, the design of a commercial aircraft represents a choice of structural materials, size and location of engines, spacing of seats, and so on; the same result could be achieved in any number of ways.

A design must satisfy a host of technical considerations and constraints because only some things are possible. In general, it must conform to the laws of natural science. To continue with the aircraft example, there are limits to the strength of metal alloys or composites and to the thrust attainable from jet engines. The creation of a good design for a system requires solid technical knowledge and competence. Engineers may take this to be self-evident, but it often needs to be stressed to upper management and political leaders, who may be motivated by what a proposed system might accomplish rather than by costs and the limitations of technology.

Economics and value must also be taken into account in the choice of design; the best configuration cannot be determined from technical qualities alone. Moreover, value per dollar spent tends to dominate the final choice of a system. As a general rule, the engineer must pick from among many possible configurations, each of which may seem equally effective from a technical point of view. The selection of the best configuration is determined by comparing the costs and relative values associated with each. The choice between constructing an aircraft of aluminum or titanium is generally a question of cost, as both can meet the required standards. For more complex systems, political or other values may be more important than costs. In planning an airport for a city, for instance, it is usually the case that several sites will be judged suitable. The final choice hinges on societal decisions regarding the relative importance of accessibility, congestion, and other environmental and political impacts, in addition to cost.

The centrality of economic considerations in the design of engineering systems needs to be stressed. The recognition that economic theory is essential to engineering practice is relatively new and thus relatively limited. This new relevance results from the evolution in engineering from the design of components and mechanisms to the design and analysis of systems.

As engineers have become increasingly involved with interoperability and integration of systems, they must deal with new issues and incorporate new methods into their analyses. Traditionally, engineering education and practice have been concerned with detailed design. At that level, technical problems dominate, with economics taking a back seat. In designing an engine for example, the immediate task—and the trademark of the engineer—is to make the device work properly. At the systems level, however, economic considerations are likely to be critical. Thus, the design of a transportation system generally assumes that engines to power vehicles will be available and focuses attention on such issues as whether service can be provided at a price low enough to generate sufficient traffic to make the enterprise worthwhile.

Systems optimization, an integral component of the field known as "operations research," is the prime example of how economic theory has been incorporated into engineering systems analysis. Many key concepts have been adapted with little modification. The production function, the basic model of the way resources are transformed to achieve objectives, comes directly from economics. So does marginal analysis, which is the basic method for solving the resource allocation, or design, problem.

3.1.1 Need for Economic Analysis

The purpose of an economic evaluation is to determine whether any project or investment is financially desirable. Specifically, an evaluation addresses two sorts of questions:

- Is any individual project worthwhile? That is, does it meet our minimum standards?
- Given a list of projects, which is the best? How does each project rank or compare with the others on the list?

This chapter shows how both of these questions should be answered when dealing strictly with cash flows. Chapters 5 and 6 add qualitative considerations to the analysis.

In practice, economic evaluations are difficult to perform correctly. This is in great part because those who are responsible for carrying out the analyses—middle-level managers or staff—necessarily have a limited view of their organization's activities and cannot realistically take into account all of the appropriate factors. The result is that most evaluations are done on the basis of assumptions that often are out of date or otherwise inaccurate for the situation at hand.

Conceptual difficulties are another source of error and confusion. A number of the standard criteria for evaluation contain biases that make them inappropriate and even wrong for particular kinds of situations. Our intention is to focus on these issues so that the practitioner will be able—to the extent possible within the constraints imposed by the employer or the client—to select the most suitable criteria.

The heart of the presentation centers on the various possible criteria that may be used for evaluation. These include net present value (NPV), rate of return (ROR), and payback period. Each method is discussed in detail and then compared with the others. The role that taxes and depreciation play in several common business situations, such as make versus buy, or rent versus own, are also examined. The chapter concludes with a discussion of utility theory that can be used to help decision makers deal with uncertain outcomes.

3.1.2 Time Value of Money

Many projects, particularly large systems, evolve over long periods. Costs incurred in one period may generate benefits for many years to come. The evaluation of whether these projects are worthwhile therefore must compare benefits and costs that occur at different times.

The essential problem in evaluating projects over time is that money has a time value. A dollar now is not the same dollar a year from now. The money represents the same nominal quantity, to be sure, but a dollar later does not have the same usefulness or buying power that it has today. The problem is one of compatibility. Because of this value differential, we cannot estimate total benefits (or costs) simply by adding dollar amounts that are realized in different periods. To make a valid comparison, we need to translate all cash flows into comparable quantities. For purposes of definition, two amounts of money or a series of monies at different points in time are said to be equivalent when they are equal to each other at a given point in time for a given interest rate.

From a mathematical point of view, the solution to the evaluation problem is simple. It consists of using a handful of formulas that depend on only two parameters: the duration, or "life," of the project, n, and the discount rate, i. These formulas are built into many pocket calculators and are routinely embedded in spreadsheet programs available on personal computers. Their results have traditionally been arrayed in extensive tables, which are standard features in engineering handbooks (e.g., see Newnan et al. 2000). In the next three sections, we present these essential formulas and examine their use.

From a practical point of view, the analytic solutions are delicate and must be interpreted with care. The values generated by the formulas are sensitive to their two parameters, which are rarely known with certainty. The results, therefore are, somewhat arbitrary, implying that the problem of evaluating projects over time is a mixture of art and science.

3.1.3 Discount Rate, Interest Rate, and Minimum Acceptable Rate of Return

A dollar today is worth more than a dollar in the future because it can be used productively between now and then. For example, you can place money in a savings account and get a greater amount back after some period. In the economy at large, businesses and governments can use money to build plants, manufacture products, grow food, educate people, and undertake other worthwhile activities.

Moreover, any given amount of money now is typically worth more than the same amount in the future because of inflation. As prices go up as a result of inflation, the current buying power of the dollar erodes. The discount rate is one way of translating cash flows in the future to the present. It is used to determine by how much any future receipt or expenditure is discounted; that is, reduced to make it correspond to an equivalent amount today. The discount rate thus is the key factor in the evaluation of projects over time. It is the parameter that permits us to compare costs and benefits incurred at different instances in time.

The discount rate is generally expressed as an annual percentage. Normally, this percentage is assumed to be constant for any particular evaluation. Because we usually have no reason to believe that it would change in any known way, we take it to be constant over time when looking at any project. It may, however, be different for various individuals, companies, or governments and may also vary among people or groups as circumstances change. Baumol (1968) discussed the effect of the discount rate on social choice, and De Neufville (1990) indicated how to select an appropriate value for both public- and private-sector investments.

The discount rate is similar to what we think of as the prevailing interest rate but is actually a different concept. It is similar in that both can be stated as a percentage per period, and both can indicate a connection between money now and money later. The difference is that the discount rate represents real change in value to a person or a group, as determined by their possibilities for productive use of the money and the effects of inflation. By contrast, the interest rate narrowly defines a contractual arrangement between a borrower and a lender. This distinction implies a general rule: *discount rate > interest rate.* Indeed, if people were not getting more value from the money that they borrow than the interest that they pay for it, then they would be silly to go to the trouble of incurring the debt.

Having said all this, it is common in the engineering economic literature to use the terms *discount rate* and *interest rate* interchangeably. A third term, *minimum acceptable rate of return* (MARR), also has the same meaning. In the remainder of the book, we follow convention and take all three terms to be synonymous unless otherwise indicated.

3.2 COMPOUND INTEREST FORMULAS

Whenever the interest charge for any period is based on the remaining principal to be repaid plus any accumulated interest charges up to the beginning of that period, the interest is said to be compound. Basic compound interest formulas and factors that assume discrete (lump-sum) payments and discrete interest periods are discussed in this section. The notation used to present the concepts is summarized below:

i =   interest rate per interest period, sometimes referred to as the discount rate or MARR; given as a decimal number in the formulas below (e.g., 12% is equivalent to 0.12)

n =   number of compounding periods

P =   present sum of money (equivalent worth of one or more cash flows at a point in time called the present)

F =   future sum of money (equivalent worth of one or more cash flows at a point in time called the future)

A_n =   discrete payment or receipt occurring at the end of some interest period n

A = end-of-period cash flow (or equivalent end-of-period value) in a uniform series continuing for n periods (sometimes called "annuity"); special case in which $A_1 = A_2 = \cdots = A_n = A$

G = gradient or amount by which end-of-period cash flows increase or decrease linearly (arithmetic gradient); $A_n = A_1 + (n - 1)G$

g = gradient or amount by which end-of-period cash flows increase or decrease geometrically; $A_n = A_1(1 + g)^{n-1}$

The compound interest formulas follow.

Single payment compound amount factor

$$(F/P, i, n) = (1 + i)^n$$

Single payment present worth factor

$$(P/F, i, n) = \frac{1}{(1 + i)^n} = \frac{1}{(F/P, i, n)}$$

Uniform series compound amount factor

$$(F/A, i, n) = \frac{(1 + i)^n - 1}{i}$$

Uniform series sinking fund factor

$$(A/F, i, n) = \frac{i}{(1 + i)^n - 1} = \frac{1}{(F/A, i, n)}$$

Uniform series present worth factor

$$(P/A, i, n) = \frac{(1 + i)^n - 1}{i(1 + i)^n}$$

Uniform series capital recovery factor

$$(A/P, i, n) = \frac{i(1 + i)^n}{(1 + i)^n - 1} = \frac{1}{(P/A, i, n)}$$

Arithmetic gradient present worth factor

$$(P/G, i, n) = \frac{(1 + i)^n - in - 1}{i^2(1 + i)^n}$$

Arithmetic gradient uniform series factor

$$(A/G, i, n) = \frac{(1 + i)^n - in - 1}{i(1 + i)^n - i}$$

Geometric gradient present worth factor

$$(P/A_1, g, i, n) = \frac{1 - (1 + g)^n(1 + i)^{-n}}{g - i} \quad \text{for } i \neq g$$

$$= \frac{n}{(1 + i)} \quad \text{for } i = g$$

Limiting Cases

As $n \rightarrow \infty$: $(F/P, i, n) \rightarrow \infty$, $(P/F, i, n) \rightarrow 0$, $(P/A, i, n) \rightarrow 1/i$, $(A/P, i, n) \rightarrow i$,

$(F/A, i, n) \rightarrow \infty$, $(A/F, i, n) \rightarrow 0$, $(P/G, i, n) \rightarrow 1/i^2$, $(A/G, i, n) \rightarrow 1/i$

For $i = 0$: $(F/P, i, n) = 1$, $(P/F, i, n) = 1$, $(P/A, i, n) = n$, $(A/P, i, n) = 1/n$,

$(F/A, i, n) = n$, $(A/F, i, n) = 1/n$, $(P/G, i, n) = n(n - 1)/2$,

$(A/G, i, n) = (n - 1)/2$

In using the compound interest formulas to solve a problem, it is useful to note that the chain rule is applicable. For example, if you want to find P given F, instead of calculating P with the expression $P = F(P/F, i, n)$, you can make use of the relationship $P = F(A/F, i, n)(P/A, i, n)$ should it be more convenient to do so.

3.2.1 Present Worth, Future Worth, Uniform Series, and Gradient Series

Figure 3.1 is a diagram that shows typical placements of P, F, A, and G over time for n periods with interest at $i\%$ per period. Upward pointing arrows usually indicate payments or disbursements, and downward pointing arrows indicate receipts or savings. As depicted in the figure, the following conventions apply in using the discrete compound interest formulas and corresponding tables:

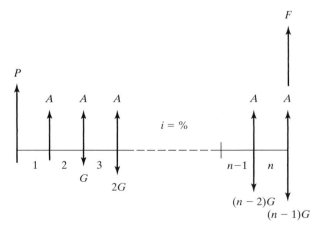

Figure 3.1   Standard cash flow diagram indicating
points in time for P, F, A, and G.

1. *A* occurs at the end of the interest period.
2. *P* occurs one interest period before the first *A*.
3. *F* occurs at the same point in time as the last *A*, and *n* periods after *P*.
4. There is no *G* cash flow at the end of period 1; hence, the total gradient cash flow at the end of period *n* is $(n - 1)G$.

Most economic analyses involve conversion of estimated or given cash flows to some point or points in time, such as the present, per annum, or the future. The specific calculations are best illustrated with the help of examples.

Example 3-1

Suppose that a $20,000 piece of equipment is expected to last 5 years and then result in a $4,000 salvage value; i.e., can be sold for $4,000. If the minimum acceptable rate of return (interest rate) is 15%, then what are the following values?

 (a) Annual equivalent (cost)
 (b) Present equivalent (cost)

Solution   Figure 3.2 shows all of the cash flows.

 (a) $A = -\$20{,}000(A/P, 15\%, 5) + \$4{,}000(A/F, 15\%, 5)$

   $= -20{,}000(0.2983) + 4{,}000(0.1483) = -\$5{,}373$

 [Note: $5,373 is sometimes called the *annual cost* (AC) or *equivalent uniform annual cost* (EUAC).]

 (b) $P = -\$20{,}000 + \$4{,}000(P/F, 15\%, 5)$

   $= -20{,}000 + 4{,}000(0.4972) = -\$18{,}011$

Alternatively, it is possible to solve part (b) by exploiting the results obtained from part (a) as follows:

$$P = A(P/A, 15\%, 5)$$

$$= -\$5{,}373(3.3522) = -\$18{,}011$$

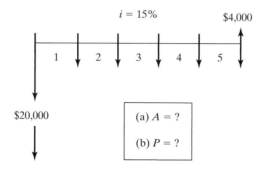

Figure 3.2   Cash flow diagram for Example 3-1.

Example 3-2   (Deferred Uniform Series and Gradient Series)

Suppose that a certain savings is expected to be $10M at the end of year 3 and to increase $1M each year until the end of year 7. If the MARR is 20%, then what are the following values?

(a) Present equivalent (at beginning of year 1)

(b) Future equivalent (at end of year 7)

Solution   Once again, the first step is to draw the cash flow diagram. Figure 3.3 shows the gradient beginning at the end of year 3 and the unknowns to be calculated (dashed arrows). In the solution, subscripts are used to indicate a point or points in time.

(a) $A_{3-7} = \$10M + \$1M(A/G, 20\%, 5)$

$\qquad = \$10M + \$1M(1.6405) = \$11.64M$

$\quad P_2 = A_{3-7}(P/A, 20\%, 5)$

$\qquad = 11.64M(2.9906) = \$34.81M$

$\quad P_0 = F_2(P/F, 20\%, 2)$

$\qquad = \$34.81M(0.6944) = \$24.17M$

Notice that in the last calculation, the value of P_2 is substituted for F_2.

(b) (Skipping intermediate calculations):

$$F_7 = [\$10M + \$1M(A/G, 20\%, 5)](F/A, 20\%, 5)$$

$$= [\$10M + \$1M(1.6405)](7.4416) = \$86.62M$$

Alternatively, one can use part (a) results to obtain F_7 as follows:

$$F_7 = P_0(F/P, 20\%, 7)$$

$$= \$24.17M(3.5832) = \$86.62M$$

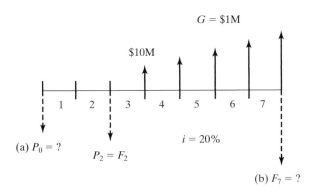

Figure 3.3   Cash flow diagram for Example 3-2
showing deferred uniform and
gradient series.

Example 3-3   (Repeating Cycle of Payments)

Suppose that the equipment in Example 3-1 is expected to be replaced three times with identical equipment, making four life cycles of 5 years each. To compare this investment correctly with another alternative that can serve 20 years, what are the following values when MARR = 15%?

(a) Annual equivalent (cost)

(b) Present equivalent (cost)

Solution   Figure 3.4 shows the costs involved. The key to this type of problem is to recognize that if the cash flows repeat each cycle, then the annual equivalent for one cycle will be the same for all other cycles.

(a) We demonstrate a slightly different way to get the same answer as in Example 3-1.

$$A = [-\$20M + \$4M(P/F, 15\%, 5)](A/P, 15\%, 5)$$
$$= [-\$20M + \$4M(0.4972)](0.2983) = -\$5,373K$$

(b) $P = -\$5,373K(P/A, 15\%, 20)$
$$= -\$5,373K(6.2593) = -\$33,629K \qquad \blacksquare$$

3.2.2 Nominal and Effective Interest Rates

Interest rates are often quoted many different ways. In standard terminology, we have

Nominal interest rate, r, is the annual interest rate without considering the effects of compounding.

Effective interest rate, i_{eff}, is the annual interest rate taking into account the effects of compounding during the year.

To work with these rates, it is necessary to know the number of compounding periods per year, denoted by p. The nominal interest rate is typically stated as a percentage compounded p times per year.

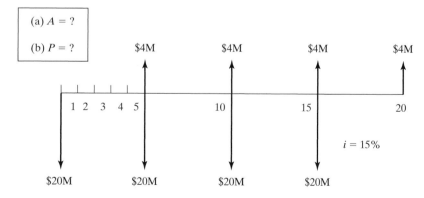

Figure 3.4   Cash flow diagram for Example 3-3.

Example 3-4

The nominal rate is 16%/year compounded quarterly. What is the effective rate?

Solution r = 16%/year divided by 4 = 4%/quarter. On an annual basis, this equals 16.99%/year. The general formula is

$$i_{\text{eff}} = (1 + r/p)^p - 1$$
$$i_{\text{eff}} = (1 + 0.16/4)^4 - 1 = (1.04)4 - 1 = 1.1699 - 1 = 0.1699 \rightarrow 16.99\% \quad \blacksquare$$

Example 3-5   (Nominal vs. Effective Rates)

A credit card company advertises a nominal rate of 16% on unpaid balances compounded daily. What is the effective interest rate per year being charged?

Solution r = 16%/year, p = 365 days/year

$$i_{\text{eff}} = (1 + 0.16/365)^{365} - 1 = 0.1735 \rightarrow 17.35\% \quad \blacksquare$$

In the beginning of this section, i was defined simply as the interest rate per interest period. A more precise definition, we now know, is that i is the effective interest rate per interest period. When compounding is continuous, we have the special case in which $i_{\text{eff}} = e^r - 1$.

3.2.3 Inflation

Inflation is a condition in the economy characterized by rising prices for goods and services. An inflationary trend makes future dollars have less purchasing power than current dollars. This helps long-term borrowers at the expense of lenders because a loan negotiated today will be repaid in the future with dollars of lesser value. Some of the principal causes of inflation are listed below. The general consensus among economists is that excessive deficit spending at the federal level and political instability are the main culprits.

- Shortages of raw materials and basic necessities (too many dollars chasing too few goods bid prices up)
- Government creates too much money that is not backed by hard currency
- Unreasonable demands by labor
- Unreasonable price increases by business
- Inflationary expectations (psychological factors lead to an inflationary spiral)
- Uncertainty about government survival and policies
- Relative strength of currency in international markets

Ways to reduce inflation are to increase the cost of borrowing money for individuals, industry, and the government and to curtail government spending. In the United States, monetary policy is the charge of the Federal Reserve Board, or "Fed," which controls the funds rate and the discount rate. These terms have the following formal meaning:

Funds rate: Rate charged by a depository institution on an overnight sale of federal funds to another depository institution; rate may vary from day to day and from bank to bank.

Discount rate: Interest rate at which an eligible depository institution may borrow funds, typically for a short period, directly from a Federal Reserve Bank. The law requires that the board of directors of each Reserve Bank establish the discount rate every 14 days subject to the approval of the Board of Governors.

Raising or lowering these rates is one of the levers that the Fed uses to keep the lid on inflation as well as to stimulate the economy. Note that a *depository institution* is a financial institution that obtains its funds mainly through deposits from the public and includes commercial banks, savings and loan associations, savings banks, and credit unions.

In an economic analysis, one approach used to compensate for inflation is first to convert all cash flows from year-*n*, or actual dollars into year-0, or real dollars. If the inflation rate is, say *f*, then this can be done by discounting or deflating future dollars to the present as follows:

$$\text{year-0 dollars} = [(1 + f)^{-n}](\text{year-}n \text{ dollars})$$

We would now proceed as before with the analysis. Alternatively, one may compute an interest rate, i', with inflation

$$i' = i + f + i \times f$$

and use it in conjunction with the present worth factors to compute the present value of future cash flows. Either approach should give the same results. The important thing to remember is that all cash flows must be expressed in the same units.

Example 3-6

1. Tuition at Big State University is $2,000 today. We expect college costs to increase at a 6% annual rate. What will tuition be in 10 years?

$$\text{Future tuition} = \$2,000(1 + 0.06)^{10} = \$4,477$$

2. If the cost of a hamburger is $3 today, then what did it cost 40 years ago? Assume the average rate of inflation during that time was 5%.

$$\text{Former price of hamburger} = 3/(1 + 0.05)^{40} = \$0.43 \qquad ■$$

When all receipts and expenses escalate at the same rate as inflation, we can ignore inflation and do the analysis in real dollars using *i*. In practice, however, cash flows may be given in both real and actual dollars, so we must select a constant frame of reference in which to perform the analysis.

Example 3-7

You are considering a $10,000 investment that has a life of 10 years and no salvage. On the basis of today's economic environment, it is estimated that

- operating costs will be $500 per year and revenue $2,000 per year
- the general inflation rate will be 5% ($f = 0.05$)
- operating costs will escalate at the same rate as general inflation
- revenues will not increase with time

For a 4% MARR without inflation ($i = 0.04$), what is the NPV of the investment?

Solution   The components of the cash flow increase at different rates than general inflation, so we must either convert all of them to actual dollars and use the MARR with inflation (i') or convert all of them to real dollars and use the MARR without inflation (i). The analysis for both approaches is presented.

1. Analysis in terms of actual dollars: We first must find the appropriate interest rate:

$$i' = 0.04 + 0.05 - 0.04 \times 0.05 = 0.092 \text{ or } 9.2\%$$

The revenues are already expressed in actual dollars, so it is necessary only to convert the costs to actual dollars. The data in the last column of the first table below represent the present worth (PW) of the cash flow at the end of year n using an MARR of 9.2%.

Time	Costs (actual $)	Revenues (actual $)	Net cash flow	PW(9.2%) (actual $)
0	10,000		−10,000	−10,000
1	525	2,000	1,475	1,351
2	551	2,000	1,449	1,215
3	579	2,000	1,421	1,091
4	608	2,000	1,392	979
5	638	2,000	1,362	877
6	670	2,000	1,330	784
7	704	2,000	1,296	700
8	739	2,000	1,261	624
9	776	2,000	1,224	554
10	814	2,000	1,186	492

NPV = −1,332

2. Analysis in terms of real dollars: For this case, we use $i = 0.04$ to compute PW. To get the net cash flows in each year, it first is necessary to convert revenues to real dollars using the formula

$$\text{Revenue in real \$ (in year } n) = \$2,000/(1.05)^n$$

Time	Costs (real $)	Revenues (real $)	Net cash flow	PW(4%) (real $)
0	10,000		−10,000	−10,000
1	500	1,905	1,405	1,351
2	500	1,814	1,314	1,215
3	500	1,728	1,228	1,091
4	500	1,645	1,145	979
5	500	1,567	1,067	877
6	500	1,492	992	784
7	500	1,421	921	700
8	500	1,354	854	624
9	500	1,289	789	554
10	500	1,228	728	492

NPV = −1,332

As expected, both sets of computations give the same NPV of −$1,332.   ∎

3.2.4 Treatment of Risk

Risk comes in many forms. If a new product is being developed, then the probability of commercial success is a major consideration. If a new technology is being pursued, then we must constantly reevaluate the probability of technical success and the availability of critical personnel and resources. Once a product is ready for the market, such factors as financing, contractual obligations, reliability of suppliers, and strength of competition must be brought into the equation.

In the private sector, projects that are riskier than others are forced to pay higher interest rates to attract capital. A speculative new company will have to pay the banks several percentage points more for its borrowing than will established, prime customers. Private companies, which always run the risk of bankruptcy, have to pay more than the government. This extra amount of interest is know as the *risk premium* and, as a practical matter, is already included in the discount rate.

When a particular project faces uncommon technical or commercial risks, the evaluation process should address each directly. Decision analysis (Chapter 5), coupled with the use of multiple criteria methodologies (Chapter 6), is the preferred way to appraise projects with a high component of risk.

3.3 COMPARISON OF ALTERNATIVES

The essence of all economic evaluation is a discounted cash flow analysis. The first step in every situation is to lay out the estimated cash flows, the sequence of benefits (returns), and costs (payments) over time. These are then discounted back to the present, using the methods shown in the previous section, either directly or indirectly in the case of the rate-of-return and payback period methods.

The relative merits of the available alternatives are determined by comparing the discounted cash flows of benefits and costs. In general, a project is considered to be worthwhile when its benefits exceed its costs. The relative ranking of the projects is then determined by one of several evaluation criteria. The methods of evaluation differ from each other principally in the way in which they handle the results of the discounted cash flow analysis. The present value method focuses on the difference between the discounted benefits and costs, the ratio methods involve various comparisons of these qualities, and the internal rate-of-return method tries to equalize them. The question of what one does with the results of the discounted cash flows is the central problem of economic evaluation.

Most methods presume that the discount rate to be used in the cash flow analysis is known. This is often a reasonable assumption, because many companies or agencies require that a specific rate be used for all of their economic evaluations. In many instances, however, the discount rate must be determined.

In carrying out an evaluation, it will be essential to remember that correct selection of the discount rate may be crucial. Its choice can easily change the ranking of projects, making one or another seem best depending on the rate used. This is because lower rates make long-term projects, with benefits in the distant future, seem much more attractive relative to short-term projects with immediate benefits than they would be if a higher rate were used.

To see this, suppose that your organization has the choice of two storage and retrieval systems, one that requires a human operator and one that is fully automated. Both will last for 10 years. The human-assisted system costs $10,000 and requires $4,200 per year of labor. The automated system has an initial cost of $18,000 and consumes an additional $3,000 per year in power. The decision is a question of whether the benefits of the annual savings ($4,200 − $3,000 = $1,200 a year) justify the additional initial cost of $8,000. Is the NPV of the upgrade to the more expensive alternative positive?

If the discount rate were zero, implying that future benefits are not discounted, then the upgrade is clearly worthwhile.

$$\text{NPV}(i = 0\%) = (\$1,200/\text{yr})(10 \text{ years}) - \$8,000 = \$4,000$$

Conversely, if the discount rate were large, then future benefits would be heavily discounted. For infinite i,

$$\text{NPV}(i = \infty) = \$1,200(0) - \$8,000 = -\$8,000$$

so the project is not worthwhile.

The variation of the NPV with the discount rate is summarized as follows:

$i\%$	0	5	10	15	∞
$\text{NPV}(i\%)$	$4,000	$1,264	−$632	−$1,976	−$8,000

The critical value of i, below which the more expensive system is preferred, is approximately 8.5%, as determined by interpolation.

As this example shows, the choice of the discount rate can steer an analysis in one direction or another. Powerful economic and political forces allied with a particular technology may encourage this. When the U.S. Federal Highway Administration promulgated a regulation in the early 1970s that the discount rate for all federally funded highways would be zero, this was widely interpreted as a victory for the cement industry over asphalt interests. Roads that are made of concrete cost significantly more than those that are made of asphalt but require less maintenance and less frequent replacement.

3.3.1 Defining Investment Alternatives

Every evaluation deals with two distinct sets of projects or alternatives: the explicit and the implicit. The explicit set consists of the opportunities that are to be considered in detail; they are the focus of the analysis. The implicit set, which can only be defined imprecisely, is important because it provides the frame of reference for the evaluation and defines the minimum standards.

Explicit Set of Alternatives.   This is a limited list of the potential projects that could actually be chosen. The list is usually defined by a manager who is concerned with a particular issue; for example,

- an official of the department of highways who is responsible for maintenance and construction of roads
- a manager of a computer center, proposing to acquire new equipment
- an investment officer for a bank, presenting a menu of opportunities for construction loans

The projects suggested by each of the preceding situations illustrate two characteristics typical of the choices considered in an evaluation. The explicit set is

1. Limited in scope, in that it includes only a portion of the projects that might be in front of the organization as a whole. Thus, the manager of the computer center is competent only in and considers only various ways to improve the information systems; whether money should be spent on developing a new product or replacing the central heating is literally not his or her department.
2. Limited in number, being only a fraction of all of the projects that could be defined over the next several years. Usually, the explicit list deals only with the immediate choices, not the ones that could arise during the next budget or decision period.

That the sets of projects that we consider explicitly are limited poses a basic problem for any organization. The difficulty is that any procedure that analyzes separate sets of projects independently can easily lead to a list of recommended choices that are not the best ones for the organization as a whole. For example, consider a company with an information systems department, a research laboratory, and a manufacturing plant: if we evaluate the projects proposed by each group, we can determine the best software, the best instrument, and the best machine tool to buy, but this plan may not be in the best interests of the company. It is possible that the second-best machine tool is a better investment than the best instrument or that none of the software is worthwhile financially.

The issue is: How does an organization ensure that the projects selected by its components are best for the organization as a whole? In addressing this question, we must recognize that the obvious answer, considering all possible projects simultaneously, is neither practical nor even possible. A large number of analyses could be done, but the level of computation is not the real obstacle.

An analysis of all alternatives at once is not practical because it would be extremely difficult for any group in an organization to be sufficiently knowledgeable both to generate the possible projects for all departments and to estimate their benefits and costs. They simply would not have sufficient knowledge of the topic, region, or clients. Furthermore, the analysis of all alternatives at once is not even conceptually feasible because we are unable to predict which options will be available in the future. We therefore can never be sure that the projects that we select from a current list, however comprehensive it may be, will include all of the opportunities that will be available over the life of the projects and that might otherwise be selected. Some degree of suboptimization is unavoidable.

To reduce the likelihood for suboptimization, it is necessary to create some means of evaluating any set of explicit alternatives that do not critically depend on future developments. This can be done by creating a substitute for the universe of possibilities. The implicit alternatives fill this role.

Implicit Set of Alternatives.   This set is intended to represent all projects that were available in the past and that might be available in the near future. Because it refers in part to unknown prospects, it can never be described in detail. It thus indicates inexactly what could be done instead of what can be done by opting for one of the explicit alternatives.

The implicit set of alternatives is of interest because it establishes the minimum standards for deciding whether any explicit project is worthwhile. To illustrate, consider the situation in which a person has consistently been able to choose investments that provide yearly profits of 12% or more and has rejected all others with smaller returns. Faced now with the problem of evaluating an explicit set of specific proposals, this person will naturally turn to past experience for guidance. If the investment possibilities have not changed fundamentally, then the person may assume that there are continued possibilities—the implicit set of alternatives—for earning at least 12% as before and should correctly conclude that any explicit choice can be worthwhile only if its profitability equals or exceeds the 12% implicitly available elsewhere.

The minimum standards suggested by the implicit alternatives can be stated in several ways. An obvious and common way is to stipulate a minimum acceptable rate of return. Minimum standards of profitability can also be expressed differently, however. In business, they are typically stated in terms of the highest number of periods that will be required for the benefits to equal the initial investment (the maximum payback period, see Section 3.4.6). Minimum standards can also be defined in terms of minimum ratios of benefits to costs (Section 5.4).

Organizations use minimum standards for the economic acceptability of projects as the way to reduce the possibility of suboptimization. These standards force each department or group to take into account the global picture. They cannot, for example, choose projects unless they are at least as good as others available elsewhere in the organization.

3.3.2 Steps in the Analysis

A systematic procedure for comparing investment alternatives can be outlined as follows:

1. Define the alternatives.
2. Determine the study period.
3. Provide estimates of the cash flows for each alternative.
4. Specify the interest rate (MARR).
5. Select the measure(s) of effectiveness (i.e., the criteria for judging success).
6. Compare the alternatives.
7. Perform sensitivity analyses.
8. Select the preferred alternative(s).

The study period defines the planning horizon over which the analysis is to be performed. It may or may not be the same as the useful lives of the equipment, facility, or project involved. In general, if the study period is less than the useful life of an asset, then an estimate of its salvage value should be provided in the final period; if the study period is longer than the useful life, then estimates of cash flows are needed for subsequent replacements of the asset.

Whenever alternatives that have different lives are to be compared, the study period is usually one of the following:

1. The organization's traditional planning horizon
2. The life of the shortest-lived alternative

3. The life of the longest-lived alternative

4. The lowest common multiple of the lives of the alternatives

When the study period for the alternatives is forced to be the same by using measures 1, 2, or 3 above or for any other reason, the so-called *coterminated assumption* is said to apply and whatever cash flows are thought appropriate are considered within that study period. When the study period is chosen by measure 4 above, the alternatives normally are assumed to satisfy the following so-called *repeatability assumptions*.

1. The period of needed service is either indefinitely long or a common multiple of the lives.

2. What is estimated to happen in the first life cycle will happen in all succeeding life cycles, if any, for each alternative.

In the upcoming subsections that illustrate the various analytic methods, when alternatives have different lives and nothing is indicated to the contrary, the repeatability assumptions are used. These assumptions are commonly adopted for computational convenience. The decision maker must decide whether they are reasonable for the situation.

3.4 EQUIVALENT WORTH METHODS

For purposes of analysis, *equivalent worth methods* convert all relevant cash flows into equivalent (present, annual, or future) amounts using the MARR. If a single project is under consideration, then it is acceptable (earns at least the MARR) if its equivalent worth is greater than or equal to zero; otherwise, it is not acceptable. These methods all assume that recovered funds (net cash inflows) can be reinvested at the MARR.

If two or more mutually exclusive alternatives are being compared and receipts or savings (cash inflows) as well as costs (cash outflows) are known, then the project that has the highest net equivalent worth should be chosen, as long as that equivalent worth is greater than or equal to zero. If only costs are known or considered (assuming that all alternatives have the same benefits), then the project that has the lowest total equivalent of those costs should be chosen. Because all three equivalent worth methods give completely consistent results, the choice of which to use is a matter of computational convenience and preference for the form in which the results are expressed.

3.4.1 Present Worth Method

Present worth (PW) denotes a lump-sum amount at some early point in time (often the present) that is equivalent to a particular schedule of receipts and/or disbursements under consideration. If receipts and disbursements are included in the analysis, then PW can best be expressed as the difference between the present worth of benefits and the present value of costs, otherwise known as NPV.

Example 3-8

Consider the following two mutually exclusive alternatives and recommend which one (if either) should be implemented.

	Machine	
	A	B
Initial cost	$20,000	$30,000
Life	5 years	10 years
Salvage value	$4,000	0
Annual receipts	$10,000	$14,000
Annual disbursements	$4,400	$8,600
Minimum acceptable rate of return = 15%		
Assume 10-year study period and repeatability		

Solution   (using PW method)

	Machine	
	A	B
Annual receipts		
$10,000(P/A, 15\%, 10)$	$50,188	
$14,000(P/A, 15\%, 10)$		$70,263
Salvage value at end of		
year 10 = $4,000(P/F, 15\%, 10)$	$989	0
Total PW of cash inflow	$51,177	$70,263
Annual disbursements:		
$4,400(P/A, 15\%, 10)$	−$22,083	
$8,600(P/A, 15\%, 10)$		−$43,162
Initial cost	−$20,000	−$30,000
Replacement:		
$($20,000 − $4,000)(P/F, 15\%, 5)$	−$7,955	0
Total PW of cash outflow	−$50,038	−$73,162
Net PW (NPV)	$1,139	−$2,899

Thus, project A has the higher NPV and represents the better economic choice. That the NPV of project B is negative makes it unacceptable in any case.   ■

3.4.2 Annual Worth Method

Annual worth (AW) is merely an "annualized" measure for assessing the financial desirability of a proposed undertaking. It is a uniform series of money over a certain period of time that is equivalent in amount to a particular schedule of receipts and/or disbursements under consideration. Any "period" can be used in the analysis, such as a month or a week. The word "annual" is viewed as generic. If only disbursements are included, then the term is usually expressed as *annual cost* (AC) or EUAC. The examples in this section include both cash inflows and outflows.

Calculation of Capital Recovery Cost.   The *capital recovery* (CR) *cost* for a project is the EUAC of the capital that is invested. It is an annual amount that covers the following two items.

1. Depreciation (loss in value of the asset)
2. Interest (MARR) on invested capital

Consider an alternative requiring a lump-sum investment P and a salvage value S at the end of n years. At interest rate i per year, the annual equivalent cost can be calculated as

$$CR = P(A/P, i, n) - S(A/F, i, n)$$

There are several other formulas for calculating the CR cost. Probably the most common is

$$CR = (P - S)(A/P, i, n) + Si$$

One might want to reverse signs so that a cost is negative, as is done in the following example, which includes CR costs in an AW comparison.

Example 3-9

Given the same machines A and B as used to demonstrate the net PW method in Example 3-8, we now compare them by the net AW method.

	Machine	
	A	B
Initial cost	$20,000	$30,000
Life	5 years	10 years
Salvage value	$4,000	0
Annual receipts	$10,000	$14,000
Annual disbursements	$4,400	$8,600
Minimum acceptable rate of return = 15%		
Assume repeatability		

Solution   (using AW method)

	Machine	
	A	B
Annual receipts	$10,000	$14,000
Annual disbursements	−$4,400	−$8,600
CR amount: −$20,000($A/P$, 15%, 5)	−$5,966	
+$4,000($A/F$, 15%, 5)	+$593	
−$30,000($A/P$, 15%, 10)		−$5,978
Net AW	$227	−$578

Thus, project A, having the higher net annual worth, which also is greater than $0, is the better economic choice. A shortcut for calculating the net AWs given the net PWs calculated in the preceding section is

$$AW(A) = \$1,139(A/P, 15\%, 10) = \$227$$
$$AW(B) = -\$2,889(A/P, 15\%, 10) = -\$578$$

One significant computational shortcut when comparing alternatives with different lives by the PW method and assuming repeatability is first to calculate AWs as above and then calculate the PWs for the lowest common multiple-of-lives study period. Thus,

$$PW(A) = \$227(P/A, 15\%, 10) = \$1,139$$
$$PW(B) = -\$578(P/A, 15\%, 10) = -\$2,899$$ ■

3.4.3 Future Worth Method

The *future worth* (FW) measure of merit is a lump-sum amount at the end of the study period which is equivalent to the cash flows under consideration.

Example 3-10

Given the same machines A and B (Examples 3-8 and 3-9), determine which is better on the basis of FW at the end of the 10-year study period.

Solution   (using FW method) Rather than calculating FWs of all of the types of cash flows involved (as was done for the PW solution above), shown below are shortcut solutions based on (a) PWs and (b) AWs calculated previously:

(a) $FW(A) = \$1,139(F/P, 15\%, 10) = \$4,608$

$FW(B) = -\$2,899(F/P, 15\%, 10) = -\$11,728$

(b) $FW(A) = \$227(F/A, 15\%, 10) = \$4,608$

$FW(B) = -\$578(F/A, 15\%, 10) = -\$11,735$

Not surprisingly, we have once again found that alternative A is preferred. The ratios of the numbers produced by each of the equivalent worth methods will always be the same. For machines A and B, $FW(A)/FW(B) = PW(A)/PW(B) = AW(A)/AW(B) = -0.393$.   ∎

Example 3-11   (Different Useful Lives: Fixed-Length Study Period)

Suppose that two measurement instruments are being considered for a certain industrial laboratory. Following are the principal cost data for one life cycle of each alternative:

	Instrument	
	M1	M2
Investment	$15,000	$25,000
Life	3 years	5 years
Salvage value	0	0
Annual disbursements	$4,400	$8,600
Minimum acceptable rate of return = 20%		
Assume no repeatability		

Which instrument is preferred?

Solution   The calculations will be done using the PW method and MARR = 20% for the following two cases:

1. If the study period is taken to be 3 years, then we need a salvage value for alternative M2 at the end of the third year. Assuming it to be, say, $6,000, the following results are obtained:

	Instrument	
	M1	M2
Investment	$15,000	$25,000
Annual disbursements:		
$8,000(A/P, 20%, 3)$	$16,852	
$5,000(A/P, 20%, 3)$		$10,533
Salvage: $-$6,000(A/F, 20%, 3)$		$-$3,472
Net PW (NPV)	$31,852	$32,061

Thus, the first alternative is slightly better. Note that "+" is used for costs.

2. If the study period is taken to be 5 years, then we need estimates of what will happen after the first life cycle of alternative M1. Let us assume that it can be replaced at the beginning of the fourth year for $18,000 and that the annual disbursements will be $9,000 for years 4 and 5. Furthermore, it will have a $7,000 salvage value at the end of year 5. In this case, we obtain

	Instrument	
	M1	M2
Investment	$15,000	$25,000
Annual disbursements:		
$8,000(A/P, 20%, 3)$	$16,852	
$9,000(P/A, 20%, 2)(P/F, 20%, 3)$	$7,975	
$5,000(A/P, 20%, 5)$		$14,953
Additional investment: $18,000(P/F, 20%, 3)$	$10,147	
Salvage: $-$7,000(P/F, 20%, 5)$	$-$2,813	
NPV	$47,413	$39,953

Thus, alternative M2 has a slightly lower net PW and hence is better with the new assumption. ■

3.4.4 Discussion of Present Worth, Annual Worth, and Future Worth Methods

Some academics and accountants assert that the net PW methods—and in particular, the NPV criterion—should be used in all economic analyses. This prescription should be resisted. NPV (and its equivalents) provides a good comparison between projects only when they are strictly comparable in terms of level of investment or total budget. This condition is rarely met in the real world. The practical consequence is that NPVs are used primarily for the analysis of investments, particularly of specific sums of money, rather than for the evaluation of projects, which come in many different sizes.

The advantage of the net PW criteria is that they focus attention on quantity of money, which is what the evaluation is ultimately concerned with. Net PW, AW, and FW differ in this respect from the other criteria of evaluation, which rank projects by ratios and hence do not directly address the bottom-line question of maximizing profit.

One disadvantage of NPV is that its precise meaning is difficult to explain; practical-minded people such as businesspeople thus tend to avoid the concept. NPV suggests profit but in fact is not profit in any usual sense of the term. In ordinary language, profit is the difference between what we receive and what we pay out. As an example, consider an investment now for a lump sum of revenue later. In crude terms,

$$\text{profit} = \text{money received} - \text{money invested}$$

More precise, if we had to borrow money to make the original investment, then the profit would be net of interest paid for n periods:

$$\text{profit} = \text{money received} - (\text{money invested})(F/P, i, n)$$

where i is the interest rate. This profit can also be placed in present value terms using the appropriate MARR for the organization concerned. Note that it is now important to make the distinction between the MARR and the interest rate:

$$\text{present value of profit} = (\text{money received})(P/F, \text{MARR}, n)$$
$$- (\text{money invested})(F/P, i, n)(P/F, \text{MARR}, n)$$

In the last calculation, it turns out that because the MARR is not, in general, equal to the interest rate, NPV $\neq$ present value of profit. Thus, even when the NPV equals zero, the project may be profitable, as understood in common language. A project with NPV $= 0$ is simply not advantageous compared with other alternatives available to the organization. NPV thus indicates "extra profitability" beyond the minimum. As a reader, you probably found it difficult to grasp this subtlety. This demonstrates the point that NPV may be a questionable measure to use.

Another difficulty with the net PW criteria is that they give no indication of the scale of effort required to achieve the result. To see this, consider the problem of evaluating projects P1 and P2 below.

Project	Benefit	Cost	NPV	NPV as % of cost
P1	$2,002,000	$2,000,000	$2,000	0.1
P2	$2,000	$1,000	$1,000	100

If one considers only NPV, then project P1 seems better. Most investors would consider that an absurd choice, however, because of the difference in scale between the projects. Taking scale into account, P2 presumably gives a much better return than P1: the money saved by investing in the former rather than the latter can be invested elsewhere for a return greater than that offered by P1. In any case, NPV by itself is not a good criterion for ranking projects.

Formally, the essential conditions for net worth to be an appropriate criterion for the evaluation and ranking of projects are that

• we have a fixed budget to invest
• projects require the same investment

These conditions do not hold with any regularity. On the contrary, it is most often the case that the list of projects consists of a variety of possibilities with varying costs. A central problem in the evaluation and choice of systems is to delimit their size and budget. Analysis of net worth is not particularly helpful in those contexts.

3.4.5 Internal Rate of Return Method

The internal rate of return (IRR) method involves the calculation of an interest rate that is compared against a minimum threshold (i.e., the MARR). As we will see, it is the interest rate for which the NPV of a project is zero. The concept is that the IRR expresses the real return on any investment (i.e., return on investment). For evaluation, the idea is that projects should be ranked from the highest IRR down.

The IRR is now used increasingly by sophisticated business analysts. The advantage of this criterion is that it overcomes two difficulties inherent in the calculation of both NPV and benefit-cost ratios. That is,

1. It eliminates the need to determine, indeed to argue about, the appropriate MARR.

2. Its rankings cannot be manipulated by the choice of a MARR.

It also focuses attention directly on the rate of return of each project, an attribute that cannot be understood from either the NPV or the benefit-cost ratio.

The IRR is known by other names, such as *investor's rate of return*, *discounted cash flow return*, and so on. We demonstrate its use for a single project and then for the comparison of mutually exclusive projects.

IRR Method for Single Project.   The most common method of calculation of the IRR for a single project involves finding the interest rate, i, at which the PW of the cash inflow (receipts or cash savings) equals the PW of the cash outflow (disbursements or cash savings forgone). That is, one finds the interest rate at which PW of cash inflow equals PW of cash outflow, or at which PW of cash inflow minus PW of cash outflow equals 0, or at which PW of net cash flow equals 0. The IRR could also be calculated by using the same procedures applied to either AW or FW.

The calculations normally involve trial and error until the correct interest rate is found or can be interpolated. Closed-form solutions are not available because the equivalent worth factors are a nonlinear function of the interest rate. The procedure is described below for several situations. (When both cash inflows and outflows are involved, the convention of using a "+" sign for inflows and a "−" sign for outflows will be followed.)

Example 3-12

Given the same machine A as in Section 3.4.1, find the IRR and compare it with a MARR of 15%.

	Machine A
Initial cost	$20,000
Life	5 years
Salvage value	$4,000
Annual receipts	$10,000
Annual disbursements	$4,400

Solution   Expressing the NPV of cash flow and setting it equal to zero results in the following:

$$\text{NPV}(i) = -\$20{,}000 + (\$10{,}000 - \$4{,}400)(P/A, i, 5) + \$4{,}000(P/F, i, 5) = 0$$

Try $i = 10\%$

$$\text{NPV}(10\%) = -\$20,000 + \$5,600(P/A, 10\%, 5) + \$4,000(P/F, 10\%, 5)$$
$$= \$3,713 > 0$$

Try $i = 15\%$

$$\text{NPV}(15\%) = -\$20,000 + \$5,600(P/A, 15\%, 5) + \$4,000(P/F, 15\%, 5)$$
$$= \$730 > 0$$

Try $i = 20\%$

$$\text{NPV}(20\%) = -\$20,000 + \$5,600(P/A, 20\% 5) + \$4,000(P/F, 20\%, 5)$$
$$= -\$1,196 < 0$$

Because we have both a positive and a negative NPV, the desired answer is bracketed. Linear interpolation can be used to approximate the unknown interest rate, i, as follows:

$$\frac{i - 15\%}{20\% - 15\%} = \frac{\$730 - 0}{\$730 - (-\$1,196)}$$

so

$$i = 15\% + \frac{\$730}{\$730 + \$1,196}(20\% - 15\%)$$

Solving gives $i = 16.9\%$.[1] Now, because 16.9% is greater than the MARR of 15%, the project is justified. A plot of NPV versus interest rate is given in Fig. 3.5.   ■

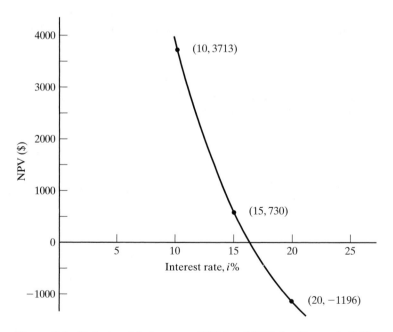

Figure 3.5   Relationship between NPV and IRR for Example 3-12.

[1]A more exact calculation gives $i\% = 16.47\%$, but we use 16.9% for the remainder of the chapter.

Because the P/A and P/F factors are nonlinear functions of the interest rate, the linear interpolation (above) causes an error, but the error is usually inconsequential in economic analyses. The narrower the range of rates over which the interpolation is done, the more accurate are the results. Finally, note that as the trial interest rate is increased, the corresponding NPV decreases.

IRR Method for Comparing Mutually Exclusive Alternatives.   When comparing alternatives by any rate of return (ROR) method when at most one alternative will be chosen, there are three main principles to keep in mind:

1. Any alternative whose IRR is less than the MARR can be discarded immediately.
2. Each increment of investment capital must justify itself (by sufficient ROR on that increment).
3. Compare a higher investment alternative against a lower investment alternative only when that lower investment alternative is justified.

The usual approach when using a ROR method is to choose the alternative that requires the highest investment for which each increment of investment capital is justified. This choice assumes that the organization wants to invest any capital needed as long as the capital is justified by earning a sufficient ROR on each increment of capital. In general, a sufficient ROR is any value greater than or equal to the MARR. The IRR on the incremental investment for any two alternatives can be found by

1. Finding the rate at which the PW (or AW or FW) of the net cash flow for the difference between the two alternatives is equal to zero
2. Finding the rate at which the PWs (or AWs or FWs) of the two alternatives are equal.

Example 3-13

Suppose that we have the same machines, A and B, as considered in Section 3.4.1. In addition, machines C and D are mutually exclusive alternatives also to be included in the comparison by the IRR method. Relevant data and the solution are presented below. Repeatability of the alternatives is assumed.

	Machine			
	A	B	C	D
Initial cost	$20,000	$30,000	$35,000	$43,000
Life	5 years	10 years	5 years	5 years
Salvage value	$4,000	0	$4,000	$5,000
Annual receipts	$10,000	$14,000	$20,000	$18,000
Annual disbursements	$4,400	$8,600	$9,390	$5,250
Net annual receipts—disbursements	$5,600	$5,400	$10,610	$12,750
IRR	16.9%	12.4%	17.9%	17.1%

Solution   As a first step, it is best to arrange the alternatives in order of increasing initial investment because this is the order in which the increments will be considered. The symbol Δ means "increment," and A → B means "the increment in going from alternative A to alternative B." Recall that an increment of investment is justified if the IRR on that increment (i.e., ΔIRR) is ≥15%. The least expensive alternative is always compared with the "do nothing" option.

	A	A → B*	A → C	C → D
ΔInvestment	$20,000	$10,000	$15,000	$8,000
ΔSalvage	$4,000	−$4,000	$0	$1,000
Δ(annual receipts − disbursements)	$5,600	−$200	$5,010	$2,140
ΔIRR	16.9%	0%	20%	13.3%
Is Δinvestment justified?	Yes	No	Yes	No

*Analysis must include $16,000 replacement cost for alternative A at end of year 5.

The analysis indicates that alternative C would be chosen because it is associated with the largest investment for which each increment of investment capital is justified. The analysis was performed without considering the IRR on the total investment for each alternative. However, when we look at the individual IRRs, we see that IRR(B) = 12.4% < 15% = MARR, so alternative B could have been discarded.   ∎

In choosing alternative C, one increment of investment was justified as follows:

Increment	Incremental investment	IRR on increment, ΔIRR (%)
A	$20,000	16.9
A → C	$15,000	20.0
Total investment	$35,000	

Coincidentally, alternative C had the largest IRR, which seems intuitive but is not always the case. If the MARR were, say, 12%, then alternative D would have been selected. As a general rule, if the most expensive alternative has the highest IRR, then it will always turn out to be preferred.

In Example 3-13, because the useful lives of A and B are different and repeatability is assumed, one should closely examine the cash flows for A → B (B minus A) for the lowest common multiple of lives. For the 10-year period, Σ(positive cash flows) = $16,000 = (replacement cost) = Σ(negative cash flows) = $10,000 + $4,000 + 10($200). Thus, ΔIRR = 0%; any $i > 0$ would produce a negative NPV.

Occasionally, situations arise in which a single positive interest rate cannot be determined from the cash flow; that is, solving for NPV = 0 yields more than one solution. Descartes' rule of signs indicates that multiple solutions can occur whenever the cash flow series reverses sign (from net outflow to net inflow, or vice versa) more than once over the study period. This is demonstrated in the following example.

Example 3-14   (No Single IRR Solution)

The Converse Aircraft Company has an opportunity to supply a wide-body airplane to Banzai Airlines. Banzai will pay $19 million when the contract is signed and $10 million 1 year later. Converse estimates its second- and third-year net cash flows at $50 million each during production. Banzai will take delivery of the plane during year 4 and agrees to pay $20 million at the end of that year and the $60 million balance at the end of year 5. Compute the ROR on this project.

Solution   Computation of NPV at various interest rates, using single-payment PW factors (for year 2 and $i = 10\%$, $PW = -50(P/F, 10\%, 2) = -50(0.826) = -41.3$) is presented:

Year	Cash flow	0%	10%	20%	40%	50%
0	+19	+19	+19	+19	+19	+19
1	+10	+10	+9.1	+8.3	+7.1	+6.7
2	−50	−50	−41.3	−34.7	−25.5	−22.2
3	−50	−50	−37.6	−28.9	−18.2	−14.8
4	+20	+20	+13.7	+9.6	+5.2	+4.0
5	+60	+60	+37.3	+24.1	+11.2	+7.9
	NPV =	+9	+0.2	−2.6	−1.2	+0.6

The NPV plot for these data is depicted in Fig. 3.6. We see that the cash flow produces two points at which NPV = 0; one at approximately 10.1% and the other at approximately 47%. Whenever multiple answers such as these exist, it is likely that neither is correct.

An effective way to overcome this difficulty and obtain a "correct" answer is to manipulate cash flows as little as necessary so that there is only one sign reversal in the net cash flow stream. This can be done by using an appropriate interest rate to move lump sums either forward or backward, and then solve in the usual manner. To demonstrate, let us assume that all money held outside the project earns 6%. (This value could be considered the external interest rate that Converse faces. If it had to borrow money, the interest rate might be different.) At both year 0 and year 1, there is an inflow of cash resulting from the advance payments by Banzai. The money will be needed later to help pay the production costs. Given an external interest rate of 6%, the $19 million will be invested for 2

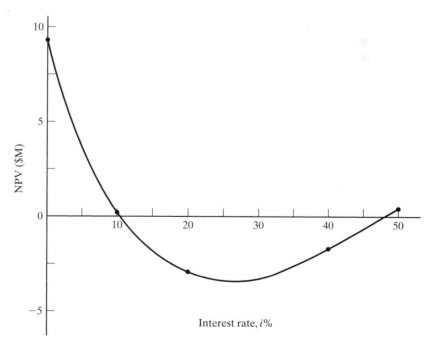

Figure 3.6   NPV plot for more than one change in sign.

years and the $10 million for 1 year. Their compounded amount at the end of year 2 will be

$$\text{FW at end of year 2} = 19(F/P, 6\%, 2) + 10(F/P, 6\%, 1)$$
$$= 19(1.124) + 10(1.06)$$
$$= 32$$

When this amount is returned to the project, the net cash flow for year 2 becomes $-50 + 32 = -18$. The resulting cash flow for the 5 years is

Year	Cash flow	0%	8%	10%
0	0	0	0	0
1	0	0	0	0
2	-18	-18	-15.4	-14.9
3	-50	-50	-39.7	-37.6
4	$+20$	$+20$	$+14.7$	$+13.7$
5	$+60$	$+60$	$+40.8$	$+37.3$
	NPV =	$+12$	$+0.4$	-1.5

This cash flow stream has one sign change, indicating that there is either zero or one positive interest rate. By interpolation, we can find the point where NPV = 0:

$$i = 8\% + 2\%\frac{0.4}{1.5 + 0.4} = 8\% + 2\%(0.21) = 8.42\%$$

Thus, assuming an external interest rate of 6%, the internal rate of return for the Banzai plane contract is 8.42%. ∎

In many situations, we are asked to compare and rank independent investment opportunities rather than a set of mutually exclusive alternatives designed to meet the same need. Portfolio analysis is such an example in which the firm is considering a number of different R&D projects and must evaluate the costs and benefits of each. Here, the IRR method will always give results that are consistent (regarding project acceptance or rejection) with those obtained from the PW, AW, or FW method. However, the IRR method may give a different ranking regarding the order of desirability than any of the others when comparing independent investment opportunities.

As an example, consider Fig. 3.7, depicting the relation of IRR to NPV for two projects, X and Y. The IRR for each project is the interest rate at which the NPV for that project is zero. This is shown for a nominal MARR. For the hypothetical but feasible relationship shown in Fig. 3.7, project Y has the higher IRR, whereas project X has the higher NPV of all IRRs except for the rate at which the NPVs are equal. This illustrates the case in which the IRR method does result in a different ranking of alternatives compared with the PW (AW or FW) method. Nevertheless, because both projects have an NPV greater than zero, the IRR for either is greater than the MARR. The determination of acceptance of both projects is shown consistently by either method. It should be noted that if X and Y had been mutually exclusive *alternatives*, then there would have been no inconsistency regarding which to choose provided an incremental IRR analysis was performed.

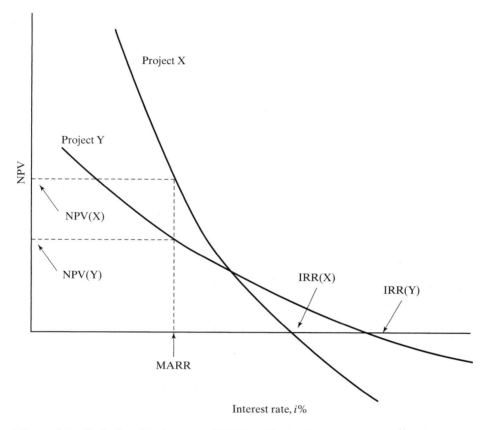

Figure 3.7   Relationship between NPV and IRR for independent investment.

3.4.6 Payback Period Method

In its simplest form, the payback period is the number of periods, usually measured in years, that it takes for the accruing net *undiscounted* benefits from the investment to equal the cost of the investment. If we assume that the benefits are equal in each future year and that depreciation and income taxes are not included into the calculations, the formula is

$$\text{payback period} = \frac{\text{initial investment}}{\text{annual net undiscounted benefits}}$$

When the benefits differ from year to year, it is necessary to find the smallest value of n such that

$$\sum_{j=1}^{n} B_j \geq P$$

where P is the initial investment and B_j is the annual net benefit in year i.

Example 3-15

The cash flows for two alternatives are as follows:

	Year					
Alternative	0	1	2	3	4	5
A	− $2,700	+1,200	+1,200	+1,200	+1,200	+1,200
B	− $1,000	+200	+200	+1,200	+1,200	+1,200

On the basis of the payback period, which alternative is best?

Solution   *Alternative A*: Because the annual benefits are uniform, the payback period can be computed from the first formula in this section; that is,

$$\frac{\$2,700}{\$1,200/\text{yr}} = 2.25 \text{ years}$$

Alternative B: The payback period is the length of time required for profits or other benefits of an investment to equal the cost of the investment. In the first 2 years, only $400 of the $1,000 cost is recovered. The remaining $600 is recovered in the first half of the third year. Thus, the answer is 2.5 years.
Therefore, to minimize the payback period, choose alternative A.   ∎

The great advantage of the payback period is that it is simple and can be applied by anyone. It thus is an excellent mechanism for allowing middle managers and technical staff to choose among proposals without going through a detailed analysis or to sort through many possibilities before resorting to a more sophisticated approach.

Situations that are suitable for the use of the payback period are often found in industry. These are projects in which a constant benefit is expected to accrue for an extended period as a result of a particular investment. A typical case would be the purchase of a new robot that would reduce operating expenses each year by a fixed amount, or some insulation or control that would regularly save on energy bills.

The weakness of this criterion is that it is crude; it does not clearly distinguish between projects with different useful lives. For any projects with identical useful lives, for which the capital recovery factor will be identical, the payback period gives as good a measure of economic desirability as the NPV or IRR. When the useful lives of projects are different, the capital recovery factors are not the same and the results can be highly misleading, as the following analysis shows:

	Project	
	P1	P2
Investment	$2,000	$2,000
Useful life	3 years	6 years
Annual receipts	$1,000	$800
Payback period	2 years	2.5 years
NPV at 10%	$487	$1,484
IRR	23.4%	32.7%

In this example, project P1 has a shorter payback period than the alternative P2 and would seem better by this criterion, yet project P2 is, in fact, more economically desirable for a wide range of discount rates. This is because P2 provides substantial benefits over a much longer period. Thus, over a 6-year cycle, P1 would have to be repeated twice for a total cost of $4,000 and benefits of $6,000, whereas P2 would cost only $2,000 and yield returns of $4,800—greater net benefits and a higher NPV for any number of discount factors.

3.5 SENSITIVITY AND BREAKEVEN ANALYSIS

Much of the data collected in solving a problem represent projections of future consequences and hence may possess a high degree of uncertainty. As the desired result of the analysis is decision making, an appropriate question is, "To what extent do the variations in the data affect the decision?" When small variations in a particular estimate would change the alternative selected, the decision is said to be *sensitive* to the estimate. To better evaluate the impact of any parameter, one should determine the amount of variation necessary in it to effect a change in outcome. This is called *sensitivity analysis*.

This type of analysis highlights the important and significant aspects of a problem. For example, one might be concerned that the estimates for annual maintenance and future salvage value in a facility modernization project vary substantially, depending on the assumptions used. Sensitivity analysis might indicate, however, that the decision is insensitive to the salvage value estimates over the full range of possibilities. At the same time, it might show that small changes in annual maintenance expenditures strongly influence the choice of equipment. Under these circumstances, one should place greater emphasis on pinning down the true maintenance costs than on worrying about salvage value estimates.

Succinctly, sensitivity analysis describes the relative magnitude of a particular variation in one or more elements of a problem that is sufficient to alter a particular decision. Closely related is *breakeven analysis*, which determines the conditions under which two alternatives are equivalent. These two evaluation techniques frequently are useful in engineering problems called *stage construction*. That is, should a facility be constructed now to meet its future full-scale requirements, or should it be constructed in stages as the need for the increased capacity arises? Three examples of this situation are as follows:

- Should we install a cable with 400 circuits now, or a 200-circuit cable now and another 200-circuit cable later?
- A 10-cm water main is needed to serve a new area of homes. Should the 10-cm main be installed now, or should a 15-cm main be installed to provide an adequate water supply later for adjoining areas when other homes are built?
- An industrial firm currently needs a 10,000-m^2 warehouse and estimates that it will need an additional 10,000 m^2 in 4 years. The firm could have a warehouse built now and later enlarged, or have a 20,000-m^2 warehouse built today.

Examples 3-16 and 3-17, adapted from Newnan et al. (2000), illustrate the principles and calculations behind sensitivity and breakeven analysis.

Example 3-16

Consider the following situation in which a project may be constructed to full capacity now or may be undertaken in two stages.

Construction Costs.

Two-stage construction
Construct first stage now	$100,000
Construct second stage *n* years from now	$120,000
Full-capacity construction	$140,000

Other Factors.

1. All facilities will last until 40 years from now, regardless of when they are installed; at that time, they will have zero salvage value.
2. The annual cost of operation and maintenance is the same for both alternatives.
3. Assume that the MARR is 8%.

Plot a graph showing "age when second stage is constructed" versus "costs for both alternatives." Mark the breakeven point. What is the sensitivity of the decision to second-stage construction 16 or more years in the future?

Solution   Because we are dealing with a common analysis period, the calculations may be either AC or PW. PW calculations seem simpler and are used here:

Construct Full Capacity Now

$$\text{PW of cost} = \$140,000$$

Two-stage Construction.   In this alternative, the first stage is constructed now with the second stage to be constructed *n* years hence. To begin, compute the PW of cost for several values of *n* (years).

$$\text{PW of cost} = \$100,000 + \$120,000(P/F, 8\%, n)$$

$n = 5$:	$PW = \$100,000 + \$120,000(0.6806) = \$181,700$
$n = 10$:	$PW = \$100,000 + \$120,000(0.4632) = \$155,600$
$n = 20$:	$PW = \$100,000 + \$120,000(0.2145) = \$125,700$
$n = 30$:	$PW = \$100,000 + \$120,000(0.0994) = \$111,900$

These data are plotted in Fig. 3.8 in the form of a breakeven chart. The horizontal axis is the time when the second stage is constructed; the vertical axis represents PW. We see that the PW of cost for two-stage construction naturally decreases as the time for the second stage is deferred. The one-stage construction (full capacity now) option is unaffected by the time variable and hence is a horizontal line on the graph.

The breakeven point on the graph is the point at which both alternatives have equivalent costs. We see that if in two-stage construction, the second stage is deferred for 15 years, the PW of that alternative is equal to the PW of the first, which is approximately $137,800. Thus, year 15 is the breakeven point. The plot also shows that if the second stage were needed before year 15, then one-stage construction, with its smaller PW of cost, would be preferred. If the second stage were not needed until after year 15, then the opposite is true.

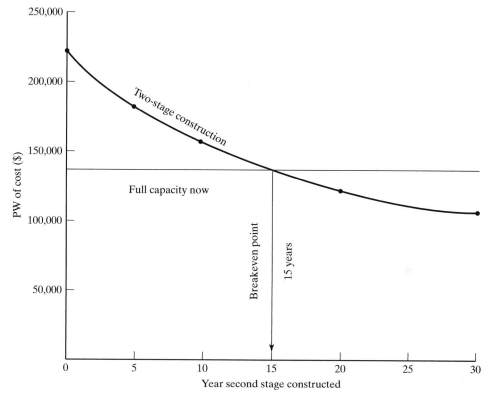

Figure 3.8   Breakeven chart diagram for Example 3-16.

The decision as to how to construct a project is sensitive to the age at which the second stage is needed only if the range of estimates includes 15 years. For example, if one estimated that the second-stage capacity would be needed sometime over the next 5 to 10 years, then the decision is insensitive to that estimate. The more economical thing to do is to build the full capacity now, but if demand for the second-stage capacity were between, say, years 12 and 18, then the decision would depend on the estimate of when full capacity would actually be needed. ∎

One question posed by Example 3-16 is how sensitive the decision is to the need for the second stage at or beyond 16 years. The graph shows that the decision is insensitive. In all cases for construction on or after 16 years, two-stage construction has a lower PW of cost.

Example 3-17

In this example, we have three mutually exclusive alternatives, each with a 20-year life and no salvage value. Assume that the MARR is 6% and

	A	B	C
Initial cost	$2,000	$4,000	$5,000
Uniform annual benefit	$410	$639	$700

Calculating the NPV of each alternative gives

$$NPV = A(P/A, 6\%, 20)$$

$$NPV(A) = \$410(11.470) - \$2,000 = \$2,703$$

$$NPV(B) = \$639(11.470) - \$4,000 = \$3,329$$

$$NPV(C) = \$700(11.470) - \$5,000 = \$3,029$$

so alternative B is preferred. Now we would like to know how sensitive the decision is to the estimate of the initial cost of B. If B is preferred at an initial cost of $4,000, then it will continue to be preferred for any smaller values, but how much higher than $4,000 can the initial cost go up and still have B as the preferred alternative?

Solution   The computations may be performed in several different ways. The first thing to note is that for the three alternatives, B will maximize NPV only as long as its NPV is greater than $3,029. Let X = initial cost of B. Thus, we have

$$NPV(B) = \$639(11.470) - X > \$3,029$$

or

$$X < \$7,329 - \$3,029 = \$4,300$$

implying that B is the best alternative if its initial cost does not exceed $4,300. The breakeven chart for the problem is displayed in Fig. 3.9. Because we are maximizing NPV, we see that B is preferred if its initial cost is less than $4,300. At an initial cost above this value, C is preferred. At the breakeven point, B and C are equally desirable. For the data given, alternative A is always inferior to alternative C.   ■

Sensitivity analysis and breakeven point calculations can be very useful in identifying how different estimates affect the decision. It must be recognized, however, that these calculations assume that all parameters except one are held constant and that the sensitivity of the decision to that parameter is what is being evaluated.

3.6 EFFECT OF TAX AND DEPRECIATION ON INVESTMENT DECISIONS

The discussion thus far referred to investment earnings as cash flows implicitly net of tax consequences. The reason for this is that only the actual cash flow produced by an investment is relevant to the decision process. Earnings before depreciation and taxes do not represent the actual benefits realized by a firm. Consequently, the expected income from an investment must be adjusted to represent the true cash inflow before ranking can take place. Note that depreciation can be viewed as an expense and thus reduces gross income for tax purposes. The procedures and schedules used to compute depreciation in any year are promulgated by the Internal Revenue Service (IRS).

Assume that a machine that costs $10,000 has a useful life of 5 years and is expected to produce gross earnings of $4,000 each year. With straight-line depreciation [amount per year = (initial cost − salvage value)/(useful life)], no salvage value, and

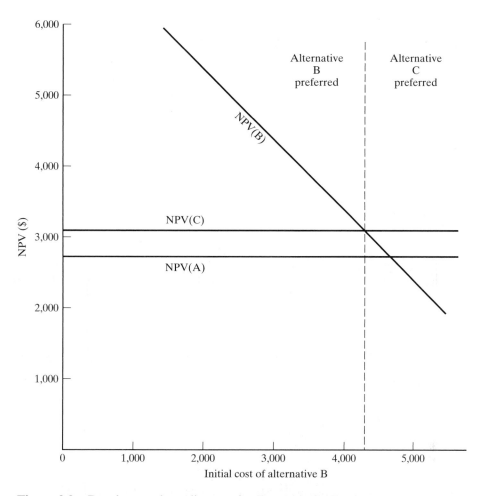

Figure 3.9   Breakeven chart diagram for Example 3-17.

a 40% tax rate, the annual cash flow in each of the 5 years will be

A.	Gross earnings		$4,000
B.	Depreciation expense	$2,000	
C.	Taxable income (A − B)	$2,000	
D.	Taxes (40% of C)		−$800
E.	Cash flow (A − D)		$3,200

Now, if the MARR for the firm is 10%, then the NPV of the investment is

$$\$3,200(P/A, 10\%, 5) - \$10,000 = \$3,200(3.708) - \$10,000 = \$2,131$$

which makes it worthwhile.

Income tax rates are specified differently for individuals and corporations and depend on the level of income. Most countries have what is called a *progress* tax system in which the more money you make, the higher your tax rate is on the additional income. In such a system, income brackets and corresponding tax rates are defined. Each dollar earned within a bracket after accounting for deductions is taxed at the corresponding rate. In 2004 in the U.S., all individual income over $297,374 was taxed at the rate of 39.1%, the highest bracket. For corporations, the situation is a bit more complicated, but all income over $15M was taxed at 38%.

The rationale for a progress tax system is based on what economists call the marginal utility of the last dollar earned. If someone is poor and struggling to pay for basic necessities such as food and housing, then an extra dollar or an extra $100 probably mean a lot to him or her. For a wealthy person, an extra $100 might be the equivalent of pocket change. Therefore, "removing" $39 of the $100 from someone who makes $300,000 per year should have much less of an impact on that person than on someone who makes only $25,000 per year. In fact, one could argue, as do the proponents of the system, that the amount that should be removed from the lower wage earner to achieve an equivalent impact is roughly $15, or 15%, the current tax bracket for $25,000. As the argument goes, the wealthier you are, the less you should miss the additional dollars earned, so taxing them at a progressively higher rate is reasonable. At some point, though, this argument breaks down because the system becomes confiscatory. This was realized in the U.S. in the mid-1960s, when the highest marginal rate peaked at 90%. Since then, the U.S. Congress has been steadily lowering all brackets for both economic and political reasons.

It should be mentioned that profits that are realized on the sale of assets such as stocks, homes, antiques, businesses, and equipment are not taxed as income but as *capital gains*. The capital gains tax rate is flat, so everyone pays the same percentage on their *net* profits. Losses can be balanced against gains in any given year, so only the net counts in computing your taxes.

When determining a depreciation allowance on an asset, it is necessary to use the method prescribed by the IRS. In the past, straight-line, sum-of-the-years digits (SOYD), and declining balance were the common methods. For all assets put into productive service in recent years, the modified accelerated cost recovery system (MACRS) must be used. This system assigns all property to a handful of classes distinguished by their tax life. For example, computers are given a 3-year life, whereas nonresidential real property is given a 31.5-year life. Depreciation is calculated as a percentage of the initial cost. The MACRS percentages for the 3-year class are 33.33%, 44.45%, 14.81%, and 7.41%; that is, a 3-year asset must be depreciated over four years according to this schedule. For the 5-year class, the percentages are 20%, 32%, 19.2%, 11.52%[*], 11.52%, and 5.76%. The 3-, 5-, 7-, and 10-year classes are based on double declining balance depreciation with conversion to the straight-line method in the appropriate year (*) to maximize the deduction.

3.6.1 Capital Expansion Decision

Example 3-18

The Leeds Corporation leases plant facilities in which expendable thermocouples are manufactured. Because of rising demand, Leeds could increase sales by investing in new equipment to expand output. The selling price of $10 per thermocouple will remain unchanged if output and sales increase. On the basis of engineering and cost estimates, the accounting department provides management with the following cost estimates based on an annual increased output of 100,000 units.

Cost of new equipment having an expected life of 5 years	$500,000
Equipment installation cost	$20,000
Expected salvage value	0
New operation's share of annual lease expense	$10,000
Annual increase in utility expenses	$40,000
Annual increase in labor costs	$160,000
Annual additional cost for raw materials	$400,000

The SOYD method of depreciation will be used, and taxes are paid at a rate of 40%. Mr. Leeds' policy is not to invest capital in projects that earn less than a 20% ROR. Should the proposed expansion be undertaken?

Solution   Compute cost of investment:

Acquisition cost of equipment	$500,000
Equipment installation costs	$20,000
Total cost of investment	$520,000

Determine yearly cash flows throughout the life of the investment. The lease expense is a sunk cost. It will be incurred regardless of whether the investment is made and therefore is irrelevant to the decision and should be disregarded. Annual production expenses to be considered are utility, labor, and raw materials. These total $600,000 per year. Annual sales revenue is $10 \times 100,000$ units of output, or $1,000,000. Yearly income before depreciation and taxes thus is $1,000,000 gross revenue less $600,000 expenses, or $400,000.

Determine the depreciation charges to be deducted from the $400,000 income each year using the SOYD method ($\Sigma = 1 + 2 + 3 + 4 + 5 = 15$). With SOYD, the depreciation in year j is (initial cost $-$ salvage value) $\times (N - j + 1)/\Sigma$ for $j = 1, \ldots, N$.

Year	Proportion of $500,000 to be depreciated		Depreciation charge
1	$5/15 \times \$500,000$	=	
$166,667		=	
2	$4/15 \times \$500,000$	=	
$133,333		=	
3	$3/15 \times \$500,000$	=	
$100,000		=	

Find each year's cash flow when taxes are 40%. Cash flow for only the first year is illustrated:

Earnings before depreciation and taxes		$400,000
Depreciation expense	$166,667	
Taxable income	$233,333	
Taxes ($0.4 \times \$233,333$)		$-$93,332
Cash flow (first year)		$306,668

Determine present value of the cash flows. Because Leeds demands at least a 20% ROR on investments, multiply the cash flows by the 20% present value factor (P/F, 20%, *j*) for each year *j*.

Year	Present-value factor		Cash flow		Present value
1	0.833	×	$306,667	=	$255,454
2	0.694	×	$293,333	=	$203,573
3	0.579	×	$280,000	=	$162,120
4	0.482	×	$266,667	=	$128,533
5	0.402	×	$253,334	=	$101,840
Total present value of cash flows					
	(discounted at 20%)			=	$851,520

Find whether NPV is positive or negative:

Total present value of cash flows	$851,520
Total cost of investment	$520,000
NPV	$331,520

Decision. NPV is positive when returns are discounted at 20%. Therefore, the proposed expansion should be undertaken. ∎

3.6.2 Replacement Decision

We now consider the case of fixed assets, such as equipment or buildings, and ask whether they should be replaced. The normal means of monitoring expenditures in industry as well as in government are by annual budgets. One important factor in budgeting is the allocation of money for new capital expenditures, either new facilities or replacement and upgrading of current facilities. Existing assets are replaced for many reasons, including deterioration, reduced performance, new requirements, increasing operations and maintenance (O&M) costs, reduced reliability, obsolescence, or more attractive leasing options. In each of these cases, the ability of a current asset to produce a desired output for the lowest cost is challenged. This adversarial situation has given rise to the terms *defender*—the existing asset—and the *challenger*—the potential replacement.

Example 3-19

For 5 years, Emetic Pharmaceuticals has been using a machine that attaches labels to bottles. The machine was purchased for $4,000 and is being depreciated over 10 years to a zero salvage value using the straight-line method. The machine can be sold now for $2,000. Emetic can buy a new labeling machine for $6,000 that will have a useful life of 5 years and cut labor costs by $1,200 annually. The old machine will require a major overhaul in the next few months. The cost of the overhaul is expected to be $300. If purchased, the new machine will be depreciated over 5 years to a $500 salvage value using the straight-line method. The company will invest in any project that earns more than the 12% cost of capital. Its tax rate is 40%. Should Emetic invest in the new machine?

Solution   Determine the cost of investment:

Price of the new machine		$6,000
Less: Sale of old machine	$2,000	
Avoidable overhaul costs	$300	
Total deductions		−$2,300
Effective cost of investment		$3,700

Determine the increase in cash flow resulting from investment in the new machine:

Yearly cost savings = $1,200.

Differential depreciation:

Annual depreciation on old machine:

$$\frac{\text{cost} - \text{salvage}}{\text{useful life}} = \frac{\$4,000 - \$0}{10} = \$400$$

Annual depreciation on new machine:

$$\frac{\text{cost} - \text{salvage}}{\text{useful life}} = \frac{\$6,000 - \$500}{5} = \$1,100$$

Differential depreciation = $1,100 − $400 = $700

Yearly net increase in cash flow into the firm:

Cost savings		$1,200
Deduct: Taxes at 40%	$480	
Add: Advantage of increase in depreciation		
(0.4 × $700)	$280	
Net deductions		−$200
Yearly increase in cash flow		$1,000

Determine the total present value of the investment:

The 5-year cash flow of $1,000 per year is an annuity.

Discounted at 12%, the cost of capital, the present value is $1,000 × 3.605 = $3,605.

The present value of the new machine, if sold at its salvage value of $500 at the end of the fifth year is $500 × 0.567 = $284.

Total present value of the expected cash flows: $3,605 + $284 = $3,889

Determine whether the NPV is positive:

Total present value	$3,889
Cost of investment	$3,700
NPV	$189

Decision   Emetic Pharmaceuticals should make the purchase because the investment will return slightly more than the cost of capital.

Note.   The importance of depreciation has been shown in this example. The present value of the yearly cash flow resulting from operations is *only*

(cost savings − taxes)   (PV factor)
($1,200 − $480)   ×   3.605   = $2,596

This figure is $1,104 less than the $3,700 cost of the investment. Only a very large depreciation advantage makes this investment worthwhile. The total present value of the advantage is $1,009; that is,

(tax rate × differential depreciation)   (PV factor)
(0.4 × $700)   ×   3.605   = $1,009   ∎

In this problem, we did a 5-year analysis based on the useful life of the new asset. In most situations, it is more appropriate first to determine the "life" of the competing assets. Types of asset lives include

1. The physical life is the period until the asset is salvaged, scrapped, or torn down.
2. The accounting life or tax life is the time over which the asset is depreciated. It may or may not reflect the physical life.
3. Useful life is the time over which the asset will provide useful service.
4. Economic life is the number of years at which the EUAC or net annual cost (NAC) of ownership is minimized.

It is often the case that the economic life is shorter than the physical or useful life of an asset as a result of increasing O&M costs in the later years of ownership. In a traditional replacement analysis, the economic lives of the defender and challenger along with the accompanying costs are used to make the decision. To conduct an analysis, let

N = useful life
P = investment at time 0
$A(n)$ = net cost in year n (i.e., O&M − revenue)
$S(n)$ = salvage value in year n
$PA(n)$ = present worth of annual costs for n years
$NAC(n)$ = net annual cost for n years

where

$$PA(n) = A(1)(P/F, i, 1) + A(2)(P/F, i, 2) + \cdots + A(n)(P/F, i, n)$$
$$NAC(n) = [P + PA(n)](A/P, i, n) - S(n)(A/F, i, n)$$

The economic life is then argmin{NAC(n): $n = 1, \ldots, N$}; that is, the value of n that minimizes NAC(n).

Example 3-20

You have purchased a router for $15,000. The machine has a useful life of 10 years and will be depreciated to zero using the SOYD method over that period of time. Assume that the salvage in year n is equal to the book value. In the first year, operating costs are expected to be $500, increasing by 40% in each subsequent year. If your MARR is 18%, then what is the economic life of the router?

Solution   The following table lists the relevant data. The last column indicates the equivalent annual cost if the router is kept for n years, $n = 1, \ldots, 10$. The minimum $NAC(n)$ occurs at year 6, which is economic life.

Time, n	Operating cost, $A(n)$	Salvage value, $S(n)$	$NAC(n)$	
0		$15,000		
1	$500	$12,273	$5,927	
2	$700	$9,818	$5,667	
3	$980	$7,636	$5,462	
4	$1,372	$5,727	$5,307	
5	$1,921	$4,091	$5,207	
6	$2,689	$2,727	$5,162	← min
7	$3,765	$1,636	$5,178	
8	$5,271	$818	$5,256	
9	$7,379	$273	$5,404	
10	$10,331	0	$5,627	

Although in this example the initial investment cost at time 0 was given, it is usually not so straightforward to figure out what value should be used for an existing asset. In general, the investment cost that should be used for the defender is the money that you give up by not disposing of it; i.e., the opportunity cost. You must also add any costs at time 0 to make it equivalent to the challenger. In summary, the investment consists of the

- current market value for the defender,
- less costs necessary for its disposal,
- less taxes on the capital gain (when taxes are considered),
- plus any real costs at time 0 necessary to keep it.

Example 3-21

Eight years ago, you bought a used car for $4,500 that has a trade-in value of $500. You are now considering a replacement for $8,250 and want to know whether to go ahead with the deal. Your minimum acceptable rate of return is 12%. Some additional cost data are given below.

Old car (defender)

Maintenance costs next year will be $800 and are expected to go up by $400 a year in the coming years ($800, $1,200, $1,600, …). The car is now a death trap, not worth more than $250. To trade it in, you're going to have to clean it up for a cost of $50. At any time in the future, net salvage value is also expected to be $200.

New car (challenger)

This car is supposed to last for 10 years with a trade-in value of $750 at the end of that time. If you sell it before the end of its useful life, you expect the trade-in value to be the same as the book value computed with straight-line depreciation. Maintenance will be $100 per year for the first 3 years and $300 per year thereafter.

Solution   For the defender, we have

Investment: $P_D = \$200$

Operating cost: $A_D(n) = \$800 + \$400(n - 1)$

Salvage value: $S_D(n) = \$200$

$\text{NAC}_D(n) = P_D(A/P, i, n) + \$800 + \$400(A/G, i, n) - 200(A/F, i, n)$

For the challenger,

Investment: $P_C = \$8{,}250$

Operating cost: $A_C(n) = \$100, \$100, \$100, \$300, \$300, \$300, \ldots$

Salvage value: $S_C(n) = \$8{,}250 - \$750n$

$\text{NAC}_C(n) = P_C(A/P, i, n) + 100 - S_C(n)(A/F, i, n)$ for $n = 1, 2, 3$

$\text{NAC}_C(n) = P_C(A/P, i, n) + 300 - 200(P/A, i, 3)(A/P, i, n) - S_C(n)(A/F, i, n)$

for $n = 4, \ldots, 10$

The investment cost specified for the defender is simply the opportunity cost of not trading it in plus the \$50 to get it working satisfactorily. It is not the book value or the actual trade-in value. The investment cost specified for the challenger is the purchase cost, which does not include the trade-in. Generally speaking, we do not use any challenger characteristics to compute the defender investment, costs, or salvage, and vice versa.

The following table lists the data used in the analysis. As can be seen, the economic life is 1 year for the defender and the corresponding cost is \$824. The economic life of the challenger is 10 years with an annual cost of \$1,632. Thus, it is optimal to keep the defender 1 more year at least.

	Defender				Challenger		
Age, n	$A_D(n)$	$S_D(n)$	$\text{NAC}_D(n)$	Age, n	$A_C(n)$	$S_C(n)$	$\text{NAC}_C(n)$
0		\$200		0		\$8,250	
1	\$800	\$200	\$824	1	\$100	\$7,500	\$1,840
2	\$1,200	\$200	\$1,013	2	\$100	\$6,750	\$1,798
3	\$1,600	\$200	\$1,194	3	\$100	\$6,000	\$1,757
				4	\$300	\$5,250	\$1,760
				5	\$300	\$4,500	\$1,747
				6	\$300	\$3,750	\$1,728
				7	\$300	\$3,000	\$1,705
				8	\$300	\$2,250	\$1,681
				9	\$300	\$1,500	\$1,657
				10	\$300	\$750	\$1,632

■

This example illustrates a common situation: namely, that the economic life of the defender is often 1 year, and the economic life of the challenger is often its useful life. Finally, we mention that when considering taxes, an after-tax cash flow analysis should be used. In such cases, there will be a tax consequence if the book value of the defender does not equal its net market value.

3.6.3 Make-or-Buy Decision

Example 3-22

The GIGO Corporation manufactures and sells computers. It makes some of the parts and purchases others. The engineering department believes that it might be possible to cut costs by manufacturing one of the parts that is currently being purchased for $8.25 each. The firm uses 100,000 of these parts each year, and the accounting department compiles the following list of annual costs based on engineering estimates:

Fixed costs will increase by $50,000.

Labor costs will increase by $125,000.

Factory overhead, currently running $500,000 per year, is expected to increase 12%.

Raw materials used to make the part will cost $600,000.

Given the estimates above, should GIGO make the part or continue to buy it?

Solution   Find the total cost per year incurred if the part were manufactured:

Additional fixed costs	$50,000
Additional labor costs	$125,000
Raw materials cost	$600,000
Additional overhead costs $= 0.12 \times \$500,000$	$60,000
Total cost to manufacturer	$835,000

Find cost per unit to manufacture:

$$\frac{\$835,000}{100,000} = \$8.35 \text{ per unit}$$

Decision   GIGO should continue to buy the part. Manufacturing costs exceed the present cost to purchase by $0.10 per unit.

Perspective   The decision to make or buy is arguably the most fundamental component of manufacturing strategy. Should a firm be highly integrated, such as Henry Ford's River Rouge plant, with raw iron ore and coal flowing in one end and a finished Model A rolling out the other? Or should they simply purchase components from capable suppliers and then perform an assembly role much like today's PC manufacturers such as Compaq and Dell?

Henry Ford's model of vertical integration slipped from favor in the early 1960s, when outsourcing became increasingly attractive. Businesses found that outsourcing had certain advantages, potentially allowing them to

- Convert fixed costs to variable costs, thereby providing flexibility in an economic downturn
- Balance workforce requirements
- Reduce capital investment requirements
- Reduce costs via suppliers' economies of scale and lower wage structures
- Accelerate new product development
- Gain access to invention and innovation from suppliers
- Focus resources on high-value-added activities

Nevertheless, recent studies have shown that many make-or-buy decisions have historically been taken with a disproportionate weight placed on unit cost and an insufficient regard for strategic or technical issues (e.g., see Dertouzos et al. 1989). This cost-focused approach has led to competitive disaster for many firms, indeed, entire industries in the United States. The list of those affected by this phenomenon is well known. Some of the most notable include consumer electronics, machine tools, semiconductors, and office equipment. As recently as 2004, General Motors reported more than 8,000 suppliers for direct material alone.   ■

3.6.4 Lease-or-Buy Decision

Example 3-23

Jeremy Sitzer is a small businessman who has need for a pickup truck in his everyday work. He is considering buying a used truck for $3,000. If he goes ahead, he believes that he will be able to sell it for $1,000 at the end of 4 years, so he will depreciate $2,000 of the truck's value on a straight-line basis. Sitzer can borrow $3,000 from the bank and repay it in four equal annual installments at 6% interest. However, a friend advises him that he may be better off to lease a truck if he can get the same terms from the leasing company that he receives at the bank. Assuming that this is so, should Sitzer buy or lease the truck? He is in the 40% tax rate bracket.

Solution   Find the cost to buy: The bank loan is an installment loan at 6% interest, so the payments constitute a 4-year annuity. Divide the amount of the loan by the present value factor for a 4-year annuity at 6% $[(P/A, 6\%, 4) = 3.465]$ to find the annual payment. Multiply the annual payments by 4 to find the total payment.

$$\frac{\$3,000}{3.465} = \$866 \text{ annual payment}$$

$$4 \times \$866 = \$3,464 \text{ total payment}$$

Next, find the present value of the cost of the loans:
Present value of salvage = $1,000 × 0.792 = $792
Present value of cost of loan = $2,127 − $792 = $1,335

(1) Year	(2) Yearly payment	(3) Interest at 6%	(4) Payment on principal	(5) Remaining balance	(6) Depreciation
1	$866	$180	$686	$2,314	$500
2	$866	$139	$727	$1,587	$500
3	$866	$95	$771	$816	$500
4	$866	$50	$816	—	$500

(7) Tax deductible expense (3) + (6)	(8) Tax saving 0.4 × (7)	(9) Cost of owning (2) − (8)	(10) Present value factor	(11) Present value (9) × (10)
$680	$272	$594	0.943	$560
$639	$256	$610	0.890	$543
$595	$238	$628	0.840	$527
$550	$220	$646	0.792	$497
			Total present value of payments =	$2,127

Find the cost to lease:

(1)	(2)	(3)	(4)	(5)	(6)
		Tax	Lease cost	Present	Present
	Lease	savings	after taxes	value	value
Year	payment	0.4 × 866	(2) − (3)	factor at 6%	(4) × (5)
1	$866	$346	$520	0.943	$490
2	$866	$346	$520	0.890	$463
3	$866	$346	$520	0.840	$437
4	$866	$346	$520	0.792	$411
				Total present value of lease payments =	$1,801

Compare present values of cost to buy and cost to lease:

Present value of cost to lease	$1,801
Present value of cost to buy	$1,335
Advantage of buying	$ 466

Decision   Mr. Sitzer should buy the truck.

Note   Again, the importance of depreciation should be mentioned. When Sitzer purchases the truck, he gains the accompanying tax advantages of ownership. If the truck were leased, then the leasor would depreciate it and thereby gain advantage. Sitzer was also aided by being able to reduce the cost of buying by the present value of the salvage (or disposal) value of the truck. In general, depreciation and salvage value reduce the cost of buying. Nevertheless, if an asset is subject to rapid obsolescence, then it may be less expensive to lease. ■

3.7 UTILITY THEORY

Decision theory is concerned with giving structure and rationale to the various conditions under which decisions are made. In general, one must choose from among an array of alternatives. These are referred to as actions (or strategies), and each results in a payoff or outcome. If decision makers knew the payoff associated with each action, then they would be able to choose the action with the largest payoff. Most situations, however, are characterized by incomplete information, so for a given action, it is necessary to enumerate all probable outcomes together with their consequences and probabilities. The degree of information and understanding that the decision maker has about a particular situation determines how the underlying problem can be approached.

Two people, faced with the same set of alternatives and conditions, are likely to arrive at very different decisions regarding the most appropriate course of action for them. What is optimal for one may not even be an attractive alternative for the other. Judgment, risk, and experience work together to influence attitudes and choices.

Implicit in any decision-making process is the need to construct, either formally or informally, a preference order so that alternatives can be ranked and a final choice made. For some problems this may be easy to accomplish, as we saw in the preceding sections, where the decision was based on a profit-maximization or cost-minimization rule. There, the preference order is adequately represented by the natural order of real numbers ($\leq$ or $\geq$). In more complex situations, in which factors other than profit maximization or cost minimization apply, it may be desirable to explore the decision maker's preference structure in an explicit manner and to attempt to construct a preference ordering directly. An important class of techniques that work by eliciting preference information from the decision maker is predicated on what is known as *utility theory*. This, in turn, is based on the premise that the preference structure can be represented by a real-valued function called a *utility function*.[2] Once such a function is constructed, selection of the final alternative should be relatively simple. In the absence of uncertainty, an alternative with the highest utility would represent the preferred solution. For the case in which outcomes are subject to uncertainty, the appropriate choice would correspond to the one that attains the highest expected utility. Thus, the decision maker is faced with two basic problems involving judgment:

1. How to quantify (or measure) utility for various payoffs
2. How to quantify judgments concerning the probability of the occurrence of each possible outcome or event

In this section, we focus on the first question—of quantifying and exploiting personal preference. The second, subjective probability estimation, falls more appropriately in the realm of elementary statistics and so is not treated here.

3.7.1 Expected Utility Maximization

Assuming the presence of uncertainty, when a decision maker is repeatedly faced with the same problem, experience often leads to a strategy that provides, on average, the best results over the long run. In technical terms, such a strategy is one that maximizes *expected monetary value* (EMV). Notationally, let A be a particular action with possible outcomes $j = 1, \ldots, n$. Also, let p_j be the probability of realizing outcome j with corresponding payoff or return x_j. The expected monetary value of A is calculated as follows:

$$\text{EMV}(A) = \sum_{j=1}^{n} p_j x_j \tag{3.1}$$

For the case in which the decision maker is faced with a unique problem, using the EMV criterion might not be such a good idea. In fact, a large body of empirical evidence suggests that it is rarely the criterion selected. To see this, assume that you must select one of the two alternatives in each of the following five situations:

Situation 1: a_1:   The certainty of receiving \$1
                    or
                    a_2:   on the flip of a fair coin, \$10 if it comes up heads or $-\$1$ if it comes up tails.

Situation 2: b_1:   The certainty of receiving \$100
                    or
                    b_2:   on the flip of a fair coin, \$1,000 if it comes up heads or $-\$100$ if it comes up tails.

[2]Technically speaking, the term *utility function* is reserved for the case in which uncertainty is present. When each alternative has only one possible outcome, the term *value function* is used. In either case, the construction procedure is the same.

Situation 3: c_1:   The certainty of receiving \$1,000

or

c_2:   on the flip of a fair coin, \$10,000 if it comes up heads or −\$1,000 if it comes up tails.

Situation 4: d_1:   The certainty of receiving \$10,000

or

d_2:   on the flip of a fair coin, \$100,000 if it comes up heads or −\$10,000 if it comes up tails.

Situation 5: e_1:   The certainty of receiving \$10,000

or

e_2:   a payment of $\$2^n$, where n is the number of times that a fair coin is flipped until heads comes up. If heads appears on the first toss, then you receive \$2; if the coin shows tails on the first toss and heads on the second, then you receive \$4 and so forth. However, you are given only one chance; the game stops with the first showing of heads.

Most people would probably choose a_2, b_2, c_1, d_1 and e_1. The choices a_2 and b_2 would be those derived from an EMV maximization criterion because $\text{EMV}(a_2) = \frac{1}{2}\$10 + \frac{1}{2}(-\$1) = \$4.5$ is greater than the return from the certain choice $a_1 = \$1$, and $\text{EMV}(b_2) = \$450$ is greater than \$100. Nevertheless, in situations 3 and 4, c_1 would probably be preferred to c_2, even though $\text{EMV}(c_2) = \$4,500$ is greater than \$1,000, and d_1 would be preferred to d_2 even though $\text{EMV}(d_2) = \$45,000$ is greater than \$10,000. In situation 5, the EMV of e_2 is infinite; that is,

$$\text{EMV}(e_2) = \frac{1}{2}(\$2) + \frac{1}{4}(\$4) + \frac{1}{8}(\$8) + \cdots$$
$$= \$1 + \$1 + \$1 + \cdots$$
$$= \infty$$

yet e_1 would be preferred to e_2 by practically everyone.

In the first four situations, most people would tend to change their decision criterion away from maximizing EMV as soon as the thought of losing a large sum of money (say \$1,000) became too painful despite the pleasure to be gained from possibly obtaining a large sum (say, \$10,000). At this point, the person faced with such a choice would not be considering EMV but would instead be thinking solely of utility. In this sense, *utility* refers to the pleasure (utility) or displeasure (disutility) that one would derive from certain outcomes. In essence, we are saying that the person's displeasure from losing \$1,000 is greater that the pleasure of winning many times that amount. In situation 5, no prudent person would choose the gamble e_2 over the certainty of a relatively modest amount obtained from e_1. This problem, known as the St. Petersburg paradox, led Daniel Bernoulli to the first investigations of utility rather than EMV as the basis of decision making.

3.7.2 Bernoulli's Principle

Logic, observed behavior, and introspection all indicate that any adequate procedure for handling choice under uncertainty must involve two components: personal valuation of consequences and personal strengths of belief about the occurrence of uncertain events. Bernoulli's principle, as refined by von Neumann and Morgenstern (1947), has the normative justification of being a logical deduction from a small number of axioms that most people find reasonable. The relevant axioms differ slightly depending on whether the decision maker (a) has a single goal, (b) has multiple goals between which he or she can establish acceptable trade-off relations, or (c) has multiple goals that are not substitutable. The first two cases lead to a one-dimensional utility measure (i.e., real number) for each alternative action; the last to a lexicographically ordered utility vector.[3] We consider only the single-goal case here; multiple goals are taken up in subsequent chapters.

Axioms.

1. *Ordering.* For the two alternatives A_1 and A_2, one of the following must be true: the person either prefers A_1 to A_2 or A_2 to A_1 or is indifferent between them.
2. *Transitivity.* The person's evaluation of alternatives is transitive: if he or she prefers A_1 to A_2 and A_2 to A_3, then he or she prefers A_1 to A_3.
3. *Continuity.* If A_1 is preferred to A_2, and A_2 to A_3, then there exists a unique probability $p, 0 < p < 1$, such that the person is indifferent between outcome A_2 with certainty, or receiving A_1 with probability p and A_3 with probability $(1 - p)$. In other words, there exists a certainty equivalent to any gamble.
4. *Independence.* If A_1 is preferred to A_2, and A_3 is some other prospect, then a gamble with A_1 and A_3 as outcomes will be preferred to a gamble with A_2 and A_3 as outcomes if the probability of A_1 and A_2 occurring is the same in both cases.

These axioms relate to choices among both certain and uncertain outcomes. That is, if a person conforms to the four axioms, then a utility function that expresses his or her preferences for both certain outcomes (more precisely, we should say value function in this case) and the choices in a risky situation can be derived. In essence, they are equivalent to assuming that the decision maker is rational and consistent in his or her preferences and imply Bernoulli's principle, or as it is also known, the *expected utility theorem*.

Expected Utility Theorem.   Given a decision maker whose preferences satisfy the four axioms, there exists a function U, called a utility function, that associates a single real number or utility index with all risky prospects faced by the decision maker. This function has the following properties:

1. If the risky prospect A_1 is preferred to A_2 (written $A_1 > A_2$), then the utility index of A_1 will be greater than that of A_2 [i.e., $U(A_1) > U(A_2)$]. Conversely, $U(A_1) > U(A_2)$ implies that A_1 is preferred to A_2.

---

[3]Given two n-dimensional vectors $\mathbf{x}$ and $\mathbf{y}$, if $x_i = y_i$, for $i = 1, \ldots, r - 1$, and $x_r > y_r$, then $\mathbf{x}$ is said to be lexicographically greater than $\mathbf{y}$.

2. If A is the risky prospect with a set of outcomes $\{\theta\}$ distributed according to the probability density function $p(\theta)$, then the utility of A is equal to the statistically expected utility of A; that is,

$$U(A) = E[U(A)] \tag{3.2}$$

If $p(\theta)$ is discrete,

$$E[U(A)] = \sum_{\theta} U(\theta)p(\theta) \tag{3.3a}$$

and if $p(\theta)$ is continuous,

$$E[U(A)] = \int_{-\infty}^{\infty} U(\theta)p(\theta)d\theta \tag{3.3b}$$

As these equations indicate, only the first moment (i.e., the mean or expected value) of utility is relevant to the choice. For a person who accepts the axioms underlying Bernoulli's principle, the variance or other higher moments of utility are irrelevant; the expected value takes full account of all of the moments (mean, variance, skewness, etc.) of the probability distribution $p(\theta)$ of outcomes.

3. Uniqueness of the function is defined only up to a positive linear transformation. Given a utility function U, any other function U^* such that

$$U^* = aU + b, \quad a > 0, \tag{3.4}$$

for scalars a and b, will serve as well as the original function. Thus, utility is measured on an arbitrary scale and is a relative measure analogous, for example, to the various scales used for measuring temperature. Because there is no absolute scale for utility and because a person's utility function reflects his or her own personal valuations, it is not possible to compare one person's utility indices with another's (for further discussion of numbers and scales, see Gass 2001).

Bernoulli's principle thus provides a mechanism for ranking risky prospects in order of preference, the most preferred prospect being the one with the highest utility. Hence, Bernoullian or statistical decision theory implies the maximization of utility, which, by the expected utility theorem, is equivalent to maximization of expected utility. Equations (3.3a) and (3.3b) provide the empirical basis of application of the theory. Two concepts are involved: degree of preference (or utility) and degree of belief (or probability).

3.7.3 Constructing the Utility Function

Utility functions must be assessed separately for each decision maker. To be of use, utility values (i.e., subjective preferences) must be assigned to all possible outcomes for the problem at hand. Usually, we define a frame of reference whose lower and upper bounds represent the worst and best possible outcomes, respectively. In many circumstances, outcomes are nonmonetary in nature. For example, in selecting a portable computer, one weighs such factors as speed, memory, display quality, and weight. It is possible to assign utility values to these outcomes; however, in most business-related problems, a monetary consequence is of major importance. Hence, we illustrate how to evaluate one's utility function for money, although the same procedure applies to non-monetary outcomes.

The assessment of a person's utility function involves pinning down, in quantitative terms, subjective feelings that may not have been thought of before in such a precise way. At least four approaches for doing this have been distinguished (Keeney and Raiffa 1993): (1) direct measurement; (2) the von Neumann-Morgenstern (NM) method, or standard reference contract; (3) the modified NM method; and (4) the Ramsey method.

The first approach involves asking a series of questions of the type, "Suppose that I were to give you an outright gift of $100. How much money would you need to make you twice as happy as the $100 would make you feel?" The answers to a sequence of such questions enable the plotting of a utility curve against whatever arbitrarily chosen utility (value) scale is desired. The drawbacks of this approach are that it is not concerned with uncertainty, and for many people, it cannot be expected to be as precise as the other methods.

The other three approaches deal with the question of risk attitude directly and ask the decision maker to compare certain gambles to sure sums of money, or gambles to gambles. For example, in a new product development problem, a question might be to have the project manager choose between receiving $200,000 for certain versus a gamble (lottery), with equal chances of winning $1,000,000 and losing $500,000. Such a situation might arise if the project manager were faced with selecting one of two technologies: the first being a sure thing, the second being much more risky. Through this type of questioning, one can find some riskless value that would make the project manager indifferent (Axiom 3). This value is called the *certainty equivalent* (CE) of the gamble. When the CE is less than the expected monetary value (CE < EMV), we say that the decision maker is risk averse. The measurement procedure is continued with different gambles until enough data points are available to plot the utility curve.

In this subsection, we discuss the modified NM method, which, in our experience, is the most easily understood. The first step in deriving the utility function is to designate two monetary outcomes as reference points. For convenience, we look at the most favorable and least favorable outcomes and then select two values greater than or equal to and less than or equal to these outcomes. The utilities of these extreme points may be selected arbitrarily; however, convention usually assigns them values of 1 and 0, respectively. For example, in the new product development problem given below, the monetary outcomes range from $-$267,000 to $750,000. For expediency, we thus might choose extreme values of $-$500,000 and $1,000,000, assigning a utility of 0 to the first and a utility of 1 to the second. That is,

$$U(-\$0.5\text{M}) = 0 \quad \text{and} \quad U(\$1\text{M}) = 1 \tag{3.5}$$

Once again, the choice of the scale 0 to 1 is arbitrary and just as well could have been -100 to 100, or 34 to 78.

The standard reference contract, or NM method, is based on the concept of certainty equivalence. If outcome x_1 is preferred to x_2, and x_2 is preferred to x_3, then by continuity there exists a probability p such that

$$pU(x_1) + (1 - p)U(x_3) = U(x_2) \tag{3.6}$$

For specified values of x_1, x_2 and x_3, the utility of x_2 can be determined by questioning to find the value of p at which x_2 is the CE of the gamble involving x_1 and x_3 (i.e., what value of p will make you indifferent to the gamble of receiving x_2 for certain?), $U(x_1)$ and $U(x_3)$ being given values on an arbitrary scale. For example, if $U(x_1)$ is set at 1 and $U(x_3)$ at 0, then $U(x_2) = p$ [i.e., $p(1) + (1 - p)(0) = U(x_2)$]. By defining the values of p corresponding to an array of values of x_2 between x_1 and x_3, the utility curve may be plotted for values of x in this range.

The difficulty that arises in applying Eq. (3.6) is that most people have no experience in specifying probabilities and consequently become extremely frustrated with the questioning. This is especially true when the appropriate value of p is small, say, less than 0.1. To overcome the biases that result, the modified NM method uses neutral probabilities of $p = 0.5 = 1 - p$. Questions are posed to determine the CE x_2 for a 50-50 lottery of x_1 and x_3. Thus, we have

$$0.5U(x_1) + 0.5U(x_3) = U(x_2). \tag{3.7}$$

If $U(x_1)$ is set at 1 and $U(x_3)$ at 0, then $U(x_2) = 0.5$. In a similar manner, the CE may be established for the 50-50 lottery of x_1 and x_2, say x_4, which will have a utility of

$$U(x_4) = 0.5U(x_1) + 0.5U(x_2) = 0.75$$

and for the 50-50 lottery of x_2 and x_3, say x_5, which will have a utility of

$$U(x_5) = 0.5U(x_2) + 0.5U(x_3) = 0.25.$$

By such further linked questions, additional points on the utility curve may be established. Now, using Equation (3.5), let's see how we can find the project manager's utility function. To do this, we formulate the following two alternatives: (1) a gamble that offers a 50-50 chance of winning $1,000,000 and losing $500,000 and (2) one that offers a sure amount of money.

Suppose that you have the choice of the gamble (call this scenario B) versus the sure thing (call this A). How much money would the sure thing have to be such that you were indifferent between A and B (i.e., the two alternatives were equally attractive)? Suppose that you said $-$250,000. Because you are indifferent to these two options, they must have the same utility or, more properly, the same expected utility. Recall that the expected utility of any set of mutually exclusive outcomes resulting from a decision is the sum of the products of the utility of each outcome and its probability of occurrence. The expected utility of the gamble B is

$$U(\text{B}) = 0.5U(\$1{,}000{,}000) + 0.5U(-\$500{,}000)$$
$$= 0.5(1) + 0.5(0) = 0.5$$

implying that $U(B) = U(A) = U(-\$250,000) = 0.5$. The basic concept is depicted in Fig. 3.10.

We now have three points on the project manager's utility curve. Additional evaluations may be made in a similar manner to obtain a more precise picture. For example, pose an alternative that offers a 50-50 chance of gaining \$1,000,000 and losing \$250,000. Find the amount that must be offered with certainty to make him or her indifferent to the gamble. Suppose that he or she says \$75,000. Then

$$U(\$75,000) = 0.5U(\$1,000,000) + 0.5U(-\$250,000)$$
$$= 0.5(1) + 0.5(0.5) = 0.75$$

Next, pose the alternative involving a 50-50 chance of losing \$250,000 or \$500,000. The project manager would clearly consider this gamble unfavorable and would surely be willing to pay some amount to be relieved of the choice (in the same way that one buys insurance to be relieved of risk). Suppose that he or she were indifferent between the gamble and paying a fixed amount of \$420,000. Then

$$U(-\$420,000) = 0.5U(-\$250,000) + 0.5U(-\$500,000)$$
$$= 0.5(0.5) + 0.5(0) = 0.25$$

We now have five points on his or her utility function, as given in Table 3.1. These can be connected by a smooth curve to approximate the "true" utility function over the entire range from $-\$500,000$ to \$1,000,000 (see Fig. 3.11).

Note that to be consistent, the project manager should, for example, be indifferent between a gamble C, which offered an equal chance of winning \$1,000,000 or losing \$500,000, and a second gamble D, which offered an equal chance of winning \$75,000 or

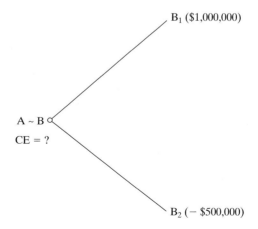

Figure 3.10   Diagram for utility assessment.

TABLE 3.1   Assessed Utilities for Project Manager

Monetary outcome, x	Utility, $U(x)$
$-\$500,000$	0.00
$-\$420,000$	0.25
$-\$250,000$	0.50
$\$75,000$	0.75
$\$1,000,000$	1.00

Figure 3.11   Utility function obtained from data in Table 3.1.

losing $420,000. That is,

$$U(\text{C}) = 0.5U(\$1,000,000) + 0.5U(-\$500,000) = 0.5(1) + 0.5(0) = 0.5$$
$$U(\text{D}) = 0.5U(\$75,000) + 0.5U(-\$420,000) = 0.5(0.75) + 0.5(0.25) = 0.5$$

If this is not true, then the manager's assessments are inconsistent and should be revised. Similar checks should be performed to gain confidence in the decision maker's responses.

To facilitate the analysis, a number of commercial products are available. These can be used to guide in the construction of the utility function, assess subjective probabilities, check for inconsistencies in judgment, and rank the alternatives.

3.7.4 Evaluating Alternatives

In the general case, we are given a set of m alternatives $A = \{A_1, \dots, A_m\}$, where each alternative may result in one of n outcomes or "states of nature." Call these $\theta_1, \dots, \theta_n$, and denote x_{ij} as the consequence realized if θ_j results when alternative i is selected. Also, let $p_j(\theta_j)$ be the probability that the state of nature θ_j occurs. Then, from Eq. (3.3a) we can compute the expected utility of alternative A_i as follows:

$$U(A_i) = \sum_{j=1}^{n} p_j(\theta_j)U(x_{ij}), \quad i = 1,\ldots,m \tag{3.8}$$

where $x_{ij} \equiv x_{ij}(\theta_j)$ is an implicit function of θ_j. For the deterministic case in which $n = 1$, implying that only one outcome is possible, Equation (3.8) reduces to $U(A_i) = U(x_i)$.

Example 3-24   (Selection of New Product Development Strategy)

As project manager of a research and development group, you have been assigned the responsibility for coming up with a new switching circuit as a modular component for a laser device. You are given a budget of $300,000 and 3 months to complete the project. Two technical approaches have been identified, one using a circuit incorporating conventional transistors and another designed around a single integrated chip.

You estimate that a successful conventional circuit design would be worth $478,300 to the company. In contrast, use of a single integrated chip would offer a simpler, more reliable circuit and one that was sufficiently easier to manufacture. Moreover, it would yield an additional cost savings of $150,000 and would be worth an additional $121,700 to the firm over and above any cost savings, for the quantity expected.

You are sure that either of the two approaches could be developed to satisfy the project's specifications given enough time and money. However, within the allotted time and budget, you estimate that there is a 30% chance that the conventional circuit would not meet specifications and a 50% chance that the integrated chip would also fail.

The end result of the project is to be a prototype built in the manufacturing shop from the drawings furnished by you. To work out the design details of the circuit and to identify and resolve unanticipated problems, you plan to design and build a breadboard model. This would take 3 months and cost (in labor, materials, and equipment) $60,000 for the conventional design and $100,000 for the integrated chip. The critical decision with which you are confronted is the choice of which design to pursue in construction of a breadboard.

Because you would be within budget, you have the additional option of pursuing the two technical approaches simultaneously. Nevertheless, if you undertake both in parallel, you will incur an additional $107,000 in expenses. What is the best course of action for conducting the development project?

Solution Let A_1 be the alternative associated with the conventional design, A_2 the alternative associated with the integrated chip, and A_3 the parallel strategy. Note that if the last is pursued and both breadboards are built, then the cost will be $267,000.

The data for this problem are displayed in Table 3.2 in the form of a payoff matrix. For each alternative, there are four possible states of nature ($n = 4$), depending on whether the respective breadboard is a success (S) or a failure (F). These outcomes, θ_j ($j = 1,\ldots,4$), are indicated in the first row of the table. The probabilities $p_j(\theta_j)$ are computed by taking the product of the two possible outcomes, S or F. For example, $p_1(\theta_1) = \text{Prob}(A_1 \text{ is a success}) \times \text{Prob}(A_2 \text{ is a success}) = 0.7 \times 0.5 = 0.35$. The monetary consequences of each action for each state of nature are determined by subtracting the costs from the returns. For example, x_{33} represents the payoff for which both designs are pursued but only the second succeeds. The cost would be $60,000 for the conventional option + $100,000 for the integrated chip + $107,000 for the duplication of effort = $267,000. The returns to the firm are $478,300 + $121,700 + $150,000 for ease of manufacturability = $750,000. Thus x_{33} = $750,000 − $267,000 = $483,000.

TABLE 3.2   Payoff Matrix for New Product Development Example

θ_j	A_1:S	S	F	F	
	A_2:S	F	S	F	
$A_i \setminus p_j(\theta_j)$	0.35	0.35	0.15	0.15	EMV ($1,000)
A_1	418.3	418.3	−60.0	−60.0	275
A_2	650.0	−100.0	650.0	−100.0	275
A_3	483.0	211.3	483.0	−267.0	275

The last column of Table 3.2 lists the EMV of each alternative. These values were obtained by repeated application of Eq. (3.1) and all are equal to $275,000. This suggests that one should be indifferent to all three alternatives, but can this really be the case? You, as the decision maker, might not be willing to tolerate the prospect of losing $100,000 or more (e.g., such a loss might cost you your job or might put the company into a difficult financial position), but you might be willing and able to bear the strain of a $60,000 loss. Hence, you would choose A_1 over the other options in that no more than $60,000 could be lost with A_1, whereas $100,000 and $267,000 could be lost with A_2 and A_3, respectively.

If we now approach this problem from a utility theory point of view, whereby our attitude toward risk is implicitly taken into account in the construction of the utility function, then the analysis is more informative. To proceed, the first step is to convert monetary outcomes to "utiles" by using the curve in Fig. 3.11. The results are displayed in Table 3.3, where now we see that A_1 is preferred to A_3, which is preferred to A_2, although only slightly. Evidently, the increased prospect for success with alternative 3 is not sufficiently high to balance the risk of losing $267,000 should both projects fail. Similarly, the $650,000 payoff associated with A_2 is not large enough for this risk-averse decision maker to compensate for the 50% chance of losing $100,000. Nevertheless, because the expected utilities for the three alternatives are so close, additional effort should go into refining the probability, cost, and return estimates. ∎

3.7.5 Characteristics of the Utility Function

The curve derived in Fig. 3.11 increases monotonically from the lower left to the upper right. In other words, it has a positive slope throughout. This is generally the characteristic of utility functions. It simply implies that people ordinarily attach greater utility to larger amounts of money than to smaller amounts (i.e., more is preferred to less). Economists refer to such a psychological trait as a *positive marginal utility for money*.

TABLE 3.3   Utility Matrix for New Product Development Example

θ_j	A_1:S	S	F	F	
	A_2:S	F	S	F	Expected
$A_i \setminus p_j(\theta_j)$	0.35	0.35	0.15	0.15	utility
A_1	0.90	0.90	0.70	0.70	0.84
A_2	0.95	0.67	0.95	0.67	0.81
A_3	0.92	0.83	0.92	0.49	0.82

Three general types of utility functions are depicted in Fig. 3.12. Of course, actual shapes may vary, and the particular application will determine the scale on the horizontal axis. Any number of combinations of the three are possible. The concave-downward shape is illustrative of a person who has a diminishing marginal utility for money, although the marginal utility is always positive (the slope is positive but decreasing as the dollar amount increases—the rate of change of the slope is negative). This type of utility function is indicative of a *risk avoider*, or someone who is risk averse. The decreasing slope implies that the utility of a given amount of gain is less than the disutility of an equal amount of loss; also, as the dollar gain increases, it becomes less valuable. This is in part the rationale for a progressive income tax system. A person characterized by such a utility function would prefer a small but certain monetary gain to a gamble whose EMV is greater but may involve a larger but unlikely gain, or a large and not unlikely loss.

The linear function in Fig. 3.12 depicts the behavior of a person who is *neutral* or indifferent to risk. For such a person, every increment of, say, $1,000 has an associated constant increment of utility (the slope of the utility curve is positive and constant). That is, he or she values an additional dollar of income just as highly regardless of whether it is the first dollar or the 100,000th dollar gained. This type of person would use the EMV criterion in making decisions because by so doing, he or she would also maximize expected utility. Government decision making usually proceeds from a risk-neutral viewpoint. Referring to Fig. 3.12, the expected utility of each alternative in Example 3-24 is 0.51.

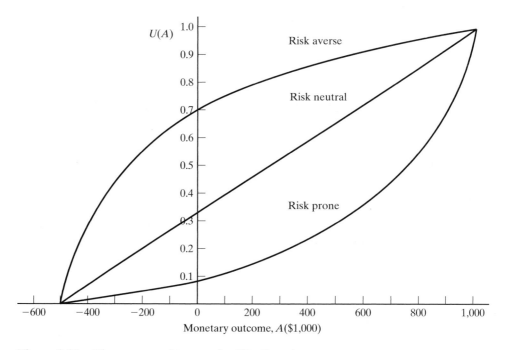

Figure 3.12   Three general types of utility functions.

The third curve in Fig. 3.12, which has a convex shape, is that of a *risk seeker*, someone who is risk prone. Note that the slope of the utility function increases as the dollar amount increases. This implies that the utility of a given gain is greater than the disutility of an equivalent loss. A risk-seeking person subjectively values each dollar of gain more highly. This type of person willingly accepts gambles that have a smaller EMV than an alternative payoff received with certainty. He or she will also take an "unfair" bet in the sense that he or she will choose an action whose EMV is negative. In the case of such a person, the attractiveness of a possibly large payoff in the gamble tends to outweigh the fact that the probability of such a payoff may indeed be exceedingly small. People who persistently buy lottery tickets fall into this category. When the risk-prone curve in Fig. 3.12 is used in Example 3-24, the expected utilities for the three alternatives are 0.155, 0.195 and 0.157, thus reversing the order of preference. Now, $A_2 > A_3 > A_1$.

Most people have utility functions whose slopes do not change very much for small changes in money, suggesting risk-neutral attitudes. In considering courses of action, however, in which one of the consequences is very adverse or in which one of the payoffs is very favorable, people can be expected to depart from the maximization of EMV criterion. In fact, most people are risk seekers for small gains and losses and risk avoiders when the stakes are high, in either direction. This explains why most of us buy insurance and stay with secure but often unexciting jobs rather than seek out risky opportunities that have the probability of making us wildly rich.

For many business decisions, for which the monetary consequences may represent only a small fraction of the total assets of the organization, maximization of EMV constitutes a reasonable approximation to the decision-making criterion of maximization of expected utility. In such cases, the utility function may be considered linear over the range of possible monetary outcomes.

TEAM PROJECT

Thermal Transfer Plant

On the basis of your excellent report and presentation, TMS has decided to approve a prototype project in the area of waste management and recycling. Because there is a need for a rotary combustor in one of the company's new plant designs, a decision was made to select this project as a prototype.

Rotary combustors are designed to burn a variety of solid combustible wastes, including municipal, commercial, industrial, and agricultural wastes. The basic component of the combustor is the rotating barrel, made out of alternating carbon steel water tubes and perforated steel bars (Fig. 3.13). The barrel assembly is set at a slope of $-6°$ and is rotated slowly [approximately 10 revolutions per hour (rph)]. Solid waste is charged from the higher end of the barrel, and the combustion air comes into the barrel through the perforated holes. As the material burns, it tumbles through the barrel and eventually comes out of the lower end as residue (Fig. 3.14). In the process, heated forced air promotes drying and burning.

Hot gases created inside the barrel convert the boiler water into steam, which is used in the generation of electricity. High thermal efficiency of up to 80% provides

Figure 3.13 Arrangement of rotary combustor.

Figure 3.14 Details of rotary combustor.

maximum energy recovery through heat transfer from all hot surfaces of the combustor/boiler. Simplified moving parts ensure ease of operation, maintenance, and servicing, as well as minimal repair costs.

The combustor capacity is targeted for 14 tons/day. Estimated costs are as follows:

Cost of material:

Combustor barrel	$10,000
Tires and trunnions	$50,000
Chutes	$10,000
Drive gears and chain	$20,000
Pushers (2)	$2,000
Enclosure and insulation	$20,000
Rotary water joint	$5,000
Hydraulic drive system (includes power unit, cylinders, and combustor drive components)	$90,000
Welding materials	$30,000

Cost of labor:

Combustor barrel fabrication 10 workers, 8 weeks at $50/hr	$160,000
Tire and trunnion installation 5 workers, 1 week	$10,000
Chute fabrication 4 workers, 2 weeks	$16,000
Gear installation 2 workers, 2 days	$1,600
Pusher fabrication 2 workers, 2 weeks	$8,000
Enclosure fabrication 10 workers, 4 weeks	$80,000
Water joint installation 2 workers, 1 day	$800

Other:

Design	$15,000
Instrumentation	$13,000
Pressure testing	$2,500
Preassembly	$7,000
Breakdown and loading for shipment	$3,000
Overhead	25%

The following factors contribute to the risk of the project:

Schedule Risks

- *NIMBY (not in my back yard).* The construction of thermal transfer plants may prove to be a long, drawn-out affair. In addition to Environmental Protection Agency requirements, local opposition must be considered.
- One option for the combustor drive is to use a single large hydraulic motor. There are two manufacturers of this type of motor, one in Sweden and one in Germany.

Cost Risks

- Costs due to delays (see first item above).
- Price increases—an entire plant is being built—estimated duration is 2 years.
- Design time—difficult to estimate.
- Fabrication time.
- Overhead is very difficult to estimate and control.

Technological Risks

- Hazardous location—a rotary combustor is a furnace, and because of fire hazards, mineral-based hydraulic fluid cannot be used. Fire-resistant fluids are an alternative but require that certain hydraulic components be down-rated.
- Speed control—the accuracy and degree of variability of speed control for the rams is yet to be determined.
- No satisfactory design exists yet for a rotary water joint.
- Satisfactory seals around the combustor are yet to be developed.
- Hydraulic leaks at other installations have been a problem, particularly at the rams and at the power unit.
- Instrumentation—there is disagreement as to the sophistication of instrumentation required, particularly on the rams.

TMS's main business is design and consulting; however, it is believed that this new area of operation may present an opportunity for the company to develop manufacturing capabilities. Management has three alternatives under consideration:

1. Design the rotary combustor at TMS based on customer needs, but subcontract all manufacturing and assembly.
2. Design the rotary combustor at TMS, subcontracting all manufacturing of parts but assembling the system at TMS facilities.
3. Design, manufacture, and assemble the combustor at TMS.

Your assignment is to compare the economic aspects, including risks.

1. For each alternative, list the risks involved and their associated costs.
2. Analyze TMS's overall financial position under each alternative.
3. Include projected differences in total expenditures and investments.

In evaluating these alternatives, you can make any assumptions necessary. Each should be stated explicitly.

DISCUSSION QUESTIONS

1. What are the shortcomings of engineering economic analysis? What difficulties and uncertainties might one face when performing such an analysis?

2. American businesses have often been criticized for short-term thinking that places too much emphasis on payback period and ROR. When Honda started making cars in the early 1970s, for example, the chief executive officer stated that the firm would be "willing to accept an ROR no greater than 2% or 3% for as long as it took to be recognized as the best car maker in the world." In light of the success of many Japanese firms, is the criticism of American business justified?

3. If a firm is short of capital, then what action might it take to conserve the capital it has and to obtain more?

4. Explain why the marginal cost for borrowing money increases. Why might the cost also be high for borrowing small amounts?

5. Are there any reasons for using present value analysis rather than future value analysis?

6. Why might a decision maker like to see the payback analysis as well as the ROR and the NPV?

7. In the 1960s, the top marginal tax rate for individuals in the United States was 90%; that is, for each dollar that a person earned above roughly $100,000, he or she had to pay 90 cents in taxes. It was argued by many economists at the time that this rate was much too high. What do you think are the negative economic and social consequences of such "confiscatory" tax rates?

8. Discuss why the comparison of alternative investment decisions is especially difficult when the investment choices have different useful lives.

9. Breakeven analysis is typically simplified by using constant-unit variable costs and revenues. What would you expect realistic costs and revenues to be, and what would a corresponding breakeven chart look like?

10. Identify a situation and set of alternatives whose outcomes are not measured on a monetary scale. Assess your utility function for this situation.

11. Give some examples for which the axioms underlying Bernoulli's principle are violated.

12. Most countries have a progressive income tax system whereby each dollar earned in incrementally higher tax brackets is taxed at an increasingly higher rate. Do you think that a flat tax system would be more fair? How about a proportional tax system? Explain your answer.

13. If you just assessed a corporate executive's utility function for a problem concerning the purchase of supercomputer, then could you use the same utility function for a problem of buying an automobile? A personal computer? Explain.

14. It has been argued that comparable interpersonal utility scales may be established on the basis of equating people's best conceivable situations at the top end and their worst conceivable situations at the bottom end. What's wrong, if anything, with this approach?

15. In situations in which wealthy employers bargain over wages and benefits with needy employees on an individual basis, the employer usually gives away much less than he actually might have been pressured into or could have afforded. Can you explain this consequence in terms of utility theory?

EXERCISES

3.1 Construct a diagram illustrating the cash flows involved in the following transactions from the borrower's viewpoint. The amount borrowed is $2,000 at 10% for 5 years.

   a. Year-end payment of interest only; repayment of principal at the end of the 5 years
   b. Year-end repayment of one fifth of the principal ($400) plus interest on the unpaid balance
   c. Lump-sum repayment at the end of year 5 of principal plus accrued interest compounded annually
   d. Year-end payments of equal-sized installments, as in a standard installment loan contract

3.2 A firm wants to lease some land from you for 20 years and build a warehouse on it. As your payment for the lease, you will own the warehouse at the end of the 20 years, estimated to be worth $20,000 at that time.

   a. If $i = 8\%$, then what is the PW of the deal to you?
   b. If $i = 2\%$ per quarter, then what is the PW of the deal to you?

3.3 In payment for engineering services, a client offers your choice between (1) $10,000 now and (2) a share in the project, which you are fairly certain you can cash in for $15,000 5 years from now. With $i = 10\%$, which is the most profitable choice?

3.4 Assume that a medium-size town now has a peak electrical demand of 105 megawatts, increasing at an annually compounded rate of 15%. The current generating capacity is 240 megawatts.

   a. How soon will additional generating capacity be needed on-line?
   b. If the new generator is designed to take care of needs 5 years past the on-line date, then what size should it be? Assume that the present generators continue in service.

3.5 A local government agency has asked you to consult regarding acquisition of land for recreation needs for the urban area. The following data are provided:

Urban population 10 years ago	49,050
Urban area population now	89,920
Desired ratio of recreation land in	
acres per 1,000 population	10 acres/1,000
Actual acres of land now held by local	
government for recreational purposes	803 acres

   a. Find the annual growth rate in the urban area by assuming that the population grew at a compounded annual rate over the past 10 years.
   b. How many years ago was the desired ratio of recreation land per 1,000 population exceeded if no more land was acquired and the population continued to grow at the indicated rate?
   c. The local government is planning to purchase more land to supply the recreational needs for 10 years past the point in time found in part (b). How many acres of land should they purchase to maintain the desired ratio, assuming that the population growth continues at the same rate?

3.6 A young engineer decides to save $240 per year toward retirement in 40 years.

   a. If he invests this sum at the end of every year at 9%, then how much will be accumulated by retirement time?
   b. If by astute investing the interest rate could be raised to 12%, then what sum could be saved?

c. If he deposits one fourth of this annual amount each quarter ($60 per quarter) in an interest-bearing account earning a nominal annual interest rate of 12%, compounded quarterly, then how much could be saved by retirement time?

d. In part (c), what annual effective interest rate is being earned?

3.7 A lump sum of $100,000 is borrowed now to be repaid in one lump sum at end of month (EOM) 120. The loan bears a nominal interest rate of 12% compounded monthly. No partial repayments will be accepted on the loan. To accumulate the repayment lump sum due, monthly deposits are made into an interest-bearing account that bears interest at 0.75% per month from EOM 1 until EOM 48. From EOM 48 until EOM 120, the interest rate changes to 0.5%. Monthly deposits of amount A begin with the first deposit at EOM 1 and continue until EOM 48. Beginning with EOM 49, the deposits are doubled at amount $2A$ and continued at this level until the final deposit at EOM 120. Draw the cash flow diagram and find the initial monthly deposit amount A.

3.8 A backhoe is purchased for $20,000. The terms are 10% down and 2% per month on the unpaid balance for 60 months.

a. How much are the monthly payments?

b. What annual effective interest rate is being charged?

3.9 Your firm owns a large earth-moving machine and has contracts to move earth for $1 per cubic yard. For $100,000, this machine may be modified to increase its production output by an extra 10 yd^3 per hour, with no increase in operating costs. The earth-moving machine is expected to last another 8 years, with zero salvage value at the end of that time. Determine whether this investment meets the company objective of earning at least 15% return. Assume that the equipment works 2,000 hours per year.

3.10 Your firm wants to purchase a $50,000 computer, no money down. The $50,000 will be paid off in 10 equal end-of-year payments with interest at 8% on the unpaid balance.

a. What are the annual end-of-year payments?

b. What hourly charge should be included to pay off the computer, assuming 2,000 hours of work per year, credited at the end of the year?

c. Assume that 5 years from now you would like to trade in the computer and purchase a new one. You expect a 5% increase in price each year. What would the new computer cost at the end of year 5?

d. What is the unpaid balance on the current computer after 5 years?

3.11 A transportation authority asks you to check on the feasibility of financing for a toll bridge that will cost $2,000,000. The authority can borrow this amount now and repay it from tolls. It will take 2 years to construct and be open for traffic at end of year (EOY) 2. Tolls will be accumulated throughout the third year and will be available for the initial annual repayment at EOY 3. In subsequent years, the tolls are deposited at the end of the year. Draw the cash flow diagram assuming a flow rate of 10,000 cars/day. How much must be charged to each car to repay the borrowed funds in 20 equal annual installments (first installment due at EOY 3), with 8% compound interest on the unpaid balance?

3.12 A firm invested $15,000 in a project that seemed to have excellent potential. Unfortunately, a lengthy labor dispute in year 3 resulted in costs that exceeded benefits by $8,000. The cash flow for the project is as follows:

Year	0	1	2	3	4	5	6
Cash flow ($)	−15,000	+10,000	+6,000	−8,000	+4,000	+4,000	+4,000

Compute the ROR for the project. Assume a 12% interest rate on external investments for purposes of moving money from one period to another.

3.13 An oil company plans to purchase for $70,000 a piece of vacant land on the corner of two busy streets. The company has four different types of businesses that it installs on properties of this type.

Plan	Cost of improvements*	Description
A	$75,000	Conventional gas station with service facilities for lubrication, oil changes, etc.
B	$230,000	Automatic car wash facility with gasoline pump island in front
C	$30,000	Discount gas station (no service bays)
D	$130,000	Gas station with low-cost, quick-car-wash facility

*Cost of improvements does not include the $70,000 cost of land.

In each case, the estimated useful life of the improvements is 15 years. The salvage value for each is estimated to be the $70,000 cost of the land. The net annual income, after paying all operating expenses, is projected as follows:

Plan	Net annual income
A	$23,300
B	$44,300
C	$10,000
D	$27,500

If the oil company expects a 10% ROR on its investments, then which plan (if any) should be selected?

3.14 A firm is considering three mutually exclusive alternatives as part of a production improvement program. The relevant data are as follows:

	A	B	C
Installation cost	$10,000	$15,000	$20,000
Uniform annual benefit	$1,625	$1,625	$1,890
Useful life (years)	10	20	20

For each alternative, the salvage value at the end of useful life is zero. At the end of 10 years, alternative A could be replaced by a copy of itself that has identical cost and benefits. The MARR is 6%. If the analysis period is 20 years, then which alternative should be selected?

3.15 Consider four mutually exclusive alternatives each having an 8-year useful life. The costs and benefits of each are given in the following table:

	A	B	C	D
Initial cost	$1,000	$800	$600	$500
Uniform annual benefit	$122	$120	$97	$122
Salvage value	$750	$500	$500	0

If the minimum acceptable ROR is 8%, then which alternative should be selected?

3.16 A project has the following costs and benefits. What is the payback period?

Year	Costs	Benefits
0	$1,400	
1	$500	
2	$300	$400
3–10		$300 per year

3.17 A motor with a 200-horsepower output is needed for intermittent use in a factory. A Teledyne motor costs $7,000 and has an electrical efficiency of 89%. An Allison motor costs $6,000 and has an 85% efficiency. Neither motor would have any salvage value after 20 years of use because the cost to remove them would equal their scrap value. The maintenance cost for either motor is estimated at $300 per year. Electric power costs $0.072/kilowatthour (1 hp = 0.746 KW). If a 10% annual interest rate is used in the calculations, then what is the minimum number of hours that the higher-initial-cost Teledyne motor must be used each year to justify its purchase? Use a 20-year planning horizon.

3.18 Lu Hodler planned to buy a rental property as an investment. After looking for several months, she found an attractive duplex that could be purchased for $93,000 cash. The total expected income from renting out both sides of the duplex would be $800 per month. The total annual expenses for property taxes, repairs, gardening, and so on are estimated at $600 per year. For tax purposes, Lu plans to depreciate the building by the SOYD method, assuming that the building has a 20-year remaining life and no salvage value. Of the total $93,000 cost of the property, $84,000 represents the value of the building and $9,000 is the value of the lot (only the former can be depreciated). Assume that Lu is in the 38% incremental income tax bracket (combined state and federal taxes) throughout the 20 years.

In this analysis, Lu estimates that the income and expenses will remain constant at their present levels. If she buys and holds the property for 20 years, then what after-tax ROR can she expect to receive on her investment, using the assumptions noted below?

a. The building and lot can be sold at the end of 20 years for the $9,000 estimated value of the lot.

b. A more optimistic estimate of the future value of the property is that it can be sold for $100,000 at the end of the 20 years.

3.19 The effective combined tax rate in an owner-managed corporation is 40%. An outlay of $20,000 for certain new assets is under consideration. It is estimated that for the next 8 years, these assets will be responsible for annual receipts of $9,000 and annual disbursements (other than for income taxes) of $4,000. After this time, they will be used only for standby purposes, and no future excess of receipts over disbursements is expected.

a. What is the prospective ROR before income taxes?

b. What is the prospective ROR after taxes if these assets can be written off for tax purposes in 8 years using straight-line depreciation?

c. What is the prospective ROR after taxes if it is assumed that these assets must be written off over the next 20 years using straight-line depreciation?

3.20 The Coma Chemical Company needs a large insulated stainless steel tank for the expansion of its plant. Coma has located one at a brewery that has just been closed. The brewery offers to sell the tank for $15,000, including delivery. The price is so low that Coma believes that it can sell the tank at any future time and recover its $15,000 investment. The outside of the tank is lined with heavy insulation that requires considerable maintenance. Estimated costs are as follows:

Year	0	1	2	3	4	5
Maintenance cost	$2,000	$500	$1,000	$1,500	$2,000	$2,500

a. On the basis of a 15% before-tax MARR, what is the economic life of the insulated tank; that is, how long should it be kept?

b. Is it likely that the insulated tank will be replaced by another tank at the end of its computed economic life? Explain.

3.21 The Gonzo Manufacturing Company is considering the replacement of one of its machine fixtures with a more flexible variety. The new fixture would cost $3,700, have a 4-year useful and depreciable life, and have no salvage value. For tax purposes, SOYD depreciation would be used. The existing fixture was purchased 4 years ago at a cost of $4,000 and has been depreciated by straight-line depreciation assuming an 8-year life and no salvage value. It could be sold now to a used equipment dealer for $1,000 or be kept in service for another 4 years. It would then have no salvage value. The new fixture would save approximately $900 per year in operating costs compared with the existing one. Assume a 40% combined state and federal tax rate and that capital gains (and losses) are taxed at 40% as well.

Hint: For the existing fixture, the "investment" cost is the opportunity cost of not selling it.

a. Compute the before-tax ROR on the replacement proposal of installing the new fixture rather than keeping the old one.

b. Compute the after-tax ROR on the proposal.

3.22 The following estimates have been made for two mutually exclusive alternatives; one must be chosen. The before-tax rate of return required is 20%.

	A	B
Installed cost	$120,000	$150,000
Estimated useful life	10 years	10 years
Salvage at retirement	$20,000	$30,000
Annual operating costs	$20,000	$15,000

Try to minimize your computations as you determine which course of action to recommend.

3.23 The following cost estimates apply to independent equipment alternatives A and B. The before-tax ROR required is 20%.

	A	B
Installed cost	$100,000	$40,000
Operating costs	$5,000 at the end of year 1 and increasing by $1,000 per year for 20 years	$10,000 at the end of year 1 and increasing by $2,000 per year for 10 years
Overhaul costs every 5 years	$10,000	None required
Economic life	20 years	10 years
Salvage value at end of life (just overhauled)	$20,000	$10,000

a. Compare the NPV of each using a study period of 20 years.

b. Compare the annual equivalent costs.

3.24 An investor requires a MARR of 12% before inflation (not considering the effect of inflation on future costs and benefits).

   a. If an inflation rate of 8% is expected, then what MARR should the investor require for an analysis that includes the effect of inflation?

   b. If the labor cost is $15 an hour today and the inflation rate is 6%, then how much would you expect the labor cost to be in 3 years?

3.25 Martha is considering the purchase of the piece of land and some new equipment adjacent to her day care center to use as a play area. Maintenance costs (e.g., mowing the lawn, repairs) are expected to be $500 a year for every year of the project. She expects that the additional lure of the play area will bring in extra business, increasing her income by $1,000 in the first year, and then by an additional $600/year thereafter ($1,600 in year 2, and so on). She plans to keep the land for 5 years, then donate it to the town (meaning no salvage value). All of these costs and revenues are estimated in today's dollars. The cash flows are expected to inflate by 7% per year. This is the same as the general rate of inflation.

   How much should she pay for the land to get a 12% ROR? The 12% includes the effect of the 7% inflation rate.

3.26 An investment of $2,000 results in the cash flow below. The amounts are expressed in constant dollars.

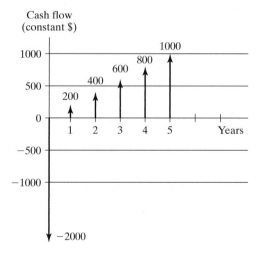

   a. The general rate of inflation is 6%, and future cash flows are expected to increase with inflation. Show the amounts in actual (year-n) dollars in the following table:

Year	0	1	2	3	4	5
Cash flow						

   b. Your minimum acceptable ROR without considering inflation is 10%. Should you accept this investment opportunity? Show your work.

3.27 For the cash flow given in the figure of the previous exercise, say that you must pay taxes on the incomes shown. The investment for the project is to be depreciated with the SOYD method. The future incomes are expected to increase with an inflation rate of 6%. The general rate of inflation is also 6%. The tax rate is 40%, the tax life is 5 years, and salvage is zero. Show in the table below the after-tax cash flows for the 5 years associated with this project. Also show the interest rate that you should use that is appropriate for these cash flows. The after-tax MARR without considering inflation is 10%.

Year	0	1	2	3	4	5
ATCF						

Should you accept or reject this project? Show your work.

3.28 Your brother needs a $5,000 loan to go to college. Because of his poverty, he will pay nothing for the next 4 years. Five years from today, he will begin paying you $2,500 a year for the next 4 years. The first payment occurs 5 years from today, and the total of the four payments will be $10,000.

  a. If your minimum ROR is 8%, then is this an acceptable investment? Explain.
  b. For the same payment schedule but with a 5% rate of inflation, is this an acceptable investment? Note that your brother pays you $2,500 a year regardless of the inflation rate. Provide quantitative justification for your decision.

3.29 You are to do an analysis of an investment with and without taxes and with and without considering inflation. The initial investment (at time 0) is $10,000. The projected benefits of the investment are $1,000 per year. After 5 years, the project will be sold for $8,000. All of these amounts are estimated in real (year-0) dollars. The MARR for the project is 20% and does not include an allowance for inflation. This MARR is to be used for both the before-tax and the after-tax analyses. In each case, you are to write the formula for the NPV of the investment. Be sure to show the appropriate interest rate. It is not necessary to evaluate the formula.

  a. Consider the investment without taxes and without inflation. Write the formula for the NPV of the investment.
  b. Consider the investment with taxes but without inflation. Write the formula for the NPV of the investment. Use straight-line depreciation with a salvage of 0. All income and capital gains are taxed at 40%.
  c. Consider the investment without taxes but with inflation. The original information given about the problem was in real dollars. The inflation rate is 10% per year for the benefits. The salvage value is also expected to be affected by inflation, growing at a rate of 10% per year. The general inflation rate is also 10% per year.
  d. Consider both taxes and inflation in this part. The general inflation rate is 10% per year, affecting both the annual benefits and the salvage value. Use straight-line depreciation with a salvage value of 0. Assume that all income and capital gains are taxed at 40%. Find the NPV of the investment.

3.30 The tables below show the operating cost and salvage value for a machine that was purchased for $50,000 and has a useful life of 3 years. Find its economic life using an MARR of 10%.

  a.

Year	Operating cost	Salvage value
1	$10,000	0
2	$40,000	0
3	$70,000	0

b.

Year	Operating cost	Salvage value
1	$10,000	$30,000
2	$10,000	$20,000
3	$10,000	0

3.31 Your company purchased a machine for $14,000 with a 6-year tax life. The SOYD method is used for depreciation, and the tax salvage value is zero.

    a. After the third year of use, the machine is sold for $10,000. How much does the company get from the sale after taxes, assuming that the tax rate on capital gains is 40%?

    b. Neglect taxes in this part. After the third year of life, the company is thinking about replacing the machine with a new one. It can be sold now for $10,000. Next year it will be worth only $6,000, and in 2 years, only $4,000. Three years from now the machine will have no resale value. The operating cost of the machine is expected to be constant for the next 3 years at $1,000 per annum. The new machine has a life of 10 years with a NAC of $5,000. Should the old machine be replaced with the new one if the company's MARR is 10%? Explain.

3.32 A milling machine (machine A) in your company's shop has a current market value of $30,000. It was bought 9 years ago for $54,000 and has since been depreciated by the straight-line method assuming a 12-year tax life. If the decision is made to keep the machine at this point it time, then it can be expected to last another 12 years (measured from today). At the end of the 12 years, it will be worthless. The operating costs of this machine are $7,500 per year and are not expected to change for its remaining life.

    Alternatively, machine A can be replaced by a smaller machine B, which costs $42,000 and is expected to last 12 years. Its operating costs are $5,000 per year and would be depreciated by the straight-line method over the 12-year period with no salvage value expected.

    Both income and capital gains are taxed at 40%. Compare the after-tax EUACs of the two machines and decide whether machine A should be retained or replaced by machine B. Use a 10% after-tax MARR in your calculations.

3.33 What is the argument for using assessment procedures based on 50-50 gambles as opposed to assessment procedures based on using reference gambles?

3.34 Explain why identification of special attitudes toward risk can simplify the utility assessment process.

3.35 Given the following information, plot four points on the person's preference curve. The maximum payoff is $1,000. The minimum payoff is $0. The CE for a 50-50 gamble between $1,000 and $0 is $400. The CE for a 50-50 gamble between $400 and $0 is $100.

3.36 As part of a decision analysis, Archie Leach provided the following information:

- He was indifferent between a 50-50 chance at +$10 million and −$10 million, and −$5 million for certain.
- His CE for a lottery offering a 0.5 chance at −$5 million and a 0.5 chance at +$10 million was $0.
- He was indifferent between a lottery with a 0.7 chance at +$10 million and a 0.3 chance at $0, and +$5 million for certain.

Sketch a preference curve for Leach on the basis of this information.

3.37 Refer to Fig. 3.15.

Figure 3.15   Preference curve for risk-averse decision maker.

a. Specify a reference gamble that is equivalent (based on this curve) to the certain amount $30,000.

b. Specify a 50-50 gamble that is equivalent (based on this curve) to the certain amount $30,000.

3.38 Beverly Silverman had long been promised a graduation present of $10,000 by her father, to be received on graduation day 3 months hence. Her father had recently offered an alternative gift of 1,000 shares of stock in Opera Systems, Inc., a consulting firm with which Beverly was slightly acquainted. He requested that she choose between the two gifts by the following day. On the day she was trying to decide, the stock was selling for $12 per share. Thus, it looked like it would be wise to take the stock because its present value was $12,000. She recognized, however, that she would not receive the stock until graduation day and that the stock price 3 months in the future was uncertain. She also recognized that her utility for money was not linear and that her risk aversion would play a major role in her decision. With these facts in mind, Beverly reached the following conclusions:

1. She believed that the stock price was more likely to rise than to fall in the intervening 3 months and that it was as likely to be above $14 per share as below that figure when she was to receive the stock.

2. She believed that there was only 1 chance in 100 that the stock price would drop to less than $6 per share and an equal chance that the price would be more than twice its current value on graduation day.

3. She also thought that there was only one chance in five that the price would be below $10 and that there was one chance in four that it would be above $16 when she received it.

In considering her preferences, Beverly decided the following:

1. That her CE for a lottery offering a 50-50 chance at $0 and $25,000 was $9,000.
2. That her CE for a lottery offering a 0.2 chance at $25,000 and a 0.8 chance at 0 was $3,000.
3. That her CE for a lottery offering a 50-50 chance at $3,000 or $25,000 was $12,000.
4. That her CE for a lottery offering a 50-50 chance at $12,000 or $25,000 was $17,000.

Determine the cumulative probability distribution that Ms Silverman has assigned to the stock price. Calculate her CE for the gift of the stock.

3.39 A manager expresses indifference between a certain profit of $5,000 and a venture with a 70% chance of making $10,000 and a 30% chance of making nothing. If the manager's utility scale is set at 1 utile for $0 and 100 utiles for $10,000, then what is the utility index for $5,000?

3.40 The manager in Exercise 3.39 is indifferent between a venture that has a 60% chance of making $10,000 and a 40% chance of making $1,000, and a sure investment that yields $5,000. Find the value of $1,000 in utiles for this manager.

3.41 Below are the results of a preference test given to an executive:

1. She is indifferent between an investment that will yield a certain $10,000 and a risky venture with a 50% chance of $30,000 profit and a 50% chance of a loss of $1,000.
2. Her utility function for money has the following shape:

Money ($)	−1,000	0	5,000	20,000	30,000
Utility	−2	0	10	20	30

A new risky venture is proposed. The possible payoffs are *either* $0 or $20,000. The probabilities of the gain cannot be determined. Find the probability combination of $0 and $20,000 that would make the executive indifferent to the certain $10,000.

3.42 Frances Gumm has an opportunity to invest $3,000 in a venture that has a 0.2 chance of making nothing, a 0.3 chance of making $2,000, a 0.2 chance of making $4,000, and a 0.3 chance of making $6,000. Her utilities for each of the outcomes are 0 for $0, 25 for $2,000, 35 for $4,000, and 40 for making $6,000. Draw Frances's utility curve and advise her on making the investment.

3.43 A plant manager has a utility of 10 for $20,000, 6 for $11,000, 0 for $0, and −10 for a loss of $5,000.

a. The plant manager is indifferent between receiving $11,000 for certain and a lottery with a 0.6 chance of winning $5,000 and a 0.4 chance of winning $20,000. What is the utility of $5,000 for the manager? Construct the manager's utility curve.
b. Using this curve, find the CE for the following gamble (i.e., the amount of cash that will make the manager indifferent to the gamble):

Payoff	Probability
−$2,000	0.2
0	0.3
$3,000	0.4
$10,000	0.1

   c. What probability combination of $0 and $20,000 would make the manager indifferent to the certain $11,000?
   d. The manager is facing a decision about buying a new production machine that can bring a net profit of $15,000 (80% chance) or a loss of $1,000 (20% chance); alternatively, the manager can use the old machine and make a $10,000 profit. Use the utility curve to find which alternative the manager should select. Specify all necessary assumptions.

BIBLIOGRAPHY

Baumol, W. J., "On the Social Rate of Discount," *American Economic Review*, Vol. 57, No. 4, pp. 778–802, 1968.

Blank, L. T. and A. Tarquin, *Engineering Economy*, Fifth Edition, McGraw-Hill, New York, 2002.

Bowman, M. S., *Applied Economic Analysis for Technologists, Engineers and Managers*, Second Edition, Prentice Hall, Upper Saddle River, NJ, 2003.

Canada, J. R. and W. G. Sullivan, *Economic and Multiattribute Evaluation of Advanced Manufacturing Systems*, Prentice Hall, Englewood Cliffs, NJ, 1989.

Collier, A. C. and C. R. Glagola, *Engineering Economic and Cost Analysis*, Third Edition, Prentice Hall, Upper Saddle River, NJ, 1999.

De Neufville, R., *Applied Systems Analysis: Engineering Planning and Technology Management*, McGraw-Hill, New York, 1990.

Dertouzos, M., R. Lester and R. Solow (Editors), *Made in America: Regaining the Productive Edge,* MIT Press, Cambridge, MA, 1989.

English, J. M., *Project Evaluation: A Unified Approach for the Analysis of Capital Investments*, Macmillan, New York, 1984.

Gass, S. I., "Model World: When Is a Number a Number?" *Interfaces*, Vol 31, No. 1, pp. 93–103, 2001.

Humphreys, K. K., *Jelen's Cost and Optimization Engineering*, Third Edition, McGraw-Hill, New York, 1991.

Keeney, R. L. and H. Raiffa, *Decisions with Multiple Objectives: Preferences and Value Tradeoffs*, Cambridge University Press, Second Edition, Cambridge, 1993.

Martino, J. P., *R&D Project Selection*, John Wiley & Sons, New York, 1995.

Miller, C. and A. P. Sage, "A Methodology for the Evaluation of Research and Development of Projects and Associated Resource Allocation," *Computers & Electrical Engineering*, Vol. 8, No. 2, pp. 123–152, 1981.

Newnan, D. G., J. P. Lavelle and T.G. Eschenbach, *Engineering Economic Analysis*, Eighth Edition, Engineering Press, Austin, TX, 2000.

Park, C. S., *Contemporary Engineering Economics*, Third Edition, Prentice Hall, Upper Saddle River, NJ, 2002.

von Neumann, J. and O. Morgenstern, *Theory of Games and Economic Behavior,* Second Edition, Princeton University Press, Princeton, NJ, 1947.

White, J. A., K. E. Case, D. B. Pratt and M. H. Agee, *Principles of Engineering Economic Analysis*, Fourth Edition, John Wiley & Sons, New York, 1997.

Chapter 4

Life-Cycle Costing

4.1 NEED FOR LIFE-CYCLE COST ANALYSIS

The total cost of ownership of a product, structure, or system over its useful life is its *life-cycle cost* (LCC). For products purchased off the shelf, the major factors are the cost of acquisition, operations, service, and disposal. For products or systems that are not available for immediate purchase, it may be necessary to include the costs associated with conceptual analysis, feasibility studies, development and design, logistics support analysis, manufacturing, and testing.

In discussing the LCC of a system or a product versus a project, a distinction is often made between the various phases of the two. The main difference is that the project usually terminates when the system or product enters its operational life. The life cycle of the system or product, however, continues far beyond that point. In Chapter 1, we introduced the five life-cycle phases of a project. Here we introduce the five life-cycle phases of a system or product:

1. Conceptual design phase
2. Advanced development and detailed design phase
3. Production phase
4. System operations and maintenance phase
5. System divestment/disposal phase

The need for life-cycle costing arises because decisions made during the early phases of a project inevitably have an impact on future outlays as the design evolves and the product matures. This need was recognized in the mid-1960s by the Logistics Management Institute, which issued a report stating that "the use of predicted logistics costs, despite their uncertainty, is preferable to the traditional practice of ignoring logistics' costs because the absolute accuracy of their quantitative values cannot be assured in advance."

TABLE 4.1 LCC Estimates for Appliances

	Air conditioners	Refrigerators	Televisions	Gas ranges
Useful life:	10 years	15 years	12 years	15 years
Cost element				
Acquisition	$204 (58.7%)	$295 (40.9%)	$400 (60.2%)	$211 (50.8%)
Operations	$131 (37.8%)	$92 (54.3%)	$178 (26.8%)	$159 (38.3%)
Service	$4 (1.2%)	$19 (2.6%)	$79 (11.9%)	$35 (8.5%)
Disposal	$8 (2.3%)	$16 (2.2%)	$7 (1.1%)	$10 (2.4%)
	$347 (100%)	$722 (100%)	$664 (100%)	$415 (100%)

An LCC analysis is intended to help managers identify and evaluate the economic consequences of their decisions. In 1978, the Massachusetts Institute of Technology (MIT) Center for Policy Alternatives published one of the first studies on LCC estimates. The focus was on appliances; some of the estimates are summarized in Table 4.1. As can be seen, the cost of acquisition was between 40.9% and 60.2%; and the rest was spent after the acquisition on operations, maintenance, and disposal. Nevertheless, the decisions made at the acquisition stage affect 100% of the LCC. Because the product's design dictates its LCC, it is of utmost importance to consider different options and their overall impact. A design that increases the production costs may be justified if it reduces the system's operational costs over its useful life.

The MIT research demonstrated the importance of considering costs that are incurred during the operational stage of a system or a product. This led the principal investigators to propose the establishment of consumer LCC data banks. Today, information on the operational costs of appliances such as energy consumption of refrigerators is posted on the units in the retail outlets. Similarly, the Environmental Protection Agency makes data on gasoline mileage of passenger cars readily available to the public.

A parallel situation exists for purchased commodities, as well as for research, development, and construction projects, in which decisions made in the early stages have a significant impact on the entire LCC. Engineering projects in which a new system or product is being designed, developed, manufactured, and tested may span years, as in the case of a new automobile, or decades in the case of a nuclear power plant. New product development takes anywhere from several months to several years. In lengthy processes of this type, decisions made at the outset may have substantial, long-term effects that are frequently difficult to analyze. The tradeoff between current objectives and long-term consequences of each decision is therefore a strategic aspect of project management that should be integrated into the project management system.

A typical example of a decision that has a long-term effect deals with the selection of components and parts for a new system at the advanced development and detailed design phase. Often, manufacturing costs can be reduced by selecting less expensive components and parts at the expense of a higher probability of failures during the operational life of the system. Another example is the decision regarding inspection and testing of components and subassemblies. Time and money can be saved at the early stages of a project by minimizing these efforts, but design errors and faulty components that surface during the operational phase may have severe cost consequences.

A third example relates to the need for logistics support. In this regard, consider the maintenance costs during the operational phase of a system. These costs can be reduced by including in the design built-in test equipment that identifies problems, locates their source, and recommends a corrective course of action. Systems of this type that combine sensors with automated checklists and expert systems logic are expensive to develop but in the long run decrease maintenance costs and increase availability.

LCC models track the costs of development, design, manufacturing, operations, maintenance, and disposal of a system over its useful life. They relate estimates of these cost components to independent (or explanatory) decision variables. By developing a functional representation [known as a *cost estimating relationship* (CER)] of the cost components in terms of the decision variables, the expected effect of changing any of the decision variables on one or more of the cost components can be analyzed.

A typical example of a CER is the effect of work design on the cost of labor. One aspect of this effect is the learning phenomenon discussed in Chapter 9. Because the slope of the learning curve depends on the type of manufacturing technology used, a CER can help the design engineers select the most appropriate technology. This situation is depicted in Fig. 4.1, where two manufacturing technologies are considered. Technology 1 requires lower labor cost for the first unit produced but has a slower learning rate than that of technology 2. The decision to adopt either technology depends on the number of units required and the cost of capital (assuming that everything else is equal). For a small number of units, technology 1 is better, as labor costs are lower in the early stages of the corresponding learning curve. Also, if the cost of labor is high, then technology 1 might be preferred because it displaces a substantial portion of the labor cost into the future. Finally, for a large number of units, technology 2 is preferred. In Fig. 4.1, the point where the two technologies yield the same total cost is called the breakeven point.

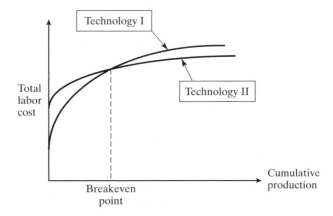

Figure 4.1   Learning curves for two technologies.

In this example (as in many others), the importance of the LCC model increases when the proportion of manufacturing, operations, and maintenance costs is greater than the proportion of design and development costs over the lifetime of the product or system.

The development and widespread use of LCC models is particularly justified when a number of alternatives exist in the early stages of a project's life cycle and the selection of an alternative has a noticeable influence on the total LCC. At the outset of a project, they provide a means of evaluating alternative designs; as work progresses, they may be called on to evaluate proposed engineering changes. These models are also used in logistics planning, where it is necessary, for example, to compare different maintenance concepts, training approaches, and replenishment policies. At a higher level, model results support decisions regarding logistic and configuration issues, the selection of manufacturing processes, and the formulation of maintenance procedures. By proper use, engineers and managers can choose alternatives so that the LCC is minimized while the required system effectiveness is maintained. The development and application of LCC models therefore is an essential part of most engineering projects.

As another example, let us consider a project involving the construction of an office building in which the windows can be either single- or double-pane glass. Material and installation costs make the initial investment in the second option greater than in the first; however, if an LCC analysis is conducted, then the cash flow over the useful life of the windows should be evaluated. The aim would be to consider not only the initial investment but also the intermittent and recurrent costs resulting from the decision, such as the loss of energy as a result of differences in isolation abilities. Taking qualitative factors into account, though, presents a problem. Although double-pane windows have technical advantages, such as better noise isolation, it is difficult if not impossible to translate these types of advantages in monetary terms. If this is the case, then the multi-criteria methods for project evaluation discussed in Chapters 5 and 6 should be used.

4.2 UNCERTAINTIES IN LIFE-CYCLE COST MODELS

In the conceptual design phase, when LCC models are usually developed, little may be known about the system, the activities required to design and manufacture it, its modes of operation, and the maintenance policies to be used. Consequently, LCC models are subject to the highest degrees of uncertainty at the beginning of a project. This uncertainty declines as progress is made and additional information becomes available.

Because decisions taken in the early stages of a project's life cycle have the potential to affect the overall costs more than decisions taken later, the project team faces a situation in which the most critical decisions are made when uncertainty is highest. This is illustrated in Figs. 4.2 and 4.3 where the potential effect of decisions on cost and the corresponding level of uncertainty are plotted as a function of time. From these graphs, the importance of a good LCC model in the early phases of a system's life cycle is evident.

There are two principal types of uncertainty that LCC model builders should consider: (1) uncertainty regarding the cost-generating activities during the system's life cycle and (2) uncertainty regarding the expected cost of each of these activities. The first type of

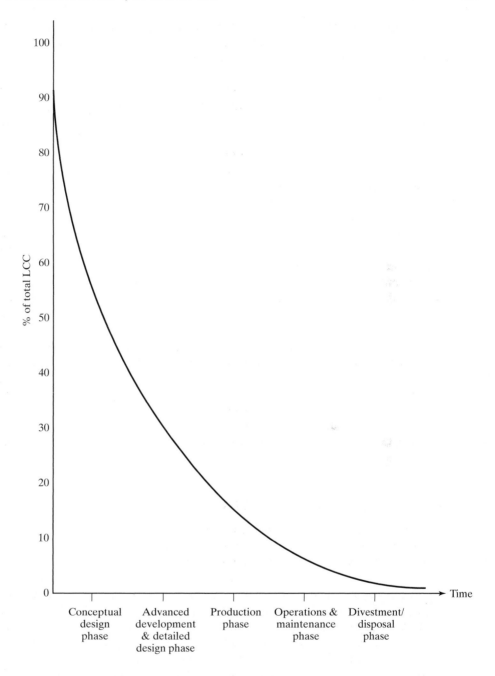

Figure 4.2   Percentage of budget affected by decision made is life-cycle
phase of a system.

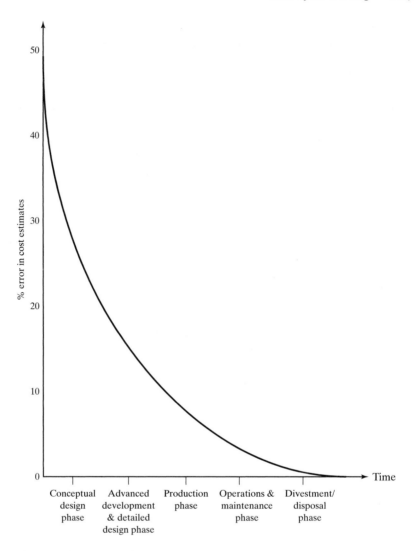

Figure 4.3   Cost estimate errors over time.

uncertainty is typically present when a new system is being developed and few historical data points exist. The equipment used on board several of the early earth-orbiting satellites and the first space shuttle, *Columbia*, fall into this category. There was a high level of uncertainty with respect to maintenance requirements for this equipment as well as the procedures for operating and maintaining the launch vehicles and supporting facilities. Maintenance practices were finalized only after sufficient operational experience was accumulated. The reliability and dependability of these systems were studied carefully to determine the required frequency of scheduled maintenance.

Nevertheless, the accuracy of LCC models in which this type of uncertainty is present is relatively low, implying that their benefits may be somewhat limited to providing a framework for enumerating all possible cost drivers and promoting consistent data collection efforts throughout the life of the system. But even if this were the only use of the model, benefits would accrue from the available data when the time came to upgrade or build a second-generation system.

The second type of uncertainty, estimating the magnitude of a specific cost-generating activity, is common to all LCC models. There are multiple sources of this type of uncertainty, such as future inflation rates, the expected efficiency and utilization of resources, and the failure rate of system components. Each affects the accuracy of the cost estimates. To obtain better results, sophisticated forecasting techniques are often used, fueled by a wide array of data sources. Analysts who build LCC models should always trade off the desired level of accuracy with the cost of achieving that level. Most engineering projects are associated with improving current systems or developing new generations of existing systems. For such projects, it is frequently possible to increase the accuracy of cost estimates by investing more effort in collecting and analyzing the underlying data. Therefore, it is important to determine when the point of diminishing returns has been reached. More sophisticated models may pose an increasingly problematic challenge to their intended users and may become more expensive or complicated than the quality that the input data can justify.

The accuracy of cost estimates changes over the life cycle of the system. During the conceptual design phase, a tolerance of -30% to $+50\%$ may be acceptable for some factors. By the end of the advanced development and detailed design phase, more reliable estimates are expected to be available. Further improvement is realized during the production and system operations phases when field data are collected.

4.3 CLASSIFICATION OF COST COMPONENTS

The selection of a specific design alternative, the adoption of a maintenance or training policy, or the analysis of the impact of a proposed engineering change is based on the tradeoff between the expected costs and the expected benefits of each candidate. To ensure that the economic analysis is complete, the LCC model should include all significant costs that are likely to arise over the system's life cycle. In this effort, it is essential for the model builder to consider the type of system being developed. On the basis of the logical design of the project, common management concerns, and supporting data requirements, the cost classifications and structures can be defined.

Many ways of classifying costs are possible in an LCC analysis. Some are generic, whereas others are tailored to meet individual circumstances. In the following discussion, we present several commonly used schemes. Each can be modified to fit a specific situation, but a particular application may require a unique approach.

One way to classify costs is by the five life-cycle phases:

1. *Cost of the conceptual design phase.* This category highlights the costs associated with early efforts in the life cycle. These efforts include feasibility studies, configuration analysis and selection, systems engineering, initial logistic analysis, and initial design.

    The cost of the conceptual design phase usually increases with the degree of innovation involved. In projects aimed at developing new technologies, this phase tends to be long and expensive. For example, consider the development of a new drug for AIDS or the development of a permanently manned lunar base. In such projects, high levels of uncertainty motivate in-depth feasibility studies, including the development of models, laboratory tests, and detailed analyses of alternatives. When a modification or improvement of an existing system is being weighed, the level of uncertainty is lower, and consequently, the cost associated with the conceptual design phase is lower. This is the case, for example, with many construction projects in which the use of new techniques or technologies is not the main issue.

The LCC model can be used in this phase to support benefit-cost analyses. One must proceed with caution, however, because initial LCC estimates may be subject to large errors. A comparison of alternatives is appropriate only when the cost difference between them is measurably larger than the estimation errors and hence can be detected by the LCC models.

2. *Cost of the advanced development and detailed design phases.* Here the cost of planning and detailed design is presented. This includes product and process design; preparation of final performance requirements; preparation of the work breakdown structure, schedule, budget, and resource management plans; and the definition of procedures and management tools to be used throughout the life cycle of the project.

These phases are labor intensive. Engineers and managers design the product and plan the project for smooth execution. Attempts to save time and money by starting implementation before a satisfactory completion of these phases can lead to future failures. The development of a good product design and a comprehensive project plan are preconditions for successful implementation. In the advanced development and detailed design phase of the LCC analysis, accurate estimates of cost components are required. These estimates are used, in part, to support decisions regarding the selection of alternative technologies and the logistic support system for the product.

3. *Cost of the production phase.* This category consists of the costs associated with the execution of the design, including the construction of new facilities or the remodeling of existing facilities for assembly, testing, production, and repair. Also included are the actual costs of equipment, labor, and material required for operations, as well as blueprint reproduction costs for engineering drawings and the costs associated with documenting production, assembly, and testing procedures.

In many projects and systems, this is the highest cost phase. The quality of the requirements and design decisions made earlier in the project determine the actual cost of production. By accumulating and storing the actual costs in appropriate databases, LCC analysis can be improved for similar future projects. The LCC model in this phase becomes increasingly accurate, making detailed cost analysis of alternative operations and maintenance policies possible.

4. *Cost of operating and maintaining the system.* This category identifies the costs surrounding the activities performed during the operational life of the system. These include the cost of personnel required for operations and maintenance together with the cost of energy, spare parts, facilities, transportation, and inventory management. Design changes and system upgrade costs also fall into this category.

5. *Cost of divestment/disposal phase.* When the end of the useful life of a system has been reached, it must be phased out. Parts and subassemblies must be inventoried, sold for scrap, or discarded. In some cases, it is necessary to take the system apart and dispose of its components safely. The phasing out or disposal of a system might have a negative cost (i.e., produce revenue) when it is sold at the end of its useful life, or it might have a positive cost (often high), as in the case of a nuclear reactor that has to be carefully dismantled and its radioactive components safely discarded.

The relative importance of each phase in the total LCC model is system specific. Figure 4.4 presents a comparison for two generic systems by life-cycle phase. In general, when alternative projects are being considered, the relative magnitude and timing of the different cost components figure prominently in the analysis. In Fig. 4.4, system A requires substantial research and development efforts. The conceptual design phase and the advanced development phase account for 50% of the LCC. In system B, these two phases account for only 30% of the total cost. Thus, system B can be thought of more as a production/implementation project, whereas system A represents more of a design/development project.

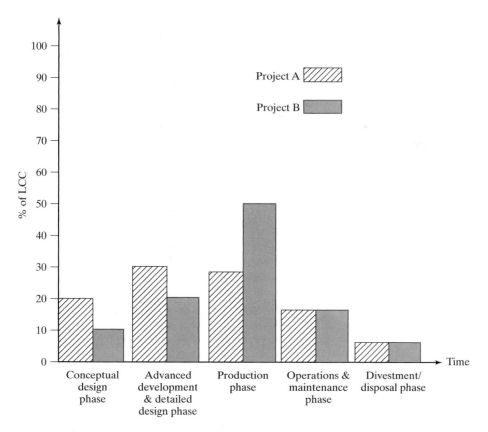

Figure 4.4   Cost comparison of two projects by life-cycle phase.

A second classification scheme has its origins in manufacturing and is based on cost type; that is, direct labor versus indirect labor, subcontracting, overhead allocations, and material (direct and indirect), as illustrated in Fig. 4.5. These categories parallel those traditionally found in cost accounting, so data should be readily available for many applications.

A third means of classification is based on the time period in which each cost component is realized. To make this scheme operational, it is necessary to define a minimum time period, such as 1 month or 1 quarter, in the system's life cycle. All costs that are incurred in this predetermined time period are grouped together. This is illustrated in Fig. 4.6, where the graphs provide a 12-month history of costs. This type of classification scheme is important when cash flow constraints are considered. Two projects with the same total cost may have a different cost distribution over time. In this case, because of cash flow considerations (the time value of money), the project for which cost outlays are delayed may be preferred.

Figure 4.5   Cost classification for manufacturing.

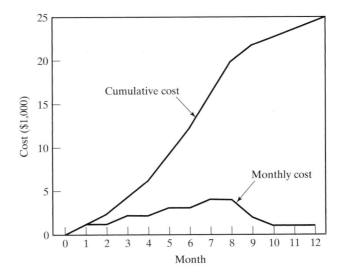

Figure 4.6   LCC as a function of time.

A fourth classification scheme is by work breakdown structure (WBS). In this approach, the cost of each element is estimated at the lowest level of the WBS. If more detail is desired, then each element can be disaggregated further by life-cycle phase (first classification), cost type (second classification), or time period (third classification).

As the situation dictates, other schemes, perhaps based on the bill of material, the product structure, or the organization breakdown structure (OBS), might be used. In particular, classification based on the OBS has proved useful as a bridge between the LCC model and the project budget, which traditionally is prepared along organizational lines.

It goes without saying that the scheme chosen should directly support the kinds of analyses to be undertaken. Thus, if future cash flow analyses are required, then the timing of each cost component is important. If, however, a system is developed by one organization (a contractor) for use by another (the client) and the customer is scheduled to deliver some of the subsystems, as in the case of *government-furnished equipment* in government contracts, then classification of cost based on the organization responsible for each cost component might be appropriate.

Sophisticated LCC models apply several classification schemes in the cost breakdown structure (CBS) so that each cost component can be categorized by the life-cycle phase and time period in which it arises, the WBS element in which it appears, and the class type from an accounting point of view. The cost of developing and maintaining such models depends on the desired resolution (number of subcategories in each classification scheme) and accuracy of the cost estimates, the updating frequency, and the number of classification schemes used. LCC model builders should strive to balance development costs with maintenance and data collection requirements.

An example of an LCC model for a hypothetical system in which a simple three-dimensional cost structure is used is given next. In this classification scheme, costs are broken down by (1) the life-cycle phase, (2) the quarter in which they occur, and (3) labor and material. The data are presented in Table 4.2.

In the example, we assume that three different models of the same system are being developed during the first 2 years (8 quarters). Production starts on the first model before detailed design of the other two is finalized. Thus during quarters 6 through 8, advanced development and detailed design as well as production costs are present. Similarly, the first model becomes operational before the completion of the production phase of the other models, implying overlapping costs in these categories in quarters 9 and 4. The three models are phased out in quarters 14, 15, and 17 as noted by divestment costs and reduced operations and maintenance costs in these periods.

The LCC data in Table 4.2 can be used to produce several views, each giving a different perspective and highlighting different aspects of the project. For example, in Fig. 4.7, we plot the cumulative LCC of the system over time, as well as the cost that is incurred in each quarter. The LCC can also be presented by life-cycle phase. This is illustrated in Fig. 4.8. A third possibility is labor cost versus material cost, as shown in Fig. 4.9. Although the periodic and total LCCs are the same in Figs. 4.8 and 4.9, the breakdown of these costs is different and can serve different purposes, as discussed in the next section.

TABLE 4.2   Example of a LCC Model ($1,000)

| | System life-cycle phase | | | | | | | | | |
| | Conceptual design | | Advanced development & detailed design | | Production | | Operations & maintenance | | Divestment/ disposal | | |
Quarter	Labor	Mat'l	Labor	Mat'l	Labor	Mat'l	Labor	Mat'l	Labor	Mat'l	Total
1	2										2
2	3										3
3	3										3
4	1		3								4
5			4	1							5
6			5	1	10	3					19
7			5	1	12	4					22
8			3	1	15	6					25
9					10	5	3	1			19
10					7	3	4	2			16
11							5	3			8
12							5	3			8
13							5	3			8
14							5	3	1		9
15							4	2	1		7
16							4	2			6
17							3	1	1		5
18											
Total	9	—	20	4	54	21	38	20	3	—	169

Figure 4.7   Total LCC of the system.

In the example, a fourth classification (or dimension) might correspond to the WBS and a fifth to the OBS. By using a five-dimensional grid, questions such as, "What is the expected cost of software development by the main contractor for the real-time control system during the third quarter of the project?" can be answered. The type of questions and scenarios for which the LCC model is to be exercised is the principal consideration in its design.

Figure 4.8   LCC by phase.

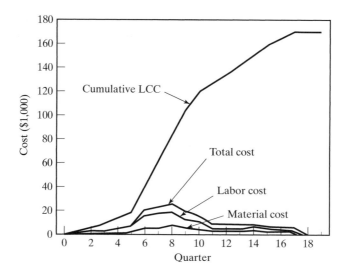

Figure 4.9   Cost breakdown by labor and material.

4.4 DEVELOPING THE LCC MODEL

The first step in the design of an LCC model is to identify the types of analyses that it is intended to support. The following is a list of several common applications:

- *Strategic or long-range budgeting.* Because the LCC model covers the entire life cycle of a system, it can be used to coordinate investment expenditures over the system's useful life or to adjust the requirement for capital for one system or project with capital needed or generated by other systems or projects. Such long-range budget planning is important for strategic investment decisions.

- *Strategic or long-range technical decisions.* Strategic decision making as it relates to such issues as the redesign of a system or the early termination of a research and development (R&D) project is difficult to support. The LCC model can be used to monitor changes in cost estimates as the project evolves. Revised estimates of production, operations, or maintenance costs that are substantially higher than the baseline figures may serve as a trigger for unscheduled design reviews, major changes in system engineering, or even a complete shutdown of the project. Because LCC estimates improve over time, rough projections made in the early phases of a project's life cycle may be updated later and provide managers with more accurate data to support the technical decision-making process.

- *Data analysis and processing.* LCC models routinely serve as a framework for the collection, storage, and retrieval of cost data. By using an appropriate data structure (e.g., LCC breakdown structure), the cost components of current or retired systems can be analyzed simultaneously to yield better estimates for future systems.

- *Logistic support analysis.* Logistics is generally concerned with transportation, inventory and spare parts management, database systems, maintenance, and training.

Questions such as which maintenance operations should be performed and at what frequency, how much to invest in spare parts, how to package and ship systems and parts, which training facilities are required, and which type of courses should be offered to the operators and maintenance personnel are examples of decisions supported by LCC analyses.

Once agreement is reached on the types of analyses that will be conducted, LCC model development can proceed. The following steps should be carried out:

1. *Classification*. In this step the classification schemes are developed. Major activities that generate cost are listed and major cost categories (labor, material, etc.) are identified. For example, the LCC data presented in Table 4.2 can be classified by the organizational unit responsible for each cost component and the activities performed by that unit.

2. *CBS*. Next, a coding system is selected to keep track of each cost component. To gain further insights, the latter may be organized in a multidimensional hierarchical structure based on the system chosen in step 1. Each component at each level of the hierarchy is assigned an identification number. The CBS enables the cost components to be aggregated on the basis of the classification scheme. Thus, with the proper scheme, the labor cost of a specific activity in a given period or the cost of a specific subsystem during its operational phase can be determined. The CBS links cost components to organizational units, to WBS elements, and to the system's bill of material.

   As an example, consider the CBS of a project aimed at developing a new radar system. The system is composed of a transmitter, receiver, antenna, and computer. The plan is to subcontract the computer design and its software as well as part of the antenna servo, while developing the rest of the components in-house. The coding scheme for the CBS is as shown in Table 4.3.

TABLE 4.3 Coding and Classification Scheme for LCC

Digit	Classification	Code assignment	
1	Who performs the work	Performed in-house	1
		Subcontracted	2
2	System part	Transmitter	1
		Receiver	2
		Antenna	3
		Computer	4
3	Life-cycle phase	Conceptual	1
		Detailed design	2
		Production	3
		Operations & maintenance	4
		Divestment	5
4	Type of cost	Direct labor	1
		Direct material	2
		Overhead	3

Using this simple four-digit code, a question such as, "What is the direct cost of material to be used during the production phase of the receiver?" can be answered by retrieving all cost components with the following LCC codes:

first digit	1 or 2
second digit	2
third digit	3
fourth digit	2

Thus, we would search for the LCC codes 1232 and 2232. The corresponding cost components might represent the cost at different months of the project, assuming that cost is estimated on a monthly basis. Other situations are possible.

3. *Cost estimates.* After the various cost components are identified and organized within the chosen classification scheme, the final step is to estimate each cost component. The American Association of Cost Engineers (AACE 1986) has proposed three classifications for this purpose:

- *Order of magnitude:* accuracy of −30% to +50%. An estimate that is made without any detailed engineering data.
- *Budget:* accuracy of −15% to +30%. This estimate is based on preliminary layout design and equipment details and is performed by the client to establish a budget for a new project (at the request for proposal (RFP) stage).
- *Definitive:* accuracy of −5% to +15%. This cost estimate is based on well-defined engineering data and a complete set of specifications.

The work involved in preparing cost estimates is a function of the required accuracy and the size and cost of the project. In the process industries, the typical costs for preparing estimates were estimated by Pikulik and Diaz (1977):

- *Order-of-magnitude estimates*

Project cost ($ million)	Cost of estimate ($ thousand)
Up to 1	7.5 to 20
1 to 5	17.5 to 45
5 to 50	30 to 60

- *Budget estimates*

Project cost ($ million)	Cost of estimate ($ thousand)
Up to 1	20 to 50
1 to 5	45 to 85
5 to 50	70 to 130

- *Definitive estimates*

Project cost ($ million)	Cost of estimate ($ thousand)
Up to 1	35 to 85
1 to 5	85 to 175
5 to 50	150 to 330

A variety of estimation procedures is used in industry, all of which are based on the assumption that past experience is a valid predictor of future performance. Estimation procedures fall into one of two categories: (1) causal, whereby the aim is to derive CERs; and (2) noncausal, or direct. Causal estimates follow from an assumed functional relationship between the cost component and one or more explanatory variables. For example, the cost of fuel required during the operational life of a car might be estimated as a function of the distance driven, the weight of the car, the car's engine size, and the expected road conditions. An equation, relating the cost of fuel to the explanatory variables, can be developed by using regression analysis or any other curve-fitting technique (see Section 9.2.5). With the use of CERs, the expected effect of changing any explanatory variable on the LCC can be analyzed. To develop CERs, past data on the values of the cost component under investigation and the explanatory variables are required.

As an example, consider the equipment CER proposed by Fabrycky and Blanchard (1991),

$$C = C_r \times \left(\frac{Q_c}{Q_r}\right)^{\beta} \tag{4.1}$$

where

$$
\begin{aligned}
C &= \text{cost for a new design size } Q_c \\
C_r &= \text{cost for existing reference design } Q_r \\
Q_c &= \text{design size—new design} \\
Q_r &= \text{design size—existing reference design} \\
\beta &= \text{correlation parameter; } 0 < \beta \le 1
\end{aligned}
$$

Taking the logarithm of both sides of Eq. (4.1) gives the CER

$$\log C - \log C_r = \beta(\log Q_c - \log Q_r) \tag{4.2}$$

where β is to be determined from a regression analysis.

Suppose that a cost estimate for a new 750-gallon water desalination system is required and that information on the actual cost of five systems is available. These data are presented below:

Reactor	Cost	Size (gallons)
1	$14,000	200
2	$18,000	300
3	$21,500	400
4	$25,000	500
5	$28,000	600

A pairwise comparison between the five systems yields the following data in the form needed for Eq. (4.2):

C_r	C	Q_r	Q_c	$\log C - \log C_r$	$\log Q_c - \log Q_r$
\$14,000	\$18,000	200	300	0.109	0.176
\$18,000	\$21,500	300	400	0.077	0.125
\$21,500	\$25,000	400	500	0.066	0.096
\$25,000	\$28,000	500	600	0.049	0.079

A regression analysis using the first three systems yields the CER

$$\log C - \log C_r = 0.628(\log Q_c - \log Q_r)$$

with $R^2 = 0.983$. Now, using the fourth system as a reference (Q_r), the estimated cost for a new 750-gallon (Q_c) system (same type) is

$$C = \$25,000 \times \left(\frac{750}{500}\right)^{0.628} = \$32,249$$

This type of CER is useful for a company that has to estimate the cost of new systems that differ from existing systems mainly by size.

Cost estimates can alternatively be derived using noncausal methods, such as

- Judgment and experience, rules of thumb, or the use of organizational standards for similar activities. These techniques are informal, inexpensive, and therefore appropriate when formal LCC models and cost estimates with high levels of accuracy are not essential.
- Analogy to a similar system or component and an appropriate adjustment of cost components according to the difference between the systems.
- Technical estimation based on drawings, specifications, time standards, and values of parameters such as mean time between failure and mean time to repair.
- Value of contracts for similar systems, such as office cleaning contracts and maintenance contracts. It is also possible to estimate costs on the basis of bids from contractors who respond to RFPs.

Each technique requires a combination of resources, such as time, data, equipment, and software, and may call on the expertise and experience of people within or external to the organization. From the data and resources available, the required accuracy, and the cost of using each cost estimating technique, the most suitable approach for each application can be selected. For each cost component, one or more cost estimating techniques might be appropriate. In the early stages of the life cycle, technical estimation is usually not feasible as drawings and other information are not available. For new systems, analogy might not be feasible if similar systems have not been developed or previously deployed.

Let us demonstrate the derivation of a CER for a project related to the development of a training course. Stark Awareness, Inc., is a company that specializes in developing such courses for its customers and wishes to estimate the labor hours required for putting together a new course. The deliverable is a packet of materials that will include all of the documents and slides required for conducting the class. Dr. Stark, the chief statistician for the company, decided to develop a CER based on expert judgment, in this case a team of instructors who have wide experience in this type of project. The experts identified the relevant parameters and the labor hours associated with each. For example, for the parameter "number of lecture hours" for the course, it was agreed that for every new lecture hour, there is a need to spend 15 labor hours on activities such as reading new material, summarizing the main points, and preparing PowerPoint slides.

The above process led to the following equation:

$$LH = 15L + 4E + 20T + 10P$$

where

$$LH = \text{number of labor hours required to develop new course}$$
$$L = \text{number of lecture hours for new course}$$
$$E = \text{number of exercises that students will be assigned}$$
$$T = \text{number of tests to be given}$$
$$P = \text{number of course projects}$$

For example, if there is a need to develop a training program that consists of 12 lecture hours, three exercises, and one project, then the estimated number of labor hours required to organize the class is

$$LH = (15 \times 12) + (4 \times 3) + (10 \times 1) = 202 \text{ hours}$$

LCC models are relatively mature in the areas of software development and maintenance planning. Several exist for estimating labor requirements for different tasks as a function of system characteristics and the level of experience of the project team. One such model, called COCOMO II, is based on the analysis of data collected from approximately 160 projects (Bohem et al. 2000). To estimate the resource requirements (independent variable) for a software project, the authors proposed using the following parameters (dependent variables):

- Project size, expressed by the number of old and new line codes
- Technical complexity of the new system
- Risk level
- Size of the databases required for the system
- Experience of the project team
- Complexity of communication channels
- Previous experience of the organization on projects of similar nature
- Organizational ability in the application of project management methodology
- Availability of advanced programming tools
- Organizational turnover

Obviously, it is impractical to use the same model for every project; however, it is not uncommon for an organization to use similar estimation techniques and models for similar projects.

The selection of a cost estimating procedure depends on data availability, required accuracy, and cost. The analyst should consider all three aspects in the process of model design and application. To demonstrate further the process of developing an LCC model, consider the problem of estimating energy costs in residential buildings. It is possible to reduce the cost of energy by proper design, the use of insulation and improved ventilation, and the selection of efficient heating and cooling devices. The following is an example of a basic LCC model for such a project. The model has only two classifications: the first centers on the activities that generate cost, and the second is based on time. Table 4.4 depicts levels 1 and 2 of the CBS for the cost-generating activities.

A time dimension is added to the model by introducing the timing of each cost component. For example, the structural design (1.1) may take 3 months. Assuming that the cost of the first month is $500, the cost of the second month is $1,100, and the cost of the last month is $400, the total cost of structural design is $500 + $1100 + $400 = $2000 over a 3-month period. By assigning the cost of each cost component in Table 4.4 to a specific month, the time aspect of this LCC model is introduced.

If more detail is needed, then the model can be expanded to three or four levels. For example, consider item 2.1, equipment, which can be broken down further by air conditioning system, heater, and so on. Once the lowest level is identified and the data elements are defined, the model can be used to estimate the cost of each component for each design alternative on a periodic basis, if necessary. Alternatives might differ in their total LCC, in the allocation of costs over the life cycle, and in the allocation of costs among different system components. As discussed in Chapters 5 and 6, the selection of the best alternative depends on the evaluation criteria specified. System reliability, maintenance requirements, and safety are common criteria, but LCC usually plays a predominant role. In particular, if the minimum net present cost is the criterion chosen between two design alternatives with the same total LCC, then the one that delays monetary outlays the longest would be preferred. In the above example, it should not be surprising that this might lead to an energy-inefficient house—one that is less expensive to build but more expensive to maintain.

A possible CER for the example might be a linear equation relating the cost of heating to the insulation used and the difference between the desired temperature inside

---

TABLE 4.4   Partial CBS for Residential Building Example

1. Cost of engineering	2. Cost of construction	3. Cost of operations
1.1 Structural design	2.1 Equipment	3.1 Energy
1.2 Interior design	2.2 Contractors	3.2 Maintenance
1.3 Drawing preparation	2.3 Material	3.3 Consumables
1.4 Supervision	2.4 Labor	3.4 Subcontractors
1.5 Management	2.5 Energy	
	2.6 Inspection	
	2.7 Management	

the house and the ambient temperature outside. Additional explanatory variables that might be included are the area of windows and the type of glass used.

The CBS can be as detailed as required to capture the impacts of decisions on overall cost and performance. Continuing with item 2.1, equipment can be broken down further to the level of components used in the air-conditioning system if it were thought that the selection of these components would measurably affect the LCC.

4.5 USING THE LIFE-CYCLE COST MODEL

The integration of the CBS with estimates of each component produces the aggregate LCC model for the system. This model (distributed over time) is the basis for several types of analyses and decision making.

1. *Design evaluations.* In the planning stages of a project, alternative designs for the entire system or its components have to be evaluated. The LCC model combined with a measure of system effectiveness produce a basis for cost-effectiveness analysis during various stages of the development cycle. Methodological details are provided in Chapters 5 and 6, where issues related to risk, benefit estimation, and criteria selection are discussed.

2. *Evaluation of engineering change requests (ECRs).* As explained in Chapter 8, the process of ECR approval or rejection is based on estimates of cost and effectiveness with and without the proposed change. The LCC model provides the foundation for conducting the analysis.

3. *Sensitivity analysis and risk assessment.* In the development of CERs, parameters that affect the LCC of the system are used as the explanatory variables. A sensitivity analysis should always be conducted to see how the LCC changes as each parameter is varied over its feasible range. Depending on the nature of the project and the time horizon, some typical explanatory variables might be the rate of inflation, the cost of energy, and the minimum acceptable rate of return.

4. *Logistic support analysis.* The evaluation of policies for maintenance, training, stocking of spare parts, inventory management, shipping, and packaging is supported by appropriate LCC models. By estimating the cost of different alternatives for logistic support, decision makers can trade off the cost and benefits of each scenario under consideration.

5. *Pareto, or ABC, analysis.* This analysis is used to identify the most important cost components of a project. The first step is to sort each component by cost and then to place them into one of the following three groups:

Group A:	small percentage of the top cost components (10% to 15%) which together account for roughly 60% or more of the total cost
Group B:	all cost components that are not members of group A or C
Group C:	large percentage of the bottom cost components (approximately 50%), which account for 10% or less of the total cost

In the sorted list, the first 10% to 15% of the cost components are members of group A, and the last 50% are members of group C. The remaining components in the middle range of the list are assigned to group B. This clustering scheme is the basis for management control. The strategy is to monitor closely those items that account for the largest percentage of the total LCC (group A components). Conversely, group C components, which represent a relatively large number of items but account for a relatively small portion of the total cost, require the least amount of attention.

6. *Budget and cash flow analysis.* Here the concern is staying within budget and cash flow constraints and estimating future capital investment needs. By combining the LCC models of all projects in an organization, the net cash flow for each future period can be forecast. The results then may be used to support feasibility analyses, decisions regarding the acceptance of new projects, and recommendations for rescheduling or abandoning ongoing projects.

The LCC model is an important project management tool for strategic financial planning, logistics analysis, and technology-related decision making. Properly designed and maintained LCC models help the project manager in both planning and control by linking together the cost and technological aspects of a project. By using CERs, the impact that different alternatives have on the system's LCC can be analyzed and used as a basis for technology evaluation and selection, resource acquisition, and configuration management.

TEAM PROJECT

Thermal Transfer Plant

Your plans for the prototype rotary combustor project have been approved. TMS management is now weighing the possibility of investing in a plant for manufacturing the combustors. There is a feeling, however, that the degree of subcontracting associated with producing the prototype may not be appropriate for the repetitive manufacturing environment of the new plant.

Your team has been requested to perform an LCC analysis to help determine which parts and components of the rotary combustor to manufacture in-house and which to buy or subcontract. Design your models to answer these "make or buy" questions, keeping in mind that the expected life of a rotary combustor is approximately 25 years and TMS would like to support these units throughout their life cycle. State any assumptions that you believe are necessary to estimate costs and risks. Discuss the sensitivity of your results, assumed parameter values, timing of costs, levels of risk, and so on.

DISCUSSION QUESTIONS

1. Estimate the LCC for a passenger car. In so doing, select an appropriate CBS and explain your cost estimates.
2. Explain how the design of a car affects its LCC.
3. Compare the cost of ownership of a new car with that of a used car of similar type.

4. Explain the design factors that affect the LCC of an elevator in a New York City office building.

5. What are the sources of uncertainty in Question 4?

6. What do you think are the principal cost drivers in designing a permanently manned lunar base? What non-cost factors would you want to consider?

7. Identify a potential consumer product that is not yet on the market, such as video telephones, and list the major costs in each phase of its life cycle. How might these costs be estimated?

8. Pick an R&D project of national scope, such as mapping all of the genes on a human chromosome (the human genome project). First, sketch a potential OBS for the project and identify the tasks that might fall within each organizational unit. Then develop a CBS and relate it to the OBS.

9. Develop an LCC model to assist you in selecting the best heating system for your house. Discuss the alternatives and explain the cost structure that you have selected.

10. Discuss the effect of taxes on the LCC of passenger cars. Compare domestic and imported cars.

11. Discuss the effect of LCC on the decision to locate a new warehouse.

12. Discuss a project in which the first phase of the life cycle accounts for more than 50% of the LCC.

13. Discuss a project in which the detailed design phase accounts for more than 50% of the LCC.

EXERCISES

4.1 The cost of a used car is highly correlated with the following variables:

t = age of the car $\qquad$ $1 \leq t \leq 5$ (years)
V = volume of engine $\qquad$ $1{,}000 \leq V \leq 2{,}500$ (cubic centimeters)
D = number of doors $\qquad$ $D = 2, 3, 4, 5$
A = accessories and style $\qquad$ $A = 1, 2, 3, 4, 5, 6$ (qualitative)

Using regression analysis, the following relationship between the cost of a car and the four independent variables was found:

$$\text{purchase cost} = \left(1 + \frac{1}{t}\right) \times V \times \left(\frac{D}{2} + A\right)$$

a. Plot the purchase cost as a function of the four variables.
b. Which variable has the greatest effect on cost?
c. You have a total of $5,000. List the different types of cars (combinations of the parameters) that you can afford.
d. Develop a model by which you select the best car for your needs.
e. Operations and maintenance costs for the car are estimated as follows:

$$\text{annual maintenance cost} = \frac{t}{2} \times V \times \frac{s}{1{,}000}$$

$$\text{annual operating cost} = \left(D \times t + \frac{V}{1{,}000}\right) \times \frac{s}{250}$$

where s is the number of miles driven annually. What is the best car (combination of parameters) for a person who drives 12,000 miles every year?

4.2 A construction project consists of 10 identical units. The cost of the first unit is $25,000, and a learning curve of 90% applies to the cost and the duration of consecutive units. Assume that the first unit takes 6 months to finish and that the project is financed by a loan taken at the beginning of the project at an annual interest rate of 10%.

    a. Should the units be constructed in sequence (to maximize learning) or in parallel (to minimize the cost of the loan)?

    b. Find the schedule for the 10 units that minimizes the total cost of the project.

4.3 Develop three cost classifications for the LCC of an office building.

4.4 Develop a CBS for the cost of an office building. Estimate the cost of each component.

4.5 Show a cash flow analysis for the LCC of an office building.

4.6 Perform a Pareto (ABC) analysis on the data of the LCC of an office building.

4.7 Develop an estimate for the cost of a 3-week vacation in Europe.

4.8 Develop an LCC model to support the decision to buy or rent a car.

4.9 Natasha Gurdin is debating which of two possible models of a car to buy (A or B), being indifferent with regard to their technical performance. She has been told that the average monthly cost of owning model A, based on an LCC analysis, is $500.

    a. Using the following data for model B, calculate its LCC and determine which model is the better choice for Natasha:

Purchase price	$23,000
Life expectancy	4 years
Resale value	$13,000
Maintenance	$1,100 per year
Operational cost (gas, etc.)	$90 per month
Car insurance	$1,400 per year
Mean time between failures	14 months
Repair lost per failure	$650

    b. Develop a general model that can be used to calculate the LCC for a car.

4.10 Your company has just taken over an old apartment building and is renovating it. You have been appointed manager and must decide which brand of refrigerator to install in each apartment unit. Your analysis should consider expenses such as purchase price, delivery charges, operational costs, insurance for service, and selling price after 6 years of use. Identify two brands of 18-cubic foot refrigerators and compare them.

4.11 You have been told that even warehouse location decisions should be based, at least in part, on the results of an LCC analysis. Discuss this issue.

4.12 Maurice Micklewhite has decided to replant his garden. Show him what the cost is of making an erroneous decision at various stages of the project, starting with conceptual design and ending with the ongoing maintenance of the garden.

4.13 The relative cost of each stage in the project life cycle is a function of the nature of the project or product. Generate a list of possible projects and group them by the similarities in their relative cost profile.

4.14 Different organizations and customers look at different aspects of the LCC data. Select five projects and identify the relevant LCC aspects for each organization and customer involved.

4.15 Develop a list of cost components for two projects and estimate their values. Identify the components that represent approximately 80% of the projects' costs, and discuss possible alternatives to reduce the LCC of one particular component. What might be the expected impact of the suggested alternatives?

BIBLIOGRAPHY

Life-Cycle Cost

Blanchard, B. S., *Design and Manage to Life Cycle Cost*, Matrix Press, Chesterland, OH, 1978.

Dhillon, B. S., *Life Cycle Costing: Techniques, Models and Applications,* Gordon and Breach Science Publishers, New York, 1989.

Earls, U. E., *Factors, Formulas and Structures for Life Cycle Costing*, Second Edition, Eddins-Earles, Concord, MA, 1981.

Emblemsvag, J., *Life-Cycle Costing: Using Activity-Based Costing and Monte Carlo Methods to Manage Future Costs and Risks*, John Wiley & Sons, New York, 2003.

Fabrycky, J. W. and B. S. Blanchard, *Life Cycle Cost and Economic Analysis*, Prentice Hall, Englewood Cliffs, NJ, 1991.

Perera, H., N. Nagarur and M. Tabucanon, "Component Part Standardization: A Way to Reduce the Life-Cycle Costs of Products," *International Journal of Production Economics*, Vol. 60–61, pp. 109–117, 1999.

Riggs, J. L. and D. Jones, "Flowgraph Representation of Life-Cycle Cost Methodology: A New Perspective for Project Managers," *IEEE Transactions on Engineering Management*, Vol. 37, No. 2, pp. 147–152, 1990.

Spence, G., "Designing for Total Life Cycle Costs," *Printed Circuit Design*, Vol. 6, No. 8, pp. 14–17, 1989.

Cost Estimation

AACE, *Standard Cost Engineering Terminology*, American Association of Cost Engineers, Morgantown, WV, 1986.

Augustine, N. R., *Augustine's Laws*, Viking, Penguin, New York, 1997.

Bledsoe, J. D., *Successful Estimating Methods: From Concept to Bid*, RSMeans, Kingston, MA, 1991.

Bohem, B. W., E. Horowitz, R. Madachy, D. Reifer, B. K. Clark, B. Steece, A. W. Brown, S. Chulani and C. Abts, *Software Cost Estimation with COCOMO II*, Prentice Hall, Upper Saddle River, NJ, 2000.

Coombs, P., *IT Project Estimation: A Practical Guide to the Costing of Software*, Cambridge University Press, Cambridge, England, 2003.

Emblemsvag, J., *Life Cycle Costing*, John Wiley & Sons, New York, 2003.

Neil, J. M. (Editor), *Skills and Knowledge of Cost Engineering*, Second Edition, American Association of Cost Engineers, Morgantown, WV, 1988.

Ostwald, P., *Construction Cost Analysis and Estimating*, Prentice Hall, Upper Saddle River, NJ, 2000.

Pikulik, A. and H. E. Diaz, "Cost Estimating for Major Process Equipment," *Chemical Engineering*, Vol. 84, p. 106, 1977.

Puerifoy, R., *Estimating Construction Costs*, Fifth Edition, McGraw-Hill, New York, 2001.

Stewart, R. D. and R. M. Wyskida, *Cost Estimator's Reference Manual,* John Wiley & Sons, New York, 1987.

Chapter 5

Project Screening and Selection

5.1 COMPONENTS OF THE EVALUATION PROCESS

Every new project starts with an idea. Typically, new ideas arrive continuously from a variety of sources, such as customers, suppliers, upper management, and shop floor personnel. For organizations that work in the private sector, the details of the steps involved in processing these ideas and the related analyses are highlighted in Fig. 5.1. A similar diagram can be drawn for other classes of organizations.

Depending on the scope and estimated costs, management may simply be interested in determining the merit of the idea, or it may want to determine how best to allocate a budget among a portfolio of projects. If the organization is a consulting firm or an outside contractor, then it may want to decide on the most advantageous strategy for responding to requests for proposals (RFPs).

Of course, there are many different types of projects, so the evaluation criteria and accompanying methodology should reflect the peculiar characteristics of the sponsoring or respondent organization. The usual divisions are public sector versus private sector, research and development (R&D) versus operations, and internal customer versus external customer. Project size, expected duration, underlying risks, and required resources are some of the factors that must weigh on the decision.

Regardless of the source or nature of the customer, screening is usually the first step. Here the proposed project is analyzed in a preliminary manner in light of the most prominent criteria or prevailing conditions. This should be a quick and inexpensive exercise. The results may suggest, for example, that no further effort is warranted as a result of uncertainty in the technology or the lack of a well-defined market. If some promise exists, then the project may be temporarily backlogged in deference to more attractive contenders. At some time in the future when conditions are more favorable, it may be desirable to resurrect it, or the project may be deemed so urgent or

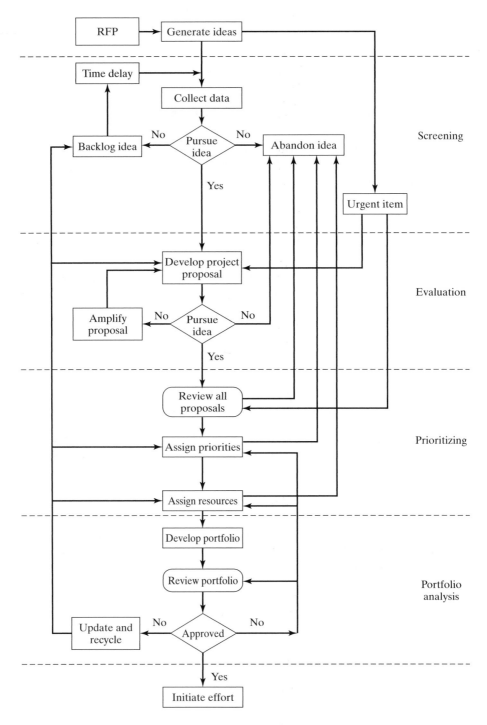

Figure 5.1 Project evaluation and selection process.

beneficial to the organization that it is placed at the top of the priority list. Alternatively, the results of the screening may indicate that the proposed project possesses some merit and deserves further investigation.

If this is the case, then a more in-depth analysis should be performed with the goal of narrowing the uncertainties associated with the project's costs, benefits, and risks. This evaluation process usually involves extensive data collection and reduction, the solicitation of expert opinion, sample computations, and perhaps technological forecasting. As with the screening process, several courses of action might be suggested. The proposal may be rejected or abandoned for lack of merit, it may be backlogged for later retrieval and analysis, or it may be found to be acceptable and placed on a candidate list for a comparative analysis. In some cases, it may be initiated immediately.

When the results of the evaluation process indicate that a proposal passes an acceptance threshold but that it is not clearly superior to the other candidates, each should be assessed and ranked competitively. In this prioritizing process, the relative strengths and weaknesses of each candidate are examined carefully, and a weighted ranking is obtained. Ideally, the ranking would indicate not only the most preferred project but also the degree to which it is preferred over the other contenders. A number of assessment methodologies are presented in Sections 5.3 through 5.7 and Chapter 6.

If the ranking of a particular proposal is high enough, then resources may tentatively be assigned. However, the decision to fund and initiate work on a proposal involves the full consideration of the available human and financial resources within the organization. The level of available funds and personnel skill types and the commitments to the current portfolio of activities all must be factored into the decision. It may be that the new idea is so meritorious that it should replace one or more of the ongoing projects. If this is the case, then some ongoing project(s) will be terminated or halted temporarily so that resources can be freed up for the new project. Portfolio models have been developed to aid in making these decisions. A portfolio model determines the best way to allocate available resources among the competing alternatives, including the new candidates and the ongoing projects. An example of such a model is presented in Chapter 13.

Portfolio models should be used only when multiple projects compete for the same resources. When a contractor with excess capacity is approached by a potential customer with a project, the selection process is simple—just sign the contract as long as there is a profit in it above a predetermined rate of return (ROR). This is a common situation in times of recession. At the other extreme, a contractor may find him- or herself overburdened with projects, should he or she win more jobs than expected. In the remainder of this chapter, we take up the middle ground and discuss methods for screening and prioritizing alternatives when resources limit the size of the portfolio.

5.2 DYNAMICS OF PROJECT SELECTION

As Fig. 5.1 suggests, project selection can be a very dynamic process. Screening, evaluation, prioritizing, and portfolio analysis decisions may be made at various points, and new ideas may not even go through these steps in sequence. An idea may be shelved or abandoned at any point in time. New information and changed circumstances may call for a previous decision to reject or abandon a project to be reevaluated. For example, efforts to develop lightweight portable computers were given a new impetus with the dramatic improvement in flat-screen display technology. Alternatively, new information or changed circumstances may cause a previously backlogged project to be rejected. The drastic reduction in the price of imported oil in the early 1980s dealt a death blow to the more exotic alternative energy projects, such as coal gasification and shale oil reclamation.

The available budget or labor skills within an organization may constrain the project selection process. If the budget is inadequate to fund a particular project that seems meritorious, then it may be necessary to backlog it. Alternatively, the project may be divided up and certain portions initiated while the remainder is shelved until the economic situation becomes more favorable. Customer complaints, competitive threats, or unique opportunities may occasion an urgent need to pursue a particular idea. Depending on the urgency, the project may receive only a cursory screening and evaluation and may go directly into the portfolio.

Screening, evaluation, prioritizing, and portfolio decisions may be repeated several times over the life cycle of a project in response to emerging technologies and changing environmental, financial, or commercial circumstances. The advent of a new RFP, a change in competitive pressures, and the appearance of a new technology are some factors that may cause management to reevaluate an ongoing project. Moreover, with each advance that is recorded, new technical information that may influence other efforts and proposed ideas will be forthcoming. As current projects near completion, key personnel and equipment may be released so that they can be used on another project, perhaps one that was previously backlogged for lack of appropriate resources.

In general, the evaluation and selection of new product ideas and project proposals is a complex process, consisting of many interrelated decisions. The complexities involve the variety of data that must be collected and the difficulty of unequivocally measuring and assessing candidate projects on the basis of information derived from these data. Much of the resultant information is subjective and uncertain in nature. Many ideas and proposals exist only as embryonic thoughts and are propelled forward by the sheer force of the sponsor's enthusiasm, but selecting the best idea cannot be done in a political vacuum. The presence of various organizational and behavioral factors tends to politicize the decision-making process. In many cases, the potential costs and benefits of a project play only a small role in the final decision. For example, an extensive 2-year analysis of LANDSAT, an earth-orbiting satellite with advanced resource monitoring capabilities, concluded that the benefits to the user community would fall significantly short of the expected costs associated with operating and maintaining the system over its 10-year lifetime, even under the most optimistic of scenarios (Bard 1984). Nevertheless, pressure from the National Aeronautics and Space Administration (NASA) and its congressional allies, who saw LANDSAT as a high-profile nonmilitary application of space technology that might actually return some benefits, persuaded the U.S. Department of the Interior to provide funding.

The more sophisticated analytical and behavioral tools that have been developed to aid managers in evaluating projects variously take into account the nonquantitative aspects of the decision. As might be expected, the more comprehensive the underlying techniques, the more data and effort that are needed for the analysis.

5.3 CHECKLISTS AND SCORING MODELS

The idea-generation stage of a project, when done properly, will often lead to more proposals than can realistically be pursued. Thus, a screening procedure designed to eliminate those proposals that are clearly infeasible or without merit must be established. Compatibility with the organization's objectives and resources is a primary concern. It is also important to keep in mind that when comparing alternatives early on, a wide range of criteria should be introduced in the analysis. The fact that these criteria are often measured on incommensurate scales makes the screening and evaluation much more difficult.

Of the several techniques available to aid in the screening process, perhaps the most commonly used is rating checklists. They are appropriate for eliminating the most undesirable proposals from further consideration. Because they require a relatively small amount of information, they can be used when the available data are limited or when only rough estimates have been obtained. Such methods should be viewed as expedient; they do not provide a great deal of depth and should be used with this caveat in mind.

Table 5.1 presents an illustration of a checklist. In constructing a checklist, it is necessary to identify the criteria or set of requirements that will be used in making the decision. In the next step, a (arbitrary) scoring scale is developed to measure how well a project does with respect to each criterion. Words such as "excellent" and "good" may be associated with the numerical values (see Gass 2001 for a more complete discussion of several issues related to the choice of scales and their effect on rankings).

In the example displayed in Table 5.1, the criteria include profitability, time to market, development risks, and commercial success. Each candidate is evaluated subjectively and scored using a three-point scale. The built-in assumption is that each criterion is weighted equally. Total scores are displayed in the rightmost column. Typically, a cutoff point or threshold is specified below which the project is abandoned. Of those that exceed the threshold, the top contenders are held for further analysis, whereas the remainder are backlogged or shelved temporarily. Here, if 7 is specified as the threshold, then only projects A and C would be pursued.

An alternative means of displaying the information in Table 5.1 is a multidimensional diagram known as a polar graph (Canada et al. 1996), shown in Fig. 5.2. In one sense, this type of representation is more efficient than a table because it allows the analyst quickly to ascertain the presence of dominance. For example, by noting that the

TABLE 5.1   An Example of a Checklist for Screening Projects

	Criteria											
	Profitability			Time to market			Development risks			Commercial success			
Score:	3	2	1	3	2	1	3	2	1	3	2	1	Total score
Project A		×		×			×				×		10
Project B		×			×				×			×	6
Project C	×					×		×			×		8

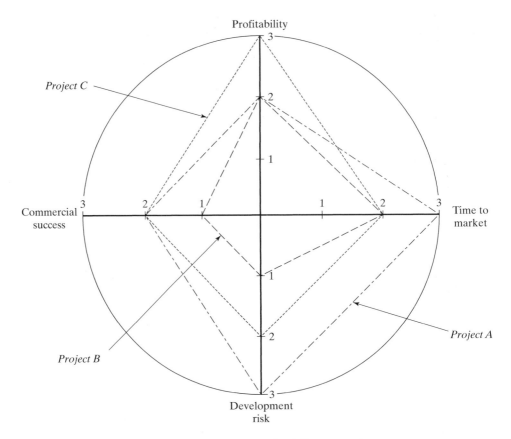

Figure 5.2 Multidimensional diagram for checklist example.

performance measure surface of project B is completely within that of project A, we can conclude that B is no better than A on any dimension and thus can be discarded or backlogged.

Scoring models extend the logic of checklists by assigning a weight to each criterion that signifies the relative importance of one to the other (Baker 1974, Hobbs 1980, Souder and Mandakovic 1986). A weighted score is then computed for each candidate. In deriving the weights, a team approach should be used to head off disagreement after the assessment. One way of accomplishing this is to list all criteria in descending order of importance. Next, assign the least important (last-listed) criterion a value of 10, and assign a numerical weight to each criterion on the basis of how important it is relative to this one. A criterion considered to be twice as important as the least important criterion would be assigned a weight of 20. If team members cannot agree on specific values, then sensitivity analysis should be performed.

An example of the use of a scoring model for screening projects associated with the development of new products is shown in Table 5.2. Here eight criteria are to be rated on a numerical scale of 0 to 30, where 0 means poor and 30 means excellent. Because this scale is arbitrary, no significance should be placed on relative values. For convenience, the weights are scaled between 0 and 1. In general, the factor score

TABLE 5.2   An Example of a Scoring Model for Screening Projects

		Rating				
Criteria	Relative weight	Excellent 30	Good 20	Fair 10	Poor 0	Factor score
Marketability	0.20	×				6
Risk	0.20		×			4
Competition	0.15		×			3
Value added	0.15				×	0
Technical opportunities	0.10	×				3
Material availability	0.10			×		1
Patent protection	0.05				×	0
Current products	0.05		×			1
Total	1.00					18

for project j, call it T_j, is obtained by multiplying the relative weights, w_i for criterion i, by the ratings, s_{ij}, and summing. That is,

$$T_j = \sum_i w_i s_{ij} \tag{5.1}$$

In this example, the project under consideration received a factor score of 18.

A variety of other formulas have been proposed for deriving the relative weights. Three of the simplest are presented below. More elaborate schemes are discussed in the next chapter.

1. *Uniform or equal weights.* Given N criteria, the weight for each is

$$w_i = \frac{1}{N}$$

2. *Rank sum weights.* If R_i is the rank position of criterion i (with 1 as the highest rank) and there are N criteria, then rank sum weights for each criterion may be calculated as

$$w_i = \frac{N - R_i + 1}{\sum_{k=1}^{N}(N - R_k + 1)}$$

where the denominator is the sum of the first N integers; i.e., $N(N + 1)/2$.

3. *Rank reciprocal weights.* These weights may be calculated as

$$w_i = \frac{1/R_i}{\sum_{k=1}^{N} 1/R_k}$$

The advantage of a scoring model is that it takes into account the tradeoffs among the criteria, as defined by the relative weights. The disadvantage is that it lacks precision and relies on an arbitrary scoring system. More sophisticated models should lead to better decisions.

One area in which the use of multiattribute scoring models has increased rapidly in the United States over the last few years is in planning studies. Specific applications can be found in regulatory proceedings and in bidding systems used by some utilities to acquire capacity from independent power producers. An environmental scoring form developed by Niagara Mohawk, a New York utility, is depicted in Table 5.3. Note that the procedure for assigning points is specified.

A typical rationale for the interest shown by regulatory commissions is offered by Mintzer (1990), who asserted that the "scaled scoring models are easy to use, facilitate comparisons of environmental impacts measured in different units, and are more comprehensive than economic analysis. In addition, they provide a rank from the lowest to the highest cost on the basis of all economic, environmental, and social factors that can be quantified." These are very impressive claims, but unfortunately, many of the applications reported have paid little attention to methodological issues, with the consequence that the validity of the results is highly uncertain.

5.4 BENEFIT-COST ANALYSIS

Within the private sector, evaluating the merits of alternative investment opportunities begins with technical feasibility. The next step involves a comparison at some minimum attractive rate of return (MARR) of the estimated stream of costs over the expected economic life of each project. Engineering studies must be undertaken to establish the fundamental data. The estimated benefits and costs are then compared, usually on a present value basis, using a predetermined discount rate.

In the private sector, the firm generally pays all of the costs and receives all of the benefits, both quantitative and qualitative. Replacing an outdated piece of equipment is an example in which the returns are measurable, whereas constructing a new company cafeteria illustrates the opposite case. Where the activities of government are concerned, however, a different situation arises. Revenues are received through various forms of taxation and are supposed to be spent "in the public interest." Thus, the government pays but receives very few, if any, benefits. This can present all sorts of problems. For one, it means that the intended beneficiaries of a federal project will be very anxious to get the project approved and funded. Such situations may induce otherwise virtuous people to redefine the standards of acceptable ethical behavior. A second problem concerns the measurement of benefits, which are often widely disbursed. Other difficulties include the selection of an interest rate and choosing the correct viewpoint from which the analysis should made. Finally, in the benefit-cost (B/C) analysis, where the B/C ratio is used to rank competing projects, there may be legitimate ambiguity in deciding what goes in the numerator and what goes in the denominator of the ratio.

At first glance, it would seem to be a simple matter of sorting out the consequences into benefits (for the numerator) or costs (for the denominator). This works satisfactorily when applied to projects for a firm or a person. In government projects, it may be considerably more difficult to classify the various consequences, as shown in Example 5-1.

TABLE 5.3   Environmental Scoring Form Used by Niagara Mohawk

Environmental attributes	Weight, W	Points, P						Score, $W \times P$
		0	1	2	3	4	5	
Air emissions								
Sulfur oxides (lb/MWh)	7	>6	4.0–6.0	2.5–3.9	1.5–2.4	0.5–1.4	<0.5	
Nitrogen oxides (lb/MWh)	16	>6	4.0–6.0	2.5–3.9	1.5–2.4	0.5–1.4	<0.1	
Carbon dioxide (lb/MWh)	3	>1500	1050–1500	650–1049	250–649	100–249	<100	
Particulates (lb/MWh)	1	>0.3	0.2–0.3	0.1–0.199	0.05–0.099	0.01–0.049	<0.01	
Water effects								
Cooling water flow (annual intake as % of lake volume)	1	80–100	60–79	40–59	20–39	5–19	<5	
Fish protection	1	None		Operational restrictions		Fish protection	No public water used provided	
NY State water quality classification of receiving water	1	A or better	B	C+	C+	D	No water use or municipal water/waste water utilized	
Land effects								
Acreage required (acres/MW)	1	0.3–0.5	0.2–0.29	0.1–0.19	0.05–0.09	0.01–0.05	<0.01	
Terrestrial	1	Unique ecological or historical value		Rural or low-density suburban		Industrial area	No land used	
Visual aesthetics	1	Highly visible		Within existing developed area		Not visible from public roads		
Transmission	2	New OH >5 miles	New OH 1–5 miles	New UG >5 miles	New UG 1–5 miles	Use existing facilities	Energy conservation	
Noise (L_{eq} − backgrd L_{90})	2	5–10			0–4.9		<0	
Solid waste disposal (lb/MWh)	2	>300	200–300	100–199	50–99	10–49	<10	
Solid waste as fuel (% of total Btu)	1	0	1–30	31–50	51–80	81–90	91–100	
Fuel delivery method	1	New RR spur	Truck and existing RR	New pipeline	Barge	Use existing pipeline	No fuel use	
Distance from receptor area (km)	1	<10	10–39	40–69	70–100	>100	Energy conservation	
							Total score (210 maximum) =	

Example 5-1

On a proposed government project, the following consequences have been identified:

- Initial cost of project to be paid by government is $100K.
- Present worth (PW) of future maintenance to be paid by government is $40K.
- PW of benefits to the public is $300K.
- PW of additional public users costs is $60K.

Show the various ways of computing the B/C ratio.

Solution   Putting the benefits in the numerator and all costs in the denominator gives

$$\text{B/C ratio} = \frac{\text{All benefits}}{\text{All costs}} = \frac{300}{100 + 40 + 60} = \frac{300}{200} = 1.5$$

An alternative computation is to consider user costs as disbenefits and to subtract them in the numerator rather than add them in the denominator:

$$\text{B/C ratio} = \frac{\text{Public benefits} - \text{Public costs}}{\text{Government costs}} = \frac{300 - 60}{100 + 40} = \frac{240}{140} = 1.7$$

Still another variation would be to consider maintenance costs as disbenefits:

$$\text{B/C ratio} = \frac{300 - 60 - 40}{100} = \frac{200}{100} = 2.0$$

It should be noted that although three different B/C ratios may be computed, the net present value (NPV) does not change:

$$\text{NPV} = \text{PW of benefits} - \text{PW of costs} = 300 - 60 - 40 - 100 = 100. \quad ■$$

There is no inherently correct way to compute the B/C ratio. Using the notation of Chapter 3, two commonly used formulations are given below:

1. *Conventional B/C*

$$\text{B/C} = \frac{\text{PW of benefits to user}}{\text{PW of total costs to supplier}} = \frac{\text{PW}(B)}{\text{PW}[CR + (O + M)]} \tag{5.2a}$$

or

$$\text{B/C} = \frac{\text{Annual worth (AW) of benefits to user}}{\text{AW of total costs to supplier}} = \frac{B}{CR + (O + M)} \tag{5.2b}$$

where

B = AW of benefits to user
CR = capital recovery cost (equivalent annual cost of initial investment, considering any salvage value)
O = equivalent uniform annual operating cost
M = equivalent uniform maintenance cost

2. *Modified B/C*

$$B/C = \frac{PW[B - (O + M)]}{PW(CR)} \quad \text{or} \quad B/C = \frac{B - (O + M)}{CR} \qquad \blacksquare$$

The modified method has become more popular with governmental agencies and departments over the last decade. Although both methods yield the same recommendation when comparing mutually exclusive alternatives, they may yield different rankings for independent investment opportunities. In either case, using PW, AW, or future worth (FW) should always provide the same results.

Example 5-2   (Single-Project Analysis)

An individual investment opportunity is deemed to be worthwhile if its B/C ratio is greater than or equal to 1. Consider the project of installing a new inventory control system with the following data:

Initial cost	$20,000
Project life	5 years
Salvage value	$4,000
Annual savings	$10,000
O&M disbursements	$4,400
MARR	15%

By interpreting annual savings as benefits, the conventional and modified B/C ratios based on annual equivalents are computed as follows:

$$CR = \$20,000(A/P, 15\%, 5) - \$4,000(A/F, 15\%, 5)$$
$$= 20,000(0.2983) - 4,000(0.1483) = \$5,373$$

$$\text{conventional B/C} = \frac{B}{CR + (O + M)} = \frac{\$10,000}{\$5,373 + \$4,400} = 1.02$$

$$\text{modified B/C} = \frac{B - (O + M)}{CR} = \frac{\$10,000 - \$4,400}{\$5,373} = 1.04$$

Because either B/C is greater than 1, the investment is worthwhile. Nevertheless, there is an opportunity cost associated with the investment that may preclude other possibilities. The fact that the B/C of a project is greater than 1 does not necessarily mean that it should be pursued.   ■

Example 5-3   (Comparing Mutually Exclusive Alternatives)

As was true for ROR calculations, when comparing a set of mutually exclusive alternatives by any B/C method, an incremental approach is preferred. The principles and criterion of choice as explained in Chapter 3 apply equally to B/C methods, the only difference being that each increment of cost (the denominator) must be justified by a B/C ratio ≥ 1.

Consider the data in Table 5.4a associated with the four alternative projects used in Example 3-9 to demonstrate the internal ROR (IRR) method. Each is listed in increasing

TABLE 5.4   Input Data and Results for Incremental Analysis

(a) Input data	Project			
	A	B	C	D
Initial cost	$20,000	$30,000	$35,000	$43,000
Useful life	5 years	10 years	5 years	5 years
Salvage value	$4000	0	$4000	$5000
Annual receipts	$10,000	$14,000	$20,000	$18,000
Annual disbursements	$4,400	$8,600	$9,390	$5,250
Net annual receipts − disbursements	$5,600	$5,400	$10,610	$12,750

(b) Results	A	A → B	A → C	C → D
ΔInvestment	$20,000	$10,000	$15,000	$8,000
ΔSalvage	4,000	−4,000	0	1,000
ΔCR = ΔC	5,373	605	4,477	2,386
Δ(annual receipts − disbursements) = ΔB	5,600	−200	5,010	2140
Δ(B/C) = ΔB/ΔC	1.04	−0.33	1.12	0.90
Is Δinvestment justified?	Yes	No	Yes	No

order of investment. The symbol Δ(B/C) means that the B/C ratio is being computed on the incremental cost. Once again, a MARR of 15% is used.

The output data in Table 5.4b confirm the results previously found using the IRR method. Alternative C would be chosen given that it is the most expensive project for which each increment of cost is justified (by B/C ratio $\geq$ 1). ∎

B/C studies within the public sector in particular may be approached from several points of view. The perspective taken may have a significant impact on the outcome of the analysis. Possible viewpoints include

1. That of the governmental agency conducting the study
2. That of the local area (e.g., town, municipality)
3. The nation as a whole
4. The targeted industry

Thus, it is essential that the analyst have clearly in mind which group is being represented before proceeding with the study. If the objective is to promote the general welfare of the public, then it is necessary to consider the impact of alternative policies on the entire population, not merely on the income and expenditures of a selected group. Practically speaking, however, without regulations, the best that can be hoped for is that the broader interests of the community will be taken into account. Most would agree, for example, that without environmental and health regulations and the attendant threat of prosecution, there would be little incentive for firms to treat their waste products before discharging them into local waterways.

The national viewpoint would seem to be the correct one for all federally funded public works projects; however, most such projects provide benefits only to a local area, making it difficult, if not impossible, to trace and evaluate quantitatively the national effects. The following example parallels an actual case history.

Example 5-4

The government wants to decide whether to give a $5,000,000 subsidy to a chemical man- ufacturer who is interested in opening a new factory in a depressed area. The factory is ex- pected to generate jobs for 200 people and further stimulate the local economy through commercial ventures and tourist trade. The benefits as a result of jobs created and im- proved trade in the area are estimated at $1,000,000 per year. Six percent is considered to be a fair discount rate. The study period is 20 years. Calculate the B/C ratio to determine whether the project is worthwhile.

Solution   PW of benefits $= \$1,000,000(P/A, 6\%, 20) = \$11,470,000$

$$\text{B/C ratio} = \frac{\$11,470,000}{\$5,000,000} = 2.3$$

Outcome.   The plant was funded on the basis of the foregoing study, but pollution control equipment was not installed. During operations, raw by-products were dumped into the river, causing major environmental problems downstream. Virtually all of the fish died, and the river became a local health hazard. The retrofitting of pollution control equipment sometime later made the entire project uneconomical, and the plant eventually closed.

Conclusion.   Because the full costs of the project were not taken into account orig- inally, the results were overly optimistic and misleading. Had the proper viewpoint been established at the outset and all of the factors considered, the outcome might not have been so unfortunate.   ∎

5.4.1 Step-by-Step Approach

To conduct a B/C analysis for an investment project, it is important to complete the fol- lowing steps:

1. Identify the problem clearly.
2. Explicitly define the set of objectives to be accomplished.
3. Generate alternatives that satisfy the stated objectives.
4. Identify clearly the constraints (e.g., technological, political, legal, social, finan- cial) that exist with the project environment. This step will help narrow the alter- natives generated.
5. Determine and list the benefits and costs associated with each alternative. Specify each in monetary terms. If this cannot be done for all factors, then this should be stated clearly in the final report.
6. Calculate the B/C ratios and other indicators (e.g., present value, ROR, initial in- vestment required, payback period) for each alternative.
7. Prepare the final report comparing the results of the evaluation of each alterna- tive examined.

5.4.2 Using the Methodology

As with any decision-making process, the first two steps above are to define the problem and related goals. This may involve identifying a particular problem to be solved (e.g., pol- lution) or agreeing on a specific program, such as landing an astronaut on the moon. Once this is done, it is necessary to devise a solution that is feasible, not only technically and economically but also politically.

Implicit in these steps is a twofold selection process: a macro-selection process whereby we choose from among competing opportunities or programs (should more federal funds be expended on space research or pollution cleanup and control?) and a micro-selection process whereby we strive to find the best of several alternatives (should we build a nuclear- or coal-fired plant?). In the public sector, it has often been claimed that we as a society are ruefully inept in conducting the selection process. Usually, goals and options are chosen in the thick of political debate, and benefits and costs are viewed so narrowly that we end up with projects that are not truly desirable when the needs of society as a whole are considered.

One of the most dramatic examples of such a failure is the East St. Louis public housing project that was torn down only a few years after it was erected. When this project was being planned, the main consideration was apparently to maximize the ratio of bricks to dollars; there is no sign that sociological factors, such as the possible wishes and concerns of the potential inhabitants, entered into the analysis. The result was that the project became badly crime ridden and vandalized, many people refused to live in it, and bankruptcy quickly ensued.

The potential for such mistakes can be greatly minimized if an external as well as an internal B/C analysis is made. For a housing project, the planners might examine such external factors as prevailing social conditions (crime rate, poverty levels, family structure, etc.) and the availability of public transportation, schools, and employment. Then the tradeoffs that are involved in such internal factors as the type of construction material to use, the size of the rooms versus the number of rooms, and cabinetry in the kitchen versus the size of the appliances must be established. The internal and external analyses are interdependent, but most large public-sector engineering projects can be reduced to five or six alternatives.

5.4.3 Classes of Benefits and Costs

Once a set of alternatives has been established, the detailed analysis can begin. The benefits and costs may be broken down into four classes: primary, secondary, external, and intangible. Primary refers to benefits and costs that are a direct result of a particular project. If a corporation manufactures videocassette recorders, then the primary costs are in production and the primary benefits are in profits. In building a canal, the construction costs and the revenues generated from water charges are the primary elements.

"Secondary" benefits and costs are not those that are less important but rather the marginal benefits and costs that accrue when an imperfect market mechanism is at work. In such instances, the market prices of a project's final goods and services do not reflect the "true" prices. The use of government funds to build and maintain airports is a good example. There is a hidden cost to society as well as a hidden benefit to the airlines and their more frequent customers. Increased noise pollution and traffic congestion around the airport are illustrative of the costs; benefits can be measured by lower airfares.

External benefits and costs are those that arise when a project produces a spillover effect on someone other than the intended group. Thus, a government subsidy to airports produces external benefits by indirectly boosting the local economy. Massive government spending on space has yielded extensive benefits to medical science and the microelectronics industry. Similarly, there are spillover effects of pollution that produce disbenefits in the form of health costs and the loss of recreational facilities.

Intangible benefits and costs are those that are difficult, if not impossible, to measure on a monetary scale. Trademarks and goodwill are intangibles that have always been of concern, whereas the cost of increased urban congestion and the benefits of advanced automation and robots in the workplace are factors that engineers have more recently been forced to consider. When intangibles dominate the decision process, the value of multiple-criteria methods such as multiattribute utility theory and the analytic hierarchy process, each discussed in Chapter 6, becomes persuasively self-evident.

After categorizing the benefits and costs in this manner, they should be allocated to the various project time periods in which they are expected to occur. These periods include the planning stage, the implementation stage, the operation stage, and the close-out stage. This distinction is necessary for proper quantitative evaluation. For example, the costs associated with noise, traffic disruption, and hazards of subway construction may occur only in the implementation stage and must be discounted accordingly.

5.4.4 Shortcomings of the Benefit-Cost Methodology

Upon completion of the quantitative assessment of the various costs and benefits, the actual desirability of the project can be determined. Use of the B/C ratio to rank or ascertain the best alternative can be deceptive, however, because it disguises the problem of scale. Two projects may have the same ratio yet involve benefits and costs that differ by millions of dollars, or one project may have a lower ratio than another and still possess greater benefits. Sometimes, therefore, projects will be selected simply on the basis of whether their benefits exceed their costs; yet again, scale must be considered, for two projects obviously can have the same net benefit, but one may be far more costly than the other.

As mentioned, another way to evaluate projects is to compare the expected ROR on investment with the interest rate on an alternative use of the funds. This criterion is implicit in most private-sector decisions but generally is neglected in the public sector, where tangible financial returns are not the sole criterion for investment allocations. Moreover, there is rarely a consensus on which discount rate should be used. Economists invariably dispute the choice, some arguing for the social rate of time preference, whereas others lean toward the prevailing interest rate. Except when a particular rate is specified by the decision maker, the NPV calculations should be repeated using several values to ascertain sensitivity effects.

The difficulty in agreeing on a discount rate is usually secondary to the problem of determining future costs and benefit streams. Uncertainties in long-term consequences may be large for extended time horizons of more than a few years, although frequently, all alternatives will suffer from a similar fate. Investigating questions of inter-temporal equity and methods for dealing with uncertain outcomes are central problems of research, and their logic must be pursued relentlessly. Moreover, all forms of decision making must resolve these questions, regardless of whether they are dealt with explicitly.

In practice, it is rare that any one criterion will suffice for making a sound decision. Several criteria, as well as their many variations, must be examined in the analysis.

The important point, however, is that even if all relevant factors are addressed, the analysis will still possess a high degree of subjectivity, leaving room for both conscious and unacknowledged bias. This leads to the two major shortcomings of B/C analysis.

The first is the need and general failure to evaluate those items that are unquantifiable in monetary terms. The type of question that continually gets raised is, "How do you measure the value of harmony between labor and management?" or "What is the value of a pollution-free environment?" The development of indicators other than those that reflect dollar values explicitly present a considerable challenge to analysts. They must depart from the familiar criteria of economic efficiency as a prime mechanism of evaluation and venture into the unknown areas of social and environmental concerns. Interesting enough, the nonquantifiable elements bear equally on the governmental, business, and consumer sectors of the economy. In short, these "unmeasurables" may be of utmost significance, as system indicators must be developed to evaluate their impact on the program. It is here where judgment and subjectivity come into play.

The second weakness in the practice of B/C analysis arises from the "judge and jury" characteristic. Invariably, the same government agency that proposes and sponsors a particular project undertakes the analysis. Whether this is done internally or by a subcontractor is not important. Rather, the agency and its contractors will usually display similar attitudes and biases in their approach to a problem. Independent, unbiased assessments are needed if the process is to work correctly and produce believable results.

5.5 COST-EFFECTIVENESS ANALYSIS

When comparing two projects that have the same B/C ratio, the one that costs more will provide greater returns. In some situations, though, there may be a fixed or upper limit on the budget, so a project that is technically feasible may not be economically feasible even if it has a high B/C ratio. Economic barriers to entry are common in many fields, such as automotive or semiconductor manufacturing, where the required initial investment may be as high as $1 billion.

In the case in which the budget is the limiting factor, we would like to know what is the most effective use of our money. To answer this question, *cost-effectiveness* (C-E) studies are often performed. In these studies, the concern is not so much the ROR as the performance of the resultant system as measured by a composite index that is necessarily subjective in nature. This is because incommensurable and qualitative factors such as development risk, maintainability, and ease of use all must be evaluated collectively.

In general, system effectiveness can be thought of as a measure of the extent to which a system may be expected to achieve a set of specific mission requirements. It is often denoted as a function of the system availability, dependability, and capability.

- *Availability* is defined as a measure of the system condition at the start of a mission. It is a function of the relationship among hardware, personnel, and procedures.
- *Dependability* is defined as a measure of the system condition at one or more points during mission operations.
- *Capability* accounts specifically for the performance spectrum of the system.

The term *effectiveness* possesses a high order of abstraction. Because of its generality, it is subject to many interpretations, which makes it difficult to define precisely. For a product or service, one definition would be the ability to deliver what is called for in the technical specification. Among the terms that are related to (or have been substituted for) *effectiveness* are *value, worth, benefit, utility, gain,* and *performance.* Unlike cost, which can be measured in dollars, effectiveness does not possess an intrinsic measure by which it can be uniquely expressed.

Government agencies, in particular, the U.S. Department of Defense, have been the primary exponents of C-E analyses. The following eight steps represent a common blueprint for conducting a C-E study:

1. Define the desired goals.
2. Identify the mission requirements.
3. Develop alternative systems.
4. Establish system evaluation criteria.
5. Determine capabilities of alternative systems.
6. Analyze the merits of each.
7. Perform sensitivity analysis.
8. Document results and make recommendations.

A critical step in the procedure is in deciding how the merits of each alternative will be judged. After the evaluation criteria or attributes are established, a mechanism is needed to construct a single measure of performance. Scoring models, such as those described in Section 5.3, are commonly used. Here we assess the relative importance of each system attribute and assign a weight to each. Next, a numerical value, say between 0 and 100, is assigned to represent the effectiveness of each attribute for each system. Once again, these values are subjective ratings but may actually be based on simple mathematical calculations of objective measures, subjective opinion, or engineering judgments. Where an appropriate physical scale exists, the maximum and minimum values can be noted and a straight line between those boundaries can be used to translate outcomes to a scale of 0 to 100. The analyst must ensure that the actual value of the attribute corresponds to the subjective description; for example, $100 \geq$ excellent ≥ 80; $80 >$ good ≥ 60.

In many cases, it is useful to compare attribute relative values graphically to determine whether any obvious errors exist in data entry or logic. Figure 5.3 provides a visual comparison of the ratings of each of five attributes for four systems. The corresponding data are displayed in Table 5.5.

At this point in the analysis, two sets of numbers have been developed for each attribute i: the normalized weights, w_i, and the perceived effectiveness assigned to each system j for each attribute i, s_{ij}. To arrive at a composite measure of effectiveness, T_j, for each system j, we could use Equation (5.1). The highest value of T would indicate the system with the best overall performance.

If this system were within budget and none of its attribute values was below a predetermined threshold, then it would represent the likely choice. Nevertheless, effectiveness alone does not tell the entire story, and whenever possible, the analysis should be extended to include costs as well. In a similar manner, cost factors can be combined

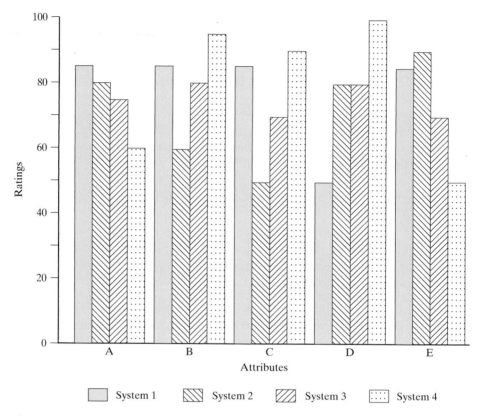

Figure 5.3   Relative effectiveness of systems.

TABLE 5.5   Data for C-E Analysis

Attribute	Weight	System 1		System 2		System 3		System 4	
		EFF	WT	EFF	WT	EFF	WT	EFF	WT
A. Efficiency	0.32	85	27.2	80	25.6	75	24.0	60	19.2
B. Speed	0.24	85	20.4	60	14.4	80	19.2	95	22.8
C. User friendly	0.24	85	20.4	50	12.0	70	16.8	90	21.6
D. Reliability	0.12	50	6.0	80	9.6	80	9.6	99	11.9
E. Expandability	0.08	85	6.8	90	7.2	70	5.6	50	4.0
Total effectiveness			80.8		68.8		75.2		79.5
Costs			$450K		$250K		$300K		$350K

into a single measure to compare with effectiveness. Typically, procurement, installation, and maintenance costs are considered. When the planning horizon extends beyond 1 year, the effects of time should be included through appropriate discounting. Table 5.5 contains this information.

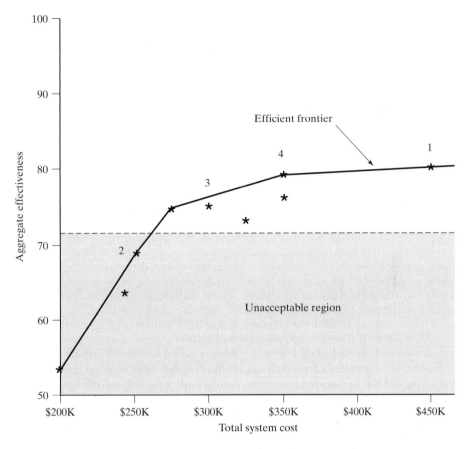

Figure 5.4   Relationship between system effectiveness and cost.

The final step in an extended version of the C-E methodology compares system effectiveness and costs. A graphical representation may be helpful in this regard. Figure 5.4 plots the two variables for each system (the unlabeled points represent systems not contained in Table 5.5). The outer envelope denotes the *efficient frontier*. Any system that is not on this curve is dominated by one or a combination of two or more systems, implying that it is inferior from both a cost and an effectiveness point of view. Systems that fall below the dashed line (predetermined threshold) are arbitrarily deemed unacceptable. Finally, note the relationship between systems 1 and 4. Although system 1 has the highest effectiveness rating, it is only marginally better than system 4. The fact that it is almost 30% more expensive, however, makes its selection problematic, as an incremental analysis would indicate.

5.6 ISSUES RELATED TO RISK

In designing, building, and operating large systems, engineers must face up to such questions as, "What can go wrong, and how likely is it to happen?" "What range of consequences might there be, when, and how could they be averted or mitigated?" "How much risk should be tolerated or accepted during normal operations, and how can it be measured, reduced, and managed?"

Formal risk analysis attempts to pin down and, whenever possible, to quantify the answers to these questions (Bell 1989, Kaplan and Garrick 1981). In new systems, it is coming to be accepted as a way of comparing the risks inherent in alternative designs, spotlighting the high-risk portion of a system, and pointing up techniques for attenuating those risks. For older systems, risk analysis conducted after they have been built and operated have often revealed crucial design faults. One such fault cost the lives of 167 workers on the British oil production platform Piper Alpha in the North Sea several years ago. A simple gas leak in the $3 billion rig led to a devastating explosion. The platform had a vertical structure, and risk analysis was not done on the design. Workers' accommodations were on top, above the lower compartments, which housed equipment for separating oil from natural gas. The accommodations were thought to be immune to mishap, but as a post-accident computer simulation revealed, the energy from the explosion in the lower level coupled to the platform's frame. Stress waves were dissipated effectively into the water below, but in short order, reflections at the steel–air interface at the upper levels expanded, weakened, and shattered the structure. In contrast, Norwegian platforms, which are designed using government-mandated risk analysis, are long and horizontal like aircraft carriers, with workers' accommodations at the opposite end of the structure from the processing facilities and insulated from them by steel doors.

Analysts define risk as a combination of the probability of an undesirable event and the magnitude of every foreseeable consequence (e.g., damage to property, loss of money, delay in implementation). The consequences considered can range in seriousness from mild setback to catastrophic. Some related definitions are given in Table 5.6.

The first step in risk analysis is to tabulate the various stages or phases of a system's mission and list the risk sensitivities in each phase, be they technical, human, or economic. The time at which a failure occurs may mitigate its consequences. For example, a failure in an air traffic control system at a major airport would disrupt local air traffic far more at weeknight rush hour than on a Sunday morning. Similarly, a failure in a chemical processing plant would be more dangerous if it interfered with an intermediate reaction that produced a toxic chemical than if it occurred at a stage when the by-products were more benign.

Next, for each phase of the mission, the system's operation should be diagrammed and the logical relationships of the components and subsystems during that phase determined. The most useful techniques for the job are failure modes and effects analysis, event tree analysis, and fault tree analysis (Kumamoto and Henley 2001). The three complement one another and, when taken together, help engineers identify the hazards of a system and the range of potential consequences. The interactions are particularly important because one piece of equipment might be caused to fail by another's failure to, say, supply fuel or current.

For engineers and managers, the chief purpose of risk analysis—defining the stages of a mission, examining the relationships between system parts, and quantifying failure probabilities—is to highlight any weakness in a design and identify those that contribute most heavily to delays or losses. The process may even suggest ways of minimizing or mitigating risk.

TABLE 5.6   Some Definitions Related to Risk

Term	Definition
Failure	Inability of a system, subsystem, or component to perform its required function.
Quality assurance	Probability that a system, subsystem, or component will perform its intended function when tested.
Reliability	Probability that a system, subsystem, or component will perform its intended function for a specified period of time or under normal conditions.
Risk	Combination of the probability of an abnormal event or failure and the consequences of that event or failure to a project's success or a system's performance.
Risk assessment	Process and procedures of identifying, characterizing, quantifying, and evaluating risks and their significance.
Risk management	Any techniques used either to minimize the probability of an accident or to mitigate its consequences with, for instance, good engineering design, good operating practices, or preventive maintenance.
Uncertainty	Measure of the limits of knowledge in a technical area, expressed as a distribution of probabilities around a point estimate. The four principal elements of uncertainty are statistical confidence (a measure of sampling accuracy), tolerance (a measure of the relevance of available information to the problem at hand), incompleteness and inaccuracy of the input data, and ambiguity in modeling the problem.

Source: Dougherty and Fragola (1988).

A case in point is the probabilistic risk analysis on the U.S. space shuttle's auxiliary power units, completed for NASA in December 1987 by the engineering consulting firm Pickard, Lowe & Garrick. The auxiliary power units, among other tasks, throttle the orbiter's main engines and operate its wing ailerons. NASA engineers and managers, using qualitative techniques, had formerly judged fuel leaks in the three auxiliary fuel units "unlikely" and the risks acceptable, without fully understanding the magnitude of the risks that they accepted, even though a worst-case consequence could be the loss of the vehicle. One of the problems with qualitative assessment is that subjective interpretation of words such as "likely" and "unlikely" allows opportunity for errors in judgment about risk. For example, NASA had applied the word "unlikely" to risks that ranged from 1:250 to 1:20,000.

The probabilistic risk analysis revealed that although the probability of individual leaks was low, there were so many places where leaks could occur that five had in fact occurred in the first 24 shuttle missions. Moreover, in the ninth mission on November 28, 1983, the escaping fuel self-ignited while the orbiter was hurtling back to earth and exploded after it had landed.

The probabilistic analysis pinpointed the fact that an explosion was more likely to occur during landing than during launch, when the auxiliary power units are purged with nitrogen to remove combustible atmospheric oxygen. It also suggested several ways of reducing the risk, such as changing the fuels or placing fire barriers between the power units.

5.6.1 Accepting and Managing Risk

Once the risks are determined, managers must decide what levels are acceptable on the basis of economic, political, and technological judgments. The decision can be controversial because it necessarily involves subjective judgments about costs and benefits of the project, the well-being of the organization, and the potential damage or liability.

Naturally, risk is tolerated at a higher level if the payoffs are high or critical to the organization. In the microcomputer industry, for example, where product lifetimes may be no greater than 1 or 2 years and new products and upgrades are being introduced continually, companies must keep pace with the competition or forfeit market share. Whatever the level of risk finally judged acceptable, it should be compared with and, if necessary, used to adjust the risks calculated to be inherent in the project. The probability of failure may be reduced further by redundant or standby subsystems or by parallel efforts during development. Also, managers should prepare to counter the consequences of failure or setbacks by devising contingency plans or emergency procedures.

5.6.2 Coping with Uncertainty

Two sources of uncertainty still need to be considered: one intrinsic in probability theory and the other born of all-too-human error. First, the laws of chance exclude the prediction of when and where a particular failure may occur. That remains true even when enough statistical information about the system's operation exists for a reliable estimate of how likely it is to fail. The probability of failure, itself, is surrounded by a band of uncertainty that expands or shrinks depending on how much data are available and how well the system is understood. This statistical level of confidence is usually expressed as a standard deviation about the mean or a related measure. Finally, if the system is so new that few or no data have been recorded for it and analogous data from similar systems must be used to get a handle on potential risks, then there is uncertainty over how well the estimate resembles the actual case.

At the human interface, the challenge is to design a system so that it will not only operate as it should but also leave the operator little room for erroneous judgment. Additional risk can be introduced if a designer cannot anticipate which information an operator may need to digest and interpret under the daily pressures of the job, especially when an emergency starts to develop.

From an operational point of view, poor design can introduce greater risk, sometimes with tragic consequences. After the U.S.S. *Vincennes* on July 3, 1988, mistook Iran Air Flight 655 for an enemy F-14 and shot down the airliner over international waters in the Persian Gulf, Rear Admiral Eugene La Roque blamed the calamity on the bewildering complexity of the Aegis radar system. He is quoted as saying that "we have scientists and engineers capable of devising complicated equipment without any thought of how it will be integrated into a combat situation or that it might be too complex to operate. These machines produce too much information and don't sort the important from the unimportant. There's a disconnection between technical effort and combat use."

All told, human behavior is not nearly as predictable as that of an engineered system. Today, there are many techniques for quantifying with fair reliability the probability of slips, lapses, and misperceptions. Still, remaining uncertainty in the prediction of individual behavior contributes to residual risk in all systems and projects.

5.6.3 Nonprobabilistic Evaluation Methods When Uncertainty Is Present

When considering a capital investment, there are four major sources of uncertainty that are nearly always present in engineering economic studies:

1. Inaccuracy of the cash flow estimates, especially benefits related to new products or technology.
2. Relationship between type of business and future health of the company. Certain lines of business are inherently unstable, such as oil drilling, entertainment, and luxury goods.
3. Type of physical plant and equipment involved. Some structures have definite economic lives and market values, whereas others are unpredictable. The cost of specialized plants and equipment is often difficult to estimate, especially for first-time projects.
4. Length of the project and study period. As the length increases, so does the variability in the estimates of operations and maintenance costs, as well as presumed benefits.

As discussed in Chapter 3, breakeven analysis and sensitivity analysis are two simple ways of addressing uncertainty. Other approaches include *scenario analysis, risk-adjusted MARR,* and *reduction of useful life.* Breakeven analysis is commonly used when the selection process is dependent on a single factor, such as capacity, sales, or ROR, and only two alternatives are being considered. In this case, we identify the one whose marginal benefit is greater and solve for the value of the factor that makes the two alternatives equally attractive. Above the breakeven point, the alternative with the greater marginal benefit is preferable.

Sensitivity analysis is aimed at assessing the relative magnitude of a change in the measure of interest, such as NPV, caused by one or more changes in estimated factors, such as interest rate and useful life. The results can often be visualized graphically, as shown in the following example.

Example 5-5   (Sensitivity Analysis)

Your office is considering the acquisition of a new workstation, but there is some uncertainty about which model to buy and the expected cash flows. Before making the investment, your supervisor has asked you to investigate the NPV of a generic system over a range of $\pm\$40\%$ with respect to (a) capital investment, (b) annual net cash flow, (c) salvage value, and (d) useful life. The following data characterize the investment

Capital investment	$-\$11,500$
Annual revenues	$\$5,000$
Annual expenses	$-\$2,000$
Estimated salvage value	$\$1,000$
Useful life	6 years
MARR	10%

Solution   The first step is to compute the NPV for the given data.

Baseline NPV $= -\$11,500 + \$3,000(P/A, 10\%, 6) + \$1,000(P/F, 10\%, 6) = \$2,130$

a. When initial investment varies by $\pm p\%$,
$$\text{NPV}(p) = -(1 + p/100)(\$11{,}500) + \$3{,}000(P/A, 10\%, 6)$$
$$+ \$1000(P/F, 10\%, 6)$$

b. When revenues vary by $\pm p\%$,
$$\text{NPV}(p) = -\$11{,}500 + (1 + p/100)(\$3{,}000)(P/A, 10\%, 6)$$
$$+ \$1{,}000(P/F, 10\%, 6)$$

c. When salvage value varies by $\pm p\%$,
$$\text{NPV}(p) = -\$11{,}500 + \$3{,}000(P/A, 10\%, 6)$$
$$+ (1 + p/100)(\$1{,}000)(P/F, 10\%, 6)$$

d. When the useful life varies by $\pm p\%$,
$$\text{NPV}(p) = -\$11{,}500 + \$3{,}000[P/A, 10\%, 6(1 + p/100)]$$
$$+ \$1{,}000[P/F, 10\%, 6(1 + p/100)]$$

Plotting the functions NPV(p) for $-40\% \le p \le +40\%$ gives rise to what is known as a spider chart, as shown in Fig. 5.5. A frame of references is provided by the baseline result.   ■

Scenario analysis, or optimistic-pessimistic estimation, is used to establish a range of values for the measure of interest. Typically, the optimistic estimate is defined to have only a 5% chance of being exceeded by the actual outcome, whereas the pessimistic estimate is defined so that it is exceeded approximately 95% of the time.

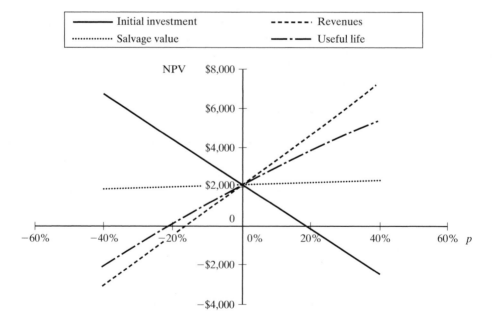

Figure 5.5   Spider chart for sensitivity analysis.

Example 5-6   (Scenario Analysis)

An ultrasound inspection device for which optimistic, most likely, and pessimistic estimates are given below is being considered for purchase. If the MARR is 8%, then what course of action would you recommend? Base your answer an net annual worth (NAW).

Measure	Optimistic (O)	Most likely (M)	Pessimisti (P)
Capital investment	−$150,000	−$150,000	−$150,000
Annual revenues	$110,000	$70,000	$50,000
Annual costs	−$20,000	−$43,000	−$57,000
Salvage value	$0	$0	$0
Useful life	18 years	10 years	8 years
NAW	$73,995	$4,650	−$33,100

Solution   Whether to accept or reject the purchase is somewhat arbitrary and would depend strongly on the decision maker's attitude toward risk. A conservative approach would be to

accept the investment if NAW(P) > 0
reject the investment if NAW(O) < 0
or do more analysis

Applying this rule tells us that more information is needed. One possible approach at this point is to evaluate all combinations of outcomes and see how many are above some threshold, say $50,000, and below, say $0. Following this idea, we note that annual revenues, annual costs, and the useful life are the independent inputs that vary from one scenario to another. This means that there are $3^3 = 27$ possible outcomes. The NAW of each is listed in the table below rounded to the nearest $1,000. For example, the first block of nine data entries represents the results when the annual revenues and useful life are varied over the three scenarios, whereas the annual costs are held fixed at the optimistic estimate.

Annual revenues	Annual costs								
	O			M			P		
	Useful life			Useful life			Useful life		
	O	M	P	O	M	P	O	M	P
O	74	68	64	51	45	41	37	31	27
M	34	28	24	11	5	1	−3	−9	−13
P	14	8	4	−9	−15	−19	−23	−29	−33

The computations indicate that the NAW > $50,000 in 4 of 27 scenarios and NAW < $0 in 9 of 27. Coupled with the results for the strictly optimistic, most likely, and pessimistic scenarios, this might not be sufficient for a positive decision.   ∎

The risk-adjusted MARR method involves the use of higher discount rates for those alternatives that have a relatively high degree of uncertainty and lower discount rates for projects that are at the other end of the spectrum. A higher-than-usual MARR implies that distance cash flows are less important than current or near-term cash flows. This approach is widely used in practice but contains many pitfalls, the most serious being that the uncertainty is not made explicit. As a consequence, the analyst should first try other methods.

Example 5-7   (Risk-Adjusted MARRs)

As an analyst for an investment firm, you are considering two alternatives that have the same initial cost and economic life but different cash flows, as indicated in the table below. Both are affected by uncertainty to some degree; however, alternative P is thought to be more uncertain than alternative Q. If the firm's risk-free MARR is 10%, then which is the better investment?

End-of-year, k	Alternative P	Alternative Q
0	−$160,000	−$160,000
1	$120,000	$20,827
2	$60,000	$60,000
3	$0	$120,000
4	$60,000	$60,000

Solution   At the risk-free MARR of 10%, both alternatives have the same NPV = $39,659. All else being equal, alternative Q should be chosen because it is less uncertain. To take into account the degree of uncertainty, we now use a prescribed risk-adjusted MARR of 20% for P and 17% for Q. Performing the same computations, we get

$$\text{NPV}_P(20\%) = -\$160,000 + \$120,000(P/F, 20\%, 1) + \$60,000(P/F, 20\%, 2)$$
$$+ \$60,000(P/F, 20\%, 4) = \$10,602$$
$$\text{NPV}_Q(17\%) = -\$160,000 + \$20,827(P/F, 17\%, 1)$$
$$+ \$60,000(P/F, 17\%, 2) + \$120,000(P/F, 17\%, 3)$$
$$+ \$60,000(P/F, 17\%, 4) = \$8,575$$

implying that alternative P is preferable. This is a reversal of the first result.

Figure 5.6 plots the NPV of the two alternatives as a function of the MARR. The breakeven point is 10%. For MARRs beyond 10%, P is always the better choice.   ■

Another technique used to compensate for uncertainty is based on truncating the project life to something less than its estimated useful life. By dropping from consideration those revenues and costs that may occur after the reduced study period, heavy emphasis is placed on rapid recovery of investment capital in the early years. Consequently, this method is closely related to the payback technique discussed in Chapter 3.

Implementation can be carried out in one of two ways. The first is to reduce the project life by some percentage and discard all subsequent cash flows. The NPV of the alternatives are then compared for the shortened life. The second is to determine the minimal life of the project that will produce an acceptable ROR. If this life is within the expectations

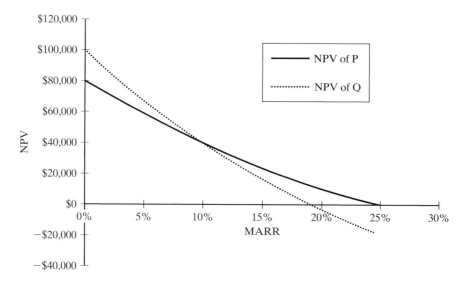

Figure 5.6   NPV comparisons for risk-adjusted MARRs.

of the decision maker, say, in terms of the maximum payback period, then the project is viewed as acceptable.

Example 5-8   (Reduction of Useful Life)

A proposed new product line requires $2,000,000 in capital over a 2-year period. Estimated revenues and expenses over the product's anticipated 8-year commercial life are shown in Table 5.7. The company's maximum payback period is 4 years (after taxes), and its effective tax rate is 40%. The investment will be depreciated by the modified accelerated cost recovery system (MACRS) using a 5-year class life.

The company's management is concerned about the financial attractiveness of this venture should unforeseen circumstances arise (e.g., loss of market or technological breakthroughs by the competition). They are very leery of investing a large amount of capital in this product because competition is fierce and companies that wait to enter the market may be able to purchase improved technology. You have been given the task of assessing the downside profitability of the product when the primary concern is its staying

TABLE 5.7   Data and Results for Reduction of Useful Life Example

Cash flows	\-1	0	1	2	3	4	5	6	7	8
					End of year ($M)					
Initial investment	\-0.9	\-1.1	0	0	0	0	0	0	0	0
Annual revenues	0	0	1.8	2	2.1	1.9	1.8	1.8	1.7	1.5
Annual expenses	0	0	\-0.8	\-0.9	\-0.9	\-0.9	\-0.8	\-0.8	\-0.8	\-0.7
After-tax cash flow	\-0.9	\-1.1	0.76	0.92	0.88	0.7	0.7	0.65	0.54	0.48
ROR	—	—	—	—	10.3%	18.6%	23.6%	26.6%	28.3%	29.4%

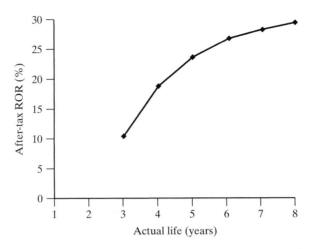

Figure 5.7   After-tax parametric analysis for product.

power (life) in the marketplace. If the after-tax MARR is 15%, then what do you recommend? State any necessary assumptions.

Solution   The first step is to compute the after-tax cash flow (ATCF). To do this, we assume that the salvage value of the investment is zero, that the MACRS deductions are unaffected by the useful life of the product, and that they begin in the first year of commercial operations (year 1). The results are given in Table 5.7.

Next we compute the ROR of the investment as a function of the product's presumed life. For the first 2 years, the undiscounted ATCF is negative, so there is no ROR. In year 3, the ROR is 10.3% and climbs to 29.4% if the full commercial life is realized. A plot of the after-tax ROR versus the actual life of the product line is shown in Fig. 5.7. To make at least 15% per year after taxes, the product line must last 4 or more years. It can be quickly determined from the data in the table that the simple payback period is 3 years. Consequently, this venture would seem to be worthwhile as long as its actual life is at least 4 years.   ∎

5.6.4 Risk-Benefit Analysis

Risk-benefit analysis is a generic term for techniques that encompass risk assessment and the inclusive evaluation of risk, costs, and benefits of alternative projects or policies. Like other quantitative methods, the steps in risk-benefit analysis include specifying objectives and goals for the project options, identifying constraints, defining the scope and limits for the study itself, and developing measures of effectiveness of feasible alternatives. Ideally, these steps should be completed in conjunction with an accountable decision maker, but in many cases, this is not possible. It therefore is incumbent upon the analyst to take exceptional care in stating the assumptions and limitations of each assessment, especially because risk-benefit analysis is frequently controversial.

The principal task of this methodology is to express numerically, insofar as possible, the risks and benefits that are likely to result from project outcomes. Calculating these outcomes may require scientific procedures or simulation models to estimate the likelihood of an accident or a mishap and its probable consequences. Finally, a composite assessment that aggregates the disparate measures associated with each alternative is carried out. The conclusions should incorporate the results of a sensitivity analysis in which each significant assumption or parameter is varied in turn to judge its effect on the aggregated risks, costs, and benefits.

One approach to risk assessment is based on the three primary steps of systems engineering, as shown in Fig. 5.8 (Sage and White 1980). These involve the *formulation, analysis,* and *interpretation* of the impacts of alternatives on the needs, and the institutional and value perspectives of the organization. In risk formulation, we determine or identify the types and scope of the anticipated risks. A variety of systemic approaches, such as the nominal group technique, brainstorming, and the Delphi method, are especially useful at this stage (Makridakis et al. 1997). It is important to identify not only the risk elements but also the elements that represent needs, constraints, and alterables associated with possible risk reduction with and without technological innovation. This can be done only in accordance with a value system.

In the analysis step, we forecast the failures, mishaps, and other consequences that might accompany the development and implementation of the project. This will include estimation of the probabilities of outcomes and the associated magnitudes. Many methods, such as cross-impact analysis, interpretive structural modeling, economic modeling, and mathematical programming, are potentially useful at this step. The inputs are those elements determined during problem formulation.

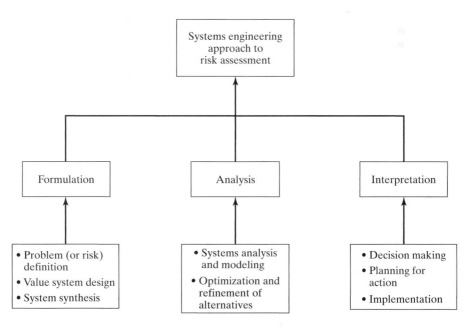

Figure 5.8   Systems engineering approach to risk assessment.

In the final step, we attempt to give an organizational or political interpretation to the risk impacts. This includes specification of individual and group utilities for the final evaluation. Decision making follows. The economic methods of B/C analysis are most commonly used at this point. Extension to include the results of the risk assessment, however, is not trivial. A principal problem is that risks and benefits may be measured in different units and therefore may not be strictly additive. Rather than trying to convert everything into a single measure, it may be better simply to present the risks and net benefits in their respective units or categories. This leaves the decision maker free to impose his or her own values on the results of the analysis.

To aid in interpreting the results, risk-return graphs, similar to the C-E graph displayed in Fig. 5.4, can be drawn to highlight the efficient frontier. Risk profiles may also be useful. For example, Fig. 5.9 illustrates a perspective provided by a risk analysis profile. Projects 1 and 2 are most likely to yield lifetime profits of $100,000 and $200,000, respectively. So, for some decision makers, project 2 might be considered superior if the B/C ratio were favorable. Nevertheless, it is worth probing the data a bit

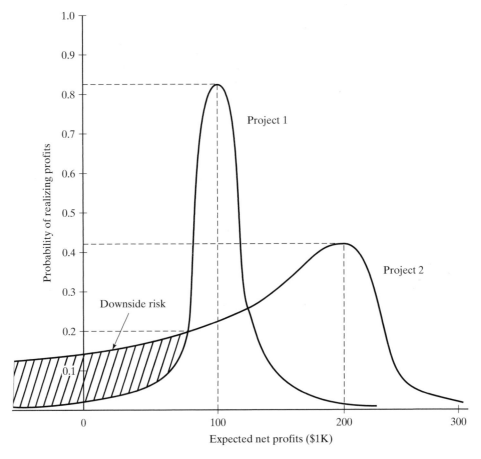

Figure 5.9   Illustration of risk profile.

more. Project 2 has a finite probability of returning a loss but a higher expected profit than project 1. The probability that project 2 will yield lower profits than project 1 is known as the downside risk and can be found by a breakeven analysis. Given these data, a risk-averse person would be inclined to select project 1, which has a big chance (0.50) of realizing a moderate profit of at least $100K, with little chance of anything much less or much greater; that is, project 1 has a small variance. A gambler would lean toward project 2, which has a small chance at a very large profit.

The kinds of risk profiles contained in Fig. 5.9 make the consequences of outcomes more visible and thus permit the decision maker consciously to operate in a manner consistent with his or her attitude toward risk, be it conservative or freewheeling. Generally speaking, the amount of data needed to construct a graph such as Fig. 5.9 is small and relatively easy to obtain if a historical database exists. It can be solicited from the engineers and marketing personnel who are familiar with the projects. If no collective experience can be found within the organization, then more subjective or arbitrary procedures would be required. A number of software packages is available to help with the construction effort.

5.6.5 Limits of Risk Analysis

The ultimate responsibility for project selection and implementation goes beyond any risk assessment and rests squarely on the shoulders of top management. Although formal analysis can point up unexpected vulnerabilities in large complex projects, it remains an academic exercise unless the managers take the results seriously and ensure that the project is managed conscientiously. Safety must be designed into a system from the beginning, and good operating practice is essential to the success of any continuing program of risk management. Controversy still rages, for example, over whether the vent-gas scrubber—a key element in the safety system of the Union Carbide pesticide plant in Bhopal, India, that exploded in 1984, killing more than 3,000 people—was designed adequately to handle a true emergency. But even if it had been, neither it nor a host of other safety features were maintained in working order.

For risks to be ascertained at all, project managers must agree on the value of assessing them in engineering design. It has often been said that you can degrade the performance of a system by poor quality control, but you cannot enhance a poor design by good quality control. At the point at which project managers are responsible for crucial decisions, risk assessment is one more tool that can help them weigh alternatives so that their choices are informed and deliberate rather than isolated, or worse, repetitions of past mistakes.

5.7 DECISION TREES

Decision trees, also known as decision flow networks and decision diagrams, are powerful means of depicting and facilitating the analysis of problems that involve sequential decisions and variable outcomes over time. They have great usefulness in practice because they make it possible to look at a large, complicated problem in terms of a series of smaller simple problems while explicitly considering risk and future consequences.

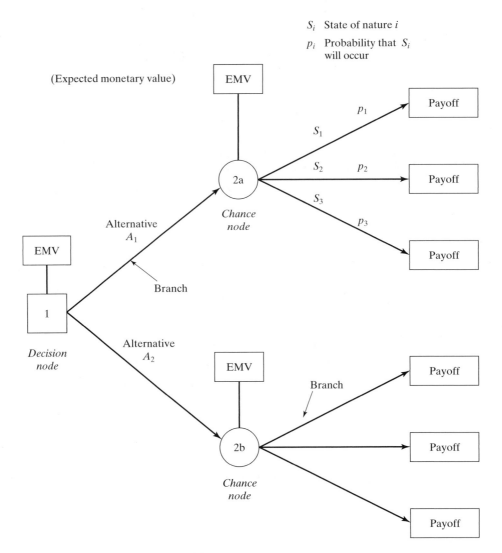

Figure 5.10 Structure of decision tree.

A decision tree is a graphical method of expressing, in chronological order, the alternative actions that are available to the decision maker and the outcomes determined by chance. In general, they are composed of the following two elements, as shown in Fig. 5.10.

1. *Decision nodes*. At a decision node, usually designated by a square, the decision maker must select one alternative course of action from a finite set of possibilities. Each is drawn as a branch emanating from the right side of the square. When there is a cost associated with an alternative, it is written along the branch. Each alternative branch may result in a payoff, another decision node, or a chance node.

2. *Chance nodes*. A chance node, designated as a circle, indicates that a random event is expected at this point in the process; that is, one of a finite number of states of nature may occur. The states of nature are shown on the tree as branches to the right of the chance nodes. The corresponding probabilities are similarly written above the branches. The states of nature may be followed by payoffs, decision nodes, or more chance nodes.

Constructing a Tree.   A tree is started on the left of the page with one or more decision nodes. From these, all possible alternatives are drawn branching out to the right. Then a chance node or a second decision node, associated with either subsequent events or decisions, respectively, is added. Each time a chance node is added, the appropriate states of nature with their corresponding probabilities emanate rightward from it. The tree continues to branch from left to right until the final payoffs are reached. The tree shown in Fig. 5.10 represents a single decision with two alternatives, each leading to a chance node with three possible states of nature.

Finding a Solution.   To solve a tree, it is customary to divide it into two segments: (1) chance nodes with all of their emerging states of nature (Fig. 5.11a) and (2) decision nodes with all their alternatives (Fig. 5.11b). The solution process starts with those segments that end in the final payoffs, at the right side of the tree, and continues to the left, segment by segment, in the reverse order from which it was drawn.

1. *Chance node segments*. The expected monetary value (EMV) of all of the states of nature that emerge from a chance node must be computed (multiply payoffs by probabilities and sum the results). The EMV is then written above the node inside a rectangle (labeled a "position value" in Fig. 5.10). These expected values are considered as payoffs for the branch to the immediate left.

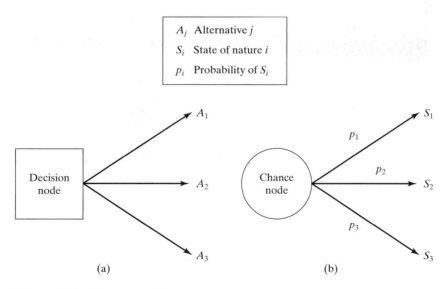

Figure 5.11   Segments of tree.

2. *Decision node segments*. At a decision point, the payoffs given (or computed) for each alternative are compared and the best one is selected. All others are discarded. The corresponding branch of a discarded alternative is marked by the symbol $\parallel$ to indicate that the path is suboptimal.

This procedure is based on principles of dynamic programming and is commonly referred to as the "rollback" step. It starts at the endpoints of the tree where the expected value at each chance node and the optimal value at each decision node are computed. Suboptimal choices at each decision node are dropped, with the rollback continuing until the first node of the tree is reached. The optimal policy is recovered by identifying the choices made at each decision node that maximize the value of the objective function from that point onward.

Example 5-9   (Deterministic Replacement Problem)

The most basic form of a decision tree occurs when each alternative results in a single outcome; that is, when certainty is assumed. The replacement problem defined in Fig. 5.12 for a 9-year planning horizon illustrates this situation. The numbers above the branches represent the returns per year for the specified period should the replacement be made at the corresponding decision point. The numbers below the branches are the costs associated with that decision. For example, at node 3, keeping the machine results in a return of $3K per year for 3 years and a total cost of $2K.

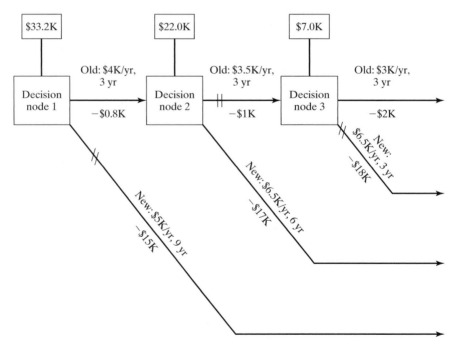

Figure 5.12   Deterministic replacement problem.

As can be seen, the decision as to whether to replace the old machine with the new machine does not occur just once but recurs periodically. In other words, if the decision is made to keep the old machine at decision point 1, then later, at decision point 2, a choice again has to be made. Similarly, if the old machine is chosen at decision point 2, then a choice has to be made at decision point 3. For each alternative, the cash inflow and duration of the project are shown above the branch, and the cash investment opportunity cost is shown below the branch. At decision point 2, for example, if a new machine is purchased for the remaining 6 years, then the net benefits from that point on are (6 yr)($6.5K/yr) returns − $17.0K opportunity cost = $22.0K net benefits. Alternatively, if the old machine is kept at decision point 2, then we have ($3.5K/yr)(3 yr) returns − $1.0K opportunity cost + $7K net benefits associated with decision point 3 = $16.5K net benefits.

For this problem, one is concerned initially with which alternative to choose at decision point 1, but an intelligent choice here should take into account the later alternatives and decisions that stem from it. Hence, the correct procedure in analyzing this type of problem is to start at the most distant decision point, determine the best alternative and quantitative result of that alternative, and then roll back to each successive decision point, repeating the procedure until finally the choice at the initial or present decision point is determined. By this procedure, one can make a present decision that directly takes into account the alternatives and expected decisions of the future.

For simplicity in this example, timing of the monetary outcomes first will be neglected, which means that a dollar has the same value regardless of the year in which it occurs. Table 5.8 displays the necessary computations and implied decisions. Note that the monetary outcome of the best alternative at decision point 3 ($7.0K for the "old") becomes part of the outcome for the old alternative at decision point 2. That is, if the decision at node 2 is to continue to use the current machine rather than replace it, then the monetary value associated with this decision equals the EMV at node 3 ($7K) plus the transition benefit from node 2 to 3 ($3.5/yr × 3 yr − $1K = $9.5K), or $16.5K. Similarly, the best alternative at decision point 2 ($22.0K for the "new") becomes part of the outcome for the "old" alternative at decision point 1.

By following the computations in Table 5.7, one can see that the answer is to keep the old now and plan to replace it with the new at the end of 3 years (at decision point 2). But this does not mean that the old machine should necessarily be kept for a full 3 years and then a new machine bought without question at that time. Conditions may change anywhere along the way, necessitating a fresh analysis that is based on estimates that are reasonable in light of the current conditions.

TABLE 5.8   Computational Results for Replacement Problem in Fig. 5.12

Decision point	Alternative	Monetary outcome		Choice
3	Old	($3K/yr)(3 yr) − $2K	= $7.0 K	Old
	New	($6.5K/yr)(3 yr) − $18K	= $1.5 K	
2	Old	$7K + ($3.5K/yr)(3 yr) − $1K	= $16.5K	
	New	($6.5K/yr)(6 yr) − $17K	= $22.0K	New
1	Old	$22.0K + ($4K/yr)(3 yr) − $0.8K	= $33.2K	Old
	New	($5K/yr)(9 yr) − $15K	= $30.0K	

Example 5-10   (Timing Considerations)

For decision tree analyses, which involve working from the most distant decision point to the nearest decision point, the easiest way to take into account the timing of money is to use the present value approach and thus discount all monetary outcomes to the decision points in question. To demonstrate, Table 5.9 gives the computations for the same replacement problem of Fig. 5.9 using an interest rate of 12% per year.

Note from Table 5.8 that when taking into account the effect of timing by calculating PWs at each decision point, the indicated choice is not only to keep the old at decision point 1 but also to keep the old at decision points 2 and 3. This result is not surprising, because the high interest rate tends to favor the alternatives with lower initial investments, and it also tends to place less weight on long-run returns. When the interest rate drops to 10%, the solution is the same as that for Example 5-9.   ∎

Example 5-11:   (Automation Decision Problem with Random Outcomes)

In this problem, the decision maker must decide whether to automate a given process. Depending on the technological success of the automation project, the results will turn out to be poor, fair, or excellent. The net payoffs for these outcomes (expressed in NPVs and including the cost of the equipment) are $-\$90K$, $\$40K$ and $\$300K$, respectively. The initially estimated probabilities that each outcome will occur are 0.5, 0.3, and 0.2. Figure 5.13 is a decision tree depicting this simple situation. The calculations for the two alternatives are

Automate: $-\$90K(0.5) + \$40K(0.3) + \$300K(0.2) = \$27K$

Don't automate: $0

These calculations show that the best choice for the firm is to automate on the basis of an expected NPV of $27K versus $0 if it does nothing. Nevertheless, this may not be a

TABLE 5.9 Computations for Replacement Problem with 12% Interest Rate

Decision point	Alternative	Monetary outcome		Choice
3	Old	$3K(P/A, 12\%, 3) - \$2K$		
		$= \$3K(2.402) - \$2K$	$= \$5.21K$	Old
	New	$6.5K(P/A, 12\%, 3) - \$18K$		
		$= \$6.5K(2.402) - \$18K$	$= -\$2.39K$	
2	Old	$3.5K(P/A, 12\%, 3) - \$1K$		
		$\quad + \$5.21K(P/F, 12\%, 3)$		
		$= \$3.5K(2.402) - \$1K$	$= \$11.11K$	Old
		$\quad + \$5.21K(0.7118)$		
	New	$6.5K(P/A, 12\%, 6) - \$17K$		
		$= \$6.5K(4.111) - \$17K$	$= \$9.72K$	
1	Old	$4K(P/A, 12\%, 3) - \$0.8K$		
		$\quad + \$11.11K(P/F, 12\%, 3)$		
		$= \$4K(2.402) - \$0.8K$	$= \$16.71K$	Old
		$\quad + \$11.11K(0.7118)$		
	New	$5.0K(P/A, 12\%, 9) - \$15K$		
		$= \$5.0K(5.328) - \$15K$	$= \$11.64K$	

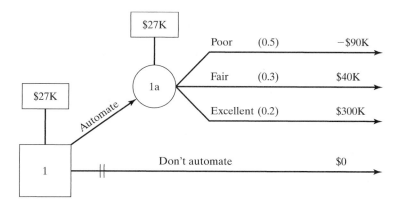

Figure 5.13   Automation problem before consideration of technology study.

clear-cut decision because of the possibility of a $90K loss. Depending on the decision maker's attitude toward risk and his or her confidence in the given data, he or she might want to gather more information.

Suppose that it is possible for the decision maker to conduct a technology study for a cost of $10K. The study will disclose that the enabling technology is "shaky," "promising," or "solid" corresponding to ultimate outcomes of "poor," "fair," and "excellent," respectively. Let us assume that the probabilities of the various outcomes, given the technology study findings, are as shown in Fig. 5.14, which is a decision tree for the entire problem. This diagram shows expected future events (outcomes), along with their respective cash flows and probabilities of occurrence. The calculation of these probabilities requires the use of Bayes' theorem given in Appendix 5A at the end of this chapter and is discussed in a later subsection. To use Bayes' theorem, it is necessary to know all conditional probabilities of the form $P(\text{study outcome}|\text{state})$; e.g., $P(\text{shaky}|\text{poor})$ or $P(\text{excellent}|\text{promising})$.

The rectangular blocks represent (decision) points in time at which the decision maker must elect to take one and only one of the paths (alternatives) available. These decisions are normally based on a quantifiable measure, such as money, which has been determined to be the predominant "cost" or "reward" for comparing alternatives. As mentioned, the general approach is to find the action or alternative that will maximize the expected NPV equivalent of future cash flows at each decision point, starting with the furthest decision point(s) and then rolling back until the initial decision point is reached.

Once again, the chance (circular) nodes represent points at which uncertain events (outcomes) occur. At a chance node, the expected value of all paths that lead (from the right) into the node can be calculated as the sum of the anticipated value of each path multiplied by its respective probability. (The probabilities of all paths that lead into a node must sum to 1.) As the project progresses through time, the chance nodes are automatically reduced to a single outcome on the basis of the "state of nature" that occurs at that time.

The solution to the problem in Fig. 5.14 is given in Table 5.10. It can be noted that the alternative "technology study" is shown to be best with an expected NPV of $34.62K. (To check the solution in Table 5.10, perform the rollback procedure on Fig. 5.14, indicating which branches should be eliminated.)

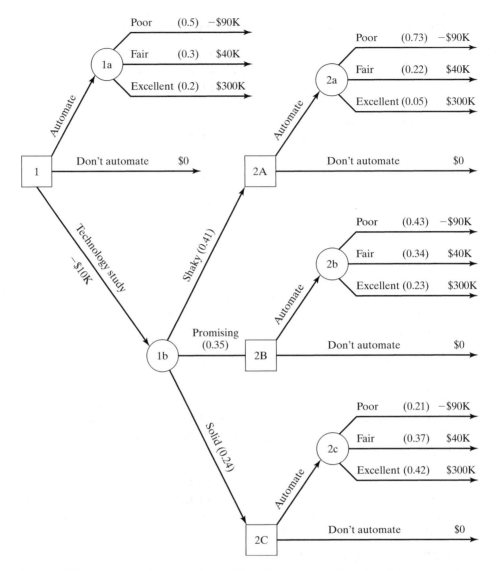

Figure 5.14   Automation problem with technology study taken into account.

5.7.1 Decision Tree Steps

Now that decision trees (diagrams) have been introduced and the mechanics of using them to arrive at an initial decision have been illustrated, the steps involved can be summarized as follows:

1. Identify the points of decision and alternatives available at each point.
2. Identify the points of uncertainty and the type or range of possible outcomes at each point (layout of decision flow network).

TABLE 5.10   Expected NPV Calculations for the Automation Problem

Decision point	Alternative	Expected monetary outcome		Choice
2A	Automate	$-\$90K(0.73) + \$40K(0.22)$ $+ \$300K(0.05)$	$= -\$41.9K$	
	Don't automate		$= \$0$	Don't automate
2B	Automate	$-\$90K(0.43) + \$40K(0.34)$ $+ \$300K(0.23)$	$= \$43.9K$	Automate
	Don't automate		$= \$0$	
2C	Automate	$-\$90K(0.21) + \$40K(0.37)$ $+ \$300K(0.42)$	$= \$121.9K$	Automate
	Don't automate		$= \$0$	
1	Automate	(see calculations above)	$= \$27K$	
	Don't automate		$= \$0$	
	Technology study	$\$0(0.41) + \$43.9K(0.35)$ $+ \$121.9K(0.24) - \$10K$	$= \$34.62K$	Technology study

3. Estimate the values needed to conduct the analysis, especially the probabilities of different outcomes and the costs/returns for various outcomes and alternative actions.

4. Remove all dominated branches.

5. Analyze the alternatives, starting with the most distant decision point(s) and working back, to choose the best initial decision.

In Example 5-10, we used the expected NPV as the decision criterion. However, if outcomes can be expressed in terms of utility units, then it may be appropriate to use the expected utility as the criterion. Alternatively, the decision maker may be willing to express his or her certain monetary equivalent for each chance outcome node and use that as the decision criterion.

Because a decision tree can quickly become unmanageably large, it is often best to start out by considering only major alternatives and outcomes in the structure to get an initial understanding or feeling for the issues. Secondary alternatives and outcomes can then be added if they are significant enough to affect the final decision. Incremental embellishments can also be added if time and resources are available.

5.7.2 Basic Principles of Diagramming

The proper diagramming of a decision problem is, in itself, very useful to the understanding of the problem, as well as being essential to performing the analysis correctly. The placement of decision points and chance nodes from the initial decision point to any subsequent decision point should give an accurate representation of the information that will and will not be available when the decision maker actually has to make the choice associated with the decision point in question. The tree should show the following:

1. All initial or immediate alternatives among which the decision maker wishes to choose.

2. All uncertain outcomes and future alternatives that the decision maker wishes to consider because they may directly affect the consequences of initial alternatives.

3. All uncertain outcomes that the decision maker wishes to consider because they may provide information that can affect his or her future choices among alternatives and hence, indirectly affect the consequences of initial alternatives.

It should also be noted that the alternatives at any decision point and the outcomes at any payoff node must be:

1. Mutually exclusive; that is, no more than one can possibly be chosen.
2. Collectively exhaustive; that is, when a decision point or payoff node is reached, some course of action must be taken.

Figure 5.14 reflects these points. For example, decision nodes 2A, 2B, and 2C are each reached only after one of the mutually exclusive results of the technology study is known; and each decision node reflects all alternatives to be considered at that point. Furthermore, all possible outcomes to be considered are shown, as evidenced by the fact that the probabilities sum to 1.0 for each chance node.

5.7.3 Use of Statistics to Determine the Value of More Information

An alternative that frequently exists in an investment decision is to conduct further research before making a commitment. This may involve such action as gathering more information about the underlying technology, updating an existing analysis of market demand, or investigating anew future operating costs for particular alternatives.

Once this additional information is collected, the concepts of Bayesian statistics provide a means of modifying estimates of probabilities, as well as a means of estimating the economic value of further investigation study. To illustrate, consider the one-stage decision situation depicted in Fig. 5.15, in which each alternative has two possible chance outcomes: "high" or "low" demand. It is estimated that each outcome

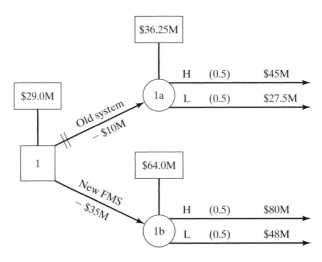

Figure 5.15   One-stage FMS replacement problem.

is equally likely to occur and that the monetary result expressed as PW is shown above the arrow for each outcome. Again, the amount of investment for each alternative is written below the respective lines. On the basis of these amounts, the calculation of the expected monetary outcomes minus the investment costs (giving expected NPV) is as follows:

Old system: $E[\text{NPV}] = \$45\text{M}(0.5) + \$27.5\text{M}(0.5) - \$10\text{M} = \$26.25\text{M}$

New FMS: $E[\text{NPV}] = \$80\text{M}(0.5) + \$48\text{M}(0.5) - \$35\text{M} = \$29.0\text{M}$

which indicates that the new flexible manufacturing system (FMS) should be selected.

To demonstrate the use of Bayesian statistics, suppose that one is considering the advisability of undertaking a fresh intensive investigation before deciding on the "old system" versus the "new FMS." Suppose also that this new study would cost $2.0M and will predict whether the demand will be high (h) or low (ℓ). To use the Bayesian approach, it is necessary to assess the conditional probabilities that the investigation (technology study) will yield certain results. These probabilities reflect explicit measures of management's confidence in the ability of the investigation to predict the outcome. Sample assessments are

$$P(h|H) = 0.70, P(\ell|H) = 0.30, P(h|L) = 0.20, \text{ and } P(\ell|L) = 0.80,$$

where H and L denote high and low actual demand as opposed to predicted demand. As an explanation, $P(h|H)$ means the probability that the predicted demand is high (h), given that the actual demand will turn out to be high (H).

A formal statement of Bayes' theorem is given in Appendix 5A along with a tabular format for ease of computation. Tables 5.11 and 5.12 use this format for revision of probabilities based on the assessment data above, and the prior probabilities of 0.5 that the demand will be high and 0.5 that the demand will be low [i.e., $P(H) = P(L) = 0.5$]. These probabilities are now used to assess the technology study alternative. Figure 5.16 depicts the complete decision tree. Note that demand probabilities are entered on the branches according to whether the investigation indicates high or low demand.

The next step is to calculate the expected outcome for the technology study alternative. This is done by the standard decision tree rollback principle, as shown in Table 5.11. Note that the 0.45 and 0.55 probabilities that the investigation-predicated demand will

TABLE 5.11   Computation of Posterior Probabilities Given That Investigation-Predicted Demand Is High (h)

(1)	(2)	(3)	(4) = (2) × (3)	(5) = (4)/Σ(4)
State (actual demand)	Prior probability, P(state)	Confidence assessment, P(h|state)	Posterior joint probability	Probability, P(state|h)
H	0.5	0.70	0.35	0.78
L	0.5	0.20	0.10	0.22
			0.45	

TABLE 5.12   Computation of Posterior Probabilities Given That Investigation-Predicted Demand Is Low (ℓ)

(1) State (actual demand)	(2) Prior probability, P(state)	(3) Confidence assessment, P(ℓ|state)	(4) = (2) × (3) Posterior joint probability	(5) = (4)/Σ(4) Probability, P(state|ℓ)
H	0.5	0.30	0.15	0.27
L	0.5	0.80	0.40	0.73
			0.55	

be high and low, respectively, are obtained from the totals in column (4) of the Bayesian revision calculations depicted in Tables 5.11 and 5.12.

Thus, from Table 5.13, it can be seen that the "new FMS" alternative with an expected NPV of $29.0M is the best course of action by a slight margin. (As an exercise, perform the calculations on Fig. 5.16 and indicate the optimal path.) Although the figures used here do not reflect any advantages to this technology study, the benefit of gathering additional information can potentially be great.

5.7.4 Discussion and Assessment

The unique feature of decision trees is that they allow management to view the logical order of a sequence of decisions. They afford a clear graphical representation of the various courses of action and their possible consequences. By using decision trees, management can also examine the impact of a series of decisions (over many periods) on the goals of the organization. Such models reduce abstract thinking to a rational visual pattern of cause and effect. When costs and benefits are associated with each branch and probabilities are estimated for each possible outcome, analysis of the tree can clarify choices and risks.

On the down side, the methodology has several weaknesses that should not be overlooked. A basic limitation of its representational properties is that only small and relatively simple models can be shown at the level of detail that makes trees so descriptive. Every variable added expands the tree's size multiplicatively. Although this

TABLE 5.13   Expected NPV Calculations for Replacement Problem in Fig. 5.13

Decision point	Alternative	Expected monetary outcome		Choice
2A	Old system New FMS	$45M(0.78) + $27.5M(0.22) − $10M $80M(0.78) + $48M(0.22) − $35M	= $31.15M = $37.96M	 New FMS
2B	Old system New FMS	$45M(0.27) + $27.5M(0.73) − $10M $80M(0.27) + $48M(0.73) − $35M	= $22.23M = $21.64M	Old system
1	Old system New FMS Technology study	(see calculations above) (see calculations above) $37.96M(0.45) + $22.23M(0.55) − $2M	= $26.25M = $29.00M = $27.31M	 New FMS

Figure 5.16   Replacement problem with alternative of technology study.

problem can be overcome to some extent by generalizing the diagram, significant information may be lost in doing so. This loss is particularly acute if the problem structure is highly dependent or asymmetric.

Regarding the computational properties of trees, for simple problems in which the endpoints are precalculated or assessed directly, the rollback procedure is very efficient. However, for problems that require a roll-forward procedure, the classic tree-based algorithm has a fundamental drawback: it is essentially an enumeration technique. That is, every path through the tree is traversed to solve the problem and generate the full range of outputs. This feature raises the "curse of dimensionality" common to many stochastic models: for every variable added, the computational requirements increase multiplicatively. This implies that the number of chance variables that can be included in the model tends to be small. There is also a strong incentive to simplify the value model, because it is recalculated at the end of each path through the tree.

Nevertheless, the enumeration property of tree-based algorithms in theory can be reduced dramatically by taking advantage of certain structural properties of a problem. Two such properties are referred to as "asymmetry" and "coalescence." For more discussion and some practical aspects of implementation, consult Call and Miller (1990).

5.8 REAL OPTIONS

NPV remains the most commonly used decision-making tool in project evaluation but has been criticized for not properly accounting for uncertainty and flexibility—that is, multistage development funding and abandonment options. Decision trees more accurately capture the multistage nature of development by using probability-based EMVs but can be time consuming and overly complex when all potential courses of action are included. An emerging alternative to decision trees is real options, a technique that applies financial options theory to nonfinancial assets and encourages managers to consider the value of strategic investments in terms of risks that can be held, hedged, or transferred.

Seen through a real options lens, NPV always undervalues potential projects, often by several hundred percent. Real-options analysis offers the flexibility to expand, extend, contract, abandon, or defer a project in response to unforeseen events that drive the value of a project up or down through time. It is good practice to consider these options at the outset of an investment analysis rather than only when trouble arises.

Recall that the NPV of a project is estimated by forecasting its annual cash flows during its expected life, discounting them back to the present at a risk-adjusted weighted average cost of capital, then subtracting the initial start-up capital expenditure. There's nothing in this calculation that captures the value of flexibility to make future decisions that resolve uncertainty.

Financial managers often overrule NPV by accepting projects with negative NPVs for "strategic reasons." Their intuition tells them that they cannot afford to miss the opportunity. In essence, they're intuiting something that has not been quantified in the project.

5.8.1 Drivers of Value

Like options on securities, real options are the right but not the obligation to take an action in the future at a predetermined price (the exercise or striking price) for a predetermined time (the life of the option). When you exercise a real option, you capture the difference between the value of the asset and the exercise price of the option. If a project is more successful than expected, then management can pay an "exercise price" to expand the project by making an additional capital expenditure. Management can also extend the life of a project by paying an exercise price. If the project does worse than expected, then it can be scaled back or abandoned. In addition, the initial investment does not have to be made today—it can be deferred.

The value of a real option is influenced by the following six variables:

1. *Value of the underlying project.* The option to expand a project (a call), for example, increases the scale of operations and therefore the value of the project at the

cost of additional investment (the exercise price). Thus, the value of the project (without flexibility) is the value of what, in real-options language, is called the underlying risky asset. If we have flexibility to expand the project—in other words, an option to buy more of the project at a fixed price—then the value of the option to expand goes up when the value of the underlying project goes up.

2. *Exercise price/investment cost.* The exercise price is the amount of investment required to expand. The value of the option to expand goes up as the cost of expansion is reduced.

3. *Volatility of the underlying project's value.* Because the decision to expand is voluntary, you will expand only when the value of expansion exceeds the cost. When the value is less than the cost and there is no variability in the value, the option is worthless, but if the value is volatile, then there's a chance that the value can rise and exceed the cost, making the option valuable. Therefore, the value of flexibility goes up when uncertainty of future outcomes increases.

4. *Time to maturity.* The value of flexibility increases as the time to maturity lengthens because there is a greater chance that the value of expansion will rise the longer you wait.

5. *Risk-free interest rate.* As the risk-free rate of interest goes up, the present value of the option also goes up because the exercise price is paid in the future, and therefore, as the discount rate increases, the present value of the exercise price decreases.

6. *Dividends.* The sixth variable is the dividends, or the cash flows, paid out by the project. When dividends are paid, they decrease the value of the project and therefore the value of the option on the project.

5.8.2 Relationship to R&D Projects

The flexible decision structure of options is valid in an R&D context. After an initial investment, management can gather more information about the status of a project and market characteristics and, on the basis of this information, change its course of action. The real option value of this managerial flexibility enhances the R&D project value, whereas a pure NPV analysis understates it. Five basic sources of flexibility have been identified (e.g., Trigeorgis 1997). A *defer option* refers to the possibility of waiting until more information has become available. An *abandonment option* offers the possibility to make the investment in stages, deciding at each stage, on the basis of the newest information, whether to proceed further or to stop (this is applied by venture capitalists). An *expansion or contraction option* represents the possibility to adjust the scale of the investment (e.g., a production facility) depending on whether market conditions turn out favorably or not. Finally, a *switching option* allows changing the mode of operation of an asset, depending on factor prices (e.g., switching the energy source of a power plant, switching raw material suppliers).

One key insight generated by the real options approach to R&D investment is that higher uncertainty in the payoffs of the investment increases the value of managerial flexibility, or the value of the real option. The intuition is clear—with higher payoff uncertainty, flexibility has a higher potential of enhancing the upside while limiting the downside. An important managerial implication of this insight is that the more uncertain the project payoff is, the more efforts should be made to delay commitments and maintain the flexibility to change the course of action. This intuition is appealing. Nevertheless, there is hardly any evidence of real options pricing of R&D projects in practice despite reports that Merck uses the method. Moreover, there is recent evidence that more uncertainty may reduce the option value if an alternative "safe" project is available.

This evidence represents a gap between the financial payoff variability, as addressed by the real options pricing literature, and operational uncertainty that pervades R&D. For example, R&D project managers encounter uncertainty about budgets, schedules, product performance, or market requirements, in addition to financial payoffs. The relationship between such operational uncertainty and the value of managerial flexibility (option value of the project) is not clear. For example, should the manager respond to increased uncertainty about product performance in the same way as to uncertainty about project payoffs, by delaying commitments? Questions such as this must be addressed on a case-by-case basis in full view the scope and consequences of the attending risks.

TEAM PROJECT

Thermal Transfer Plant

On the basis of the evaluation of alternatives, TMS management has adopted a plan by which the design and assembly of the rotary combustor will be done at TMS. Most of the manufacturing activity will be subcontracted except for the hydraulic power unit, which TMS decided to build "in-house."

There are three functions involved in charging and rotating the combustor. Two of them, the charging rams and the resistance door, naturally lend themselves to hydraulics. The third, turning the combustor, can be done either electromechanically (by an electric motor and a gearbox) or hydraulically. If the hydraulic method is chosen, then there are two alternatives: (1) use a large hydraulic motor as a direct drive or (2) use a small hydraulic motor with a gearbox. Figure 5.17 contains a schematic.

TMS engineering has produced the following specifications for the hydraulic power unit:

Applicable documents, codes, standards, and requirements

National Electric Manufacturers Association (NEMA)

American National Standards Institute (ANSI)

Pressure Vessels Code, American Society of Mechanical Engineers (ASME) Section VIII

Hydraulic rams

Two hydraulic cylinders will be provided for the rams. The cylinders will be 8 in. bore × 96 in. stroke. They will operate at 1,500 psi and will have an adjustable extension rate of 2 to 6 ft/min. They will retract in 15 seconds, will operate 180° out of phase, and will retract in the event of a power failure.

Combustor barrel drive

A single-direction, variable-speed drive will be provided for the combustor. The output of this drive will deliver up to 1.6 rpm and 7,500 ft-lb of torque.

Figure 5.17   Hydraulic power unit.

Resistance door cylinder

This cylinder will be 6 in. bore × 48 in. stroke and will operate with a constant pressure of 200 psi.

Hydraulic power unit

- The hydraulic power unit will be skid-mounted and ready for hookup to interfacing equipment. Mounting and lifting brackets will be manufactured as well.
- Hydraulic pumps will be redundant so that in the event of the failure of one, another can be started to take over its function. Accumulators will be added to retract the rams and close the resistance door in the event of a power failure.

- The hydraulic fluid is to be E. F. Houghton's Cosmolubric or equivalent. Although system operating pressure is to be 1,500 psi, the plumbing will be designed to withstand 3,000 psi. Water-to-oil heat exchangers shall be provided to limit reservoir temperature to 130°C.
- A method of controlling ram extension speed and combustor rpm within the specifications stated above will be provided. Control concepts may be analog (5 to 20 milliamperes) or digital.

Electrical

Electric motors will be of sufficient horsepower to drive the hydraulic pumps. Motors shall operate at 1,200 rpm, 220/440 volts, 3 phase, 60 hertz.

Solenoids and controls

Solenoids are to be 120 volt, 60 hertz and will have manual overrides. Any analog control function is to respond to a 5- to 20-milliampere signal.

Combustion drive

A single-direction, variable-speed drive will be provided for the combustor. The output of this drive will deliver up to 1.6 rpm and 7,500 ft-lb of torque. Three potential alternatives for the combustor drive are

- Electric motor and gearbox
- Hydraulic motor with gearbox (hydraulic power supplied by hydraulic power unit)
- Hydraulic motor with direct drive (hydraulic power supplied by hydraulic power unit)

Your team assignment is to select the most appropriate drive from these candidates. To do so, develop a scoring model or a decision tree and evaluate each alternative accordingly. State your assumptions clearly, regarding technological, economic, and other aspects and explain the methodology used to support your analysis.

Initial cost estimates available to your team are

Ram cylinders (two required)	$5,948 each
Resistance door cylinder	$1,505
Hydraulic power unit	$50,000
Low-speed, high-torque motor	$22,780
High-speed motor with gear box	$7,000

DISCUSSION QUESTIONS

1. Where would ideas for new projects and products probably originate in a manufacturing company? What would be the most likely source in an R&D organization such as AT&T Laboratories or IBM's Watson Center?

2. Assume that you work in the design department of an aerospace firm and you are given the responsibility of selecting a workstation that will be used by each group in the department.

How would you find out which systems are available? What basic information would you try to collect on these systems?

3. How can you extend a polar graph, similar to the one shown in Fig. 5.2, to the case in which the criteria are individually weighted?

4. Identify a project that you are planning to pursue either at home or at work. List all of the components, decision points, and chance events. What is the measure of success for the project? Assuming that there is more than one measure, how can you reconcile them?

5. If you were evaluating a proposal to upgrade the computer-aided design system used by your organization, what type of information would you be looking for in detail? How would your answer change if you were buying only one or two systems as opposed to a few dozen?

6. Which factors in an organization do you think would affect the decision to go ahead with a project, such as automating a production line, other than the B/C ratio?

7. For years before beginning the project to build a tunnel under the English Channel, Great Britain and France debated the pros and cons. Speculate on the critical issues that were raised.

8. The project to construct a subway in Washington, D.C., began in the early 1970s with the expectation that it would be fully operational by 1980. A portion of the system opened in 1977, but as of 2004, approximately 5% remained unfinished. What do you think were the costs, benefits, and risks involved in the original planning? How important was the interest rate used in those calculations? Speculate on who or what was to blame for the lengthy delay in completion.

9. Where does quality fit into the B/C equation? Identify some companies or products that compete primarily on the basis of quality rather than price.

10. A software company is undecided on whether it should expand its capacity by using part-time programmers or by hiring more full-time employees. Future demand is the critical factor, which is not known with certainty but can be estimated only as low, medium, or high. Draw a decision tree for the company's problem. What data are needed?

11. How could B/C analysis be used to help determine the level of subsidy to be paid to the operator of public transportation services in a congested urban area?

12. Why has the U.S. Department of Defense been the major exponent of C-E analysis? Give your interpretation of what is meant by "diminishing returns," and indicate how it might affect a decision on procuring a military system versus an office automation system.

13. In which type of projects does risk play a predominant role? What can be done to mitigate the attendant risks? Pick a specific project and discuss.

EXERCISES

5.1 Consider an important decision with which you will be faced in the near future. Construct a scoring model detailing your major criteria, and assign weights to each. Indicate which data are known for sure and which are uncertain. What can be done to reduce the uncertainty?

5.2 Use a checklist and a scoring model to select the best car for a married graduate student with one child. State your assumptions clearly.

5.3 Assume that you have just entered the university and wish to select an area of study.

   a. Using B/C analysis *only,* what would your decision be?

   b. How would your decision change if you used C-E analysis? Provide the details of your analysis.

5.4 You have just received a job offer in a city 1,000 miles away and must relocate. List all possible ways of moving your household. Use two different analytic techniques for selecting the best approach, and compare the results.

5.5 Three new-product ideas have been suggested. These ideas have been rated as shown in Table 5.14.

TABLE 5.14

| | Product[1] | | | |
Criteria	A	B	C	Weight (%)
Development cost	P	F	VG	10
Sales prospects	VG	E	G	15
Producibility	P	F	G	10
Competitive advantage	E	VG	F	15
Technical risk	P	F	VG	20
Patent protection	F	F	VG	10
Compatibility with strategy	VG	F	F	20
				100

[1] P = poor, F = fair, G = good, VG = very good, E = excellent.

a. Using an equal point spread for all five ratings (i.e., $P = 1, F = 2, G = 3, VG = 4,$ $E = 5$), determine a weighted score for each product idea. What is the ranking of the three products?

b. Rank the criteria, compute the rank-sum weights, and determine the score for each alternative. Do the same using the rank reciprocal weights.

c. What are some of the advantages and disadvantages of this method of product selection?

5.6 Suppose that the products from Exercise 5.5 have been rated further as shown in Table 5.15.

TABLE 5.15

	Product		
	A	B	C
Probability of technical success	0.9	0.8	0.7
Probability of commercial success	0.6	0.8	0.9
Annual volume (units)	10,000	8,000	6,000
Profit contribution per unit	$2.64	$3.91	$5.96
Lifetime of product (years)	10	6	12
Total development cost	$50,000	$70,000	$100,000

a. Compute the expected return on investment over the lifetime of each product.

b. Does this computation change your ranking of the products over that obtained in Exercise 5.5?

5.7 The federal government proposes to construct a multipurpose water project. This project will provide water for irrigation and for municipal uses. In addition, there will be flood control benefits and recreation benefits. The estimated project benefits computed for 10-year periods for the next 50 years are given in Table 5.16.

The annual benefits may be assumed to be one tenth of the decade benefits. The O&M cost of the project is estimated to be $15,000 per year. Assume a 50-year analysis period with no net project salvage value.

TABLE 5.16

Purpose	First decade	Second decade	Third decade	Fourth decade	Fifth decade
Municipal	$40,000	$50,000	$60,000	$70,000	$110,000
Irrigation	$350,000	$370,000	$370,000	$360,000	$350,000
Flood control	$150,000	$150,000	$150,000	$150,000	$150,000
Recreation	$60,000	$70,000	$80,000	$80,000	$90,000
Totals	$600,000	$640,000	$660,000	$660,000	$700,000

a. If an interest rate of 5% is used and there is a B/C ratio of unity, then what capital expenditure can be justified to build the water project now?

b. If the interest rate is changed to 8%, then how does this change the justified capital expenditure?

5.8 The state is considering the elimination of a railroad grade crossing by building an overpass. The new structure, together with the needed land, would cost $1,800,000. The analysis period is assumed to be 30 years on the theory that either the railroad or the highway above it will be relocated by then. Salvage value of the bridge (actually, the net value of the land on either side of the railroad tracks) 30 years hence is estimated to be $100,000. A 6% interest rate is to be used.

At present, approximately 1,000 vehicles per day are delayed as a result of trains at the grade crossing. Trucks represent 40%, and 60% are other vehicles. Time for truck drivers is valued at $18 per hour and for other drivers at $5 per hour. Average time saving per vehicle will be 2 minutes if the overpass is built. No time saving occurs for the railroad.

The installation will save the railroad an annual expense of $48,000 now spent for crossing guards. During the preceding 10-year period, the railroad has paid out $600,000 in settling lawsuits and accident cases related to the grade crossing. The proposed project will entirely eliminate both of these expenses. The state estimates that the new overpass will save it approximately $6,000 per year in expenses attributed directly to the accidents. The overpass, if built, will belong to the state.

Perform a B/C analysis to answer the question of whether the overpass should be built. If the overpass is built, how much should the railroad be asked to contribute to the state as its share of the $1,800,000 construction cost?

5.9 An existing two-lane highway between two cities is to be converted to a four-lane divided freeway. The distance between them is 10 miles. The average daily traffic on the new freeway is forecast to average 20,000 vehicles per day over the next 20 years. Trucks represent 5% of the total traffic. Annual maintenance on the existing highway is $1,500 per lane-mile. The existing accident rate is 4.58 per million vehicle miles (MVM). Three alternative plans of improvement are now under consideration.

Plan A: Add two lanes adjacent to the existing lanes at a cost of $450,000 per mile. It is estimated that this plan would reduce auto travel time by 2 minutes and truck travel time by 1 minute when compared with the existing highway. The estimated accident rate is 2.50 per MVM, and the annual maintenance is expected to be $1,250 per lane-mile for all four lanes

Plan B: Improve along the existing alignment with grade improvements at a cost of $650,000 per mile, and add two lanes. It is estimated that this would reduce auto and truck travel time by 3 minutes each compared with current travel times. The accident rate on the improved road is estimated to be 2.40 per MVM, and annual maintenance is expected to be $1,000 per lane-mile for all four lanes.

Plan C: Construct a new four-lane freeway on new alignment at a cost of $800,000 per mile. It is estimated that this plan would reduce auto travel time by 5 minutes and truck travel time by 4 minutes compared with current conditions. The new freeway would be 0.3 miles longer than the improved counterparts discussed in plans A and B. The estimated accident rate for plan C is 2.30 per MVM, and annual maintenance is expected to be $1,030 per lane-mile for all four lanes. If plan C is adopted, then the existing highway will be abandoned with no salvage value.

Useful data:

Incremental operating cost

– Autos	6 cents/mile
– Trucks	18 cents/mile

Time saving

– Autos	3 cents/minute
– Trucks	15 cents/minute

Average accident cost $1,200

If a 5% interest rate is used, then which of the three proposed plans should be adopted? Base your answer on the individual B/C ratios of each alternative. When calculating these values, consider any annual incremental operating costs due to distance, a user disbenefit rather than a cost.

5.10 A 50-meter tunnel must be constructed as part of a new aqueduct system for a city. Two alternatives are being considered. One is to build a full-capacity tunnel now for $500,000. The other alternative is to build a half-capacity tunnel now for $300,000 and then to build a second parallel half-capacity tunnel 20 years hence for $400,000. The cost of repair of the tunnel lining at the end of every 10 years is estimated to be $20,000 for the full-capacity tunnel and $16,000 for each half-capacity tunnel.

Determine whether the full-capacity tunnel or the half-capacity tunnel should be constructed now. Solve the problem by B/C ratio analysis using a 5% interest rate and a 50-year analysis period. There will be no tunnel lining repair at the end of the 50 years.

5.11 Consider the following typical noise levels in decibels (dBA):

140	threshold of pain
130	
120	four-engine jet aircraft at 500 ft unmuffled motorcycle
110	
100	rock and roll band subway train at 20 ft
90	heavy traffic at 25 to 50 ft
80	
	vacuum cleaner
70	dishwasher
60	conversational speech at 3 ft
50	business office
40	home

a. Assume that you are responsible for designing a machine shop. How would you determine an acceptable level of noise? What costs and risks should you weigh?

b. What would your answer be for the design of a commercial aircraft?

5.12 Epidemiological data indicate that only a handful of patients have contracted the AIDS (acquired immune deficiency syndrome) virus from health care workers. Many, though, have called for the periodic testing of all health care workers in an effort to protect or at least reduce the risks to the public. Identify the costs and benefits associated with such a program. Develop an implementation plan for nationwide testing. How would you go about measuring the costs of the plan? What are the costs and risks of not testing?

5.13 As chief industrial engineer in a manufacturing facility, you are contemplating the replacement of the spreadsheet procedures that you are now using for production scheduling and inventory control with a material requirements planning system. A number of options are available. You can do it all at once and throw out the old system, you can phase in the new system over time, you can run both systems simultaneously, and so on. Identify the costs, benefits, and risks with each approach. Construct a decision tree for the problem. Assume that the benefits of any option depend on the future state of the economy, which may be "good" or "bad" with probabilities 0.7 and 0.3, respectively.

5.14 The daily demand for a particular type of printed circuit board in an assembly shop can assume one of the following values: 100, 120 or 130 with probabilities 0.2, 0.3 and 0.5. The manager of the shop thus is limiting her alternatives to stocking one of the three levels indicated. If she prepares more boards than are needed in the same day, then she must reprocess those remaining at a cost price of 55 cents/board. Assuming that it costs 60 cents to prepare a board for assembly and that each board produces $1.05 in revenue, find the optimal stocking level by using a decision tree model.

5.15 In Exercise 5.14, suppose that the owner wishes to consider her decision problem over a 2-day period. Her alternatives for the second day are determined as follows. If the demand in day 1 is equal to the amount stocked, then she will continue to order the same quantity on the second day. Otherwise, if the demand exceeds the amount stocked, then she will have the options to order higher levels of stock on the second day. Finally, if day 1's demand is less than the amount stocked, then she will have the options to order any of the lower levels of stock for the second day. Express the problem as a decision tree, and find the optimal solution using the cost data given in Exercise 5.14.

5.16 Zingtronics Corp. has completed the design of a new graphic-display unit for computer systems and is about to decide on whether it should produce one of the major components internally or subcontract it to another local firm. The advisability of which action to take depends on how the market will respond to the new product. If demand is high, then it is worthwhile to make the extra investment for special facilities and equipment needed to produce the component internally. For low demand, it is preferable to subcontract. The analyst assigned to study the problem has produced the following information on costs (in thousands of dollars) and probability estimates of future demand for the next 5-year period:

Action	Future demand		
	Low	Average	High
Produce	$140	$120	$90
Subcontract	$100	$110	$160
Probability	0.10	0.60	0.30

a. Prepare a decision tree that describes the structure of this problem.

b. Select the best action on the basis of the initial probability estimates for future demand.

c. Determine the expected cost with perfect information (i.e., knowing future demand exactly).

5.17 Refer to Exercise 5.16. The management of Zingtronics is planning to hire Dr. Lalith deSilva, an economist and head of a local consulting firm, to prepare an economic forecast for the computer industry. The reliability of her forecasts based on previous assignments is provided by the following table of conditional probabilities.

| | Future demand | | |
Economic forecast	Low	Average	High
Optimistic	0.1	0.1	0.5
Normal	0.3	0.7	0.4
Pessimistic	0.6	0.2	0.1
	1.0	1.0	1.0

a. Select the best action for Zingtronics if Dr. deSilva submits a pessimistic forecast for the computer industry.
b. Prepare a decision tree diagram for the problem with the use of Dr. deSilva's forecasts.
c. What is the Bayes strategy for this problem?
d. Determine the maximum fee that should be paid for the use of Dr. deSilva's services.

5.18 Allen Konigsberg is an expert in decision support systems and has been hired by a small software engineering firm to help plan their R&D strategy for the next 6 to 12 months. The company wishes to devote up to 3 person-years, or roughly $200,000, to R&D projects. Show how Konigsberg can use a decision tree to structure his analysis. State all of your assumptions.

5.19 The management of Dream Cruises, Ltd., operating in the Caribbean, has established the need for expanding its fleet capacity and is considering what the best plan for the next 8-year planning period will be. One strategy is to buy a larger 40,000-ton cruise ship now, which would be most profitable if demand is high. Another strategy would be to start with a small 15,000-ton ship now and consider buying another medium 25,000-ton ship 3 years later. The planning department has estimated the probabilities for high and low demand for each period to be 0.6 and 0.4. If the company buys the large ship, then the annual profit after taxes for the next 8 years is estimated to be $800,000 if demand is high and $100,000 if it is low. If the company buys the small ship, then the annual profits each year will be $300,000 if demand is high and $150,000 if it is low.

After 3 years with the small vessel, a decision for new capacity will be reviewed. At this time, the firm may decide to expand by adding a 25,000-ton ship or by continuing with the small one. The annual profit after expansion will be $700,000 if demand is high and $120,000 if it is low.

a. Prepare a decision tree that shows the actions available, the states of nature, and the annual profits.
b. Calculate the total expected profit for each branch in the decision tree covering 8 years of operation.
c. Determine the optimum fleet-expansion strategy for Dream Cruises, Ltd.

5.20 Referring to Exercise 5.19, determine the optimal fleet-expansion strategy if projected annual profits are discounted at the rate of 12%.

5.21 *Pipeline Construction Model.* The following exercise is a variation of the classical "machine setup" problem. The installation of an oil pipeline that runs from an oil field to a refinery requires the welding of 1,000 seams. Two alternatives have been specified for performing the welding: (1) use a team of ordinary and apprentice welders (B-team) only, or (2) use a team of master welders (A-team) who check and rework (as necessary) the welds of the B-team. If the first alternative is chosen, then it is estimated from past experience that 5% of the seams will be defective with probability 0.30, 10% will be defective with probability 0.50, or 20% will be defective with probability 0.20. However, if the B-team is followed by the A-team, then a defective rate of 1% is almost certain.

Material and labor costs are estimated at $400,000 when the B-team is used strictly, whereas these costs rise to $530,000 when the A-team is also brought in. Defective seams result in leaks that must be reworked at a cost of $1,200 per seam, which includes the cost of labor and spilled oil but ignores the cost of environmental damage.

a. Determine the optimal decision and its expected cost. How might environmental damage be taken into account?

b. A worker on the pipeline with a Bayesian inclination (from long years of wagering on the ponies) has proposed that management consider x-ray inspections of five randomly selected seams *following* the work of the B-team. Such an inspection would identify defective seams, which would provide management with more information for the decision on whether to bring in the A-team. It costs $5,000 to inspect the five seams. Financially, is it worthwhile to carry out the inspection? If so, then what decision should be made for each possible result of the inspection?

5.22 A decision is to be made as to whether to perform a *complete audit* of an accounts receivable file. Substantial errors in the file can result in a loss of revenue to the company. However, conducting a *complete audit* is expensive. It has been estimated that the average cost of auditing one account is $6. However, if a *complete audit* is conducted, resulting in the true but *unknown* proportion p of the accounts in error being reduced, then the loss of revenue may be reduced significantly.

Andrew Garland, the audit manager, has the option of first conducting a *partial audit* before his decision on the *complete audit*. Using the prior probability distribution and payoffs (costs) given in the table below, develop a single auditing plan based on a *partial audit* of three accounts. Work with opportunity losses.

Proportion of accounts in error, p	Prior probability of p, $P(p)$	Conditional cost	
		Do not audit	Complete audit
0.05	0.2	$1,000	$10,000
0.50	0.7	$10,000	$10,000
0.95	0.1	$29,000	$10,000

a. Develop the opportunity loss matrix—the matrix derived from the payoff matrix (state of nature versus cost) by subtracting from each entry the smallest entry in its row.

b. Structure the problem in the form of a decision tree. Specify all actions, sample outcomes, and events. Indicate opportunity losses and probabilities at all points on the tree. Show all calculations.

c. Develop the conditional probability matrix, $P(X|p)$.

d. Develop the joint probability matrix.

e. Is the single auditing plan better than not conducting a partial audit?
1. What is the expected opportunity loss with no partial auditing?
2. What is the expected value of perfect information (EVPI)? Note that EVPI is the difference between the optimal EMV under perfect information and the optimal EMV under the current uncertainty (before collecting more data).

3. What is the expected value of sample information (EVSI), where EVSI = EVPI − EMV? The evaluation of EMV should take into account the results of the partial audit.

4. State how you would determine the optimal number of partial audits in a sampling plan.

5.23 A trucking company has decided to replace its existing truck fleet. Supplier A will provide the needed trucks at a cost of $700,000. Supplier B will charge $500,000, but its vehicles may require more maintenance and repair than those from supplier A. The trucking company is also considering modernizing its maintenance and repair facility either by renovation or by renovation and expansion. Although expansion is generally more expensive than renovation alone, it enables greater efficiency of repair and therefore reduced annual operating costs of the facility. The estimated costs of renovation alone and of renovation and expansion, as well as the ensuing operating costs, depend on the quality of the trucks that are purchased and the extent of the maintenance that they require. The trucking company therefore has decided on the following strategy: purchase the trucks now, observe their maintenance requirements for 1 year, then make the decision as to whether to renovate or to renovate and expand. During the 1-year observation period, the company will get additional information about expected maintenance requirements during years 2 through 5.

If the trucks are purchased from supplier A, then first-year maintenance costs are expected to be low ($30,000) with a probability of 0.7 or moderate ($40,000) with a probability of 0.3. If they are purchased from supplier B, then maintenance costs will be low ($30,000) with a probability of 0.3, moderate ($40,000) with a probability of 0.6, or high ($50,000) with a probability of 0.1. The costs of renovation, shown here, depend on the first year's maintenance experience. Probabilities of various maintenance levels in years 2 through 5 depend on the types of trucks selected and the maintenance experience during year 1 (Table 5.18).

One-year maintenance requirements	Renovation costs	Renovation and expansion costs
Low	$150,000	$300,000
Moderate	$200,000	$500,000
High	$300,000	$700,000

Expected maintenance costs for years 2 through 5 can best be estimated after observing the maintenance requirements for the first year (Table 5.17).

TABLE 5.17

Supplier	First-year maintenance	Renovate, maintenance years 2–5		Renovate and expand, maintenance years 2–5	
		Low	Moderate	Low	Moderate
A	Low	$100,000	$150,000	$40,000	$60,000
	Moderate	$100,000	$150,000	$40,000	$60,000
		Moderate	High	Moderate	High
B	Low	$150,000	$200,000	$50,000	$90,000
	Moderate	$150,000	$200,000	$50,000	$90,000
	High	$250,000	$300,000	$70,000	$100,000

TABLE 5.18

Supplier	First-year maintenance	Maintenance level, years 2–5		
		Low	Moderate	High
A	Low	0.7	0.3	—
	Moderate	0.4	0.6	—
B	Low	—	0.5	0.5
	Moderate	—	0.4	0.6
	High	—	0.3	0.7

Use decision tree analysis to determine the strategy that minimizes expected costs.

REFERENCES

General Models

Baker, N. R., "R&D Project Selection Models: An Assessment," *IEEE Transactions on Engineering Management,* Vol. EM-21, No. 4, pp. 165–171, 1974.

Davis, J., A. Fusfeld, E. Scriven and G. Tritle, "Determining a Project's Probability of Success," *Research Technology Management,* Vol. 44, No. 3, pp. 51–57, 2001.

Gass, S. I., "Model World: When Is a Number a Number?" *Interfaces,* Vol 31, No. 1, pp. 93–103, 2001.

Hobbs, B. F., "A Comparison of Weighting Methods in Power Plant Siting," *Decision Science,* Vol. 11, No. 4, pp. 725–737, 1980.

Madey, G. R. and B. V. Dean, "Strategic Planning for Investment in R&D Using Decision Analysis and Mathematical Programming," *IEEE Transactions on Engineering Management,* Vol. EM-32, No. 2, pp. 84–90, 1986.

Mandakovic, T. and W. E. Souder, "An Interactive Decomposable Heuristic for Project Selection," *Research Management,* Vol. 31, No. 10, pp. 1257–1271, 1985.

Mintzer, I., *Environmental Externality Data for Energy Technologies,* Technical Report, Center for Global Change, University of Maryland, College Park, MD, 1990.

Shachter, R. D., "Evaluating Influence Diagrams," *Operations Research,* Vol. 34, No. 6, pp. 871–882, 1986.

Souder, W. E. and T. Mandakovic, "R&D Project Selection Models," *Research Management,* Vol. 29, No. 4, pp. 36–42, 1986.

Benefit-Cost Analysis

Agogino, A. M., O. Nour-Omid, W. Imaino, and S. S. Wang, "Decision-Analytic Methodology for Cost-Benefit Evaluation of Diagnostic Testers," *IIE Transactions,* Vol. 24, No. 1, pp. 39–54, 1992.

Bard, J. F., "The Costs and Benefits of a Satellite-Based System for Natural Resource Management," *Socio-Economic Planning Sciences,* Vol. 18, No. 1, pp. 15–24, 1984.

Bordman, S. L., "Improving the Accuracy of Benefit-Cost Analysis," *IEEE Spectrum,* Vol. 10, No. 9, pp. 72–76, September 1973.

Dicker, P. F. and M. P. Dicker, "Involved in System Evaluation? Use a Multiattribute Analysis Approach to Get the Answer," *Industrial Engineering,* Vol. 23, No. 5, pp. 43–73, May 1991.

Newnan, D. G., J. P. Lavelle and T. G. Eschenbach, *Engineering Economic Analysis,* Ninth Edition, Oxford University Press, Cary, NC, 2004.

Walshe, G. and P. Daffern, *Managing Cost Benefit Analysis,* Macmillan Education, London, 1990.

Risk Issues

Bell, T. E., "Special Report on Designing and Operating a Minimum-Risk System," *IEEE Spectrum*, Vol. 26, No. 6, June 1989.

Committee on Public Engineering Policy, *Perspectives on Benefit-Risk Decision Making*, National Academy of Engineering, Washington, DC, 1972.

Dougherty, E. M. and J. R. Fragola, *Human Reliability Analysis*, John Wiley & Sons, New York, 1988.

Kaplan, S. and B. J. Garrick, "On the Quantitative Definition of Risk," *Risk Analysis*, Vol. 1, No. 1, pp. 1–23, 1981.

Kumamoto, H. and E. J. Henley, *Probablistic Risk Assessment and Management for Engineers and Scientists*, Second Edition, John Wiley & Sons, New York, 2001.

Lowrance, W. W., *Of Acceptable Risk: Science and the Determination of Safety*, William Kaufmann, Los Altos, CA, 1976.

Makridakis, S., S. C. Wheelwright and R. J. Hyndman, *Forecasting: Methods & Applications*, Third Edition, John Wiley & Sons, New York, 1997.

Sage, A. P. and E. B. White, "Methodologies for Risk and Hazard Assessment: A Survey and Status Report," *IEEE Transactions on System, Man, and Cybernetics*, Vol. SMC-10, No. 8, pp. 425–446, 1980.

Vose, D., *Risk Analysis: A Quantitative Guide*, Second Edition, John Wiley & Sons, New York, 2000.

Yates, J. F. (Editor), *Risk Taking Behavior*, John Wiley & Sons, New York, 1991.

Decision Trees

Call, J. H. and W. A. Miller, "A Comparison of Approaches and Implementations for Automating Decision Analysis," *Reliability Engineering and System Safety*, Vol. 30, pp. 115–162, 1990.

Canada, J. R., W. G. Sullivan and J. A. White, *Capital Investment Analysis for Engineering and Management*, Second Edition, Prentice Hall, Upper Saddle River, NJ, 1996.

Clemen, R. T., *Making Hard Decisions: An Introduction to Decision Analysis*, Second Edition, Duxbury Press, Belmont, CA, 1996.

Goodwin, P. and G. Wright, *Decision Analysis for Management Judgment*, Second Edition, John Wiley & Sons, New York, 2000.

Lindley, D. V., *Making Decisions*, Second Edition, John Wiley & Sons, New York, 1996.

Maxwell, D. T., "Decision Analysis: Aiding Insight VI," *OR/MS Today*, Vol. 29, No. 5, pp. 44–51, June 2002.

Raiffa, H., *Decision Analysis: Introductory Lectures on Choices under Uncertainty*, Addison-Wesley, Reading, MA, 1968.

Real Options

Amram, M. and N. Kulatilaka, *Real Options: Managing Strategic Investment in an Uncertain World*, Harvard Business School Press, Boston, MA, 1999.

Boute, R., E. Demeulemeester and W. S. Herroelen, "A Real Options Approach to Project Management," *International Journal of Projection Research*, Vol. 42, No. 9, pp. 1715–1725 (2004).

Copeland, T., "The Real-Options Approach to Capital Allocation," *Strategic Finance*, Vol. 83, No. 4, pp. 33–37, 2001.

Huchzermeier, A. and C. H. Loch, "Project Management under Risk: Using the Real Options Approach to Evaluate Flexibility in R&D," *Management Science*, Vol. 47, No. 1, pp. 85–101, 2001.

Trigeorgis, L., *Real Options*, MIT Press, Cambridge, MA, 1997.

Appendix 5A

Bayes' Theorem for Discrete Outcomes

For a given problem, let there be n mutually exclusive, collectively exhaustive possible outcomes $S_1, \ldots, S_i, \ldots, S_n$ whose prior probabilities $P(S_i)$ have been established. The laws of probability require

$$\sum_{i=1}^{n} P(S_i) = 1, \quad 0 \leq P(S_i) \leq 1, \quad i = 1, \ldots, n$$

If the results of additional study, such as sampling or further investigation, are designated as X, then where X is discrete and $P(X) > 0$, Bayes' theorem can be written as

$$P(S_i|X) = \frac{P(X|S_i)}{\sum\limits_{j=1}^{n} P(X|S_j)P(S_j)} \tag{5A.1}$$

The posterior probability $P(S_i|X)$ is the probability of outcome S_i given that additional study resulted in X. The probability of X and S_i occurring, $P(X|S_i)P(S_i)$, is the "joint" probability of X and S_i or $P(X, S_i)$. The sum of all of the joint probabilities is equal to the probability of X. Therefore, Equation (5A.1) can be written

$$P(S_i|X) = \frac{P(X|S_i)P(S_i)}{P(X)} \tag{5A.2}$$

A format for application is presented in Table 5A.1. The columns are as follows:

1. S_i: potential states of nature.
2. $P(S_i)$: estimated prior probability of S_i. (Note: This column sums to one.)

TABLE 5A.1   Format for Applying Bayes' Theorem

(1) State	(2) Prior probability	(3) Probability of sample outcome, X	(4) $= (2) \times (3)$ Joint probability	(5) $= (4)/\Sigma(4)$ Posterior probability $P(S_i\|X)$
S_1	$P(S_1)$	$P(X\|S_1)$	$P(X\|S_1)P(S_1)$	$P(X\|S_1)P(S_1)/P(X)$
S_2	$P(S_2)$	$P(X\|S_2)$	$P(X\|S_2)P(S_2)$	$P(X\|S_2)P(S_2)/P(X)$
.	.	.	.	.
.	.	.	.	.
.	.	.	.	.
S_i	$P(S_i)$	$P(X\|S_i)$	$P(X\|S_i)P(S_i)$	$P(X\|S_i)P(S_i)/P(X)$
.	.	.	.	.
.	.	.	.	.
S_n	$P(S_n)$	$P(X\|S_n)$	$P(X\|S_n)P(S_n)$	$P(X\|S_n)P(S_n)/P(X)$
	$\sum_{i=1}^{n} P(S_i) = 1$		$\sum_{i=1}^{n} P(X\|S_i)P(S_i) = P(X)$	$\sum_{i=1}^{n} P(S_i\|X) = 1$

3. $P(X\|S_i)$: the conditional probability of getting sample or added study results X, given that S_i is the true state (assumed to be known).

4. $P(X\|S_i)P(S_i)$: joint probability of getting X and S_i; the summation of this column is $P(X)$, which is the probability that the sample or added study results in outcome X.

5. $P(S_i\|X)$: posterior probability of S_i given that sample outcome resulted in X; numerically, the ith entry is equal to the ith entry of column (4) divided by the sum of the values in column (4). [Note: Column (5) sums to one.]

Chapter 6

Multiple Criteria Methods for Evaluation

6.1 INTRODUCTION

It is often the case, particularly in the public sector, that goods and services are either of a collective nature, such as those for defense and space exploration, or subsidized so that their prevailing market price is an unrealistic measure of the actual cost to the community. In these circumstances, an attempt must be made to find a suitable undistorted "price."

When the analysis turns to such intangible considerations as safety, health, and the quality of life, it is rarely possible to find a single variable whose direct measurement will provide a valid indicator. Often a surrogate is used. For example, a city's environmental character could be evaluated by means of an index composed of air pollution levels, noise levels, traffic flow rates, and pedestrian densities. Another index might include crime, fire alarms, and suicide rates. At the national level, it is common to cite unemployment percentages, the consumer and producer price indices, the level of the Dow Jones industrial stocks, and the amount of manufacturer inventories as indicators of general economic well-being. In fact, each of these measures is a composite of a multitude of elements, weighted and summed together in what many would view as an arbitrary manner. A variety of procedures for doing this were presented in Chapter 5. For evaluating large, complex projects, more systematic and rational procedures are required. In this chapter, we focus on methods that have been developed to bring greater rigor to the evaluation and selection process.

6.2 FRAMEWORK FOR EVALUATION AND SELECTION

The success of a project depends on a host of factors, the foremost being its ability to meet critical performance requirements. Success also depends on the likelihood that the project will remain within the planned schedule and budget, the technological opportunities that it offers beyond the immediate application, and the user's perception regarding its ability

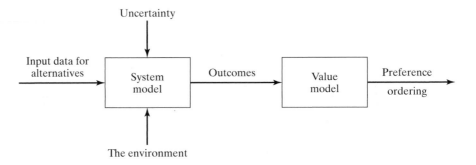

Figure 6.1   Decision analysis paradigm.

to satisfy long-term organization goals. For balancing each of these factors, a value model is needed. Such a model offers the decision maker a framework for conducting the underlying tradeoffs.

A paradigm for any decision analysis is depicted in Fig. 6.1. In the context of project management, a decision maker must pick the most "preferred" alternative from a finite set of candidates. Here, the system model may be as simple as a spreadsheet or as elaborate as a dynamic mathematical simulation. Consideration should be given to the full range of economic, technological, and political aspects of the project. Each alternative, together with the prevailing uncertainties, is fed into the system model, and a particular outcome is reported.

When the uncertainties are minimal and the data are reliable, the outcomes will be fairly accurate. When uncertainty dominates, it may not be possible to develop a valid system model. The problems in which decision analysis is most effective lie somewhere between these two extremes. For example, if an advanced energy system is to be developed, then certain engineering principles and experience with prototypes should give a good indication of performance. However, some uncertainties will still exist, such as the cost of the system in mass production or its reliability in commercial operation.

In the decision analysis paradigm, the outcomes of the system model provide the input to the value model. The output of the latter is a statement of the decision maker's preferences in terms of a rank ordering of the outcomes or as numerical values that indicate strength of preference as well as rank.

6.2.1 Objectives and Attributes[1]

The multicriteria aspect of decision analysis appears because outcomes must be evaluated in terms of several objectives (also called *goals*). These are stated in terms of properties, either desirable or undesirable, that determine the decision maker's preferences for the outcomes. For the design of an automobile, several objectives might be

---

[1]The word *attribute* is used to describe what is important in a decision problem and is often interchangeable with *objective* and *criterion*. A finer distinction can be made as follows: an *objective* represents direction of improvement or preference for one or more attributes, whereas *criterion* is a standard or rule that guides decision making.

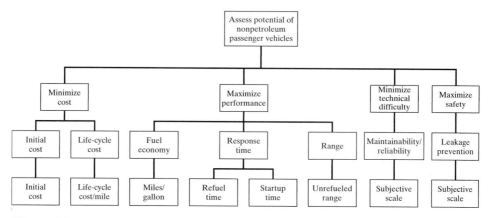

Figure 6.2 Hierarchy of objectives for advanced vehicle systems.

to (1) minimize production costs, (2) minimize fuel consumption, (3) minimize air pollution, and (4) maximize safety. The purpose of the value model is to take the outcomes of the system model, determine the degree to which they satisfy each of the objectives, and then make the necessary tradeoffs to arrive at a ranking for the alternatives that correctly express the preferences of the decision maker.

The value model is developed in terms of a hierarchy of objectives and subobjectives, as shown in Fig. 6.2 for an automobile design project. To quantify the model, a unit of measurement must be assigned to the lowest members of the hierarchy. These members are called *attributes* and may be scaled in any number of ways depending on the evaluation technique used. In Fig. 6.2, eight attributes are used to quantify the value model. They may be represented by an eight-component vector: $\mathbf{x} = (x_1, x_2, x_3, x_4, x_5, x_6, x_7, x_8)$. A specific occurrence of an attribute is called a *state*. An attribute state for the objective "minimize fuel consumption" might be $x_3 = 35$ miles per gallon.

Both theory and practice have shown that the set of attributes should satisfy the following requirements for the value model to be a valid and useful representation of the decision maker's preference structure:

1. *Completeness.* The set of attributes should characterize all of the factors to be considered in the decision-making process.
2. *Importance.* Each attribute should represent a significant criterion in the decision-making process, in the sense that it has the potential for affecting the preference ordering of the alternatives under consideration.
3. *Measurability.* Each attribute should be capable of being objectively or subjectively quantified. Technically, this requires that it be possible to establish a utility function (see Chapter 3 for a discussion of utility functions) for the attribute.
4. *Familiarity.* Each attribute should be understandable to the decision maker in the sense that he should be able to identify preferences for different states.
5. *Nonredundancy.* No two attributes should measure the same criterion, a situation that would result in double counting.

6. *Independence.* The value model should be structured so that changes within certain limits in the state of one attribute should not affect the preference ordering for states of another attribute or the preference ordering for gambles over the states of another attribute (more will be said about this later).

If an attribute does not meet these conditions, then it should either be redefined by, say, dividing its range into smaller intervals and introducing "subattributes" corresponding to these intervals or be combined with other attributes until a satisfactory situation is achieved.

6.2.2 Aggregating Objectives into a Value Model

Once attributes have been assigned to all of the objectives and attribute states have been determined for all possible outcomes, it is necessary to aggregate the states by constructing a single unit of measurement that will accurately represent the decision maker's preference ordering for the outcomes. This was achieved somewhat arbitrarily in Chapter 5 by specifying weights for each attribute or criterion. A more rigorous and defendable method of doing this is the "willingness to pay" or "pricing out" technique (Keeney and Raiffa 1976). Here, one attribute is singled out as the reference, preferably an attribute measured in dollars, and rates of substitution are determined for the others. Two procedures for operationalizing this concept will now be presented. Complementary techniques have been developed by Graves et al. (1992), Lewandowski and Wirezbicki (1989), and Lotfi et al. (1992), just to name a few.

6.3 MULTIATTRIBUTE UTILITY THEORY

If the set of attributes satisfies the requirements listed above, then it is possible to formulate a mathematical function called a *multiattribute utility function* that will assign numbers, called outcome utilities, to each outcome state. In general, the utility $U(\mathbf{x}) = U(x_1, x_2, \ldots, x_N)$, of any combination of outcomes $(x_1, x_2, \ldots, x_N)$ for N attributes can be expressed as either (1) an additive or (2) a multiplicative function of the individual attribute utility functions $U_1(x_1), U_2(x_2), \ldots, U_N(x_N)$ provided that each pair of attributes is

1. Preferentially independent of its complement; that is, the preference order of consequences for any pair of attributes does not depend on the levels at which the other attributes are held.
2. Utility independence of its complement; that is, the conditional preference for lotteries (probabilistic tradeoffs) involving only changes in the levels for any pair of attributes does not depend on the levels at which the other attributes are held.

To illustrate condition 1, suppose that four attributes for a given project are profitability, time to market, technical risk, and commercial success. Preferential independence means that if we judge technological risk, for example, to be more important than profitability, then this relationship is true regardless of whether the level of profitability is high, low, or somewhere in between and also regardless of the value of the other attributes.

The second condition, utility independence, means that if we are deciding on the preference ordering (ranking) for probabilistic tradeoffs between, for example, technological risk and time to market, then this can be done regardless of the value of profitability. An example of preference ordering of probabilistic tradeoffs between technological risk and time to market is, for instance, a 25% chance of very low risk and a 70% chance of quick time to market is preferred to, say, a 15% chance of very low risk and a 90% chance of quick time to market.

Before proceeding, it is necessary to verify that these two conditions are valid or, more correctly, to test and identify the bounds of their validity. A procedure for doing this is provided by Keeney (1977). The mathematical notation used to describe the model is given below:

x_i	state of the ith attribute
x_i^0	least preferred state to be considered for the ith attribute
x_i^*	most preferred state to be considered for the ith attribute
$\mathbf{x}$	vector $(x_1, x_2, \ldots, x_N)$ of attribute states characterizing a specific outcome
$\mathbf{x}^0$	outcome constructed from the least preferred states of all attributes; $\mathbf{x}^0 = \left(x_1^0, \ldots, x_N^0\right)$
$\mathbf{x}^*$	outcome constructed from the most preferred states of all attributes; $\mathbf{x}^* = \left(x_1^*, \ldots, x_N^*\right)$
$\left(x_i, \overline{x}_i^0\right)$	outcome in which all attributes except the ith attribute are at their least preferred state
$U_i(x_i)$	utility function associated with the ith attribute
$U(\mathbf{x})$	utility function associated with the outcome $\mathbf{x}$
k_i	scaling constant for the ith attribute; $k_i = U\left(x_i^*, \overline{x}_i^0\right)$
k	master scaling constant

Now, if the two independence conditions hold, then $U(\mathbf{x})$ assumes the following multiplicative form:

$$U(\mathbf{x}) = \frac{1}{k}\left\{\prod_{i=1}^{N}\left[1 + kk_iU_i(x_i)\right] - 1\right\} \tag{6.1a}$$

where the master scaling constant k is determined from the equation $1 + k = \Pi_i(1 + kk_i)$. If $\Sigma_i k_i > 1$, then $-1 < k < 0$; if $\Sigma_i k_i < 1$, then $k > 0$; if $\Sigma_i k_i = 1$, then $k = 0$ and Equation (6.1a) reduces to the additive form:

$$U(\mathbf{x}) = \sum_{i=1}^{N} k_iU_i(x_i) \tag{6.1b}$$

Because utility is a relative measure, the underlying theory permits the arbitrary assignment of $U_i(x_i^0) = 0$ and $U_i(x_i^*) = 1$; that is, the worst outcome for each attribute is given a utility value of 0 and the best outcome is given a utility value of 1.

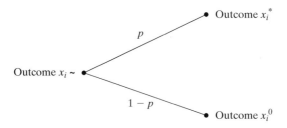

Figure 6.3 Graphical assessment of
indifference probability.

The shape of the utility function depends on the decision maker's subjective judgment
on the relative desirability of possible outcomes. A pointwise approximation of this
function can be obtained by asking a series of lottery-type questions such as the following: For attribute i, what certain outcome, x_i, would be equally desirable as realizing the highest outcome with a probability p and the lowest outcome with a probability
of $(1 - p)$? This can be expressed in utility terms using the extreme values x_i^* and x_i^0 as

$$U_i(x_i = ?) = pU_i\left(x_i^*\right) + (1 - p)U_i\left(x_i^0\right) = p$$

To construct the curve, p can be varied in fixed increments until either a continuous
function can be approximated or enough discrete points have been assessed to give an
accurate picture. Alternatively, one could specify the certain outcome x_i over a range of
values and ask questions such as, "At what p is the certain outcome x_i equally desirable
as $pU_i(x_i^*) + (1 - p)U_i(x_i^0)$?" Graphically, the assessment of p can be represented as
the lottery shown in Fig. 6.3.

Example 6-1

Suppose that we want to estimate a utility function for the relative fuel economy of an
automobile under development (attribute 3 in Fig. 6.2). The best achievable might be 80
mpg, and the worst might be 20 mpg. These outcomes would give the utility function values of 1 and 0, respectively. For $p = 0.5$ (the 50-50 lottery), the question would be, "How
many miles per gallon as a "sure thing" would be equivalent to a gamble if there were a
50% chance of realizing 80 mpg and a 50% of realizing 20 mpg?" If the answer is, say, 60
mpg, the new utility value would be calculated as

$$U(x = 60) = 0.5U(x = 80) + 0.5U(x = 20)$$
$$= 0.5(1) + 0.5(0) = 0.5$$

Note that the utility of the certain outcome equals the probability of the best outcome.
Figure 6.4 depicts the interview process. A typical utility curve that resulted from the questioning of a representative of a consumer's group is shown in Fig. 6.5 (Feinberg et al. 1985).

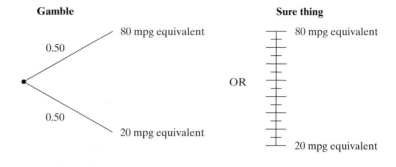

- For which value of the "sure thing" are you indifferent between the "sure thing" and the "gamble"?

      Indifference point ———

- If you knew that all other attributes were at their worst state?

      Indifference point ———

- If you knew that all other attributes were at their best state?

      Indifference point ———

Figure 6.4   Sample interview question for relative fuel economy.

Once utility functions for all attributes have been determined, the next step is to assess the scaling constants, k_i. For both the multiplicative (6.1a) and additive (6.1b) models, $k_i = U\left(x_i^*, \overline{x}_i^0\right)$, where $0 \le k_i \le 1$. That is, k_i is the utility value associated with the outcome where attribute i is at its best value, x_i^*, and all other attributes are at their worst values, $\overline{x}_i^0$. In assessing the k_i's, the following type of question is usually asked:

For what probability p are you indifferent between

1. The lottery giving a p chance at $\mathbf{x}^* \equiv \left(x_1^*, \ldots, x_N^*\right)$ and a $(1 - p)$ chance at $\mathbf{x}^0 \equiv \left(x_1^0, \ldots, x_N^0\right)$, versus

2. The consequence $\left(x_1^0, \ldots, x_{i-1}^0, x_i^*, x_{i+1}^0, \ldots, x_N^0\right)$.

The interview sheet used for determining the scaling constant associated with relative fuel economy is shown in Fig. 6.6 (the responses to the last two questions give an indication of the degree to which the independent conditions hold). The result of the assessment is that, in general, $k_i = p$. Good practice suggests that before assessing the scaling constants, the attributes should be ranked in ascending order of importance as they progress from their worst to their best states. Figure 6.7 displays the question sheet that was used for this purpose.

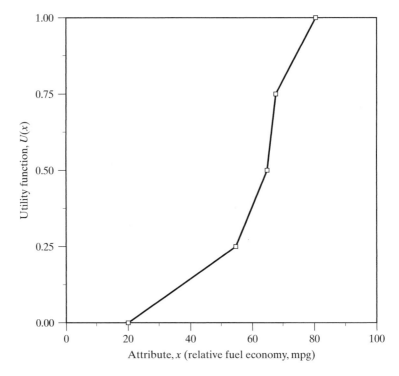

Figure 6.5 Example of utility curve for representative consumer.

The last step in the evaluation and selection process is to rank the alternatives. This is done by using the multiattribute utility function to calculate outcome utilities for each alternative under consideration. If two or more alternatives seem to be close in rank, then their sensitivity to both the scaling constants and the utility functions should be examined. Appendix 6A contains a more detailed example of the evaluation process.

A final point to make about multiattribute utility theory (MAUT) concerns the possibility that the state of an attribute may be uncertain. "Completion time of a task," "reliability of a subassembly," and "useful life of the system" are some examples of attributes whose states may take on different values with known (or, more distressingly, with unknown) probability. In these cases, x_i is really a random variable, so it is more appropriate to compute the *expected* utility of a particular outcome. For the additive model, this can be done with the following equation:

$$E[U(\mathbf{x})] = \sum_{i=1}^{N} \left[k_i \int_{-\infty}^{\infty} U_i(x_i) f_i(x_i) d(x_i) \right] \tag{6.2}$$

where $f_i(x_i)$ is the probability density function associated with attribute i, and $E[\,\cdot\,]$ is the expectation operator (Keeney and von Winterfeldt 1991). Commercial software is available for helping in the assessment of f_i, as well as the scaling constants k_i and the individual utility functions U_i.

For what value of p are you indifferent between the
"sure thing" and the "gamble"?

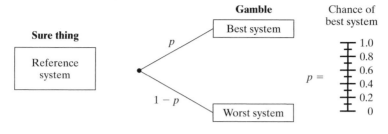

	Relative fuel economy	Initial cost	Life-cycle cost/mile	Maintain-ability	Safety	Refuel time	Unrefueled range	Maximum startup time
Ref:	80 mpg equivalent							
		$25,000	$1.00/mile	0	0	8 hours	50 miles	600 seconds
Best:	80 mpg equivalent	$5,000	$0.20/mile	10	10	0.17 hours	250 miles	5 seconds
Worst:								
	20 mpg equivalent	$25,000	$1.00/mile	0	0	8 hours	50 miles	600 seconds

Figure 6.6   Sample interview question used to determine scaling constant for the relative fuel economy attribute.

Attribute	Relative fuel economy	Initial cost	Life-cycle cost/mile	Maintain-ability	Safety	Refuel time	Unre-fueled range	Maximum startup time
Best state	80 mpg equivalent	$5,000	$0.20/mile	10	10	0.17 hours (10 min)	250 miles	5 seconds
Worst state	20 mpg equivalent	$25,000	$1.00/mile	0	0	8.0 hours	50 miles	600 seconds (10 min)
Order of importance								

Figure 6.7   Sample interview question used to determine order of importance of attributes.

6.4 ANALYTIC HIERARCHY PROCESS

The analytic hierarchy process (AHP) was developed by Thomas Saaty to provide a simple but theoretically sound multiple-criteria methodology for evaluating alternatives (Saaty and Vargas 2000). Applications can be found in such diverse fields as portfolio selection, transportation planning, manufacturing systems design, and artificial intelligence, just to name a few. The strength of the AHP lies in its ability to structure a complex, multiperson, multiattribute problem hierarchically and then to investigate each level of the hierarchy separately, combining the results as the analysis progresses. Pairwise comparisons of the factors (which, depending on the context, may be alternatives, attributes, or criteria) are undertaken using a scale that indicates the strength with which one factor dominates another with respect to a higher-level factor. This scaling process can then be translated into priority weights or scores for ranking the alternatives.

Like MAUT, the AHP starts with a hierarchy of objectives. The top of the hierarchy provides the analytic focus in terms of a problem statement. At the next level, the major considerations are defined in broad terms. This is usually followed by a listing of the criteria for each of the foregoing considerations. Depending on how much detail is called for in the model, each criterion may then be broken down into individual parameters whose values are either estimated or determined by measurement or experimentation. The bottom level of the hierarchy contains the alternatives or scenarios underlying the problem.

Figure 6.8 shows a three-level hierarchy developed for evaluating five different approaches to assembling the U.S. space station while in orbit. The focus of the problem is "selecting an in-orbit assembly system," and the four major criteria are human productivity, economics, design, and operations. The five alternatives include an astronaut with

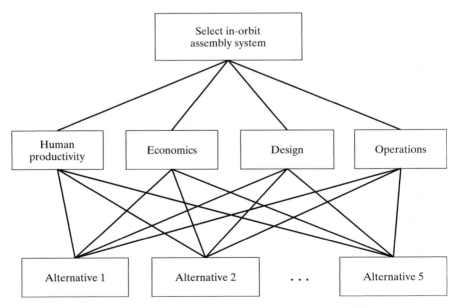

Figure 6.8   Summary three-level hierarchy for selection problem.

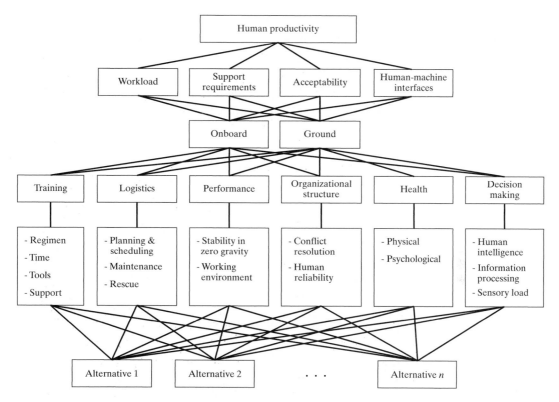

Figure 6.9   Human productivity objective hierarchy.

tools outside the spacecraft, a dexterous manipulator under human control, a dedicated manipulator under computer control, a teleoperator maneuvering system with a manipulator kit, or a computer-controlled dexterous manipulator with vision and force feedback.

In fact, in the full analysis, each of the criteria at level 2 were significantly expanded to capture the detail necessary to make accurate comparisons (Bard 1986). With regard to human productivity, workload, support requirements, crew acceptability, and issues surrounding human–machine interfaces were some of the additional factors included. Figure 6.9 depicts the full portion of the hierarchy used for this criterion.

6.4.1 Determining Local Priorities

Once the hierarchy has been structured, *local priorities* must be established for each factor on a given level with respect to each factor on the level immediately above it. This step is carried out by using pairwise comparisons between the factors to develop the relative weights or priorities. The weight of the ith factor is denoted by w_i. Because the approach is basically qualitative, it is arguably less burdensome to implement from both a data requirement and a validation point of view than by using the multiattribute utility approach of Keeney and Raiffa. That is, not all of the MAUT independence conditions need be verified or preference functions derived. Nevertheless, theory requires that the following assumptions, stated in terms of axioms, hold if the methodology is to be valid (Golden et al. 1989):

Axiom 1.   Given any two alternatives (or subcriteria) i and j from the set of alternatives $\mathcal{A}$, the decision maker is able to provide a pairwise comparison a_{ij} of these alternatives under criterion c from the set of criteria $\mathcal{C}$ on a reciprocal ratio scale; that is,

$$a_{ji} = \frac{1}{a_{ij}} \text{ for all } i, j \in \mathcal{A}$$

Axiom 2.   When comparing any two alternatives $i, j \in \mathcal{A}$, the decision maker never judges one to be infinitely better than another under any criterion $c \in \mathcal{C}$, that is, $a_{ij} \neq \infty$ for all $i, j \in \mathcal{A}$.

Axiom 3.   The decision problem can be formulated as a hierarchy.

Axiom 4.   All criteria and alternatives that have an impact on the given decision problem are represented in the hierarchy. That is, all of the decision maker's intuition must be represented (or excluded) in the structure in terms of criteria or alternatives.

These axioms can be used to describe the two basic tasks in the AHP: formulating and solving the problem as a hierarchy (3 and 4) and eliciting judgments in the form of pairwise comparisons (1 and 2). Such judgments represent an articulation of the trade-offs among the conflicting criteria and are often highly subjective in nature. Saaty suggested that a 1 to 9 ratio scale be used to quantify the decision maker's strength of feeling between any two alternatives with respect to a given criterion. The pairwise comparisons give rise to the elements a_{ij}, which are viewed as the ratio of the weights for factors i and j. In the ideal case, we have $a_{ij} = w_i/w_j$. When n alternatives are being compared, it is easy to see that

$$a_{i1}w_1 + a_{i2}w_2 + \cdots + a_{in}w_n = nw_i \quad i = 1, \ldots, n \tag{6.3}$$

In matrix form, Equation (6.3) is written as $\mathbf{A}\mathbf{w} = n\mathbf{w}$. These equations provide the basis for deriving the weights $\mathbf{w} = (w_1, w_2, \ldots, w_n)$.

An explanation of the nine-point scale is presented in Table 6.1. Depending on the context, the word *factors* means alternatives, attributes, or criteria. We also note that because a ratio scale is being used, the derived weights can be interpreted as the degree to which one alternative is preferred to another. The same cannot be said of the MAUT rankings, which have only a qualitative meaning.

Example 6-2

To illustrate the nature of the calculations, observe the three-level hierarchy in Fig. 6.8. Table 6.2 contains the input and output data for level 2.

When n factors are being compared, $n(n-1)/2$ questions are necessary to fill in the matrix $\mathbf{A} \equiv (a_{ij})$. The elements in the lower triangle are simply the reciprocal of those

TABLE 6.1   Scale Used for Pairwise Comparisons

Value	Definition	Explanation
1	Equal importance	Both factors contribute equally to the objective or criterion.
3	Weak importance of one over another	Experience and judgment slightly favor one factor over another.
5	Essential or strong importance	Experience and judgment strongly favor one factor over another.
7	Very strong or demonstrated importance	A factor is favored very strongly over another; its dominance is demonstrated in practice.
9	Absolute importance over another	The evidence favoring one factor is unquestionable.
2, 4, 6, 8	Intermediate values	Used when a compromise is needed.
0	No relationship	The factor does not contribute to the objective.

TABLE 6.2   Priority Vector for Major Criteria

Criteria	Criteria				Priority	Output parameters
	1	2	3	4		
1. Human productivity	1	3	3	7	0.521	$\lambda_{max} = 4.121$
2. Economics	0.333	1	1	5	0.205	CI = 0.040
3. Design	0.333	1	1	7	0.227	CR = 0.045
4. Operations	0.143	0.2	0.143	1	0.047	

lying above the diagonal (that is, $a_{ji} = 1/a_{ij}$, in accordance with Axiom 1) and need not be assessed. In this instance, the entries in the matrix at the center of Table 6.2 are the responses to the six ($n = 4$) pairwise questions that were asked. For example, in comparing "human productivity" with "economic" considerations (element a_{12} of the matrix), it was judged that the first "weakly" dominates the second. Note that if the elicited value for this element were 1/3 instead of 3, the opposite would have been true. Similarly, the value 7 for element a_{34} means that design considerations "very strongly" dominate those associated with operations. ∎

In general, when comparing two factors, the analyst first discerns which factor is more important and then ascertains by how much by asking the decision maker to select a value from the nine-point scale. After the decision maker supplies all of the data for the matrix, the following equation is solved to obtain the rankings denoted by **w**:

$$\mathbf{Aw} = \lambda_{max}\mathbf{w} \tag{6.4}$$

where **w** is the n-dimensional eigenvector associated with the largest eigenvalue λ_{max} of the comparison matrix **A**. The n components of **w** are then scaled so that they sum to 1. The only difference between Eq. (6.3) and Eq. (6.4) is that n has been replaced by λ_{max} on the right-hand side to allow for some inconsistency on the part of the decision maker.

In practice, the priority vector $\mathbf{w} = (w_1, w_2, \ldots, w_n)$ is obtained by raising the matrix $\mathbf{A}$ to an arbitrarily large power (16 or greater is usually sufficient). In so doing, each element in a given row i converges to the same value, call it v_i. The weights are then computed as follows:

$$w_i = \frac{v_i}{\displaystyle\sum_{k=1}^{n} v_k} \quad i = 1, \ldots, n$$

The value of λ_{max} can be found by solving each row of Eq. (6.4) for λ and averaging; that is, let λ_i be the solution to $\mathbf{A}_i \mathbf{w} = \lambda_i w_i$, where $\mathbf{A}_i$ is the ith row of $\mathbf{A}$. Then $\lambda_{max} = \frac{1}{n}\sum_{i=1}^{n}\lambda_i$. It should be noted that this procedure works only for the class of positive reciprocal matrices of which $\mathbf{A}$ belongs.

A second but less accurate way of deriving the weights is based on the geometric mean of the row elements of $\mathbf{A}$. First, we compute

$$v_i = \sqrt[n]{\prod_{j=1}^{n} a_{ij}} = \sqrt[n]{a_{i1} a_{i2} \cdots a_{in}} \quad i = 1, \ldots, n$$

and then we normalize to get $w_i = \dfrac{v_i}{v_1 + v_2 + \cdots + v_n}$ for each row i. For the example in Table 6.2,

$$\mathbf{A} = \begin{pmatrix} 1 & 3 & 3 & 7 \\ 1/3 & 1 & 1 & 5 \\ 1/3 & 1 & 1 & 7 \\ 1/7 & 1/5 & 1/7 & 1 \end{pmatrix}$$

Row 1: $v_1 = \sqrt[4]{(1)(3)(3)(7)} = \sqrt[4]{63} = 2.82$

Row 2: $v_2 = \sqrt[4]{(1/3)(1)(1)(5)} = \sqrt[4]{5/3} = 1.14$

Row 3: $v_3 = \sqrt[4]{(1/3)(1)(1)(7)} = \sqrt[4]{7/3} = 1.24$

Row 4: $v_4 = \sqrt[4]{(1/7)(1/5)(1/7)(1)} = \sqrt[4]{1/245} = 0.25$

Normalizing gives the weights

$$w_1 = \frac{2.82}{2.82 + 1.14 + 1.24 + 0.25} = \frac{2.82}{5.45} = 0.52$$

$$w_2 = \frac{1.14}{5.45} = 0.21$$

$$w_3 = \frac{1.24}{5.45} = 0.23$$

$$w_4 = \frac{0.25}{5.45} = 0.04$$

To find $\lambda_{\max}$, we solve the following equations for λ_i for each row $i = 1, \dots, n$

$$\mathbf{A}_i \mathbf{w} = \lambda_i \mathbf{w} \text{ (where } \mathbf{A}_i \text{ is the } i\text{th row of the } \mathbf{A} \text{ matrix)}$$

or

$$a_{i1} w_1 + a_{i2} w_2 + \cdots + a_{in} w_n = \lambda_i w_i.$$

For the example, we have $n = 4$:

Row 1: $\lambda_1 = 2.120/0.52 = 4.077$

Row 2: $\lambda_2 = 0.813/0.21 = 3.871$

Row 3: $\lambda_3 = 0.893/0.23 = 3.883$

Row 4: $\lambda_4 = 0.189/0.04 = 4.725$

Ideally, these values all should be the same, but because this is an approximate method, some variation is inevitable. Setting $\lambda_{\max}$ to the average of these values is a good compromise:

$$\lambda_{\max} \cong \frac{1}{n}(\lambda_1 + \lambda_2 + \cdots + \lambda_n)$$

$$= \frac{1}{4}(4.077 + 3.871 + 3.883 + 4.725)$$

$$= 4.139$$

The true value of $\lambda_{\max} = 4.121$.

6.4.2 Checking for Consistency

Consistency of response or transitivity of preference is checked by ascertaining whether

$$a_{ij} = a_{ik} a_{kj}, \text{ for all } i, j, k \tag{6.5}$$

In practice, the decision maker is only estimating the "true" elements of $\mathbf{A}$ by assigning them values from Table 6.1, so the perfectly consistent case represented by Eq. (6.5) is not likely to occur.

Therefore, as an approximation, the elements of $\mathbf{A}$ can be thought to satisfy the relationship $a_{ij} = w_i/w_j + \varepsilon_{ij}$, where ε_{ij} is the error term representing the decision maker's inconsistency in judgment when comparing factor i with factor j. As such, we would no longer expect a_{ij} to equal $a_{ik} a_{kj}$ throughout. Carrying the analysis one step further, it can be shown that the largest eigenvalue, $\lambda_{\max}$, of the matrix $\mathbf{A}$ satisfies $\lambda_{\max} \geq n$, where equality holds for perfect consistency only. This leads to the definition of a consistency index (CI)

$$CI = \frac{\lambda_{max} - n}{n - 1}$$

which can be used to evaluate the quality of the matrix **A**. To add perspective, we compare the CI to the index derived from a completely arbitrary matrix whose entries are randomly chosen. Through simulation, Saaty has obtained the following results:

n	1	2	3	4	5	6	7	8	9	10
RI	0.00	0.00	0.58	0.90	1.12	1.24	1.32	1.41	1.45	1.49

where n represents the dimension of the particular matrix and RI denotes the random index computed from the average of the CI for a large sample of random matrices. It is now possible to define the consistency ratio (CR) as

$$CR = \frac{CI}{RI}$$

Experience suggests that the CR should be less than 0.1 if one is to be fully confident of the results. (There is a certain amount of subjectivity in this assertion much like that associated with interpreting the coefficient of determination in regression analysis.) Fortunately, though, as the number of factors in the model increases, the results become less and less sensitive to the values in any one matrix.

Returning to Table 6.2, it can be seen that the priorities derived for the major considerations were 0.521 for human productivity, 0.205 for economics, 0.227 for design, and 0.047 for operations. These values tend to emphasize the first criterion over the others, probably because of the implicit mandate that the U.S. space station must eventually pay for itself. Finally, note that CR = 0.045, which is well within the acceptable range.

6.4.3 Determining Global Priorities

The next step in the analysis is to develop the priorities for the factors on the third level with respect to those on the second. In our case, we compare the five alternatives previously mentioned with each of the major criteria. For the moment, assume that the appropriate data have been elicited and that the calculations for each of the four comparison matrices have been performed, with the results displayed in Table 6.3 (note that each column sums to 1). The first four columns of data represent the local priorities derived from the inputs supplied by the decision maker. The *global priorities* are obtained by weighting each of these values by the local priorities given in Table 6.2 (and repeated at the top of Table 6.3 for convenience) and summing. The calculations for alternative 1 are as follows: $(0.066)(0.521) + (0.415)(0.205) + (0.122)(0.227) + (0.389)(0.047) = 0.165$. To see

TABLE 6.3   Local and Global Priorities for the Problem of Selecting an In-Orbit Assembly System

	Local priorities				
Alternative*	Human productivity (0.521)	Economies (0.205)	Design (0.227)	Operations (0.047)	Global priorities
1	0.066	0.415	0.122	0.389	0.165
2	0.212	0.309	0.224	0.151	0.232
3	0.309	0.059	0.206	0.178	0.228
4	0.170	0.111	0.197	0.105	0.161
5	0.243	0.106	0.251	0.177	0.214

*1. Astronaut with tools outside the spacecraft; 2. dexterous manipulator under human control; 3. dedicated manipulator under computer control; 4. teleoperator with manipulator kit; and 5. dexterous manipulator with sensory feedback.

how the calculations are performed in general, let

n_l = number of factors at level l

w_i^l = global weight at level l for factor i

w_{ij}^l = local weight at level l for factor i with respect to factor j at level $l - 1$

The global priorities at level l are obtained from the following equation:

$$w_i^l = \sum_{j=1}^{n_{l-1}} w_{ij}^i w_j^{l-1}$$

Continuing with the example, because there are no more levels left to evaluate, the values shown in the last column of Table 6.3 represent the final priorities for the problem. Thus, according to the judgments expressed by this decision maker, alternative 2 turns out to be most preferred.

To complete the analysis, it would be desirable to see how sensitive the results are to changes in judgment and criteria values; that is, to determine how changes in the **A** matrix would affect intralevel and overall priorities and consistencies. This feature is built into *Expert Choice* (Forman et al. 2004), the most popular commercial code for conducting an AHP analysis, and so can be done with little effort. *HIPRE* 3+ (Hamalainen and Mustajoki 2001) also provided this capability. When uncertainty exists in factor values, additional attributes can be defined to account for this randomness (Bard 1992).

In summary, the commonly claimed benefits of the AHP are that

1. It is simple to understand and use.
2. The construction of the objective hierarchy of criteria, attributes, and alternatives facilitates communication of the problem and solution recommendations.
3. It provides a unique means of quantifying judgment and measuring consistency.

6.5 GROUP DECISION MAKING

When more than one person is responsible for making decisions, the issues surrounding group dynamics and consensus building become paramount. Rational procedures must be developed for structuring the problem, soliciting opinions, and making use of the information collected. In general, there are two modes of operation: live sessions and some form of correspondence. In the former, the group takes time to structure its problem, usually weighing all factors and considering all inputs. Still, there is a need to trim the structure and eliminate redundancies so that the major effort can be brought to bear on the essential parts of the problem. With regard to judgments, behaviorists point out that there are four kinds of situations:

1. People are completely antagonistic to the process and do not wish to participate in a constructive way. In particular, they may believe that the outcome would dilute their own influence.
2. The participants wish to cooperate to arrive at a rational decision and in so doing wish to determine every judgment by agreement and consensus.
3. The group members are willing to have their individual judgments synthesized after some debate.
4. The group consists of experts, each of whom knows his or her mind exactly and does not wish to interact. They are willing to accept an outcome but are not willing to compromise on their judgments.

After the session in which the substance is hammered out, the group members may be willing to revise their structure and judgments by conducting additional sessions or by correspondence using questionnaires.

The second alternative is to do the entire process by correspondence without organized meetings. The question here is how to solicit opinions and interact most effectively. The Delphi method is one particular approach for doing this that has gained strong adherents.

Several researchers have pointed to the following trends in decision making:

1. Organizational decisions are much more technically and politically complex and require frequent meetings attended by a wide range of individuals.
2. Decisions must be reached quickly, usually with greater participation of low-level or staff personnel than in the past.
3. There is an increasing focus on the development of computer-based systems that support the formulation and solution of unstructured decision problems by a group [i.e., a group decision support system (GDSS)].

In what follows, we highlight some of the important considerations in the group decision-making process.

6.5.1 Group Composition

The inherent complexity and uncertainty surrounding an organization's major activities usually necessitates the participation of many people in the decision-making process. In some cases, the composition of the group is fixed (e.g., the board of directors advising the chief executive officer of a corporation), whereas in others, it is necessary to select a mix of members (e.g., choosing a panel to investigate the *Columbia* disaster). The latter selection process requires specifying the number of experts, nonexperts, staff personnel, and upper-level managers to participate, as well as choosing the appropriate people.

This process can be difficult and time consuming for many reasons. First, participants who are considered "experts" are likely to be troublesome. They may have strong ideas on the appropriate course of action and may not be easily swayed in their assessments. Second, decision makers who are considered "powerful" members of the organization might refuse to participate. These members are aware that their level of control and influence might be diminished in a group setting. They fear that the social and interactive nature of the group process might dilute their power and ability to direct policy within the organization (Saaty 1989). However, if powerful people actively participate, then they are likely to dominate the process. In contrast, results generated by a group that consists solely of "low-level" managers with little power may not be useful. The danger in all of this is that powerful managers will implement their preferred solutions without taking into account the opinions and observations of others.

One way of dealing with the "power differential" problem is to assemble a group of participants who have equal responsibility and stature within the organization. Collectively, these people can be treated as a decision-making "subgroup" that could help formulate and solve a part of the problem with which they are most knowledgeable. They could also contribute to discussions that involve higher or lower levels of management. This can be viewed as a sort of "shared" decision-making responsibility in which high-level management cooperates with subordinates. In practice, high-level management often depends on low-level employees to gather the appropriate information on which to base their decisions.

6.5.2 Running the Decision Making Session

After the group has been chosen, the members should begin preparing for the decision-making session by formalizing their agenda, structuring the allowable interactions between participants, and clearly defining the purpose of the session in advance. They can seek answers to several questions (e.g., the ones listed below) that are designed to establish the operating ground rules:

- Is the purpose of the session simply to improve the group's understanding of the problem, or is the purpose to reach a final solution?
- Are the participants committed to generating and implementing a final solution?
- What is the best way to combine the judgments of the participants on various issues to produce a united course of action?

Often we model decision problems as if the people with whom we are dealing know their minds and can give answers inspired by a clear or telling experience, but this is seldom the case. People have a habitual domain. They are conditioned and biased but also learning and adaptive. Instead of trying to cajole or coerce them prematurely, they must be given the opportunity to learn and solidify their ideas. After much experimentation and trial and error, something useful may emerge. If you hurry, then all you get is a hurried answer, no matter how scientific you try to be. People must be given an adequate chance to understand their own minds before they can be expected to commit themselves. People with different assumptions and different backgrounds, though, may never be on the same wavelength and will change their minds later if they are forced to agree. Moreover, interpersonal comparisons should be undertaken only with the utmost of care. Peer pressure, concealed and distorted preferences, and the inequalities of power all conspire to prejudice the group decision-making process.

6.5.3 Implementing the Results

After the final results have been generated, the group should evaluate the effort and cost of implementing the highest-priority outcome. It must be determined whether it is likely that the participants and their constituencies will cooperate in the implementation phase of the effort. To be useful, the decision-making process must be acceptable to the participants, and the participants must be willing to abide by the outcome. Finally, it is important for the group to view whichever GDSS was used, not as a tool for isolated, one-time applications but rather as a process that has ongoing validity and usefulness to an organization.

6.5.4 Group Decision Support Systems

A GDSS aims to improve the process of group decision making by removing common communications barriers, providing techniques for structuring decision analysis, and systematically directing the pattern, timing, and content of the discussion. The more sophisticated the GDSS technology, the more dramatic the intervention into the group's natural (unsupported) environment. Of course, more dramatic intervention does not necessarily lead to better decisions, but its appropriate design and use can produce the desired results.

Communications technologies available within a GDSS include electronic messaging, local- and wide-area networks, teleconferencing, and store-and-forward facilities. Computer technologies include multiuser operating systems, fourth-generation languages, databases, data analysis methodologies, and so on. Decision support technologies include agenda setting, decision-modeling methods (e.g., decision trees, risk assessment, forecasting techniques, the AHP, MAUT), and rules for directing discussion.

Concerning the information-exchange aspect of group decision making, DeSanctis and Gallupe (1987) proposed three levels of support. Level 1 GDSSs provide technical features aimed at removing communications barriers, such as large screens for instantaneous display of ideas, voting solicitation and compilation, anonymous input of ideas and preferences, and electronic message exchange between members. Level 1 features are found in meeting rooms normally referred to as "computer-supported conference rooms" or "electric board rooms."

Level 2 GDSSs provide decision modeling and group decision techniques that are designed to reduce the uncertainty and "noise" that occur in the group decision process. The result is an enhanced GDSS, as opposed to a level 1 system, which is a communications medium only. A Level 2 GDSS might provide automated planning tools or other aids found in individual DSSs for group members to work on and view simultaneously, again using a large, common screen. Modeling tools to support analyses that ordinarily are performed in a qualitative manner, such as social judgment formation, risk assessment, and multiattribute utility methods, can be introduced to the group via a level 2 GDSS. In addition, group structuring techniques found in the organizational development literature can be administered efficiently.

Level 3 GDSSs are characterized by machine-induced group communication patterns and can include expert advice in the selecting and arranging of rules to be applied during a meeting. As an example, Hiltz and Turoff (1985) experimented with automating the Delphi method and the nominal group technique, but to date, very little research has been done with such high-level systems.

In summary, the objective of GDSSs is to discover and present new possibilities and approaches to problems. They do this by facilitating the exchange of information among the group. Message transfer can be hastened and smoothed by removing barriers (level 1); systematic techniques can be used in the decision process (level 2); and

TABLE 6.4   Example GDSS Features to Support Six Task Types

Task purpose	Task type	GDSS level	Possible support features
General	Planning	Level 1	Large-screen display, graphical aids
		Level 2	Planning tools (e.g., program evaluation and review); risk assessment, subjective probability estimation for alternative plans
	Creativity	Level 1	Anonymous input of ideas, pooling and display of ideas; search facilities to identify common ideas, eliminate duplicates
		Level 2	Brainstorming; nominal group technique
Choose	Objective	Level 1	Data access and display; synthesis and display of rationales for choices
		Level 2	Aids to finding the correct answer (e.g., forecasting models, multiattribute utility models)
		Level 3	Rule-based discussion emphasizing thorough explanation of logic
	Preference	Level 1	Preference weighting and ranking with various schemes for determining the most favored alternative; voting schemes
		Level 2	Social judgment models; automated Delphi method
		Level 3	Rule-based discussion emphasizing equal time to present opinion
Negotiate	Cognitive conflict	Level 1	Summary and display of members' opinions
		Level 2	Using social judgment analysis, each member's judgments are analyzed by the system and then used as feedback to the individual member or the group
		Level 3	Automatic mediation; automate Roberts' rules
	Mixed motive	Level 1	Voting solicitation and summary
		Level 2	Stakeholder analysis
		Level 3	Rule base for controlling opinion expression; automatic mediation; automate parliamentary procedure

rules for controlling pattern, timing, and content of information exchange can be imposed on the group (level 3). The higher the level of the GDSS, the more sophisticated the technology and the more dramatic the intervention compared with the natural decision process. Table 6.4 highlights the major tasks of a decision-related meeting, the main activities, the corresponding level of GDSS, and the possible support features.

TEAM PROJECT

Thermal Transfer Plant

TMS management is considering the following aspects in selecting a hydraulic power unit for the rotary combustor:

- Size
- Weight
- Power consumption
- Required maintenance
- Noise
- Cost
- Reliability

The power unit provides power to operate three components of the system: feed rams, resistance door, and combustor. Three design alternatives are available:

1. Electric motor on a gearbox
2. Low-speed, high-torque hydraulic motor with direct drive
3. High-speed, low torque hydraulic motor on a gearbox

Initial data include the following:

	Electromechanical	Low speed, high torque	High speed, low torque
Delivery	90–120 days	1–6 weeks	90–120 days
Overall efficiency	96%	94%	88%
Useful life	20 years	25 years	25 years
Noise level	85 dB	78 dB	100 dB

Using the criteria above as guidance, develop an MAUT and an AHP model for evaluating the three alternatives. It will be necessary to collect data or make assumptions about the values of all of the attributes. For one of the models, perform the analysis with the help of a computer program, and give your recommendation. Be sure to justify and document your results, basing part of your recommendation on a sensitivity analysis.

DISCUSSION QUESTIONS

1. How might you measure the benefits associated with space exploration or a superconducting supercollider for investigating subatomic particles? Can you put a dollar value on these benefits? What are the real costs and opportunity costs of these types of projects?

2. Identify an advanced technology project that you believe should be undertaken, such as bio-electronic computing or coal gasification. Who should be responsible for funding the

project? The government? Industry? A consortium? What are the major attributes or criteria associated with the project?

3. What type of technical background, if any, do you think is needed to understand MAUT? The AHP?

4. You have just completed an MAUT evaluation of a number of data communications systems under consideration by your company. How would you present the results to upper management? Assuming that they know nothing about the technique, how much background would you give them? How would your answer differ if the AHP were used instead?

5. What do you think are the strengths and weaknesses of the AHP and MAUT?

6. How would you go about constructing an objective hierarchy? Who should be consulted? Identify a project from your personal experience or observations, and construct such a hierarchy.

7. When performing an evaluation using any multiple criteria method, from whose perspective should the analysis be undertaken? Would the answer differ if it were a public rather than a private project?

8. What experiences have you had with group decision making? What difficulties do you see arising when trying to perform a multiple-criteria analysis with many interested parties involved? How might these difficulties be overcome, or at least mitigated?

9. Are benefit-cost analysis and multiple-criteria analysis mutually exclusive techniques? In which circumstances is either most appropriate?

10. You just inherited a large sum of money and would like to develop a strategy to invest it. Use the AHP to fashion such a strategy. Construct an objective hierarchy listing all criteria and subcriteria and principal alternatives. What data are needed to perform the evaluation? How would you go about obtaining the data?

11. From a practical point of view, how would you verify the independence assumptions associated with MAUT?

12. Are the axioms underlying the AHP reasonable and unambiguous? In which circumstances do you think one or more of them could be relaxed?

13. Both the AHP and MAUT are value models that facilitate making tradeoffs between incommensurable criteria. Come up with your own value model or procedure for doing this.

14. In conducting a group study using a multiple-criteria method, you reach a point at which two of the participants cannot agree on a particular response. What course of action would you take to placate the parties and avoid further delay?

15. For which type of projects or problems might MAUT be more amenable than the AHP? Similarly, when is the AHP more appropriate than MAUT?

EXERCISES

6.1 Assume that you work for a company that designs and fabricates VLSI chips. You have been given the job of selecting a new computer-aided design software package for the engineering group.

a. Develop a MAUT model to assist in the selection process.
b. Develop an AHP model to assist in the selection process.

In both cases, begin by enumerating the major criteria and the associated subcriteria. Explain your assumptions. Who are the possible decision makers? How do you think the outcome of the analysis would change with each of these decision makers?

6.2 Develop a flow chart detailing input, output, and processes for a software package that supports

    a. MAUT applications
    b. AHP applications

6.3 Using MAUT and the AHP, perform an analysis to select a graduate program. Explain your assumptions, and indicate which technique you believe is most appropriate for this application.

6.4 You are the vice president of planning for Zingtronics, a small-scale manufacturer of IBM-compatible personal computers and peripherals based in Silicon Valley. Business is growing, and the company would like to open a second facility. Three options are being considered: (1) a second plant in Silicon Valley, (2) a new plant in Mexico as a Maquiladora, and (3) a new plant in Singapore. Most of the workforce will be low-skilled assembly and machine operators, but training in the use of computers and information systems will be required. It is also desirable to set up a small design group of engineers for new product and process development.

Of course, each option has its pros and cons. For example, Silicon Valley has a high-skill labor pool but is a very expensive place to do business. Singapore offers the same level of worker skills at lower cost but is distant from the market and headquarters. Mexico is the least expensive place to set up a business, as a result of favorable tax laws and cheap labor, but has a less educated workforce.

Develop two objective hierarchies, one for costs and one for benefits, that can be used to investigate the location problem. Use the AHP to rank the three alternatives on both hierarchies, and then compute the benefit/cost ratios of each. According to your analysis, which alternative is best?

6.5 Referring to Exercise 6.4, combine the two hierarchies into one so that there are no more than eight subobjectives at the bottom level. Define either a quantitative or a qualitative scale for each of these subobjectives, and construct a utility function for each. Use MAUT to evaluate and rank the three alternatives.

6.6 Use the criteria below to construct a two-level objective hierarchy (major criteria with one set of subcriteria under each) to help evaluate political candidates. Consider as alternatives the major candidates running in the last U.S. presidential election, and use the AHP to make your choice.

Criteria for choosing a national political candidate:

- *Charisma:* Personal leadership qualities inspiring enthusiasm and support
- *Glamor:* Charm, allure, personal attractiveness; associations with other attractive people
- *Experience:* Past office holding relevant to the position sought; preparation for the position
- *Economic policy:* Coherence and clarity of a national economic policy
- *Ability to manage international relations*: Coherence and clarity of foreign policy plus ability to deal with foreign leaders
- *Personal integrity:* Quality of moral standards, trustworthiness
- *Past performance:* Quality of role fulfillment—independent of what the role was—in previous public offices; public record
- *Honesty:* Lawfulness in public life, law-abidingness

6.7 Louise Ciccone, head of industrial engineering for a medium-sized metalworking shop, wants to move the CNC machines from their present location to a new area. Three distinct alternatives are under consideration. After inspecting each alternative and determining

TABLE 6.5

Attribute	Alternative			Ideal	Standard	Worst
	Area I	Area II	Area III			
A	500 ft	300 ft	75 ft	0 ft	300 ft	1,000 ft
B	Good	Very good	Good	Excellent	Good	Poor
C	Excellent	Very good	Good	Excellent	Good	Poor
D	$7,500	$3,000	$8,500	$0	$5,000	$10,000
E	60,000 ft^2	85,000 ft^2	25,000 ft^2	10,000 ft^2	25,000 ft^2	150,000 ft^2

which factors reflect significant differences among the three, Louise has decided on five independent attributes to evaluate the candidates. In *descending order of importance*, they are

A. Distance traveled from one machine to the next (more distance is worse)
B. Stability of foundation [strong (excellent) to weak (poor)]
C. Access to loading and unloading [close (excellent) to far (poor)]
D. Cost of moving the machines
E. Storage capacity

(*Note:* Once the machines have been moved, operational costs are independent of the area chosen and hence are the same for each area.) The data associated with these factors for the three alternatives are in Table 6.5.

Using the multiattribute utility methodology, determine which alternative is best. For at least one attribute, state all of the probabilistic tradeoff (lottery-type) questions that must be asked together with answers to obtain at least four utility values between the "best" and "worst" outcomes so that the preference curve can be plotted. For the other attributes, you may make shortcut approximations by determining whether each is concave or convex, upward or downward, and then sketching an appropriate graph for each. Next, ask questions to determine the scaling constants k_i, and compute the scores for the three alternatives. [*Note:* If you follow the recommended procedure for deriving the scaling constants, probably $\Sigma_i k_i \neq 1$, then so you should use the multiplicative model Equation (6.1a). After comparing alternatives by that model, "normalize" the scaling constants so $\Sigma_i k_i = 1$, and then compare the alternatives using the additive model Eq. (6.1b). (It is not theoretically correct to normalize the k_i values to enable use of the additive model.) How much difference does use of the "correct" model make?]

6.8 Starting with the environmental scoring model in Table 5.3, construct an objectives hierarchy that can be used to evaluate capital development and expansion projects being considered by an electric utility company.

6.9 The six major objectives listed below are used by the British Columbia Hydro and Power Authority to evaluate new projects. Use this list to construct an objectives hierarchy by providing subobjectives and their respective attributes where appropriate. Also, estimate the "worst" and "best" levels for all of the factors at the lowest level of the hierarchy.

1. Maximize the contribution to economic development
2. Act consistently with the public's environmental values
3. Minimize detrimental health and safety impacts
4. Promote equitable business arrangements
5. Maximize quality of service
6. Be recognized as public service oriented

TABLE 6.6

| Attribute | Alternative | | |
	Domestic	European	Japanese
Price	$8,100	$12,600	$10,300
Gas mileage	25 mpg	30 mpg	35 mpg
Type of fuel	Gasoline	Diesel	Gasoline
Aesthetic appeal	5 out of 10	7 out of 10	9 out of 10
Passengers	4	6	4
Performance on road	Fair	Very good	Very good
Ease of servicing	Excellent	Very good	Good
Stereo system	Poor	Good	Excellent
Headroom	Excellent	Very good	Poor
Storage space	Very good	Excellent	Poor

6.10 a. Use the three weighting techniques in Section 5.3 to make a selection of one of the three used automobiles for which some data are given in Table 6.6. State your assumptions regarding miles driven each year, life of the automobile (how long *you* would keep it), market (resale) value at end of life, interest cost, price of fuel, cost of annual maintenance, attribute weights, and other subjectively based determinations.

   b. Repeat the analysis using MAUT; that is, construct utility functions and scaling functions for each attribute, and determine the overall utility of each alternative. Does your answer agree with the one obtained in part (a)? Explain why they should (or should not) agree.

6.11 An aspiration level for a criterion or attribute is a level at which the decision maker is satisfied. For example, we all would like our investment portfolio to provide an annual rate of return of 30% or higher, but most of us would happily settle for a return of 5% above the Dow Jones. Develop an interactive multicriteria methodology that is based on aspiration levels of the criteria. Construct a flow chart for the logic and computations. Use your methodology to select one of the alternatives in Exercise 6.10.

BIBLIOGRAPHY

Multiattribute Utility Theory

Bard, J. F. and A. Feinberg, "A Two-Phase Methodology for Technology Selection and System Design," *IEEE Transactions on Engineering Management*, Vol. EM-36, No. 1, pp. 28–36, 1989.

Bell, D. E., R. L. Keeney and H. Raiffa (Editors), *Conflicting Objectives in Decisions*, John Wiley & Sons, New York, 1977.

Dyer, J. S. and R. F. Miles, Jr., "An Actual Application of Collective Choice Theory to the Selection of Trajectories for the Mariner Jupiter/Saturn 1977 Project," *Operations Research*, Vol. 24, pp. 220–244, 1976.

Feinberg, A., R. F. Miles, Jr. and J. H. Smith, *Advanced Vehicle Preference Analysis for Five-Passenger Vehicles with Unrefueled Ranges of 100, 150, and 250 Miles*, JPL D-2225, Jet Propulsion Laboratory, Pasadena, CA, March 1985.

Keefer, D. L., "Allocation Planning for R&D with Uncertainty and Multiple Objectives," *IEEE Transactions on Engineering Management*, Vol. EM-25, No. 1, pp. 8–14, 1978.

Keeney, R. L., "The Art of Assessing Multiattribute Utility Functions," *Organizational Behavior and Human Performance*, Vol. 19, pp. 267–310, 1977.

Keeney, R. L. and H. Raiffa, *Decisions with Multiple Objectives: Preference and Value Tradeoffs*, John Wiley & Sons, New York, 1976.

Keeney, R. L. and D. von Winterfeldt, "Eliciting Probabilities from Experts in Complex Technical Problems," *IEEE Transactions on Engineering Management*, Vol. 38, No. 3, pp. 191–201, 1991.

Shoemaker, P. J. H. and C. C. Waid, "An Experimental Comparison of Different Approaches to Determining Weights in Additive Utility Models," *Management Science*, Vol. 28, No. 2, pp. 182–196, 1982.

Vincke, P., *Multicriteria Decision-Aid*, John Wiley & Sons, New York, 2002.

Analytic Hierarchy Process

Bard, J. F., "Evaluating Space Station Applications of Automation and Robotics," *IEEE Transactions on Engineering Management*, Vol. EM-33, No. 2, pp. 102–111, 1986.

Bard, J. F. and S. F. Sousk, "A Tradeoff Analysis for Rough Terrain Cargo Handlers Using the AHP: An Example of Group Decision Making," *IEEE Transactions on Engineering Management*, Vol. 37, No. 3, pp. 222–227, 1990.

Forman, E. H., T. L. Saaty, M. A. Selly and R. Waldron, *Expert Choice, Decision Support Software*, McLean, VA, 2004 (http://www.expertchoice.com/).

Finan, J. S. and W. J. Hurley, "The Analytic Hierarchy Process: Can Wash Criteria Be Ignored?" *Computers & Operations Research*, Vol. 29, No. 8, pp. 1025–1030, 2002.

Golden, B. L., E. A. Wasil and P. T. Harker (Editors), *The Analytic Hierarchy Process: Applications and Studies*, Springer-Verlag, Berlin, 1989.

Hamalainen, R. P. and J. Mustajoki, *HIPRE 3+ Decision Support Software*, Systems Analysis Laboratory, Helsinki University of Technology, Helsinki, Finland, 2001 (http://www.hipre.hut.fi/).

Libertore, M. J., "An Extension of the Analytic Hierarchy Process for Industrial R&D Project Selection and Resource Allocation," *IEEE Transactions on Engineering Management*, Vol. EM-34, No. 1, pp. 12–18, 1987.

Saaty, T. L., "Axiomatic Foundations of the Analytic Hierarchy Process," *Management Science*, Vol. 32, No. 7, pp. 841–855, 1986.

Saaty, T. L. and L. G. Vargas, *Models, Methods, Concepts & Applications of the Analytic Hierarchy Process*, International Series in Operations Research and Management Science, Volume 34, Kluwer, Boston, 2000.

Shtub, A. and E. M. Dar-El, "A Methodology for the Selection of Assembly Systems," *International Journal of Production Research*, Vol. 27, No. 1, pp. 175–186, 1989.

Wasil, A. E. and B. L. Golden (Editors), "Focused Issue: Analytic Hierarchy Process," *Computers & Operations Research*, Vol. 30, No. 10, 2003.

Group Decision Making

Aczel, J. and C. Alsina, "Synthesizing Judgements: A Functional Equation Approach," *Mathematical Modelling*, Vol. 9, pp. 311–320, 1987.

DeSanctis, G. and Gallupe, R. B., "A Foundation for the Study of Group Decision Support Systems," *Management Science*, Vol. 33, No. 5, pp. 589–609, 1987.

Franz, L. S, G. R. Reeves and J. J. Gonzalez, "Group Decision Processes: MOLP Procedures Facilitating Group and Individual Decision Orientations," *Computers & Operations Research*, Vol. 19, No. 7, pp. 695–706, 1992.

Greenberg, J. and R. A. Baron, *Behavior in Organizations: Understanding and Managing the Human Side of Work*, Eighth Edition, Prentice Hall, Upper Saddle River, NJ, 2003.

Hiltz, S. R. and Turoff, M., "Structuring Computer-Mediated Communication Systems to Avoid Information Overload," *Communications of the ACM*, Vol. 28, No. 7, pp. 680–689, 1985.

Poole, M. S., M. Holmes and G. Desanctis, "Conflict Management in a Computer-Supported Meeting Environment, *Management Science*, Vol. 37, No. 8, pp. 926–953, 1991.

Saaty, T. L., "Group Decision Making and the AHP," in B. L. Golden, E. A. Wasil and P. T. Harker (Editors), *The Analytic Hierarchy Process: Applications and Studies*, Springer-Verlag, Berlin, pp. 59–67, 1989.

Tavana, M., "CROSS: A Multicriteria Group-Decision-Making Model for Evaluating and Prioritizing Advanced-Technology Projects in NASA," *Interfaces*, Vol. 33, No. 3, pp. 40–56, 2003.

Comparison of Methods

Bard, J. F., "A Comparison of the Analytic Hierarchy Process with Multiattribute Utility Theory: A Case Study," *IIE Transactions,* Vol. 24, No. 5, pp. 111–121, 1992.

Belton, V., "A Comparison of the Analytic Hierarchy Process and a Simple Multi-attribute Value Function," *European Journal of Operational Research*, Vol. 26, pp. 7–21, 1986.

Kamenentzky, R. D., "The Relationship between the AHP and the Additive Value Function," *Decision Science*, Vol. 13, pp. 702–713, 1982.

Additional MCDM Techniques

Belton, V. and T. J. Stewart, *Multiple Criteria Decision Analysis: An Integrated Approach*, Kluwer Academic, Dordrecht, The Netherlands, 2001.

Graves, S. B., J. L. Ringuest and J. F. Bard, "Recent Developments in Screening Methods for Nondominated Solutions in Multiobjective Optimization," *Computers & Operations Research*, Vol. 19, No. 7, pp. 683–694, 1992.

Lewandowski, A. and A. P. Wirezbicki (Editors), *Aspiration Decision Support Systems*, Vol. 331, Lecture Notes in Economics and Mathematical Systems, Springer-Verlag, Berlin, 1989.

Lotfi, V., T. J. Stewart and S. Zionts, "An Aspiration-Level Interactive Model for Multiple Criteria Decision Making," *Computers & Operations Research*, Vol. 19, No. 7 pp. 671–681, 1992.

Comparison of Multiattribute Utility Theory with the Analytic Hierarchy Process: Case Study[1]

In this appendix, we present a case study in which the AHP and MAUT are used to evaluate and select the next generation of rough terrain cargo handlers for the U.S. Army. Three alternatives are identified and ultimately ranked using the two methodologies. A major purpose of this study is to demonstrate the strengths and weaknesses of each methodology and to characterize the conditions under which one might be more appropriate than the other.

The evaluation team consisted of five program managers and engineers from the Belvoir Research, Development & Engineering Center. The objective hierarchy used for both techniques contained 12 attributes. In general, the AHP was found to be more accessible and conducive to consensus building. Once the attributes were defined, the decision makers had little difficulty in furnishing the necessary data and discussing the intermediate results. The same could not be said for the MAUT analysis. The need to juggle 12 attributes at a time produced a considerable amount of frustration among the participants. In addition, the lottery questions posed during the data collection phase had an unsettling effect that was never satisfactorily resolved.

[1]The material presented in this appendix has been excerpted from Bard (1992).

6A.1 INTRODUCTION AND BACKGROUND

In an ongoing effort to reduce risk and to boost the productivity of material-handling crews, the Army is investigating the use of robotics to perform many of the dangerous and labor-intensive functions normally undertaken by enlisted personnel. To this end, a number of programs are currently under way at several government facilities. These include the development of a universal self-deployable cargo handler (USDCH) at Belvoir Research, Development & Engineering Center (Belvoir 1987b), the testing of a field material handling robot (FMR) at the Human Engineering Laboratory, and the prototyping of an advanced robotic manipulator system (ARMS) at the Defense Advanced Research Projects Agency (more details are given in Sievers and Gordon 1986, Sousk et al. 1988).

In each of these efforts, technological risk, time, and cost ultimately intervene to limit the scope and performance of the final product, but to what extent and in what manner? To answer these questions, a model that is capable of explicitly addressing the conflicts that arise among system and organizational goals is needed. Such a model must also be able to deal with the subjective nature of the decision-making process. The two approaches examined, the AHP and MAUT, each offer an analytic framework in which the decision maker can conduct tradeoffs among incommensurate criteria without having to rely on a single measure of performance.

6A.2 THE CARGO-HANDLING PROBLEM

Although the Army is generally viewed as a fighting force, the bulk of its activity involves the movement of massive amounts of material and supplies in the field. This is achieved with a massive secondary labor force whose risk exposure is comparable to those engaged in direct combat.

From an operational point of view, cargo must be handled in all types of climates, regions, and environments. At the time of the study, this was accomplished by three different-sized rough-terrain forklifts with maximum lifting capacities of 4,000, 6,000, and 10,000 lbs each. These vehicles are similar in design and performance to those used by industry and, at best, can reach speeds of 20 mph. For the most part, this means that the fleet is not self-deployable (i.e., it cannot keep pace with the convoy on most surfaces). As a consequence, additional transportation resources are required for relocation between job sites. This restriction severely limits the unit's maneuverability and hence its survivability on the battlefield.

A second problem relates to the safety of the crew. Although protective gear is available for the operator, his or her effectiveness is severely hampered by its use. Heat exhaustion, vision impairment, and the requirement for frequent changes are the problems cited most commonly. Logistics units thus lack the ability to provide continuous support in extreme conditions.

6A.2.1 System Objectives

To overcome these deficiencies as well as to improve crew productivity, a heavy-duty cargo-handling forklift is needed. This vehicle should be capable of operating in rough terrain and of traveling over paved roads at speeds in excess of 40 mph. To permit operations in extreme conditions, internal cooling (microcooling) should be provided for the protective gear worn by the operator. As technology progresses, it is desirable that the basic functions be executable without human intervention, implying some degree of autonomy.

At a minimum, then, the vehicle should be

- Able to substitute for the existing 4,000, 6,000, and 10,000 (4K, 6K, 10K)-lb fork-lifts while maintaining current material handling capabilities
- Capable of unaided movement (self-deployability) between job sites at convoy speeds in excess of 40 mph
- Capable of determining whether cargo is contaminated by nuclear, biological, or chemical agents
- Capable of handling cargo in all climates and under all contamination conditions
- Transportable by C-130 and C-141B aircraft
- Operable in the near term as a human-machine system expandable to full autonomy
- Capable of robotic cargo engagement
- Operable remotely from up to 1 mile away

6A.2.2 Possibility of Commercial Procurement

A market survey of commercial forklift manufacturers, including those currently under contract for the 4K-, 6K-, and 10K-lb vehicles, indicates little opportunity for a suitable off-the-shelf buy. With Army needs constituting less than 15% of the overall market, lengthy procurement cycles and uneven demand work to dampen any corporate interest. In the commercial environment, the use of rough-terrain forklifts is limited to construction and logging operations; highway travel and teleoperations have no real applications. Therefore, few, if any, incentives exist for the industry to undertake the research and development (R&D) effort implied by the design requirements to build a prototype vehicle.

6A.2.3 Alternative Approaches

To satisfy the system objectives, then, the existing fleet must either be replaced outright or be substantially overhauled. However, given the low priority of logistics relative to combat needs, a full-scale R&D program is not a realistic option. A more likely approach involves an improvement in the existing system, a modification of a commercial system, or the adaptation of available technology to meet specific requirements. Each of these approaches occasions a different level of risk, cost, and performance that must be evaluated and compared before a final decision can be made. This is the subject of the remainder of the appendix, but first, the leading alternatives are defined.

Taking into account mission objectives and the fact that the Army has functioned with the existing system up until now, the following alternatives have been identified.

This set represents a consensus of the program managers and engineers at Belvoir and the customer at the Quartermaster School:

1. *Baseline:* the existing system comprising the 4K-, 6K-, and 10K-lb rough-terrain forklifts augmented with the new 6K-lb variable-reach vehicle
2. *Upgraded system:* baseline upgraded to be self-deployable
3. *USDCH:* teleoperable, robotic-assisted USDCH with microcooling for the protective gear and the potential for full autonomy

The new 6K-lb variable-reach (telescoping boom) forklift was scheduled to be introduced into the fleet in early 1990. Its performance characteristics, along with those of the USDCH, have been discussed in several reports (Belvoir 1987a, 1987b). Figure 6A.1 depicts a schematic of the robotic-assisted cargo handler. Note that the field material-handling robot and the advanced robotic manipulator system have been omitted from the list above. At this juncture, the primary interest in these systems centers on their robotic capabilities rather than on their virtues as cargo handlers. In fact, almost none of the operational deficiencies mentioned previously would be overcome by either the FMR or the ARMS. Consequently, each was dismissed from further consideration.

6A.3 ANALYTIC HIERARCHY PROCESS

The first step in any multiobjective methodology is to identify the principal criteria to be used in the evaluation. These should be expressed in fairly general terms and be well understood by the study participants. For our problem, the following four criteria were identified: performance, risk, cost, and program objectives. The next step is to add definition by associating a subset of attributes (subcriteria) with each of the above. Figure 6A.2 depicts the resultant objective hierarchy. Risk, for example, has been assigned the following attributes: system integration, technical performance, cost overrun, and schedule overrun. The alternatives are arrayed at the bottom level of the diagram. The connecting lines indicate points of comparison.

In constructing the objective hierarchy, consideration must be given to the level of detail appropriate for the analysis. This is often dictated by the present stage of the development cycle, the amount of data available on each alternative, and the relative importance of criteria and attributes. For example, if human productivity were a major concern, as it is in the space program, then a fifth criterion might have been included at the second level. The inclusion or exclusion of a particular attribute depends on the degree to which its value differs among the alternatives. Although transportability and survivability are important design considerations, all candidates for the cargo-handling mission are expected equally to satisfy basic requirements with respect to these attributes. Consequently, it is not necessary to incorporate them in the model.

To avoid too much detail, aggregation is recommended. This permits overly specific factors to be taken into account implicitly by including them in the attribute definitions. For example, "life-cycle cost" (LCC) could have been further decomposed into unit purchase price, operations and maintenance costs, spare parts, personnel and training, and so on, but at the expense of overtaxing the current database and cost

Figure 6A.1 Universal self-deployable cargo handler.

Communication system

Vehicle vision system

Control station

Vehicle system

Vehicle control electronics

Sensors

Operational vision

Boom and end effect

265

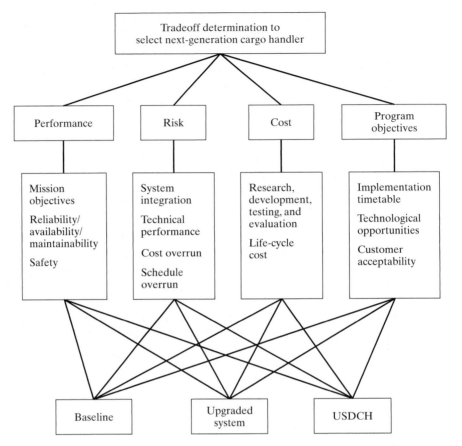

Figure 6A.2   Objective hierarchy for next-generation cargo handler.

accounting system. As a result, these factors were left undifferentiated. Similar reasoning applies to the attribute "reliability/availability/maintainability" (RAM).

6A.3.1 Definition of Attributes

Each of the attributes displayed at level 3 in Fig. 6A.2 is described in more detail below. These descriptions, in the form of instructions, were used by the analyst to elicit responses from the decision makers during the data collection phase of the study.

Performance

1. *Mission objectives.* Compare the alternatives on the basis of how close they come to satisfying mission objectives and requirements. Consideration should be given to such factors as lifting capacity, deployability, productivity improvement, and operation in a nuclear, biological, chemical (NBC) environment.
2. *RAM.* Using military standards for RAM, compare the alternatives relative to the likelihood that each will meet these standards. If possible, take into account

mean-time-between-failures, mean-time-to-repair, and the most probable failure modes.

3. *Safety*. Compare the alternatives on the basis of how well they protect the crew in all climatic conditions and in an NBC environment. Consider the probable degree of hazard exposure, the vehicle response under various driving conditions, and the ability of the crew to work effectively for extended periods.

Risk

4. *System integration*. Compare the effort required to achieve full system integration for the alternatives, taking into account the degree of upgrading and reengineering associated with each.

5. *Technical performance*. Considering the performance goals of each system, evaluate the relative likelihood that these goals will be met within the current constraints of the program. Take into account the Army's experience with similar systems and the state of commercially available technologies.

6. *Cost overrun*. Based on the maturity of the technology and the funding histories of similar programs, compare the alternatives as to whether one is more likely to go over budget than the other.

7. *Schedule overrun*. Based on the maturity of the technology and the development histories of similar programs, compare the alternatives as to whether one is more likely than the other to result in a schedule overrun.

Cost

8. *Research, development, testing, and evaluation (RDT&E)*. Compare the alternatives from the standpoint of which is likely to have the least cost impact during its development cycle. Consideration should be given to each phase of the program before implementation.

9. *LCC*. Compare the total cost of buying, operating, maintaining, and supporting each alternative over its expected lifetime. Exclude RDT&E, but take into account personnel needs, training, and the degree of standardization achieved by each system.

Program Objectives

10. *Implementation timetable*. Compare the alternatives with respect to their individual schedules for implementation. Consider the effect that the respective timetables will have on military readiness.

11. *Technological opportunities*. Compare the alternatives on the basis of what new technologies might result from their development, as well as the likelihood that new applications will be found in other areas. Consideration should be given to the prospect of spinoffs, potential benefits, and the development of long-term knowledge.

12. *Customer acceptability*. Compare the alternatives from both the user representative's and operator's points of view. Take into account the degree to which each alternative satisfies basic objectives, as well as the potential for growth, risk reduction, and the adaptation of new technologies. Also consider secondary or potential uses, operator comfort, and program politics.

6A.3.2 Analytic Hierarchy Process Computations

To illustrate the nature of the calculations, observe Fig. 6A.3, which depicts a three-level hierarchy—an abbreviated version of Fig. 6A.2 used in the analysis. Table 6A.1 contains the input and output data for level 2.

Recall that when n factors are being compared, $n(n-1)/2$ questions are necessary to fill in the matrix. The elements in the lower triangle (omitted here) are simply the reciprocal of those lying above the diagonal; that is, $a_{ji} = 1/a_{ij}$. The entries in the matrix at the center of Table 6A.1 are the responses to the 6 ($n = 4$) pairwise questions that were asked. These responses were drawn from the 9-point scale shown in Table 6.1. For example, in comparing "performance" with "risk" (element a_{12} of the matrix), it was

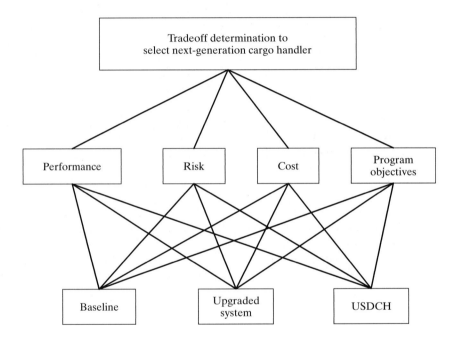

Figure 6A.3   Abbreviated version of the objective hierarchy.

TABLE 6A.1   Priority Vector for Major Criteria

Criteria	Criteria 1	2	3	4	Priority weights	Output parameters
1. Performance	1	5	3	4	0.517	$\lambda_{max} = 4.262$
2. Risk		1	1/6	1/3	0.059	
3. Cost			1	4	0.306	CR = 0.097
4. Program objectives				1	0.118	

judged that the first "strongly" dominated the second. Note that if the elicited value for this element were 1/5 instead of 5, then the opposite would have been true.

From Table 6A.1, it can be seen that the priorities derived for the major criteria were 0.517 for performance, 0.059 for risk, 0.306 for cost, and 0.118 for program objectives. Also note that the consistency ratio (0.097) is a bit high but still within the acceptable range.

The next step in the analysis is to develop the priorities for the factors on the third level with respect to those on the second. In our case, we compare the three alternatives against the major criteria. For the moment, assume that the appropriate data have been elicited and that the calculations have been performed for each of the four comparison matrices, giving the results displayed in Table 6A.2. The first four columns of data are the local priorities derived from the inputs supplied by the decision maker; note that each column sums to 1. The global priorities are found by respectively multiplying these values by the higher-level local priorities given in Table 6A.1 (and repeated at the top of Table 6A.2 for convenience) and then summing. Because there are no more levels left to evaluate, the values contained in the last column of Table 6A.2 represent the final priorities for the problem. Thus, according to the judgments expressed by this decision maker, alternative 3 turns out to be most preferred. Finally, it should be noted that other schemes are available for determining attribute weights.

6A.3.3 Data Collection and Results for AHP

In the formative stages of the study, two questions quickly arose: (1) Who should provide the responses? (2) Whose point of view should be represented? With regard to the first, it was believed that the credibility of the results depended on having a broad spectrum of opinion and expertise as input. Subsequently, five people from Belvoir's Logistics Equipment Directorate with an average of 15 years' experience in systems design, R&D program management, and government procurement practices were assembled to form the evaluation team. After some discussion, it was agreed that the responses should reflect the position of the material developer—the U.S. Army Material Command. Other candidates included the Army as a whole, the customer, and the mechanical equipment division at Belvoir.

At the first meeting, the group was introduced to the AHP methodology and examined the objective hierarchy developed previously by the analyst. Eventually, a consensus grew around the attribute definitions, and each member began to assign values to the individual matrix elements. A bottom-up approach was found to work best. Here

TABLE 6A.2   Local and Global Priorities

Alternatives	Local priorities				Global priorities
	Performance (0.517)	Risk (0.059)	Cost (0.306)	Program objectives (0.118)	
Baseline	0.142	0.704	0.384	0.133	0.248
Upgrade	0.167	0.229	0.317	0.162	0.216
USDCH	0.691	0.067	0.299	0.705	0.536

the alternatives first are compared with respect to each attribute; next, a comparison is made among the attributes with respect to the criteria; and finally, the four criteria at level 2 are compared among themselves. After the data sheets had been filled out for each criterion, individual responses were read aloud to ascertain the level of agreement. In light of the ensuing discussion, the participants were asked to revise their entries to better reflect their renewed understanding of the issues. This phase of the study took approximately 6 hours and was done in two sessions over a 5-day period.

As with the Delphi procedure, the challenge was to come as close to a consensus as possible without coercing any of the team members. Unfortunately, this proved more difficult than expected as a result of the speculative nature of much of the attribute data. In practice, many researchers have found that uniformity within a group rarely can be achieved without stretching the limits of persuasion (Greenberg and Baron 2003). Biases, insecurities, and stubbornness often develop their own constituencies. Although none of these factors was openly present at the meetings, organizational and program concerns were clearly seen to influence individual judgments.

In the extreme, when there is no possibility of reconciling conflicting perceptions, it is best to stratify responses along party lines. In our case, sufficient agreement emerged to permit the averaging of results without obscuring honest differences of opinion. Table 6A.3 highlights individual preferences for the level 2 criteria and for the problem as a whole. The numbers in parentheses represent the local weights computed for the four criteria: performance, risk, cost, and program objectives. Global weights and rankings are given in the last two columns.

Table 6A.4 summarizes the computations for each decision maker and presents two collective measures of comparison: (1) the arithmetic mean and (2) the geometric mean. (Issues surrounding the synthesis of judgments is discussed by Aczel and Alsina 1987.) The latter is obtained by a geometric averaging of the group's individual responses at each point of comparison to form a composite matrix, followed by calculation of the eigenvectors in the usual manner. As can be seen, both methods give virtually identical results and rankings. The strongest preference is shown for the USDCH, closely followed by the baseline. The upgraded system is a distant third.

6A.3.4 Discussion of the Analytic Hierarchy Process and Results

The output in Tables 6A.3 and 6A.4 represents the final judgments of the participants and was obtained only after holding two additional meetings to discuss intermediate results. All participants were given the opportunity to examine the priority weights calculated from their initial responses and to assess the reasonableness of the rankings. When their results seemed counterintuitive, they were encouraged to reevaluate their input data, determine the source of the inconsistency, and make the appropriate changes. The debate that took place during these sessions proved to be extremely helpful in clarifying attribute definitions and surfacing misunderstandings. In a few instances, well-reasoned arguments persuaded some people to reverse their position completely on a particular issue. This was more apt to occur when the advocate was viewed as an expert and was able to furnish the supporting data. Ordinarily, one- or two-point revisions were the rule and had no noticeable effect on the outcome.

TABLE 6A.3   Comparison of Responses Using the AHP

Respondent	Alternative	Local results										Global results	
		Performance		Risk		Cost		Program obj.					
		Weight	Rank	Weight	Rank	Weight	Rank	Weight	Rank			Weight	Rank
1		(0.517)		(0.059)		(0.306)		(0.118)					
	Baseline	0.142	3	0.704	1	0.384	1	0.133	3			0.248	2
	Upgrade	0.167	2	0.229	2	0.317	2	0.162	2			0.216	3
	USDCH	0.691	1	0.067	3	0.229	3	0.705	1			0.536	1
2		(0.553)		(0.218)		(0.147)		(0.082)					
	Baseline	0.144	3	0.497	1	0.432	1	0.202	3			0.268	3
	Upgrade	0.213	2	0.398	2	0.383	2	0.269	2			0.282	2
	USDCH	0.643	1	0.105	3	0.185	3	0.529	1			0.450	1
3		(0.458)		(0.240)		(0.185)		(0.117)					
	Baseline	0.252	3	0.677	1	0.467	1	0.350	2			0.405	1
	Upgrade	0.273	2	0.249	2	0.375	2	0.371	1			0.298	2
	USDCH	0.474	1	0.074	3	0.158	3	0.280	3			0.297	3
4		(0.359)		(0.315)		(0.210)		(0.116)					
	Baseline	0.214	3	0.666	1	0.602	1	0.529	1			0.474	1
	Upgrade	0.263	2	0.266	2	0.313	2	0.313	2			0.280	2
	USDCH	0.524	1	0.068	3	0.085	3	0.158	3			0.246	3
5		(0.469)		(0.252)		(0.194)		(0.085)					
	Baseline	0.184	3	0.655	1	0.565	1	0.176	3			0.376	2
	Upgrade	0.227	2	0.274	2	0.285	2	0.178	2			0.246	3
	USDCH	0.589	1	0.071	3	0.150	3	0.646	1			0.378	1

Looking at the data in Table 6A.3, a great deal of consistency can be seen across the group. In all but one instance, performance is given the highest priority, followed by risk, cost, and program objectives. For the first three criteria, each alternative has the same ordinal ranking; the only differences arise in the case of program objectives. Nevertheless, the real conflict is reflected in the magnitude of the weights. Although some variation is inevitable, it is frustrating to observe the results for "cost." In particular, there is little agreement concerning the extent to which personnel and transportation resource reductions that accompany the USDCH will be offset by increased operations and maintenance expenses or how these factors will affect the LCCs. The third and fourth decision makers were more skeptical than the first two and hence showed a greater preference for the baseline.

The results for "risk" also inform a divergence of opinion. Respondent 1 was most forthright in acknowledging its presence in the USDCH program by assigning it an extremely low weight (0.067) relative to the baseline (0.704). The effect of this assignment was minimal, though, because he judged risk to be considerably less important than the other three criteria. Compare his corresponding weight (0.059) with those derived for respondents 2 through 5 (0.218, 0.240, 0.315, 0.252). From the data in Table 6A.3, it can be seen that the last four decision makers all viewed risk as the second most important criterion. This observation was corroborated indirectly in the utility analysis.

TABLE 6A.4 Summary of Results for the AHP Analysis

	Respondent										Arithmetic mean		Geometric mean	
	1		2		3		4		5					
Alternative	Weight	Rank	Weight	Rank	Weight	Rank	Weight	Rank	Weight	Rank	Weight	Rank	Weight	Rank
Baseline	0.248	2	0.268	3	0.405	1	0.474	1	0.376	2	0.354	2	0.358	2
Upgrade	0.216	3	0.282	2	0.298	2	0.280	2	0.246	3	0.265	3	0.258	3
USDCH	0.536	1	0.450	1	0.297	3	0.246	3	0.378	1	0.381	1	0.383	1

6A.4 MULTIATTRIBUTE UTILITY THEORY

MAUT is a methodology for providing information to the decision maker for comparing and selecting among complex alternatives when uncertainty is present. It similarly calls for the construction of an objective hierarchy as depicted in Fig. 6A.2 but addresses only the bottom two levels.

6A.4.1 Data Collection and Results for Multiattribute Utility Theory

After agreeing on the attributes, the next step in model development is to determine the scaling constants, k_i, and the attribute utility functions, U_i. This is done through a series of questions designed to probe each decision maker's risk attitude over the range of permissible outcomes. Before the interviews can be conducted, though, upper and lower bounds on attribute values must be specified. Table 6A.5 lists the values elicited from respondent 1 for the 12 attributes. Notice that seven of these are measured on a qualitative (ordinal) scale, the meanings of which were made precise at the first group session. Table 6A.6 defines the range of scores for the "mission objectives" attribute and is typical of the 10-point scales used in the analysis.

To determine the scaling constants, the decision maker must specify an indifference probability, p, related to the best $(\mathbf{x}^*)$ and the worst $(\mathbf{x}^0)$ values of the attribute states. The following scenario is posed:

1. Let attribute i be at its best value and the remaining attributes be at their worst values. Call this situation the "reference."

2. Assume that a "gamble" is available such that the "best outcome" occurs with probability p and the "worst outcome" occurs with probability $1 - p$. If you can achieve the "reference" for sure, then for what value of p are you indifferent between the "sure thing" and the "gamble"?

TABLE 6A.5   Attribute Data for Decision Maker 1

No.	Attribute	Scale	Value* A1	A2	A3	Range	Order of importance[†]	Scaling constant
Performance								
1	Mission objective	Ordinal	4	4	8	4–8	1	0.176
2	RAM	Ordinal	6	4	3	3–6	11	0.044
3	Safety	Ordinal	4	4	10	4–10	2	0.162
Risk								
4	System integration	Ordinal	9	7	3	3–7	8	0.059
5	Technical performance	Ordinal	9	7	3	3–9	9	0.059
6	Cost overrun	$M	0	1	5	0–5	12	0.044
7	Schedule overrun	Years	0	2	4	0–4	7	0.059
Cost								
8	RDT&E	$M	0	6	13	0–13	6	0.059
9	LCC	$B	3.0	2.8	2.5	2.5–3.0	4	0.088
Program objectives								
10	Timetable	Years	2	6	8	2–8	10	0.044
11	Technical opportunity	Ordinal	1	2	7	1–7	5	0.074
12	Acceptability	Ordinal	1	3	9	1–9	3	0.132

* A1 = baseline, A2 = upgraded system, A3 = USDCH.

[†] Order of importance for the given *range* of attribute values.

TABLE 6A.6 Scale Used for "Mission Objectives" Attribute

Value	Explanation
10	All mission objectives are satisfied or exceeded, and some additional capabilities are provided. The design is expected to lead to significant improvements in human productivity and military readiness.
8	All basic mission objectives are met, and some improvement in productivity is expected. The design readily permits the incorporation of new technologies when they become available.
6	Minor shortcomings in system performance are evident, but the overall mission objectives will not be compromised. Some improvement in operator efficiency is expected.
4	Not all performance levels are high enough to meet basic mission objectives. However, no more than one major objective (e.g., self-deployability, microcooling) is compromised, and no threat exists to military readiness.
2	An inability to meet one or more major mission objectives exists. With the current design, it is not economically feasible to bring overall performance up to standards.
0	Significant shortcomings exist with respect to the mission objectives. Implementation or continued use could seriously jeopardize military readiness.

The resultant scaling constants for each of the five decision makers are displayed in Table 6A.7 along with the corresponding AHP weights. The former have been normalized to sum to 1 to facilitate the comparison and to permit the use of the additive model Eq. (6.1b). At a superficial level, the group showed a remarkable degree of consistency from one set of responses to the next. (Theoretically speaking, the AHP weights and the MAUT scaling constants measure different phenomena and hence

TABLE 6A.7 Comparison of AHP Weights and MAUT Scaling Constants for the Five Decision Makers

		\multicolumn{10}{c}{Respondent}								
		\multicolumn{2}{c}{1}	\multicolumn{2}{c}{2}	\multicolumn{2}{c}{3}	\multicolumn{2}{c}{4}	\multicolumn{2}{c}{5}
No.	Attribute	AHP	MAUT	AHP	MAUT	AHP	MAUT	AHP	MAUT	AHP	MAUT
\multicolumn{12}{l}{*Performance*}
1	Mission objectives	0.324	0.176	0.341	0.287	0.245	0.199	0.215	0.171	0.293	0.222
2	RAM	0.048	0.044	0.047	0.031	0.092	0.081	0.072	0.105	0.064	0.033
3	Safety	0.145	0.162	0.164	0.144	0.092	0.103	0.072	0.075	0.112	0.098
\multicolumn{12}{l}{*Risk*}
4	System integration	0.006	0.059	0.080	0.061	0.061	0.016	0.021	0.013	0.018	0.031
5	Technical performance	0.018	0.059	0.080	0.085	0.141	0.093	0.203	0.225	0.155	0.182
6	Cost overrun	0.018	0.044	0.037	0.074	0.025	0.097	0.058	0.076	0.048	0.018
7	Schedule overrun	0.018	0.059	0.023	0.023	0.013	0.016	0.033	0.047	0.031	0.018
\multicolumn{12}{l}{*Cost*}
8	RDT&E	0.038	0.059	0.018	0.025	0.023	0.038	0.023	0.013	0.024	0.046
9	Life-cycle cost	0.268	0.088	0.129	0.111	0.162	0.191	0.187	0.170	0.170	0.138
\multicolumn{12}{l}{*Program objectives*}
10	Timetable	0.012	0.044	0.027	0.025	0.066	0.094	0.079	0.032	0.015	0.018
11	Technical opportunity	0.030	0.074	0.027	0.057	0.017	0.021	0.010	0.044	0.045	0.092
12	Acceptability	0.075	0.132	0.027	0.077	0.033	0.051	0.027	0.029	0.025	0.104

cannot be given the same interpretation. In almost all cases, mission objectives, safety, technical performance, and LCC emerged as the dominant concerns. A look at individual values shows some discrepancies, but rankings and orders of magnitude are similar.

The procedure used to assess the utility functions is nearly identical to that used for the scaling constants. Not surprisingly, the respondents evidenced a slight risk aversion for the attribute ranges considered. Further explanation of the methodology is given by Bard and Feinberg (1989).

The computational results for the utility analysis are displayed in Table 6A.8 and are seen to parallel closely those for the AHP. Only decision makers 3 and 5 partially reversed themselves but without consequence; the others maintained the same ordinal rankings. Note again that it would be inappropriate to compare the final AHP priority weights with the final utility values obtained for each alternative (see Belton 1986). The former are measured on a ratio scale and have relative meaning; the latter simply indicate the order of preference.

An examination of the last four columns of Tables 6A.4 and 6A.8 shows that the two methods give the same general results. Here the geometric mean, also known as the Nash bargaining rule, is computed from the five entries in the table. In making comparisons, only the rankings (and not their relative values) should be taken into account.

6A.4.2 Discussion of the Multiattribute Theory and Results

The interview sessions in which the scaling constants and utility functions were assessed took approximately 30 minutes each and were conducted individually while the analyst and decision maker were seated at a terminal. Three difficulties arose immediately. The first related to the probabilistic nature of the questions. None of the respondents could make sense out of the relationship between the posed lotteries and the overall evaluation process. Repeated coaxing was necessary to get them to concentrate on the gambles and to give a deliberate response.

In this regard, it might have been possible to develop more perspective by using a probabilistic rather than a deterministic utility model. This would have required the attribute outcomes to be treated as random variables (which, in fact, they are) and for probability distributions to be elicited for each. It was believed, however, that this additional burden would have strained the patience and understanding of the group without producing credible results. It was difficult enough to collect the basic attribute data on each alternative without having to estimate probability distributions.

The second issue centered on the assessment of the scaling constants. Here the decision makers were asked to balance best and worst outcomes for 12 attributes at a time. This turned out to be nearly impossible to do with any degree of accuracy and created a considerable amount of tension. The problem was compounded by the fact that in most instances, the group believed that a low score on any one of the principal attributes, such as mission objectives or safety, would kill the program. This produced an unflagging reluctance to accept the sure thing unless the gamble was extremely unfavorable. Because most people are unable to deal intelligently with low-probability events, this called into question, at least in our minds, the validity of the accompanying results.

The third concern relates to the use of ordinal scales to gauge attribute outcomes. Although time and cost have a common frame of reference, ordinal scales generally

TABLE 6A.8 Summary of Results for MAUT Analysis

| Alternative | Respondent | | | | | | | | | | Arithmetic mean | | Geometric mean | |
| | 1 | | 2 | | 3 | | 4 | | 5 | | | | | |
	Weight	Rank	Weight	Rank	Weight	Rank	Weight	Rank	Weight	Rank	Weight	Rank	Weight	Rank
Baseline	0.302	2	0.299	3	0.481	1	0.539	1	0.482	1	0.421	2	0.408	2
Upgrade	0.273	3	0.328	2	0.261	3	0.426	2	0.378	3	0.333	3	0.327	3
USDCH	0.595	1	0.567	1	0.337	2	0.273	3	0.432	2	0.441	1	0.422	1

defy intuition. This was the case here. None of the respondents felt comfortable with this part of the interview, even when they were willing to accept the overall methodology.

6A.5 ADDITIONAL OBSERVATIONS

The level of abstraction surrounding the use of MAUT strongly suggests that the AHP is more acceptable to decision makers who lack familiarity with either method. For problems characterized by a large number of attributes, most of whose outcomes can be measured only on a subjective scale, the AHP once again seems best. When the data are more quantifiable, the major attributes are few, and the alternatives are well understood, MAUT may be the better choice.

This is not to say that the AHP does not have its drawbacks. The most serious relates to the definition and use of the nine-point ratio scale. At some point in the analysis, each of the decision makers found it difficult to reconcile that by expressing a "weak" preference for one alternative over another, they were saying that they preferred it by a factor of 3:1. Although this might have seemed reasonable in some instances, in others, they believed that a score of 2 was equivalent to showing a "strong" preference. Perhaps this problem could be alleviated by the use of a logarithmic scale.

From the standpoint of consensus building, the AHP methodology provides an accessible data format and a logical means of synthesizing judgment. The consequences of individual responses are easily traced through the computations and can quickly be revised when the situation warrants. In contrast, the MAUT methodology hides the implications of the input data until the final calculations. This makes intermediate discussions difficult because no single point of focus exists. Sensitivity analysis offers a partial solution to this problem but in a backward manner that undercuts its theoretical rigor.

As a final observation, we note that the enthusiasm and degree of urgency that the participants brought to the study varied directly with their involvement in the program. Those with vested interests were eager to grasp the methodologies and were quick to respond to requests for data. The remainder viewed each new request as a frustrating and unnecessary ordeal that was best dealt with through passive resistance.

6A.6 CONCLUSIONS FOR THE CASE STUDY

The collective results of the analysis indicated that the group had a modest preference for the USDCH over the baseline. The tradeoff between risk and performance for the upgraded system did not seem favorable enough to make it a serious contender for the cargo-handling mission. We therefore recommended that work continue on the development of the basic USDCH technologies, including self-deployability and robotic cargo engagement, to demonstrate the underlying principles. If more supportive data are needed, then the place to start would be with a full-scale investigation of LCCs and some of the more quantifiable performance measures, such as reliability. The effort required to gather these statistics would be considerable, though, and does not seem justified in light of the overall findings.

In summary, the group believed that the idea of imposing new technologies on an existing system would probably increase its LCC without achieving the desired capabilities.

The extensive improvements in performance ultimately sought could best be realized through a structured R&D program that fully exploited technological advances and innovative thinking in design. Such an approach would significantly reduce risk while permitting full systems integration. In fact, this is the approach now being pursued.

REFERENCES

Bard, J. F., "A Comparison of the Analytic Hierarchy Process with Multiattribute Utility Theory: A Case Study," *IIE Transactions,* Vol. 24, No. 5, pp. 111–121, 1992.

Belvoir RD&E Center, *Test and Evaluation Master Plan for the Variable Reach Rough Terrain Forklift*, U.S. Army Troop Support Command, Logistics Equipment Directorate, Fort Belvoir, VA, 1987a.

Belvoir RD&E Center, *Universal Self-Deployable Cargo Handler*, Contract DAAK-70-87-C-0052, U.S. Army Troop Support Command, Fort Belvoir, VA, Sept. 25, 1987b.

Sievers, R. H. and B. A. Gordon, *Applications of Automation Technology to Field Material Handling*, SAIC-86/1987, Science Applications International Corporation, McLean, VA, December 1986.

Sousk, S. F., H. L. Keller and M. C. Locke, *Science and Technology for Cargo Handling in the Unstructured Field Environment,* U.S. Army Belvoir RD&E Center, Logistics Equipment Directorate, Fort Belvoir, VA, 1988.

Chapter 7

Scope and Organizational Structure of a Project

7.1 INTRODUCTION

Project management deals with one-time efforts to achieve a specific goal within a given set of resource and budget constraints. It is essential to use a project organization when the work content is too large to be accomplished by a single person. The fundamentals of project management involve the identification of all work required to be performed, the allocation of work to the participating units at the planning stage, the continuous integration of output through the execution stage, and the introduction of required changes throughout the project life cycle. How the efforts of the participants are coordinated to accomplish their assigned tasks and how the final assembly of their work is achieved on time and within budget are as much an art as they are a science. Adequate technical skills and the availability of resources are necessary but rarely sufficient to guarantee project success. There is a need for coordinated teamwork and leadership—the essence of sound project management.

Three types of "structures" are involved in the overall process. Each is derived from the project scope. They include (1) the work breakdown structure (WBS), which defines the way the work content is divided into small, manageable work packages that can be allocated to the participating units; (2) the organizational structure of each unit participating in the project (the client, the prime contractor, subcontractors, and perhaps one or more government agencies); and (3) the organizational breakdown structure (OBS) of the project itself, which specifies the relationship between the organizations and people doing the work.

Organizations set up management structures to facilitate the achievement of their overall mission as defined in both strategic and tactical terms. In so doing, compromise is needed to balance short-term objectives with long-term goals. As a practical matter, the project manager has very little say in the final design of the organization or in any restructuring that might occur from time to time. Organizations may be involved in many activities and cannot be expected to reorient themselves with each new project. Nevertheless, both the project OBS and the WBS should be designed to achieve the project's objectives and therefore should be directly under project management control. The thoughtful design and implementation of these structures are critical because of their effect on project success.

The design of a project organizational structure is among the early tasks of the project manager. In performing this task, issues of authority, responsibility, and communications should be addressed. The project organizational structure should fit the nature of the project, the nature of the participating organizations, and the environment in which the project will be performed. For example, the transportation of U.S. forces to remove Saadam from Iraq in 2003 required a project organization that was capable of coordinating logistical activities across three continents (North America, Europe, and the Arab Peninsula). The authority to decide which forces to transport, when, and by what means, as well as the channels through which such decisions were communicated, had to be defined by the project organizational structure. The participating parties were many, including all branches of the U.S. armed services and countries such as England, Australia, and Turkey that were involved in one way or another. To facilitate coordination among these parties, a well-structured project organization with clear definitions of authority, responsibility, and communication channels was needed.

The issue of scope underlies the execution of every project. Scope management includes the processes required to ensure that only the work necessary to complete the project successfully is identified. It is the project manager's responsibility to inform and update the scope at each stage of a project, starting with the initiation phase, continuing with the introduction of change requests, and ending with the acceptance of the final deliverables. The work content of the project, referred to in shorthand as the WBS, can usually be structured in a variety of ways. For example, if the project is aimed at developing a new commercial aircraft, then the WBS can be structured around the main systems, including the body, wings, engines, avionics, and controls. Alternatively, it can be broken down according to the life-cycle phases of the project; that is, design, procurement, execution, testing, and so on. The first critical step after a project is approved is the design of the WBS by the project manager. The "best" WBS structure is a function of the work content and the organizational structure used to perform the required tasks. To reach an optimal design, the project manager needs to know what types of structures are common, their strengths and weaknesses, and under what conditions each structure is most effective. These issues are taken up in the remainder of the chapter.

7.2 ORGANIZATIONAL STRUCTURES

Projects are performed by organizations using human, capital, and other resources to achieve a specific goal. Many projects cut across organizational lines, so to understand the organizational structure of a project, it first is necessary to understand the general nature of organizations.

Theorists have devised various ways of partitioning an organization into subunits to improve efficiency and to decentralize authority, responsibility, and accountability. The mechanism through which this is accomplished is called *departmentalization*. In all cases, the objective is to arrive at an orderly arrangement of the interdependent components. Departmentalization is integral to the delegation process. Examples include:

1. *Functional.* The organizational units are based on distinct common specialties, such as manufacturing, engineering, and finance.
2. *Product.* Distinct units are organized around and given responsibility for a major product or product line.
3. *Customer.* Organizational units are formed to deal explicitly with a single customer group, such as the Department of Defense.
4. *Territorial.* Management and staff are located in units defined along geographical lines, such as a southern U.S. sales zone.
5. *Process.* Human and other resources are organized around the flow of work, such as in an oil refinery.

Thus, organizations may be structured in different ways based on functional similarity, types of processes used, product characteristics, customers served, and territorial considerations.

7.2.1 Functional Organization

Perhaps the most widespread organizational structure found in industry is designed around the technical and business functions performed by the organization. This structure derives from the assumption that each unit should specialize in a specific functional area and perform all of the tasks that require its expertise. Common functional organizational units are engineering, manufacturing, information systems, finance, and marketing. The engineering department is responsible for such activities as product and process design, whereas marketing is responsible for advertising, sales, etc. The division of labor is based on the function performed, not on the specific process or product. Figure 7.1 depicts a typical functional structure.

When the similarity of processes is used as a basis for the organizational structure, departments such as metal cutting, painting, and assembly are common in manufacturing, and departments such as new policy development, claim processing, and information systems are common in the service sector. When similar processes are performed by the same organizational elements, capital investment is minimized and expertise is built through repetition within the particular group.

The problems that arise in the functional organization revolve around the fact that there is no strong central authority that worries about the details of each project. Major decisions relating to resource allocation and budgets are seldom based on what is best for a particular project but rather on how they affect the strongest functional unit. In addition, considerable time is spent in evaluating alternative courses of action, because each project decision requires coordination and approval of all functional groups, in addition to upper management. Finally, there is no single point of contact for the customer.

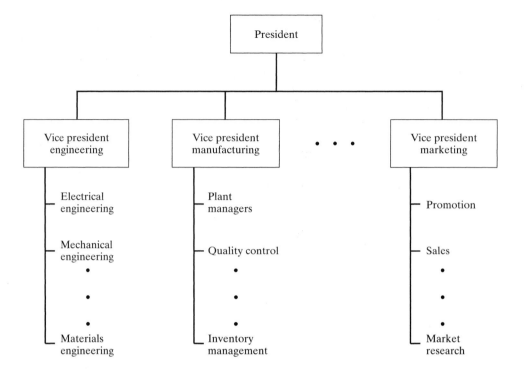

Figure 7.1 Portion of a typical functional organization.

Despite these limitations, the functional organization offers the most fundamental and stabilizing arrangement for large concerns, be they electronic manufacturers, brokerage houses, or research laboratories. Advantages and disadvantages are as follows:

Advantages

Efficient use of collective experience and facilities

Institutional framework for planning and control

All activities receive benefits from the most advanced technology

Allocates resources in anticipation of future business

Effective use of production elements

Career continuity and growth for personnel

Well suited for mass production of items

Disadvantages

No central project authority

Little or no project planning and reporting

Weak interface with customer

Poor horizontal communications across functions

Difficult to integrate multidisciplinary tasks

Tendency of decisions to favor strongest functional group

7.2.2 Project Organization

In this type of structure, each project is assigned to a single organizational unit and the various functions, such as engineering and finance, are performed by personnel within the unit. This results in a significant duplication of resources. Because similar activities and processes are performed by different organizational elements on any particular project there could be a widespread disparity in methods and results. Another disadvantage that can be attributed to the limited life span of projects is that work assignments and reporting hierarchies are subject to continuous change. This can have a detrimental effect on career paths and professional growth.

Figure 7.2 depicts the project-oriented organizational structure. As can be seen, functional units are duplicated across projects. These units are coordinated indirectly by the corresponding central functional unit, but the degree of coordination may vary sharply. The higher the level of coordination, the closer the organizational structure is to a pure functionally oriented structure. Low levels of coordination represent organizational structures closer to the project-oriented structure. For example, consider an

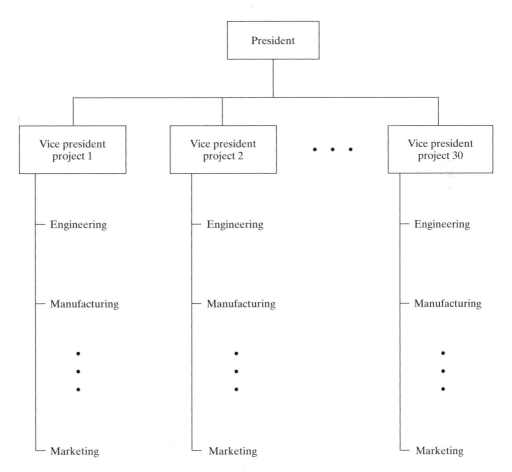

Figure 7.2   Project-oriented organizational structure.

organization that has to select a new CAD/CAM (computer-aided design/computer-aided manufacturing) system. In a functional organization, the engineering department might have the responsibility of selecting the most appropriate system. In a project-oriented organization, each engineering group will select the system that fits its needs best. If, however, it is desirable to achieve commonality and have all engineering groups use the same system, then the central engineering department will have to solicit input from the various groups and, on the basis of this input, make a decision that balances the concerns of each. The characteristics of a fully "projectized" organization are highlighted below.

Advantages

Strong control by a single project authority

Rapid reaction time

Encourages performance, schedule, and cost tradeoffs

Personnel loyal to a single project

Interfaces well with outside units

Good interface with customer

Disadvantages

Inefficient use of resources

Does not develop technology with an eye on the future

Does not prepare for future business

Less opportunity for technical interchange among projects

Minimal career continuity for project personnel

Difficulty in balancing workloads, as projects phase in and out

In addition to the functional organization and project organization, the following structures are also common.

7.2.3 Product Organization

In a mass production environment where large volumes are the norm, such as in consumer electronics or chemical processing, the organizational structure may be based on the similarity among products. An organization specializing in domestic appliances, for example, may have a refrigerator division, washing machine division, and small appliances division. This structure facilitates the use of common resources, marketing channels, and subassemblies for similar products. By exploiting commonality, it is possible for mixed model lines and group technology cells handling a family of similar products, to achieve performance that rivals the efficiency of dedicated facilities designed for a unique product.

7.2.4 Customer Organization

Some organizations have a few large customers. This is frequently the case in the defense industry, where contractors deal primarily with one branch of the service. By structuring the contractor's organization around its principal client, it is much easier to establish good working relationships. In many such organizations, as exemplified by consulting firms and architecture and engineering firms, there is a tendency to hire veteran employees from the customer's organization to smooth communications and exploit personal friendships.

7.2.5 Territorial Organization

Organizational structures can be based on territorial considerations, too. Service organizations that have to be located close to the customer tend to be structured along geographical lines. With the push toward reduced inventories and just-in-time delivery, large manufacturers are encouraging their suppliers to set up plants, or warehouses, in the neighborhood of the main facility. The same rationale applies to advertising agencies that need to be in close contact with specific market segments, although this need continues to shrink with the widespread use of both the Internet and video conferencing.

7.2.6 The Matrix Organization

A hybrid structure known as the matrix organization provides a sound basis for balancing the use of human resources and skills, as workers are shifted from one project to another. The matrix organization can be viewed as a project organization superimposed on a functional organization, with well-defined interfaces between project teams and functional elements. In the matrix organization, duplication of functional units is eliminated by assigning specific resources of each functional unit to each project. Figure 7.3 depicts an organization that is performing several projects concurrently. Each project has a manager who must secure the required skills and resources from the functional groups. Technical support, for example, is obtained from the engineering department, and the marketing department provides sales estimates. The project manager's request for support is handled by the appropriate functional manager who assigns resources on the basis of their availability, the project's need, and the project's priority as compared with other projects. Project managers and functional managers must act as partners to coordinate operations and the use of resources. It is the project manager, though, who is ultimately responsible for the success or failure of the project. Important advantages of the matrix organization are

1. *Better utilization of resources.* Because the functional manager assigns resources to all projects, he or she can allocate resources in the most efficient manner. The limited life span of projects does not reduce utilization of resources, because they can be reassigned to other projects and tasks as the need arises.
2. *State-of-the-art technology.* The knowledge gained from various projects is accumulated at the functional level. The most sophisticated projects are sources of new technology and skills that can be transferred to other projects and activities performed by the organization. Therefore, the functional departments become knowledge centers.
3. *Adaptation to changing environment.* The matrix organization can adapt to changing conditions, including the arrival of new competition in the market, the termination of existing projects, and the realignment of suppliers and subcontractors. The functional skeleton is not affected by such changes, and resources can be

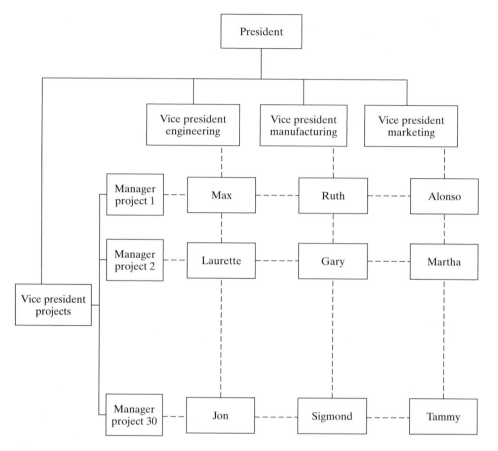

Figure 7.3 Typical matrix structure.

reallocated and rescheduled as needed. No loss of knowledge is experienced when projects terminate, because the experts are kept within the functional units.

The matrix organization benefits from having focused effort in both the functional and the project dimensions. However, this advantage may be offset by several potential difficulties.

1. *Authority*. Whereas the resources are under the control of the functional manager in the long run, they perform day-to-day work for the project, which may lead the project manager to the belief that he or she can instruct them. In a matrix organization, this can lead to a conflict of interest and to a "dual boss" phenomenon.

2. *Technical knowledge*. The project manager is not an expert in all technical aspects of a project. He or she has to rely on the functional experts and the functional managers for their inputs but, once again, must take responsibility for the overall outcome.

3. *Communications.* Workers have to report to their functional manager and to the project manager for whom they perform specific tasks. Double reporting and simultaneous horizontal/vertical communication channels are difficult to develop, manage, and maintain.

4. *Goals.* The project manager tends to see the short-term objectives of the project most clearly, whereas the functional manager typically focuses on the longer-term goals, such as accumulation of knowledge and the acquisition and efficient use of resources. These different perspectives frequently conflict and create friction within an organization.

The design and operation of a matrix organization are complicated, time-consuming tasks. A well-conceived and well-managed structure is necessary if the impact of the problems listed above is to be minimized.

In general, each project and functional unit has a set of objectives that must be balanced against a set of mutually agreed-on performance measures. This balance depends on the weight given to each objective and is an important determinant in selecting the organizational structure. For example, if the successful completion of projects on time and within budget is considered most important, then the matrix organization will be more project oriented. In the case in which functional goals are emphasized, the matrix organization can be designed to be functionally oriented.

The orientation of a matrix organization can be measured to some degree by the percentage of workers who are fully committed to single projects. If this number is 100%, then the organization has a perfect project-oriented structure. If none are fully committed, then the organization has a functional structure. A range of matrix organizations can be defined between these two extremes as depicted in Fig. 7.4. In this figure, functional organizations are located on the left-hand side, and project-oriented organizations are on the right. Those in between are hybrids of varying degree. An organizational

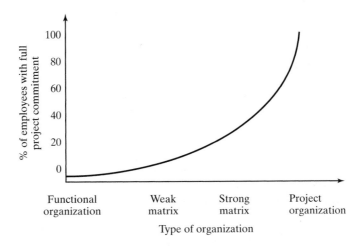

Figure 7.4   Level of employee commitment as a function of organizational structure.

structure that is based on one part-time person managing each project while everyone else is a member of a functional unit represents a very weak matrix structure with a strong functional orientation. Conversely, if the common arrangement is project teams with only a few shared experts among them, then we have a matrix organization with a strong project orientation, sometimes called a "strong matrix" structure.

In summary, the principal advantages and disadvantages of the matrix organization are

Advantages

Effective accumulation of know-how

Effective use of resources

Good interface with outside contacts

Ability to use multidisciplinary teams

Career continuity and professional growth

Perpetuates technology

Disadvantages

Dual accountability of personnel

Conflicts between project and functional managers

Profit-and-loss accountability difficult

7.2.7 Criteria for Selecting an Organizational Structure

The decision to adopt a specific organizational structure is based on several criteria, as discussed below.

1. *Technology.* A functional organization and a process-oriented organization have one focal point for each type of technology. The knowledge gained in all operations, projects, and products is accumulated at that focal point and is available to the entire organization. Furthermore, experts in different areas can be used efficiently because they, too, are a resource available to the whole organization.

2. *Finance and accounting.* These functions are easier to perform in a functional organization, where the budgeting process is controlled by one organizational element that is capable of understanding the "whole picture." Such an entity is in the best position to develop a budget that integrates the organizational goals within individual project objectives.

3. *Communications.* The functional organization has clear lines of communication that follow the organizational structure. Instructions flow from the top down, whereas progress reports are directed over the same channels from the bottom up. The functional organization provides a clear definition of responsibility and authority and thus minimizes ambiguity in communications.

   Product-, process-, or project-oriented structures have vertical as well as horizontal lines of communication. In many cases, communication between units that are responsible for the same function on different projects, processes, or product lines might not be well defined. The organizational structure itself is subject to frequent changes as new projects or products are introduced, existing projects are terminated, or obsolete lines are discontinued. These changes affect the flow of information and cause communications problems.

4. *Responsibility to a project/product.* The product- or project-oriented organization removes any ambiguity over who has responsibility for each product manufactured or project performed. The project manager has complete control over all resources allocated to the project, along with the authority to use those resources as he or she sees fit. The one-to-one relationship between an organizational element and a project or product eliminates the need for coordination of effort and communication across organizational units and thus makes management easier and more efficient.

5. *Coordination.* As mentioned, the project/product-oriented structure reduces the need for coordination of activities related to the project or product; however, more coordination is required between organizational units that perform the same function on different products.

6. *Customer relations.* The project/product-oriented organization provides the customer with a single point of contact. Any need for service, documentation, or support can be handled by the same organizational unit. Accordingly, this structure supports better communications and frequently better service for the customer, compared with the functional structure. Its performance closely approximates that of a pure customer-oriented organizational structure.

This partial list demonstrates that there is no single structure that is optimal for all organizations, in all situations. Therefore, each organization must analyze its own operations and select the structure that best fits its needs, be it functional, process oriented, customer oriented, project/product oriented, or a combination thereof.

7.3 ORGANIZATIONAL BREAKDOWN STRUCTURE OF PROJECTS

The OBS should be designed as early as possible in the project's life cycle. An unambiguous definition of communication channels, responsibilities, and the authority of each participating unit is a key element that affects project success. The most appropriate structure depends on the nature of the project, on the environment in which the work is performed, and on the structure of the participating organizations. For example, if a computer company believes that the development of a lighter laptop is crucial to maintaining its market share, then it is likely that either a project structure or a strong matrix structure would be used for this purpose. In these structures, team members report directly to the project manager and, as a result, are able to maintain a strong identification with the project, thus increasing the probability that the project will be completed successfully.

In most projects, it is not enough to adopt the organizational structure of the prime contractor. At a minimum, both the client and the contractor organizations must be considered. The client organization usually initiates the project by defining its specific needs, whereas the contractor is responsible for developing the plan to satisfy those needs. The two may be elements of the same organization (e.g., an engineering department that develops a new product "for" the marketing department), or they may be unrelated (e.g., a contractor for the National Aeronautics and Space Administration). In either case, the relationship between these organizations is defined by the project organizational structure. This definition should specify the responsibility of each party; the client's responsibility to supply information or components for the project, such as government-furnished equipment; and the contractor's responsibility to perform certain tasks, to provide progress reports, to consult periodically with the client, and so on.

7.3.1 Factors in Selecting a Structure

The primary factors that should be taken into consideration when selecting an organizational structure for managing projects are as follows.

1. *Number of projects and their relative importance.* Most organizations are involved in projects. Common examples are the installation of a new enterprise resource planning system, the integration of a new acquisition into the company structure, or the cultivation of a new market. If an organization is dealing with projects only infrequently, then a functional structure supported by ad hoc project coordinators may be best. As the number of projects increases and their relative importance (measured by the budget of all projects as a percentage of the organizational budget, or any other method) increases, the organizational structure should adapt by moving to a matrix structure with a stronger project orientation.

2. *Level of uncertainty in projects.* Projects may be subject to different levels of uncertainty that affect cost, schedule, and performance. To handle uncertainty, a feedback control system is used to detect deviations from original plans and to detect trends that might lead to future deviations. It is easier to achieve tight control and to react faster to the effects of uncertainty when each project manager controls all of the resources used in the project and gets all of the information regarding actual performance directly from those who are actively involved. Therefore, a project-oriented structure is preferred when high levels of uncertainty are presented.

3. *Type of technology used.* When a project is based on a number of different technologies and the effort required in each area does not justify a continuous effort throughout the project life cycle, the matrix organization is preferred. When projects are based on several technologies and the work content in each area is sufficient to employ at least one full-time person, then a strong matrix or a project-oriented structure is preferred.

    Research and development projects in which new technologies or processes are developed are subject to high levels of uncertainty. The uncertainty is expressed through parameters such as task completion times, the likelihood of a contemplated breakthrough, or simply the chances that the project's components can be integrated successfully. Therefore, to struggle better with this high uncertainty, stronger commitment for the project is needed, calling for the use of a project-oriented structure.

4. *Project complexity.* High complexity that requires very good coordination among the project team is best handled in a project-oriented structure. Here communication is most rapid and unobstructed. Low-complexity projects can be handled

effectively in a functional organization or a matrix arrangement with a functional orientation.

5. *Duration of projects.* Short projects do not justify a dedicated project organization and are best handled within the matrix organization. Long projects that span many months or years justify a project-oriented structure.

6. *Resources used by projects.* When common resources are shared by two or more projects, the matrix arrangement with a functional orientation tends to be best. This is the case when expensive resources are used or when each project does not need a fully devoted unit of a resource. If the number of common resources among projects is small, then the project-oriented structure is preferred.

7. *Overhead cost.* By sharing facilities and services among projects, the overhead cost of each project is reduced. A matrix organization should be preferred when an effort to reduce overhead cost is required.

8. *Data requirements.* If many projects have to share the same databases and it is desirable to make available as quickly as possible the information generated by a set of projects to other elements in the organization not directly involved in these projects, then a weak matrix structure is preferred.

In addition to the above factors, the organizational structures of the client and the contractor must be taken into account. If both have a functional orientation, then direct communication between similar functions in the two organizations might be best. If both are project/product oriented, then an arrangement that supports direct communication links between project managers in their respective organizations would be most efficient.

The situation is complicated when the contractor and the client do not have similar organizational structures or when there are several participating units. If the organizational structure of the contractor is functionally oriented, then the client project manager may have to deal simultaneously with many departments as well as a host of subcontractors, government agencies, and private consultants.

7.3.2 The Project Manager

The success of a project is highly correlated with the qualities and skills of the project manager. In particular, a project manager must be capable of dealing with a wide range of issues that include refining and promoting project objectives, translating those objectives into plans, and obtaining the required resources to execute each phase of the project. On a day-to-day basis, he or she must cope with issues related to budgeting, scheduling, and procurement. He or she must also be able to minister to the needs and expectations of the stakeholders, whether they be the customer, a subcontractor, or a government agency. It is often the case that the project manager has most of the responsibilities of a general manager but almost none of the authority.

In Section 1.4.2, we highlighted some of the important attributes that a project manager should have if he or she is to grapple successfully with the above issues. These attributes are now discussed in detail.

Leadership. The most essential attribute of a project manager is leadership. The project manager has to lead the project team through each phase of its life cycle, dealing swiftly and conclusively with any number of problems as they arise along the way.

This is made all the more difficult given that the project manager usually lacks full control and authority over the participants. His or her ability to guide the project team smoothly from one stage to the next depends on the person's stature; temperament; skills of persuasion, and the degree of commitment, self-confidence, and technical knowledge. A manager who possesses these characteristics in some measure is more likely to be successful even when his or her formal authority is limited.

Interpersonal Skills.   The project manager (as any manager) has to achieve a given set of goals through other people. The manager must deal with his or her own superiors, the members of the project team, the functional managers, and perhaps, an array of clients. In addition, the manager frequently must interact with representatives from other organizations, including subcontractors, laboratories, and government agencies. To achieve the goals of the project, the ability to develop and maintain good personal relationships with all parties is crucial.

Communication Skills.   The interaction between groups involved in a project and the project manager takes place through a combination of verbal and written communications. The project manager must be kept abreast of progress and be able to transmit directions in a succinct and unambiguous manner. By building reliable communication channels and by using the best channel for each application, the project manager can achieve a fast, accurate response from the team with some degree of confidence that his or her directions will be carried out correctly. The more up to date and comprehensive the information, the smoother the implementation route will be.

Decision-Making Skills.   The project manager has to establish procedures for documenting and dealing with problems as they arise. Once the source and the nature of a problem are identified, the manager must evaluate alternative solutions, select the best corrective action, and ensure that it is implemented. These are the fundamental steps in project control.

In some instances, the project manager gets involved early enough to participate in discussions regarding the organizational structure of the project and the choice of technology to be used. An understanding of the basic technical issues gives the project manager the credibility needed to influence resource allocation, budget, and schedule decisions before they are finalized. His or her input on these matters in the initial stages increases the probability that the project will get started in the right direction.

Negotiation and Conflict Resolution.   Many of the problems that the project manager faces do not have a "best solution," for example, when a conflict of interest exists between the project manager and the client over a contract issue contingent on various interpretations. There are many sources of conflict, including

Scheduling	Disagreements that develop around the timing, sequencing, and duration of projects and feasibility of schedule for project-related tasks or activities.
Managerial and administrative procedures	Disagreements that develop over how the project will be managed: the definition of reporting relationships and responsibilities, interface relationships, project scope, work design, plans of execution, negotiated work agreements with other groups, and procedures for administrative support.

Communication	Disagreements resulting from poor information flow among staff or between senior management and technical staff, including such topics as misunderstanding of project-related goals, the strategic mission of the organization, and the flow of communication from technical staff to senior management.
Goal or priority	Disagreements arising from lack of goals or poorly defined project goals, including disagreements regarding the project mission and related tasks, differing views of project participants over the importance of activities and tasks, or the shifting of priorities by superiors/customers.
Resource allocation	Disagreements resulting from the competition for resources (e.g., personnel, materials, facilities, equipment) among project members or across teams or from lack of resources or downsizing of organizations.
Reward structure/ performance appraisal	Disagreements that originate from differences in understanding the reward structure or from the insufficient match between the project team approach and the performance appraisal system.
Personality and interpersonal relations	Disagreements that focus on interpersonal differences rather than "technical" issues; includes conflicts that are ego-centered, personality differences, or conflicts caused by prejudice or stereo typing.
Costs	Disagreements that arise from the lack of cost control authority within the project office or with a functional group. Disagreements related to the allocation of funds.
Technical opinion	Disagreements that arise, particularly in technology-oriented projects, over technical issues, performance specifications, technical tradeoffs, and the means to achieve performance.
Politics	Disagreements that center on issues of territorial power (not-invented-here attitudes) or hidden agendas.
Poor input or direction from leaders	Disagreements that arise from a need for clarification from upper management on project-related goals and the strategic mission of the organization.
Ambiguous roles/structure	Disagreements, especially in the matrix structure, in which two or more people or sections have related or overlapping assignments or roles.

Tradeoff Analysis Skills.   Because most projects have multidimensional goals (e.g., performance, schedule, budget), the project manager often has to perform tradeoff analyses to reach a compromise solution. Questions such as, "Should the project be delayed if extra time is required to achieve the performance levels specified?" or, "Should more resources be acquired at the risk of a cost overrun to reduce a schedule delay?" are common and must be resolved by trading off one objective for another.

In addition to these skills and attributes, a successful project manager will embody good organizational skills, the ability to manage time effectively, a degree of open mindedness, and loyalty to his or her charge. The correct selection of the project manager and the project organizational structure are two important decisions that are made early in the life cycle of a project and have a lasting impact.

A major difficulty that a project manager faces in a matrix structure (which is the most common one) is related to the nature of the relationship with the functional managers. To understand the sources of the difficulties, let us compare the roles of the two by referring to the four following domains: responsibility, authority, time horizon, and communication.

Responsibility. The project manager is responsible for ensuring that the project is completed successfully, as measured by time, cost, system or product performance, and stakeholder satisfaction. The functional manager is responsible for running his department so that all of his or her customers are served efficiently and effectively. To be successful, he or she must continuously upgrade the technical ability of the department and take care of the needs of his or her staff.

Inherent in these responsibilities is the following conflict: Assume that a project manager needs a certain job done by one of the functional departments in the organization. The project manager would like a specific individual to do the work because he knows that the person in question is the most skilled. However, the functional manager plans to assign another person to do the job because the preferred employee is needed elsewhere. For example, she could be scheduled for training or she might be working on another job of higher priority. In these situations, the functional manager is inclined to do what's best for the department, and not necessarily what's best for a particular project.

Authority. Authority is measured by the amount of resources that a manager can allocate without the need to get an approval from his or her manager. Whenever external contractors are used, the project manager is the one who approves payment in accordance with the terms of the contract. This is not the case when the work is performed by a functional department within the organization, particularly in a matrix environment, because payment is little more than an accounting entry. This means that if the functional department is late with a deliverable, then the project manager cannot withhold payment, implying that he has little leverage over his functional counterpart. In situations such as this, in which unresolved internal conflicts hurt the chances of the project being completed on time, the project manager should seek resolution with higher-level management. In contrast, the functional manager has the authority over all of the resources that belong to his department, including material, equipment, and employees. His implicit obligation is to use his authority in a manner that will best serve the overall goals of the company.

Time Horizon. Because projects have a limited time horizon, the project manager is necessarily short-term oriented. As such, he is interested in immediate impacts. A functional manager has an ongoing department to run, and his mission remains in effect after satisfying the needs of his current customers. A functional manager sees work orders that have to be executed for different customers; he does not see projects or even fully understand their role within the organization. A project can be viewed as a small business within a larger enterprise whose ultimate goal is to go out of business when all tasks are completed. At the same time, functional departments should be viewed as permanent entities striving to maximize the benefits that they provide to the organization.

Communication.   In allocating work, a project manager has to interact with many individuals, often from different companies. With some individuals, such as a contractor or consultant, he has a formal relationship established through a signed, legally binding contract. With others, such as functional managers within the organization undertaking the project, he does not have a formal contract, although there is generally an explicit agreement on the work to be performed. In most cases, specific tasks are carried out not by the person who negotiated the scope of work, be it a contractor or a functional manager, but by his or her subordinates. Depending on the established line of communications, the project manager may not able to communicate directly with those charged with the work; however, in many cases, there is a continuing need for communication and coordination between two individuals who belong to two different organizational units. Using formal communication channels, the project manager should approach those individuals through their managers. Unfortunately, this process may complicate the communications and increase the response time to unacceptable levels. To circumvent this difficulty, the execution of projects in a matrix environment often requires that the project manager communicate informally with those who are working on his project.

Projects are essentially horizontal, whereas the functional organization, as exemplified by the traditional organization chart, is vertical. The basic dichotomy between the two can be better understood by comparing the types of questions that project and functional managers ask. Table 7.1 highlights the differences.

TABLE 7.1   Concerns of Project and Functional Managers

Project manager	Functional manager
What is to be done?	How will the task be done?
When will the task be done?	Where will the task be done?
What is the importance of the task?	Who will do the task?
How much money is available to do the task?	How well has the functional input been integrated into the project?
How well has the total project been done?	

7.3.3 Project Office

The project office is a functional department that specializes in the development and implementation of project management methodologies and processes. This department offers its services to all other units in the organization in the same manner as any other functional department. It may be directly under the general manager or may be a subunit in, say, the research and development (R&D) department or the information systems department. These two departments are the ones typically involved in most projects, especially in technology-oriented companies.

The following is a list of project-related tasks that fall within the scope of the project office:

- Support in data entry, presentation, and analysis
- Development and introduction of project management body of knowledge (PMBOK)-related methods, tools, and techniques
- Training project and functional managers
- Supplying professional project managers to the organization
- Multiproject management support
- Maintaining the company's project management know-how
- Coordination between organizational strategy and project portfolio
- Contract management
- Developing infrastructure required for effective project management

Increased reliance of the use of a project office within large organizations over the last decade can be traced to the need to overcome the following problems:

- High failure rate of project completion with respect to budget and schedule
- Constant complaints of overwork by project teams
- Departments within the same organization manage projects differently, making it complicated to integrate interdepartmental projects
- Insufficient correlation between organizational strategy and the project portfolio
- Lack of a standardized way to perform projects

A major concern of many organizations is the process by which data and information are collected and stored. If this process is handled diligently, then its output can be used as a vehicle for improving future project planning and execution. To be effective, the data processing procedures should be standardized for all departments. This is often not the case when data processing is not centralized; different project managers have different management styles. One of the most important tasks of the project office is to develop, install, and maintain standard archives for all projects within an organization.

The development of a project office is not a straightforward job and should be treated as a project in and of itself. The following may serve as guidelines for such a project:

- The project office should be developed in stages, beginning with the most painful problems faced by the organization. Long-term objectives can be deferred until the structure is in place, a manager and staff have been chosen, and operational procedures have been put in place.
- In the early stages, the office may offer support on issues such as report design, tracking progress, budgeting, methods for analyzing performance, and standardizing processes by developing templates.
- There is a need to meet with different stakeholders, such as project managers and functional managers, and identify their immediate needs.

- A list of current projects along with their status should be developed to help determine the most pressing organizational needs.
- A respected officer in the organization who believes in the need for a project office should be recruited to champion its development.

A project office is typically called on to support one or more of the following activities:

1. *Developing a performance measure and control system.* Monitoring the use of resources such as money, labor hours, and material is a basic need of any project.

2. *Developing project managers.* It is common for a technically competent person to be nominated to be a project manager without having any training or experience in management. A technical perspective is likely to be much different than the perspective needed to plan, schedule, monitor, and control the various aspects of a project. One of the primary functions of a project office is to offer training programs for inexperienced project managers.

3. *Formulating project management processes.* Training effectiveness depends highly on the organizational commitment to implement standard methods for managing projects. Therefore, the organization should first make a decision on which project management processes it wishes to adopt. If the project is to be managed with the help of software, for example, then it will be necessary to plan for the acquisition, installation, training, and maintenance of the selected product.

4. *Developing technological infrastructure.* As with any process, project management processes require a technological infrastructure for their implementation. For example, an intranet (internal organizational Internet) is an infrastructure that facilitates the integration of information and effort across all projects within an organization.

5. *Developing processes used to manage contractors.* Managing work performed by contractors is different from managing work performed by internal units. Because many organizations outsource a significant portion of a project, there is a need to develop a standard process for contract management that will be used by all projects.

6. *Continuous improvement.* To compete effectively in open markets, there is an ongoing need to improve product performance and quality. This translates into a continuing need for an organization to learn and improve the way it initiates, manages, and administers projects. The development of systematic procedures for incorporating the experience and knowledge gained at the project level and accumulated over time falls within the domain of the project office.

The specific unit within an organization that carries out the above functions may be called by one of several names rather than the "project office." The name chosen may better characterize its responsibilities. Table 7.2 presents a list of names and their common meaning.

The first column in the table specifies the sophistication level of the departmental activities: level 1 means that the project management department performs very basic tasks, whereas level 7 is associated with the most complicated tasks. Project management

TABLE 7.2   Similar Organizational Units That Perform Project Management–Related Tasks

Level	Organizational unit	Major Activity
1	Project Support Office	Administrative support for projects
2	Project Tool Support Office	Support for tools and techniques
3	Project Office	Overall project management support
4	Project Management Office	Overall project management support
5	Program Office	Program and project management support
6	Master Program Office	Same as above but with more authority
7	Enterprise Project Management Office	Project and portfolio management
—	Virtual Project Management Office	Project management via the Internet

departments that belong to levels 1 to 4 focus mostly on managing single projects, whereas departments that belong to levels 5 to 7 deal not only with single projects but also with the coordination and integration of project activities with organizational strategy. No level is specified for the virtual project management office because it may be anywhere from 1 to 7, depending on the organization. This type of office is becoming more and more common as "virtual companies" set up shop in a single office and do all of their business with subcontractors over the Internet and with telecommuting employees. Projects are typically managed with templates that are used by all participants.

Although one may see the obvious advantages of a project office, it is difficult to quantify the benefit that it offers in monetary terms alone. The phrase "cost is a fact for which benefit is an opinion" is the guiding principle here. Therefore, without the sponsorship and ongoing support of upper management, the chances of establishing and maintaining an effective project office are slim. In reality, though, an increasing number of large corporations are finding it impossible to function without them.

7.4 PROJECT SCOPE

This section highlights issues and concepts associated with the project scope. We begin with the following definitions.

Project scope. The work that must be done to deliver a product that is able to perform a specified set of functions and incorporates a predetermined set of features. If all of the required work is not delineated, then some of the deliverables may be excluded. If more than the required work is delineated, then unplanned and unbudgeted items will be delivered. This will have a negative impact on the cost and schedule of the project and may lead to excessive delays.

Project scope management. The processes required to ensure that the project includes all of the work required and only the work required for successful completion. The scope plays a role at each stage of a project, starting with initiation, continuing with change orders, and terminating with the approval of the deliverables. The following is an outline of the scope-related concepts that arise throughout the project life cycle.

Scope in the initiation stage. When a need for a project is identified, possible technical alternatives are explored, their feasibility is evaluated, and a "go/no go" decision is made. At this point, the work required to design, build, and implement a system that responds to the defined need has to be estimated. The end result of the initiation stage is a project charter that provides a summary description of the project content, the project sponsor, and the management approach that should be used. A project charter for an internal project is similar to but not necessarily as detailed as a contract signed with an outside vendor.

Scope planning. This process includes a short description of the project scope, called a scope statement, which is used as the basis for future project decisions and for establishing an understanding between the project team and the customer. The primary components of the scope statement are:

1. Justification for the project
2. Project objectives
3. Sponsor of project
4. Major stakeholders
5. Project manager
6. Major project deliverables
7. Success criteria

The seventh component is used to determine whether each major phase, as well as the project as a whole, has been completed successfully. If a request for proposal (RFP) has already been issued, then it may serve as the basis for the scope statement document, because it includes most of the required information. An example of a scope statement is given in Fig. 7.5.

Composing the scope statement starts during the final phase of project initiation and ends before the start of any significant planning efforts.

Scope definition. The project manager has full responsibility for defining the scope. The major output of this process is the WBS, which is developed right after scope planning. Details are given in the next section.

Scope verification. This process consists of comparing the planned scope with the actual outputs. As a result, the outputs are accepted, rejected, or modified as required. It is performed throughout the life cycle of the project.

Scope change. Because no project of any consequence is completed as originally planned, there is a need for a mechanism that will govern the way scope changes are introduced and implemented throughout the project life cycle.

7.4.1 Work Breakdown Structure

The scope definition process involves subdividing the major project deliverables into smaller, manageable components called work packages, which can be assigned to organizational units that are then responsible for their execution. As stated in the beginning

Project justification:

The lack of qualified managers within the region is one of the principal reasons that economic growth has stagnated over the past decade. After evaluating a variety of alternatives, community leaders decided that the best way to respond to this problem was to create a college.

Project objectives:

1. To open a top management school within a year, equipped with advanced computer systems and high-tech teaching facilities.
2. The school will run two major programs: (a) an MBA program and (b) focused seminars that will serve managers who wish to improve their leadership and communications skills.
3. The school will use an existing building that will be renovated to fit its needs.

Sponsor of the project:

The local mayor is the chief supporter and fundraiser.

Major stakeholders:

1. The mayor.
2. Big State University, an internationally renowned institution situated in the region that will help structure the program. Dr. Knowly has been nominated to be the coordinator on behalf of the university.
3. Regional Management Association, which will be involved in identifying the region's management needs and in helping to promote the program. Ms. Simpson has been nominated to be the coordinator on behalf of the association.
4. Regional industry—organizations that wish to upgrade the managerial skills of their current and future employees. There is an emerging high-tech concentration in the area on which to draw students.

The project manager:

The mayor has nominated Seymour Smyles as the project manager. Dr. Smyles has 10 years of project experience in the telecommunications industry and has recently earned an MBA.

Major project deliverables:

1. Recognized MBA program
2. Published catalog with courses and instructors
3. Web presence
4. Registered students for the first year
5. High-tech classroom facilities
6. Administrative staff
7. Faculty offices and teaching resources

Success criteria:

1. On-time completion within budget
2. Number of students registered for the first year of the program
3. Number of advanced seminars offered the first year
4. Operating costs for first year

Figure 7.5   Scope statement for a project.

of the chapter, the desegregation of the work content into lower level components is called the WBS. According to the PMBOK, the WBS is a deliverable-oriented grouping of project elements that organizes and defines the total scope of the project. Each descending level represents an increasingly detailed definition of project components.

Figure 7.6   Two-level WBS for curriculum development project.

The notion of a WBS was initiated by the U.S. Department of Defense, which also has published guidelines relating to the design of military systems. In particular, MIL-STD-881A states that "a Work Breakdown Structure (WBS) is a product-oriented family tree composed of hardware, services and data which result from project engineering efforts during the development and production of a defense material item, and, which completely defines the project/program. A WBS displays and defines the product(s) to be developed or produced and relates the elements of work to be accomplished to each other and to the end product."

The concept of a "WBS dictionary" is widely used as well and consists of a set of documents that includes the WBS and a detailed description of each work package. The conscientious development, maintenance, and use of the WBS contribute significantly to the probability that a project will be completed successfully.

The WBS provides a common language for describing the work content of a project. This language centers on the work package definitions and a hierarchical coding scheme for representing each WBS element. It enables all stakeholders, such as customers, suppliers, and contractors to communicate effectively throughout a project.

The resources required for a project can be determined by summing the resources required to execute each work package and the level-of-effort (LOE) resources used to maintain the project infrastructure. Typical LOE resources are project management, quality assurance personnel, and information systems.

The first level of the WBS hierarchy represents the entire project. Subsequent levels reflect the decomposition of the project according to a number of possible criteria, such as product components, organization functions, or life-cycle stages. Different WBSs are obtained by applying the criteria at different levels of the hierarchy.

The division of the work content into work packages should reflect the way in which the project will be executed. If, for example, a university initiates a project to create an executive MBA program, then the development of a specific course for the program can be defined as a task and the organizational unit responsible for that course (a professor) can be associated with the task to form a work package. There are, however, different ways to decompose the work content of this project. One way is to divide the entire project directly into work packages. If there are 30 courses required in the program and each course is developed by one professor, then there will be 30 work packages in the WBS. This is illustrated in Fig. 7.6. The following coding scheme can also be used:

1. Development of an MBA program curriculum

      1.1   Introduction to Finance

      1.2   Introduction to Operations

        .

        .

        .

      1.30 Corporate Accounting

Alternatively, the project manager may decide to disaggregate the project work content by functional area and have each such area divide the work content further into specific courses assigned to professors. This situation is illustrated in Fig. 7.7. Using an expanded coding scheme, the WBS in this case might take the following form:

1. Development of an MBA program curriculum

    1.1 Development of courses in finance

        1.1.1 Introduction to Finance

        1.1.2 Financial Management

         .

         .

         .

    1.2 Development of courses in operations

        1.2.1 Introduction to Operations

        1.2.2 Practice of Operations Management

         .

         .

         .

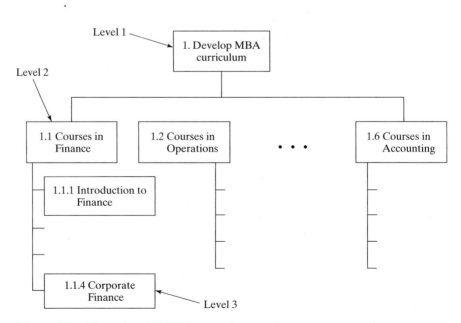

Figure 7.7   Three-level WBS for curriculum development project.

1.6 Development of courses in accounting
    1.6.1   Fundamentals of Accounting

      ·

      ·

      ·

    1.6.4   Corporate Accounting

A third option that the project manager might consider is to divide the work content according to the year in the program in which the course is taught and then divide it again by functional areas. This WBS is illustrated in Fig. 7.8 and might take the following form:

I. Development of an MBA curriculum
    1.1 First-year courses
        1.1.1   Development of courses in finance
            1.1.1.1   Introduction to Finance

          ·

          ·

          ·

    1.2 Second-year courses
        1.2.1   Development of courses in finance
            1.2.1.1   Financial Management

          ·

          ·

          ·

    1.7.6 Development of courses in accounting
        1.7.6.1   Management Information Systems in Accounting

        ·

        ·

        ·

    1.7.6.4 Corporate Accounting

For all three WBSs, the same 30 tasks are performed at the lowest level by the same professors. However, each WBS represents a different approach to organizing the project. The first structure is "flat." There are only two levels, and from the organizational point of view, all of the professors report directly to the project manager, who has to deal with the integration of all 30 work packages. In the second WBS, consisting of three levels, there is one intermediate level—the functional committee–in which each functional committee is responsible for integration of the work packages that are directly under them. In the third example of the WBS chart, there are four levels; that is, two intermediate levels that deal with integration.

As a second example, let us consider the construction of a new assembly line for an existing product. To capitalize on experience and minimize risk, the design may be identical to that of the existing facilities; alternatively, a new design that exploits more advanced technology may be sought. In the latter case, the WBS might include automated

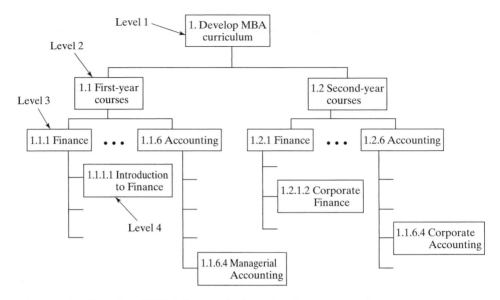

Figure 7.8   Four-level WBS for curriculum development project.

material handling equipment, an updated process design, and the development of production planning and control systems. One possible WBS follows:

1. New assembly line
    1.1 Process design
        1.1.1 Develop a list of assembly operations
        1.1.2 Estimate assembly time for each operation
        1.1.3 Assignment of operations to workstations
        1.1.4 Design of equipment required at each station
    1.2 Capacity planning
        1.2.1 Forecast of future demand
        1.2.2 Estimates of required assembly rates
        1.2.3 Design of equipment required at each station
        1.2.4 Estimate of labor requirements
    1.3 Material handling
        1.3.1 Design of line layout
        1.3.2 Selection of material handling equipment
        1.3.3 Integration design for the material handling system
    1.4 Facilities planning
        1.4.1 Determination of space requirements
        1.4.2 Analysis of energy requirements
        1.4.3 Temperature and humidity analysis
        1.4.4 Facility and integration design for the whole line

    1.5 Purchasing
        1.5.1 Equipment
        1.5.2 Material-handling system
        1.5.3 Assembly machines
    1.6 Development of training programs
        1.6.1 For assembly line operators
        1.6.2 For quality control personnel
        1.6.3 For foremen and managers
    1.7 Actual training
        1.7.1 Assembly line operators
        1.7.2 Quality control
        1.7.3 Foremen, managers
    1.8 Installation and integration
        1.8.1 Shipment of equipment and machines
        1.8.2 Installations
        1.8.3 Testing of components
        1.8.4 Integration and testing of line
        1.8.5 Operations
    1.9 Management of project
        1.9.1 Design and planning
        1.9.2 Implementation monitoring and control

The decision on how to disaggregate the work content of a project is related to the decision on how to structure the project organization. In making these decisions, the project manager not only establishes how the work content will be decomposed and then integrated but also lays the foundation for the project planning and control systems.

The WBS of a project can be defined in several ways. The choice depends on a number of factors, such as the complexity of the project, duration of the project, the work content of the project, risk levels, the organizational structure, resource availability, and management style, so there is no one "correct" way. Nevertheless, the WBS selected should be complete in the sense that it captures all of the work to be performed during the project. It should be detailed in the sense that at its lowest level, executable work packages with specific objectives, resources, budgets, and durations are specified; and it should be accurate in the sense that it represents the way management envisions first decomposing the work content and then integrating the completed tasks into a unified whole.

The following general guidelines may be used when considering a WBS:

- The WBS represents work content and not an execution sequence.
- The second level of the WBS may be components, functions, and geographical locations.
- Managerial philosophy often influences the structure.
- The WBS and its derived work packages should be compatible with organizational working procedures.

- The WBS should be generic in nature so that it may be used in the future for similar projects.
- The WBS is not a product structure tree or bill of materials, both of which refer to a hierarchy of components that are physically assembled into a product.

7.4.2 Work Package Design

Each work package (WP) requires a certain amount of planning, reporting, and control. Hence, decomposition of the project into smaller work packages increases the workload on the project manager and on the project team. Nevertheless, it may support better planning and control. As shown by Raz and Globerson (1998), organizations use general guidelines to size WPs. These guidelines are typically expressed in terms of effort (e.g., person-days, dollar value) or in terms of elapsed time (e.g., days, weeks). One possible principle is that a WP should last not more than 4 weeks.

Ideally, the project manager should ensure that each WP is assigned to a single person or organizational unit and that this unit has the capabilities required to execute it. Smaller WPs mean more frequent deliveries to the customer and earlier payments, reducing finance charges to the contractor and increasing them for the customer.

The definition of a WP—the lowest level of the WBS—should include the following elements:

Objectives. A statement of what is to be achieved by performing this WP. The objectives may include tangible accomplishments, such as the successful production of a part or a successful integration of a system. Nontangible objectives are also possible, such as learning a new computer language.

Deliverables. Every WP has deliverables, which may be hardware components, software modules, reports, economic analyses, or a recommendation made after evaluating different alternatives.

Responsibility. The organizational unit that is responsible for proper completion of each WP has to be defined. This unit may be a component of the organization or be an outside contractor.

Required inputs. These include data, documents, and other material needed for the execution of the WP. They are provided by various sources, such as the stakeholders, company records, contractors, and marketing studies. The information derived from these inputs is used by the project manager to establish the order in which all of the WPs will be executed.

Resources. The unit that is responsible for executing the WP should estimate resources that are required for the task (e.g., labor hours, material, equipment).

Duration. After estimating the resource required for each WP, the responsible party should estimate the duration required for its completion. Resource availability and possible delays must be taken into account.

Budget. A time-phased budget should be prepared for each WP. The budget is a function of the resources allocated to the WP and the duration that each will be used.

Performance measures. Whether a WP has been completed successfully is determined by a predefined set of performance measures and standards. These elements are used during project execution to compare actual versus planned performance and to establish project control.

Because a WP is the smallest manageable unit of a project, the success of the project depends to a large extent on the ability of the project manager to deal properly with each WP. A powerful tool for this purpose is the WP description form, which contains a description of all relevant WP attributes. It is also used as the basis for a contract, either formal or informal, between the project manager and the supplier of the WP. Figure 7.9 depicts a sample form for the MBA project. The form is generic and may be used for

---

WP identification:

Project name: *MBA Curriculum*   Project code: *MBA3*   Project manager: *Smith*
WP name: *OM Course*   WP code: *MBA3-1.3.2*   WP owner: Ribson
WP deliverables: *Syllabus, PowerPoint lectures, 6 exercises, 2 examinations, 1 term project*
Revision no.: *3*   Date: *07-07-05*

Resources required:

Labor		Other resources		
Type	Labor days	Type	Quantity	Cost
Instructor	8	Simulation	1	$2,000
Assistant	20	Software A	8	$1,000
Secratery	3	Equipment	....	....
Programmer	....	Facility	....	....
Others	....	Other	....	....

Required prerequisites: *Overall program, WP code MBA3-1.1.2*
Acceptance tests: *Review by two colleagues from the same area of expertise. Also see attachment MBA3-1.1.2-A2*
Number of working days required for completing the WP: *30*
Possible risk events that may impair the successful completion of the WP: *Lack of knowledge concerning the needs of other courses, different statistical knowledge of students starting the class*

TO BE COMPLETED AFTER SCHEDULING THE PROJECT:

Earliest start of the WP: *07.07.05* **Earliest finish of the WP:** *08.25.05*
Review meeting according to milestones:

Milestone	Deliverables	Meeting date	Participants	
Completion of content	Draft material	07.15.05	Smith, Ribson, Nakamura	
Course completion	PP slides, documents	08.25.05	Smith, Ribson, Nakamura	
....	....		....	
....	....		....	

Design approval of the WP:
WP owner: Name: *Ribson*   Signature: ....   Date: ....
WP customer: Name: *Forman*   Signature: ....   Date: ....
Project manager: Name: *Smith*   Signature: ....   Date: ....

Completion approval of the WP:
WP owner: Name: *Ribson*   Signature: ....   Date: ....
WP customer: Name: *Forman*   Signature: ....   Date: ....
Project manager: Name: *Smith*   Signature: ....   Date: ....

Figure 7.9   Work package definition form.

different WPs. The nature of the required resources, for example, will obviously change from one WP to another.

Points to remember when defining a WP:

- A WP is the lowest level in the WBS.
- A WP always has a deliverable associated with it.
- A WP should have one responsible party, called the WP owner.
- A WP may be considered by the WP owner as a project in itself.
- A WP may include several milestones.
- A WP should fit organizational procedures and culture.

If we think of a company as being in a certain line of business, then many of its projects are likely to be similar in nature. In such cases, developing a generic approach to defining WPs and constructing WBSs can prove extremely advantageous. Although no two projects are identical, many will have enough similarities to allow the same WBS template to be used as a starting point with the necessary modifications made as the requirements unfold. Using this approach will enable a company to improve its performance and perhaps gain a competitive edge.

7.5 COMBINING THE ORGANIZATIONAL AND WORK BREAKDOWN STRUCTURES

The two structures—the OBS and the WBS—form the basis for project planning, execution, and control. Building blocks, called work packages, are formed at the intersection of the lowest levels of these structures. A specific organizational unit is assigned a specific WP that includes tasks that reside at the lowest level of the WBS. The WP is further divided by the organizational unit into specific activities, each defined by its work content, expected output, required resources, time table, and budget. The hierarchical nature of these structures provides for a *roll-up* mechanism wherein the information gathered and processed at any level can be aggregated and rolled up to its higher level.

In operational terms, the WP is the smallest unit used by the project manager for planning and control, although internal milestones may be defined to allow for better visibility of progress. Further disaggregation of a WP is undertaken by the person who is charged with getting the work done (e.g., a group leader) and converts the WP into a set of basic tasks and activities. For example, "Introduction to Operations" is a WP in the project outlined in Fig. 7.6. Let's assume that the corresponding execution responsibilities have been assigned to an operations management instructor. To complete the assignment properly, the instructor must divide the WP into tasks and activities. These might include collecting syllabi from institutions that offer a similar course, establishing a list of possible topics, deciding what material to cover on each topic, developing a detailed bibliography, evaluating case studies, generating exercises and discussion questions, and so on.

The person who is responsible for a WP is responsible for the detailed resource planning, budgeting, and scheduling of its constituent tasks. The development of the OBS-WBS relationship is a major step in the responsibility assignment task faced by the project manager. By planning, controlling, and managing the execution of a project at the WP level, lines of responsibility are clarified and the effect of each decision made on each element of the project can be traced to any level of the OBS or the WBS.

7.5.1 Linear Responsibility Chart

An important tool for the design and implementation of the project's work content is the *linear responsibility chart* (LRC). The LRC, also known as the *matrix responsibility chart* or *responsibility interface matrix*, summarizes the relationships between project stakeholders and their responsibilities in each project element. An element can be a specific activity, an authorization to perform an activity, a decision, or a report. The columns of the LRC represent project stakeholders; the rows represent project elements performed by the organization. Each cell corresponds to an activity and the organizational unit to which it is assigned. The level of participation of the organizational unit is also specified.

By reading down a column of the LRC, one gets a picture of the nature of involvement of each stakeholder; reading across a row gives an indication of which organizational unit is responsible for that element, as well as the nature of involvement of other stakeholders with that element. An example of an LRC is shown in Table 7.3. The notation used in the table is defined as follows:

A   *Approval.* Approves the WP or the element.

P   *Prime responsibility.* Indicates who is responsible for accomplishing the WP.

R   *Review.* Reviews output of the WP. For example, the legal department reviews a proposal of a bid submitted by the team leader.

N   *Notification.* Notified of the output of the WP. As a result of this notification, the person makes a judgment as to whether any action should be taken.

O   *Output.* Receives the output of the WP and integrates it into the work being accomplished—in other words, the user of that package. For example, the contract administrator receives a copy of the engineering change orders so that the effects of changes on the terms and conditions of the contract can be determined.

I   *Input.* Provides input to the WP. For example, a "bid/no bid" decision on a contract cannot be made by a company, unless inputs are received from the manufacturing manager, financial manager, contract administrator, and the marketing manager.

B   *Initiation.* Initiates the WP. For example, new product development is the responsibility of the R&D manager, but the process generally is initiated with a request from the marketing manager.

If A, R, and B are not separately identified, then P is assumed to include them. The LRC in Table 7.3 corresponds to a single project. Similar charts can be constructed for each project in the portfolio, as well as for each WP in a project.

The LRC clarifies authority, responsibility, and communication channels among project stakeholders. Taken as a whole, it is a blueprint of the activity and information flows that occur at the interfaces of an organization. Once the LRC for a project is developed, it can be sorted for each organizational unit by the nature of its involvement. When

TABLE 7.3 Example of an LRC

Activity	Engineering	Manufacturing	Contracts	Project manager	Marketing	Quality assurance
Respond to RFP	I	I	O, A	P	B	A
Negotiating contract	I, N	I, N	I, R	P		A
Preliminary design	P	A	R	O, B		A
Detailed design	P	A	R	O		A
Execution	R	P		O, B		R
Testing	I	I		O, B		P
Delivery	N	N	P	A	N	A

a manager reviews the sorted WPs associated with his unit, he can identify those activities for which he has direct responsibility and others in which he plays a supportive role.

The LRC conveys information on job descriptions and organizational procedures. It provides a means for all stakeholders in a project to view their responsibilities and agree on their assignments. It shows the extent or type of authority exercised by each participant in performing an activity in which two or more parties have overlapping involvement, and it clarifies supervisory relationships that may otherwise be ambiguous when people share work.

To generate the LRC, the OBS should be complete, detailed, and accurate: complete in the sense that it should depict all of the stakeholders and organizational units that will participate in the project; detailed in the sense that each organizational unit is represented down to the level at which the work is actually being performed; and accurate in the sense that it reflects the true lines of authority, responsibility, and communication. The LRC integrates the two structures by assigning bottom-level WBS elements to bottom-level OBS elements. This can be done only when the WBS and the OBS are accurate and comprehensive.

Although both the LRC and WPs are formed from elements at the lowest levels of the WBS and the OBS, they take different forms and serve different purposes. The LRC defines the nature of the organizational interaction associated with each major WP. For example, it identifies the responsible stakeholders who have to be consulted with regard to each WP and indicates who should be notified when the WP is completed. Each row in the LRC represents the decision-making process for the specific WP, and each column represents the job description of a specific organizational unit/stakeholder with regard to the project.

The integration of the WBS and the OBS, along with the LRC, is the cornerstone of project management. It provides the framework for developing and integrating the tools needed for scheduling, budgeting, management, and control. It also aids in defining the relationship among the project manager, client representatives, functional managers, and other stakeholders.

7.6 MANAGEMENT OF HUMAN RESOURCES

Of the many types of resources used in projects (people, equipment, machinery, data, capital), human resources are the most difficult to manage. Unlike other resources, human beings seek motivation, satisfaction, and security and need an appropriate climate and culture to achieve high performance. The problem becomes even more complicated in a project environment because the successful completion of the project is primarily dependent on team effort. Working groups, or teams, are the common organizational units within which individual efforts are coordinated to achieve a common goal. A team is well integrated when information flows smoothly, trust exists among its members, each person knows his or her role in the project, morale is high, and the desire is for a high level of achievement.

7.6.1 Developing and Managing the Team

In a project environment where workers from many disciplines join to perform multifunctional tasks, the importance of teamwork is paramount. The issues center on how to build a team, how to manage it, and which kind of leadership is most appropriate for a project team. The objective of team building is to transform a collection of individuals with different objectives and experiences into a well-integrated group in which the objectives of each person promote the goals of the group. The limited life of projects and the frequent need to cross the functional organizational lines make team building a complicated task.

Members of a new project team may come from a variety of organizational units or may be new employees. To build an efficient team, personal and organizational uncertainty and ambiguity must be reduced to a minimum. This is done by clearly defining, as early as possible, the project, its goals, its organizational structure (organizational chart), and the procedures and policies that will be followed during execution.

Each person who joins the project must be given a job description that defines reporting relationships, responsibilities, and duties. Task responsibilities must also be defined. Each person needs to know the tasks in which he or she is expected to participate and in what capacity. The linear responsibility chart is a useful tool for defining individual tasks and responsibilities. Once the roles of all team members have been established, they should be introduced to each other properly and their functions explained. Continuous efforts on the part of the project manager are required to keep the team organized and highly motivated. An ongoing effort is also required to detect any problems and to ensure that appropriate correction measures are taken.

The roles of team members tend to change over time as the project moves from one phase of its life cycle to the next. Because confusion and uncertainty cause conflict and inefficiency, the project manager should frequently update team members regarding their roles in the project. Furthermore, the manager should detect any morale or image problems as early as possible in an effort to identify and eliminate the cause of such problems. For example, the appearance of cliques or isolated members should serve as a signal that the team is not being managed properly.

The project manager should also help in reducing anxieties and uncertainty related to "life after the project." When a project reaches its final stages, the project manager should discuss the future role in the organization of each team member and prepare a plan that ensures a smooth transition to that new role. By providing a stable environment and a clear project goal, team members can focus on the job at hand.

A recommended practice for management is to conduct regular team meetings throughout the life cycle of the project but more frequently in the early phases, when uncertainty is highest. In a team meeting, plans, problems, operating procedures, and policies should be discussed and explained. By identifying future problems and preparing an agreed-on plan, the probability of success is increased and the probability of conflicts is reduced or eliminated altogether.

Despite the pragmatic guidelines specified above, if the team is not properly developed, then there is a high probability that it will not perform its functions effectively. If, for the moment, we associate an iceberg with the processes of a project, then we might see something similar to relationships depicted in Fig. 7.10.

The tip of the iceberg, the part first to be seen and supported by the submerged structure, is the deliverables—what the project manager and his team have committed to deliver. The middle of the iceberg, still above water (and supporting the tip), contains all of the supporting project management tools and processes. Finally, below the surface lie all of the human processes. These are hidden from the eye in the sense that we can see their results but not their essence; that is, we can see the product of a committed team or an unmotivated team, but we cannot see the commitment or the lack of motivation itself. Like the iceberg base, any movement below the surface will affect the entire structure. The stability of the iceberg as a whole is only as strong as the stability of its base, yet although the human processes are of critical importance, they are often left relatively unattended, at least until they rumble and threaten to undermine the project.

One of the paradoxes of project management is that the project manager is chosen for his technical/professional skills rather than for his leadership skills but is then given the task of leading a group of people to achieve collaboratively what may be a set of unfamiliar and conflicting goals. The following paragraphs outline typical team development stages. By recognizing these stages, the project manager will be in a better position to bring out the full potential of the team.

Figure 7.10 Iceberg model of project processes.

When individuals get together to form a team, they are concerned with four issues:

1. *Identity:* Who will they be in the team? What role will they play? Will their role be meaningful?
2. *Power:* How much power and influence will they have in the team? Will their voice be heard? Will they be able to change the course of events and influence team decisions?
3. *Interface* (conflict or overlap) between their needs as individuals and the needs of the team: Will they benefit from working in this team (materially, professionally)? What will they have to give up to stay in line with the team?
4. *Acceptance:* Will they be accepted and liked? Will they fit in? Will they belong?

At any given point, individuals may be concerned with one or more of these issues, although it is unlikely that they will formulate and express them precisely. A project manager will be better able to respond to a team member who is dissatisfied with what is happening if he or she is aware that behind complaints related to, say, scheduling/workload/role definitions lie concerns of identity/acceptance/power and so on.

At the same time as all individuals are concerned with the above issues, the team as a whole tends to go through the following four stages: forming, storming, norming, and performing. These stages give rise to what is known as a *performance model.* As the team moves from one stage to the next, its competence in performing its task grows. More precisely, we have the following:

Forming

- task performance at a lower level
- lack of clarity regarding roles and expectations
- lack of norms governing team interactions
- relatively low commitment to both team and task
- low trust
- high dependence on project manager
- high curiosity, expectations
- boundaries begin to form (who is/is not a part of the team)

Storming

- roles and responsibilities understood (accepted or challenged)
- open confrontations and power struggles
- open expression of disagreement
- high competition
- "subgroups" formed
- little or no team spirit
- lots of testing of authority
- feeling of being "stuck"
- low motivation

Norming

- roles and responsibilities accepted
- purpose clear
- agreement on working procedures
- trust built
- confidence rises
- openness to give and receive feedback
- conflict resolution strategies formed
- task orientation
- feeling of belonging
- very strong norms may suffocate individual expression and creativity

Performing

- cooperation and coordination
- strong sense of team identity
- high commitment to task
- mutual support
- high confidence in team ability
- high task performance
- networks created with other teams/parts of the organization
- leadership role moves informally between members
- high motivation (with occasional dips)

How can this model benefit the project manager? First, many project managers find a familiarity with this model helpful in that it can predict and explain some of the phenomena that they may be observing in their team. Most salient is the storming stage, which project managers often view with distress and come to the conclusion that "something is wrong with the team" or "we'll never be able to work together," rather than viewing it as an integral—even necessary—part of team development.

Second, there are operational implications associated with the model; i.e., the project manager can, to a certain extent, manage the process of team development. With this in mind, his or her role becomes one of leading the team through the first three stages as smoothly as possible so that they all arrive at the performing stage at the earliest possible time.

In the ambiguity of the forming stage, the project manager may facilitate the team process by being directive and ensuring clarity; that is, by setting a clear mission and set of objectives for the team, by establishing clear roles and reporting procedures, by defining human resource processes, and, in general, by being the authority for the team's uncertainty and questions.

In the storming stage, the project manager's role calls for a more supportive and flexible attitude: supporting members, facilitating and reconciling differences, setting boundaries through persuasion, spending time building trust between team members, and constantly reminding the team of their superordinate goals and mission—which tend to get lost in the day-to-day struggles.

In the norming stage, the project manager must constantly be aware of the team norms that are being created regarding planning and schedules, feedback loops, meetings, communication (quantity and quality), expressing disagreement, and changing priorities as some examples. At this stage, the team forms its own particular style of working, or, in other words, its own culture, which can sometimes be effective and sometimes serve as a real obstacle to effectiveness. (An example of ineffective norms might concern meetings: "We have far too many meetings, people come unprepared for the most part, and the first 15 minutes are spent on socializing—no wonder people are no longer coming as frequently.") It is important for the project manager to remember that it is much easier to set a desired norm than it is to change an undesirable one.

Finally, in the performing stage, the project manager is called on to become more of a coach: delegating responsibilities as team members become more proficient at taking them on, giving feedback on performance and advice on problems, generating team spirit and motivation, and, generally directing and supporting the team's work.

A revision of the model added a fifth stage, "adjourning," which is especially relevant in project management because the team is, a priori, a temporary one. Although this is not really a stage like the others, it is sometimes characterized by lowered motivation, by people moving on to the next project (in their minds, if not in reality), and by a scattering of focus and attention. The project manager needs to be aware when he or she sees these things happening and to take steps in two directions. The first is to encourage people to "run the last leg," mainly through motivational techniques and encouragement. The second is to make sure that the project ends on a positive note—both in the sense of joint celebration and in a process of "lessons learned." This is particularly important in organizations that are based on project structures because the end of each project leaves all involved with either a positive experience and an enthusiasm to go on to the next project or, the contrary, a negative experience that generates a lack of energy and will to commit to the next project.

7.6.2 Encouraging Creativity and Innovation

The one-time nature of projects requires solutions to problems that have not been dealt with in the past. The ability to apply past solutions to present problems may be limited. The human ability to innovate and create new ideas thus should be exploited properly by the project manager and maintained at top performance by encouraging team members to think, create, and innovate.

To flourish, creativity and innovation require the appropriate climate. The various ways and means by which management has tried to establish the proper conditions have been well documented in literature and include quality circles, suggestion boxes, and rewards for new ideas that are implemented. Sherman (1984) interviewed key executives in eight leading U.S. companies to study the techniques used to encourage innovation. Following are some of his findings:

Organizational level

- The search for new ideas is part of the organizational strategy. Continuous effort is encouraged and supported at all levels.
- Innovation is seen as a means for long-term survival.
- Small teams of people from different functions are used frequently.
- New organizational models such as quality circles, product development teams, and decentralized management are tested frequently.

Individual level

- Creative and innovative team members are rewarded.
- Fear that the status quo will lead to disaster is a common motivator for individual innovation.
- The importance of product quality, market leadership, and innovation is stressed repeatedly and thus is well known to employees.

To put it more succinctly, innovation and creativity should be encouraged and properly managed. To enhance innovation, a systematic process that starts by analyzing the sources of new opportunities in the market is required; namely, users' needs and expectations. Techniques such as *quality function deployment* and the *house of quality* have proved to be very effective in this regard (Cohen 1995, Hauser and Clausing 1988).

Once a need is identified, a focused effort is required to fulfill that need. Such an effort is based on knowledge, ingenuity, free communication, and well-coordinated hard work. The entire process should aim at a solution that will be the standard and trend setter for that industry. Techniques that support individual creativity and innovation are usually designed to organize the process of thinking and include

1. A list of questions regarding the problem, or the status quo
2. Influence diagrams that relate elements of a problem to each other
3. Models that represent a real problem in a simplified way, such as physical models, mathematical programs, and simulation models

A project manager can enhance innovation by selecting team members who are experts in their technical fields with a good record as problem solvers and innovators in past projects. The potential of individuals to innovate is further enhanced by teamwork and the application of proper techniques, such as brainstorming and the Delphi method.

Brainstorming is used as a tool for developing ideas by groups of individuals headed by a session chairman. The session starts by the chairman presenting a clear definition of the problem at hand. Group members are invited to present ideas, subscribing to the following rules:

- Criticism of an idea is barred absolutely.
- Modification of an idea or its combination with another idea is encouraged.

- Quantity of ideas is sought.
- Unusual, remote, or wild ideas are encouraged.

A major function of the chairman is to stimulate the session with new ideas or direction. A typical session lasts up to an hour and is brought to an end at the onset of fatigue.

The Delphi technique is used to structure intuitive thinking. It was developed by the Rand Corporation as a tool for the systematic collection of informed opinions from a group of experts. Unlike brainstorming, the members of the group need not be in the same physical location. Each member gets a description of the problem and submits a response. These responses are collected and fed back anonymously to the group members. Each person then considers whether he or she wants to modify earlier views or contribute more information. Iterations continue until there is convergence to some form of consensus.

In addition to these two approaches, a number of other techniques are available to support creativity and innovation by groups. For a comprehensive review, see Warfield et al. (1975). As a final example, we mention the *nominal group technique*, which works as follows:

1. A problem or topic is given and each team member is asked to prepare a list of ideas that might lead to a solution.
2. Participants present their ideas to the group, one at a time, taking turns. The team leader records the ideas until all lists are exhausted.
3. The ideas are presented for clarification. Team members can comment on or clarify each of the ideas.
4. Participants are asked to rank the ideas.
5. The group discusses the ranked ideas and ways to expand or implement them.

7.6.3 Leadership, Authority, and Responsibility

Because of the cross-functional nature of most project teams, organizations tend to be matrix oriented. This means that at any given moment, each team member may have two bosses—the project manager and his functional manager. Often a person is also a part of two or more project teams. As a result, he is likely to be faced with conflicting priorities and demands and has to decide where his first commitment lies. Similarly, the project manager may find that he is severely constrained by the limited options available to him for managing his team (e.g., he usually lacks control over compensation and other types of rewards). In the absence of full authority, managing teams becomes both more complex and more challenging. Often the only way a project manager can achieve outstanding results is if he is able to motivate his team through a sense of pride, belonging, and commitment. Whereas in other areas such as scheduling and budgeting, a project manager is able to manage, in the "people management" area, he is actually expected to "lead" rather than to "manage." Indeed, one definition of "leadership" is precisely the ability to motivate people to achieve a goal through the use of informal motivational techniques, rather than those associated with formal authority. An alternative definition is the use of noncoercive influence to direct the activities of members of a group to accomplish its collective goals.

One way of differentiating between management and leadership would be to consider the sources or bases of power that a project manager has. In general, we tend to speak of five main power bases:

1. **Formal/position:** the power that a manager has over subordinates given to him or her by the organization—to hire and fire, to compensate, to promote, and so on.
2. **Reward/coercive:** the power to use the "carrot and stick" method. Although there is a large overlap with the first power base, the two are not identical. People have the ability to punish and reward others even when they are not formally responsible for them, for example, by withholding valuable information or resources.
3. **Professional expertise:** the power to influence people or events through in-depth knowledge, skills, and experience in a certain discipline.
4. **Interpersonal skills:** the power to create and maintain relationships, which includes the ability to listen, to empathize, and to resolve conflicts.
5. **Ability to create identification/commitment:** the power to create a sense of meaningfulness for people through a connecting of their own wishes, desires, and ambitions to the task in question.

In a matrix environment, a project manager rarely has the first source of power (formal) at his disposal. The second (reward/coercive) is one that he can use to a certain extent, but he must be aware of its limits. Coercion, whether implicit or explicit, creates a type of "transactional" relationship whereby a subordinate will perform according to his perception of the value of the reward that he will receive for successful results—or conversely, according to his fear of possible punishment for not performing well (e.g., not being assigned to a desired project in the future). The obvious problem is that team members will be cooperative as long as the promise of significant reward or punishment holds out; when neither is there, motivation disappears.

Professional expertise is and has always been a prime power base used by project managers. This is frequently the reason they are chosen for the role in the first place, and it is in using their expertise that they usually feel the most comfortable, seeing themselves and being seen by others as adding value. Although this is both a necessary and an effective power base, it is most often not sufficient by itself. It enables the project manager to manage and control task processes but not necessarily people.

Interpersonal skills are also a critical power base at the disposal of the project manager, provided that he understands how to balance the time and energy that he invests in dealing with people's whims and follies. One common misperception concerning this power base is that it is inborn, i.e., either you have it or you don't. Although some people may have a head start in interpersonal skills, anyone can acquire a good understanding of them through focus and attention, training, practice, and the intelligent use of several commercial methodologies.

It is, however, the ability to create identification/commitment that differentiates between a good project manager and an outstanding one. This is where "intangible" motivational abilities come into play, first to bring out team members' inner need to excel and to be a part of a team that is doing something meaningful and, second, to generate the commitment that can lead people to perform above and beyond their normal levels. These abilities include

- Giving meaning to the tasks by linking them to the project and to the larger organizational picture. This involves generating an ongoing dialogue concerning the "what," the "how," and especially the "why" of the project.
- Setting an example: being a role model is one of the most difficult but effective ways in which the project manager can motivate his team. He must set standards of behavior, integrity, commitment and sensitivity to others, which he must both demand and adhere to himself. There is probably nothing as demotivating as a manager who does not "walk his talk."
- Creating trust: this relates to the fact, consistently upheld by research, that mutual trust is the primary condition under which people will commit themselves—their knowledge, skills, and spirit—to a team project. When trust does not exist, an inordinate amount of energy is channeled from task-related issues to political or power issues or toward self-justification and protection from criticism.
- Creating intellectual and emotional stimuli: both of these relate to the question that each team member asks him- or herself at the beginning of the project: "What's in it for me?" The answer lies not on the material level but rather in terms of challenge, professional growth, experience, and development in more generic project management areas as well as in a member's specific professional field. If a project manager can create an environment in which team members can both contribute to and learn from others and take on meaningful responsibilities, and in which each individual's unique voice will be heard and heeded, then he will have gone a long way toward ensuring the project's success, for his team will give it the best they have.

Leading a team to the successful completion of a project is no simple task. Whereas prediction and control have always been the staples of effective management, they are not easy to implement in today's turbulent and constantly changing environment. The "grand paradox" of management, as management theorist Peter Vaill (1990) sees it, is that being a manager in our complex reality is taking responsibility for what is less and less stable and controllable. In the same vein, project managers are expected to work within a paradoxical framework: they need to predict and control the many variables that affect their project, at the same time as planning for the inevitable changes and surprises that cannot be predicted and controlled.

This becomes very clear in the team leadership role of a project manager. He needs to understand that effective teamwork does not "just happen" automatically. It requires attention to and engagement in human processes that are often "messy," emotional, and sometimes irrational. It requires knowledge of group processes and individual preferences and tendencies, together with the understanding that there is no model that can completely capture the complexity of thought processes, behavior, and interaction. It requires an understanding that people are motivated to do their best only when their heart and spirit are involved in the project, rather than only their professional and technical expertise.

Finally, perhaps the biggest paradox of all lies in the fact that although project managers need to be adept in the theory and practice of "people management," "it is the ability to meet each situation armed not with a battery of techniques but with openness that permits a genuine response. The better managers transcend technique. Having acquired many techniques in their development as professionals, they succeed precisely by leaving technique behind." (Farson 1996).

The responsibility of a project manager is typically to execute the project in such a way that the prespecified deliverables will be ready within the time and budget planned. This responsibility must come with the proper level of legal authority, implying that leadership and authority are related. A manager cannot be a leader unless he or she has authority. Authority is the power to command or direct other people. There are two sources of authority: *legal authority* and *voluntarily accepted authority*. Legal authority is based on the organizational structure and a person's organizational position. It is delegated from the owners of the organization to the various managerial levels and is usually contained in a document. Voluntarily accepted authority is based on personal knowledge, interpersonal skills, or a person's experience that enables him or her to exercise influence over and above the legal authority. The project manager should have well-defined legal authority in the organization and over the project. However, a good project manager will seek voluntarily accepted authority from the team members and organizations involved in the project on the basis of his or her personal skills.

The importance of legal authority is most pronounced in a matrix organization in which the need to work with functional managers and to utilize resources that "belong" to functional units can trigger conflicts. Reduction of these conflicts depends on the formal authority definition, as well as on the ability of both the project manager and the functional manager to be flexible.

7.6.4 Ethical and Legal Aspects of Project Management

The legal authority of a project manager and his or her role as a leader require proper understanding of the legal and ethical aspects of project management. The Project Management Institute (PMI)[1] developed a code of ethics that states,

> "As a professional in the field of project management, PMI members pledge to uphold and abide by the following:
>
> I will maintain high standards of integrity and professional conduct
>
> I will accept responsibility for my actions
>
> I will continually seek to enhance my professional capabilities
>
> I will practice with fairness and honesty
>
> I will encourage others in the profession to act in an ethical and professional manner."

The PMI *Member Standards of Conduct* describes the obligations and expectations associated with membership in the PMI. All members must conduct their activities consistent with these standards.

I. Professional obligations

    A. Professional behavior

        1. PMI members will fully and accurately disclose any professional or business-related conflicts or potential conflicts of interest in a timely manner.

        2. PMI members will refrain from offering or accepting payments, or other forms of compensation or tangible benefits, which: (a) do not conform

---

[1]PMI Member Ethical Standards, Project Management Institute Inc., 2000. Copyright and all rights reserved. Material from this publication has been reproduced with the permission of PMI.

with applicable laws; and (b) may provide unfair advantage for them-selves, their business or others they may represent.

3. PMI members who conduct research or similar professional activities will do so in a manner that is fair, honest, accurate, unbiased, and other-wise appropriate, and will maintain appropriate, accurate, and complete records with respect to such research and professional activities.

4. PMI members will respect and protect the intellectual property rights of others, and will properly disclose and recognize the professional, in-tellectual, and research contributions of others.

5. PMI members will strive to enhance their professional capabilities, skills, and knowledge; and will accurately and truthfully represent and advertise their professional services and qualifications.

B. Relationship with customers, clients, and employers

1. PMI members will provide customers, clients, and employers with fair, honest, complete, and accurate information concerning: (a) their qualifi-cations; (b) their professional services; and (c) the preparation of esti-mates concerning costs, services, and expected results.

2. PMI members will honor and maintain the confidentiality and privacy of customer, client, employer, and similar work information, including the confidentiality of customer or client identities, assignments under-taken, and other information obtained throughout the course of a pro-fessional relationship, unless: (a) granted permission by the customer, client, or employer; or (b) the maintenance of the confidentiality is oth-erwise unethical or unlawful.

3. PMI members will not take personal, business, or financial advantage of confidential or private information acquired during the course of their professional relationships, nor will they provide such information to others.

C. Relationship with the public and the global community

1. PMI members will honor and meet all applicable legal and ethical obligations, including the laws, rules, and customs of the community and nation in which they function, work, or conduct professional activities.

2. PMI members will perform their work consistent and in conformance with professional standards to ensure that the public is protected from harm.

II. Obligations to PMI

A. Responsibilities of PMI membership

1. PMI members will abide by the bylaws, policies, rules, requirements, and procedures of the Project Management Institute, and will not knowingly engage or assist in any activities intended to compromise the integrity, reputation, property, and/or legal rights of the institute.

2. PMI members will abide by the laws, regulations, and other require-ments of their respective communities and nations, and will not knowingly

engage in, or assist in, any activities intended to have negative implications, including criminal conduct, professional misconduct, or malfeasance.

3. PMI members will cooperate with the institute concerning the review of possible ethics violations, and other PMI matters, completely, consistent with applicable policies and requirements.

4. PMI members will accurately, completely, and truthfully represent information to PMI.

This code establishes guidelines for the ethical responsibilities of a project manager who is a member of PMI. In case of violations, PMI will initiate nonlegal procedures to deal with them, although an attorney may represent the parties involved. PMI Ethics Review and the Ethics Appeals Committees were established to deal with ethics complaints. For details, see "PMI Member Ethical Standards Member Code of Ethics" (http://www.PMI.org).

Similar guidelines are required for the project manager's legal responsibilities. These, however, depend on the specific organizations involved, the contract, and the laws of the country where the project is performed. The following legal aspects are common to most projects:

- Contractual issues regarding clients, suppliers, and subcontractors
- Government laws and regulations
- Labor relations legislation

As a rule of thumb, whenever the project manager is not sure of the legal aspects of a decision or a situation, he or she should consult the legal staff of the organization.

Legalities are very important when an organization contracts to carry out a project or parts of a project for a customer or when an organization uses subcontractors. A large variety of contract types exist, commonly classified into fixed-cost and cost-reimbursable contracts, and each requires a different legal orientation. Among the first class, two major subclasses can be identified: (1) firm fixed price (FFP) contracts and (2) fixed price incentive fee (FPIF) contracts. Under FFP contracts, the contractor assumes full responsibility for cost, schedule, and technical aspects of the project. This type of contract is suitable only when the levels of uncertainty are low, technical specifications are well defined, and schedule and cost estimates are subject to minimal errors. The FPIF contract is designed to encourage performance above a preset target level. Thus, if the project is completed ahead of schedule or under cost, then an incentive is paid to the contractor. In some FPIF contracts, a penalty is also specified in case of cost overruns or late deliveries. By specifying a target that can be achieved with high probability, the risk that the contractor takes is minimized, while the incentive motivates the contractor to try to do better than the specified target.

Cost-reimbursable contracts are also classified into two major types: (1) cost plus fixed fee and (2) cost plus incentive fee (CPIF) contracts. The former are designed for projects in which most of the risk associated with cost overrun is borne by the customer. This type of contract is appropriate when it is impossible to estimate costs accurately, as, for example, in R&D projects. On top of the actual cost of performing the work, an agreed-on fee is paid to the contractor. CPIF contracts are designed to guarantee a minimum profit to the contractor while motivating the contractor to achieve superior cost, schedule, and technical performance. This is done by paying an incentive for performance higher than expected and tying the level of incentive to the performance level.

Within the four types of contracts, there are many variations. The proper contract for a specific project depends on the levels of risk involved, the ability of each party to assume part of the risk, and the relative negotiating power of the participants. Although the legal staff is usually responsible for contractual arrangements, the project manager has to execute the contract, so his or her ability to establish good working relationships with the client, suppliers, and subcontractors within the framework of the contract is extremely important.

In addition to the contracts, the project manager should be familiar with government laws and regulations in areas such as labor relations, safety, environmental issues, patents, and trade regulations. Whenever a question arises, the project manager should consult the legal staff. It is highly recommended that the project manager be trained in the basics of labor relations legislation, as an important part of his or her work is to manage the human resources.

Each country has its own labor relations legislation, and managers of international projects must not assume that these regulations are the same or even similar from one country to the next. Typically, these regulations have to do with minimum wages, benefits, work conditions, equal employment opportunity, the employment of the handicapped, and occupational safety and health.

To summarize, the management of human resources is probably the most difficult aspect of project management. It requires the ability to create a project team, to manage it, to encourage creativity and innovation without being threatened, and to deal with human resources in and out of the organization. The project manager can learn some of these skills, but a majority of them come only with experience, common sense, and inherent leadership qualities.

TEAM PROJECT

Thermal Transfer Plant

At the last TMS board meeting, approval was given to develop a new area of business: recycling and waste management. Because your supporting analysis was the determining factor, your team has been asked to develop for TMS an organizational structure that will integrate this new area with its current business. You are also required to develop a detailed OBS and WBS for a project aimed at designing and assembling a prototype rotary combustor for which only the power unit will be manufactured in-house; other parts will be purchased or subcontracted. In developing the OBS and WBS for the project, clearly identify the corresponding hierarchies and show who has responsibility at each level.

In your report, explain your objectives and the criteria used in reaching a decision. Show why the selected structure is superior to the alternatives considered, and explain how this structure relates to the TMS organization as a whole. Your report will be submitted to TMS management for review. Be prepared to present the major points to your management and to defend your recommendations.

DISCUSSION QUESTIONS

1. Describe the organizational structure of your school or company. What difficulties have you encountered working within this structure?

2. Explain how a matrix organization can perform a project for a functional organization. What are the difficulties, contact points, and communication channels?

3. In the matrix management structure, the functional expert on a project has two bosses. What considerations in a well-run organization reduce the potential for conflict?

4. Write a job description for a project manager in a matrix organization. Assume that only the project manager is employed full time by the project.

5. How does the WBS affect the selection of the OBS of a project?

6. Under what conditions can a functional manager act as a project manager?

7. Develop a list of advantages and disadvantages of the following structures:

    a. Product organization
    b. Customer organization
    c. Territorial organization

8. Which kind of OBS is used in the company or organization to which you now or used to belong? What are the limitations that you have perceived?

9. What are the activities and steps involved in developing an LRC?

10. Describe the "team building" inherent in the development of an LRC. How is team building accomplished on large projects? How does this relate to development of the LRC?

11. Discuss the applicability of the nominal group technique, the Delphi method, and brainstorming to the process of scheduling and budgeting a project.

12. Compare the advantages and disadvantages of the four types of contracts discussed in this chapter.

13. Of the types of leadership discussed, which is most appropriate for a high-risk project?

EXERCISES

7.1 Develop an organizational structure for a project performed in your school (e.g., the development of a new degree program). Explain your assumptions and objectives.

7.2 You are in charge of designing and building a new solar heater. Develop the OBS and the WBS. Explain the relationship between the two.

7.3 Develop an OBS for an emergency health care unit in a hospital. How should this unit be related to the other departments in the hospital?

7.4 Develop a WBS for a construction project.

7.5 Consider the development of a new electric car by an auto manufacturer and a manufacturer of high-capacity batteries.

    a. Develop an appropriate four-level WBS.
    b. Develop the OBS.
    c. Define several WPs to relate the WBS elements to the OBS.

7.6 Suggest three approaches (OBS-WBS combinations) for the development of a new undergraduate program in electrical engineering.

7.7 Develop an LRC for a project done for a client who has a functional organization by a contractor who has a customer-oriented organization.

    a. Describe the project and its WBS.

    b. Describe the OBS of the client and the contractor.

7.8 You are the president of a startup company that specializes in computer peripherals such as optical backup units, tape drives, signature verifications systems, and data transfer devices. Construct two OBSs, and discuss the advantages and disadvantages of each.

7.9 List two activities that you have recently performed with two or more other people. Explain the role of each participant using an OBS, a WBS, and an LRC.

7.10 Give an example of an organization with an ineffective or cumbersome structure. Explain the problems with the current structure and how these problems could be solved.

7.11 You have been awarded the contract to set up a new restaurant in an existing building at a local university (i.e., there is no need for external construction). The WBS for the project, as developed by the planning team, is presented in Fig. 7.11. Using this WBS, carry out the following exercises:

    a. Develop a coding system for the project.

    b. Identify other types of projects that could use this coding system. For which types of projects would it be inappropriate? Explain.

    c. If you wish to use a more general coding system that deals with construction, what would be the differences between the latter and the more specific coding system developed in part (a)?

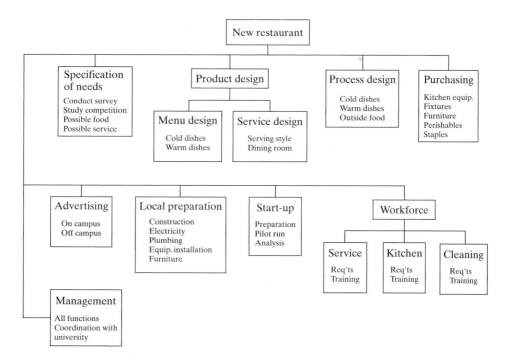

Figure 7.11 WBS for new restaurant.

7.12 You have been offered a contract to undertake the restaurant project in Exercise 7.11 at several campuses that belong to the same university.
   a. Suggest an OBS for these projects.
   b. Generate three WPs, and assign them to the appropriate organizations.
   c. Identify some areas that will require coordination among the organizations included in the OBS to ensure that the three WPs will be completed properly.
   d. Construct a linear responsibility chart for coordinating the work among the various functions that are to be carried out.

7.13 For the restaurant project in Exercise 7.11:
   a. Develop another WBS, making sure that it includes the same WPs that are shown in the original WBS in Fig. 7.11.
   b. Generate additional WPs for the project, and add them to the new WBS.

7.14 You have been assigned the task of developing a network representation of the project in Exercise 7.11 (network construction is taken up in much greater detail in Chapter 9).
   a. Design the network for the WBS in Fig. 7.11. In so doing, each WP in the WBS should correspond to a node in the network, and each arc should indicate a precedence relation. Include in your diagram a dummy start node and a dummy end node.
   b. Extend your network by including several activities for each WP.

7.15 Prepare a Delphi session for selecting the best project manager for a given project.

7.16 Develop a set of guidelines for project managers in international projects that deal with legal and ethical issues.

7.17 Generate an example of project management–related ethical issue, and discuss possible ways to resolve it.

7.18 Generate a WP template, and test it on a selected WP.

BIBLIOGRAPHY

Organizational Structures

Anderson, C. C. and M. M. K. Fleming, "Management Control in an Engineering Matrix Organization: A Project Engineer's Perspective," *Industrial Management,* Vol. 32, No. 2, pp. 8–13, 1990.

Chambers, G. J., "The Individual in a Matrix Organization," *Project Management Journal,* Vol. 20, No. 4, pp. 37–42, 1989.

DiMarco, N., J. R. Goodson and H. F. Houser, "Situational Leadership in a Project/Matrix Environment," *Project Management Journal,* Vol. 20, No. 1, pp. 11–18, 1989.

Kerzner, H. and D. I. Cleland, *Project/Matrix Management Policy and Strategy: Cases and Situations*, Van Nostrand Reinhold, New York, 1997.

McCollum, J. K. and J. D. Sherman, "The Effects of Matrix Organization Size and Number of Project Assignments on Performance," *IEEE Transaction on Engineering Management*, Vol. 38, No. 1, pp. 75–78, 1991.

Nader, D. and M. Gerstein, *Organizational Architectures: Design for Changing Organizations*, Jossey Bass, San Francisco, 1992.

Takahashi, N., "Sequential Analysis of Organization Design: A Model and a Case of Japanese Firms," *European Journal of Operational Research*, Vol. 36, No. 3, pp. 297–310, 1988.

Project Organization

Ashly, P. and T. Edwards, *Introduction to Human Resource Management*, Oxford University Press, New York, 2000.

Carmel, E., *Global Software Teams*, Prentice Hall, Upper Saddle River, NJ, 1999.

Craig, S. and J. Hadi, *People and Project Management for IT*, McGraw-Hill, Boston, 1999.

Globerson, S. and A. Korman, "The Use of Just-in-Time Training in a Project Environment," *International Journal of Project Management*, Vol. 19, pp 279–285, 2001.

Hallows, J., *Project Management Office Toolkit*, Amacom, London, 2001.

Haywood, M., *Managing Virtual Teams: Practical Techniques for High-Technology Project Managers*, Artech House, Norwood, MA, 1998.

Humphrey, W. S., *Managing Technical People: Innovation, Teamwork, and the Software Process*, Addison-Wesley, Reading, MA, 1996.

Meredith, J. R. and S. J. Mantel, Jr., *Project Management: A Managerial Approach*, Fifth Edition, John Wiley & Sons, New York, 2003.

O'Conell, F., *How to Run Successful High-Tech Project Based Organization*, Artech House, Norwood, MA, 2002.

Peters, L., C. R. Greer and S. A. Youngblood (Editors), *The Blackwell Encyclopedic Dictionary of Human Resource Management*, Blackwell Publishers, Malden, MA, 1997.

Pinto, J. (Editor), *Project Leadership: From Theory to Practice*, Project Management Institute, Newtown Square, PA, 1998.

Shapira, A., A. Laufer and A. Shenhar, "Anatomy of Decision Making in Project Teams," *The International Journal of Project Management*, Vol. 12, No. 3, pp. 172–182, 1994.

Williams, J., *Team Development for High-Tech Project Managers*, Artech House, Norwood, MA, 2002.

Work Breakdown Structure

Bohem, B. W., E. Horowitz, R. Madachy, D. Reifer, B. K. Clark, B. Steece, A. W. Brown, S. Chulani and C. Abts, *Software Cost Estimation with COCOMO II*, Prentice Hall, Upper Saddle River, NJ, 2000.

Globerson, S., "Impact of Various Work Breakdown Structure on Project Conceptualization," *International Journal of Project Management*, Vol. 12, No. 3, pp, 165–171, 1994.

Globerson, S., and A. Shtub, "Estimating the Progress of Projects," *Engineering Management Journal*, Vol. 7, No. 3, pp. 39–44, 1995.

Globerson, S., "Scope Management," in J. Knutson (Editor), *Project Management for Business Professionals*, pp. 49–62, John Wiley & Sons, New York, 2001.

Haugan, G., *Effective Work Breakdown Structures*, Management Concepts, Vienna, VA, 2001.

ISO 10007, "Quality Management—Guidelines for Configuration Management," International Organization for Standardization, Geneva, 1995.

Luby, R. E., D. Peel and W. Swahl, "Component Based Work Breakdown Structure," *Project Management Journal*, Vol. 26, No. 4, pp. 38–43, 1995.

Luon, D., *Practical CM: Best Configuration Management Practices for the 21st Century*, Fourth Edition, Raven Publishing, Pittsfield, MA, 2003.

MIL-STD-881, *A Work Breakdown Structure for Defense Military Items*, U.S. Department of Defense, Washington, DC, 1975.

PMI Standards Committee, *A Guide to the Project Management Body of Knowledge (PMBOK)*, Project Management Institute, Newtown Square, PA, 2000 (http://www.PMI.org).

Rad, P., *Project Estimation and Cost Management*, Management Concepts, Vienna, VA, 2002.

Raz, T., "An Iterative Screening Methodology for Selecting Project Alternatives," *Project Management Journal*, Vol. 28, No. 4, pp. 34–39, 1997.

Raz, T. and S. Globerson, "Effective Sizing and Content Definition of Work Packages," *Project Management Journal*, Vol. 29, No. 4, pp. 17–23, 1998.

Shtub, A. and T. Raz, "Optimal Segmentation of Projects—Schedule and Cost Considerations," *European Journal of Operational Research*, Vol. 95, No. 2, pp. 278–283, 1996.

Human Resources

Adams, J., *Conceptual Blockbusting: A Guide to Better Ideas*, Perseus Publishing, New York, 2001.

Carmel, E., *Global Software Teams*, Prentice Hall, Upper Saddle River, NJ, 1999.

Cohen, L., *Quality Function Deployment*, Prentice Hall, Upper Saddle River, NJ, 1995.

Farson, R., *Management of the Absurd*, Simon & Schuster, New York, 1996.

Flannes, S. and G. Levin, *People Skills for Project Managers*, Management Concepts, Vienna, VA, 2001.

Hackman, R., *Leading Teams*, Harvard Business School Press, Boston, 2002.

Hauser, J. R. and D. Clausing, "The House of Quality," *Harvard Business Review*, Vol. 66, No. 3, pp. 62–73, 1988.

Kotter, J., *Leading Change*, Harvard Business School Press, Boston, 1996.

Rahin, A., *Managing Conflicts in Organizations*, Third Edition, Greenwood Publishing/Quorum Books, Westport, CT, 2001.

Sherman, P. S., "Eight Big Masters of Innovation," *Fortune*, pp. 66–81, October 15, 1984.

Vaill, P., *Managing as a Performing Art*, Jossey-Bass, San Francisco, 1990.

Verna, V., *Managing the Project Team*, Project Management Institute, Newtown Square, PA, 1997.

Warfield, J. N., H. Geschka and R. Hamilton, *Methods of Idea Management,* Battelle Institute and Academy of Contemporary Problems, Columbus, OH, 1975.

Chapter 8

Management of Product, Process, and Support Design

8.1 DESIGN OF PRODUCTS, SERVICES, AND SYSTEMS

Design is the conversion of an idea or a need into information from which a new service, product, or system can be developed. It is the "transformation from vague concepts to defined objects, from abstract thoughts to the solution of detailed problems" (Hales 1993). Design is an important part of the life cycle of any product or system. It is also part of any project, either as a phase in the project life cycle or as a process used to introduce changes in existing designs as a result of new information and changes in the environment. Design has an impact on the deliverables of the project as well as on its cost, schedule, and risk. Furthermore, the satisfaction of the project stakeholders depends to a large extent on the management of the design process and its results.

The project manager should not assume that good engineers are guaranteed to produce good designs. It is the project manager's responsibility to implement an appropriate design process and to manage the design effort throughout the life cycle of the project to maximize the technological competitive edge that the project yields.

A good design starts with the selection of the right technology, where "right" connotes the following two primary benefits. First, it provides a market advantage through differentiation of value added, and second, it provides a cost advantage through improved overall system economies. To use technology effectively, companies must be explicit about its role. This requires answering four elementary questions: (1) What is the basis of competition in our industry? (2) To compete, which technologies must we master? (3) How competitive are we in these areas? (4) What is our technology strategy? In embryonic and growth industries, technology frequently drives the strategy, whereas in more mature fields, technology must be an enabling resource for manufacturing, marketing, and customer service. The United States excels at technology-driven innovation that creates whole new enterprises. By contrast, Japan excels at incremental advances in existing products and processes.

In the following sections, general purpose tools and techniques for managing the design process are presented. Specific applications, such as CASE (Computer-Aided Software Engineering) tools for software design, though interesting in their own right, fall outside the scope of the text and will not be discussed.

8.1.1 Principles of Good Design

The success of products, services, and systems is heavily dependent on the quality of the design process. We saw in Chapter 4 that the life-cycle cost (LCC) of a product is determined to a large extent in the design phase. In a similar way, most product characteristics and the corresponding performance measures are also determined in the design phase, including

1. *Operational or functional capability.* This is a measure of the system's ability to perform tasks and satisfy the market's or customer's needs. For example, the range of an electric passenger vehicle, its payload, and its speed are possible measures of operational or functional capabilities. In software selection, the ability to perform all required functions within acceptable time standards is an operational performance measure.

2. *Timeliness.* This measure relates to the time at which the system is available to perform its mission (i.e., the successful completion of acceptance tests and the start of regular operations).

3. *Quality.* The measure of quality relates to the degree that the system's design reflects the market or the customer needs and to the degree that the product or service meets its design specifications. Therefore, the quality of an alternative refers to the system's components, the integration of those components, and the compatibility of the proposed system with the environment in which it will interact. Quality is defined in specific terms for military systems (known as MIL-STD, or military standards); for nonmilitary systems such as planes, boats, buildings, and computers, a host of national and international standards exist. The Institute of Electrical and Electronics Engineers is in the forefront of setting standards for electrical equipment and devices. If adequate standards are not available, then desired quality levels should be specified for both the operational (functional) and the technical (design and workmanship) aspects of the system. The Software Engineering Institute, based at Carnegie-Mellon University, has taken the lead in setting standards for software quality and reliability.

4. *Reliability.* This measure relates to the probability that a product, system, or service will operate properly for a specified period of time under specified conditions without failure. In the simplest form, two factors—the mean time between failures (MTBF) and the mean time to repair (MTTR) the system—can be combined to calculate the proportion of time that the system is available

$$\text{Reliability} = \frac{\text{MTBF}}{\text{MTBF} + \text{MTTR}} \times 100\%$$

There is a correlation between reliability and quality, as a high quality of design, workmanship, and integration usually leads to a high level of reliability. However, reliability also depends on the type of technology used and the operating environment.

5. *Compatibility.* This measure corresponds to the system's ability to operate in harmony with existing or planned systems. For example, a new management information system has a higher degree of compatibility if it can use existing databases. Electronic systems are said to be compatible when they can operate without interference from the electromagnetic radiation put out by other systems in the same vicinity. A new software package is compatible when it has the ability to import and export data from other information systems and databases.

6. *Adaptability.* This measure evaluates a system's ability to operate in conditions other than those initially specified. For example, a communication system that is designed for ground use would be considered a highly adaptable system if it could be used in high-altitude supersonic aircraft without losing any of its functionality. Systems with high adaptabilities are preferred when future operating conditions are difficult to forecast. A highly adaptable software package is one that can run on different computer types under a variety of operating systems in addition to the computer and operating system specified.

7. *Life span.* This measure has a direct impact on both cost and effectiveness. Because of learning and efforts at continued process improvement, systems with a longer life span tend to improve over time. This eliminates the need for frequent capital investments and hence reduces total LCC.

8. *Simplicity.* The process of learning a new system while it is being introduced into an organization depends on its simplicity. A system that is easy to maintain and operate is usually accepted faster and creates fewer difficulties for the user. Furthermore, complicated systems may not be maintained and exercised adequately, especially during startup or periods of change when there is high turnover in the organization. A software package that is simple to operate and maintain is one that is developed according to software engineering standards regarding modularity, documentation, and so on.

9. *Safety.* The methods by which a system will be operated and maintained should be considered in the advanced development phase. Safety precautions should be introduced and evaluated to minimize the risk of accidents. As with quality, designing a safe system from the start can provide significant benefits over the long run.

10. *Commonality.* A high level of commonality with other systems either used by or produced by the organization should be a driving force in the design. Commonality has many facets, such as common parts and subsystems, input sources, communication channels, databases, and equipment for troubleshooting and maintenance. Many airlines insist that all aircraft that they buy within a particular class, regardless of manufacturer, have the same engines. Southwest airlines has taken this one step further and buys only one type of aircraft—Boeing 737s. In a similar vein, the U.S. Department of Defense developed the computer language Ada in the late 1970s and for many years required that all programs commissioned by any of its branches be written in Ada.

11. *Maintainability*. Providing adequate maintenance for a system is essential. There is a question, though, as to how much preventive maintenance should be scheduled. When system is out of service, it cannot perform its assigned tasks. The loss in operational time must be weighed against the probability of system failure and the need for unscheduled maintenance, which, in turn, reduces the system's overall effectiveness. Higher levels of maintainability lead to better labor utilization and lower personnel training costs. Part of maintainability is testability—the ability to detect a system failure and pinpoint its source in a timely manner. Higher levels of maintainability and testability contribute to the effectiveness of a system. In the design of software, a well-documented source code, as well as clearly defined interfaces between the modules of the software package, helps in the detection and correction of bugs.

12. *Friendliness*. This performance measure quantifies the effort and time required to learn how to operate and maintain a system. A friendly system requires less time and skill to learn and hence reduces both direct and indirect labor costs. In software, the use of menus, on-line help, and pointing devices such as a mouse can increase the friendliness of the software package.

8.1.2 Management of Technology and Design in Projects

Although some projects do not have a design phase in their life cycle (these are known as built-to-print projects), almost every project must have a mechanism for addressing design changes. Configuration management systems that deal with design changes will be discussed later in the chapter. Design changes are common in all projects because new information that was not available during the design phase may call for a reassessment of the original assumptions and decisions.

Design activities begin with "the voice of the customer," an analysis of the client's or organization's needs, which are translated into technical factors and operation and maintenance plans. A common tool for this process is quality function deployment, or the house of quality (see Section 8.4). Once approved by the client or upper management, these requirements are transformed into functional and technical specifications. The last link in the chain is detailed product, process, and support design. Product design centers on the structure and shape of the product. Performance, cost, and quality goals all must be defined. Process design deals with the preparation of a series of plans for manufacture, integration, testing, and quality control. In the case of an item to be manufactured, this means selecting the processes and equipment to be used during production, setting up the part routings, defining the information flows, and ensuring that adequate testing procedures are put into place.

Support design is responsible for selecting the hardware and software that will be used to track and monitor performance once the system becomes operational. This means developing databases, defining report formats, and specifying communication protocols for the exchange of data. A second support function concerns the preparation of manuals for operators and maintenance personnel. Related issues center on the design of maintenance facilities and equipment and the development of policies for inventory management. Both process design and support design include the design of training for those who manufacture, test, operate, and maintain the system.

Design efforts are relevant to many nonengineering projects. Such efforts are required to transform needs into the blueprint of the final product. For example, consider the design of a new insurance policy or a change in the structure of an organization. In the first case, new needs may be detected by the marketing department—for example, a need to provide insurance for pilots of ultra-light airplanes. The designer of the new policy should consider the various risks involved in flying ultra-lights and the cost and probability of occurrence associated with each risk. In addition to the risk to the pilot as a result of accidents, damage to the ultra-light or to a third party must be considered. The designer of the new policy has to decide which options should be available to the customer and how the different options should be combined.

In the case of new products, changes in the business environment and new technologies may generate a need to restructure an organization. For example, if a new product is very successful in a traditional organization and the business associated with this product becomes critical to the financial well-being of the organization, then a special division may be needed to manufacture, market, and support this product. The designer of the new organizational structure should consider questions related to the size of the new division and its mission and relationship with the existing parts of the organization.

In some projects, the design effort represents the most important component of the work. Examples are an architect who is designing a new building and a team of communication experts who are designing a satellite relay network. Usually, design is the basis for production or implementation, depending on the context. In many situations, the design effort may consume only a small portion of the assigned budget and resources. Nevertheless, decisions made in the conceptual design and advanced development phases are likely to have a significant effect on the total budget, schedule, resource requirements, performances, and overall success of the project.

Management of the design effort, from identifying a specific need to implementation of the end product, is the core of the technological aspect of project management. That design takes place in the early stages of most projects does not imply that technological management efforts cease once the blueprints are drawn. Changes in design are notoriously common throughout the life cycle of a project and have to be managed carefully.

8.2 ROLE OF THE PROJECT MANAGER

The project manager is responsible for assigning the total work content specified in the statement of work (SOW) to the participating units. In Chapter 7, we explained how work packages are constructed from the work breakdown structure (WBS) and assigned to the lowest level units in the organizational breakdown structure (OBS). Design efforts are part of the statement of work (SOW) and are similarly allocated to members of the performing organization or outsourced. In either case, it is the responsibility of the project manager to oversee both the design process and the change process throughout the project life cycle. In so doing, five major factors must be considered: quality, cost, time, risk, and performance, the last being measured by the functional attributes of the system. The tools for assessing each of these factors in the initial stages of a project were discussed in Chapter 3, Engineering Economic Analysis; Chapter 5, Project Screening and Selection; and Chapter 6, Multiple-Criteria Methods for Evaluation. In Chapter 4, we discussed life-cycle costing and showed how (design) decisions made early in the project affect the total LCC. To underscore the importance of a good design, we cite a National Science Foundation study that showed that more than 70% of the LCC of a product is defined at the conceptual and preliminary design stages. Information and decision support systems play a dynamic role in these stages by focusing management's efforts on technology and providing feedback to the design team in the form of assessment data.

Our aim here is to discuss how the techniques discussed previously can be used throughout the life cycle of a project to manage its design processes and thus its technological aspects. Frequently, the design is subject to change as a result of newly identified needs, changing business conditions, and the evolution of the underlying technology. Therefore, the management of the design (or technological management) is a continuing process that ends only with delivery of the finished product to the customer and perhaps not even then. Manufacturer warranties and an insistent desire for product improvement in some markets may keep a project alive well after delivery of the product(s).

8.3 IMPORTANCE OF TIME AND THE USE OF TEAMS

In the global market, successful companies will be those that learn to make and deliver goods and services faster than their competitors. These "turbo marketers," as Kotler and Stonich (1991) term them, will have a distinct advantage in markets where customers value time compression enough to pay a premium or to increase purchases. Moreover, in certain high-tech areas, such as semiconductor manufacturing and telecommunications, where performance is increasing and price is dropping almost daily, survival depends on the rapid introduction of new technologies.

Once a company has examined the demand for its product, it can begin to reduce cycle time. In general, three principles can be applied: (1) reorganize the work, (2) organize and reward to encourage time compression, and (3) pursue cycle time reduction aggressively. Although the implementation effort and cost required to reduce cycle time will be substantial, the payoff can be great. To create a sustainable advantage, companies must couple the so-called "soft" aspects of management with programs aimed at achieving measurable time-based results.

In this regard, a trend in technology management is to perform all major components of design concurrently. This approach, aptly known as *concurrent engineering*, is based on the concept that the parallel execution of the major design components will shorten project life cycles and thus reduce the time to market for new products. In an era of time-based competition, when the shelf life of some high-tech items may be as short as 6 months, this can make the difference between mere survival and material profits.

Studies by the consulting firm McKinsey & Co. have shown repeatedly that being a few months late to market is even worse than having a 30% development cost overrun. Figure 8.1 points out the difference in revenue when a product is on time or late. The model underlying the graph assumes that there are three phases in the product's commercial life: a growth phase (when sales increase at a fixed rate regardless of entry time), a stagnation phase (when sales level off), and a decline phase (when sales decrease to

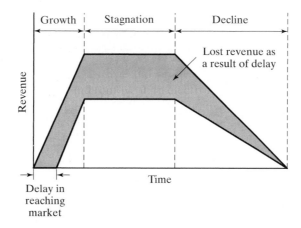

Figure 8.1   Lost revenue as a result of delay in reaching market.

zero). Figure 8.1 shows that a delay causes a significant decline in revenue. Suppose that a market has a 6-month growth period followed by a year of stagnation and a decline to zero sales in the succeeding 8 months. Then, being late to market by 3 months would reduce revenues by 36%. Thus, a delay of one eighth of the product lifetime reduces income by more than one third. Such a loss can be especially severe because the largest profits are usually realized during the growth phase.

The application of concurrent engineering principles to technology management requires thoughtful planning and oversight. There is a clear need to inform the product engineers, process engineers, and support specialists of the current status of the design and to keep them updated on all change requests. This is accomplished by the configuration management systems discussed later in the chapter. Because of the rapid propagation of errors, the risk of cost and schedule overruns, faltering performance, and team bickering is greatly increased when control is lax. An error in one aspect of the design may have repercussions that quickly extend to all functional areas.

In the following sections, we explore the issues surrounding concurrent engineering, configuration management, and describe the risk and quality aspects of technological management.

8.3.1 Concurrent Engineering and Time-Based Competition

The ability to design and produce high-quality products that satisfy a real need at a competitive price was, for many years, almost a sure guarantee for commercial success. With the explosion of electronic and information technology, a new factor—time—has become a critical element in the equation. The ability to reduce the time required to develop new products and bring them to market is considered by many the next industrial battleground. For example, the Boeing 777 transport design took a year and half less than its predecessor the 767, permitting the company to introduce it in time to stave off much of the competition from the European Airbus. Similarly, John Deere's success in trimming development time for new products by 60% has enabled it to maintain its position as world leader in farm equipment in the face of a growing challenge from the Japanese. This was done using the concurrent engineering (CE) approach to support time-based competition. Griffin (1997a,b) found that 64% of the projects that she surveyed used cross-functional teams. CE's major advantage is in creating more manufacturable designs (Fleischer and Liker 1997).

The basic idea of CE is to use project scheduling and resource management techniques in the design process. These techniques, discussed in Chapters 9 and 10, have always been common to the production phase but are now recognized as vital to all life-cycle phases of a project from start to finish. In a CE environment, teams of experts from different disciplines work together to ensure that the design progresses smoothly and that all of the participants share the same, most recent information.

The CE approach replaces the conventional sequential engineering approach in which new product development starts by one organizational unit (e.g., marketing), which lays out product specifications on customer needs. These specifications are used by engineers to come up with a product design, which in turn serves as the basis for manufacturing engineering to develop the production processes and flows. Only when this last step is approved does support design begin.

Sequential engineering takes longer because all of the design activities are strictly ordered. Furthermore, cycles are common throughout the project's life cycle. This is the case when product specifications prepared by marketing cannot be met by the available technology (unless, perhaps, a risky or costly research and development [R&D] effort is undertaken). Similarly, manufacturing engineering may not be able to translate product design into process design, as a result of technological difficulties or the absence of adequate support (e.g., it may not be economically practical to develop test equipment for a product that has not been designed with testing in mind). In each of these examples, primary activities have to be repeated, creating cycles and thus lengthening the entire design process, making it that much more expensive.

Put succinctly, concurrent engineering depends on designing, developing, testing, and building prototype parts and subsystems concurrently, not serially, while designing and developing the equipment to fabricate the new product or system. This does not necessarily mean that all tasks are performed in parallel but rather that the team members from the various departments make their contribution in parallel. A prime objective of CE is to shorten the time from conception to market (or deployment in the case of government or military systems), so as to be more competitive or responsive to evolving needs.

The basis of CE is teamwork, parallel operations, information sharing, and constant communication among team members. In recent years, the terms *integrated product team* (IPT) and *integrated product development* have been used to describe a team that is responsible for the whole design and support process. The IPT concept is discussed in more detail in the next subsection. To be most effective, the team should be multidisciplinary, composed of one or more representatives from each functional area of the organization. The watchword is cooperation. After a century of labor–management confrontation and sequestering employees in job categories, hierarchies, and functional departments, many manufacturers are now seeking teamwork, dialogue, and barrier bashing, if only for survival. By performing product, process, and support design in parallel, there is a much greater likelihood that misunderstandings and problems of incompatibility will be averted over the project's life cycle. By reducing the length of the design process, overhead and management costs are reduced proportionally, while the elimination of design cycles reduces direct costs as well. These cost-related issues are discussed in detail in Chapter 11. From a marketing point of view, a shorter design process results in the ability to introduce new models more frequently and to target specific models to specific groups of customers. This strategy leads to a higher market share and, consequently, to higher sales and profits.

The implementation of CE is based on shared databases, good management of design information (this is the subject of configuration management), and computerized design tools such as CAD/CAM (computer-aided design/computer-aided manufacturing) and CASE (computer-aided software engineering). It is also important to understand that CE is risky and that without proper technological and risk management, the results can be calamitous. The two most prominent risks are

1. *Organizational risks.* The attempt to cross the lines of functional organizations and to introduce changes into the design process is usually met with resistance. One way to overcome this resistance, often manifested by inertia and subtle acts of neglect, is to form project teams (IPTs) that are made up of people from the various functional areas before the implementation of CE. In addition, an educational effort aimed at teaching the advantages and the logic of CE can create a positive atmosphere for this new approach.

2. *Technological risks.* The simultaneous effort of product, process, and support design should be well coordinated to ensure that the information that is used by all of the designers is current and correct. Configuration management systems are the key to ensure that the information that is used by all of the designers is current and correct. The risks associated with a failure to manage this design information in the CE environment is much higher than in sequential engineering, where it is possible to freeze product design once process design starts and to freeze process design once support design starts.

Companies that are thinking about using CE techniques for the first time should consider projects that have the following characteristics:

1. The project can be classified as developmental (novel applications of known technology) or applied (routine applications of known technology).

2. The team has experience with the technology.

3. The team has received training in quality management and has had the opportunity to apply the concepts in its work.

4. The scale of the project falls somewhere in the range of 5 to 35 full-time staff members for a period of 3 to 30 months.

5. The goal is a product or family of products with clearly defined features and functions.

6. Success is not dependent on invention or significant innovation.

8.3.2 Time Management

As mentioned, one of the goals of CE is to reduce the time that it takes to develop and market new products. Before we can say that a reduction has been achieved, we must have some idea of what the current standards are and what controls them. This is not as clear-cut as it sounds, because few projects proceed smoothly without interference from outside forces. Also, most companies modify their goals as work progresses, making it that much more difficult to measure project length.

Every industry and its constituent firms are in continuous flux, but they all are limited in their flexibility to achieve change. A number of inhibiting factors combine to create a rhythm or tempo in a company that is very difficult to break. Table 8.1 lists some of these factors for manufacturing companies, although each may not be universally applicable at all times. Thoughtful engineering managers develop a feeling for the important factors in their business and how these affect their operations. As far as possible, they quantify them. This provides a baseline against which improvement can be measured. It is clear that many time-sensitive decisions have an impact on the successful operation of a business and that focusing on only one or two factors to the exclusion of the others is rarely optimal. CE is a business activity, not just an engineering activity. Market success is a function of a firm's ability to improve all of its key tempo factors by integrating current engineering decisions with business decisions. Important issues are

TABLE 8.1   Factors That Affect the Tempo of Manufacturing Firms

Technology life	Market forces
Product lifetime costs	Product life
Product development cycle	Process development cycle
Market development cycle	Economic cycle
Workforce hiring/training	Capital/loan acquisition
Long-lead items	Access to limited resources
Manufacturing capacity planning	Competitive product introductions

IPT. Many people have written about time management for individuals. CE requires time management for organizations. The principles are the same, but their implementations are somewhat different. Two notorious time wasters are senior people doing junior work and everyone repeating the same tasks. These are both addressed by the IPT approach—forming a multifunctional project team from the appropriate departments and carefully assigning responsibilities to the members. Not everyone is needed full time on every team, but the organizing plan should indicate where to get resources when needed on a part-time basis. All team members, whether active or not, should be kept informed of progress so that they do not have to waste time catching up when called into play. Examples of people who fall into this category are patent attorneys, illustrators, and technical specialists needed for tricky problems.

The participation of staff from all major functions—marketing, development, manufacturing, finance, and so on—from the first day of the project makes a direct contribution to the reduction of duplicate effort. The marketing person can immediately comment on the desirability of some feature before the development person has spent time on it. Similarly, the development staff can get immediate feedback from manufacturing on the producibility of a particular design.

Tools. The team organization will lose effectiveness if the members are not provided with appropriate tools. Today this usually means access to personal computers, applications software, and system support for CAD, CAE, CIM, CASE, and other computer-aided disciplines. Team members must also be trained in the effective use of the tools. Just as the craftsman can do better work than the journeyman, so can the trained specialist with a detailed understanding of the capabilities of computer-aided systems compared with an untrained person using the same tools.

Team empowerment. The IPT organization will also lose effectiveness if there are unnecessary delays in decision making. This is another major source of time wasting. The solution is the well-known empowerment approach, which gives the team the authority to make the majority of the decisions. This is not to say that upper management should not be informed of those decisions on a regular basis, but the natural tendency to second guess those who are doing the work should be restricted. The initial program plan should include some major review points, called *design reviews*, when upper management and peer evaluation can influence the course of the project. These meetings should not be determined by the calendar but rather by progress. The same principle is true of meetings among team members. Setting them up every Tuesday at 8:00 a.m. usually leads people to spend all day Monday preparing for Tuesday and all day Wednesday responding to Tuesday. Have frequent team meetings, but schedule them at short notice to deal with issues as they arise. To use the project scheduling terminology, team meetings are activities, not events. Many companies have difficulty implementing the empowerment requirement because it encroaches on established lines of authority. This is one area where CE can actually increase risks, not reduce them, unless special attention is paid to it.

If there is an important role for upper management to play during the course of day-to-day activities, then it is in assigning access to limited resources. If two or more teams need access to a special piece of equipment, say, for production trials, then there has to be a responsive mechanism in place to set priorities. Again, the initial project plan must cover this situation.

Use of design authorities. Another approach to facilitate decision making is to appoint design authorities in various areas. For example, there could be a technology design authority, a product design authority, a process design authority, and an equipment design authority. The authorities must be legitimate experts in their fields. They do not necessarily do the design work and may not, in fact, be full-time members of the team. Their role is to help the project manager make the final decision when two or more conflicting approaches have been recommended and to provide peer evaluation and review when needed. The design authority should not be called in until the competing approaches have been documented in equivalent detail. He or she is a last resort to help resolve sticky issues. By having them available and identified in the plan with their role clearly spelled out, it is possible to facilitate decision making even in complex situations. Nevertheless, the ultimate decision maker is the project manager. The design authorities are consultants who are called on only to evaluate competing solutions and offer their expertise.

Quality. A major time waster is repeating work because of poor quality. Every person on the team must realize that he or she has "customers," many of which are fellow team members, whereas some are outsiders who will use their products. Developing procedures and habits that focus on delivering satisfaction to the customers, both internal and external, goes a long way in reducing the need to correct or redo work. Obviously, careful selection of team members also goes a long way in ensuring high-quality results. Here is where the best interests of a CE team can conflict with the best interests of individuals. Unless the company implementing the procedures takes special steps to prevent it, working on a CE team can limit growth opportunities for individuals and even eliminate career paths. The project manager wants to be assured of high-quality work in all areas and will tend to select people who have already demonstrated their ability to deliver. The problem can be especially acute for junior staff members who have demonstrated their skills in one area but are not given a chance to expand into other areas because they are continually asked to work on projects that require their known skills.

Bureaucracy. The final time waster of note is lengthy administrative and bureaucratic procedures. Eberhardt Rechtin, a former vice president of engineering at Hewlett-Packard, once said that an approval takes $2n$ days, where n is the number of levels of approval needed. The obvious solution to this problem is to empower the project team in advance with all of the necessary approval authority. Again, this means that the initial project plan must be prepared very carefully. Another approach to shortening the time required for administration is to provide the team leader with the authority to eliminate competitive bidding procedures on certain development items involving known vendors. Other bureaucratic red tape should also be eliminated, although this makes sense even in the absence of CE. Many companies assign a full-time administrator/facilitator to CE teams to relieve the project manager of the burden of handling all of the details.

External participation. The best users of CE also extend the concept of the project team to involve key vendors and customers. The customers can help minimize the time required to define and specify the product, facilitate product acceptance procedures, and reduce project risk by either ordering early or at least indicating through a letter of intent what their purchases may be. Vendors can be extraordinarily helpful members of the team by providing technical support for the application of their products and materials and by providing preferential access to scarce resources. In return, they get some indication of likely sales. If a company uses formal vendor certification procedures, they should extend them to "certifying" selected key vendors as participants in CE development programs.

Toyota Example.   To cut the length of the design cycle and to improve the quality of the design, Toyota implemented a design process in which IPT plays a major role. Each IPT is headed by a *shusa*, or big boss, whose name becomes synonymous with the project. Members are assigned to the project for its life but retain ties with the functional area (continuity) from which they were drawn. Team member performance is evaluated by the shusa and is used to determine subsequent assignments. Team members sign pledges to do exactly what everyone has agreed on as a group and try to resolve critical design tradeoffs early. The number of team members is highest at the outset of a project. As development proceeds, the number dwindles as certain specialties (e.g., market assessment) are no longer needed.

8.3.3 Guideposts for Success

On the surface, the idea of multifunctional product design and development teams along with self-managing work groups seems unassailable. Nevertheless, a critical issue remains: How do you keep such teams from becoming committees with plenty of talk but little action? Tom Peters (1991), a well-know management consultant, postulated the following guideposts to help organizations implement the team concept:

1. *Set goals, deadlines, or key subsystem tests.* Committees deliberate. Project teams do. Successful project teams are characterized by a clear goal, although the exact path is left unclear to induce creativity. Also, three to six strict due dates for subsystem technical and market tests/experiments are set and adhered to religiously.

2. *Insist on 100% assignment to the team.* Members must be obsessed by the project. Forget "one fifth obsession": key function members must be assigned full time for the project's duration.

3. *Place key functions on board from the outset.* Members from sales, distribution, marketing, finance, purchasing, operations/manufacturing, and design/engineering should be part of the project team from day 1. Legal, personnel, and others should provide full-time members for part of the project.

4. *Give members authority to commit their function.* With few exceptions, each member should be able to commit resources from his or her function to project goals and deadlines without second-guessing from higher-ups. Top management must establish and enforce this rule from the start. If commitments from members' primary functional areas (e.g., engineering) are conditional, then you have a committee.

5. *Keep team-member destiny in the hands of the project leader.* For consulting firms such as Booz, Allen & Hamilton and McKinsey & Co., life is a series of projects. The team leader might be from San Francisco or Sydney, Australia; either way, his or her evaluation of team members' performance will make or break a career. In general, then, the project boss rather than the functional boss should evaluate team members. Otherwise, the project concept falls flat.

6. *Make careers a string of projects.* A career in a "project-minded company" is viewed as a string of multifunction tasks. How one does on these determines career prospects.

7. *Live together.* Project teams should be sequestered from headquarters as much as possible. Team camaraderie and commitment depend to a surprising extent on "hanging out" together, isolated from one's normal set of functional colleagues.

8. *Remember the social element.* Spirit is important: "We're in it together." "Mission impossible." High spirits are not accidental. The challenge of the task per se is central. Beyond that, the successful team leader facilitates what psychologists call "bonding." This can take the form of "signing up" ceremonies upon joining the team, frequent (at least monthly) milestone celebrations, and humorous awards for successes and setbacks alike.

9. *Allow outsiders in.* The product development team notion is incomplete unless outsiders participate. Principal vendors, distributors, and "lead" (future test-site) customers should be full-time members. Outsiders not only contribute directly but also add authenticity and enhance the sense of distinctiveness and task commitment.

10. *Construct self-contained systems.* At the risk of duplicating equipment and support, the engaged team should have its own workstations, local area network, database, and so on. This is necessary to foster an "its-up-to-us-and-we've-got-the-wherewithal" environment. However, the additional risk created by too much isolation must be balanced with the need for self-sufficiency. Problems may arise when it comes time to integrate the project with the rest of the firm.

11. *Permit the teams to pick their own leader.* A champion blessed by management gets things under way, but successful project teams usually select *and alter* their own leaders as circumstances warrant. It is expected that leadership will shift over the course of the project, as one role and then another dominates a particular stage (engineering first, then manufacturing, distribution later).

12. *Honor project leadership skills.* No less than a wholesale reorientation of the firm is called for away from "vertical" (functional specialists dominate) and toward "horizontal" (cross-functional teams are the norm). In this environment, horizontal project leadership becomes the most cherished skill in the firm, rewarded by dollars and promotions. Good team skills, for junior members, are also valued and rewarded.

Few experts or practitioners disagree: To halve product development time and constantly improve quality and service, all companies must destroy the walls between functions and commit to perpetual "horizontal" improvement projects, but to become project focused requires more than appointing teams. Teams and task forces have often ended up adding to rather than subtracting from bureaucracy. Care must be taken to avoid the project-turned-committee trap.

8.3.4 Industrial Experience

The success stories of CE implementation in companies such as Boeing, Hewlett-Packard, Raytheon, and John Deere have been amply documented and reported at professional conferences, including those sponsored by the Computer-Aided Acquisition and Logistics Support Society, the Society for Computer-Aided Engineering, the Institute of Industrial Engineers, and the Society of Manufacturing Engineers. We cite a few short examples to gain a better appreciation of the issues.

For Cadillac, a winner of the Malcolm Baldrige National Quality Award, CE has come to mean a new culture and a new way of designing and building its extraordinary, complex product—luxury cars. Engineers, designers, and assemblers are now members of vehicle, vehicle-systems, and product (parts) teams that work in close coordination rather than belonging to separate, isolated functional areas as before. Assembly line workers, dealers, repair shop managers, and customers provide insight to engineers involved in all stages of design. To inspire cultural change, Cadillac created a position of champion of simultaneous engineering (a role that combines keeping the process on track, preaching to the believers, and motivating the recalcitrant) and sent 1,400 employees to seminars on quality management. They also established an "Assembly Line Effectiveness Center," where production workers rub shoulders with engineers, critiquing prototypes for manufacturability.

John Deere's Industrial Equipment Division in Moline, Illinois, has had two concurrent engineering efforts. The first, begun in 1984, failed because management retained the traditional manufacturing departments. Designers and process engineers who were assigned to task groups remained loyal to the interests of their disciplines rather than to the overall enterprise. In 1988, the division reorganized. Staff members now report to product teams and answer to team leaders, not functional department heads. Early in the design stage, teams create a product definition document that describes the product precisely, sets deadlines, and lays out the manufacturing plan. Products no longer change as departments work on them. The result has been gradual improvements in manufacturing processes. There are now fewer experimental designs, and it is possible to produce prototypes in the production environment. The advantage of this is that in addition to checking for flaws in the prototypes themselves, engineers can simultaneously perfect the manufacturing process.

The third example comes from Federal-Mogul, a precision parts manufacturer in Southfield, Michigan. The first Federal-Mogul unit to adopt concurrent engineering was its troubled oil-seal business. Other units quickly followed.

Success in the oil-seal business, in which products are simple but must meet exacting standards, requires rapid turnaround on bids and prototypes and strong customer service. By providing estimates to customers in minutes instead of weeks and producing sample seals in 20 working days instead of 20 weeks, market share soared. Federal-Mogul accomplished this by adopting a cross-functional product team approach to manufacturing, encouraging consensus building and empowerment, and introducing new information technologies. Key applications include networks that allow all plants to share CAD drawings and machine tools, a scheduling system that automatically notifies appropriate team members when a new order comes in, an engineering data management system, and an on-line database of past orders.

8.3.5 Unresolved Issues

From a technical point of view, what makes CE possible are the recent advances in hardware and software, database systems, electronic communications, and the various components of computer-integrated manufacturing. At the first International Workshop on Concurrent Engineering Design, sponsored by the National Science Foundation (Hsu et al. 1991), four themes emerged from the discussions: models, tools, training, and culture. Participants identified measurement issues and tradeoffs that will inform future models of new product development. They concluded that tools must focus on expanded CAD/CAM/CAPP capabilities with strong interfaces. Training is needed for multiple job stations, in the impact of design on downstream tasks, and in teamwork and individual responsibility. Corporate culture—and how to change it—must be better understood. Important aspects of culture to be clarified include incentives and performance, myths that inhibit an organization's progress, and the management of change.

One of the primary roles of CE is identifying the interdependencies and constraints that exist over the life cycle of a product and ensuring that the design team is aware of them. Nevertheless, care must be taken in the early stages to avoid overwhelming the design team with constraints and stifling their creativity for the sake of simplicity. A truly creative design that satisfies customer requirements in a superior manner may justify the expense of relaxing some of the development and process guidelines.

Although a basic tenet of CE is that input to the design process should come from all life cycle stages, there is much ambiguity about how to achieve this. At exactly what point in the CE process should discussion of assembly, sequences, tolerances, and support requirements be introduced? Also, tradeoffs abound. For example, consolidation of parts is desirable, yet too much consolidation implies costly and inefficient procurement and inventorying. A balance must be struck between meeting the customer's specifications, designing for manufacturability, and LCC. This means that cost information should be available to the design teams, not just the accounting department, throughout the project.

8.4 SUPPORTING TOOLS

8.4.1 Quality Function Deployment

A quality product is one that meets or exceeds stakeholders' needs and expectations. Thus, the design quality is the degree to which product, process, and support design meets or exceeds stakeholders' needs and expectations, and the quality of conformance is the degree to which the product, service, or system delivered meets the design specifications.

Clearly, a quality design is the translation of needs and expectations into the blueprints of the product, process, and support system. An important technique that accompanies quality design and CE is quality function deployment (QFD), introduced by Yoji Akao. QFD is based on using interdisciplinary teams. The members of the teams study the market (customers) to determine the required characteristics of the product or system. These characteristics are classified into customer attributes and are listed in order of their relative importance to the customer.

The ranked attributes, also called the "whats," are the input to a second step in which the team members translate the attributes into technical specifications, or "hows." Thus, an attribute such as "a tape recorder that is easy to carry around" can be translated into physical dimensions and weight that can be used to guide product development. This example, of course, led to Sony's Walkman. The joint effort by the team members promotes CE while ensuring better communication and easier integration of the basic functions.

A matrix called the *quality chart* is used in the QFD process. The rows of the quality chart list in hierarchical order the attributes (the "whats"); the design characteristics (the "hows") are similarly listed across the columns. Each cell in the resulting matrix corresponds to a lower-level attribute intersection with a lower-level design characteristic. Entries indicate the correlation between the corresponding attribute and design characteristic. From the matrix, the team members can infer the relative importance of the attributes along with their correlated design characteristics and the degree of correlation. On the basis of this information, a weight, w_i, is calculated for each design characteristic, i. This weight is the sum of all attribute weights, a_j, multiplied by the corresponding correlation, c_{ij}, between the specific design characteristic and the particular attribute. The formula for calculating w_i is

$$w_i = \sum_j a_j c_{ij}$$

QFD is a powerful tool that helps the CE team focus on the design characteristics that influence the attributes viewed as most important by customers. The weights derived as part of the process serve this purpose directly. To illustrate the ideas behind QFD, consider a project aimed at designing a new cross-country bicycle. By using market research, the project team can identify the most important attributes of this product for its potential customers. Suppose that the four top-ranking attributes were found to be durability, convenience, speed, and cost. Next, the team considers the three major components of the new bicycle: the frame, the gears, and the wheels. Table 8.2 illustrates the relationship between the attributes required by the customers and the design characteristics.

TABLE 8.2   Quality Chart for New Bicycle Design

			Design characteristics				
			1. Frame		2. Gears		3. Wheels	
Attributes		Weight (a_j)	1.1 Material	1.2 Design	2.1 Material	2.2 Design	3.1 Material	3.2 Design
1. *Durability*	1.1 Corrosion	2	H	L	H	M	H	M
	1.2 Impact	1	H	H	H	H	H	H
	1.3 Pressure	3	H	H	H	M	H	H
	1.4 Wear	2	M	L	H	H	H	M
2. *Convenience*	2.1 Carrying	3	H	M	L	L	H	H
	2.2 Riding	3	M	M	M	H	H	H
	2.3 Maintenance	2	L	M	H	H	H	H
3. *Speed*	3.1 Flat surface	1	M	H	M	H	L	H
	3.2 Up hill	3	M	H	M	H	L	H
	3.3 Down hill	2	M	H	M	H	L	H
4. *Cost*	4.1 Purchase	2	H	H	M	H	H	M
	4.2 Maintenance	2	M	M	H	H	H	M
	4.3 Salvage value	1	H	H	M	H	H	M

H = high correlation; M = medium correlation; L = low correlation

Now, assuming that the correlations used are H = 0.9, M = 0.5, L = 0.3, the weight of, say, the frame material (w_1) is

$$w_1 = \sum_{j=1}^{13} a_j c_{1j} = 2 \times 0.9 + 1 \times 0.9 + 3 \times 0.9 + 2 \times 0.5 + 3 \times 0.9 + 3 \times 0.5$$

$$+ 2 \times 0.3 + 1 \times 0.5 + 3 \times 0.5 + 2 \times 0.5 + 2 \times 0.9$$

$$+ 2 \times 0.5 + 1 \times 0.9 = 17.9$$

In Table 8.2, only two levels of attributes and design characteristics are presented. Lower levels, such as the dimensions and shape of the frame and the size of each gear in the transmission, can be added if more detail is deemed necessary. Additional information frequently found in the quality chart is the relative importance of each attribute, target value of design characteristics, information about similar products available in the market, and the correlation between design characteristics.

In general terms, QFD uses four "houses" to integrate the informational needs of marketing, engineering, R&D, manufacturing, and management. The best known is the first, the *house of quality*, shown conceptually in Fig. 8.2. For new-product development, the team begins by obtaining the "voice of the customer" in the form of 200 to 300 detailed customer needs, such as (on-screen programming) "a menu appears on the TV screen with easy-to-read instructions." These customer needs are grouped hierarchically into a relatively few primary needs (to establish the strategic position), 20 to 30 secondary needs (to design the basic product and its marketing), and 150 to 250 tertiary needs (to provide specific design direction to engineers). Customer perceptions of competitive products provide goals and opportunities for new products. The importance of customer needs establishes design priorities.

The relationship matrix translates customer needs, the language of marketing, into engineering language. Engineering design attributes, such as an automatic shutoff time delay, provide the means to satisfy customer needs. Performance measures of the design attributes (seconds of delay, etc.) establish competitor capabilities. Finally, the "roof matrix" (upper triangle in Fig. 8.2) quantifies the physical interrelations among the design attributes—instructions must be succinct and correlate with the design.

The house of quality encourages cooperation and communication among functions by requiring input from marketing (the customer's voice) and from engineering

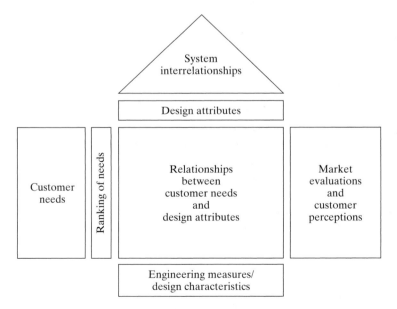

Figure 8.2   House of quality.

(engineering measures and the roof matrix), and agreement on interrelationships. The entire team should participate with all members understanding and accepting these inputs and relationships. Once the house of quality is complete, the other "houses" link design attributes to part characteristics, part characteristics to manufacturing processes, and manufacturing processes to the production line. A complete set of QFD houses represents the customer's needs through every product development function. Further discussion on these ideas can be found in the work of Hauser and Clausing (1988).

8.4.2 Configuration Selection

Configuration is a term that refers to the complete description of the physical and functional characteristics of a product or a system. Configuration is the output of the design process. In large technologically sophisticated projects, selection of the best design by a direct comparison among the functional efficiencies of the alternatives is difficult and sometimes impossible, as a result of technological uncertainties, the absence of a single agreed-on objective, the size of the system, and the system's complexity. In such projects, it might not be appropriate to make a decision solely on the basis of the cost of development and manufacturing. Once the system is put into place, its operations and maintenance costs may be significant enough, even after discounting over the useful life, to warrant consideration when the original decision is being made.

Cost-effectiveness and benefit-cost (B/C) analyses are intended to assist in the selection of the most appropriate design alternative for system development or system modification–type projects. These techniques are supported by a variety of models used to estimate the functional efficiency, the risk, and the LCC of each technological alternative.

The selection process may be driven by the available budget or by the functional requirements. In the first case, the available budget for the project is viewed as a binding constraint, and an effort is made to design a system with the best possible capabilities without exceeding the budget. This is known as the *design-to-cost* approach. In the second case, the design effort is aimed at minimizing the ratio between the cost of the system and its effectiveness. This is known as the *cost-effectiveness* approach. In either case, there is a need to define and estimate the value of some performance measures for cost and effectiveness. Both approaches are used in the process of configuration selection. This process takes place before and during the detailed design phase, when the exact configuration of the system and each of its components are selected.

The techniques discussed earlier in this book for project selection are used for configuration selection as well. Checklists and scoring models, B/C analysis, cost-effectiveness analysis, and multiple-criteria methods all have a role. In the configuration selection process, each alternative design (configuration) is analyzed with respect to its LCCs and is evaluated with respect to its expected performance. Performance measures are project dependent (they would be different for the development of a new car and for the construction of a new building), but some are common to many systems. Those discussed in Section 8.1.1 are general indicators that should be taken into account when evaluating a system from a technological point of view. By combining them with specific project objectives related to budget and schedule, they provide a framework for selecting the design configuration and foreshadow the capabilities of the final system.

For a particular project, each measure should be subdivided until the desired level of detail is reached. For example, compatibility might be broken down by hardware, software, operations and maintenance personnel, training requirements, and logistics support. Software then might be decomposed into databases, controls, interface protocols, and applications. Quantifying each element in the resultant hierarchy for each alternative is the first step in the analysis. The selection process itself can be supported by scoring models, multiattribute utility theory–based models, or the analytic hierarchy process, as discussed in Chapters 5 and 6.

The cost of each alternative must also be evaluated. The notion of LCC is widely used for this purpose. Recall that the LCC of a system is defined as its total cost from the start of the conceptual design phase until it completes active service. Related methodologies and techniques are discussed in Chapter 4.

Along with a B/C analysis, a risk analysis of each alternative design should be conducted. Risk analysis includes the following steps:

- Identification of risk drivers
- Estimation of probabilities of undesired outcomes
- Evaluation of the impact of each undesired outcome (on cost, schedule, quality, and operational and technological capabilities)
- Elimination and reduction of risks
- Preparation of contingency plans

The procedures used for selecting the best design alternative can also be adopted for managing configuration changes. This is discussed later, but first we offer some guidelines for system definition. The selection process is complete when the specifications of the proposed system are robust enough to at least answer the following questions:

Technological specifications
- *Operational/functional*: What tasks should the system perform and what performance levels are expected?
- *Timeliness*: When should the system be operational?
- *Quality*: Which standards are applicable? Which customer needs are to be supported by the system, and to what extent?
- *Reliability*: What are the expected MTBF and MTTR in the environment in which the system has to operate?
- *Compatibility*: With which other systems must the system contemplated operate in harmony? What interfaces are required?
- *Adaptability*: Under what environmental conditions is the system designed to operate, be maintained, and be stored? Under what conditions is the system required to operate, be maintained, and be stored?
- *Life span*: For how long is the system expected to be in service?
- *Simplicity*: What level of training is required to operate and to maintain the system?
- *Safety*: What safety standards are applicable to the system?

- *Commonality*: What level of commonality is required with each existing or planned system?
- *Maintainability*: What logistics support is required: spare parts, training, technical manuals, test equipment, and so on?
- *Friendliness*: What features should be included in the system to enhance its friendliness?

LCC

- What are the estimated costs of design, manufacture, operation, maintenance, and phaseout for the system?
- What is the expected timing of each cost component?

Risk assessment

- What are the major risk drivers?
- What are the probabilities of undesired outcomes?
- What is the expected impact of each undesired outcome?
- What are the plans to handle undesired outcomes?

The selected design alternative defines the technological aspects of the project. Based on the specifications, estimates of cost and schedule are made and the proposed project is either approved or rejected. Project approval is a management decision that may affect the entire organization. When several projects are being considered, the final choice is based on strategic and tactical considerations, including

General considerations

- Organizational goals
- Current or pending projects
- Existing and future products and markets
- Introduction of new technologies
- Image of the organization
- Organizational growth

R&D

- Availability of required technology
- Future use of new technologies developed or acquired for the project
- Development risks
- Opportunity to acquire new technologies and new knowledge
- Availability of resources required
- Future use of new resources acquired for the project

Logistics and production

- Project's need for logistics support
- Future use of investment in logistics support

- Project's production resource requirements
- Availability of production resources needed
- Effect on utilization of existing resources
- Need for new facilities
- Future use of facilities required for the project

Marketing

- Potential markets
- Estimate of future sales or business
- Availability of marketing resources
- Effect on existing products markets

Finance

- Project net present value
- Project rate of return
- Project payback period
- Project budgetary risks
- Project cash flow

This partial list, together with any specific considerations unique to the organization, underlies the selection process. Once again, actual decision making can be based on multicriteria techniques or any of the other methods discussed for evaluating and selecting alternatives.

8.4.3 Configuration Management

Configuration management (CM) concentrates on the management of technology by identifying and controlling the physical and functional characteristics of a product or a system as well as its supporting documentation. The medium of implementation is a set of tools designed to provide accurate information on what is to be built, what is currently being built, and what has been built in the past. The mission of CM is to support CE and to assist management in evaluating and controlling proposed technological changes. Through quality assurance activities, CM ensures the integrity of the design and engineering documentation and supports production, operation, and maintenance of the system.

Lager (2002) explained, "There is no mystery to CM. It is simply an amalgamation of a set of best practices, many of which have been used for centuries. The Parthenon in ancient Greece is a prime example. This elegantly curved marble block structure was built over the span of a century without a single straight line. Surely, identification of each piece and its ultimate location took place." Eli Whitney, the inventor of the cotton gin, is acknowledged as an early user of a well-documented change proposal. He proposed a radical change to the way muskets were manufactured, introducing the concept of interchangeable parts. His approach, which changed the specifications and created a need for logistics support, reduced the cost of manufacture as well as total life-cycle cost.

In configuration management, a baseline is established in each phase of the system's life cycle with well-defined procedures for handling proposed deviations. The initial baseline, known as the *functional* (or *program requirements*) *baseline*, is prepared in the first phase of the life cycle—the conceptual design phase. This baseline contains technical data regarding functional characteristics, demonstration tests, interface and integration characteristics, and design constraints imposed by operational, environmental, and other considerations. Approval is subject to a preliminary design review (PDR). The PDR and other design reviews serve as gates for subjecting projects to peer evaluation and stakeholder "go/no go" decisions. Gating is critical when it comes to project termination. Because it is unlikely that the project team will decide to terminate a project, design reviews or gates should serve as "kill points" for the stakeholders to assess performance and evaluate the probability of successful completion.

The advanced development phase, also known as the definition phase, produces the second baseline, the *allocated* (or *design requirements*) *baseline*. This document contains performance specifications guiding the development of subsystems and components, including characteristics derived from the system's design. Laboratory or computer simulation may be used to demonstrate achievement of functional characteristics, interface requirements, and design constraints. This baseline is subject to a critical design review.

The *product* (or *product configuration*) *baseline* is last and includes information on the system as built, including results of acceptance tests for a prototype, supporting literature, operation and maintenance manuals, and part lists. Acceptance is subject to a physical configuration audit. In addition to these three baselines, other baselines and additional design reviews are frequently needed when complicated systems are involved. Examples are a baseline that defines the initial design and a baseline that defines the detailed design of the system. The transition from one baseline to the next is controlled by design reviews.

The CM system ensures smooth transition and provides updated information on the configuration of the system and all pending change requests at all times. To function properly, it should perform the tasks discussed in the following subsections.

Configuration Identification.   This function is at the heart of the CM system. It starts with the selection of configuration items, both software and hardware, that have one or more of the following characteristics:

- End-use function
- New or modified design
- Technical risk or technical complexity
- Many interfaces with other items
- High rate of future design changes expected
- Logistic criticality

The selection of configuration items is a critical task of systems engineering. Too few configuration items will not provide adequate management control, and too many may overload the system, sparking a waste of time and money.

Next, a coding system is adopted and configuration identification numbers are assigned. These numbers are designed to assist in providing the following information on each configuration item or a lower-level item:

1. Technical requirements that form the basis for detail design. These are provided by *specification numbers*.
2. Identification of the equipment that is designed and built to the applicable specification. These are provided by *equipment numbers*.
3. Technical descriptions for the equipment and its lower-level items. These are provided by *drawing and part numbers*.
4. Description of the sequence of manufacturing the equipment and its lower-level items. These are provided by equipment and item *serialization numbers*.
5. Change documents. These are provided by *change identification numbers*.
6. Sources of manufacture at all levels. These are provided by *manufacturer's code identification numbers*.

As an example, consider configuration item 123. For this configuration item, the following identification numbers are defined:

Specification number	SPEC 123
Equipment number	CI 123
Drawing number	123A
Serial number	123 SN5
Manufacturer number	00375
Change identification numbers:	
Engineering change request	ECR 123 N 005
Engineering order	EO 123 N 005

To control the allocation of numbers, they should be assigned with reference to a single point, and a standard procedure should be established to prevent errors in identification.

Configuration Change Control.   This function involves the development of procedures that govern the following three steps.

1. *Preparation of a change request.* This step requires that a formal change request be prepared and submitted. The initiation of a change can be internal (the project team) or external (any other stakeholder, e.g., the customer, a subcontractor, or a supplier). The change request specifies the reason for the modification and forewarns management of increases in cost, schedule, and risk, as well as changes in quality, contractual arrangements, and system performance. Each change request is assigned an identification number and is evaluated after input is received from all organizational units affected. The principal aim is to collect the relevant data on each proposed change and to assess its expected impact.

A typical change request form will include the following information:

- Change request number _____
- Originator _____

- Date issued _____
- Contract or project number _____
- Configuration items affected by the change _____
- Type of changes: temporary _____ permanent _____
- Description of change _____
- Justification for change _____
- From serial number _____ through serial number _____
- Priority _____

Effect on:

    Cost _____
    Schedule _____
    Resource requirements _____
    Operational aspects _____
    Timeliness _____
    Quality _____
    Reliability _____
    Compatibility _____
    Life span _____
    Simplicity _____
    Safety _____
    Commonality _____
    Maintainability _____
    Friendliness _____

Remarks:

    Engineering _____
    Marketing _____
    Manufacturing _____
    Logistics support _____
    Configuration management _____
    Other organizational units _____

CCB decision:

    Accept _____ Reject _____ More information needed _____
    Acceptance date _____
    Rejection date _____

2. *Evaluation of a change request.* A team of experts representing the different organizational functions and the project stakeholders are responsible for the evaluation of change requests. This team, known as a change control board (CCB) or configuration management board, evaluates each proposed change on the basis of its effect on the form, fit, and function of the system, logistics (manuals, training, support equipment, spare parts, etc.), and project cost and schedule. This review leads to a decision to approve or reject the change request or to reconsider it after more data are collected.

Changes are classified as either permanent or temporary. A temporary change might be needed for test programs or debugging software. Approval can usually be obtained in a short time compared with a request for a permanent change.

Changes are also classified by type of change. Major changes are handled by the CCB, whereas minor changes can be approved by the project manager or a subcommittee that consists of some of the CCB members. This classification can be based on the effect of the proposed change on the form, fit, and function of the system or product as well as on the effect on the cost schedule and risk of the project.

All information regarding each proposed change is accumulated and analyzed by CM, which also functions as a central repository for historical records. The decision to accept a proposed change is based on cost-effectiveness and risk analysis in which the need for the change and its expected benefits are weighed against implementation and project LCCs, its impact on project quality and schedule, and the expected risks associated with implementation.

3. *Management of the implementation of approved changes.* Approved changes are integrated into the design. This is accomplished by preparing and distributing a change approval form or an engineering change order to all parties involved, including engineering, manufacturing, quality control, and quality assurance.

The CCB is responsible for the pivotal task of conducting a comprehensive impact analysis of each change proposed. A well-functioning change control system ensures tight control of the technological aspects of a project. In addition, it provides accurate configuration records for the smooth, coordinated implementation of changes and effective logistics support during the life cycle of the system.

Configuration Status Accounting.   This task provides for the updated recording of

- Current configuration identification, including all baselines and configuration items
- Historical baselines and the registration of approved changes
- Register and status of all pending change requests
- Status of implementation of approved changes

Configuration status accounting provides the link between different baselines of the system. It is the tool that supports the CCB in its analysis of new change requests. The effect of these changes on the current baseline must be evaluated and their relationship to all pending change requests must be determined before a decision can be made.

Review and Audits.   This CM task provides all stakeholders (e.g., the contractor, the customer) with the assurance that test plans demonstrate the required performance and that test results prove conformance to requirements. Functional configuration audit includes a review of development test plans and test results, as well as a list of required tests not performed, deviations from the plan, and waivers. In this task, the relationship between quality assurance and CM is established. CM provides the baselines and a record of incorporated and outstanding changes. Quality assurance first checks the configuration documentation to gauge requirements; then it verifies that the system conforms to the approved configuration.

CM is a tool designed to help the project team know what they are developing, producing, testing, and delivering so that the appropriate support and maintenance can be given to the product throughout its life cycle. It specifies the procedures and information required for the project to be carried out in the most cost-effective manner.

8.4.4 Risk Management

Risk is a major factor in the management of projects because of their one-time nature and the uniqueness of the deliverables. The highest levels of uncertainty and, hence, risk appear early in the project life cycle. Whenever the design process or the design itself deviates from current procedures and established techniques, technological risks are introduced. These risks can be related to the product design, to the process design, or to the design of the support system and can vary widely in magnitude. For example, in product design, a low-level risk might be one associated with the modification of an existing subassembly. A moderate-level risk would concern the design of a new product based on currently used technologies and parts (integration risks); a third, even higher level of risk is related to the use of new materials, such as ceramics, in a product that was previously fabricated out of conventional metal alloys.

The development of the first transistor was a high-risk project involving a completely new technology. Sony's work on the first radio transistor was also a high-risk project because this technology was being implemented in a new product—the portable radio. However, development of subsequent models of the transistor radio represented much lower risks, as both the technology and the basic product were known.

The probability of success (or the risk of failure) should be estimated and monitored throughout the life cycle of a project. The selection of projects for implementation, the evaluation of alternative designs for a specific project, the decision to adopt or to reject proposed design changes, and the implementation of such changes measurably affect outcomes. Risk management is therefore an important part of the project manager's responsibilities. The scope of activities associated with risk management includes

- Risk management planning
- Risk identification
- Risk analysis
- Risk response planning
- Risk monitoring and control

Risk can be measured as a function of the probability of an undesirable event and the severity of the consequences of that event. In general, high risk corresponds to a strongly adverse event that has a high probability of occurrence, whereas low risk corresponds to a low probability of occurrence and low severity. Moderate levels of risk correspond to combinations of probabilities and consequences that fall between these extremes.

Consider, for example, the risk associated with flying. The possible outcome of an accident is death, but because of high safety standards in the airline industry, the probability of accidents is very low, and therefore the overall risk is low. This is evidenced by the cost of traveler insurance policies. When the probability of an undesirable event is higher (e.g., with parachuting or hang gliding), insurance policies that cover the same outcome (death) are much more expensive. Thus, the level of risk depends on both the severity of an adverse outcome and its probability of occurrence.

It is possible to develop a scale for assessing the level of risk based on these two measures. Each risk, however, may affect one or more of the dimensions of project success. Thus, a project may face a schedule risk related to the event of delays, a cost risk associated with the event of a budget overrun, one or more performance risks accompanying the failure to achieve technical/operational goals, and a program risk related to the success of the project as perceived by the stakeholders.

The multiple sources of risks and the different aspects of a project that are subject to failure or delay make risk management a demanding, time-consuming activity. Because technological risks affect performance, as well as cost and schedule, we shall discuss the effect that these risks have on overall project success. However, political risks, environmental risks, and marketing/business risks are as important as technological risks and should be managed in the same way that technological risks are managed throughout the life cycle of the project.

To demonstrate the problems faced by management during the various project phases, consider an organization that has decided to initiate a project aimed at automating its production planning and control system. Among the large number of available options, the organization focuses on two alternatives: (1) purchasing the most suitable system off the shelf and modifying it according to its individual needs or (2) developing a system that will support all of the specific production planning policies and procedures currently in use. In this example, the first alternative represents a project of relatively low development risk; however, the benefits may be minimal. This is because most off-the-shelf software packages have limited flexibility and can only rarely be made 100% compatible with the existing work environment. The second alternative offers a higher chance of achieving the technological and functional goals but involves a significant software development effort. As such, development and integration risks and, consequently, the risk of schedule delays and budget overruns are higher.

To perform a tradeoff analysis between the two alternatives, the techniques presented in earlier chapters can be implemented. This should be done in such a way that all parties feel involved in arriving at the final choice and are satisfied with the decision-making process. Consensus building is the key. Achieving a high level of satisfaction depends on the process used in selecting and implementing the alternative. When management, potential users, and future operators of the new system select the alternative and define its specific configuration, the probability that the project will be successful is greatly increased.

In addition to the economic, scheduling, and cost aspects that have to be analyzed, risk analysis is part of the selection process. Risk analysis starts with the identification of all possible events that might have a negative impact on the project. In the example above, typical negative events for the first alternative are an inability to modify the software to accommodate a given need and an inability to integrate the package with existing management information systems and databases. Negative events for the second alternative include unexpected difficulties in integrating the modules of the new software package and excessive CPU time requirements that slow down information processing and retrieval.

In the next stage of the analysis, the severity of each event is estimated and the level of risk (based on the severity of the event and the probability of occurrence) is calculated. The events are then ranked, with those exhibiting the highest risks placed at the top of the list. Next, the source of high-risk events is investigated, and, if needed, actions are taken to eliminate, reduce, or mitigate the risk. In some cases, it may be appropriate to contract with an outside consultant to undertake the assessment. By initiating a risk management activity at the outset of the project, unnecessary risks can be avoided, whereas those that are deemed necessary can be minimized or transformed. A formal description of the processes involved in risk management follows.

Risk Management Planning.   Major sources of risk require special attention. The risk management plan starts by identifying each of these sources and their magnitude, their relation to the various design stages, and their possible effects on cost, schedule, quality, and performance. The next step is to develop a plan to manage, monitor, and control these risks. One component of the plan includes the identification of modifications or alternatives that would either reduce or eliminate some of the risks altogether. Continuing with the example above, the thoughtful selection of a computer language or an operating system may reduce some of the integration risks. If management decides to develop a new software package, then contingency plans that cut expenses and development time at the cost of lower performance should be prepared. These plans would be used in case one or more undesired events take place. By preparing contingency plans in advance, time is saved when the anticipated problem surfaces.

Risk Identification.   Risks are caused by several factors and can affect different aspects of the project. A list of such factors can help the project manager focus on potential risks. In organizations that perform similar projects, it is possible to develop a checklist of risk sources based on past occurrences of such risks.

1. *Technology.* The rapid pace with which technology (e.g., information systems and integrated circuits) is expanding may make a new product obsolete the day the first unit rolls off the production line. To avoid this risk, design engineers prefer to use the latest technologies available, which frequently are immature and unproved. This increases the risk of technological failure. Simple lack of experience heightens the chances that the project will be saddled with unforeseen problems. The tradeoff between well-proven technologies with lower performance levels and new, unproven technologies requires detailed risk analysis. When NASA decided to build a new space shuttle in 1987 to replace the *Challenger*, which exploded on launch, it opted for a design that was nearly identical to the original. Rather than exploit recent advances in microelectronics, expert systems, and robotics, 20-year-old technology was used to avoid additional risks.

2. *Complexity and integration.* The adoption of well-known technologies for a project reduces the risk of component failure but may do little to mitigate the risk

of integration failure. Modern, complex systems are based on the integration of parts and subsystems, the compatibility of software modules, and integration of hardware and software. The interfaces between components of a system are a source of integration problems and risks. For example, problems related to RFI (radio-frequency interference) or EMI (electromagnetic interference) should be considered in the design of electrical devices. Parts of the same system may affect each other in an undesired and unexpected manner. Complex interfaces within a system, between systems, and between systems and humans are sources of risk that need management's attention throughout the project.

3. *Changes.* Virtually all projects are subject to design changes throughout their life cycle. A reassessment of needs, revitalized competition, and emerging technologies are some of the factors that may call the original design into question. Design changes are risky, as each change may have a different effect on the system or its components. As a result, the risks of integration may go up sharply. A control system that evaluates each proposed change and its possible consequences is required. This system should provide information on approved changes to the design engineers in an effort to reduce the risk of integration failure. The same system should provide updated design information to manufacturing and quality control so that the product is manufactured and tested according to the most recent configuration.

4. *Supportability.* Good design and workmanship are not enough to guarantee a successful project. The ultimate test of success is customer or end-user satisfaction. To achieve this goal, the design should be based on the customer's needs, and the product should conform to the design. At the conclusion of the project, the product or system delivered should be operational (i.e., all of the support required for maintenance and operations should be available). In the case of the rough-terrain cargo handler, for example, this includes trained personnel, transportation, storage and maintenance facilities, spare parts, and manuals. To prepare for worst-case contingencies, the design effort should cover the risks of a system delivered without adequate logistics support.

To summarize, technological risks are usually generated by one or more of the following factors:

- Unproven technology
- System complexity
- Integration requirements
- Physical or chemical properties
- Modeling assumptions
- Interfacing with other systems
- Interfacing with operators, service personnel, and so on
- Operating environment

In addition to technological risks, other sources of risk should be identified, including political risks, environmental risks, and marketing/business risks.

Risk Analysis.   Risk identification, when done properly in complex projects, may produce a long list of risk events or sources of risk. The most important should be singled out for in-depth analysis. A simple yet effective way of doing this is to classify each risk event according to the impact that it has on the project, e.g., separating schedule risks from budget risks from performance-related risks. Another classification is to distinguish between "known unknowns" versus "unknown unknowns." Known unknowns are risk events that occurred in past projects, so information on their probability and severity is available. Unknown unknowns are risk events associated with a new technology, a new market, or a new environment for which no past information is available.

The next step is to assess the magnitude of each type of risk and identify those that seem to be the most serious. Special techniques for risk analysis include fault tree analysis, event tree analysis, synergistic contingency evaluation and review technique, and reliability analysis evaluation and review. The specifics can be found in several of the risk management references at the end of the chapter. The analysis of risk is based on experience gathered in past projects, expert opinion, and physical or mathematical models. If the project manager does not have the technical expertise to perform the job, then he or she should call on those in the organization who are more qualified.

The simplest approach is to estimate the probability of each risk event and the potential severity of its impact by category: schedule, cost, performance, and quality. A high risk is one with high probability of occurrence and high impact. Low risk has low probability of occurrence and low impact. Anything in between can be classified as a medium risk. This approach produces a ranked ordering of risks by category, which can be used to prioritize the reduction efforts.

Organizations that perform similar projects over time can use historical databases to estimate the probability of each risk event on the basis of past frequency. This is limited, though, to known unknowns only.

Response Planning.   The next step in the analysis is to decide how to handle the risks identified. Possible alternatives are

- *Information gathering*. Because risk is generated by uncertainty, an effort to collect information and to reduce the level of uncertainty can reduce or eliminate the risk. Such an effort in the form of literature search, feasibility studies, purchasing of knowledge or patents, reverse engineering, hiring of new employees that have the needed know-how, and designing and executing experiments all are common in the high-tech industry.
- *Risk elimination*. Eliminating the probability of occurrence (bringing it to zero) or eliminating the impact, for example, by selecting a different technology.
- *Risk reduction*. Reducing the probability of occurrence, say, by redundancy (e.g., having two independent R&D groups each develop a new component) or by reducing the impact of the risk event should it happen (or doing both).
- *Risk sharing*. Sharing the risk with another stakeholder in the project, such as a partner or a client.
- *Risk transfer*. Transferring the risk to a third party; for example, by purchasing insurance that pays any penalties associated with schedule delays.

- *Risk buffering.* Adding a buffer of extra time to the schedule or a buffer of management reserve to the budget to protect the project from risk by absorbing it.
- *Contingency planning.* Preparing plans that will be used as soon as a risk event occurs, thus reducing the response time and the impact of the risk on the project.

The problem of how to handle risk is a function of the degree to which it can undermine performance, the cost to the organization, and the tolerance of the stakeholders. If the stakeholders are not sensitive to schedule delays, for example, then all that needs to be done is to identify and monitor the related risks; if the stakeholders are highly concerned about delays, however, then staying on schedule should be a top priority.

Risk Monitoring and Control.   Throughout the life cycle of a project, new information is collected, leading to a better understanding of the hurdles faced by the project team. As new risks are identified, the probability and impact of existing risks may change, and the stakeholders may realign their tolerances and expectations. It is important to continuously monitor the existing risks and to identify new risks as soon as possible to keep the risk management plan updated. In fact, risk management is a critical component of project management and deserves a prominent place in the budget. Without sufficient resources dedicated to analyzing and mitigating risk, all but the simplest of projects will continually be in jeopardy.

8.5 QUALITY MANAGEMENT

The industrial world saw a quality revolution brought on by the Japanese. The introduction of the just-in-time philosophy supported by Kanban for production and inventory control, continuous process improvement on the shop floor, and the general goal of zero part and product defects has allowed Japanese firms to capture the bulk of the consumer electronics market, a large share of the semiconductor market, and a troublesome proportion of the U.S. automobile market. This success, which has come in less than two decades, can be attributed to a knack for squeezing a few more percentage points of performance out of a system or process after logic and economics indicate that diminishing returns have long set in, but such an explanation is too glib. At the heart of Japanese manufacturing is an emphasis on education and training, a cross-functional workforce, teamwork, and a commitment to excellence; these are some of the basic components of quality management.

8.5.1 Philosophy and Methods

Quality management is a system that combines quality planning, quality assurance, and quality control techniques. It is a logical evolution of management by objectives, strategic planning, quality circles, and many other systems. It is built on the assumption that 90% of our problems are process related, rather than employee related. The three major components are

- *Quality planning*: identifying which quality standards are relevant to the project and determining how to satisfy them

- *Quality assurance*: all of the planned and systematic activities implemented to provide confidence that the project will satisfy the quality standards
- *Quality control*: monitoring of specific project results to determine whether they comply with relevant standards and identifying ways to eliminate causes of unsatisfactory results

Quality management typically involves one or more of the following approaches developed by such leaders in the field as W. Edwards Deming, Joseph Juran, Philip Crosby, and Masaaki Imai. Their message is basically the same:

- Commit to quality improvement throughout the organization.
- Attack the process, not the employees.
- Strip down the process to find and eliminate problems that diminish quality.
- Identify your customers, and satisfy their requirements.
- Instill teamwork, and create an atmosphere for innovation and permanent quality improvement.

The leitmotif is worker enablement and empowerment; that is, train the workers, and give them responsibility. In the project context, the leitmotif is enablement and empowerment of the IPT.

In the remainder of this section, we highlight the main points made by each of these pioneers and mention how they can be applied to project management. Like any discipline, a unique vocabulary has grown around quality management.

Deming Approach.   Deming, originally a physicist with a Ph.D. from Yale, after many years in industry came to believe, "Improve quality and you automatically improve productivity. You capture the market with lower prices and better quality. You stay in business and you produce jobs. It's so simple." In his work, he stresses statistical process control, statistical quality control, and a 14-point plan for managers that emphasizes the human element. The philosophy is to treat people as intelligent human beings who want to do a good job. Although statistical control methods are difficult to implement in a project environment as a result of the one-of-a-kind nature of projects, the 14 points are readily adoptable.

Deming was the American who took his message to Japan in 1950 after being shown the door by most major U.S. corporations. It was a time when U.S. firms dominated international markets; there was virtually no competition from abroad, so as long as the product worked, the concern for quality was minimal. Deming was instrumental in changing this attitude and in turning Japanese industry into an economic world power. His 14 principles for achieving competitiveness through quality are as follows (Deming 1986):

1. *Create constancy of purpose toward improvement of products and services; emphasize long-term needs rather than short-term objectives.* This principle should guide management throughout the life cycle of a project. In early stages of project selection, long-term goals should be emphasized. The acquisition of new knowledge and the ability to master new technologies are leading considerations.

Furthermore, the specific configuration selected for a project should support these long-term objectives. The required constancy can be achieved only by a learning process that promotes improvement from one project to the next. Whatever was learned during project execution is as important as the final results and deliverance. Top management has to facilitate the diffusion of knowledge throughout the organization and the transfer of technology between different projects. This calls for an investment in resources and the development of procedures to support these activities.

2. *Adopt a new philosophy.* The philosophy that productivity and cost are the most important performance measures should be modified based on the recognition that improved quality can reduce cost and improve productivity while increasing customer satisfaction. Thus, quality is the most important performance measure. Defects are unacceptable, and problem-solving tools should be used at all levels of the organization to eliminate their sources.

3. *Cease dependence on mass inspection.* Quality should be built into the product design, the process design, and the support design. The responsibility for quality should not be with quality control and quality assurance but rather with all members of the organization regardless of function and level. Advanced presentation analysis should be used to support group problem solving so that improved process capability is maintained.

4. *Reduce the number of vendors; don't select vendors on the basis of cost.* The decision on project structure and selecting subcontractors should be based on quality considerations; i.e., employ a limited number of high-quality subcontractors with whom long-term relationships, predicated on loyalty and trust, can be established. Quality should be the predominant factor in choosing a subcontractor, rather than price tag alone.

5. *Search for problems and improve constantly.* Successful project management is based on good design and good planning and a dogged determination to remain on course. Thus, an ongoing effort to identify and solve problems is the key to smooth implementation. The earlier a problem is detected, the easier it is to correct. Control systems should be established with this adage in mind. One way of doing this is with trend analysis in areas such as cost, schedule, and quality, as discussed in Chapter 12.

6. *Institute on-the-job training to make better use of human resources.* Instituting training in technological and managerial fields supports continuous improvement in the process. Training employees in new technologies developed in one project enhances the likelihood of success for future projects. It is an investment that will pay for itself many times over. Promulgating the philosophy of built-in quality enables the whole organization to move in the direction of quality improvement. Training in managerial techniques used for planning, scheduling, budgeting, and control is important for the project manager and the project team. Input from the various team members on all problems that are relevant to their expertise should be continually sought, and the reasons behind all decisions should be made explicit.

7. *Improve supervision.* The role of supervision is leadership aimed at helping people do a better job. Because recognition and reinforcement are critical to good job performance, supervisors should be trained to support this continued improvement process by providing leadership, example, and training to their teams. Managers should become coaches rather than feudal lords.

8. *Drive out fear.* Encourage open communication. Open communication lines and the ability to report problems without fearing the consequences are essential to the ongoing improvement process. Employees are the first to know about problems in their specific areas of responsibility. Problems can be resolved early in the project life cycle by encouraging open discussion. Furthermore, employees usually know their part of the project better than anybody else. By encouraging them to initiate change in the product, process, or support design when they see fit, a continuous improvement is likely to take place. Management should institute an "open door" policy and a "How can I help you in doing your job?" approach to promote communication and to effectively use its most important resource—people.

9. *Break down barriers and promote communication among the different organizations that are participating in the project.* By eliminating communication barriers between functional areas, departments, and subcontractors, concurrent engineering can be implemented. All of the participants in the project should be viewed as a team with a common goal. The OBS should clearly define the formal communication channels within the team. However, informal communication between the members of the project should also be encouraged. Each organization that participates in a project should learn to view the other organizations as its customers (or suppliers), striving to understand their needs in performing their tasks. By adopting the customer-provider point of view, integration between the various elements of the WBS assigned to different organizations in the OBS greatly increases the likelihood that it will be smooth and error-free.

10. *Eliminate slogans, posters, and targets for the workforce that ask for a new level of productivity without appropriate methods and solutions.* The focus should be on the process as well as the outcome. An effort to improve the process of design and implementation will result in higher levels of achievement. Management should help employees develop better ways of performing their tasks; i.e., provide leadership in problem identification and problem-solving methodologies.

11. *Use work standards (quotas) carefully.* Work standards that are used in a project environment can be dangerous, especially when they depend on environmental factors external to the project. Standards and quotas are important in the planning process (they can be used for time and cost estimates as explained in Chapters 9 and 11) but should be used carefully as a foundation for performance evaluations. When standard time or cost goals are not achieved, the source of the problem should be determined. It is rarely a good idea to apply sanctions solely on the basis of cost or schedule overruns, as the cause may be outside the worker's control.

12. *Remove barriers that eliminate the worker's pride of workmanship. The responsibility of supervisors must be changed from sheer numbers to quality.* Employees should be

permitted to evaluate their own work and to take pride in it. This means the abolishment of annual or merit rating and of management by objectives. By assigning the responsibility of better quality to the employees who perform the work, a link is established between their satisfaction and the improvement process. This link is necessary to promote improvement in quality.

13. *Institute an education and training program to teach workers new skills as new technologies are developed or assimilated by the organization.* Technologies that are developed or acquired for one project can serve the whole organization in future projects if proper training regimens are established. In addition to on-the-job training, a training program should be instituted to transfer knowledge between different parts of the organization.

14. *Everyone in the organization should team up in the quality improvement process.* This process should not be an isolated effort of the quality control or quality assurance departments. Everyone in the organization should be involved in the transformation to quality. Too often, advice and opinions of low-level staff are either not sought or ignored. Too many times, managers act as if they know the answer to every problem. Top management must set the example in implementing a quality management program by insisting that the basic principles be adopted by each unit in the organization.

Juran Approach.   Juran (1998) believes that management must establish top-level plans for annual improvement and encourage projects as a means to achieve this end. The underlying philosophy seems to appeal to boss-type managers, because it gives them a strong sense of control. Juran asserts that poor planning by management results in poor quality. His approach for improving quality, known as the *Juran trilogy*, is to (1) plan, (2) control, and (3) improve. More specifically:

- *Quality planning.* In preparing to meet organizational goals, the end result should be a process that is capable of meeting those goals under operating conditions. Quality planning might include identifying internal and external customers, determining customer needs, developing a product or service that responds to those needs, establishing goals that meet the needs of customers and suppliers at a minimum cost, and proving that the process is capable of meeting quality goals under operating conditions. A necessary step is for managers to engage cross-functional teams and openly supply data to team members so that they may work together with unity of purpose.

- *Quality control.* At the heart of this process is the collection and analysis of data for the purpose of determining how best to meet project goals under normal operating conditions. One may have to decide on control subjects, units of measurement, standards of performance, and degrees of conformance. To measure the difference between the actual performance before and after the process or system has been modified, the data should be statistically significant and the processes or system should be in statistical control. Task forces that work on various problems need to establish baseline data so that they can determine whether the implemented recommendations are responsible for the observed improvements.

- *Quality improvement*. This process is concerned with breaking through to a new level of performance. The end result is that the particular process or system is obviously at a higher level of quality in delivering either a product or a service.

Juran's approach, like those of his colleagues, stresses the involvement of employees in all phases of a project. The philosophy and procedures require that managers listen to employees and help them rank the processes and systems that require improvement. This can be done with the help of any of the techniques described in Chapters 5 and 6.

Crosby Approach.   Crosby's philosophy seems to appeal to the human resources type of manager. He enforces the belief that quality is a universal goal and that management must provide the leadership to compel an enterprise in which quality is never compromised. Crosby defines quality as conformance to requirements and asserts that the mechanism for attaining quality is prevention (i.e., the first mission is appraisal). He encourages a performance standard of zero defects and says that a casualness toward quality is the price of nonconformance—doing something over rather than doing it right the first time. He believes that managers should be facilitators and should be considered as such by employees, rather than as punishment sent from heaven.

Like Deming, Crosby (1984) has 14 steps for quality improvement. They are

1. Management commitment
2. Quality improvement teams
3. Measurement
4. Cost of quality
5. Quality awareness
6. Corrective action
7. Zero-defect planning
8. Employee education
9. Zero-defect day
10. Goal setting
11. Error-cause removal
12. Recognition
13. Quality councils
14. Doing it over again

Imai Approach.   Imai (1986) supports the continuous improvement process, whereby people are encouraged to focus on the environment in which they work rather than on the results. He believes that by continually improving processes and systems, the end result will be a better product or service. This has become known as the "P," or *process approach*, rather than the "R," or *results approach* of Frederick Taylor, a pioneer in work measurement and the father of industrial management. The process approach is also known as the *Kaizen approach*.

In the "R" approach, management examines the anticipated result(s), usually specified by a management-by-objectives plan, and then rates the performance of the individual(s). A person's performance is influenced by reward and punishment; that is, the use of "carrot and stick" motivation. In the "P" approach, management supports individual and team efforts to improve the processes and systems that lead to the end result.

The effects of the continuous improvement, or Kaizen approach, can be elusive because they are long term and often undramatic. Change is gradual and consistent. The approach involves everyone, with the group effort focused on processes and systems rather than on one person's performance evaluation. Although the monetary investment is low, a great deal of management support is required to maintain the momentum of the group. The Kaizen approach is people oriented.

8.5.2 Importance of Quality in Design

By integrating product design, process design, and support design, producibility and inspectability are built into the product and the process by which it is manufactured. Producibility is achieved when the product design has been verified through prototypes and qualification testing. Issues related to good process design include the use of standard equipment and tooling for fabrication, assembly, and test. Inspectability is achieved when all possible defects that can be created as a result of design errors or manufacturing problems are detectable by those who perform the actual work.

A major goal of quality management is defect prevention. To achieve this end, design should be started only after the requirements are clearly understood. Product, process, and support design should be integrated so that manufacturing technology is compatible with product complexity, and all training requirements are identified and performed before the production phase. The configuration management system provides the project manager with updated configuration and engineering information needed as references for quality control. When applying quality management, the detection of a defect not only is a trigger for rework but also initiates a study aimed at eliminating future defects; that is, a study of the process and product design, as well as the processes and methods used in manufacturing that might be the source of the problem. Again, quality management tries to eliminate the source of defects so that defect detection and rework do not become the normal mode of operation.

When a project consists of building several identical units in series, product trend analysis is used to avoid repeating mistakes. This is done by monitoring the performance of consecutive units and studying related trends. When the trend is toward higher performance as a result of learning, no special action is required. If, however, deterioration (or simply no improvement) in performance is observed, then the source of such a trend should be identified and corrective action should be taken.

The integration of quality management with CE and CM greatly facilitates the design of quality into new products and their manufacturing processes. This minimizes dependence on inspection and the need for costly rework. High quality is achieved by doing things right from the beginning, not by removing defects that should not have been there in the first place.

8.5.3 Quality Planning

Quality planning is based on the philosophy that quality should be designed into the product and process and that defects should be avoided at almost all cost. This is because defect detection by itself is expensive and prone to error. Once a defect is created, it might be a nightmare to find and remove it. In electronic assembly, for example, an often-cited rule of thumb is that the cost of finding a defective component goes up by a factor of 10 for each level of assembly: device, board, system, and field installation. Furthermore, even if the defect is found, correction is not only expensive and time-consuming but also is likely to reduce the quality of the product. A reworked part will often not measure up to the same standards of one manufactured properly the first time.

8.5.4 Quality Assurance

There are many definitions of quality, such as "meeting or exceeding customer requirements" or "fitness for use," but these can be vague and even troublesome when it comes time for action. In the conceptual design phase of a system, quality is often undervalued, as a result of the difficulty we have in quantifying it. However, even if this problem is remedied, there is another that catches most people unaware—the lack of planning. To rephrase a point made above, quality cannot be added to a system upon completion; it must be built in.

The vehicle for doing this is the quality assurance (QA) plan. This is a before-the-fact document that states the rules that will be followed during project execution. Of course, whenever there is a plan, there must be a way to verify that it is being carried out correctly. This is the function of the QA review, which is an after-the-fact checkpoint. The QA plan and the QA review provide a means for close monitoring of a project, in terms of both meeting requirements and conformance to standards.

The necessity for quality planning is much the same as the necessity for any planning activity. The underlying rationale and expected benefits are outlined below:

1. A plan is needed to make something happen. Conversely, without a plan, objectives are likely to be shortchanged. For example, during development, if all levels of testing (parts, subassemblies, integration, system, acceptance) are not mentioned explicitly, then one of them could easily be overlooked. Or if no procedure has been defined for updating all documentation after a change is made, then blueprints and manuals may become dangerously out of date.

2. A plan is needed to prevent corners from being cut. The idea here is an extension of what was said above. For example, there may be an implicit requirement to conduct a walk-through on test plans, but with a project behind schedule, the temptation may be great to skip over this step and thus lose the benefit of peer criticism on the testing procedures.

3. A plan is a statement of procedures. It describes how quality will be examined and measured. If prototypes are to be subjected to quality inspection, for example, then the people involved should know beforehand what is going to be examined and measured so that there are no surprises after the fact. It is easier to play the game when one knows all of the rules.

4. A plan states the amount of time and money required. Thus, quality is less susceptible to cuts when it is planned for explicitly. It becomes a stated requirement of the system being developed for which resources must be allocated.

5. A plan becomes a yardstick for measuring improvement. After quality planning becomes an integral step in the system development life cycle, the degree to which expectations are met can be weighed against the amount of planning undertaken. This comparison should reveal whether an increase in overall quality planning is required or it is simply necessary to shift the emphasis of observation and measurement from one phase of the system life cycle to another.

6. A QA plan tends to generate uniform quality. Differing levels of experience, ability, style of work, and even attitude can cause variations in quality levels within the same company or department, but if quality plans are mandatory and are produced according to standard guidelines, then the variations in quality should diminish.

7. Finally, quality plans encourage attention to standards. The problem is not that standards do not exist but simply that they frequently fall into disuse. People rarely read manuals from cover to cover, but if at the start of a project they were told what the relevant standards were and exactly where they could be found, then the chances of the standards being applied correctly would increase.

Plans must be tailored. No single quality plan will suit all project environments and circumstances. The *IEEE Standard for Software Quality Assurance Plans* is a comprehensive document that can provide guidance for software development. For two-party contractual arrangements, the International Standards Organization (ISO) has propounded a series of standards known as ISO 9000. Coverage includes the selection and use of equipment, the development, installation, and servicing of facilities, final inspection and test, and general management responsibilities. ISO 9000 certification is critical for companies that wish to compete in the European marketplace. Additional references for military system standards are given in the reference list at the end of the chapter.

A customized QA plan can be developed easily by asking some fundamental "what–who–how" questions: What has to be accomplished? Who has the responsibility? How are the tasks to be done? Consolidating answers to these questions into a concise, practical format yields a simple yet effective plan for ensuring a smooth, problem-free transition from one phase of a project to the next. A common format is the QA matrix, which arrays standards for each task against the three headings "what," "who," and "how." It is similar to the linear responsibility chart discussed in Chapter 7.

Generally, the QA matrix is developed by the QA team if one exists or, alternatively, by the project manager. Regardless of who prepares it, agreement must be obtained from all parties mentioned before work begins. Consensus carries with it a number of automatic benefits:

- It verifies responsibility and identifies the type of involvement for each of the participants.
- It presents a complete picture of responsibility, such that one party can see the involvement of other responsible parties.
- It is a forewarning of required standards knowledge.
- It is an explicit sign of acceptance of shared responsibility for deliverable quality.

A QA matrix can be developed at several different levels: deliverables, project phase, or the complete system life cycle. In each case, the elements remain the same.

8.5.5 Quality Control

Quality control is based on the collection and analysis of data for the purpose of determining whether project results comply with the selected quality standards. Quality control should be performed throughout the project life cycle to detect problems as early as possible and to eliminate them.

Every step in the project, including design and execution, should be subject to quality control. During the design phase, peer evaluation in the form of design reviews, and laboratory and field tests are used to detect faulty design. In the implementation phase, acceptance testing of parts, modules, and complete systems serves as a major building block of quality control. In software development, for instance, quality control starts with unit testing, whereby each program or module in a program is tested. Integration testing is the next step whenever two or more modules are integrated. The final step is to verify that the entire system performs as it should. Although the cost of testing is high, the alternative—releasing a defective product to the market—is more expensive, as we shall now see.

8.5.6 Cost of Quality

The modeling and analysis of tradeoffs are at the very foundation of decision making. In manufacturing, one of the tradeoffs most enshrined in our thinking has been the perceived relation between quality and cost. Vaughn (1990) pointed out that when people go to buy a product, they usually want it to be perfect at a minimum price. However, defect-free products are impossible to attain in any production environment at any cost.

The traditional view holds that approaches to zero-defect operations are too expensive for manufacturers of most products to attempt to reach. When the manufacturer must work to such high quality standards, production costs require that the price charged be outrageously high. As a consequence, a balance is struck between cost and quality, as shown in Fig. 8.3. This frequently leads to the distribution of goods and services that fail to meet customer expectations.

What drives the tradeoff according to this traditional view? Vaughn explained that efforts to reduce rework, repairs, warranty costs, and liability losses generate increasing costs associated with the time, materials, engineering, and overhead required to achieve these ends. From an economic perspective, the point at which the marginal cost of improving quality 1 unit equals the marginal loss as a result of poor quality is the point at which the optimum is achieved. Even Joe Juran, the guru mentioned previously who has long been at the forefront of the quality improvement movement, encouraged this kind of thinking. In his optimization model, he showed how failure costs decline until they are overtaken by the increasing costs of appraisal and prevention. At this point, total quality costs begin to rise.

Why, then, have the Japanese been so successful in increasing quality while simultaneously bringing down production costs? As Cole (1992) asked, "Have they abolished the laws of economics?" Hardly, but they have made us realize that the point at which total quality costs start to rise again as failure costs are driven down has shifted sharply to the right in Fig. 8.3. Moreover, continuous improvement makes perfect economic

Figure 8.3   Relationship between quality and cost.

sense as long as the search follows a minimum cost path. In terms of organizational dynamics, it has long been observed that quality achievements tend to regress over time. If one is not going forward, then one is going backward. Thus, to press for continuous improvement at least helps ensure that no ground is lost.

According to Cole, the Japanese achievement has been sixfold. First, Japanese managers realized that the traditional calculations dramatically underestimated the costs of poor quality. Typically, such calculations ignored the customers who were lost or who had never bought the product. A declining reputation among customers and the effects of negative word-of-mouth publicity were never considered, partly because they were difficult to quantify. There is every reason to believe that these effects are substantial. Japanese managers recognize these costs. They stress the fragility of their reputations with their customers and the importance of winning the customer's trust. They find it entirely appropriate to spend generously for this purpose. In short, once one recognizes the high costs associated with poor quality, one sees that it is economically rational to invest more in quality improvement.

Second, the traditional approach vastly underestimated the payback that a corporate-wide quality improvement culture yields in terms of worker motivation and a broad array of performance indicators. A 1991 study undertaken by the U.S. General Accounting Office (GAO) of the 1988 and 1989 Baldrige Award finalists revealed that companies that adopted total quality management (TQM) practices achieved better employee relations, higher productivity, greater customer satisfaction, increased market share, and improved profitability. The GAO calculated that, on average, these measures increased 4.5% per year from the mid-1980s on. Other measures, related to employee turnover, product reliability, number of employee suggestions, on-time delivery, order processing time, number of defects, production lead times, customer complaints, and inventory turnover, improved at even greater rates. Although these findings are still preliminary (no control groups were included, and some data were missing), they are suggestive of the broad impact that a quality initiative can have.

Third, the Japanese pursuit of quality is accompanied by intense pressure to minimize the attending costs. In the United States, some of the quality zealots have made the mistake of separating the two and regarding support for any quality initiative as a kind of litmus test of enlightened management. This misses the point altogether and substitutes an unthinking repetition of the quality mantra for real understanding. The widespread mobilization of production workers, equipped with elementary but powerful statistical problem-solving methods to improve quality, is a concrete illustration of this low-cost approach. Such employees are a lot less expensive than design engineers, and there are a lot more of them to work on an endless supply of problems. The incremental costs of their involvement in quality improvement are extremely modest, as found in a study by Schneiderman (1986).

Fourth, preventing problems at the source has become the preferred approach to improving quality. The Japanese gradually recognized that the costs of poor quality could be reduced more effectively by moving their efforts "upstream." In practice, this means concentrating on the process of new product development. This approach dramatically reduces appraisal costs and has the beneficial side effect of eliminating white-collar rework (e.g., downstream engineering changes).

Fifth, Japanese managers came to see quality improvement not as a matter of adding product attributes (which inevitably add costs) but as a matter of improving the quality of all business processes. By doing things right the first time, massive amounts of rework could be avoided and costs could actually be reduced. Those who were involved in the business processes were trained and given responsibility for improving them. Proceeding along these lines, Japanese firms actually eliminated a good deal of the traditional quality–cost tradeoff.

Finally, the traditional tradeoff model assumed that what the customer wanted in quality and was willing to pay for did not change over time. In fact, what Japanese manufacturers discovered was that by achieving the highest quality standards, they could charge a premium for their products, and in so doing, they educated consumers to demand higher and higher quality. As the company that changed customers' tastes, they were then in a unique market position to satisfy those new tastes. This in turn could be translated into higher prices or a greater share of the market.

Cole's analysis has a resonance that is being felt by all players in the global marketplace. New attitudes toward quality improvement and the results that have been achieved have made the traditional quality–cost tradeoff model obsolete. The Japanese did not abolish the economics of quality, but they did change the way we approach, perceive, and measure the relevant variables.

TEAM PROJECT

Thermal Transfer Plant

The approved rotary combustor project is now in the detailed design phase. Recently, the chief operating officer (COO) at TMS was exposed to the following three concepts: time-based competition, TQM, and configuration management. Because a task force under his supervision is now examining the potential benefits and risks of the rotary combustor project, you have been asked to explain how these three concepts will be implemented in the project's production phase to maximize its probability of success.

Specifically, the COO would like to know how the configuration will be managed, what level of CE will be implemented, and which aspects of and by what means TQM will be designed into the project. Your analysis is part of the detailed design phase, and the COO is expecting a thoroughly documented report that at least answers the following questions:

1. Which forms will be used for change requests?
2. Who should sit on the CCB?
3. How can continuous improvement be encouraged? Be specific.

Submit a detailed report that can be implemented within TMS's current organizational structure. Discuss the costs and benefits of introducing each of these ideas into the project on the basis of your assumptions and analysis.

DISCUSSION QUESTIONS

1. What are the design aspects of writing a term paper?
2. Describe a design process with which you are familiar and that is performed sequentially. Explain how CE could be implemented (if possible) in this case. If, in your opinion, CE is not possible, explain why.
3. Give an example in which CE cannot be applied.
4. What is the difference between the communication needs in sequential engineering and CE?
5. What is the relationship between CM and quality?
6. In what ways does CE affect quality?
7. What are the similarities and differences between Deming's 14 points and Crosby's 14 points?
8. The Kaizen approach of Imai stresses gradual, long-term improvement. In what situations or under what conditions might this approach not work very well? Under what conditions is this approach best?
9. Contrast Juran's approach with the Kaizen approach. Identify situations in which either would be more or less appropriate.
10. Is it possible to implement the idea of training workers and giving them responsibility for improving the processes with which they are involved in a project environment?
11. Henry Ford invented mass production. In so doing, he perfected the assembly line concept in which each worker does only one job or a handful of jobs and is given little other responsibility. This worked well for 70 years; however, it became apparent in the 1990s that an increasing number of U.S. companies could not produce a high-quality product by sticking to the assembly line model. What has changed?
12. U.S. manufacturers spend approximately 80% of their R&D budgets on new technology, whereas their Japanese counterparts spend approximately 80% on process improvement. What do you think have been the positive and negative impacts of these allocations on product quality? What, in your opinion, is the best division of the R&D budget? Your answer should be industry specific.
13. Discuss the problem of assigning weights and estimating correlations in QFD. Suggest a way to solve this problem.
14. Discuss the risks involved in the project "buying a used car." Develop a risk management plan for this project.

15. One of the requirements for graduating with a B.S. in engineering is the successful completion of a design project. Discuss the criteria and the logic that a student should use in selecting a project.

16. What are the risks associated with the project in Question 15?

EXERCISES

8.1 Prepare a risk management plan for the project of finding a job after graduation.

8.2 Select a project with which you are familiar and explain the most important factors that affect the configuration selection decisions of this project.

8.3 Prepare a configuration identification system for the project you have selected in Exercise 8.2.

8.4 Prepare a form for a configuration change request for the project selected in Exercise 8.2.

8.5 Write a job description for the configuration manager of a project.

8.6 Develop a flow diagram for the data handling and data processing required for CM, including

    i. definition of files
    ii. sources of data
    iii. data processing requirement
    iv. required output

8.7 Assume that you are an instructor in either an engineering or a business college. Interpret the meaning of and indicate how you would apply each of Deming's 14 points to a typical class that you teach.

8.8 Do the same as in Exercise 8.7 for Crosby's 14 points.

8.9 Quality principles are only now being adopted by universities. Develop a plan for the administration in your college for implementing Juran's approach.

8.10 Do the same as in Exercise 8.9 for the chairman of an academic department.

8.11 Develop a reward system for motivating IPT members to do their jobs more conscientiously and to take on more responsibility.

8.12 How would the reward system developed in Exercise 8.11 be different for (a) matrix organization and (b) project organization?

8.13 Use QFD to analyze the project "developing a new course in project management."

8.14 List the major risks of a military operation such as the United States' effort to oust Saadam Hussein from power in Iraq in 2003. Outline a risk management plan for such projects.

8.15 Explain the relationship among time-based competition, cost-based competition, and CE.

8.16 Explain why configuration management is needed when concurrent engineering is used.

8.17 List the pros and cons of concurrent engineering.

BIBLIOGRAPHY

Concurrent Engineering

Clausing, D., *Total Quality Development: A Step-By-Step Guide to World Class Concurrent Engineering*, ASME Press, New York, 1994.

Cleland, D. I., "Product Design Teams: The Simultaneous Engineering Perspective," *Project Management Journal*, Vol. 22, No. 4, pp. 5–10, 1991.

Delchambre, A., *CAD Method for Industrial Assembly: Concurrent Design of Products, Equipment, and Control Systems*, John Wiley & Sons, Chichester, England, 1996.

Fleischer, M. and J. Liker, *Concurrent Engineering Effectiveness*, Hanser Gardner Publications, Cincinnati, OH, 1997.

Griffin, A., "PDMA Research on New Product Development Practices," *Journal of Product Innovation Management*, Vol. 14, No. 6, pp. 429–458, 1997a.

Griffin, A., "The Effect of Project and Process Characteristics on Product Development Cycle Time," *Journal of Marketing Research*, Vol. 34, No. 1, pp. 24–35, 1997b.

Hauptman, O. and K. K. Hirji, "The Influence of Process Concurrency on Project Outcomes in Product Development: An Empirical Study of Cross-Functional Teams," *IEEE Transactions on Engineering Management*, Vol. 43, No. 2, pp. 153–164, 1996.

Hsu, J. P., J. S. Gervais and F. Y. Phillips, *International Workshop on Concurrent Engineering Design, Final Report*, National Science Foundation, Washington, DC, September 1991.

King, N. and A. Majchrzak, "Concurrent Engineering Tools: Are the Human Issues Being Ignored?" *IEEE Transactions on Engineering Management*, Vol. 43, No. 2, pp. 189–202, 1996.

O'Grady, P. and J. S. Oh, "A Review of Approaches to Design for Assembly," *Concurrent Engineering*, pp. 5–11, May-June 1991.

Peters, T., "Get Innovative or Get Dead," *California Management Review*, Vol. 33, No. 2, pp. 9–23, 1991.

Salomone, A., *What Every Engineer Should Know about Concurrent Engineering*, Marcel Dekker, New York, 1995.

Smith, P. and D. G. Reinertsen, *Developing Products in Half the Time*, John Wiley, New York, 1998.

Ulrich, K. and S. Eppinger, *Product Design and Development*, McGraw-Hill, New York, 2000.

Configuration Selection

Blanchard, B. S. and W. J. Fabrycky, *Systems Engineering and Analysis,* Third Edition, Prentice Hall, Upper Saddle River, NJ, 1998.

Canada, J. R., W. G. Sullivan and J. A. White, *Capital Investment Analysis for Engineering and Management,* Prentice Hall, Upper Saddle River, NJ, 1996.

Design to Cost, Directive 5000.28, U.S. Department of Defense, Washington, DC, 1975.

Krishnan, V. and K. T. Ulrich, "Product Development Decisions: A Review of the Literature," *Management Science*, Vol. 47, No. 1, pp. 1–21, 2001.

Ostwald, P. F. and T. S. McLaren, *Cost Analysis and Estimating for Engineering and Management*, Prentice Hall, Upper Saddle River, NJ, 2004.

Configuration Management

Berlack, H. R., *Software Configuration Management*, John Wiley & Sons, New York, 1991.

Bersoff, E. H. and A. M. Davis, "Impacts of Life Cycle Models on Software Configuration Management," *Communications of the ACM*, Vol. 34, No. 8, pp. 104–118, 1991.

Buckley, F. J., *Implementing Configuration Management: Hardware, Software, and Firmware*, IEEE Computer Society Press, Los Alamitos, CA, 1996.

Eggerman, W. V., *Configuration Management Handbook*, TAB Professional and Reference Books, Blue Ridge Summit, PA, 1990.

Lager, A. E., "The Evolution of Configuration Management Standards," *Logistics Spectrum*, Vol. 36, No. 1, pp. 9–12, 2002.

Lyon, D. D., *Practical CM: Best Configuration Management Practices*, Butterworth-Heinemann, Woburn, MA, 2000.

Stevens, C. A. and K. Wright, "Managing Change with Configuration Management," *National Productivity Review*, Vol. 10, No. 4, pp. 509–518, 1991.

Sweetman, S. L., "Utilizing Expert Systems to Improve the Configuration Management Process," *Project Management Journal*, Vol. 21, No. 1, pp. 5–12, 1990.

Standards

EIA STANDARD 836, *Configuration Management Data Exchange and Interoperability*, Government Electronics and Information Technology Association, Arlington, VA, 2002.

DOD-STD-480A, *Engineering Changes, Deviations and Waivers*, U.S. Department of Defense, Washington, DC, 1978.

Goetsch, D. L. and S. B. Davis, *Understanding and Implementing ISO 9000 and ISO Standards*, Prentice-Hall, Upper Saddle River, NJ, 1998.

MIL-STD-482A, *Configuration Status Accounting, Data Elements, and Related Features*, U.S. Department of Defense, Washington, DC, 1974.

MIL-STD-483, *Configuration Management for Systems, Equipment, Munitions and Computer Programs*, U.S. Department of Defense, Washington, DC, 1985.

Quality Management and Quality Assurance Standards, International Organization for Standardization, Geneva, Switzerland, 2001.

Management of Technology

Babcock, D. and L. Morse, *Managing Engineering and Technology*, Third Edition, Prentice Hall, Upper Saddle River, NJ, 2002.

Fleming, S. C., "Using Technology for Competitive Advantage," *Research-Technology Management*, Vol. 34, No. 5, pp. 38–41, 1991.

Hales, C., *Managing Engineering Design*, Longman Scientific & Technical, Harlow, Essex, England, 1993.

Kotler, P. and P. J. Stonich, "Turbo Marketing through Time Compression," *Journal of Business Strategy*, Vol. 12, No. 5, pp. 24–29, 1991.

Levy, N. S., *Managing High Technology and Innovation*, Prentice Hall, Upper Saddle River, NJ, 1998.

Narayanan, V. K, *Managing Technology and Innovation for Competitive Advantage*, Prentice Hall, Upper Saddle River, NJ, 2001.

Risk Management

Barton, T. L., W. G. Shenkir and P. L. Walker, *Making Enterprise Risk Management Pay Off: How Leading Companies Implement Risk Management*, Prentice Hall, Upper Saddle River, NJ, 2002.

Chapman, C. and S. Ward, *Managing Project Risk and Uncertainty: A Constructively Simple Approach to Decision Making*, John Wiley & Sons, New York, 2002.

Davis, C. R., "Calculated Risk: A Framework for Evaluating Product Development," *MIT Sloan Management Review*, Vol. 43, No. 4, pp. 71–77, 2002.

Karolak, D. W., *Software Engineering Risk Management*, IEEE Computer Society Press, Los Alamitos, CA, 1996.

Culp, C. L., *The Risk Management Process: Business Strategy and Tactics*, John Wiley & Sons, New York, 2001.

Rasmussen, N. C., "The Application of Probabilistic Risk Assessment Techniques to Energy Technologies," *Annual Review of Energy*, Vol. 6, pp. 123–138, 1981.

Royer, S. R., *Project Risk Management: A Proactive Approach*, Management Concepts, Vienna, VA, 2002.

Quality Management

CEB Task Group, *Quality Management: Guidelines*, Quality Assurance Systems, Telford, London, 1998.

Cole, R., "The Quality Revolution," *Production and Operations Management*, Vol. 1, No. 1, pp. 118–120, 1992.

Crosby, P., *Quality without Tears: The Art of Hassle-Free Management*, McGraw-Hill, New York, 1984.

Deming, W. E., *Out of the Crisis*, MIT Center for Advanced Engineering, Cambridge, MA, 1986.

Gitlow, H. S., A. Oppenheim and R. Oppenheim, *Quality Management*, Second Edition, McGraw-Hill, New York, 1995.

General Accounting Office, *Management Practices: U.S. Companies Improve Performance through Quality Efforts*, U.S. Government Printing Office, Washington, DC, 1991.

Imai, M., *Kaizen: The Key to Japan's Competitive Success*, Productivity Press, Cambridge, MA, 1986.

Juran, J., *Juran's Quality Handbook*, Fifth Edition, McGraw-Hill, New York, 1998.

NIST, *Award Criteria: Malcolm Baldrige National Quality Award*, U.S. Department of Commerce, National Institute of Standards and Technology, Gaithersburg, MD, 1993.

Schneiderman, A., "Optimum Quality Costs and Zero Defects: Are They Contradictory Concepts?" *Quality Progress*, Vol. 19, pp. 28–31, 1986.

Vaughn, R., *Quality Assurance*, Iowa State University Press, Ames, IA, 1990.

Quality Function Deployment

Akao, Y. (Editor), "Quality Function Deployment," in *Integrating Customer Requirements into Product Design*, Productivity Press, Cambridge, MA, 1990.

Cohen, L., *Quality Function Deployment: How to Make QFD Work for You*, Addison-Wesley, Reading, MA, 1995.

Griffen, A. and J. R. Hauser, "Patterns of Communication among Marketing, Engineering and Manufacturing: A Comparison between Two New Product Teams," *Management Science*, Vol. 38, No. 3, pp. 360–373, 1992.

Hauser, J. R. and D. Clausing, "The House of Quality," *Harvard Business Review*, Vol. 66, No. 3, pp. 62–73, 1988.

King, B., *Better Designs in Half the Time: Implementing Quality Function Deployment (QFD) in America*, GOAL/QPC, Methuen, MA, 1987.

Maddux, G. A., R. W. Amos and A. R. Wyskida, "Organizations Can Apply Quality Function Deployment as Strategic Planning Tool," *Industrial Engineering*, Vol. 23, No. 9, pp. 33–37, 1991.

Teminko, J., *Step-by-Step QFD: Customer-Driven Product Design*, St. Lucie Press, Boca Raton, FL, 1997.

Chapter 9

Project Scheduling

9.1 INTRODUCTION

Project scheduling deals with the establishment of timetables and dates during which various resources, such as equipment and personnel, will be used to perform the activities required to complete the project. Schedules are the cornerstone of the planning and control system and, because of their importance, are often written into the contract by the customer.

The scheduling activity integrates information on several aspects of the project, including the estimated duration of activities, the technological precedence relations among activities, constraints imposed by the availability of resources and the budget, and, if applicable, due-date requirements. This information is processed into an acceptable schedule with the help of a decision support system that may include network models, a resource database, cost-estimating relationships, and options for accelerating performance. The aim is to answer the following questions:

1. If each activity goes according to plan, then when will the project be completed?
2. Which tasks are most critical to ensure the timely completion of the project?
3. Which tasks can be delayed, if necessary, without delaying project completion, and by how much?
4. More specifically, at what times should each activity begin and end?
5. At any given time during the project, how much money should have been spent?
6. Is it worthwhile to incur extra costs to accelerate some of the activities? If so, then which ones?

The first four questions relate to time, which is the chief concern of this chapter; the last two deal with the possibility of trading off time for money and are taken up in Chapter 11.

The schedule itself can be presented in several ways, such as a timetable or a Gantt chart, which is essentially a bar chart that shows the relationship of activities over time. Different schedules can be prepared for the various participants in the project. A functional manager may be interested in a schedule of tasks performed by members of his or her group. The project manager may need a detailed schedule for each work breakdown structure (WBS) element and a master schedule for the entire project. The vice president of finance may need a combined schedule for all projects that are under way in the organization to plan cash flows and capital requirements. Each person involved in the project may need a schedule with all of the activities in which he or she is involved.

Schedules provide an essential communications and coordination link between the individuals and organizations that are participating in the project. They facilitate the coordination of effort among people who are coming from different organizations and working on different elements of the WBS in different locations at different times. By developing a schedule, the project manager is *planning* the project. By authorizing work according to the scheduled start of each task, he or she triggers execution of the project; and by comparing the actual execution dates of tasks with the scheduled dates, he or she *monitors* the project. When actual performance deviates from the plan to such an extent that corrective action must be taken, the project manager is exercising *control*.

Although schedules come in many forms and levels of detail, they all should relate to the master program schedule, which gives a time-phased picture of the principal activities and highlights the major milestones associated with the project. For large programs, a modular approach that reduces the prospects of getting bogged down in the excess detail that necessarily accompanies work assignments is recommended. To implement this approach, the schedule should be partitioned according to its functions or phases and then disaggregated to reflect the various work packages (WPs). For example, consider the WBS shown in Fig. 9.1 for the development of a microcomputer. One possible modular array of project schedules is depicted in Fig. 9.2. The details of each module would have to be worked out by the individual project leaders and then integrated by the project manager to gain the full perspective.

Schedules are working tools for program planning, evaluation, and control. They are developed in many iterations with project team members and continuing feedback from the client. The reality of changing circumstances requires that they remain dynamic throughout the project life cycle. Every project has unique management requirements. When preparing the schedule, it is important that the dates and time allotments for the WPs be in precise agreement with those set forth in the master schedule. These times are control points for the project manager. It is his or her responsibility to insist on and maintain consistency, but the actual scheduling of tasks and WPs is usually done by those who are responsible for their accomplishment—after the project manager has approved the due dates. This procedure ensures that the final schedule reflects the interdependencies among all of the tasks and participating units and that it is consistent with available resources and upper management expectations.

It is worth noting that the most comprehensive schedule is not necessarily best in all situations. In fact, too much detail can impede communications and divert attention from critical activities. Nevertheless, the quality of a schedule has a major impact on the success of the project and frequently affects other projects that compete for the same resources.

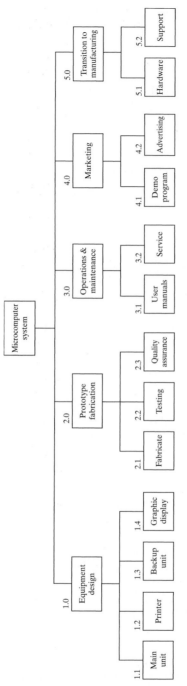

Figure 9.1 WBS for a microcomputer.

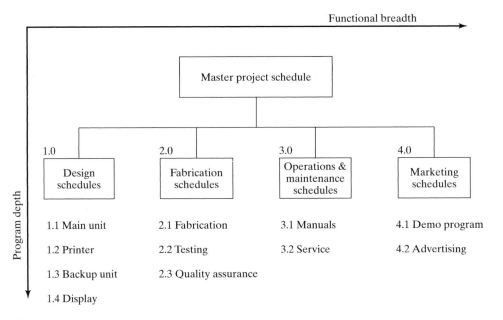

Figure 9.2   Modular array of project schedules.

9.1.1 Key Milestones

A place to begin the development of any schedule is to define the major milestones for the work to be accomplished. For ease of viewing, it is often convenient to array this information on a time line depicting events and their due dates. Once agreed on, the resultant milestone chart becomes the skeleton for the master schedule and its disaggregated components.

A key milestone is defined as an important event in the project life cycle and may include, for instance, the fabrication of a prototype, the start of a new phase, a status review, a test, or the first shipment. Ideally, the completion of these milestones should be easily verifiable, but in reality, this may not be the case. Design, testing, and review tend to run together. There is always a desire to do a bit more work to correct superficial flaws or to extract a marginal improvement in performance. This blurs the demarcation points and makes project control that much more difficult.

Key milestones should be defined for all major phases of the project before start-up. Care must be taken to arrive at an appropriate level of detail. If the milestones are spread too far apart, continuity problems in tracking and control can arise. Conversely, too many milestones can result in unnecessary busywork, overcontrol, confusion, and increased overhead costs. As a guideline for long-term projects, four key milestones per year seem to be sufficient for tracking without overburdening the system.

The project office, in close cooperation with the customer and the participating organizations, typically has the responsibility for defining key milestones. Selecting the right type and number is critical. Every key milestone should represent a checkpoint for a collection of activities at the completion of a major project phase. Some examples with well-defined boundaries include

- Project kickoff
- Requirements analysis complete
- Preliminary design review
- Critical design review
- Prototype fabricated
- Integration and testing completed
- Quality assurance review
- Start volume production
- Marketing program defined
- First shipment
- Customer acceptance test complete

9.1.2 Network Techniques

The basic approach to all project scheduling is to form an actual or implied network that graphically portrays the relationships between the tasks and milestones in the project. Several techniques evolved in the late 1950s for organizing and representing this basic information. Best known today are the program evaluation and review technique (PERT) and the critical path method (CPM). PERT was developed by Booz, Allen & Hamilton in conjunction with the U.S. Navy in 1958 as a tool for coordinating the activities of more than 11,000 contractors involved with the Polaris missile program. CPM was the result of a joint effort by DuPont and the UNIVAC division of Remington Rand to develop a procedure for scheduling maintenance shutdowns in chemical processing plants. The major difference between the two is that CPM assumes that activity times are deterministic, whereas PERT views the time to complete an activity as a random variable that can be characterized by an optimistic, a pessimistic, and a most likely estimate of its durations. Over the years, a host of variants has arisen, mainly to address specific aspects of the tracking and control problem, such as budget fluctuations, complex intertask dependencies, and the multitude of uncertainties found in the research and development (R&D) environment.

PERT/CPM is based on a diagram that represents the entire project as a network of arrows and nodes. The two most popular approaches are either to place the activities on the arrows (AOA) and have the nodes signify milestones or to place activities on the nodes (AON) and let the arrows show precedence relations among activities. A precedence relation states, for example, that activity X must be completed before activity Y can begin, or that X and Y must end at the same time. It allows tasks that must precede or follow other tasks to be clearly identified, in time as well as in function. The resulting diagram can be used to identify potential scheduling difficulties, to estimate the time needed to finish the entire project, and to improve coordination among the participants.

To apply PERT/CPM, a thorough understanding of the project's requirements and structure is needed. The effort spent in identifying activity relationships and constraints yields valuable insights. In particular, four questions must be answered to begin the modeling process:

1. What are the major project activities?
2. What are the sequencing requirements or constraints for these activities?
3. Which activities can be conducted simultaneously?
4. What are the estimated time requirements for each activity?

PERT/CPM networks are an integral component of project management and have been shown to provide the following benefits (Clark and Fujimoto 1989, Meredith and Mantel 1999):

- They furnish a consistent framework for planning, scheduling, monitoring, and controlling projects.
- They illustrate the interdependencies of all tasks, WPs, and work units.
- They aid in setting up the proper communications channels between participating organizations and points of authority.
- They can be used to estimate the expected project completion dates as well as the probability that the project will be completed by a specific date.
- They identify so-called critical activities that, if delayed, will delay the completion of the entire project.
- They also identify activities that have slack and so can be delayed for specific periods of time without penalty or from which resources may temporarily be borrowed without negative consequences.
- They determine the dates on which tasks may be started or must be started if the project is to stay on schedule.
- They illustrate which tasks must be coordinated to avoid resource or timing conflicts.
- They also indicate which tasks may be run or must be run in parallel to achieve the predetermined completion date.

As we shall see, PERT and CPM are easy to understand and use. Although computerized versions are available for both small and large projects, manual calculation is suitable for many everyday situations. Unfortunately, though, some managers have placed too much reliance on these techniques at the expense of good management practice. For example, when activities are scheduled for a designated time slot, there is a tendency to meet the schedule at all costs. This may divert resources from other activities and cause much more serious problems downstream, the effects of which may not be felt until a near-catastrophe has set in. If tests are shortened or eliminated as a result of time pressure, design flaws may be discovered much later in the project. As a consequence, a project that seemed to be under control is suddenly several months behind schedule and substantially over budget. When this happens, it is convenient to blame PERT/CPM even though the real cause is poor management.

In the remainder of this chapter, we discuss and illustrate the techniques used to estimate activity durations, to construct PERT/CPM networks, and to develop the project schedules. The focus is on the timing of activities. Issues related to resource and budget constraints as they affect the project's schedule are taken up in Chapters 10 and 11.

9.2 ESTIMATING THE DURATION OF PROJECT ACTIVITIES

A project is composed of a set of tasks. Each task is performed by one organizational unit and is part of a single WP. Most tasks can be broken down into activities. Each activity is characterized by its technological specifications, drawings, list of required materials, quality control requirements, and so on. The technological processes selected for each activity affect the resources required, the materials needed, and the timetable. For example, to move a heavy piece of equipment from one point to another, resources such as a crane and a tractor-trailer might be called for, as well as qualified operators. The time required to perform the activity may also be regarded as a resource. If the piece of equipment is mounted on a special fixture before moving, then the required resources and the performance time might be affected. Thus, the schedule of the project as well as its cost and resource requirements are a function of the technological decisions.

Some activities cannot be performed unless certain activities are completed beforehand. For example, if the piece of equipment to be moved is very large, then it might be necessary to disassemble it or at least remove a few of its parts before loading it onto the truck. Thus, the "moving" task has to be broken down into activities with precedence relations among them.

The process of dividing a task into activities and dividing activities into subactivities should be performed carefully to strike a proper balance between size and duration. The following guidelines are recommended:

1. The length of each activity should be approximately in the range of 0.5% to 2% of the length of the project. Thus, if the project takes approximately 1 year, then each activity should be between a day and a week.
2. Critical activities that fall below this range should be included. For example, a critical design review that is scheduled to last two days on a 3-year project should be included in the activity list because of its pivotal importance.
3. If the number of activities is very large (e.g., above 250), then the project should be divided into subprojects, perhaps by functional area as suggested in Section 9.1, and individual schedules should be developed for each. Schedules with too many activities quickly become unwieldy and are difficult to monitor and control.

We start our discussion with techniques commonly used to estimate the length of activities. We then describe the effects that precedence relations among activities have on the overall schedule.

Two approaches are used for estimating the length of an activity: the deterministic approach and the stochastic approach. The deterministic approach ignores uncertainty and thus results in a point estimate. The stochastic approach addresses the probabilistic elements in a project by estimating both the expected duration of each activity and its corresponding variance. Although tasks are subject to random forces and other uncertainties, the majority of project managers prefer the deterministic approach because of its simplicity and ease of understanding. A corollary benefit is that it yields satisfactory results in most instances.

9.2.1 Stochastic Approach

Only in rare circumstances is the exact duration of a planned activity known in advance. Therefore, to gain an understanding of how long it will take to perform the activity, it is logical to analyze past data and to construct a frequency distribution of related activity durations. An example of such a distribution is illustrated in Fig. 9.3. From the plot, we observe that previously the activity under consideration was performed 40 times and required anywhere from 10 to 70 hours. We also see that in 3 of the 40 observations, the actual duration was 45 hours and that the most frequent duration was 35 hours. That is, in 8 out of the 40 repetitions, the actual duration was 35 hours.

The information in Fig. 9.3 can be summarized by two measures: the first is associated with the center of the distribution (commonly used measures are the mean, the mode, and the median), and the second is related to the spread of the distribution (commonly used measures are the variance, the standard deviation, and the interquartile range). The mean of the distribution in Fig. 9.3 is 35.25, its mode is 35, and its median is also 35. The standard deviation is 13.3 and the variance is 176.89.

When working with empirical data, it is often desirable to fit the data with a continuous distribution that can be represented mathematically in closed form. This approach

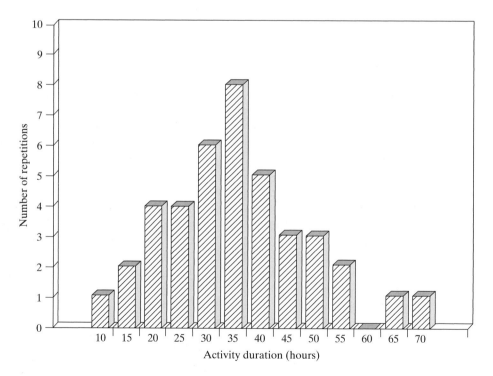

Figure 9.3 Frequency distribution of an activity duration.

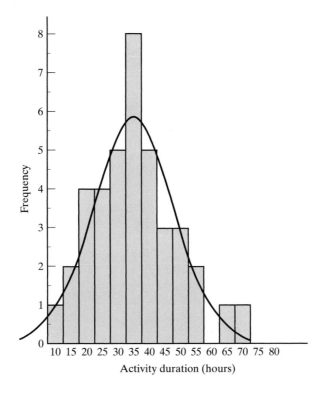

Figure 9.4   Normal distribution fitted to the data.

facilitates the analysis. Figure 9.4 shows the superposition of a normal distribution with the parameters $\mu = 35.25$ and $\sigma = 13.3$ on the original data.

Whereas the normal distribution is symmetrical and easy to work with, the distribution of activity durations is likely to be skewed. Furthermore, the normal distribution has a long left-hand tail, whereas actual performance time cannot be negative. A better model of the distribution of activity lengths has proved to be the beta distribution, which is illustrated in Fig. 9.5.

A visual comparison between Figs. 9.4 and 9.5 reveals that the beta distribution provides a closer fit to the frequency data depicted in Fig. 9.3. The left-hand tail of the beta distribution does not cross the zero duration point, neither is it necessarily symmetric. Nevertheless, in practice, a statistical test (e.g., the chi-square goodness-of-fit test or the Kolmogorov-Smirnov test; Banks et al. 2001) must be used to determine whether a theoretical distribution is a valid representation of the actual data.

In project scheduling, probabilistic considerations are incorporated by assuming that the time estimate for each activity can be derived from three different values:

a = optimistic time, which will be required if execution goes extremely well

m = most likely time, which will be required if execution is normal

b = pessimistic time, which will be required if everything goes badly

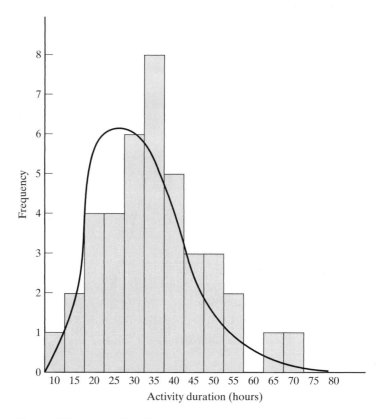

Figure 9.5   Beta distribution fitted to the data.

Statistically speaking, a and b are estimates of the lower and upper bounds of the frequency distribution, respectively. If the activity is repeated a large number of times, then only in approximately 0.5% of the cases would the duration fall below the optimistic estimate, a, or above the pessimistic estimate, b. The most likely time, m, is an estimate of the mode (the highest point) of the distribution. It need not coincide with the midpoint $(a + b)/2$ but may occur on either side.

To convert m, a, and b into estimates of the expected value $\hat{d}$ and variance $\hat{v}$ of the elapsed time required by the activity, two assumptions are made. The first is that the standard deviation, $\hat{s}$ (square root of the variance) equals one sixth the range of possible outcomes; that is,

$$\hat{s} = \frac{b - a}{6} \tag{9.1}$$

The rationale for this assumption is that the tails of many probability distributions (e.g., the normal distribution) are considered to lie approximately 3 standard deviations from the mean, implying a spread of approximately 6 standard deviations between tails. In industry, statistical quality control charts are constructed so that the spread between the upper and lower control limits is approximately 6 standard deviations

(a) Symmetric

(b) Skewed to right

(c) Skewed to left

Figure 9.6   Three cases of the beta distribution: (a) symmetric, (b) skewed to the right, and (c) skewed to the left.

(6σ). If the underlying distribution is normal, then the probability is 0.9973 that $\hat{d}$ falls within $b - a$. In any case, according to Chebyshev's inequality, there is at least an 89% chance that the duration will fall within this range (see, e.g., Banks et al. 2001).

The second assumption concerns the form of the distribution and is needed to estimate the expected value, $\hat{d}$. In this regard, the definition of the three time estimates above provide an intuitive justification that the duration of an activity may follow a beta distribution with its unimodal point occurring at m and its end points at a and b. Figure 9.6 shows the three cases of the beta distribution: (a) symmetric, (b) skewed to the right, and (c) skewed to the left. The expected value of the activity duration is given by

$$\hat{d} = \frac{1}{3}\left[2m + \frac{1}{2}(a + b)\right] = \frac{a + 4m + b}{6} \tag{9.2}$$

Notice that $\hat{d}$ is a weighted average of the mode, m, and the midpoint $(a + b)/2$, where the former is given twice as much weight as the latter. Although the assumption of the beta distribution is an arbitrary one and its validity has been challenged from the start (Grubbs 1962), it serves the purpose of locating $\hat{d}$ with respect to m, a, and b in what seems to be a reasonable way (Hillier and Lieberman 2001).

The following calculations are based on the data in Fig. 9.3 from which we observe that $a = 10, b = 70$, and $m = 35$:

$$\hat{d} = \frac{10 + (4)(35) + 70}{6} = 36.6 \quad \text{and} \quad \hat{s} = \frac{70 - 10}{6} = 10$$

Thus, assuming that the beta distribution is appropriate, the expected time to perform the activity is 36.6 hours with an estimated standard deviation of 10 hours.

9.2.2 Deterministic Approach

When past data for an activity similar to the one under consideration are available and the variability in performance time is negligible, the duration of the activity may be estimated by its mean; that is, the average time that it took to perform the activity in the past. A problem arises when no past data exist. This problem is common in organizations that do not have an adequate information system to collect and store past data and in R&D projects in which an activity is performed for the first time. To deal with this situation, three techniques are available: the modular technique, the benchmark job technique, and the parametric technique. A discussion of each follows.

9.2.3 Modular Technique

This technique is based on decomposing each activity into subactivities (or modules), estimating the performance time of each module, and then totaling the results to get an approximate performance time for the activity. As an example, consider a project to install a new flexible manufacturing system (FMS). A training program for employees has to be developed as part of the project. The associated task can be broken down into the following activities:

1. Definition of goals for the training program
2. Study of the potential participants in the program and their qualifications
3. Detailed analysis of the FMS and its operation
4. Definition of required topics to be covered
5. Preparation of a syllabus for each topic
6. Preparation of handouts, transparencies, and so on
7. Evaluation of the proposed program (a pilot study)
8. Improvements and modifications

If possible, the time required to perform each activity is estimated directly. If not, then the activity is broken into modules, and the time to perform each module is estimated based on past experience. Although the new training task may not be wholly identical to previous tasks undertaken by the company, the modules themselves should be common to many training programs, so historical data may be available.

9.2.4 Benchmark Job Technique

This technique is best suited for projects that contain many repetitions of some standard activities. The extent to which it is used depends on the performing organization's diligence in maintaining a database of the most common activities along with estimates of their duration and resource requirements.

To see how this technique is used, consider an organization that specializes in construction projects. To estimate the time required to install an electrical system in a new building, the time required to install each component of the system would be multiplied by the number of components of that type in the new building. If, for example, the installation of an electrical outlet takes on average 10 minutes and there are 80 outlets in the new building, then a total of $80 \times 10 = 800$ minutes is required for this type of component. After performing similar calculations for each component type or job, the total time to install the electrical system would be determined by summing the resultant times.

The benchmark job technique is most appropriate when a project is composed of a set of basic elements whose execution time is additive. If the nature of the work does not support the additivity assumption, then another method—the parametric technique—should be used.

9.2.5 Parametric Technique

This technique is based on cause–effect analysis. The first step is to identify the independent variables. For example, in digging a tunnel, an independent variable might be the length of the tunnel. If it takes on average 20 hours to dig 1 ft, then the time to dig

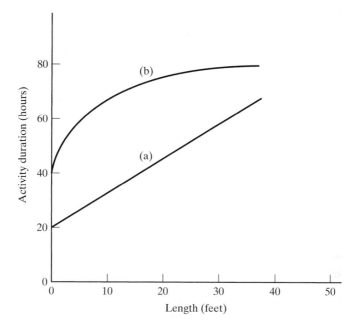

Figure 9.7   Two examples of activity duration as a
function of length.

a tunnel of length L can be estimated by $T(L) = 20 \times L$, where time is considered the dependent variable and the length of the tunnel is considered the independent variable.

When the relationship between the dependent variable and the independent variable is known exactly, as it is in many physical systems, one can plot a response curve in two dimensions. Figure 9.7 depicts two examples of length versus time: line (a) represents a linear relationship between the independent and dependent variables, and line (b) is a nonlinear one. In general, if the dependent variable, Y, is believed to be a linear function of the independent variable, X, then regression analysis can be used to estimate the parameters of the line $Y = b_0 + b_1 X$. Otherwise, either a transformation is performed on one or both of the variables to establish a linear relationship and then regression analysis applied, or a nonlinear curve-fitting technique is used.

In the simple case, we have n pairs of sample observations on X and Y, which can be represented on a scatter diagram as in Fig. 9.8. Because the line $Y = b_0 + b_1 X$ is unknown, we hypothesize that

$$Y_i = b_0 + b_1 X_i + u_i, \qquad i = 1, \ldots, n$$

$$E[u_i] = 0, \qquad\qquad\quad i = 1, \ldots, n$$

$$E[u_i u_j] = \begin{cases} 0, & \text{for } i \neq j; \; i, j = 1, \ldots, n \\ \sigma_u^2, & \text{for } i = j; \; i, j = 1, \ldots, n \end{cases}$$

where $E[\,\cdot\,]$ is the expected value operator and b_0, b_1, and σ_u^2 are unknown parameters that must be estimated from the sample observations $X_1, \ldots, X_n$ and $Y_1, \ldots, Y_n$. It is usually assumed that $u_i \sim N(0, \sigma_u^2)$; i.e., u_i is normally distributed with mean 0 and variance σ_u^2.

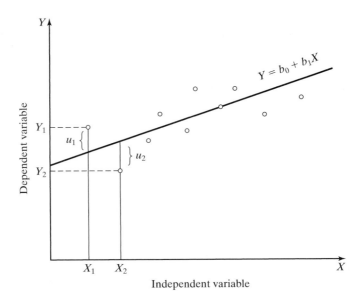

Figure 9.8 Typical scatter diagram.

To begin, denote the regression line by

$$\hat{Y} = \hat{b}_0 + \hat{b}_1 X$$

where $\hat{b}_0$ and $\hat{b}_1$ are estimates of the unknown parameters b_0 and b_1, and $\hat{Y}$ is the value of the dependent variable for any given value of X. To fit such a line, we must develop formulas for $\hat{b}_0$ and $\hat{b}_1$ in terms of the sample observations. This is done by the principle of least squares (Draper and Smith 1998) as discussed in Appendix 9A.

With some activities, more than one independent variable is required to estimate the performance time. For example, consider the activity of populating a printed circuit board. The use of three independent variables might be appropriate, the first being the number of components to be inserted, the second being the number of setups or tool changes required, and the third being the type of equipment used (here a qualitative rather than a quantitative measure is called for).

In general, if we start with m independent variables, then the regression line is

$$Y = b_0 + b_1 X_1 + b_2 X_2 + \cdots + b_m X_m + u$$

The coefficients $b_0, b_1, \ldots, b_m$ are also estimated by using the principle of least squares. Goodness of fit is measured by the R^2 value, which ranges from 0 (no correlation) to 1 (perfect correlation). The formula used in its calculation is given in Appendix 9A. However, some analysts prefer to use a normalized version of R^2 known as *adjusted* R^2 given by

$$R_a^2 = 1 - (1 - R^2)\left(\frac{n - 1}{n - m - 1}\right)$$

where n is the total number of observations and $m + 1$ is the number of coefficients to be estimated. By working with the adjusted R^2, it is possible to compare regression models used to estimate the same dependent variable using different numbers of independent variables.

Guidelines for developing a regression equation include the following steps:

- Identify the independent variables that affect activity duration.
- Collect data on past performance time of the activity for different values of the independent variables.
- Check the correlation between the variables. If necessary, use appropriate transformations and only then generate the regression equation.

In the case that several potential independent variables are considered, a technique called *stepwise regression analysis* can be used. This technique is designed to select the independent variables to be included in the model. At each step, at most one independent variable is added to the model. In the first step, a simple regression equation is developed with the independent variable that is the best predictor of the dependent variable (i.e., the one that yields the highest value of R^2). Next, a second variable is introduced. This process continues until no improvement in the regression equation is observed. The final form of the model includes only those independent variables that entered the regression equation during the stepwise iterations.

The quality of a regression model is assessed by analysis of residuals. These residuals ($e_i = Y_i - \hat{Y}_i$) are assumed to be normally distributed with a mean of zero. If this is not the case or a trend in the value of the residuals as a function of any independent variable exists, then the dependent variable or some of the independent variables may require a transformation.

Example 9-1

An organization decides to use a regression equation to estimate the time required to develop a new software package. The candidate list of independent variables includes

X_1 = number of subroutines in the program
X_2 = average number of lines of code in each subroutine
X_3 = number of modules or subprograms

Table 9.1 summarizes the data collected on 10 software packages. The time required in person-months denoted by Y is the dependent variable (the duration is given by the number of person-months divided by the number of programmers assigned to the project). Running a stepwise regression on the data yields the following equation:

$$Y = -0.76 + 0.13X_1 + 0.045X_2$$

with $R^2 = 0.972$ and $R_a^2 = 0.964$. Figure 9.9 plots the data points and the fitted line. The value of R_a^2 is lower than R^2 because

$$R_a^2 = 1 - (1 - R^2)\left(\frac{n-1}{n-m-1}\right) = 1 - (1 - 0.972)\left(\frac{9}{7}\right) = 0.964$$

TABLE 9.1   Data for Regression Analysis

Package number	Time required, Y	X_1	X_2	X_3
1	7.9	50	100	4
2	6.8	30	60	2
3	16.9	90	120	7
4	26.1	110	280	9
5	14.4	65	140	8
6	17.5	70	170	7
7	7.8	40	60	2
8	19.3	80	195	7
9	21.3	100	180	6
10	14.3	75	120	3

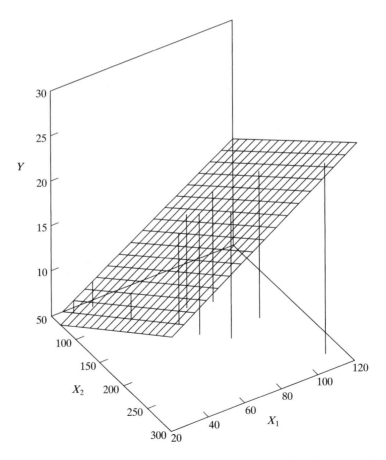

Figure 9.9   Data points and regression surface for the example.

By introducing the third candidate X_3 into the regression model the value of R_a^2 is reduced to 0.963; consequently, it is best to use only the independent variables X_1 and X_2 as predictors, although the difference is negligible.

If a new software package similar to the previous 10 is to be developed and it contains $X_1 = 45$ subroutines with an average of $X_2 = 170$ lines of code in each, then the estimated development time is

$$Y = -0.76 + (0.13)(45) + (0.045)(170) = 12.7 \text{ person-months} \quad \blacksquare$$

In general, the following points should be taken into account when using and evaluating the results of a regression analysis:

- For the activity under investigation, only data collected on similar activities performed by the same work methods should be used in the calculations.
- When the value of R^2 or R_a^2 is low (below 0.5), the independent variables may not be appropriate.
- If the distribution of the residuals is not close to normal or there is a trend in the residuals as a function of any independent variable, then the regression model may not be appropriate.

9.3 EFFECT OF LEARNING

The ability to learn is translated into improved performance as experience is gained, at both the organizational and individual levels. Improved performance can be measured by reductions in activity times or lower direct costs per repetition. Experience is usually measured by the number of repetitions of a given activity.

Most organizations have the potential to improve performance. This potential will be realized, however, only if sufficient motivation exists on the part of management and the workforce. Improvement at the individual level stems from the ability of a person to move faster and more accurately as experience is gained. Details of the work to be performed are memorized, and the time spent on reading instructions, looking at drawings, and experimenting with different procedures decreases. At the organizational level, the potential for improvement is found largely in the areas of communications and logistics and may be achieved with the use of more efficient equipment and work methods.

The relationship between performance time and experience (number of repetitions) can conveniently be represented by a learning curve. The underlying model relates the direct labor required to perform an activity to the experience gained in its execution. The basic learning curve equation (Wright 1936) is

$$T(n) = T(1)n^\beta \tag{9.3}$$

where $T(n)$ = expected number of direct labor hours required to perform the activity in the nth repetition

n = repetition number

$T(1)$ = expected number of direct labor hours required to perform the activity the first time

β = learning coefficient

A common practice is to describe this learning curve by the percentage decline of labor hours required for repetition $2n$ compared with the required labor hours for repetition n. A 90% learning curve means that the time required for repetition $2n$ is 90% of that required for n; thus

$$\frac{T(2n)}{T(n)} = \frac{T(1)(2n)^\beta}{T(1)(n)^\beta} = 2^\beta = 0.9$$

so

$$\beta \log_{10} 2 = \log_{10} 0.9$$

or

$$\beta = \frac{\log_{10} 0.9}{\log_{10} 2} = -0.15$$

If we assume a $100 \times L$ percent learning curve (where L is a fraction between 0 and 1), then

$$\beta = \frac{\log_{10} L}{\log_{10} 2} \tag{9.4}$$

Other learning curve models are discussed in Yelle (1979) and Smunt (1986).

The effect of learning is most important during startup when the cumulative number of repetitions is small. This is because the same relative improvement takes place whenever the number of repetitions is doubled; that is,

$$\frac{T(2n)}{T(n)} = 2^\beta$$

Thus, the relative improvement between the first and second repetitions is the same as the improvement between the 10th and the 20th repetitions.

This observation suggests that in projects in which a small number of identical units are to be produced, the careful assignment of workers to activities is crucial. By assigning the same workers to perform an activity on all units, direct labor costs and time can be saved as a result of learning. The scheduling of projects under learning is discussed in detail by Shtub (1991) and LeBlanc et al. (1992).

The learning process in projects may be interrupted if there are long breaks between consecutive repetitions of activities. Such breaks may cause forgetting. The relationship between learning and forgetting was investigated by Globerson et al. (1989), who developed an empirical learning-forgetting model based on the results of a field study.

To demonstrate the effect of learning in task planning, consider the following example: An activity is to be repeated four times in a project. Its duration is estimated to be 100 hours if performed by a single worker. The learning percentage defined is estimated as 80%. Solving Eq. (9.4) for β, we get

$$\beta = \frac{\log_{10} 0.8}{\log_{10} 2} = -0.322$$

Based on the initial estimate, the time to perform this activity is as follows:

Repetition number	Performance time
1	100
2	$100 \times 2^{-0.322} = 80$
3	$100 \times 3^{-0.322} = 70$
4	$100 \times 4^{-0.322} = 64$
	$\overline{314}$

Tables 9B.1 and 9B.2 in Appendix 9B can replace the calculations above. In Table 9B.1, the values of n^{β} are given for different values of n and $100 \times L\%$. Using Table 9B.1, the performance time for the activity when $n = 3$ (and assuming an 80% learning curve) is $100 \times 0.7021 = 70$. Using Table 9B.2, the total time for the four repetitions is $100 \times 3.142 = 314$.

Thus, in this example, the total time to perform the activity is 314 hours if the same worker is assigned to the activity and learning takes place. If, however, the four repetitions are assigned to four different workers, then the total time required would be $100 \times 4 = 400$ hours.

The learning curve can also be used to update time and cost estimates. Suppose that the actual time for the first repetition were 105 hours, whereas the actual time for the second repetition were 90 hours. In this case $T(1) = 105$ and $T(2) = 90$, so from Eqs. (9.3) and (9.4)

$$2^{\beta} = \frac{T(2)}{T(1)} = \frac{90}{105} = 0.857 \quad \text{or} \quad \beta = \frac{\log_{10} 0.857}{\log_2 2} = -0.22$$

By using the learning curve model for time and cost estimation and by scheduling workers so that learning is maximized, the project manager can take advantage of the learning effect.

9.4 PRECEDENCE RELATIONS AMONG ACTIVITIES

The schedule of activities is constrained by the availability of resources required to perform each activity and by technological constraints known as *precedence relations*. Four general types of precedence relations exist among activities. The most common, termed "finish to start," requires that an activity can start only after its predecessor has been completed. For example, it is possible to lift a piece of equipment by a crane only after the equipment is secured to the hoist.

A "start to start" relationship exists when an activity can start only after a specified activity has already begun. For example, in projects in which concurrent engineering is applied, logistic support analysis starts as soon as the detailed design phase begins. The "start to finish" connection occurs when an activity cannot end until another activity has begun. This would be the case in a project of building a nuclear reactor and charging it with fuel, in which one industrial robot transfers radioactive material to another. The first robot can release the material only after the second robot achieves a tight enough grip.

The "finish to finish" connection is used when an activity cannot terminate unless another activity is completed. Quality control efforts, for example, cannot terminate before production ceases, although the two activities can be performed at the same time.

A lag or time delay can be added to any of these connections. In the case of the "finish to finish" arrangement, there might be a need to spend 2 days on testing and quality control after production shuts down. In the case of the "finish to start" connection, a fixed setup may be required between the two activities. In some situations, the relationship between activities is subject to uncertainty. For example, after testing a printed circuit board that is to be part of a prototype communications system, the succeeding activity might be to install the board on its rack, to repair any defects found, or to scrap the board if it fails the functionality test.

The four types of precedence relations are illustrated in Fig. 9.10. A formal definition of each follows:

FS_{AB} (finish to start): This relation specifies that activity B cannot start until at least FS time units after the completion of activity A. Note that the PERT/CPM approaches use $FS_{AB} = 0$ for network analysis.

SS_{AB} (start to start): In this case, activity B cannot start until activity A has been in progress for at least SS time units.

FF_{AB} (finish to finish): Here, activity B cannot finish until at least FF time units after the completion of activity A.

SF_{AB} (start to finish): There must be at least SF time units between the start of activity A and the completion of activity B.

The leads or lags may be expressed alternately in percentages rather than time units. For example, we may specify that 20% of the work content of activity A must be completed before activity B can start. If percentage of work completed is used for determining lead-lag constraints, then a reliable procedure must be used for estimating the percentage of completion. If the project work is broken up properly in the WBS, then it will be much easier to estimate percentage of completion by evaluating the work completed at the elementary task levels. The lead-lag relationships may also be specified in

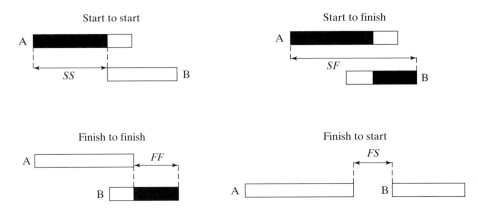

Figure 9.10   Lead-lag relationships in precedence diagramming.

terms of *at most* relationships instead of *at least* relationships. For example, we may have at most an *FF* lag requirement between the finish time of one activity and the finish time of another activity.

In the following sections, we concentrate on the analysis of "finish to start" connections, the most prevalent. Other types of connections are examined in Section 9.8, and the effect of uncertainty on precedence relations is discussed in Section 9.11. Uncertainty gives rise to probabilistic networks.

The large number of precedence relations among activities makes it difficult to rely on verbal descriptions alone to convey the effect of technological constraints on scheduling, so graphical representations are frequently used. In subsequent sections, a number of such representations are illustrated with the help of an example project. Table 9.2 contains the relevant activity data.

TABLE 9.2   Data for Example Project

Activity	Immediate predecessors	Duration (weeks)
A	–	5
B	–	3
C	A	8
D	A, B	7
E	–	7
F	C, E, D	4
G	F	5

In this project, only "finish to start" precedence relations are considered. From Table 9.2, we see that activities A, B, and E do not have any predecessors and thus can start at any time. Activity C, however, can start only after A finishes, whereas D can start after the completion of A and B. Further examination reveals that F can start only after C, E, and D are finished and that G must follow F. Because activity A precedes C, and C precedes F, A must also precede F by transitivity. Nevertheless, when using a network representation, it is necessary to list only immediate or direct precedence relations; implied relations are taken care of automatically.

The three models used to analyze precedence relations and their effect on the schedule are the Gantt chart, CPM, and PERT. As mentioned, the last two are based on network techniques in which the activities are placed either on the nodes or on the arrows, depending on which is more intuitive for the analyst.

9.5 GANTT CHART

The most widely used management tool for project scheduling and control is a version of the bar chart developed during World War I by Henry L. Gantt. The Gantt chart, as it is called, enumerates the activities to be performed on the vertical axis and their corresponding duration on the horizontal axis. It is possible to schedule activities by either early-start or late-start logic. In the early-start approach, each activity is initiated as early as possible without violating the precedence relations. In the late-start approach, each activity is delayed as much as possible as long as the earliest finish time of the project is not compromised.

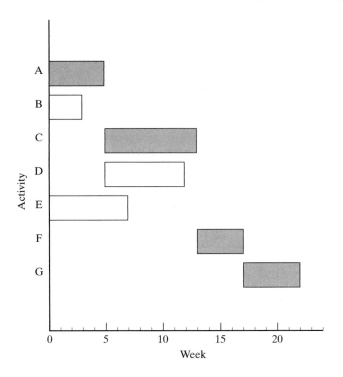

Figure 9.11   Gantt chart for an early-start schedule.

A range of schedules is generated on the Gantt chart when a combination of early and late starts is applied. The early-start schedule is performed first and yields the earliest finish time of the project. That time is then used as the required finish time for the late-start schedule. Figure 9.11 depicts the early-start Gantt chart schedule for the example above. The bars denote the activities; their location with respect to the time axis indicates the time over which the corresponding activity is performed. For example, activity D can start only after activities A and B finish, which happens at the end of week 5. A direct output of this schedule is the earliest finish time for the project (22 weeks for the example).

On the basis of the earliest finish time, the late-start schedule can be generated. This is done by shifting each activity to the right as much as possible while still starting the project at time 0 and completing it in 22 weeks. The resultant schedule is depicted in Fig. 9.12. The difference between the start (or the finish) times of an activity on the two schedules is called the slack (or float) of the activity. Activities that do not have any slack are denoted by a shaded bar and are termed *critical*. The sequence of critical activities connecting the start and end points of the project is known as the *critical path*, which logically turns out to be the *longest path* in the network. A delay in any activity along the critical path delays the entire project. Put another way, the sum of durations for critical activities represents the *shortest* possible time to complete the project.

Gantt charts are simple to generate and interpret. In the construction, there should be a one-to-one correspondence between the listed tasks and the WBS and its numbering scheme. As shown in Fig. 9.13, which depicts the Gantt chart for the microcomputer

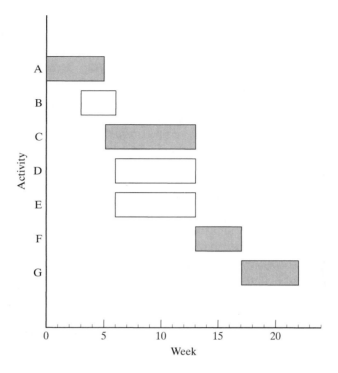

Figure 9.12   Gantt chart for a late-start schedule.

Master schedule

No.	Task/milestone	WBS no.	Dec	Jan	Feb	Mar	Apr	May	Jun	Jul	Aug	Sep	Oct	Nov	Dec	Jan	Feb
1	Project kickoff	–															
2	Equipment design	1.0															
3	Critical design review	–															
4	Prototype fabrication	2.0															
5	Test and integration	2.2															
6	Opers. and maintenance	3.0															
7	Marketing	4.0															
8	Transition to manufacturing	5.0															

↑
Review date

Figure 9.13   Gantt chart for the microcomputer development example.

development project, a separate column can be added for this purpose. In fact, the schedule should not contain any tasks that do not appear in the WBS. Often, however, the Gantt chart includes milestones such as project kickoff and design review, which are listed along with the tasks.

In addition to showing the critical path, Gantt charts can be modified to indicate project and activity status. In Fig. 9.13, a bold border is used to identify a critical activity, and a shaded area indicates the approximate completion status at the August review. Accordingly, we see that tasks 2, 5, and 8 are critical, falling on the longest path. Task 2 is 100% complete; task 4 is 65% complete; task 7 is 55% complete; tasks 5, 6 and 8 have not yet been started.

Gantt charts can be modified further to show budget status by adding a column that lists planned and actual expenditures for each task. This is taken up in Chapter 11. Many variations of the original bar graph have been developed to provide more detailed information for the project manager. One commonly used variation that replaces the bars with lines and adds triangles to indicate project status and revision points is shown in Fig. 9.14. To explain the features, let us examine task no. 2, equipment design. According to the code given in the lower left-hand corner of the figure, this task was rescheduled three times, finally starting in February and finishing at the end of June. Note the two rescheduled start milestones and the two rescheduled finish milestones.

The problem with adding features to the bar graph is that they take away from the clarity and simplicity of the basic form. Nevertheless, the additional information conveyed to the user may offset the additional effort required in generating and interpreting the data. A common modification of the analysis is the case when a milestone

Figure 9.14   Extended Gantt chart with task details.

has a contractual due date. Consider, for example, activity 8 (WBS no. 5.0) in Fig. 9.14. If management decides that the required due date for the termination of this activity is the end of February (instead of the end of January), then a slack of 1 month will be added to each activity in the project. If, however, the due date of activity 8 is the end of December, then the schedule in Fig. 9.14 is no longer feasible because the sequence of activities 2, 5, and 8 (the critical sequence) cannot be completed by the end of December. In Section 9.13, scheduling conflicts and their management are discussed in detail.

The major limitation of bar graph schedules is their inability to show task dependencies and time–resource tradeoffs. Network techniques are often used in parallel with Gantt charts to compensate for these shortcomings.

9.6 ACTIVITY-ON-ARROW NETWORK APPROACH FOR CRITICAL PATH METHOD ANALYSIS

Although the AOA model is most closely associated with PERT, it can be applied to CPM as well (it is sometimes called *activity-on-arc*). In constructing the network, an arrow is used to represent an activity, with its head indicating the direction of progress of the project. The precedence relations among activities are introduced by defining events. An event represents a point in time that signifies the completion of one or more activities and the beginning of new ones. The beginning and ending points of an activity thus are described by two events known as the head and the tail. Activities that originate from a certain event cannot start until the activities that terminate at the same event have been completed.

Figure 9.15a shows an example of a typical representation of an activity (i, j) with its tail event i and its head event j. Figure 9.15b depicts a second example, in which activities $(1, 3)$ and $(2, 3)$ must be completed before activity $(3, 4)$ can start. For computational purposes, it is customary to number the events in ascending order so that, compared with the head event, a smaller number is always assigned to the tail event of an activity.

The rules for constructing a diagram are summarized below.

Rule 1.   Each activity is represented by one and only one arrow in the network.

No single activity can be represented twice in the network. This is to be differentiated from the case in which one activity is broken down into segments wherein each segment may then be represented by separate arrows. For example, in designing a new computer architecture, the controller might first be developed followed by the arithmetic unit, the I/O processor, and so on.

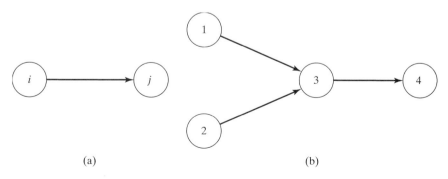

(a)   (b)

Figure 9.15   Network components.

Rule 2. No two activities can be identified by the same head and tail events.

A situation such as this may arise when two or more activities can be performed in parallel. As an example, consider Fig. 9.16a, which shows activities A and B running in parallel. The procedure used to circumvent this difficulty is to introduce a dummy activity between either A or B. The four equivalent ways of doing this are shown in Fig. 9.16b, where D_1 is the dummy activity. As a result of using D_1, activities A and B can now be identified by a unique set of events. It should be noted that dummy activities do not consume time or resources. Typically, they are represented by dashed lines in the network.

Dummy activities are also necessary in establishing logical relationships that cannot otherwise be represented correctly. Suppose that in a certain project, tasks A and B must precede C, whereas task E is preceded only by B. Figure 9.17a shows an incorrect

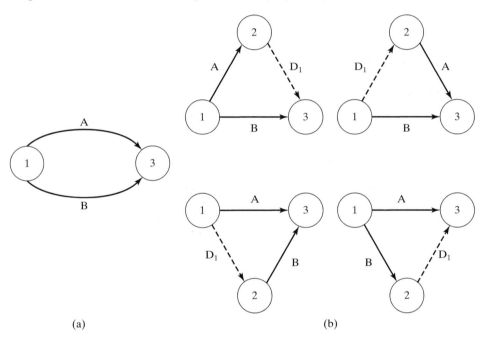

(a)   (b)

Figure 9.16   Use of a dummy arc between two nodes.

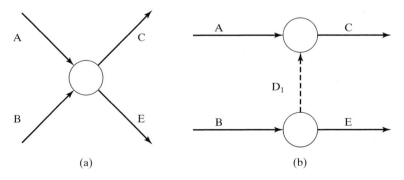

(a)   (b)

Figure 9.17   (a) Incorrect and (b) correct representation.

but common way that many beginners would draw this part of the network. The difficulty is that although the relationship among A, B, and C is correct, the diagram implies that E must be preceded by both A and B. The correct representation using dummy D_1 is depicted in Fig. 9.17b.

Rule 3.   To ensure the correct representation in the AOA diagram, the following questions must be answered as each activity is added to the network:

1. Which activities must be completed immediately before this activity can start?
2. Which activities must immediately follow this activity?
3. Which activities must occur concurrently with this activity?

This rule is self-explanatory. It provides guidance for checking and rechecking the precedence relations as the network is constructed.

The following examples further illustrate the use of dummy activities.

Example 9-2

Draw the AOA diagram so that the following precedence relations are satisfied:

1. E is preceded by B and C.
2. F is preceded by A and B.

Solution   Consider Fig. 9.18. Part (a) shows an incorrect precedence relation for activity E. According to the requirements, B and C are to precede E, and A and B are to precede F. The dummy D_1 therefore is inserted to allow B to precede E. Doing so, however, implies that A *also* must precede E, which is incorrect. Part (b) in the figure shows the correct relationships. ∎

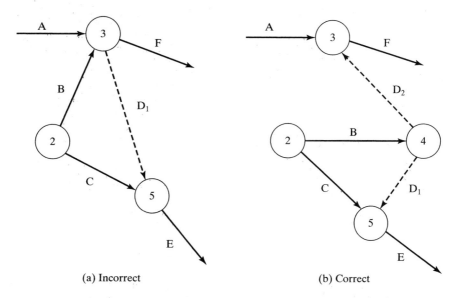

(a) Incorrect   (b) Correct

Figure 9.18   Subnetwork with two dummy arcs: (a) incorrect, (b) correct.

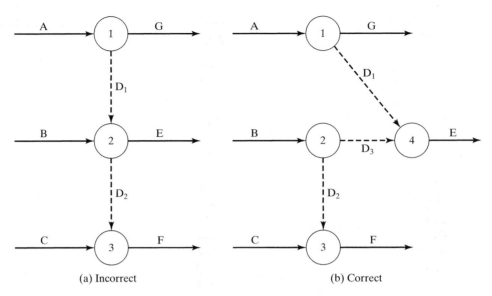

Figure 9.19   Subnetwork with complicated precedence relations: (a) incorrect, (b) correct.

Example 9-3

Draw the precedence diagram for the following conditions:

1. G is preceded by A.
2. E is preceded by A and B.
3. F is preceded by B and C.

Solution   An incorrect and correct representation is given in Fig. 9.19. The diagram in part (a) of the figure is wrong because it implies that A precedes F. ∎

It is good practice to have a single start event common to all activities that have no predecessors and a single end event for all activities that have no successors. The actual mechanics of drawing the AOA network are illustrated using the data in Table 9.2.

The process begins by identifying all activities that have no predecessors and joining them to a unique start node. This is shown in Fig. 9.20. Each activity terminates at a

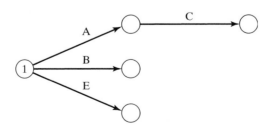

Figure 9.20   Partial plot of the example AOA network.

node. Only the first node in the network is assigned a number (1); all other nodes are labeled only when network construction is completed, as explained presently. Because activity C has only one predecessor (A), it can be added immediately to the diagram (see Fig. 9.20).

Activity D has both A and B as predecessors; thus, there is a need for an event that represents the completion of A and B. We begin by adding two dummy activities D_1 and D_2. The common end event of D_1 and D_2 is now the start event of D, as depicted in Fig. 9.21. As we progress, it may happen that one or more dummy activities are added that really are not necessary. To correct this situation, a check will be made at completion and redundant dummies will be eliminated.

Before starting activity F, activities C, E, and D must be completed. Therefore, an event that represents the terminal point of these activities should be introduced. Notice that C, E, and D are not predecessors of any other activity but F. This implies that we can have the three arrows representing these activities terminate at the same node (event)—the tail of F. Activity G, which has only F as a predecessor, can start from the head of F (see Fig. 9.22).

Once all of the activities and their precedence relations have been included in the network diagram, it is possible to eliminate redundant dummy activities. A dummy activity is redundant when it is the only activity that starts or ends at a given event. Thus, D_2 is redundant and is eliminated by connecting the head of activity B to the event that marked the end of D_2. The next step is to number the events in ascending order, making sure that the tail always has a lower number than the head. The resulting network is illustrated in Fig. 9.23. The duration of each activity is written next to the corresponding arrow. The dummy D_1 is shown like any other activity but with a duration of zero.

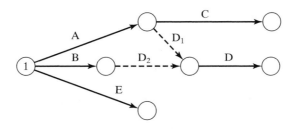

Figure 9.21   Using dummy activities to represent precedence relations.

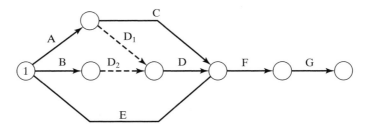

Figure 9.22   Network with activities F and G included.

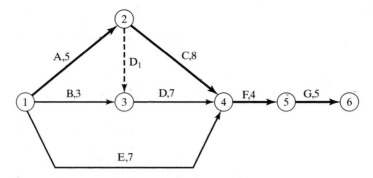

Figure 9.23   Complete AOA project network.

Example 9-4

Construct an AOA diagram that comprises activities A, B, C, ..., L such that the following relationships are satisfied:

1. A, B, and C, the first activities of the project, can start simultaneously.
2. A and B precede D.
3. B precedes E, F, and H.
4. F and C precede G.
5. E and H precede I and J.
6. C, D, F, and J precede K.
7. K precedes L.
8. I, G, and L are the terminal activities of the project.

Solution   The resulting diagram is shown in Fig. 9.24. The dummy activities D_1 and D_2 are needed to establish correct precedence relations. D_3 is introduced to ensure that the

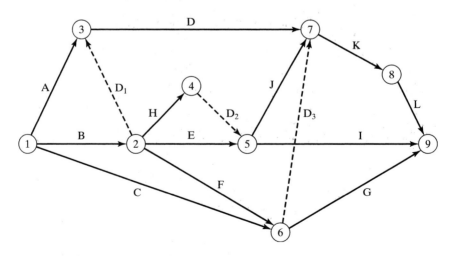

Figure 9.24   Network for Example 9-4.

Finishing event

		1	2	3	4	5	6
	1		×	×	×		
	2			×	×		
Starting	3				×		
event	4					×	
	5						×
	6						

parallel activities E and H have unique finish events. Note that the events in the project are numbered in such a way that if there is a path connecting nodes i and j, then $i < j$. In fact, there is a basic result from graph theory that states that a directed graph is acyclic if and only if its nodes can be numbered so that for all arcs (i, j), $i < j$.   ∎

Once the nodes are numbered, the network can be represented by a matrix whose respective rows and columns correspond to the start and finish events of a particular activity. The matrix for the example in Fig. 9.23 is as follows: where the entry "×" means that there is an activity connecting the two events (instead of a ×, it may be more efficient to use the activity number or its duration). For example, the × in row 3, column 4 indicates that an activity starts at event 3 and finishes at event 4, that is, activity D. The absence of an entry in the second row and fifth column means that no activity starts at event 2 and finishes at event 5.

Because the numbering scheme used ensures that if activity (i, j) exists, then $i < j$, it is sufficient to store only that portion of the matrix that is above the diagonal. Alternatively, the lower portion of the matrix can be used to store other information about an activity, such as resource requirements or budget. This conveniently represents computer input.

For complex projects, it may not be obvious how to label the nodes in the desired manner. Suppose that we have a graph that is described by its adjacency matrix $\mathbf{A}$, where $a_{ij} = 1$ if node i immediately precedes j and 0 otherwise and that the rows and columns of this matrix are ordered according to the given arbitrary numbering of the nodes. Let $v(j)$ denote the new number of node j, and define the in-degree of a node as the number of arcs that enter it. Let $d_j^{(in)}$ be the in-degree of node j. Initially, $d_j^{(in)}$ is computed for all nodes j, by forming the sum of the entries in column j of matrix $\mathbf{A}$. A node k for which $d_k^{(in)} = 0$ is found, and $v(k)$ is set to 1. The in-degrees are revised by subtracting the entries in row k of $\mathbf{A}$ and repeating the process. The accompanying algorithm is summarized below:

Step 0 (Start)

$$\text{Set } d_j^{(in)} = \sum_{i=1}^{n} a_{ij}, \quad j = 1, 2, \ldots, n.$$

$$\text{Set } N = \{1, 2, \ldots, n\}.$$

$$\text{Set } m = 1.$$

Step 1 (Detection of node with zero in-degree)

Find $k \in N$ such that $d_k^{(in)} = 0$. If there is no such k, then stop; the network is not acyclic—it contains one or more cycles.

Set $v(k) = m$.

Set $m = m + 1$.

Set $N = N - \{k\}$.

If $N = \emptyset$, then stop; all nodes have been correctly labeled.

Step 2 (Revision of in-degrees)

Set $d_j^{(in)} = d_j^{(in)} - a_{kj}$, for all $j \in N$.

Return to step 1.

If it is not possible to assign node numbers so that each activity starts at an event with a number lower than its finish event, then there is a logical error in the definition of precedence relations and a closed loop of activities exists in the network. This problem must be solved before the analysis can proceed.

From the network diagram, it is easy to see the sequences of activities that connect the start of the project to its terminal node. As explained earlier, the longest sequence is called the *critical path*. The total time required to perform all of the activities on the critical path is the minimum duration of the project because these activities cannot be performed in parallel as a result of precedence relations among them.

To simplify the analysis, it is recommended that in the case of multiple activities that have no predecessors, a common start event be used for all of them. Similarly, in cases in which multiple activities have no successors, a common finish event should be defined.

In the example network of Fig. 9.23, there are four sequences of activities connecting the start and finish nodes. Each is listed in Table 9.3.

TABLE 9.3   Sequences in the Network

Sequence number	Events in the sequence	Activities in the sequence	Sum of activity times
1	1-2-4-5-6	A, C, F, G	22
2	1-2-3-4-5-6	A, D₁, D, F, G	21
3	1-3-4-5-6	B, D, F, G	19
4	1-4-5-6	E, F, G	16

The last column of the table contains the duration of each sequence. As can be seen, the longest path (critical path) is sequence 1, which includes activities A, C, F, and G. A delay in completing any of these (critical) activities because of, say, a late start or a longer performance time than initially expected will cause a delay in project completion.

Activities that are not on the critical path(s) have slack and can be delayed temporarily on an individual basis. Two types of slack are possible: free slack (free float) and total slack (total float). *Free slack* denotes the time that an activity can be delayed without delaying both the start of any succeeding activity and the end of the project. *Total slack* is the time that the completion of an activity can be delayed without delaying the end of the project. A delay of an activity that has total slack but no free slack reduces the slack of other activities in the project.

A simple rule can be used to identify the type of slack. A noncritical activity whose finish event is on the critical path has both total and free slack, and the two are equal. For example, noncritical activity E, whose event 4 is on the critical path, has total slack = free slack = 6, as we will see shortly. In contrast, the head of noncritical activity B is not on the critical path; its total slack = 3, and its free slack = 2. The head of activity B is the start event of activity D, which is also noncritical. The difference between the length of the critical sequence (A-C) and the noncritical sequence (B-D), which runs in parallel to (A-C), is the total slack of B and D and is equal to $(5 + 8) - (3 + 7) = 3$. Any delay in activity B will reduce the remaining slack for activity D. Therefore, the person responsible for performing D should be notified.

The roles of the total and free slacks in scheduling noncritical activities can be explained in terms of two general rules:

1. If the total slack *equals* the free slack, then the noncritical activity can be scheduled anywhere between its early start and late finish times.

2. If the free slack is *less than* the total slack, then the noncritical activity can be delayed relative to its early start time by no more than the amount of its free slack without affecting the schedule of those activities that immediately succeed it.

Further elaboration and an exact mathematical expression for calculating activity slacks are presented in the following subsections.

9.6.1 Calculating Event Times and Critical Path

Important scheduling information for the project manager is the earliest and latest times when each event can take place without causing a schedule overrun. This information is needed to compute the critical path. The *early time* of an event i is determined by the length of the longest sequence from the start node (event 1) to event i. Denote t_i as the early time of event i, and let $t_1 = 0$, implying that activities without precedence constraints begin as early as possible. If a starting date is given, then t_1 is adjusted accordingly.

To determine t_i for each event i, a **forward** pass is made through the network. Let L_{ij} be the duration or length of activity (i, j). The following formula is used for the calculations:

$$t_j = \max_i\{t_i + L_{ij}\} \quad \text{for all } (i, j) \text{ activities defined} \tag{9.5}$$

where $t_1 = 0$. Thus, to compute t_j for event j, t_i for the tail events of all incoming activities, (i, j) must be computed first. In words, the early time of each event is the latest of the early times of its immediate predecessors plus the duration of the connecting activity.

The forward-pass calculations for the example network in Fig. 9.23 will now be given. The early time for event 2 is simply

$$t_2 = t_1 + L_{12} = 0 + 5 = 5$$

where $L_{12} = 5$ is the duration of the activity connecting event 1 to event 2 (activity A).

Early-time calculations for event 3 are a bit more complicated because event 3 marks the completion of the two activities D_1 and B. By implication, there are two sequences connecting the start of the project to event 3. The first comprises activities A and D_1 and is of length 5; the second includes activity B only and has $L_{13} = 3$. Using Eq. (9.5), we get

$$t_3 = \max\left\{\begin{matrix} t_1 + L_{13} \\ t_2 + L_{23} \end{matrix}\right\} = \max\left\{\begin{matrix} 0 + 3 \\ 5 + 0 \end{matrix}\right\} = 5$$

so the early time of event 3 is $t_3 = 5$.

The remaining calculations are performed as follows:

$$t_4 = \max\left\{\begin{matrix} t_1 + L_{14} \\ t_2 + L_{24} \\ t_3 + L_{34} \end{matrix}\right\} = \max\left\{\begin{matrix} 0 + 7 \\ 5 + 8 \\ 5 + 7 \end{matrix}\right\} = 13$$

$$t_5 = t_4 + L_{45} = 13 + 4 = 17$$
$$t_6 = t_5 + L_{56} = 17 + 5 = 22$$

This confirms that the earliest that the project can finish is in 22 weeks.

The late time of each event is calculated next by making a **backward** pass through the network. Let T_i denote the late time of event i. If n is the finish event, then the calculations are generally initiated by setting $T_n = t_n$ and working backward toward the start event using the following formula:

$$T_i = \min_j\{T_j - L_{ij}\} \quad \text{for all } (i, j) \text{ activities defined} \tag{9.6}$$

If, however, a required project completion date is given that is later than the early time of event n, then it is possible to assign that time as the late time for the finish event. If the required date is earlier than the early time of the finish event, then no feasible schedule exists. This case is discussed later in the chapter.

In our example, $T_6 = t_6 = 22$. The late time for event 5 is calculated as follows:

$$T_5 = T_6 - L_{56} = 22 - 5 = 17$$

Similarly,

$$T_4 = T_5 - L_{45} = 17 - 4 = 13$$
$$T_3 = T_4 - L_{34} = 13 - 7 = 6$$

Event 2 is connected by sequences of activities to both events 3 and 4. Thus, applying Eq. (9.6), the late time of event 2 is the minimum among the late times dictated by the two sequences; that is,

$$T_2 = \min\left\{\begin{matrix} T_3 - L_{23} \\ T_4 - L_{24} \end{matrix}\right\} = \min\left\{\begin{matrix} 6 - 0 \\ 13 - 8 \end{matrix}\right\} = 5$$

The late time of event 1 is calculated in a similar manner:

$$T_1 = \min\left\{\begin{array}{l} 6 - 3 = 3 \\ 5 - 5 = 0 \\ 13 - 7 = 6 \end{array}\right\} = 0$$

The results are summarized in Table 9.4.

TABLE 9.4   Summary of Event Time Calculations

Event, i	Early time, t_i	Late time, T_i
1	0	0
2	5	5
3	5	6
4	13	13
5	17	17
6	22	22

The critical activities can now be identified by using the results of the forward and backward passes. An activity (i, j) lies on the critical path if it satisfies the following three conditions:

$$t_i = T_i$$

$$t_j = T_j$$

$$t_j - T_i = T_j - T_i = L_{ij}$$

These conditions actually indicate that there is no float or slack time between the earliest start (completion) and the latest start (completion) of the critical activities. In Fig. 9.23, activities $(0, 2), (2, 4), (4, 5)$, and $(5, 6)$ define the critical path forming a chain in the network from node 1 (start) to node 6 (finish).

9.6.2 Calculating Activity Start and Finish Times

In addition to scheduling the events of a project, detailed scheduling of activities is performed by calculating the following four times (or dates) for each activity (i, j):

ES_{ij} = *early start* time: the earliest time when activity (i, j) can start without violating any precedence relations

EF_{ij} = *early finish* time: the earliest time when activity (i, j) can finish without violating any precedence relations

LS_{ij} = *late start* time: the latest time when activity (i, j) can start without delaying the completion of the project

LF_{ij} = *late finish* time: the latest time when activity (i, j) can finish without delaying the completion of the project

The calculations proceed as follows:

$$\begin{aligned}
\text{ES}_{ij} &= t_i & &\text{for all } i \\
\text{EF}_{ij} &= \text{ES}_{ij} + L_{ij} & &\text{for all } (i, j) \text{ defined} \\
\text{LF}_{ij} &= T_j & &\text{for all } j \\
\text{LS}_{ij} &= \text{LF}_{ij} - L_{ij} & &\text{for all } (i, j) \text{ defined}
\end{aligned}$$

Thus, the earliest time when an activity can begin is equal to the early time of its start event; the latest an activity can finish is equal to the late finish of its finish event. For activity D in the example, which is denoted by arc (3, 4) in the network, we have $\text{ES}_{34} = t_3 = 5$ and $\text{LF}_{34} = T_4 = 13$.

The earliest time when an activity can finish is given by its ES plus its duration; the latest time when an activity can start is equal to its LF minus its duration. For activity D, this implies that $\text{EF}_{34} = \text{ES}_{34} + L_{34} = 5 + 7 = 12$, and $\text{LS}_{34} = \text{LF}_{34} - L_{34} = 13 - 7 = 6$. The full set of calculations is presented in Table 9.5.

TABLE 9.5 Summary of Start and Finish Time Analysis

Activity	(i, j)	L_{ij}	$\text{ES}_{ij} = t_i$	$\text{EF}_{ij} =$ $\text{ES}_{ij} + L_{ij}$	$\text{LF}_{ij} = T_j$	$\text{LS}_{ij} =$ $\text{LF}_{ij} - L_{ij}$	$\text{TS}_{ij} =$ $\text{LS}_{ij} - \text{ES}_{ij}$	$\text{FS}_{ij} =$ $t_j - t_i - L_{ij}$
A	(1, 2)	5	0	5	5	0	0	0
B	(1, 3)	3	0	3	6	3	3	2
C	(2, 4)	8	5	13	13	5	0	0
D	(3, 4)	7	5	12	13	6	1	1
E	(1, 4)	7	0	7	13	6	6	6
F	(4, 5)	4	13	17	17	13	0	0
G	(5, 6)	5	17	22	22	17	0	0
D_1	(2, 3)	0	5	5	6	6	1	0

9.6.3 Calculating Slacks

As mentioned, there are two types of slack associated with an activity: total slack and free slack. Information about slack is important to the project manager, who may have to adjust budgets and resource allocations to stay on schedule. Knowing the amount of slack in an activity is essential if he or she is to do this without delaying the completion of the project. In a multiproject environment, slack in one project can be used temporarily to free up resources needed for other projects that are behind schedule or overly constrained.

Because of the importance of slack, project management is sometimes referred to as slack management. We will elaborate on slack management in the chapters that deal with resources and budgets. The total slack TS_{ij} (or total float TF_{ij}) of activity (i, j) is equal to the difference between its late start (LS_{ij}) and its early start (ES_{ij}) or the difference between its late finish (LF_{ij}) and its early finish (EF_{ij}); that is,

$$\text{TS}_{ij} = \text{TF}_{ij} = \text{LS}_{ij} - \text{ES}_{ij} = \text{LF}_{ij} - \text{EF}_{ij}$$

This is equivalent to the difference between the maximum time available to perform the activity $(T_j - t_i)$ and its duration (L_{ij}). The total slack of activity D $(3, 4)$ in the example is $TS_{34} = LS_{34} - ES_{34} = 6 - 5 = 1$.

The free slack (or free float) is defined by assuming that all activities start as early as possible. In this case, the free slack, FS_{ij}, for activity (i, j) is the difference between the early time of its finish event j and the sum of the early time of its start event i plus its length; that is,

$$FS_{ij} = t_j - (t_i + L_{ij}).$$

For the example, the free slack for activity D $(3, 4)$ is $FS_{34} = t_4 - (t_3 + L_{34}) = 13 - (5 + 7) = 1$. Thus, it is possible to delay activity D by 1 week without affecting the start of any other activity. The times and slacks for the events and activities of the example are summarized in Table 9.5.

Activities with a total slack equal to zero are critical because any delay in these activities will lead to a delay in the completion of the project. The total slack is either equal to or larger than the free slack because the total slack of an activity is composed of its free slack plus the slack shared with other activities. For example, activity B denoted by $(1, 3)$ has a free slack of 2 weeks. Thus, it can be delayed up to 2 weeks without affecting its successor D. If, however, B is delayed by 3 weeks, then the project can still be finished on time provided that D starts immediately after B finishes. This follows because activities B and D share 1 week of total slack. Finally, notice that activity D_1 has a total slack of 1 and a free slack of 0, implying that noncritical activities may have zero free slack.

In an AOA network, the length of the arrows is not necessarily proportional to the duration of the activities. When developing a graphical representation of the problem, it is convenient to write the duration of each activity on the corresponding arrow. Most software packages that are based on the AOA model follow this convention. In addition, they typically provide the user with the option of placing a subset of activity parameters above or below the arrows. We have intentionally omitted placing this information on our diagrams because of the clutter that it occasions. Nevertheless, it is good practice when manually performing the forward and backward calculations to write the early and late start times above the corresponding nodes.

9.7 ACTIVITY-ON-NODE NETWORK APPROACH FOR CRITICAL PATH METHOD ANALYSIS

The AON model is an alternative approach to representing project activities and their interrelationships. It is most closely associated with CPM analysis and is the basis for most computer implementations. In the AON model, the arrows are used to denote the precedence relations among activities. Its basic advantage is that there is no need for dummy arrows and it is very easy to construct. In developing the network, it is convenient to add a single start node and a single finish node that uniquely identify these milestones. This is illustrated in Fig. 9.25 for the example.

Some additional network construction rules include:

1. All nodes, with the exception of the terminal node, must have at least one successor.
2. All nodes, except the first, must have at least one predecessor.

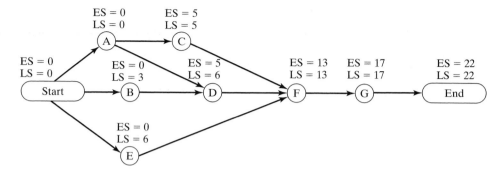

Figure 9.25   AON network for the example project.

3. There should be only one initial and one terminal node.
4. No arrows should be left dangling. Notwithstanding rules 1 and 2, every arrow must have a head and a tail.
5. An arrow specifies only precedence relations; its length has no significance with respect to the time duration accompanying either of the activities that it connects.
6. Cycles or closed-loop paths through the network are not permitted. They imply that an activity is a successor of another activity that depends on it.

As with the AOA model, the computational procedure involves forward and backward passes through the network. This is discussed next.

9.7.1 Calculating Early Start and Early Finish Times of Activities

A forward pass is used to determine the earliest start time and the earliest finish time for each activity. During the forward pass, it is assumed that each activity begins as soon as possible; that is, as soon as the last of its predecessors is completed. Thus, the early start (ES) time of an activity is equal to the maximum early finish (EF) time of all of the activities immediately preceding it. The ES time of the initial activity is assumed to be zero, as is its EF. For all other activities, the EF time is equal to its early start time plus its duration.

Using slightly different notation to distinguish the AON calculations from those prescribed for the AOA model, we have

$$\text{ES}(K) = \max\{\text{EF}(J) : J \text{ an immediate predecessor of } K\} \qquad (9.7)$$

$$\text{EF}(K) = \text{ES}(K) + L(K) \qquad (9.8)$$

where $L(K)$ denotes the duration of activity K.

Returning once again to the example, activities A, B, and E do not have predecessors (except the start node), and thus their early start times are zero; that is, $\text{ES}(A) = \text{ES}(B) = \text{ES}(E) = 0$. The early finish time of these activities is equal to their early start time plus their duration, so $\text{EF}(A) = 0 + 5 = 5$, $\text{EF}(B) = 0 + 3 = 3$, and $\text{EF}(E) = 0 + 7 = 7$.

From Eq. (9.7), the early start of any other activity is determined by the latest (the maximum) early finish time of its predecessors. For activity D, the calculations are

$$ES(D) = max\begin{Bmatrix} EF(A) \\ EF(B) \end{Bmatrix} = max\begin{Bmatrix} 5 \\ 3 \end{Bmatrix} = 5$$

The early start and early finish times of the remaining activities are computed in a similar manner. Table 9.6 summarizes the results.

TABLE 9.6 Early Start and Early Finish of Project Activities

Activity	Early start	Early finish
A	0	5
B	0	3
C	5	13
D	5	12
E	0	7
F	13	17
G	17	22

9.7.2 Calculating Late Start and Finish Times of Activities

The calculation of late times on the AON network is performed in the reverse order of the calculation of early times. As with the AOA model, a backward pass is made beginning at the expected completion time and concluding at the earliest start time. To complete the project as soon as possible, the late finish (LF) of the last activity is set equal to its early finish (EF) time calculated in the forward pass. Alternatively, the latest allowable completion time may be fixed by a contractual deadline, if one exists, or some other rationale.

In general, the late finish time of an activity with more than one successor is the earliest of the succeeding late start times. The late start (LS) time of an activity is its LF time minus its duration. Computational expressions for LF and LS are

$$LF(K) = min\{LS(J) : J \text{ is a successor of } K\} \tag{9.9}$$

$$LS(K) = LF(K) - L(K) \tag{9.10}$$

To begin the calculations for the example network in Fig. 9.23, we set $LF(G) = EF(G) = 22$ and apply Eq. (9.10) to get $LS(G) = LF(G) - L(G) = 22 - 5 = 17$. The late finish of any other activity is equal to the earliest (or the minimum) among the late start time of its succeeding activities. Because activity F has only one successor (G), we get

$$LF(F) = LS(G) = 17 \quad and \quad LS(F) = 17 - 4 = 13$$

Continuing with activities C and D yields

$$LF(C) = LS(F) = 13 \quad \text{and} \quad LS(C) = 13 - 8 = 5$$
$$LF(D) = LS(F) = 13 \quad \text{and} \quad LS(D) = 13 - 7 = 6$$

Because A has two successors, we get

$$LF(A) = \min\left\{\begin{matrix} LS(C) \\ LS(D) \end{matrix}\right\} = \min\left\{\begin{matrix} 5 \\ 6 \end{matrix}\right\} = 5$$

and

$$LS(A) = LF(A) - L(A) = 5 - 5 = 0$$

The late start and late finish times of activities in the example project are summarized in Table 9.7. As expected, these results are identical to those of the AOA model.

TABLE 9.7   Late Finish and Late Start of Project Activities

Activity	Late finish	Late start
A	5	0
B	6	3
C	13	5
D	13	6
E	13	6
F	17	13
G	22	17

The total slack of an activity is calculated as the difference between its late start (or finish) and its early start (or finish). The free slack of an activity is the difference between the earliest among the early start times of its successors and its early finish time. That is, for each activity K,

$$TS(K) = LS(K) - ES(K)$$
$$FS(K) = \min\{ES(J): J \text{ is successor of } K\} - EF(K)$$

Activities with zero total slack fall on the critical path. When performing the calculations manually, it is convenient to write the corresponding ES and LS times above each node to help identify the critical path.

9.8 PRECEDENCE DIAGRAMMING WITH LEAD–LAG RELATIONSHIPS

When lead or lag constraints exist between the start and finish of activities or when precedence relations other than "finish to start" are present, it is often possible to split activities to simplify the analysis. Some of the factors that determine whether an activity can be split are technical or logical limitations, setup times required to restart split tasks, difficulty involved in managing resources for split tasks, loss of consistency of work, and management policy about splitting jobs.

Figure 9.26 presents a simple AON network that consists of three activities. The two top numbers on either side of the nodes correspond to early start and early finish times, whereas the two bottom numbers correspond to late start and late finish times. The activities are to be performed serially, and each has an expected duration of 10 days. The conventional CPM analysis indicates that the duration of the network is 30 days.

The Gantt chart for the example is shown in Fig. 9.27. For comparison, Fig. 9.28 displays the same network but with lead–lag constraints. For example, there is an *SS*

Figure 9.26   Serial activities in simple CPM network.

Figure 9.27   Gantt chart for serial network.

Figure 9.28   Serial network with lead and lag constraints.

constraint of 2 days and an *FF* constraint of 2 days between activities A and B. Thus, activity B can start as early as 2 days after activity A starts, but it cannot finish until 2 days after the completion of A. In other words, *at least* 2 days must separate the start times of A and B. Likewise, at least 2 days must separate the finish times of A and B. A similar precedence relation exists between activities B and C. The earliest and latest times obtained by considering the lag constraints are indicated in Fig. 9.28.

The calculations show that if B is started just 2 days after A is started, then it can be completed as early as 12 days as opposed to the 20 days required in the case of conventional CPM. Similarly, activity C can finish in 14 days, which is considerably less than the 30 days calculated by conventional CPM. The lead–lag constraints allow us to compress or overlap activities. Depending on the nature of the tasks involved, an activity does not have to wait until its predecessor finishes before it can start. Figure 9.29 depicts the Gantt chart for the example incorporating the lead–lag constraints. As we see, a portion of a succeeding activity can be performed simultaneously with a portion of a preceding activity.

The portion of an activity that overlaps another can be viewed as a distinct component of the required work. Thus, partial completion of an activity may be evaluated. Figure 9.30 shows how each of the three activities is partitioned into contiguous parts. Even though there is no physical break or termination of work in any activity, the distinct parts are

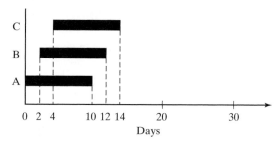

Figure 9.29   Gantt chart for network with lead and lag constraints.

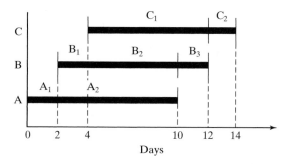

Figure 9.30   Partitioning of overlapping activities.

determined on the basis of the amount of work that must be completed before or after another activity, as dictated by the lead–lag relationships. In Fig. 9.30, activity A is partitioned into the segments A_1 and A_2. The duration of A_1 is 2 days because there is an $SS = 2$ relationship between activity A and activity B. Because the original duration of A is 10 days, the duration of A_2 is then calculated to be $10 - 2 = 8$ days.

Likewise, activity B is partitioned into segments B_1, B_2, and B_3. The duration of B_1 is 2 days because there is an $SS = 2$ relationship between activity B and activity C. The duration of B_3 is also 2 days because there is an $FF = 2$ relationship between activities A and B. Because the original duration of B is 10 days, the duration of B_2 is calculated to be $10 - (2 + 2) = 6$ days. In a similar manner, activity C is partitioned into C_1 and C_2. The duration of C_2 is 2 days because there is an $FF = 2$ relationship between activity A and activity C. Given that the original duration of C is 10 days, the duration of C_1 is then calculated to be $10 - 2 = 8$ days. Figure 9.31 shows a conventional AON network drawn for the three activities after they are partitioned into distinct parts. The conventional forward and backward passes reveal that all of the activity parts are on the critical path. This makes sense, because the original three activities are performed serially and none of them has been physically split. Note that there are three critical paths in Fig. 9.31, each with a length of 14 days. It should also be noted that the distinct segments of each activity are performed contiguously.

Figure 9.32 depicts a second example of three serial activities. The conventional CPM analysis shows that the earliest finish time is 30 days. When lead–lag constraints are introduced, as shown in Fig. 9.33, the network duration is compressed to 18 days.

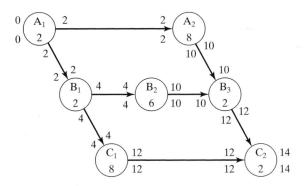

Figure 9.31   AON network of partitioned activities.

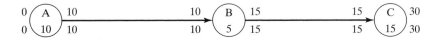

Figure 9.32   Second example of an AON network with serial activities.

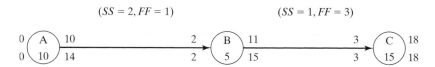

Figure 9.33 Compressed network for second example.

In the forward-pass computations in Fig. 9.33, the earliest completion time of B is 11 because there is an $FF = 1$ restriction between activities A and B. Because A finishes at time 10, B cannot finish until at least time 11. Even though the earliest starting time of B is 2 and its duration is 5 days, its earliest completion time cannot be earlier than 11 days. Also note that C can start as early as time 3 because there is an $SS = 1$ relationship between B and C. Thus, given a duration of 15 days for C, the earliest completion time of C and the earliest completion time of B is $18 - 11 = 7$ days, which satisfies the $FF = 3$ relationship between B and C.

In the backward pass, the latest completion time of B is 15 (i.e., $18 - 3 = 15$), because there is an $FF = 3$ relationship between activities B and C. The latest start time for B is 2 (i.e., $3 - 1 = 2$), because there is an $SS = 1$ relationship between activities B and C. If we are not careful, then we may erroneously set the latest start time of B to 10 (i.e., $15 - 5 = 10$), but that would violate the $SS = 1$ restriction between B and C. The latest completion time of A is found to be 14 (i.e., $15 - 1 = 14$), because there is an $FF = 1$ relationship between A and B. All of the earliest times and latest times at each node must be evaluated to ensure that they conform to all of the lead–lag constraints. When computing earliest start or earliest completion times, the largest possible value that satisfies the lead–lag constraints should be used.

Manual evaluations of the lead–lag precedence relations can become very tedious for large networks, so software is necessary for analyzing projects of any significant size. If manual analysis is the only option, then it is suggested that the network be partitioned into more manageable segments. The segments may then be linked after the computations are performed. The expanded AON network in Fig. 9.34 was developed on the basis of the precedence network in Fig. 9.33. It is seen that activity A is divided into two parts, activity B into three parts, and activity C into two parts. The forward and backward passes show that only the first parts of activities A and B are on the critical path, whereas both parts of C are on the critical path.

Figure 9.35 shows the corresponding early-start Gantt chart for the expanded network. Looking at the earliest start times, one can see that activity B is physically split at the boundary of B_2 and B_3 in such a way that B_3 is separated from B_2 by 4 days. This implies that work on activity B is temporarily stopped at time 6 after B_2 is finished and is not started again until time 10. Note that despite the 4-day delay in starting B_3, the entire project is not delayed. This is because B_3, the last part of activity B, is not on the critical path. In fact, B_3 has a total slack of 4 days. In a situation such as this, the duration of activity B can actually be increased from 5 days to 9 days without any adverse effect on the project duration. It should be recognized, however, that increasing the duration of an activity may have negative implications for project cost and personnel productivity.

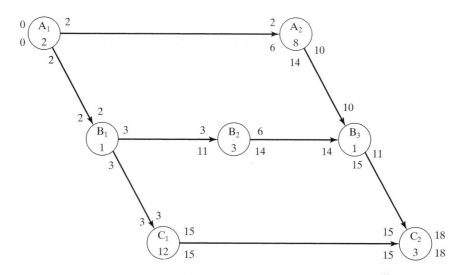

Figure 9.34   AON expansion of second example.

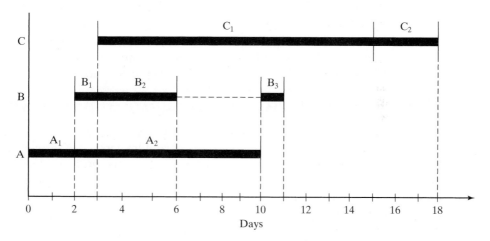

Figure 9.35   Compressed schedule for second example based on earliest start times.

   If the physical splitting of activities is not permitted, then the best option available in Fig. 9.35 is to stretch the duration of B_2 so as to fill up the gap from time 6 to time 10. An alternative is to delay the start time of B_1 until time 4 so as to use up the 4-day slack right at the beginning of activity B. Unfortunately, delaying the start time of B_1 by 4 days will delay the overall project by 4 days, because B_1 is on the critical path (see Fig. 9.34). The project analyst will need to evaluate the appropriate tradeoffs among splitting activities, delaying activities, increasing activity durations, and incurring higher project costs. The prevailing project scenario should be considered when making such tradeoff

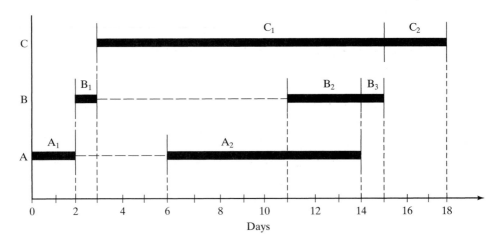

Figure 9.36   Compressed schedule for second example based on latest start times.

decisions. Figure 9.36 shows the Gantt chart for the compressed schedule based on latest start times. In this case, it will be necessary to split both activities A and B even though the total project duration remains the same at 18 days. If activity splitting is to be avoided, then we can increase the duration of activity A from 10 to 14 days and the duration of B from 5 to 13 days without adversely affecting the entire project duration. The important benefit that one gains from this type of precedence diagramming is the ability to overlap activities. This permits more flexibility in manipulating individual activity times and the greater possibility of compressing the project duration.

9.9 LINEAR PROGRAMMING APPROACH FOR CRITICAL PATH METHOD ANALYSIS

Many classical network problems can be formulated as linear programs and solved using standard algorithms. Finding the shortest and longest paths through a network are two such examples. Of course, the latter is exactly the problem that is solved in CPM analysis. To see its linear programming representation, we make use of the following notation and assume an AOA model:

i, j = indices for nodes in the network; each node corresponds to an event; $i = 1$ is the unique project start node

N = set of nodes or events

n = number of events in the network; n is the unique node marking the end of the project

A = set of arcs in the network; each arc (i, j) corresponds to a project activity, where i denotes its start event and j its end event

L_{ij} = the length of the activity that starts at node i and terminates at node j

t_i = decision variable associated with the start time of event $i \in N$

The following linear program (LP) schedules all events and all activities in a feasible manner such that the project finishes as early as possible, assuming that work begins at time $t_1 = 0$:

$$\text{Minimize} \quad t_n \tag{9.11a}$$

$$\text{subject to} \quad t_j - t_i \geq L_{ij} \qquad \text{for all activities } (i, j) \in A \tag{9.11b}$$

$$t_1 = 0, t_i \geq 0 \qquad \text{for all } i \in N \tag{9.11c}$$

Note that the nonnegativity condition $t_i \geq 0$ is redundant and that the last event t_n denotes the completion time of the project.

The slack associated with a nonbinding constraint in (9.11b) represents the slack of the corresponding activity given the start times t_i found by the LP. These values may not coincide with the CPM calculations. To find the total slack of an activity, it is necessary to perform sensitivity (ranging) analysis on the LP solution. The amount that each right-hand side (L_{ij}) can be increased without changing the optimal solution is equivalent to the total slack of activity (i, j).

The LP formulation for the example project is

$$\text{Minimize } t_6$$

subject to

$$
\begin{array}{ll}
t_2 - t_1 \geq 5 & \text{activity A} \\
t_3 - t_1 \geq 3 & \text{activity B} \\
t_4 - t_2 \geq 8 & \text{activity C} \\
t_4 - t_3 \geq 7 & \text{activity D} \\
t_4 - t_1 \geq 7 & \text{activity E} \\
t_5 - t_4 \geq 4 & \text{activity F} \\
t_6 - t_5 \geq 5 & \text{activity G} \\
t_3 - t_2 \geq 0 & \text{dummy } D_1 \\
t_1 = 0 &
\end{array}
$$

Using the Excel add-ins that come with the book by Jensen and Bard (2003), we find the solution to be $\mathbf{t} = (0, 5, 6, 13, 17, 22)$. The slack vector for the first eight rows is $(0, 3, 0, 0, 6, 0, 0, 1)$. Notice that these results differ slightly from those in Tables 9.4 and 9.5. To guarantee that the LP (9.11a)–(9.11c) finds the earliest time when each event can start, as was done in Section 9.6.1, the following penalty term must be added to the objective function (9.11a):

$$\varepsilon \sum_{i=2}^{n-1} t_i$$

where $\varepsilon > 0$ is an arbitrarily small constant. Conceptually, in the augmented formulation, the computations are done in two stages. First, t_n is found. Then, given this value, a search is conducted over the set of alternative optima to find the minimum values of $t_i, i = 2, \ldots, n - 1$. In reality, the computations all are done in one stage, not two.

9.10 AGGREGATING ACTIVITIES IN THE NETWORK

The detailed network model of a project is very useful in scheduling and monitoring progress at the operational (short-term) level. Management concerns at the tactical or strategic level, however, create a need for a focused presentation that eliminates unnecessary clutter. For projects that span a number of years and include hundreds of activities, it is likely that only a portion of those activities will be active or require close control at any point in time. To facilitate the management function, there is a need to condense information and aggregate tasks. The two common tools used for this purpose are hammock activities and milestones.

9.10.1 Hammock Activities

When a group of activities has a common start and a common end point, it is possible to replace the entire group with a single activity, called a hammock activity. For example, in the network depicted in Fig. 9.37, it is possible to use a hammock activity between events 4 and 6. In so doing, activities F and G are collapsed into FG whose duration is the sum of L_{45} and L_{56}.

In general, the duration of a hammock activity is equal to the duration of the longest sequence of activities that it replaces. If another hammock activity is used to represent A, B, C, D, and E, then its length would be

$$\max\begin{Bmatrix} L_{12} + L_{24} \\ L_{13} + L_{34} \\ L_{12} + L_{23} + L_{34} \\ L_{14} \end{Bmatrix} = \max\begin{Bmatrix} 5 + 8 \\ 3 + 7 \\ 5 + 0 + 7 \\ 7 \end{Bmatrix} = 13$$

Hammock activities reduce the size of a network while preserving, in general, information on precedence relations and activity durations. By using hammock activities, an upper-level network that presents a synoptic view of the project can be created. Such networks are useful for medium (tactical) and long-range (strategic) planning. The common practice is to develop a hierarchy of networks in which the various levels

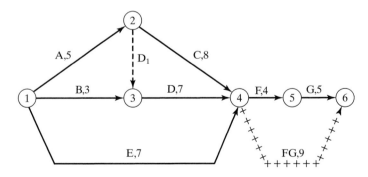

Figure 9.37   Example of a hammock activity.

correspond to the levels of either the WBS or the organizational breakdown structure (OBS). Higher-level networks contain many hammock activities and provide upper management with a general picture of flows, milestones, and overall status. Lower-level networks consist of single activities and provide detailed schedule information for team leaders. Proper use of hammock activities can help in providing the right level of detail to each participant in the project.

9.10.2 Milestones

A higher level of aggregation is also possible by introducing milestones to mark the completion of significant activities. As explained in Section 9.1.1, milestones are commonly used to mark the delivery of goods and services, to denote points in time when payments are due, and to flag important events such as the successful completion of a critical design review. In the simplest case, a milestone can mark the completion of a single activity, as event 2 in our example marks the completion of activity A. It can also mark the completion of several activities as exemplified by event 4, which denotes the completion of C, D, and E.

By using several levels of aggregation—that is, networks with various layers of hammock activities and milestones—it is possible to design the most appropriate decision support tool for each level of management. Such an exercise should take into account the WBS and the OBS. At the lowest levels of these structures, a detailed network is essential; at higher levels, aggregation by hammock activities and milestones is the norm.

9.11 DEALING WITH UNCERTAINTY

CPM assumes either that the duration of an activity is known and deterministic or that a point estimate such as the mean or mode can be used in its place. It makes no allowance for activity variance. When fluctuations in performance time are low, this assumption is logically justified and has empirically been shown to produce accurate results. When high levels of uncertainty exist, however, CPM may not provide a very good estimate of the project completion time. In these situations, there is a need to account explicitly for the effects of uncertainty. Monte Carlo simulation and PERT are the two most common approaches that have been developed for this purpose.

9.11.1 Simulation Approach

This approach is based on simulating the project by randomly generating performance times for each activity from their perceived distributions. In most cases, it is assumed that activity times follow a beta distribution as discussed in Section 9.2.1. In each simulation run, a sample of the performance time of each activity is taken and a CPM analysis is conducted to determine the critical path and the project finish time for that realization. By repeating the process a large number of times, it is possible to construct a frequency distribution or histogram of the project completion time. This distribution then may be used to calculate the probability that the project finishes by a given date, as well as the expected error of each such estimate.

A single simulation run would consist of the following steps:

1. Generate a random value for the duration of each activity from the appropriate distribution.
2. Determine the critical path and its duration using CPM.
3. Record the results.

The number of times that this procedure must be repeated depends on the error tolerances deemed acceptable. Standard statistical tests can be used to verify the accuracy of the estimates.

To understand the calculations, let us focus on the AOA network in Fig. 9.23 for the example project and assume that each activity follows a beta distribution with parameter values given in Table 9.8. After performing 10 simulation runs, the results listed in Table 9.9 for activity durations, critical path, and project completion time were obtained. Additional data collected but not presented include the earliest and latest start and completion times of each event and activity slacks.

Looking at the first run in Table 9.9, we see that the realized duration of activity A is 6.3, whereas the duration of activity B is 2.2. In the second run, the duration of A is 2.1, and so on. Note that the critical path differs from one replication to the next depending

TABLE 9.8 Statistics for Example Activities

Activity	Optimistic time, a	Most likely time, m	Pessimistic time, b	Expected value, $\hat{d}$	Standard deviation, $\hat{s}$
A	2	5	8	5	1
B	1	3	5	3	0.66
C	7	8	9	8	0.33
D	4	7	10	7	1
E	6	7	8	7	0.33
F	2	4	6	4	0.66
G	4	5	6	5	0.33

TABLE 9.9 Summary of Simulation Runs for Example Project

Run number	A	B	C	D	E	F	G	Critical path	Completion time
1	6.3	2.2	8.8	6.6	7.6	5.7	4.6	A-C-F-G	25.4
2	2.1	1.8	7.4	8.0	6.6	2.7	4.6	A-D-F-G	17.4
3	7.8	4.9	8.8	7.0	6.7	5.0	4.9	A-C-F-G	26.5
4	5.3	2.3	8.9	9.5	6.2	4.8	5.4	A-D-F-G	25.0
5	4.5	2.6	7.6	7.2	7.2	5.3	5.6	A-C-F-G	23.0
6	7.1	.4	7.2	5.8	6.1	2.8	5.2	A-C-F-G	22.3
7	5.2	4.7	8.9	6.6	7.3	4.6	5.5	A-C-F-G	24.2
8	6.2	4.4	8.9	4.0	6.7	3.0	4.0	A-C-F-G	22.1
9	2.7	1.1	7.4	5.9	7.9	2.9	5.9	A-C-F-G	18.9
10	4.0	3.6	8.3	4.3	7.1	3.1	4.3	A-C-F-G	19.7

Activity duration spans columns A–G.

on the randomly generated durations of the activities. In the 10 runs reported, the sequence A-D-F-G is the longest (critical) in two replications, whereas the sequence A-C-F-G is critical in the other eight. Activities A, F, and G are critical in 100% of the replications, whereas activity C is critical in 80% and activity D is critical in 20%.

A principal output of the simulation runs is a frequency distribution of the project length (the length of the critical path). Figure 9.38 plots the results of some 50 replications for the example. As can be seen, the project length varied from 17 to 29 weeks, with a mean of 22.5 weeks and a standard deviation of 2.9 weeks. Now let X be a random variable associated with project completion time. The probability of finishing the project within, say, τ weeks can be estimated from the following ratio:

$$P(X \leq \tau) = \frac{\text{number of times project finished in} \leq \tau \text{ weeks}}{\text{total number of replications}}$$

For the example, if $\tau = 20$ weeks, then the number of runs in which the length of the critical path was ≤ 20 weeks is seen to be 13, so $P(X \leq 20) = \frac{13}{50} = 26\%$.

In addition, it is possible to estimate the criticality of each activity. The *criticality index* (CI) of an activity is defined as the proportion of runs in which the activity was on the critical path (i.e., it had a zero slack). Dodin and Elmaghraby (1985) provided some theoretical background on this problem as well as extensive test results for large PERT networks.

The simulation approach is easy to implement and has the advantage that it produces arbitrarily accurate results as the number of runs increases. However, for problems

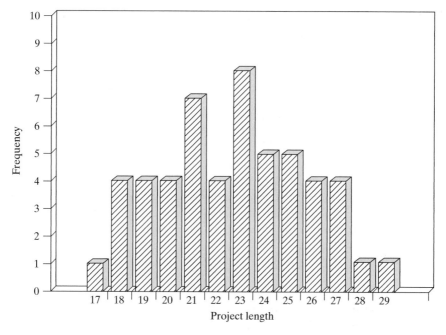

Figure 9.38   Distribution of project length for simulation runs.

of realistic size, the computational burden may be significant for each run, so a balance must be reached between accuracy and effort.

9.11.2 PERT and Extensions

Two common analytical approaches are used to assess uncertainty in projects. Both are based on the *central limit theorem*, which states that the distribution of the sum of independent random variables is approximately normal when the number of terms in the sum is sufficiently large.

The first approach yields a rough estimate and assumes that the duration of each project activity is an independent random variable. Given probabilistic durations of activities along specific paths, it follows that elapsed times for achieving events along those paths are also probabilistic. Now, suppose that there are n activities in the project, k of which are critical. Denote the durations of the critical activities by the random variables d_i with mean $\overline{d}_i$ and variance $s_i^2, i = 1, \ldots, k$. Then the total project length is the random variable

$$X = d_1 + d_2 + \cdots + d_k$$

It follows that the mean project length, $E[X]$, and the variance of the project length, $V[X]$, are given by

$$E[X] = \overline{d}_1 + \overline{d}_2 + \cdots + \overline{d}_k$$
$$V[X] = s_1^2 + s_2^2 + \cdots + s_k^2$$

These formulas are based on elementary probability theory, which tells us that the expected value of the sum of any set of random variables is the sum of their expected values, and the variance of the sum of independent random variables is the sum of the variances.

Now, invoking the central limit theorem, we can use normal distribution theory to find the probability of completing the project in less than or equal to some given time τ as follows:

$$P(X \leq \tau) = P\left(\frac{X - E[X]}{V[X]^{1/2}} \leq \frac{\tau - E[X]}{V[X]^{1/2}}\right) = P\left(Z \leq \frac{\tau - E[X]}{V[X]^{1/2}}\right) \qquad (9.12)$$

where Z is the standard normal deviate with mean 0 and variance 1. The desired probability in Eq. (9.12) can be looked up in Table 9C.1 in Appendix 9C.

Continuing with the example project, if (based on the simulation) the mean time of the critical path is 22.5 weeks and the variance is $(2.9)^2$, then the probability of completing the project within 25 weeks is found by first calculating

$$z = \frac{25 - 22.5}{2.9} = 0.86$$

and then looking up 0.86 in Table 9C.1. Doing so, we find that $P(Z \leq 0.86) = 0.805$, so the probability of finishing the project in 25 weeks or less is 80.5%. This solution is depicted in Fig. 9.39.

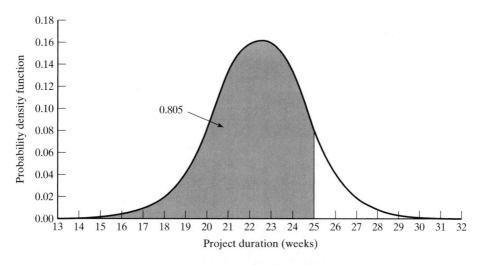

Figure 9.39   Example of probabilistic analysis with PERT.

If, however, the mean project length, $E[X]$, and the variance of the project length, $V[X]$, are calculated using the assumption that the critical activities are only those that have a zero slack in the deterministic CPM analysis (A-C-F-G), we get

$$E[X] = 5 + 8 + 4 + 5 = 22$$

$$V[X]^{1/2} = \sqrt{1^2 + 0.33^2 + 0.66^2 + 0.33^2} = 1.285$$

On the basis of this assumption, the probability of completing the project within 25 weeks is

$$P\left(Z \le \frac{25 - 22}{1.285}\right) = P(Z \le 2.33) = 0.99$$

This probability is higher than 0.805, which was computed using data from the simulation in which both sequences A-C-F-G and A-D-F-G were critical.

The procedure above is, in essence, PERT. Summarizing for an AON network:

1. For each activity i, assess its probability distribution or assume a beta distribution and obtain estimates of a_i, b_i and m_i. These values should be supplied by the project manager or experts who work in the field.

2. If a beta distribution is assumed for activity i, then use the estimates a, b and m to compute the variance $\hat{s}_i^2$ and mean $\hat{d}_i$ from Eqs. (9.1) and (9.2) in Section 9.2.1. These values then are used in place of the true but unknown values of s_i^2 and $\bar{d}_i$, respectively, in the above formulas for $V[X]$ and $E[X]$.

3. Use CPM to determine the critical path given $\hat{d}_i$, $i = 1, \ldots, n$.

4. Once the critical activities are identified, sum their means and variances to find the mean and variance of the project length.

5. Use Eq. (9.12) with the statistics computed in step 4 to evaluate the probability that the project finishes within some desired time.

Using PERT, it is possible to estimate completion time for a desired completion probability. For example, for a 95% probability, the corresponding z value is $z_{0.95} = 1.64$. Solving for the time τ for which the probability to complete the project is 95%, we get

$$z_{0.95} = \frac{\tau - 22.5}{2.9} = 1.64 \quad \text{or} \quad \tau = (1.64)(2.9) + 22.5 = 27.256 \text{ weeks}$$

A shortcoming of the standard PERT calculations is that they ignore all activities that are not on the critical path. A more accurate analytical approach is to identify each sequence of activities that lead from the start node of the project to the finish event and then to calculate separately the probability that the activities that compose each sequence will be completed by a given date. This step can be done as above by assuming that the central limit theorem holds for each sequence and then applying normal distribution theory to calculate the individual path probabilities. It is necessary, though, to make the additional assumption that the sequences themselves are statistically independent to proceed. This means that the time to traverse each path in the network is independent of what happens on the other paths. Although it is easy to see that this is rarely true because some activities are sure to be on more than one path, empirical evidence suggests that good results can be obtained if there is not too much overlap.

Once these calculations are performed, assuming that the various sequences are independent of each other, the probability of completing the project by a given date is set equal to the product of the individual probabilities that each sequence is finished by that date. That is, given n sequences with completion times $X_1, X_2, \ldots, X_n$, the probability that $X \leq \tau$ is found from

$$P(X \leq \tau) = P(X_1 \leq \tau)P(X_2 \leq \tau) \cdots P(X_n \leq \tau) \qquad (9.13)$$

where now the random variable $X = \max\{X_1, X_2, \ldots, X_n\}$.

Example 9-5

Consider the simple project in Fig. 9.40. If no uncertainty exists in activity durations, then the critical path is A-B, and exactly 17 weeks are required to finish the project. Now if we assume that the durations of all four activities are normally distributed (the corresponding means and standard deviations are listed under the arrows in Fig. 9.40), then the durations of the two sequences are also normally distributed [i.e., $N(\mu, \sigma)$], with the following parameters:

$$\text{length(A-B)} = X_1 \sim N(17, 3.61)$$
$$\text{length(C-D)} = X_2 \sim N(16, 3.35)$$

The accompanying probability density functions are plotted in Fig. 9.41. It should be clear that the project can end in 17 weeks only if both A-B and C-D are completed within that time. The probability that A-B finishes within 17 weeks is

$$P(X_1 \leq 17) = P\left(Z \leq \frac{17 - 17}{3.61}\right) = P(Z \leq 0) = 0.5$$

Figure 9.40   Stochastic network.

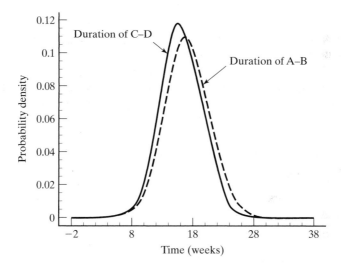

Figure 9.41   Performance time distribution for the two sequences.

and similarly for C-D,

$$P(X_2 \leq 17) = P\left(Z \leq \frac{17 - 16}{3.35}\right) = P(Z \leq 0.299) = 0.62$$

Using Eq. (9.13), we now can find the probability that both sequences finish within 17 weeks:

$$P(X \leq 17) = P(X_1 \leq 17)P(X_2 \leq 17) = (0.5)(0.62) = 0.31$$

Thus, the probability that the project will finish by week 17 is approximately 31%. A similar analysis for 20 weeks yields $P(X \leq 20) = 0.7$ or 70%.   ■

The approach that is based on calculating the probability of each sequence to complete by a given due date is accurate only if the sequences are independent. This is

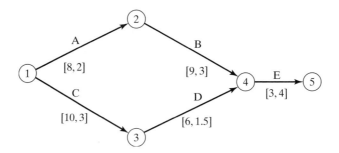

Figure 9.42   Stochastic network with dependent sequences.

not the case when one or more activities are members of two or more sequences. Consider, for example, the project in Fig. 9.42. Here, activity E is a member of the two sequences that connect the start of the project (event 1) to its termination node (event 5). The expected lengths and standard deviations of these sequences are

Sequence	Expected length	Standard deviation
A-B-E	$8 + 9 + 3 = 20$	$\sqrt{2^2 + 3^2 + 4^2} = 5.39$
C-D-E	$10 + 6 + 3 = 19$	$\sqrt{3^2 + 1.5^2 + 4^2} = 5.22$

The probability that the sequence A-B-E will be completed in 17 days is calculated as follows:

$$z = \frac{17 - 20}{5.39} = -0.5565 \quad \text{implying that } P = 0.29$$

which is obtained from Table 9C.1 by noting that

$$P(Z \leq -z) = 1 - P(Z \leq z)$$

Similarly, the probability that the sequence C-D-E will be completed in 17 days is calculated by determining $z = (17 - 19)/5.22 = -0.383$ and then using Table 9C.1 to find $P = 0.35$.

Thus, the simple PERT estimate (based on the critical sequence A-B-E) indicates that the probability of completing the project in 17 days is 29%. If both sequences A-B-E and C-D-E are taken into account, then the probability of completing the project in 17 days is estimated as

$$P(X_{\text{ABE}} \leq 17)P(X_{\text{CDE}} \leq 17) = (0.29)(0.35) = 0.1 \text{ or } 10\%$$

assuming that the two sequences are independent. However, because activity E is common to both sequences, the true probability of completing the project in 17 days is somewhere between 10 and 29%.

The next question that naturally arises is what to do if only the parameters of the distribution are known but not its form (e.g., beta, normal), and the number of activities is too small to rely on the central limit theorem to give accurate results. In this case, Chebyshev's inequality can be used to calculate project duration probabilities (see Montgomery and Runger 2003). The underlying theorem states that if X is a random variable with mean μ and variance σ^2, then for any $k > 0$,

$$P(|X - \mu| \geq k\sigma) \leq \frac{1}{k^2}$$

An alternative form is

$$P(|X - \mu| < k\sigma) \geq 1 - \frac{1}{k^2}$$

Based on the second inequality, the probability of a random variable being within ± 3 standard deviations of its mean is at least $\frac{8}{9}$, or 89%. Although this might not be a tight bound in all cases, it is surprising that such a bound can be found to hold for all possible discrete and continuous distributions.

To illustrate the effect of uncertainty, consider the example project. Four sequences connect the start node to the finish node. The mean length and the standard deviation of each sequence are summarized in Table 9.10.

TABLE 9.10   Mean Length and Standard Deviation for Sequences in Example Project

Sequence	Mean length	Standard deviation
A-C-F-G	22	1.285
A-D-F-G	21	1.595
B-D-F-G	19	1.407
E-F-G	16	0.808

The probability of completing each sequence in 22 weeks is computed next and summarized in Table 9.11.

TABLE 9.11   Probability of Completing Each Sequence in 22 Weeks

Sequence	z value	Probability
A-C-F-G	$\dfrac{22 - 22}{1.285} = 0$	0.5
A-D-F-G	$\dfrac{22 - 21}{1.595} = 0.626$	0.73
B-D-F-G	$\dfrac{22 - 19}{1.407} = 2.13$	0.98
E-F-G	$\dfrac{22 - 16}{0.808} = 7.42$	1.0

Based on the simple PERT analysis, the probability to complete the project in 22 weeks is 0.5. If both sequences A-C-F-G and A-D-F-G are considered and assumed to be independent, the probability is reduced to $(0.5)(0.73) = 0.365$.

Because three activities (A, F, G) are common to both sequences, the actual probability to complete in 22 weeks is closer to 0.5 than to 0.365. Based on the data in Fig. 9.38, we see that in 24 of 50 simulation runs, the project duration was 22 weeks or less. This implies that the probability of completing the project in 22 weeks is 24/50 = 0.48, or 48%.

Continuing with this example, if the Chebyshev's inequality is used for the critical path ($\mu = 22, \sigma = 1.285$), then the probability of completing the project in, say, $22 + (2)(1.285) = 24.57$ weeks is approximately

$$1 - \left(\frac{1}{2}\right)^2 = \frac{3}{4} = 0.75$$

By way of comparison, using the normal distribution assumption, the corresponding probability is

$$P\left(Z \leq \frac{24.57 - 22}{1.285}\right) = P(Z \leq 2) = 0.97$$

Of the two, the Chebyshev estimate is likely to be more reliable given that there are only a few activities on the critical path.

Because uncertainty is bound to be present in most activities, it is possible that after determining the critical path with CPM, a noncritical activity may become critical as certain tasks are completed. From a practical point of view, this suggests the basic advantage of early-start schedules. Starting each activity as soon as possible reduces the chances of a noncritical activity becoming critical and delaying the project.

9.12 CRITIQUE OF PERT AND CPM ASSUMPTIONS

PERT and CPM are models of projects and hence are open to a wide range of technical criticism including (1) the difficulty in accurately estimating durations, variances, and costs; (2) the validity of using the beta distribution in representing durations; (3) the validity of applying the central limit theorem; and (4) the heavy focus on the critical path for project control. Table 9.12 highlights some of the more significant shortcomings. In addition, PERT and CPM analysis is based on the precedence graph, which contains only two types of information: activity times and precedence constraints. The results may be highly sensitive to the data estimates and defining relationships.

In addition to the points made in Table 9.12, Schonberger (1981) showed that a PERT estimate that is based on the assumption that the variance of a sequence of activities is equal to the sum of the activity variances (i.e., that activities and sequences are independent) can lead to a consistent error in estimating the completion time of a project.

A related problem, investigated by Britney (1976), concerns to the cost of over- and underestimating activity duration times. He found that underestimates precipitate the reallocation of resources and, in many cases, engender costly project delays. Overestimates, on the other hand, result in inactivity and tend to misdirect management's

---

TABLE 9.12   Principal Assumptions and Criticisms of PERT/CPM

---

1. *Assumption*: Project activities can be identified as entities; that is, there is a clear beginning and ending point for each activity.

   Criticism: Projects, especially complex ones, change in content over time, and therefore a network constructed in the planning phase may be highly inaccurate later. Also, the very fact that activities are specified and a network is formalized tends to limit the flexibility that is required to handle changing situations as the project progresses.

2. *Assumption*: Project activity-sequence relationships can be specified and arranged in a directed network.

   Criticism: Sequence relationships cannot always be specified beforehand. In some projects, in fact, the ordering of certain activities is conditional on previous activities. (PERT and CPM, in their basic form, have no provision for treating this problem, although some other techniques have been proposed that present the project manager with several contingency paths, given different outcomes from each activity.)

3. *Assumption*: Project control should focus on the critical path.

   Criticism: It is not necessarily true that the longest path obtained from summing activity expected duration values will ultimately determine project completion time. What often happens as the project progresses is that some activity that is not on the critical path becomes delayed to such a degree that it extends the entire project. For this reason, it has been suggested that a critical activity concept replace the critical path concept as the focus of managerial control. Under this approach, attention would center on those activities that have a high potential variation and lie on a *near-critical path*. A near-critical path is one that does not share any activities with the critical path and, although it has slack, could become critical if one or a few activities along it become delayed. Obviously, the more parallelism in a network, the more likely that one or more near-critical paths will exist. Conversely, the more a network approximates a single series of activities, the less likely it is to have near-critical paths.

4. *Assumption*: The activity times in PERT follow the beta distribution, with the variance of the project assumed to be equal to the sum of the variances along the critical path.

   Criticism: As mentioned in the discussion in Section 9.2.1, the beta distribution was selected for a variety of good reasons. Nevertheless, each component of the statistical treatment in PERT has been brought into question. First, the formulas are in reality a modification of the beta distribution mean and variance, which, when compared with the basic formulas, could be expected to lead to absolute errors on the order of 10% for the mean and 5% for the individual variances. Second, given that the activity-time distributions have the properties of unimodality, continuity, and finite positive endpoints, other distributions with the same properties would yield different means and variances. Third, obtaining three "valid" time estimates to put into the PERT formulas presents operational problems: it is often difficult to arrive at one activity-time estimate, let alone three, and the somewhat subjective definitions of a and b do not help the matter. (How optimistic and pessimistic should one be?)

Source: Adapted from Chase et al. (2003).

attention to relatively unfruitful areas, causing planning losses. (Britney recommends a modification of PERT called BPERT, which uses concepts from Bayesian decision theory to consider these two categories of cost explicitly in deriving a project network plan.)

Another problem that sometimes arises, especially when PERT is used by subcontractors who work with the government, is the attempt to "beat" the network in order to get on or off the critical path. Many government contracts provide cost incentives for finishing a project early or are negotiated on a "cost-plus-fixed-fee" basis. The contractor who is on the critical path generally has more leverage in obtaining additional funds from these contracts because he or she has a major influence in determining the duration of the project. In contrast, some contractors deem it desirable to be less "visible" and therefore adjust their time estimates and activity descriptions in such a way as to ensure that they will not be on the critical path. This criticism, of course, reflects more on the use of the method than on the method itself, but PERT and CPM, by virtue of their focus on the critical path, enable such ploys to be used.

Finally, the cost of applying critical path methods to a project is sometimes used as a basis for criticism. However, the cost of applying PERT or CPM rarely exceeds 2% of total project cost. Thus, this added cost is generally outweighed by the savings from improved scheduling and reduced project time.

As with any analytic technique, it is important when using CPM and PERT to understand fully the underlying assumptions and limitations that they impose. Management must be sure that the people who are charged with monitoring and controlling activity performance have a working knowledge of the statistical features of PERT as well as the general nature of critical path scheduling. Correct application of these techniques can provide a significant benefit in each phase of the project's life cycle as long as the abovementioned pitfalls are avoided.

9.13 CRITICAL CHAIN PROCESS

Partially in response to these criticisms, Goldratt (1997) developed the critical chain buffer management (CCBM) process, which is an application of his theory of constraints to managing and scheduling projects. With CCBM, several alterations are made to traditional PERT. First, all individual activity slack, or "buffer," becomes project buffer. Each team member, responsible for his or her component of the activity network, creates a duration estimate free from any padding—one, say, that is based on a 50% probability of success. All activities on the critical chain (path) and feeder chains (noncritical chains in the network) then are linked with minimal time padding. The project buffer now is aggregated, and some proportion of the saved time (Goldratt uses a 50% rule of thumb) is added to the project.

Even adding 50% of the saved time significantly reduces the overall project schedule while requiring team members to be concerned less with activity padding and more with task completion. Even if they miss their delivery date (as they are likely to do) 50% of the time, the overall effect on the project's duration is minimized because of the downstream aggregated buffer.

The same approach can also be used for tasks that are not on the critical chain. Accordingly, all feeder path activities are reduced by the same order of magnitude and a feeder buffer is constructed for the overall noncritical chain of activities. Finally, CCBM distinguishes between its use of buffer and the traditional PERT use of project slack. With the PERT approach, project slack is a function of the overall completed activity network. In other words, slack is an outcome of the task dependencies, whereas CCBM's buffer is used as an *a priori* planning input that is based on a reasoned cut in each activity and the application of aggregated project buffer at the end.

Proponents of CCBM argue that it is more than a new scheduling technique, representing instead a different paradigm by which project management should be viewed. The CCBM paradigm argues for truth in activity duration estimation, a "just in time" approach to scheduling noncritical activities, and greater discipline in project scheduling and control as a result of more open communication among internal project stakeholders.

The newness of CCBM is a point refuted by some who see the technique as either ill-suited to many types of projects or simply a reconceptualization of well-understood scheduling methodologies (e.g., PERT). Nevertheless, a growing body of case studies and proponents is emerging to champion the CCBM process as it continues to diffuse throughout project organizations.

Nevertheless, critical chain project management is not without its critics. Several arguments against the process include the following charges and perceived weaknesses in the methodology:

1. Lack of project milestones makes coordinated scheduling, particularly with external suppliers, highly problematic. Critics contend that the lack of in-process project milestones adversely affects the ability to coordinate schedule dates with suppliers who provide the external delivery of critical components.

2. Although it may be true that CCBM brings increased discipline to project scheduling, efficient methods for applying this technique to a firm's portfolio of projects are unclear; that is, CCBM seems to offer benefits on a project-by-project basis, but its usefulness at the program level has not been proved. Furthermore, because CCBM argues for dedicated resources in a multiproject environment where resources are shared, it is impossible to avoid multitasking, which severely limits its power.

3. Evidence of its success is still almost exclusively anecdotal and based on single-case studies. Debating the merits and pitfalls of CCBM has remained largely an intellectual exercise among academics and writers of project management theory. No large-scale empirical research exists to either confirm or refute its efficacy.

4. Critics also charge that Goldratt's evaluation of duration estimation is overly negative and critical, suggesting that his contention of huge levels of activity duration estimation "padding" is exaggerated.

Of course, it must be remembered that models, whether associated with CPM, PERT or CCBM, are simplifications of reality designed to support analysis and decision making by focusing on the most important aspects of the problem. They should be judged not so much by their fidelity with the actual system but by the insight that they provide, by the certainty with which they show the correct consequences of the working assumptions, and by the ease with which the problem structure can be communicated.

9.14 SCHEDULING CONFLICTS

The discussion so far assumed that the only constraints on the schedule are precedence relations among activities. On the basis of these constraints, the early and late time of each event and the early and late start and finish of each activity are calculated.

In most projects, there are additional constraints that must be addressed, such as those associated with resource availability and the budget. In some cases, ready time and due-date constraints also exist. These constraints specify a time window in which an activity must be performed. In addition, there may be a target completion date for the project or a due date for a milestone. If these due dates are earlier than the corresponding dates derived from the CPM analysis, then the accompanying schedule will not be feasible.

There are several ways to handle these type of infeasibilities, such as

- Reducing some activity durations by allocating more resources to them. This approach is discussed in Chapter 10.
- Eliminating some activities or reducing their lengths by using a more effective technology. For example, conventional painting, which requires the application of several layers of paint and a long drying time, may be replaced by anodizing—a faster but more expensive process.
- Replacing some precedence relations of the "finish to start" type by other precedence relations, such as "start to start," without affecting quality, cost, or performance. When this is possible, a significant amount of time may be saved.

It is common to start the scheduling analysis with each activity being performed in the most economical way and assuming "finish to start" precedence relations. If infeasibility is detected, then one or more of the foregoing courses of action can be used to circumnavigate the cause of the problem.

TEAM PROJECT

Thermal Transfer Plant

A detailed schedule is now required for the project. Major milestones suggested by TMS's contract department follow:

Milestones	Time from project start (weeks)
Initial drawing	2
Order parts and materials	3
Initial drawing approval or revisions	4
Drawings revised and approved	5
Schedule production	5
Begin production	6
Document final testing procedures	6
Finish assembly/begin testing	9
Documentation, maintenance, and user manuals	9
Ship tested unit to site	11
Install on site	13
Final testing and operator personnel training	14
Customer satisfaction check	16

Your assignment is to prepare a list of activities and a detailed schedule (on a daily basis) for the project team and an upper-level schedule for TMS management.

The detailed schedule should consist of up to 50 activities; the upper-level schedule should contain approximately 20 activities.

In your report, explain each task and activity and its corresponding WBS and OBS units, the type of precedence relations among activities, the way activity duration was estimated, and your confidence in these estimates. Use a network model to develop the schedule and a linear responsibility chart to identify its relationship to OBS units. Present the schedule as a Gantt chart and as a table of activities and events with their corresponding times and slacks.

Discuss the range of schedules that can be adopted for this project, and explain the methodology by which your team has selected the most appropriate schedule. Present a "what if" analysis for your final choice, testing its sensitivity to important sources of uncertainty.

DISCUSSION QUESTIONS

1. What objectives, variables, and constraints should be considered in developing a project schedule?

2. If a project, by definition, is something that is not performed on a regular basis, then how can activity times be estimated?

3. What are the advantages and disadvantages of the five project activity-duration estimation techniques presented in Section 9.2?

4. What are the major characteristics that must be present in a project to use network techniques?

5. The "finish to start" precedence relation is the most common found in projects. Give some examples in which "start to start," "end to end," and "start to finish" precedence relations arise.

6. Identify some projects in which PERT and CPM are inappropriate. Explain.

7. How can the LP model in Section 9.9 be expanded to include resource constraints that might arise as a result of, say, the limited availability of equipment or technical personnel?

8. Discuss a project in which scheduling is not important. Explain why this project is not sensitive to scheduling decisions.

9. Compare and list the relative advantages of (a) the Gantt chart, (b) CPM analysis, and (c) the basic PERT approach to scheduling.

10. Is it possible for a project team to achieve high efficiency without scheduling tasks and activities? Discuss.

11. "To excel in time-based competition, the early-start schedule should always be implemented." Discuss.

12. "To maximize the net present value of a project, all cash-generating activities should begin on their early start, whereas all cost-generating activities should begin on their late start." Discuss.

EXERCISES

9.1 A project is defined by the list of activities in Table 9.13.

TABLE 9.13

Activity	Immediate predecessors	Duration (days)
A	–	3
B	–	4
C	–	3
D	C	2
E	B	1
F	A	5
G	B	2
H	B	3
I	C	11
J	D, E	3
K	F, G	1
L	K	4
M	J, H	4

a. Draw the AOA network.
b. Draw the AON network.
c. Find the critical path.
d. Find the total slack and free slack of each activity.
e. Suppose that activities A, C, I are subject to uncertainty and that only the following time estimates are available:

Activity	a	m	b
A	2	4	5
C	1	3	4
I	8	11	15

Calculate the probability that the project will be completed in d days, for $d = 10, 12, 14, 16, 18, 20$. Plot the probability as a function of d.

9.2 Estimate the time that it will take you to learn a new computer software package that combines a spreadsheet with statistical analysis. Explain how the estimate was made and what accuracy you think it has.

9.3 Use the modular technique to estimate the time required to prepare a proposal or business plan for manufacturing a new medical device that analyzes blood enzymes.

9.4 Use the benchmark job technique to estimate the time required to type a 50-page paper and prepare figures using a computer graphics package.

9.5 Develop a linear regression model to estimate the dependent variable "time to type a paper" as a function of two or more independent variables.

9.6 Develop a list of activities for the project "designing a new house." Estimate the duration of each activity, and define the precedence relations among them. How much uncertainty exists in each activity? The project ends when the plans and documents have been finalized.

9.7 Develop an early-start and a late-start schedule for the project in Exercise 9.6 using a Gantt chart. Identify the critical path, and calculate the slack of noncritical activities.

9.8 Develop the AOA network for the project in Exercise 9.6. Calculate the early time and the late time of each event and the early start, early finish, late start, and late finish of each activity.

9.9 Develop an AON network model for the project in Exercise 9.6.

9.10 Develop a linear program that generates the schedule for the project in Exercise 9.6.

9.11 Develop a high-level AOA model for the project "designing and building a new house."

9.12 Suppose that the project mentioned in Exercise 9.11 must be finished 2 months before the early finish time. How would you solve this scheduling conflict?

9.13 Caryn Johnson is in charge of relocating ("reconductoring") 1,700 ft of 13.8-kilovolt over-head primary line as a result of the widening of the road section in which the line is presently installed. Table 9.14 summarizes the activities for the project. Draw the network model for her, and carry out the critical path computations.

TABLE 9.14

Activity	Description	Immediate predecessors	Duration (days)
A	Job review	–	1
B	Advise customers of temporary outage	A	0.5
C	Requisition stores	A	1
D	Scout job	A	0.5
E	Secure poles and materials	C, D	3
F	Distribute poles	E	3.5
G	Pole location coordination	D	0.5
H	Re-stake	G	0.5
I	Dig holes	H	3
J	Frame and set poles	F, I	4
K	Cover old conductors	F, I	1
L	Pull new conductors	J, K	2
M	Install remaining material	L	2
N	Sag conductor	L	2
O	Trim trees	D	2
P	De-energize and switch lines	B, M, N, O	0.1
Q	Energize and phase new line	P	0.5
R	Clean up	Q	1
S	Remove old conductor	Q	1
T	Remove old poles	S	2
U	Return material to stores	R, T	2

9.14 Thomas Cruise wants to buy a new motorboat and has summarized the associated activities in Table 9.15. Draw the AOA network model and carry out the critical path computations for him.

9.15 For Exercise 9.14, compute the total slacks and free slacks, and summarize the critical path calculations using the format in Table 9.5.

9.16 Determine the critical path(s) for projects (a) and (b) in the AOA networks in Fig. 9.43.

9.17 For Exercise 9.16, compute the total slacks and free slacks, and summarize the critical path calculations in a tabular format.

TABLE 9.15

Activity	Description	Immediate predecessors	Duration (days)
A	Conduct feasibility study	–	3
B	Find potential customer for present boat	A	14
C	List possible models	A	1
D	Research all possible models	C	3
E	Conduct interviews with mechanics	C	1
F	Collect dealer propaganda	C	2
G	Compile and organize all pertinent information	D, E, F	1
H	Choose top three models	G	1
I	Test-drive all three choices	H	3
J	Gather warranty and financing information	H	2
K	Choose one boat	I, J	2
L	Compare dealers and choose dealer	K	2
M	Search for desired color and options	L	4
N	Test-drive chosen model once again	L	1
O	Purchase new boat	B, M, N	3

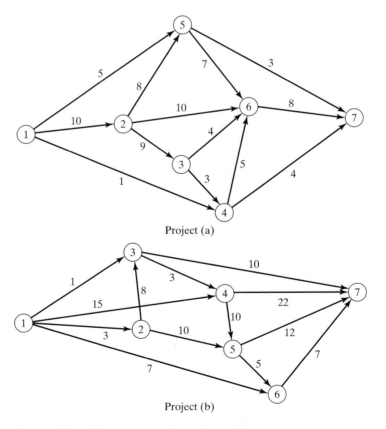

Project (a)

Project (b)

Figure 9.43   Networks for Exercise 9.16.

9.18 In Exercise 9.16, suppose that the estimates (a, b, m) are given in Table 9.16 and that activity times follow a beta distribution. Use the data in the table to calculate the expected activity times, $\hat{d}_{ij}$, and then compute the critical path for each event using $\hat{d}_{ij}$ as the completion time for activity (i, j). Assume that the solution that you obtain is the "planned" time to complete each event, and then find the probabilities that the events will occur without delay.

TABLE 9.16

Project (a)

Activity	(a, b, m)	Activity	(a, b, m)
1, 2	$(5, 8, 6)$	3, 6	$(3, 5, 4)$
1, 4	$(1, 4, 3)$	4, 6	$(4, 10, 8)$
1, 5	$(2, 5, 4)$	4, 7	$(5, 8, 6)$
2, 3	$(4, 6, 5)$	5, 6	$(9, 15, 10)$
2, 5	$(7, 10, 8)$	5, 7	$(4, 8, 6)$
2, 6	$(8, 13, 9)$	6, 7	$(3, 5, 4)$
3, 4	$(5, 10, 9)$		

Project (b)

Activity	(a, b, m)	Activity	(a, b, m)
1, 2	$(1, 4, 3)$	3, 7	$(12, 14, 13)$
1, 3	$(5, 8, 7)$	4, 5	$(10, 15, 12)$
1, 4	$(6, 9, 7)$	4, 7	$(8, 12, 10)$
1, 6	$(1, 3, 2)$	5, 6	$(7, 11, 8)$
2, 3	$(3, 5, 4)$	5, 7	$(2, 8, 4)$
2, 5	$(7, 9, 8)$	6, 7	$(5, 7, 6)$
3, 4	$(10, 20, 15)$		

9.19 *Product Development.* Consider the simplified set of activities in Table 9.17 for the development of a consumer product from initiation through the market test phase.

a. Draw the AOA network for this project.

b. Calculate total slacks and free slacks, and interpret their meaning.

TABLE 9.17

Activity	Symbol	Immediate predecessors	Time estimate (weeks)
Investigate demand	A	–	3
Develop pricing strategy	B	–	1
Design product	C	–	5
Conduct promotional cost analysis	D	A	1
Manufacture prototype models	E	C	6
Perform product cost analysis	F	E	1
Perform final pricing analysis	G	B, D, F	2
Conduct market test	H	G	8

c. Determine the critical path, and interpret its meaning.

d. Construct a Gantt chart, and mark the latest start times for each activity.

9.20 For the product development project in Exercise 9.19, consider the detailed time estimates given in Table 9.18. Note that the time estimates in Exercise 9.19 are equivalent to modal time estimates in this exercise.

TABLE 9.18

	Time estimate (weeks)		
Activity	Optimistic	Most likely	Pessimistic
A	1	3	4
B	1	1	2
C	4	5	9
D	1	1	1
E	4	6	12
F	1	1	2
G	1	2	3
H	6	8	10

a. Relabel your network in Exercise 9.19 to include $\hat{d}_{ij}$ (in place of d_{ij}) and $\hat{s}_{ij}$. Use Eqs. (9.1) and (9.2).

b. Compare total slacks and free slacks to Exercise 9.19.

c. Has the critical path changed?

d. Determine the following probabilities:

 1. That the project will be completed in 22 weeks or less

 2. That the project will be completed by the date obtained from the critical path calculations using $\hat{d}_{ij}$ as the activity durations

 3. That the project takes more than 30 weeks to complete

9.21 Criticism of the traditional PERT equations in Section 9.2.1 for estimating the means and standard deviations of activities has led to the development of alternative formulas by Perry and Greig (1975):

$$\hat{d}_{ij} = \frac{a_{ij} + 0.95m_{ij} + b_{ij}}{2.95} \tag{9.14}$$

$$\hat{s}_{ij} = \frac{b_{ij} - a_{ij}}{3.25} \tag{9.15}$$

where a_{ij} and b_{ij} are estimates for the 5 and 95 percentiles of the probability distribution of activity (i, j), and m_{ij} is the mode. Use these equations to recalculate $\hat{d}_{ij}$ and $\hat{s}_{ij}$ and answer the same questions as in Exercise 9.19. Compare the results.

9.22 *Space Module Assembly.* An aerospace company has received a contract from NASA for the final assembly of a space module for an upcoming mission. A team of engineers has determined the activities, precedence constraints, and time estimates as given in Table 9.19.

TABLE 9.19

Activity	Symbol	Immediate predecessors	Time estimate (days)
Construct shell of module	A	–	30
Order life support system and scientific experimentation package from same supplier	B	–	15
Order components of control and navigational system	C	–	25
Wire module	D	A	3
Assemble control and navigational system	E	C	7
Preliminary test of life support system	F	B	1
Install life support in module	G	D, F	5
Install scientific experimentation package in module	H	D, F	2
Preliminary test of control and navigational system	I	E, F	4
Install control and navigational system in module	J	H, I	10
Final testing and debugging	K	G, J	8

    a. Draw the AOA network for this project. (*Hint:* You should have 10 events and two dummy activities.)

    b. Calculate total slacks and free slacks, and interpret their meaning.

    c. Determine the critical path and interpret its meaning.

    d. Construct a Gantt chart and identify scheduling flexibilities.

9.23 A more careful analysis of time estimates for the space module assembly of the preceding exercise is given in Table 9.20. Note that the "most likely estimates" are identical to the "time estimates" in Exercise 9.22.

TABLE 9.20

Activity	Time estimate (weeks)		
	Optimistic	Most likely	Pessimistic
A	25	30	45
B	10	15	20
C	20	25	35
D	3	3	5
E	5	7	12
F	1	1	1
G	4	5	7
H	2	2	3
I	4	4	6
J	8	10	14
K	6	8	15

a. Relabel your network in Exercise 9.22 to include $\hat{d}_{ij}$ (in place of d_{ij}) and $\hat{s}_{ij}$. Use Eqs. (9.1) and (9.2).

b. Compare total slacks and free slacks to Exercise 9.22.

c. Has the critical path changed?

d. Determine the following probabilities:

   1. That the project will be completed in 54 days or less

   2. That the project will be completed by the date obtained from the critical path calculations using $\hat{d}_{ij}$ as the activity durations

   3. That the project takes more than 70 days to complete

9.24 Use Eqs. (9.14) and (9.15) to recalculate $\hat{d}_{ij}$ and $\hat{s}_{ij}$ and answer the same questions as in Exercise 9.23. Compare the results.

9.25 As part of an R&D project, it is required to produce 60 circuit boards using a specific piece of equipment. According to the equipment specification, its design capacity is 0.4 board per hour. However, past experience indicates that significantly more time will be required. In particular, the following frequency data were collected over a 1-week period when the machine was working on other jobs.

Activity	Frequency
Machine is working on a job	67
Parts are being fed to the machine	6
Maintenance is being performed	9
Machine is waiting for parts	22

a. Estimate the actual machine capacity.

b. How long will it take to complete the 60 boards?

c. If you want the capacity estimate to be within ±5% of the true value with a 95% level of confidence, then what should the sample size be? Assume that the capacity estimate is normally distributed.

9.26 The project manager did not accept the approach that you proposed in Exercise 9.25 and suggested the use of a parametric equation to estimate the machine's capacity.

a. Give an example of the type of data that should be collected to develop such an equation.

b. Furnish an example of such an equation and demonstrate how to use it.

c. State the assumptions used in employing this approach.

9.27 Consider the precedence relations given in Table 9.21.

a. Draw an early-start Gantt chart.

b. Draw the AON network for this project.

c. Draw the AOA network.

d. Generate all possible paths for the AOA network, calculate their duration, and analyze the findings.

e. Calculate ES, EF, LF, and LS for each activity.

f. Calculate the slacks for the activities.

TABLE 9.21

Activity	Immediate predecessors	Weeks
A	–	1
B	A	4
C	A	3
D	A	7
E	B	6
F	C, D	2
G	E, F	7
H	D	9
I	G, H	4

9.28 There is uncertainty regarding the duration of activities D and E in the project described in Exercise 9.27 expressed by the following data:

Activity	Time (weeks)		
	Optimistic	Most likely	Pessimistic
D	6	7	8
E	5	6	9

a. Using an early-start approach, calculate the probability of completing the project within 22 weeks or less.

b. Repeat part (a) using a late-start approach. State your assumptions in both cases.

BIBLIOGRAPHY

Estimating the Duration of Project Activities

Banks, J., J. S. Carson, B. L. Nelson and D. M. Nicol, *Discrete-Event System Simulation*, Third Edition, Prentice Hall, Upper Saddle River, NJ, 2001.

Britney, R. R., "Bayesian Point Estimation and the PERT Scheduling of Stochastic Activities," *Management Science*, Vol. 22, No. 9, pp. 938–948, 1976.

Dodin, B., "Bounding the Project Completion Time Distribution in PERT Networks," *Operations Research*, Vol. 33, No. 4, pp. 862–881, 1985.

Grubbs, F., "Attempts to Validate Certain PERT Statistics or 'Picking on PERT,'" *Operations Research*, Vol. 10, pp. 912–915, 1962.

Hershauer, J. C. and G. Nabielsky, "Estimating Activity Times," *Journal of Systems Management*, Vol. 23, No. 9, pp. 17–21, 1972.

Montgomery, D. C. and G. C. Runger, *Applied Statistics and Probability for Engineers*, Third Edition, John Wiley & Sons, New York, 2003.

Perry, C. and I. D. Greig, "Estimating the Mean and Variance of Subjective Distributions in PERT and Decision Analysis," *Management Science*, Vol. 21, No. 12, pp. 1477–1480, 1975.

Effect of Learning

Badiru, A. B., "Computational Survey of Univariate and Multivariate Learning Curve Models," *IEEE Transactions on Engineering Management*, Vol. 39, No. 2, pp. 176–188, 1992.

Dar-El, E., *Human Learning*, Kluwer, Norwell, MA, 2000.

Hancock, W. M. and F. H. Bayha, "The Learning Curve," in *Handbook of Industrial Engineering*, John Wiley & Sons, New York, 1982.

Marmaras, N. and T. Kontogiannis, "Cognitive Tasks," in G. Salvendy (Editor) *Handbook of Industrial Engineering: Technology and Operations Management*, Third Edition, John Wiley & Sons, New York, 2001.

Smunt, T. L., "A Comparison of Learning Curve Analysis and Moving Average Ratio Analysis for Detailed Operations Planning," *Decision Science*, Vol. 17, No. 4, pp. 475–495, 1986.

Wright, T. P., "Factors Affecting the Cost of Airplanes," *Journal of Aeronautical Sciences*, Vol. 3, No. 4, pp. 122–128, 1936.

Yelle, L. E., "The Learning Curve: Historical Review and Comprehensive Survey," *Decision Sciences*, Vol. 10, pp. 302–328, 1979.

Forgetting

Globerson, S., N. Levin and A. Shtub, "The Impact of Breaks on Forgetting When Performing a Repetitive Task," *IIE Transactions*, Vol. 21, No. 4, pp. 376–381, 1989.

LeBlanc, L. J., A. Shtub and Z. Cai, *Project Planning with Learning: Models and Computational Testing*, Working Paper 91–2, Graduate School of Management, Vanderbilt University, Nashville, TN, 1992.

Shtub, A., "Scheduling of Programs with Repetitive Projects," *Project Management Journal*, Vol. XXII, No. 6, pp. 49–53, 1991.

Project Scheduling

Clark, K. B. and T. Fujimoto, "Overlapping Problem Solving in Product Development," in K. Ferdows (Editor), *Managing International Manufacturing*, North Holland, New York, 1989.

Goldratt, E., *Critical Chain*, North River Press, Great Barrington, MA, 1997.

Hartley, K. O., "The Project Schedule," in R. L. Kimmon and J. H. Lowree (Editors), *Project Management: A Reference for Professionals*, Marcel Dekker, New York, 1989.

Hillier, F. S. and G. J. Lieberman, *Introduction to Operations Research*, Seventh Edition, McGraw Hill, Boston, 2001.

Meredith, J. R. and S. J. Mantel, Jr., *Project Management: A Managerial Approach*, Fourth Edition, John Wiley & Sons, New York, 1999.

Neumann, K., C. Schwindt and J. Zimmermann, *Project Scheduling with Time Windows and Scarce Resources: Temporal and Resource Constrained Project Scheduling with Regular and Nonregular Objective Functions*, Lecture Notes in Economics and Mathematical Systems, Vol. 508, Springer, Amsterdam, 2002.

Steyn, H., "An Investigation into the Fundamentals of Critical Chain Project Scheduling," *International Journal of Project Scheduling*, Vol. 19, pp. 363–369, 2000.

Vazsonyi, A., "The History of the Rise and Fall of the PERT Method," *Management Science*, Vol. 16, No. 8, pp. B449–B455, 1970.

Webster, F. M., *Survey of CPM Scheduling Packages and Related Project Control Programs*, Project Management Institute, Drexel Hill, PA, 1991.

CPM Approach

Cornell, D. G., C. C. Gotlieb and Y. M. Lee, "Minimal Event-Node Network of Project Precedence Relations," *Communications of the ACM*, Vol. 16, No. 5, pp. 296–298, 1973.

Jewell, W. S., "Divisible Activities in Critical Path Analysis," *Operations Research*, Vol. 13, No. 5, pp. 747–760, 1965.

Kelley, J. E., Jr. and M. R. Walker, "Critical Path Planning and Scheduling," *Proceedings of the Eastern Joint Computer Conference*, Boston, pp. 160–173, 1979.

PERT Approach

Burgher, P. H., "PERT and the Auditor," *The Accounting Review*, Vol. 39, pp. 103–120, 1964.

Dodin, M. B., "Determining the K Most Critical Paths in PERT Networks," *Operations Research*, Vol. 32, No. 4, pp. 859–877, 1984.

Dodin, M. B. and S. E. Elmaghraby, "Approximating the Criticality Indices of the Activities in PERT Networks," *Management Science*, Vol. 31, No. 2, pp. 207–223, 1985.

Fazar, W., "Program Evaluation and Review Technique," *American Statistician*, Vol. 13, No. 2, p. 10, 1959.

Fisher, D. L., D. Saisi and W. M. Goldstein, "Stochastic PERT Networks: OP Diagrams, Critical Paths and the Project Completion Time," *Computers & Operations Research*, Vol. 12, No. 5, pp. 471–482, 1985.

PERT, *Program Evaluation Research Task, Phase I Summary Report*, Vol. 7, Special Projects Office, Bureau of Ordinance, Department of the Navy, Washington, DC, pp. 646–669, 1958.

Van Slyke, R. M., "Monte Carlo Methods and the PERT Problem," *Operations Research*, Vol. 11, No. 5, pp. 839–860, 1963.

PERT and CPM Assumptions

Chase, R. B., F. R. Jacobs and N. J. Aquilano, *Operations Management for Competitive Advantage*, Tenth Edition, McGraw Hill, Boston, 2003.

Golenko-Ginzburg, D., "On the Distribution of Activity Time in PERT," *Journal of the Operational Research Society*, Vol. 39, No. 8, pp. 767–771, 1988.

Littlefield, T. K. and P. H. Randolph, "PERT Duration Times: Mathematics or MBO," *Interfaces*, Vol. 21, No. 6, pp. 92–95, 1991.

Sasieni, M. W., "A Note on PERT Times," *Management Science*, Vol. 16, No. 8, pp. 1652–1653, 1986.

Schonberger, R. J., "Why Projects Are Always Late: A Rationale Based on Manual Simulation of a PERT/CPM Network," *Interfaces*, Vol. 11, No. 5, pp. 66–70, 1981.

Wiest, J. D. and F. K. Levy, *A Management Guide to PERT/CPM*, Second Edition, Prentice Hall, Englewood Cliffs, NJ, 1977.

Computational Issues

Draper, N. and H. Smith, *Applied Regression Analysis*, Third Edition, John Wiley & Sons, New York, 1998.

Jensen, P. A. and J. F. Bard, *Operations Research: Models and Methods*, John Wiley & Sons, New York, 2003.

Hindelang, T. J. and J. F. Muth, "A Dynamic Programming Algorithm for Decision CPM Networks," *Operations Research*, Vol. 27, No. 2, pp. 225–241, 1979.

Kulkarni, V. G. and J. S. Provan, "An Improved Implementation of Conditional Monte Carlo Estimation of Path Lengths in Stochastic Networks," *Operations Research*, Vol. 33, No. 6, pp. 1389–1393, 1985.

Least-Squares Regression Analysis

In the least squares method, we define the residual, e_i, or deviation from the estimated line, $\hat{Y} = \hat{b}_0 + \hat{b}_1 X$, for each point i as follows:

$$e_i = Y_i - \hat{Y}_i$$

These residuals will be positive or negative depending on whether the actual point lies above or below the line. If they are squared and summed, the resultant quantity must be nonnegative and will vary directly with the spread of the points from the line. Different pairs of values for $\hat{b}_0$ and $\hat{b}_1$ will give different lines and hence different values for the sum of the squared residuals about the line. Thus, we have

$$\sum_{i=1}^{n} e_i^2 = f(\hat{b}_0, \hat{b}_1)$$

where the function $f(\cdot, \cdot)$ depends on the model being considered.

The principle of least squares is that the parameter estimates $\hat{b}_0$ and $\hat{b}_1$ should be chosen to make $\sum_{i=1}^{n} e_i^2$ as small as possible; that is,

$$\min \sum_{i=1}^{n} e_i^2 = \min \sum_{i=1}^{n} (Y_i - \hat{Y}_i)^2 = \min \sum_{i=1}^{n} (Y_i - \hat{b}_0 - \hat{b}_1 X_i)^2$$

From calculus, we know that the first-order necessary (and sufficient, in this case) condition for optimality is that the partial derivatives with respect to $\hat{b}_0$ and $\hat{b}_1$ must be zero. Taking partial derivatives, setting the results to zero and solving yields

$$\hat{b}_1 = \frac{\sum_{i=1}^{n} (X_i - \bar{X})(Y_i - \bar{Y})}{\sum_{i=1}^{n} (X_i - \bar{X})^2} \quad \text{and} \quad \hat{b}_0 = \bar{Y} - \hat{b}_1 \bar{X}$$

where

$$\overline{X} = \frac{1}{n}\sum_{i=1}^{n} X_i \quad \text{and} \quad \overline{Y} = \frac{1}{n}\sum_{i=1}^{n} Y_i$$

Given these estimates, an important question is: How good are they? Elementary treatment of the relationship between two variables usually emphasizes their *correlation coefficient*, R, which is computed as follows:

$$R = \frac{\sum_{i=1}^{n}(X_i - \overline{X})(Y_i - \overline{Y})}{\sqrt{\sum_{i=1}^{n}(X_i - \overline{X})^2 \sum_{i=1}^{n}(Y_i - \overline{Y})^2}}$$

This value can vary between -1 and $+1$. The closer it is to either extreme, the better the fit. A related value is R^2, sometimes known as the *coefficient of determination*, which can be calculated variously as

$$R^2 = \frac{\sum_{i=1}^{n}(\hat{Y}_i - \overline{Y})^2}{\sum_{i=1}^{n}(Y_i - \overline{Y})^2} = 1 - \frac{\sum_{i=1}^{n}e_i^2}{\sum_{i=1}^{n}(Y_i - \overline{Y})^2}$$

From the right-hand expression, it should be clear that the maximum value of R^2 is unity. This can occur only when $\sum_{i=1}^{n}e_i^2 = 0$; that is, when every e_i is zero, so that all of the points on the scatter diagram lie on a straight line. The minimum value of R^2 is zero, which occurs when $\sum_{i=1}^{n}e_i^2 = \sum_{i=1}^{n}(Y_i - \overline{Y})^2$; that is, when each point on the regression line $\hat{Y}_i = \overline{Y}$ so the explained variation is zero.

The coefficient of determination is equivalent to the proportion of the Y variance explained by the linear influence of X. An R value of 0.9 therefore indicates that the least-squares regression of Y on X accounts for 81% of the variance in Y.

Appendix 9B

Learning Curve Tables

TABLE 9B.1   Learning Curve Values for n^β

	Percent learning curve							
Repetitions	60%	65%	70%	75%	80%	85%	90%	95%
1	1.0000	1.0000	1.0000	1.0000	1.0000	1.0000	1.0000	1.0000
2	0.6000	0.6500	0.7000	0.7500	0.8000	0.8500	0.9000	0.9500
3	0.4450	0.5052	0.5682	0.6338	0.7021	0.7729	0.8462	0.9219
4	0.3600	0.4225	0.4900	0.5625	0.6400	0.7225	0.8100	0.9025
5	0.3054	0.3678	0.4368	0.5127	0.5956	0.6857	0.7830	0.8877
6	0.2670	0.3284	0.3977	0.4754	0.5617	0.6570	0.7616	0.8758
7	0.2383	0.2984	0.3674	0.4459	0.5345	0.6337	0.7439	0.8659
8	0.2160	0.2746	0.3430	0.4219	0.5120	0.6141	0.7290	0.8574
9	0.1980	0.2552	0.3228	0.4017	0.4930	0.5974	0.7161	0.8499
10	0.1832	0.2391	0.3058	0.3846	0.4765	0.5828	0.7047	0.8433
12	0.1602	0.2135	0.2784	0.3565	0.4493	0.5584	0.6854	0.8320
14	0.1430	0.1940	0.2572	0.3344	0.4276	0.5386	0.6696	0.8226
16	0.1296	0.1785	0.2401	0.3164	0.4096	0.5220	0.6561	0.8145
18	0.1188	0.1659	0.2260	0.3013	0.3944	0.5078	0.6445	0.8074
20	0.1099	0.1554	0.2141	0.2884	0.3812	0.4954	0.6342	0.8012
22	0.1025	0.1465	0.2038	0.2772	0.3697	0.4844	0.6251	0.7955
24	0.0961	0.1387	0.1949	0.2674	0.3595	0.4747	0.6169	0.7904
25	0.0933	0.1353	0.1908	0.2629	0.3548	0.4701	0.6131	0.7880
30	0.0815	0.1208	0.1737	0.2437	0.3346	0.4505	0.5963	0.7775
35	0.0728	0.1097	0.1605	0.2286	0.3184	0.4345	0.5825	0.7687
40	0.0660	0.1010	0.1498	0.2163	0.3050	0.4211	0.5708	0.7611
45	0.0605	0.0939	0.1410	0.2060	0.2936	0.4096	0.5607	0.7545
50	0.0560	0.0879	0.1336	0.1972	0.2838	0.3996	0.5518	0.7486
60	0.0489	0.0785	0.1216	0.1828	0.2676	0.3829	0.5367	0.7386
70	0.0437	0.0713	0.1123	0.1715	0.2547	0.3693	0.5243	0.7302
80	0.0396	0.0657	0.1049	0.1622	0.2440	0.3579	0.5137	0.7231
90	0.0363	0.0610	0.0987	0.1545	0.2349	0.3482	0.5046	0.7168
100	0.0336	0.0572	0.0935	0.1479	0.2271	0.3397	0.4966	0.7112
120	0.0294	0.0510	0.0851	0.1371	0.2141	0.3255	0.4830	0.7017
140	0.0262	0.0464	0.0786	0.1287	0.2038	0.3139	0.4718	0.6937
160	0.0237	0.0427	0.0734	0.1217	0.1952	0.3042	0.4623	0.6869
180	0.0218	0.0397	0.0691	0.1159	0.1879	0.2959	0.4541	0.6809
200	0.0201	0.0371	0.0655	0.1109	0.1816	0.2887	0.4469	0.6757
250	0.0171	0.0323	0.0584	0.1011	0.1691	0.2740	0.4320	0.6646
300	0.0149	0.0289	0.0531	0.0937	0.1594	0.2625	0.4202	0.6557
350	0.0133	0.0262	0.0491	0.0879	0.1517	0.2532	0.4105	0.6482
400	0.0121	0.0241	0.0458	0.0832	0.1453	0.2454	0.4022	0.6419
450	0.0111	0.0224	0.0431	0.0792	0.1399	0.2387	0.3951	0.6363
500	0.0103	0.0210	0.0408	0.0758	0.1352	0.2329	0.3888	0.6314
600	0.0090	0.0188	0.0372	0.0703	0.1275	0.2232	0.3782	0.6229
700	0.0080	0.0171	0.0344	0.0659	0.1214	0.2152	0.3694	0.6158
800	0.0073	0.0157	0.0321	0.0624	0.1163	0.2086	0.3620	0.6098
900	0.0067	0.0146	0.0302	0.0594	0.1119	0.2029	0.3556	0.6045
1,000	0.0062	0.0137	0.0286	0.0569	0.1082	0.1980	0.3499	0.5998
1,200	0.0054	0.0122	0.0260	0.0527	0.1020	0.1897	0.3404	0.5918
1,400	0.0048	0.0111	0.0240	0.0495	0.0971	0.1830	0.3325	0.5850
1,600	0.0044	0.0102	0.0225	0.0468	0.0930	0.1773	0.3258	0.5793
1,800	0.0040	0.0095	0.0211	0.0446	0.0895	0.1725	0.3200	0.5743
2,000	0.0037	0.0089	0.0200	0.0427	0.0866	0.1683	0.3149	0.5698
2,500	0.0031	0.0077	0.0178	0.0389	0.0806	0.1597	0.3044	0.5605
3,000	0.0027	0.0069	0.0162	0.0360	0.0760	0.1530	0.2961	0.5530

TABLE 9B.2   Cumulative Learning Curve Values for n^β

	Percent learning curve							
Repetitions	60%	65%	70%	75%	80%	85%	90%	95%
1	1.000	1.000	1.000	1.000	1.000	1.000	1.000	1.000
2	1.600	1.650	1.700	1.750	1.800	1.850	1.900	1.950
3	2.045	2.155	2.268	2.384	2.502	2.623	2.746	2.872
4	2.405	2.578	2.758	2.946	3.142	3.345	3.556	3.774
5	2.710	2.946	3.195	3.459	3.738	4.031	4.339	4.662
6	2.977	3.274	3.593	3.934	4.299	4.688	5.101	5.538
7	3.216	3.572	3.960	4.380	4.834	5.322	5.845	6.404
8	3.432	3.847	4.303	4.802	5.346	5.936	6.574	7.261
9	3.630	4.102	4.626	5.204	5.839	6.533	7.290	8.111
10	3.813	4.341	4.931	5.589	6.315	7.116	7.994	8.955
12	4.144	4.780	5.501	6.315	7.227	8.244	9.374	10.62
14	4.438	5.177	6.026	6.994	8.092	9.331	10.72	12.27
16	4.704	5.541	6.514	7.635	8.920	10.38	12.04	13.91
18	4.946	5.879	6.972	8.245	9.716	11.41	13.33	15.52
20	5.171	6.195	7.407	8.828	10.48	12.40	14.61	17.13
22	5.379	6.492	7.819	9.388	11.23	13.38	15.86	18.72
24	5.574	6.773	8.213	9.928	11.95	14.33	17.10	20.31
25	5.668	6.909	8.404	10.19	12.31	14.80	17.71	21.10
30	6.097	7.540	9.305	11.45	14.02	17.09	20.73	25.00
35	6.478	8.109	10.13	12.72	15.64	19.29	23.67	28.86
40	6.821	8.631	10.90	13.72	17.19	21.43	26.54	32.68
45	7.134	9.114	11.62	14.77	18.68	23.50	29.37	36.47
50	7.422	9.565	12.31	15.78	20.12	25.51	32.14	40.22
60	7.941	10.39	13.57	17.67	22.87	29.41	37.57	47.65
70	8.401	11.13	14.74	19.43	25.47	33.17	42.87	54.99
80	8.814	11.82	15.82	21.09	27.96	36.80	48.05	62.25
90	9.191	12.45	16.83	22.67	30.35	40.32	53.14	69.45
100	9.539	13.03	17.79	24.18	32.65	43.75	58.14	76.59
120	10.16	14.11	19.57	27.02	37.05	50.39	67.93	90.71
140	10.72	15.08	21.20	29.67	41.22	56.78	77.46	104.7
160	11.21	15.97	22.72	32.17	45.20	62.95	86.80	118.5
180	11.67	16.79	24.14	34.54	49.03	68.95	95.96	132.1
200	12.09	17.55	25.48	36.80	52.72	74.79	105.0	145.7
250	13.01	19.28	28.56	42.08	61.47	88.83	126.9	179.2
300	13.81	20.81	31.34	46.94	69.66	102.2	148.2	212.2
350	14.51	22.18	33.89	51.48	77.43	115.1	169.0	244.8
400	15.14	23.44	36.26	55.75	84.85	127.6	189.3	277.0
450	15.72	24.60	38.48	59.80	91.97	139.7	209.2	309.0
500	16.26	25.68	40.58	63.68	98.85	151.5	228.8	340.6
600	17.21	27.67	44.47	70.97	112.0	174.2	267.1	403.3
700	18.06	29.45	48.04	77.77	124.4	196.1	304.5	465.3
800	18.82	31.09	51.36	84.18	136.3	217.3	341.0	526.5
900	19.51	32.60	54.46	90.26	147.7	237.9	376.9	587.2
1,000	20.15	34.01	57.40	96.07	158.7	257.9	412.2	647.4
1,200	21.30	36.59	62.85	107.0	179.7	296.6	481.2	766.6
1,400	22.32	38.92	67.85	117.2	199.6	333.9	548.4	884.2
1,600	23.23	41.04	72.49	126.8	218.6	369.6	614.2	1001.0
1,800	24.06	43.00	76.85	135.9	236.8	404.9	678.8	1116.0
2,000	24.83	44.84	80.96	144.7	254.4	438.9	742.3	1230.0
2,500	26.53	48.97	90.39	165.0	296.1	520.8	897.0	1513.0
3,000	27.99	52.62	98.90	183.7	335.2	598.9	1047.0	1791.0

Normal Distribution Function

TABLE 9C.1 Cumulative Probabilities of the Normal Distribution (areas under the standardized normalized curve from $-\infty$ to z)

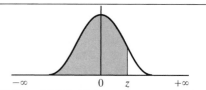

z	0.00	0.01	0.02	0.03	0.04	0.05	0.06	0.07	0.08	0.09
0.0	0.5000	0.5040	0.5080	0.5120	0.5160	0.5199	0.5239	0.5279	0.5319	0.5359
0.1	0.5389	0.5438	0.5478	0.5517	0.5557	0.5596	0.5636	0.5675	0.5714	0.5753
0.2	0.5793	0.5832	0.5871	0.5910	0.5948	0.5987	0.6026	0.6064	0.6103	0.6141
0.3	0.6179	0.6217	0.6255	0.6293	0.6331	0.6368	0.6406	0.6443	0.6480	0.6517
0.4	0.6554	0.6591	0.6628	0.6664	0.6700	0.6736	0.6772	0.6808	0.6844	0.6879
0.5	0.6915	0.6950	0.6985	0.7019	0.7054	0.7088	0.7123	0.7157	0.7190	0.7224
0.6	0.7257	0.7291	0.7324	0.7357	0.7389	0.7422	0.7454	0.7486	0.7517	0.7549
0.7	0.7580	0.7611	0.7642	0.7673	0.7704	0.7734	0.7764	0.7794	0.7823	0.7852
0.8	0.7881	0.7910	0.7939	0.7967	0.7995	0.8023	0.8051	0.8078	0.8106	0.8133
0.9	0.8159	0.8186	0.8212	0.8238	0.8264	0.8289	0.8315	0.8340	0.8365	0.8389
1.0	0.8413	0.8438	0.8461	0.8485	0.8508	0.8531	0.8554	0.8577	0.8599	0.8621
1.1	0.8643	0.8665	0.8686	0.8708	0.8729	0.8749	0.8770	0.8790	0.8810	0.8830
1.2	0.8849	0.8869	0.8888	0.8907	0.8925	0.8944	0.8962	0.8980	0.8997	0.9015
1.3	0.9032	0.9049	0.9066	0.9082	0.9099	0.9115	0.9131	0.9147	0.9162	0.9177
1.4	0.9192	0.9207	0.9222	0.9236	0.9251	0.9265	0.9279	0.9292	0.9306	0.9319
1.5	0.9332	0.9345	0.9357	0.9370	0.9382	0.9394	0.9406	0.9418	0.9429	0.9441
1.6	0.9452	0.9463	0.9474	0.9484	0.9495	0.9505	0.9515	0.9525	0.9535	0.9545
1.7	0.9554	0.9564	0.9573	0.9582	0.9591	0.9599	0.9608	0.9616	0.9625	0.9633
1.8	0.9641	0.9649	0.9656	0.9664	0.9671	0.9678	0.9686	0.9693	0.9699	0.9706
1.9	0.9713	0.9719	0.9726	0.9732	0.9738	0.9744	0.9750	0.9756	0.9761	0.9767
2.0	0.9772	0.9778	0.9783	0.9788	0.9793	0.9798	0.9803	0.9808	0.9812	0.9817
2.1	0.9821	0.9826	0.9830	0.9834	0.9838	0.9842	0.9846	0.9850	0.9854	0.9857
2.2	0.9861	0.9864	0.9868	0.9871	0.9875	0.9878	0.9881	0.9884	0.9887	0.9890
2.3	0.9893	0.9896	0.9898	0.9901	0.9904	0.9906	0.9909	0.9911	0.9913	0.9916
2.4	0.9918	0.9920	0.9922	0.9925	0.9927	0.9929	0.9931	0.9932	0.9934	0.9936
2.5	0.9938	0.9940	0.9941	0.9943	0.9945	0.9946	0.9948	0.9949	0.9951	0.9952
2.6	0.9953	0.9955	0.9956	0.9957	0.9959	0.9960	0.9961	0.9962	0.9963	0.9964
2.7	0.9965	0.9966	0.9967	0.9968	0.9969	0.9970	0.9971	0.9972	0.9973	0.9974
2.8	0.9974	0.9975	0.9976	0.9977	0.9977	0.9978	0.9979	0.9979	0.9980	0.9981
2.9	0.9981	0.9982	0.9982	0.9983	0.9984	0.9984	0.9985	0.9985	0.9986	0.9986
3.0	0.9987	0.9987	0.9987	0.9988	0.9988	0.9989	0.9989	0.9989	0.9990	0.9990
3.1	0.9990	0.9991	0.9991	0.9991	0.9992	0.9992	0.9992	0.9992	0.9993	0.9993
3.2	0.9993	0.9993	0.9994	0.9994	0.9994	0.9994	0.9994	0.9995	0.9995	0.9995
3.3	0.9995	0.9995	0.9995	0.9996	0.9996	0.9996	0.9996	0.9996	0.9996	0.9997
3.4	0.9997	0.9997	0.9997	0.9997	0.9997	0.9997	0.9997	0.9997	0.9997	0.9998

Chapter 10

Resource Management

10.1 EFFECT OF RESOURCES ON PROJECT PLANNING

In project scheduling, we have thus far assumed that the precedence relations among activities are the sole constraints. Based on this assumption, each activity could start as soon as all of its predecessors were completed (assuming finish-to-start precedence relations). This type of analysis is based on the implicit assumption that there are enough resources available to permit any number of activities to be scheduled simultaneously. As we will see, this is rarely the case.

Resource planning is the process by which the project manager decides which resources to obtain, from which sources, when to obtain them, how to use them, and when and how to release them. Therefore, project resource planning is mainly concerned with the tradeoff analysis between (1) the cost of alternative schedules designed to accommodate resources shortages and (2) the cost of using alternative resources; for example, overtime to meet a schedule or subcontracting to accommodate a schedule change. This analysis may be subject to constraints on resource availability, budget allocations, and task deadlines.

An important function of the project manager is to monitor and control resource use and performance during project execution. If technical personnel are scarce or if materials and equipment are in short supply, then rescheduling becomes a top management priority. Shortages and uncertainty can wreak havoc on the best of plans; however, the efficient use of resources goes a long way in reducing both the cost and the duration of a project at each stage of its life cycle.

Project resources are aggregated through the budget and expended over time. The relationship between the project budget and schedule will be discussed in Chapter 11. Money is used to acquire the resources needed for the project, but in some financial organizations such as banks and insurance companies, money itself is a resource used for operations. Information is also an important resource in projects. This can be confusing, so to plan for and track resource use, some type of classification system is needed. This is taken up next.

10.2 CLASSIFICATION OF RESOURCES USED IN PROJECTS

Project resources can be classified in several ways. One approach is based on accounting principles, which distinguish between labor costs (human resources), material costs, and other "production" costs, such as subcontracting and borrowing. This classification scheme is very useful for budgeting and accounting. Its major drawbacks are that it does not specifically include the cost of the less tangible resources such as information (blueprints, databases), and it does not capture the main aspect of project resource management (i.e., the availability of resources).

A second approach is based on resource availability. Some resources are available at the same level in every time period (e.g., a fixed workforce). These are *renewable* resources. A second class consists of resources that come in a lump sum at the beginning of the project and are used up over time. These are *depletable* resources, such as material or computer time. A third class of resources is available in limited quantities each period. However, their total availability throughout the project is also circumscribed. These are called *doubly constrained* resources. The cash available for a project is a typical example of a doubly constrained resource. Based on this classification, one objective in using renewable resources is to minimize idle time or to maximize utilization. An objective in using depletable resources is to maximize "effectiveness"—the ratio between output and input.

A third classification scheme is similarly based on resource availability. The first class includes all "nonconstrained" resources—those that are available in unlimited quantities for a cost. A typical example is untrained labor or general-purpose equipment. The second class includes resources that are very expensive or impossible to obtain within the time span of the project. Special facilities, such as the use of a supercomputer, and technical experts who work on many projects are two such examples. This class also includes resources of which a given quantity is available for the entire project, such as a rare type of material that has a long lead time. The quantity ordered at the beginning of the project must last throughout, because of its limited supply.

This scheme is characteristic of an ABC inventory management system. Resources of the first class (C category) are available in unlimited quantities and so do not require continuous monitoring. Nevertheless, they still might be expensive, so their efficient use will help keep project costs down. Resources in the second class (A category) have high priority and should be monitored closely because shortages might significantly affect the project schedule and success. In general, depletable resources and those limited by periodic availability should be considered individually during the planning process. This means that project schedules should be designed to ensure optimal use of nonconstrained resources and that tight controls should be placed on the consumption of constrained resources.

In addition to availability considerations, the cost of resources should be weighed when developing project schedules. This is critical whenever activities can be performed by various resources. The combination of resources (often called the "mode") assigned to an activity affects both the duration and the cost of the activity and may affect the schedule and the cost of the entire project.

Often, it is not possible to allocate resources to activities accurately at the early stages of a project. This is because of the underlying uncertainty that initially shrouds resource requirements. Therefore, resource planning monitoring and control is a continuous process that takes place throughout the life cycle of the project.

In a multiproject environment, the specific resource alternative selected also affects other ongoing projects. It is common sense to start the planning process by assuming that each activity is performed by the minimum cost resource alternative. This mode of operation is known as the "normal" mode, and it is associated with the "normal" time and "normal" cost of the activity. To identify this alternative, the following points should be considered:

- The selection of resources should be designed for maximum flexibility so that resources that are not essential for one project can be used simultaneously on other projects. This flexibility can be achieved by buying general-purpose equipment and by broadly training employees.
- Up to a certain point, the more of a particular resource used, the less expensive it is per unit of time (as a result of savings in setup cost, greater learning, and economies of scale).
- The marginal contribution of a resource decreases with usage. Frequently, when increasing the quantity of a resource type assigned to an activity, a point at which additional resources do not shorten the activity's duration is reached. That is, inefficiencies and diminishing returns set in.
- Some resources are discrete. When this is the case, decreasing resource levels, necessarily in integer quantities, could result in a sharp decline in productivity and efficiency.
- Resources are organizational assets. Resource planning should take into consideration not only what is best for an individual project but also what is best for the organization as a whole.
- The organization has better control over its own resources. When the choice of acquiring or subcontracting for a resource exists, the degree of availability and control should be weighed against cost considerations.

The output of each resource is measured by its capacity, which is commonly defined in two ways:

1. *Nominal capacity*: maximum output achieved under ideal conditions. The nominal capacity of equipment is usually contained in its technical manual. Nominal capacity of labor can be estimated with standard work measurement techniques commonly used by industrial engineers.
2. *Effective capacity*: maximum output taking into account the mixture of activities assigned, scheduling and sequencing constraints, maintenance aspects, the operating environment, and other resources used in combination.

Resource planning is relatively easy when a single resource is used in a single project. When the coordinate use of multiple resources in multiple projects is called for, planning and scheduling become more complicated, especially when dependencies exist among several projects. In some cases, it is justified to use excessive levels of inexpensive readily available resources (type C in the ABC classification) to maximize the utilization of resources that are expensive or in limited supply (type A in the ABC classification).

The life cycle of a project affects its resource requirements. In the early stages, the focus is on design. Thus, highly trained personnel such as system analysts, design engineers, and financial planners are needed. In subsequent stages, execution becomes dominant, and machines and material requirements increase. A graph of resource requirements as a function of time is called a *resource profile*. An example of labor and material profiles as a function of a project's life-cycle stages is presented in Fig. 10.1. Curve (a) depicts the requirements for engineers as a function of time. As can be seen, demand peaks during the advanced development phase of the project. Curve (b) displays the requirements for technicians. In this case, the maximum is reached during the detailed design and production phases. This is also true for material requirements, as shown in curve (c).

The general shape of the profiles depicted in Fig. 10.1 can be modified somewhat by careful planning and control. Slack management is one way to reshape resource requirements. Because it is always possible to start an activity within the range defined by its early- and late-start schedules, it may be possible to achieve higher resource utilization and lower costs by exploring different assignment patterns. In some projects, limited resource availability forces the delay of activities beyond their late start. When this happens, project delays are inevitable unless corrective action can be taken immediately.

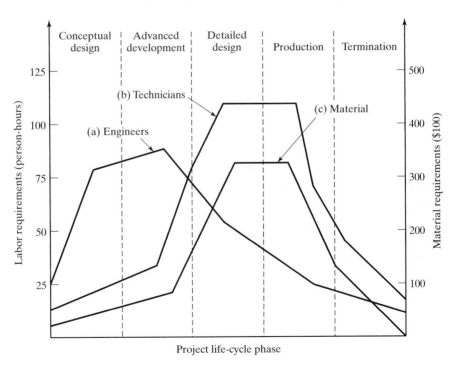

Figure 10.1 Typical resource requirement profiles.

10.3 RESOURCE LEVELING SUBJECT TO PROJECT DUE-DATE CONSTRAINTS

To discuss the relationship between resource requirements and the scheduling of activities, consider the example project that was introduced in Table 9.2. Assuming that only a single resource is used (unskilled labor) in the project, Table 10.1 lists the resource requirements for each of the seven activities.

The data in Table 10.1 are based on the assumption that performing an activity requires that the resource be used at a constant rate. Thus, activity A requires 8 unskilled labor-days in each of its 5 weeks. When the usage rate is not constant, resource requirements should be specified for each time period (a week in our example).

The Gantt chart for the early-start schedule is shown in Fig. 10.2a; the corresponding resource requirement profile is depicted in Fig. 10.2b. As can be seen, the early-start schedule produces a high level of resource use at the early stages of the project. During the first 3 weeks, there is a need for 17 labor-days each week. Assuming 5 working days per week, the requirement during the first 3 weeks is $17/5 = 3.4$ unskilled workers per day. The fractional component of demand can be met with overtime, second-shift, or part-time workers. The lowest resource requirements occur in week 13, when only 3 labor-days are needed. Thus, the early-start schedule generates a widely varying profile, with a high of 17 labor-days per week and a low of 3 labor-days per week; the range is $17 - 3 = 14$.

The Gantt chart and resource requirement profile associated with the late-start schedule are illustrated in Fig. 10.3. Because of the effect that scheduling decisions have on resource requirements, there is a difference between the profiles associated with the late-start and early-start schedules. In the example, the late-start schedule moves the maximum resource usage from weeks 1 through 3 to weeks 3 through 5. Furthermore, maximum usage is reduced from 17 labor-days per week to 12 labor-days per week, giving a range of $12 - 3 = 9$. It is important to note that the reduction in range while moving from the early-start to the late-start schedule is not necessarily uniform over the intermediate cases.

Resource leveling can be defined as the reallocation of total or free slack in activities to minimize fluctuations in the resource requirement profile. It is assumed that a more steady usage rate leads to lower resource costs. For labor, this assumption is based on the proposition that costs increase with the need to hire, fire, and train personnel. For materials, it is assumed that fluctuating consumption rates mean an increase in storage

TABLE 10.1   Resource Requirements for the Example Project

Activity	Duration (weeks)	Required labor (days per week)	Total labor (days required)
A	5	8	40
B	3	4	12
C	8	3	24
D	7	2	14
E	7	5	35
F	4	9	36
G	5	7	35

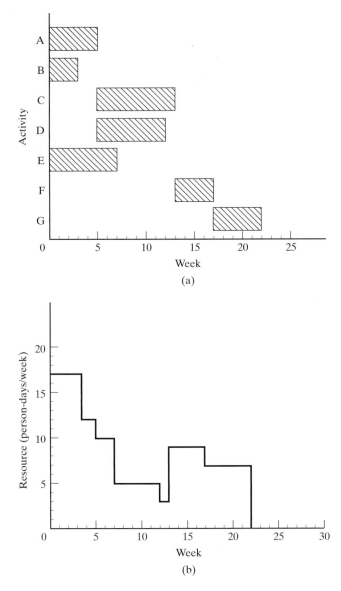

Figure 10.2 (a) Gantt chart and (b) resource profile for the early-start schedule.

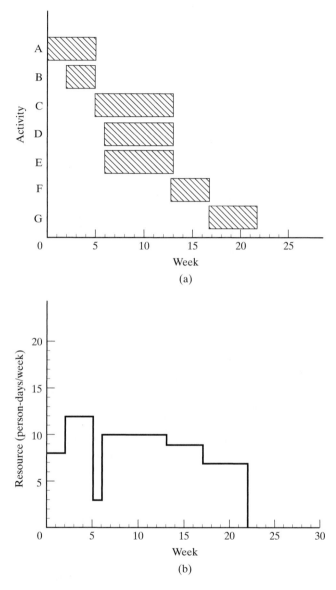

Figure 10.3 (a) Gantt chart and (b) resource profile for the late-start schedule.

requirement (perhaps to accommodate the maximum expected inventory) and more effort invested in material planning and control.

Resource leveling can be performed in a variety of ways, some of which are described in the references listed at the end of the chapter. A generic resource-leveling procedure is illustrated next and used to solve the example project.

1. Calculate the *average* number of resource-days per period (e.g., week). In the example, a total of 196 resource-days or labor-days are required. Because the project duration is 22 weeks, 196/22 = 8.9 or approximately 9 labor-days per week are required on the average.
2. With reference to the early-start schedule and noncritical activities, gradually delay activities one at a time, starting with those activities that have the largest free slack. Check the emerging resource requirement profile after each delay. Select the schedule that minimizes resource fluctuations by generating daily resource requirements close to the calculated average.

Continuing with the example, we see from Table 9.5 that activity E has the largest free slack (6 weeks). The first step is to delay the start of E by 3 weeks until the end of activity B. This reduces resource requirements in weeks 1 through 3 by 5 units. The emerging resource profile is

Week	1	2	3	4	5	6	7	8	9	10	11
Load	12	12	12	13	13	10	10	10	10	10	5

Week	12	13	14	15	16	17	18	19	20	21	22
Load	5	3	9	9	9	9	7	7	7	7	7

This profile has a maximum of 13 and a minimum of 3 labor-days per week. Because the maximum occurs in weeks 4 and 5 and activity E can be delayed further, consider a schedule in which E starts after A is finished (after week 5). The resource requirements profile in this case is

Week	1	2	3	4	5	6	7	8	9	10	11
Load	12	12	12	8	8	10	10	10	10	10	10

Week	12	13	14	15	16	17	18	19	20	21	22
Load	10	3	9	9	9	9	7	7	7	7	7

The maximum resource requirement is now 12 and occurs in weeks 1 through 3. The minimum is still 3, giving a range of 12 − 3 = 9. The next candidate for adjustment is activity B with a free slack of 2 weeks. However, delaying B by 1 or 2 weeks will only increase the load in weeks 4 and 5 from 8 to 12, yielding a net gain of zero. Therefore, we turn to the last activity with a positive free slack—activity D, which is scheduled to start at week 5. Delaying D by 1 week results in the following resource requirement profile:

Week	1	2	3	4	5	6	7	8	9	10	11
Load	12	12	12	8	8	8	10	10	10	10	10

Week	12	13	14	15	16	17	18	19	20	21	22
Load	10	5	9	9	9	9	7	7	7	7	7

The corresponding graph and Gantt chart are depicted in Fig. 10.4. Note that this profile has a range of $12 - 5 = 7$, which is smaller than that associated with any of the other candidates, including the early-start and late-start schedules. This is as far as we can go in minimizing fluctuations without causing a delay in the entire project.

For small projects, the foregoing procedure works well but cannot always be relied on to find the optimal profile. To improve the results, a similar procedure can be executed by starting with the late-start schedule and checking the effect of moving activities with slack toward the start of the project. In some projects, the objective may be to keep the maximum resource utilization below a certain ceiling rather than merely leveling the resources. If this objective cannot be met by rescheduling the critical activities, then one or more of them would have to be expanded to reduce the daily resource requirements.

The analysis is more complicated when several types of resources are used, the number of activities is large, and several projects share the same resources. Sophisticated heuristic procedures have been developed for these cases, some of which are listed in the references. Most project management software packages use such procedures for resource leveling.

10.4 RESOURCE ALLOCATION SUBJECT TO RESOURCE AVAILABILITY CONSTRAINTS

Most projects are subject to resource availability constraints. This is common when resources are limited and suitable substitutes cannot be found. As a consequence, any delay or disruption in an activity may render the original project schedule infeasible. Cash flow difficulties may limit the availability of all resource types: renewable, depletable, and nonconstrained. Some resources may be available in unlimited quantities, but as a result of cash flow problems, their use may have to be cut back in a specific project or over a specific period of time.

Under resource availability constraints, the project completion date calculated in the critical path analysis may not be achieved. This is the case when the resources required exceed the available resources in one or more time periods and the slack of noncritical activities is not sufficient to solve the problem.

Of course, resource availability constraints are not always binding on the schedule. This can be illustrated with the example project. If 17 or more labor-days are available every week, then either an early-start or a late-start schedule can be used to complete the project within 22 weeks. The leveled resource profile derived above requires at most 12 labor-days per week. Therefore, as long as this number is available, no delays will be

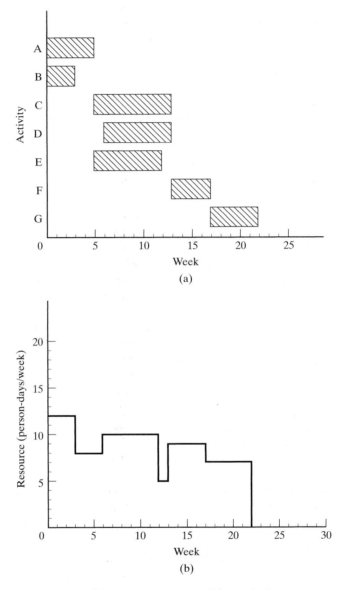

Figure 10.4 (a) Gantt chart and (b) leveled resource profile for the example project.

experienced. If fewer resources are available in some weeks, however, then the project may have to be extended beyond its earliest completion date. Activities A and B require a total of 12 labor-days per week when performed in parallel. Despite low resource availability, the project manager can try using one or more of the following strategies to avoid an extension:

1. *Performing activities at a lower rate using available resource levels.* This technique is effective only when the duration of an activity can be extended by performing it with fewer resources. Consider activity B in the example. Assuming that only 11 labor-days are available each week and activity A (which is critical) is scheduled to be performed using 8 of those days, only 3 days a week are left for activity B. Because B requires a total of (3 weeks) $\times$ (4 labor-days per week) = 12 labor-days of the resource, it may be possible to schedule B for 3 days per week for 4 weeks. If this is not satisfactory, then extending B to 5 weeks at 3 days per week may provide the solution.

   This technique may not be applicable if a minimum level of resources are required each period (week) in which the activity is performed. Such a requirement might result from technological or safety considerations.

2. *Activity splitting.* It might be possible to split some activities into subactivities without significantly altering the original precedence relations. For example, consider splitting activity A into two subactivities: A_1, which is performed during weeks 1 and 2, and A_2, which is performed after a break of 4 weeks. It is possible then to complete the project within 22 weeks, using only 11 labor-days each week. This technique is attractive whenever an activity can be split, the setup time after the break is relatively short, and the activities that succeed the first subactivity can be performed in accordance with the original plan; that is, the second subactivity has no effect on the original precedence relations.

3. *Modifying the network.* Whenever the network is based solely on end-to-start precedence relations, the introduction of other types of precedence relations might help manage the constrained resources. For example, if an end-to-start connection on the critical path is replaced by a start-to-start connection, then the delay caused by lack of resources may be eliminated. By considering the real precedence constraints among activities and modeling these constraints using all types of precedence relations defined in Chapter 9, some conflicts can be resolved.

4. *Use of alternative resources.* This option is available for some resources. Subcontractors or personnel agencies, for example, are possible sources of additional labor. However, the corresponding costs may be relatively high, so a cost overrun versus a schedule overrun tradeoff analysis may be appropriate.

If these strategies cannot solve the problem, then one or more activities will have to be delayed beyond their total slack, causing a delay in the completion of the project. To illustrate, consider the example project under a resource constraint of 11 labor-days per week. Because activity A requires 8 of these 11 days, activity B can start only when A finishes. The precedence relations force a delay of activity D—the successor of B, as well as F and G. The new schedule and resource profile are depicted in Fig. 10.5.

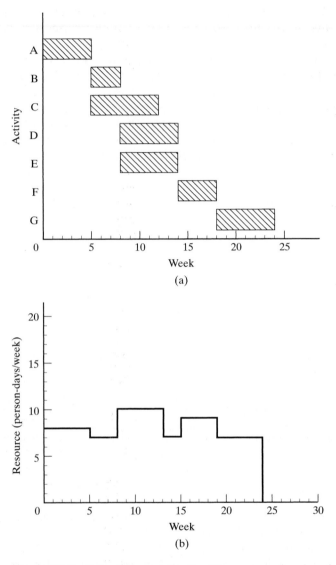

Figure 10.5 Scheduling under the 11 resource days/week constraint: (a) Gantt chart; (b) resource profile.

It is interesting to note that the maximum level of resources used in the new schedule is 10 labor-days. Thus, in the example project, a reduction of the available resource level from 11 to 10 labor-days per week does not result in a change in the schedule. A further reduction to 9 labor-days each week will cause a further delay of the project because the concurrent scheduling of activities C, D, and E requires a total of 10 resource-days. A feasible schedule in this case and the accompanying resource profile are shown in Fig. 10.6.

It is impossible to reduce the resource level below 9 labor-days per week because activity F must be performed at that level. Table 10.2 summarizes the relationship between the resource level available and the project duration.

TABLE 10.2   Implications of Resource Availability

Resource availability (work-days/week)	Project duration (weeks)	Resource utilization
12	22	0.74
11	24	0.74
10	24	0.82
9	29	0.75

In his book *Critical Chain*, Goldratt (1997) called the resource that is responsible for a project delay the *critical resource* or *bottleneck*. The activities that are performed by this resource are part of a sequence of activities that connect the start of the project to its end and constitute the "critical chain."

Resource utilization is defined as the proportion of time that a renewable resource is used. For example, if 12 labor-days are available each week and the project duration is 22 weeks, a total of $12 \times 22 = 254$ resource days are available. Because only 196 days are used to perform all of the project's activities, the utilization of this resource is $196/254 = 0.74$. Resource utilization is an important performance measure, particularly for renewable resources in a multiproject environment. Resource leveling and resource allocation techniques can be used to achieve high levels of utilization over all projects and resources. Matrix organizational structures help organizations achieve high utilization by taking advantage of pooled resources.

The analysis of multiple projects in which several types of resources are used in each is a complicated scheduling problem. In most real-life applications, the problem is solved with heuristics using priority rules to make the allocations among activities. Some of these rules are discussed in the following section.

10.5 PRIORITY RULES FOR RESOURCE ALLOCATION

A common approach to resource allocation is to begin with a simple critical path analysis assuming unlimited resources. Next, a check is made to determine whether the resultant schedule is infeasible. This would be the case whenever a resource requirement exceeds its availability. Infeasibilities are addressed one at a time starting with the first activity in the precedence graph and making a forward pass toward the last. A priority

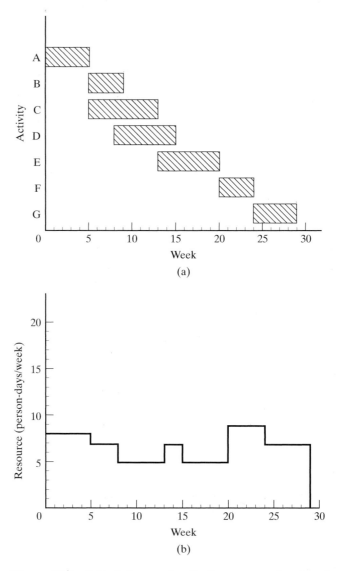

Figure 10.6 Scheduling under the 9 resource-days/week constraint: (a) Gantt chart; (b) resource profile.

measure is calculated for each activity competing for a scarce resource. The activity with the lowest priority is delayed until sufficient resources are available. This procedure is used to resolve each infeasibility.

Examples of common priority rules are as follows:

- Activity with the smallest slack
- Activity with minimum late finish time (as determined by critical path analysis)
- Activity that requires the greatest number of resource units (or the smallest number of resource units)
- Shorter activities (or longer activities)

A priority rule based on the late start of the activity and the project duration calculated by a critical path analysis is also possible. For example, define

$$\text{CPT} = \text{earliest completion time of the project (based on critical path analysis)}$$

$$\text{LS}(i) = \text{late start of activity } i \text{ (based on critical path analysis)}$$

$$\text{PT}(i) = \text{priority of activity } i, \text{ where PT}(i) = \text{CPT} - \text{LS}(i)$$

This rule gives high priority to activities that should start early in the project life cycle. In the case of multiple-project scheduling, the value of CPT is calculated for each project.

Next, we look at a priority rule that is based on each activity's resource requirements. Let

$$\text{AT}(i) = \text{duration of activity } i$$

$$\text{R}(i, k) = \text{level of resource } k \text{ required per unit of time for activity } i$$

$$\text{PR}(i, k) = \text{priority of activity } i \text{ with respect to resource type } k,$$
$$\text{where PR}(i, k) = \text{AT}(i) \times \text{R}(i, k)$$

In this rule, high priority is given to the activity that requires the maximum use of resource k.

A rule that is based on aggregated resources is used when some activities require more than a single resource. Define

$$\text{PSUMR}(i) = \text{priority of activity } i \text{ based on all of its required resources}$$

$$= \text{AT}(i) \times \Sigma_k \text{R}(i, k)$$

To operationalize this rule, it is necessary to define a common resource unit such as a resource-day.

A weighted time-resource requirement priority rule can be fashioned from two of the previous rules; for example, let

$$\omega = \text{weight between 0 and 1}$$

$$\text{PTR}(i) = \text{the weighted priority of activity } i,$$
$$\text{where PTR}(i) = \omega \, \text{PT}(i) + (1 - \omega) \, \text{PSUMR}(i)$$

By controlling the value of ω, emphasis can be shifted from the time dimension, PT(i), to the resource dimension, PSUMR(i).

Many of the priority rules above can be modified to take into account a variety of additional factors, including

- Slack of the activity (total slack, free slack)
- Early start, late start, early finish, and late finish of the activity
- Duration of the activity
- Number of succeeding/preceding activities
- Length of the longest sequence of activities that contain the activity
- Maximum resource requirement sequence of activities that contain the activity

10.6 CRITICAL CHAIN: PROJECT MANAGEMENT BY CONSTRAINTS

Goldratt (1997) extended the notion of bottlenecks used in job-shop and flow-shop scheduling to project resource management. Critical resources or bottlenecks delay activities on the critical chain as a result of their limited availability. In a multiresource project, bottlenecks whose capacity is relatively inexpensive to increase may cause low utilization of expensive or scarce resources. For example, a leased crane is an expensive resource that might be idle if an operator is not available because both resources are required simultaneously to perform an activity. From an economic point of view, it is preferable to maximize the utilization of the expensive resource at the risk of underutilizing the inexpensive one. Therefore, if the leased crane is available and needed 14 hours each day but an operator can work only between 8 and 10 hours a day, then it would be advisable to hire two operators for a total of 16 hours a day, allowing for 2 hours of operator idle time.

Of course, idle resources signal inefficiencies that should be brought to the attention of management to determine whether they can be put to alternative use. Resource utilization is a key factor, sharing center stage with cost and on-time performance during project evaluation. Each of these factors figures prominently in the planning and review process.

Because the critical chain is the longest sequence of activities that connect the start of the project to its end under resource constraints and because any delay in the critical chain will cause a delay of the entire project, Goldratt suggested using buffers to hedge against uncertainty. In particular, a time buffer can be used to protect the critical resource and the critical chain.

10.7 MATHEMATICAL MODELS FOR RESOURCE ALLOCATION

Project scheduling under resource availability constraints has been the subject of much research (e.g., see Demeulemeester and Herroelen 1997, Herroelen et al. 1999, Tavares 1990). Most of the related studies assume that the scheduling objective is to complete the project as early as possible (the scheduling approach) or to maximize the net present value (NPV) (minimize the net present cost) of the project (the budgeting approach). An early model proposed by Patterson et al. (1989, 1990) can handle both objectives.

The following notation is used to describe the model; an activity-on-node (AON) network is assumed:

Indices and sets

d = index for number of time periods that an activity is in progress

j = index for project activity $(j = 1, 2, \ldots, J)$

k = index identifying resources that are available in a fixed quantity each period [i.e., renewable resources $(k = 1, 2, \ldots, K)$]

m = index for mode of an activity; i.e., the combination of resources assigned to perform a particular project activity

t = index for time periods $(t = 1, 2, \ldots, T)$

P = set of all pairs of immediate predecessor relations; $(a, b) \in P$ denotes that activity a is an immediate predecessor of activity b

Parameters

C_{jmd} = cash flow of activity j if performed in mode m during its dth period in progress $(d = 1, 2, \ldots, D_{jm})$; if $C_{jmd} < 0$, then there is a cash withdrawal; if $C_{jmd} > 0$, then there is a cash inflow

C_{jmv}^{*} = nonnegative cash inflow v periods after the completion of activity j $(v \geq 1)$ (completion of a payment milestone)

C_t = net cash position in period t; C_0 is the cash available at the start of the project

D_{jm} = Duration of activity j if performed in mode m

$E_j(L_j)$ = Earliest (latest) completion time for activity j determined from critical path analysis based on shortest (longest) completion time mode for activities in the network

J = unique terminal activity (may be a dummy) that has only one mode $(m = 1; J$ also represents the number of activities in the project)

M_j = number of modes associated with activity j $(m = 1, 2, \ldots, M_j)$

R_{kt} = amount of resource k available in period t

r_{jmk} = per period amount of renewable resource k required to perform activity j in mode m

T = due date for project

α_t = single payment, present value discount factor for t periods at interest rate i; $\alpha_t = \left(\dfrac{1}{1+i}\right)^{t-1}$

Decision variables

$$x_{jmt} = \begin{cases} 1 & \text{if activity } j \text{ in mode } m \text{ is completed in period } t \\ 0 & \text{otherwise} \end{cases}$$

The problem formulation for the case in which project duration is minimized follows:

$$\text{Minimize} \quad \sum_{t=E_J}^{L_J} t x_{J1t} \tag{10.1a}$$

$$\text{subject to} \quad \sum_{m=1}^{M_j} \sum_{t=E_j}^{L_j} x_{jmt} = 1, \quad j = 1, \dots, J \tag{10.1b}$$

$$-\sum_{m=1}^{M_a} \sum_{t=E_a}^{L_a} t x_{amt} + \sum_{m=1}^{M_b} \sum_{t=E_b}^{L_b} (t - D_{bm}) x_{bmt} \geq 0, \text{ for all } (a, b) \in P \tag{10.1c}$$

$$\sum_{j=1}^{J} \sum_{m=1}^{M_j} \sum_{q=t}^{t+D_{jm}-1} r_{jmk} x_{jmq} \leq R_{kt}, \quad k = 1, \dots, K; \ t = 1, \dots, T \tag{10.1d}$$

$$C_{t-1} + \sum_{j=1}^{J} \sum_{m=1}^{M_j} \sum_{q=t}^{t+D_{jm}-1} \left(C_{jm(D_{jm}+t-q)} x_{jmq} \right.$$
$$\left. + \sum_{v=1}^{t-1} C^*_{jmv} x_{jm(t-v)} \right) = C_t, \quad t = 1, \dots, T \tag{10.1e}$$

$$x_{jmt} = 0 \text{ or } 1, \quad \text{for all } j, m, t \tag{10.1f}$$

In the model, the objective [Eq. (10.1a)] of minimizing the duration of the project is achieved by scheduling the unique terminal activity J as early as possible subject to the following constraints:

- Ensuring that each activity will be completed in exactly one time period using only one activity mode [Eq. (10.1b)]
- Maintaining the precedence relations among activities [Eq. (10.1c)]
- Imposing resource restrictions [Eq. (10.1d)]
- Ensuring that an activity mode is selected only if sufficient cash is available during each period of its duration [Eq. (10.1e)]

To maximize the NPV of the project, the objective function (10.1a) is replaced by

$$\text{Maximize} \quad \sum_{t=1}^{T} \alpha_t (C_t - C_{t-1}) + C_0 \tag{10.2}$$

Problem (10.1) and its variant (10.2) are formally known as *zero-one integer programs*. In practice, it is not realistic to try to solve this type of problem to optimality when projects with several hundred activities are considered or when several projects that share the same resources are scheduled in parallel. Nevertheless, good solutions can be obtained with a variety of heuristics. For example, Patterson et al. (1990) developed a backtracking algorithm that makes initial allocations and then tries to improve on the solution by shifting around resources, starting with the last node and working backward.

10.8 PROJECTS PERFORMED IN PARALLEL

The resource allocation and resource leveling techniques discussed so far are based on the assumption that each project undertaken by an organization is managed separately. This assumption is problematic if one or more of the following conditions exist:

- Technological dependency between projects
- Resource dependency between projects
- Budget dependency between projects

1. *Technological dependency.* Technological dependencies arise when precedence relations among projects are present. Consider, for example, an electronics firm that is involved in two projects: (1) the development of a new microprocessor and (2) the development of a notebook computer. If a decision is made to use the new microprocessor in the notebook, then the success of the computer project is dependent on the completion of the microprocessor. If this seems too risky, then the new computer might be designed alternatively with an existing microprocessor as well as with the new one. This reduces the degree of dependency between the two original parallel projects.

2. *Resource dependency.* Resource dependencies occur when two or more projects compete for the same resources. In the previous example, an electrical engineer might be involved in both projects, so management must decide how best to allocate his or her time. One way to make this decision is to examine the priority rules discussed earlier. Other factors that should be considered are technological dependencies, the due date of each project, and the economic consequences attending late completion.

3. *Budget dependency.* Budget dependencies exist when several projects compete for the same dollars or when the income from one group of projects is expected to cover the costs of some other group. In this case, coordination between the various projects is required.

The techniques developed for single-project scheduling can usually be used when dealing with parallel projects. A single network constructed by connecting all projects according to the precedence relations among them or by assuming that all projects have the same start node and the same end node may be used as a single project model for the multiproject situation. Once all projects are combined into a single network, the techniques developed for resource management in a single project are applicable.

Goldratt suggested buffer management as a tool for managing projects that are performed in parallel. In this approach, the time buffers that protect the critical chain of each project are used as the basis for the allocation of scarce resources among the projects. Higher priority is given to the project that consumed the highest proportion of its time buffer (with respect to the actual progress made). For example, assume that two projects are performed simultaneously, each having an initial time buffer of 2 weeks and a critical chain of 10 weeks. At a given point in time, half of the work content of the first project has been completed and 1 week of its time buffer has been consumed. At the same point in time, 60% of the second project has been completed (4 weeks to go) and 1 week of its time buffer has also been consumed. Based on this information, priority will be given to the first project.

TEAM PROJECT
Thermal Transfer Plant

With the approved schedule, it is time to assemble the resources needed to execute the rotary combustor project. Your team has been requested to submit a detailed plan indicating all of the resources required and an initial schedule for each. Be sure to define the different resources (e.g., electrical engineers, mechanical engineers, material, a crane and operator).

Assume that resources are available but that management's policy is to level their use throughout the life cycle of each project. Develop a leveled resource plan. Explain the differences between your initial resource plan and the new one. In particular, discuss the benefits and costs associated with the leveled plan.

DISCUSSION QUESTIONS

1. Consider a project with which you are familiar and describe it briefly. For each classification scheme discussed in Section 10.2, classify each resource used in the project.

2. Discuss an example of a project that is not subject to resource constraints. Is this project subject to other constraints?

3. Discuss the importance of information as a resource in a technological project. Give an example in which availability of information is a major constraint.

4. Select a classification scheme and classify the resource "information" required by a technologically advanced country that is trying to develop a manned space program.

5. Develop a flow diagram for a resource leveling procedure that can be translated into a computer program. What are your objectives, and what are the input, output, and data processing requirements?

6. Modify the flow diagram developed in Question 5 so that it can handle resource allocation problems.

7. Give an example of a bottleneck resource in a project. Under what conditions should this constraint be removed?

8. In the fall of 2002, a coalition force under the auspices of the United States moved massive amounts of equipment, matériel, and troops into the Persian Gulf area in a prelude to the war with Iraq to remove Saddam Hussein from power. This logistical operation was followed in the spring of 2003 with a large-scale military operation. Discuss the dependencies between these two projects.

9. What are the difficulties involved in leveling a schedule, particularly when the activities consume multiple resources?

10. How much does a project manager need to know about a scheduling or resource leveling computer program to use the output intelligently?

11. Why is the impact of scheduling and resource allocation generally more significant in multi-project organizations? How do large fluctuations in demand affect the situation?

12. What difficulties do you foresee in assigning technical personnel such as software engineers to multiple projects?

EXERCISES

10.1 The following project is performed with a single type of resource (labor), which is assumed to be available in unlimited quantities. The resource usage rate is constant throughout the duration of each activity. Thus, if the duration of an activity is 5 days and it requires 60 hours of the resource, then $60/5 = 12$ hours of the resource are required each day that the activity is performed. The project data are shown in Table 10.3. Develop a schedule that minimizes resource fluctuations.

TABLE 10.3

Activity	Duration (days)	Immediate predecessors	Resource requirements (hours)
A	3	—	12
B	4	—	16
C	3	—	9
D	2	C	10
E	1	B	6
F	5	A	15
G	2	B	16
H	3	B	12
I	11	C	44
J	3	D, E	30
K	1	F, G	10
L	4	K	16
M	4	J, H	8

10.2 Assume that daily resource availability is 2 hours less than the daily resource requirement indicated by the schedule derived in Exercise 10.1.

a. Use two different priority rules to allocate the available resources to activities.
b. Comment on the performance of the rules selected.

10.3 Each activity in a project can be performed by two different resource combinations (Table 10.4). Assume that the usage rate of each resource is constant throughout the duration of each activity. Now find a schedule that minimizes the time required to complete the project. Resources I and II both are available at a level of 12 hours each day.

TABLE 10.4

	Activity					
	A	B	C	D	E	F
Immediate predecessors	—	A	A	—	B, C	D, E
Mode 1						
Duration (days)	2	3	5	3	2	1
Resource I required (hours/activity)	0	9	10	6	8	4
Resource II required (hours/activity)	5	6	5	9	6	3
Mode 2						
Duration (days)	1	2	4	2	1	1
Resource I required (hours/activity)	12	12	8	6	9	4
Resource II required (hours/activity)	7	8	16	12	5	3

10.4 Develop a resource plan and a schedule for the project "cleaning and resupplying a passenger plane between flight legs." Which resource is the bottleneck?

10.5 The precedence relations and crew size required to complete a project are given in Table 10.5. For example, activity E, which comes after activity C, requires 10 weeks for its completion by a crew of six people.

   a. Construct an early-start Gantt chart and identify the critical path.
   b. Calculate and chart the labor profile required to complete the project for both an early-start and a late-start schedule.
   c. Level the required labor as much as possible with the goal of completing the project within the time period specified in part (a).

TABLE 10.5

Activity	Immediate predecessors	Time (weeks)	Crew size
A	—	4	4
B	A	2	5
C	A	6	3
D	B	3	7
E	C	10	6
F	—	2	5
G	D	5	6
H	F	7	2
I	D, E, G	1	8
J	H	10	2

10.6 a. Referring to Exercise 10.5, assume that 10 people are assigned to work on the project until it is finished. In light of the following assumptions, schedule the project and calculate labor utilization:

   1. No activities are allowed to be interrupted.
   2. The crew size that performs an activity cannot be reduced, but it is possible to increase the project's completion time.
   3. It is impossible to change the network.
   4. It is not possible to increase the size of the crew and reduce the time to complete an activity. The durations stated in the table are the lower bounds; extra resources will just be wasted.

   b. Repeat part (a) now assuming that you can reduce the crew size and increase its duration (the number of person-weeks required for each activity is constant).
   c. Repeat part (b) now assuming that you may interrupt each activity before it is completed and reschedule the remaining tasks at a later time.

10.7 The required labor profile for Exercise 10.5 is not of constant rate but resembles a symmetric trapezoid, with the peak lasting 1 week. As an example, consider activity G. Because a crew of six must work for a period of 5 weeks to complete this activity, a total of 30 personweeks is required. To calculate the labor requirement during the peak period, assuming a trapezoid profile, one should substitute the proper values into the following equation.

$$\text{lbrq} = \text{peak} \times \left(\frac{\text{dur}}{2} + 0.5 \right)$$

where lbrq = total labor required to perform the activity

peak = peak labor required during the one week peak time

dur = activity duration

Solving the equation for activity G, we obtain

$$\text{peak} = \frac{\text{lbrq}}{(\text{dur}/2) + 0.5} = \frac{30}{5/2 + 0.5} = 10$$

That is, during the 1-week peak period, there is need for a crew of 10 employees. Moreover, the required labor profile for the first 2 weeks is linear starting from 0 and ending at 10. The labor profile for the last 2 weeks is in the opposite direction; it starts at 10 and ends at 0 at the end of the fifth week. Assuming a symmetric trapezoid profile for each activity, generate an early-start resource profile for the project.

10.8 A trapezoid profile is a common shape used to describe labor requirements over time. Assuming that the permanent crew size is equal to the peak requirement, develop a model to calculate the crew utilization for an activity as a function of the peak duration. In so doing, assume that each activity i should be completed within a prespecified duration, say D_i days, and requires L_i labor-days.

10.9 A second project, identical to the one described in Exercise 10.5, is planned to start 1 week after the first. That is, the company intends to work on the two projects at the same time.
   a. Generate the early-start resource profile for the two projects.
   b. Schedule the two projects so that the required labor profile will be as level as possible.
   c. Discuss the significance of the differences observed in the schedules found in parts (a) and (b).

10.10 The following data concern an activity that has to be performed as part of a project:

Expected duration (days)	10
Standard deviation of the duration	2
Expected labor-days	30
Standard deviation of labor-days	3

   a. What is the probability that completing the activity on time will require at least a 10% addition to the expected labor-days?
   b. A crew of three workers is assigned to this activity. What is the probability that it will be completed in fewer than 11 days?

State your assumptions for both parts.

10.11 Suppose that in Exercise 9.16 personnel requirements are specified for the various activities in projects (a) and (b) as shown in Table 10.6.

   a. Draw the early-start Gantt chart for projects (a) and (b), and plot the required number of workers as a function of time.
   b. Level the resources for projects (a) and (b) as much as possible without extending their durations. Plot the corresponding manpower requirements over time.

TABLE 10.6

	Activity (i, j)	Number of workers	Activity (i, j)	Number of workers
Project (a):	(1, 2)	5	(3, 6)	9
	(1, 4)	4	(4, 6)	1
	(1, 5)	3	(4, 7)	10
	(2, 3)	1	(5, 6)	4
	(2, 5)	2	(5, 7)	5
	(2, 6)	3	(6, 7)	2
	(3, 4)	7		
Project (b):	(1, 2)	1	(3, 7)	9
	(1, 3)	2	(4, 5)	8
	(1, 4)	5	(4, 7)	7
	(1, 6)	3	(5, 6)	2
	(2, 3)	1	(5, 7)	5
	(2, 5)	4	(6, 7)	3
	(3, 4)	10		

10.12 Table 10.7 below gives the results of a critical path analysis; Table 10.8 lists worker requirements for each of the project's activities.

a. Draw the precedence graph for the project.
b. Draw the Gantt charts for the early- and late-start schedules. What is the maximum number of workers required?
c. Draw the resource requirement profiles for the early- and late-start schedules.

TABLE 10.7

Activity (i, j)	Duration, L_{ij}	Earliest Start, ES_{ij}	Earliest Finish, EF_{ij}	Latest Start, LS_{ij}	Latest Finish, LF_{ij}	Total slack, TS_{ij}	Free slack, FS_{ij}
(0, 1)	2	0	2	2	4	2	0
(0, 2)	3	0	3	0	3	0	0
(1, 3)	2	2	4	4	6	2	2
(2, 3)	3	3	6	3	6	0	0
(2, 4)	2	3	5	4	6	1	1
(3, 4)	0	6	6	6	6	0	0
(3, 5)	3	6	9	10	13	4	4
(3, 6)	2	6	8	17	19	11	11
(4, 5)	7	6	13	6	13	0	0
(4, 6)	5	6	11	14	19	8	8
(5, 6)	6	13	19	13	19	0	0

TABLE 10.8

Activity	Number of workers	Activity	Number of workers
(0, 1)	0	(3, 5)	2
(0, 2)	5	(3, 6)	1
(1, 3)	0	(4, 5)	2
(2, 3)	7	(4, 6)	5
(2, 4)	3	(5, 6)	6

d. Try to level the resource requirements (workers needed) as much as possible by applying the leveling procedure discussed in the text. [Note that activities (0, 1) and (1, 3) require no manual labor, which is indicated by assigning zero workers to each activity. As a result, the scheduling of (0, 1) and (1, 3) can be made independent of the resource leveling procedure.]

e. Suppose that activities (0, 1) and (1, 3) require eight and two workers, respectively. Perform resource leveling and redraw the Gantt chart and profile graph.

10.13 A project has 11 activities that can be accomplished either by one person working alone or by several people working together. The activities, precedence constraints, and time estimates are given in Table 10.9. Suppose that you have up to five people who can be assigned on any given day. A person must work full days on each activity, but the number of people working on an activity can vary from day to day.

a. Prepare an AOA network diagram, and calculate the critical path, total slacks, and free slacks assuming that one person (independently) is working on each task.

b. Prepare an early-start Gantt chart.

c. Prepare a daily assignment sheet for personnel with the goal of finishing the project in the minimum amount of time.

d. Prepare a daily assignment sheet to "best" balance the workforce assigned to the project.

e. By how many days could the project be compressed if unlimited personnel resources were available?

TABLE 10.9

Activity	Immediate predecessors	Person-days required
A	—	10
B	A	8
C	A	5
D	B	6
E	D	8
F	C	7
G	E, F	4
H	F	2
I	F	3
J	H, I	3
K	J, G	2

BIBLIOGRAPHY

Resource Allocation and Leveling

Boctor, F. F., "Some Efficient Multi-heuristic Procedures for Resource-Constrained Project Scheduling," *European Journal of Operational Research*, Vol. 49, pp. 3–13, 1990.

Christofides, N., R. Alvarex-Valdes and J. M. Tamarit, "Project Scheduling with Resource Constraints: A Branch and Bound Approach," *European Journal of Operational Research*, Vol. 29, pp. 262–273, 1987.

Demeulemeester, E. and W. S. Herroelen, "New Benchmark Results for the Resource Constrained Project Scheduling Problem," *Management Science*, Vol. 43, pp. 1485–1492 (1997).

De Reyck, B. and W. S. Herroelen, "A Branch-and-Bound Procedure for the Resource-Constrained Project Scheduling Problem with Generalized Precedence Relations," *European Journal of Operational Research*, Vol. 111, pp. 125–174, 1998.

Drexel, A., "Scheduling of Project Networks by Job Assignment," *Management Science*, Vol. 37, No. 12, pp. 1590–1602, 1991.

Goldratt, E. M., *Critical Chain*, North River Press Publishing, Great Barrington, MA, 1997.

Herroelen, W. S., E. Demeulemeester and B. De Reyck, "A Classification Scheme for Project Scheduling Problems," in J. Weglarz (Editor), *Handbook on Recent Advances in Project Scheduling*, pp. 1–26, Kluwer Academic Publishers, Dordrecht, The Netherlands, 1999.

Herroelen, W. S. and R. Leus, "On the Merits and Pitfalls of Critical Chain Scheduling," *Journal of Operations Management*, Vol. 19, No. 5, pp. 559–577, 2001.

Icmeli, O. and S. S. Erengüç, "A Branch-and-Bound Procedure for the Resource-Constrained Project Scheduling Problem with Discounted Cash Flows," *Management Science*, Vol. 42, No. 10, pp. 1395–1408, 1996.

Khattab, M. and F. Choobineh, "A New Heuristic for Project Scheduling with a Single Resource Constraint," *Computers & Industrial Engineering*, Vol. 20, No. 3, pp. 381–387, 1991.

Özdamar, L. and G. Ulusoy, "A Survey on the Resource-Constrained Project Scheduling Problem," *IIE Transactions on Scheduling & Logistics*, Vol. 27, No. 5, pp. 574–586, 1995.

Patterson, J. H., R. Slowinski, F. B. Talbot and J. Weglarz, "An Algorithm for a General Class of Precedence and Resource Constrained Scheduling Problems," in R. Slowinski and J. Weglarz (Editors), *Advances in Project Scheduling*, pp. 3–28, Elsevier, Amsterdam, 1989.

Patterson, J. H., F. B. Talbot, R. Slowinski and J. Weglarz, "Computational Experience with a Backtracking Algorithm for Solving a General Class of Precedence and Resource-Constrained Scheduling Problems," *European Journal of Operational Research*, Vol. 49, pp. 68–79, 1990.

Shtub, A., "The Integration of CPM and Material Management in Project Management," *Construction Management and Economics*, Vol. 6, pp. 261–272, 1988.

Slowinski, R. and J. Weglarz (Editors), *Advances in Project Scheduling*, Elsevier, Amsterdam, 1989.

Tavares, V. L., "A Multi-stage Non-deterministic Model for Project Scheduling under Resources Constraints," *European Journal of Operational Research*, Vol. 49, pp. 92–101, 1990.

Ulusoy, G. and L. Ozdamar, "Heuristic Performance and Network/Resource Characteristics in Resource-Constrained Project Scheduling," *Journal of the Operational Research Society*, Vol. 40, No. 12, pp. 1145–1152, 1989.

Multiple Projects

Dean, B. V., D. R. Denzler and J. J. Watkins, "Multiproject Staff Scheduling with Variable Resource Constraints," *IEEE Transactions on Engineering Management*, Vol. 39, No. 1, pp. 59–72, 1992.

Deckro, R. F., E. P. Winkofsky, J. E. Hebert and R. Gagnon, "A Decomposition Approach to Multi-project Scheduling," *European Journal of Operational Research*, Vol. 51, No. 1, pp. 110–118, 1991.

Kim, S. O. and M. J. Schniederjans, "Heuristics Framework for the Resource Constrained Multi-project Scheduling Problem," *Computers & Operations Research*, Vol. 16, No. 6, pp. 541–556, 1989.

Shtub, A., "Scheduling of Programs with Repetitive Projects," *Project Management Journal*, Vol. 22, No. 4, pp. 49–53, 1991.

Shtub, A., L. J. LeBlanc and Z. Cai, "Scheduling Programs with Repetitive Projects: A Comparison of Simulated Annealing, a Genetic and Pair-Wise Swap Algorithm," *European Journal of Operational Research*, Vol. 88, No. 1, pp. 124–138, 1996.

Shtub, A. and T. Raz, "Optimal Segmentation of Projects—Schedule and Cost Considerations," *European Journal of Operational Research*, Vol. 95, No. 2, pp. 278–283, 1996.

Shtub, A., "Project Segmentation—A Tool for Project Management," *International Journal of Project Management*, Vol. 15, No. 1, pp. 15–19, 1997.

Weglarz, J., "Project Scheduling with Continuously-Divisible Double Constrained Resources," *Management Science*, Vol. 27, No. 9, pp. 1040–1053, 1981.

Appendix 10A

Estimating Peak Resource Requirements

Overall resource requirements are estimated in the initial stage of a project's life cycle, even before there is a commitment to undertake the project. When responding to a request for proposals or pitching a new idea to management, rough estimates must be included in the presentation. After the project has been approved, there is a need for more accurate planning. At this point, a usage profile is developed for each resource. For example, an aggregate estimate may specify that a certain design activity or work package requires 50 person-months over a 10-month period. With this information, the usage profile over the activity's duration can be developed. If one assumes a constant rate of depletion, then there is a need for a permanent crew of 50/10 = 5 workers. However, constant usage is rarely the case. Labor requirements typically increase gradually until they hit a peak, remain at the peak for some time, and then decrease back to zero. This pattern is represented by the trapezoid in Fig. 10.A1.

Continuing with the example, assume that the manager responsible for the foregoing activity estimates that it will take 3 months to reach the peak usage rate and that the decline back to zero will take 2 months. The total labor required is equal to the area under the trapezoid; that is,

$$\text{TOT} = \frac{P \times a}{2} + P \times b + \frac{P \times c}{2}$$

where

TOT = total labor (person-months) required

P = peak person-months per month

a = time taken to reach peak usage

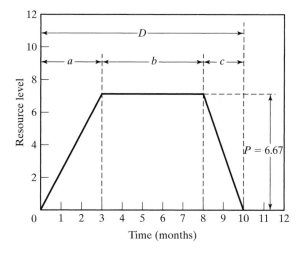

Figure 10.A1   Required labor profile with a trapezoidal pattern.

b = length of time that resource level is at its peak

c = time taken to reduce the resource level from its peak back to zero

Rearranging terms gives

$$P = \frac{\text{TOT}}{\dfrac{a}{2} + b + \dfrac{c}{2}}$$

Thus, knowing the total labor required for an activity, TOT, the duration (D) of the activity D, and the shape of the labor profile, it is possible to estimate peak labor requirements. To demonstrate the calculations for the trapezoidal case, let TOT = 50 person-months, D = 10 months, a = 3 months, and c = 2 months. We can now determine b, the length of the peak period, as follows:

$$b = D - (a + c) = 10 - (3 + 2) = 5 \text{ months}$$

so

$$P = \frac{50}{\dfrac{3}{2} + 5 + \dfrac{2}{2}} = 6.67 \text{ workers/month}$$

That is, during the 5 peak months, there will be a need for 6.67 workers every month.

Chapter 11

Project Budget

11.1 INTRODUCTION

An organization's budget (usually expressed in dollars) represents management's long-range, midrange, and short-range plans. The budget should contain a statement of prospective investments, management goals, resources necessary to achieve those goals, and a timetable. Its structure should match that of the organization. In particular, a functional structure shows an organization's investments and expenditures grouped three ways: (1) development of new products (engineering), (2) production of existing products (manufacturing), and (3) campaigns for new or existing products (advertising, marketing). A project-oriented structure, conversely, reveals the organization's planned costs and expected revenues for each project, whereas a matrix structure partially supports both the functional and project-based components of an organization's budget. This is explained presently.

The budget of any specific project is tied to the sponsoring organization's budget. In some organizations, a project budget includes only expenditures (e.g., government agencies such as the Department of Defense are engaged in projects strictly as clients). In other organizations, the project budget includes both income and expenditures (e.g., contractors whose expenditures for labor, materials, and subcontracting are covered by their clients). When an organization is involved in several projects, the budgets of these projects are coordinated centrally. It is important to combine the budget of each project to avoid the risk of steering the organization into financial difficulties. This issue should be considered when selecting new projects because it provides a hard constraint in the decision-making process.

In a matrix organization, the budget links the functional units to the projects. On a specific project, the cost of resources invested by the functional unit is charged against the project's budget. This link is one of the interfaces between the functional structure and the project aspect of the matrix organization. In this chapter, we discuss the principles used in developing, presenting, and using the budget in a project environment. The major focus is on the relationship between the organizational and the individual budgets of each project undertaken.

A well-designed budget is an efficient communication channel for management. Through this instrument, managers (at all levels) are advised of their organization's goals and the resources allocated to their units. A detailed budget defines expected costs and expenditures, thus setting the framework of constraints within which each manager is expected to operate. These constraints represent organizational policy and goals. The well-structured budget is a yardstick that can be used to measure the performance of organizational units and their managers. Managers who participate in the budget development process commit themselves, their subordinates, and their unit's resources to the goals specified in the budget as well as the constraints implied by the negotiated funding levels. A successful manager is one who can achieve the budget goals with the resources allocated to his or her project; that is, one who can successfully execute the organization's policy. The well-structured budget is also a useful tool for identifying deviations from plans, the magnitude of these deviations, and their source. Therefore, it is part of the baseline for cost and schedule control systems. In addition, the budget's structure depends on the organizational structure, whereas its level of detail depends on the planning horizon for which it was prepared.

The *long-range*, or *strategic*, budget defines an aggregate level of activity for the organization over a period of several months to several years. For example, in a functional organization, this budget might define a goal of selling 100,000 units in the coming year with a 15% increase in sales in each of the following 4 years. The expected marketing cost in the budget is $50,000 for the first year with 8% increases in each subsequent year. In an organization with a project structure, the strategic budget will define the total budget for each project. For example, assume that for project X, the design stage has a 1-year completion due date and a $500,000 budget. A critical design review is scheduled accordingly. In 2 years, a prototype will be tested in the lab. The associated budget is $600,000. The final product will be tested in the third year for a cost of $550,000. The long-range budget is typically updated annually.

By using the budgeting process, management establishes long-range goals, schedules to achieve these goals, and the available resources. When the actual expenditures, income and results are compared to the original budget, management can monitor the organization's performance. Also, when necessary, management can change the budget to control both goal setting and resource allocation.

A *midrange*, or *tactical*, budget is a detailed presentation of the long-range budget and covers 12 to 24 months. It is updated quarterly. The tasks to be performed within each work package (WP) provide the basis of the entries. A rolling planning horizon is used so that every time (e.g., quarterly) the midrange budget is updated, a budget for the ensuing quarter is added while the budget for the recently completed quarter is deleted. The tactical budget details the expected monthly costs of resources, including labor and materials, as well as overhead. In a functional organization, the tactical budget projects the expected costs and revenues of each product family and the expected costs of each functional department.

A *short-range*, or *operational*, budget lists specific activities, the resources assigned to them and their costs. This budget spans a period up to 1 year and covers the detailed costs of resources (e.g., labor and material) required to perform each activity. For example, the short-range budget of a project might specify that the design of a prototype be done on a $10,000 computer-aided design system that runs on a $5,000 piece of equipment. Lead times are 3 and 2 weeks, respectively, for the hardware and software. Installation starts as soon as both items are delivered. The expected cost of installation and training is $2,000. This short-term (operational) budget relates project costs to project activities through the work breakdown structure (WBS), organizational breakdown structure (OBS), and the project's lower-level network model.

A project's budget contains several dimensions. The first relates to the tasks and activities to be performed. The primary effort is to establish the relationship among cost, resources, and time for scheduled tasks and activities. The second dimension is based on the OBS. Each task is assigned to an organizational unit in the OBS. The third dimension is the WBS. Each task is assigned to a WBS element in the lowest level of the hierarchy. Over time, however, they are distributed among the WBS elements at their corresponding levels.

As each organization develops its own budgeting procedures, several points can help make the budget an efficient vehicle for planning, as well as a standard channel of communication:

- The budget should present management's objectives stated in terms of measurable outputs: for example, the successful completion of a test or the development of a new software module. These outputs should be presented with their budgetary constraints. Thus, the budget presents available resources and the goals to be achieved using these resources. The presentation can be based on a functional structure, a project's organizational structure, or a combination of the two if a matrix structure is assumed.

- The budget should be presented quantitatively (e.g., in monetary units or sometimes in person-hours) as a function of time. The presentation should facilitate a periodic and cumulative comparison between actual and planned performance levels.

- The budget should be divided into long-range (strategic), midrange (tactical), and short-range (operational) levels. Each level should contain a detailed breakdown of the budget at the preceding level for the planning horizon. A rolling horizon approach should be used in developing the budgets of new periods and in updating the budgets of previous periods.

A management reserve may be included at strategic and tactical levels. This reserve acts as a buffer against uncertainty and should be consumed by transforming it into specific line items in the mid- and short-range budgets.

11.2 PROJECT BUDGET AND ORGANIZATIONAL GOALS

The budget of an organization reflects management's goals. These goals and organizational constraints determine decisions on project selection, resource allocation, modes of operation, and the desired rate of progress for each project. The budget depends on the perceived organizational mission and the sector to which the organization belongs (private, government, or nonprofit). It also depends on internal and external environmental factors. The following are seven common factors that affect project selection and budget structure:

1. *Competition.* Most organizations in the private sector need a competitive edge to survive. External challenges force continued improvement within the organization and occur in various ways, such as the following:

   - *Time-based competition.* Spurs the implementation of concurrent engineering with the goal of shortening new product development cycles and improving customer service. It is also instrumental in reducing customer lead times. A major emphasis is on achieving project milestones and goals in a timely manner.
   - *Cost-based competition.* In a cost-based environment, the project budget includes smaller, tightly controlled reserves; an effort is made to perform activities in the normal (least expensive) mode and to trim overhead cost.
   - *Quality-based competition.* Quality management including quality planning, quality assurance, and quality control is emphasized.

2. *Profit.* The ability to generate profits in the short and long run is essential to most organizations in the private sector. Selection decisions are frequently based on a project's expected profits. A project can be tentatively evaluated by any of the techniques discussed in Chapter 3, including net present value (NPV), internal rate of return, and payback period.

3. *Cash flow.* The organizational cash flow is an aggregate of all routine activities combined with other ongoing projects. When unexpected cash flow problems arise, projects that generate quick cash become high-priority items in the budget allocation process. In some cases, an organization may prefer projects that begin to produce revenues immediately, albeit small, rather than projects that generate a slow cash flow and higher profits in the distant future. In the short run, to improve the cash position of the firm, activities that generate income (e.g., payment milestones) may be budgeted earlier than other activities that have the same or an even shorter slack.

4. *Risk.* Uncertainty and risk may influence budgetary decisions. An organization that tries to avoid the risk of delays may budget its projects according to an early-start schedule. This, in turn, may lead to early expenditures and cash flow problems. Organizations that try to minimize the risk of cost overruns sometimes budget each activity at its lowest level (normal mode of operation). If longer activity duration occurs, then the lowered risk of a cost overrun can translate into an increased risk of delays. The selection of new projects may also be influenced by risk assessment. In this case, the project's portfolio, to which the organization is committed, is affected by the organization's perceived risk level.

5. *Technological ability.* Some organizations in the public sector are willing to budget high-tech projects to acquire new, more advanced technologies. In the private sector (including such industries as computers, microelectronics, nanotechnology,

genetic engineering, and aerospace), an organization's technological ability is an important aspect of its competitive edge. To outdistance competitors, technologically advanced projects are selected and budgeted to ensure progress.

6. *Resources.* Each project's budget is a monetary representation of the value of resources allocated to perform that project. If adequate resources are not available, then little can be accomplished, so whatever effort is expended will have negligible effect. Therefore, it is important to classify and track resources according to their availability on the basis of the detailed classification scheme presented in Chapter 10. In the long- and midrange budgets, organizational plans for acquiring new resources are put forth. The short-range budget addresses plans to use these resources. In preparatory stages of a project, it is important to remember that some resources may not be available even if budgeted adequately. Therefore, in preparing the budget, resource availability (both internal and external to the organization) and resource lead time needs to be coordinated with the planned costs of these resources.

7. *Perceived needs.* Project selection and budgeting depend largely on organizational goals. In the government sector, especially in defense, perceived needs (or new threats) are a driving force. Cost and risk considerations might be secondary when national security or public health is considered.

These seven factors link organizational goals and the internal and external aspects of the operational environment with each project's budget. Clearly, developing an organizational budget and a budget for each project requires a coordinated effort among management, accounting, marketing, and the other functional areas. This issue is the subject of the following section.

11.3 PREPARING THE BUDGET

Budget preparation is the process by which organizational goals are translated into a plan that specifies the allocated resources, the selected processes, and the desired schedule for achieving these goals. The budget must integrate information and objectives from all functional areas of the organization with information and objectives from the various project leaders. Although upper management sets the long-range (strategic) objectives, lower-level management is responsible for establishing the detailed (operational) plans and must clearly articulate and understand the short-range objectives before executing the budget.

In a project or a matrix organization, lower-level managers, who are concerned primarily with the daily operations, should be most knowledgeable in the technical details regarding the most appropriate way to perform each project. They should also be up to date on expected activity durations and costs. Thus, it is important to integrate upper-level management inputs with the knowledge of the functional and project managers.

The organizational budget consists of both ongoing activities, such as the production and marketing of existing products, and one-time efforts or projects. It is easier to budget ongoing activities, because past budgets for these activities can serve as a reference point for planning. By adjusting for anticipated demand, the expected inflation rate, and the effect of learning, the financial planners can develop the new budget based on past information. Project budgeting is more difficult, though, because previous budgets are often unavailable. Cost estimation (Chapter 4), the project schedule (Chapter 9), and the effect of resource availability (Chapter 10) should be considered in developing the project budget.

The building blocks of the project's budget are the WPs in which tasks performed on the lowest-level WBS elements are assigned to organizational units at the lowest level of the OBS. A budget is developed for each WP. Budgets are then developed for each WBS element at each level in the hierarchy and for each organizational unit at each OBS level.

Thus, the process of integrating single-project budgets and the budgets of ongoing activities into an acceptable organizational budget requires planning and coordination. The final budget should embody sound, workable programs for each functional area and coordinate the efforts of functional units and project managers to achieve their goals. Three procedures are commonly used in budgeting: the top-down approach, the bottom-up approach, and the iterative-mixed approach.

11.3.1 Top-Down Budgeting

The trigger for the budgeting process is the strategic long-range plan that is developed by top management on the basis of its experience and perception of the organization's goals and constraints. The long-range plan is then passed to the functional unit managers and the project managers, who develop the tactical (midrange) and detailed operational (short-range) budgets, respectively.

One problem with top-down budgeting is the translation of long-range budgets into short-range budgets. The former can be spread in any number of ways over the budgets of projects and functional units. The best combination that yields the most efficient schedule for each of the projects involved is not easy to construct given the constraints imposed by the long-range budget. Therefore, the question is how to schedule projects in a "suboptimal way" to meet the strategic goals. This suboptimality is a result of top management's limited knowledge of the specifics of each project, task, and activity—knowledge that is unavailable when preparing the long-range budget using the top-down approach.

A second problem with this approach is the competition for funds among lower-level managers who try to secure adequate funding for their operations, but because top management fixes the total budget, the only way for lower-level managers to gain an advantage is to undercut their counterparts. Such a situation does not promote cooperation and understanding and does not guarantee the optimal allocation of funds. Table 11.1 illustrates the top-down budgeting process.

11.3.2 Bottom-up Budgeting

To overcome the disaggregation problem of top-down budgeting, many organizations adopt an approach that begins at the project manager level. Each project manager is asked to prepare a budget proposal that supports efficient and on-schedule project execution. On the basis of this input, functional managers prepare the budgets for their units, considering the resources required in each period. Finally, top management streamlines and integrates the individual project and functional unit budgets into a strategic long-range organizational budget.

TABLE 11.1   The Top-Down Approach to Budget Preparation

Step	Organizational level	Prepared budget at each step
1	Top management	Strategic budget based on organizational goals, constraints, and policies
2	Functional management	Tactical budget for each functional unit
3	Project managers	Detailed budgets for each project, including the cost of labor, material, subcontracting, overhead, etc.

The advantages of this approach are the clear flow of information and the use of detailed data available at the project management level as the basic source of cost, schedule, and resource requirement information. The disadvantage is that top management has limited influence over the budgeting process, because the functional and project managers prepare most of the short- and midrange budgets. Nevertheless, top management can influence the outcome by issuing a statement to the lower-level managers as they prepare the short- and midrange budgets that outlines organizational policies and goals. Also, top management can steer the budgeting process by selecting projects based on its perception of organizational needs and goals. Table 11.2 illustrates the bottom-up budgeting process.

As stated, the major problem with the bottom-up approach is the reduced level of control that it offers top management. Because the aggregate budget is developed on the basis of input obtained from the project and functional managers, the gap between strategic and operational objectives may be wide. This creates a need to fine-tune the organizational budget. The process is carried out iteratively through adjustment and review until a satisfactory compromise is achieved.

TABLE 11.2   Bottom-up Approach to Budget Preparation

Step	Organizational level	Budget prepared at each step
1	Top management	Setting goals and selection of projects (a framework for budget)
2	Project management	Detailed budget proposals for projects including costs of material, labor, subcontracting, etc.
3	Functional management	Midrange budget for each functional unit
4	Top management	Adjustments and approval of the aggregate long-range budget resulting from the process

11.3.3 Iterative Budgeting

The two budgeting approaches presented above are "pure" in that the process flows in one direction, either bottom-up or top-down. Some of the shortcomings of these approaches can be eliminated by combining the information flows in an iterative manner. A typical iterative approach starts with top management setting a budget framework for each year in its strategic plan. This framework then directs the selection of new projects and serves as a guideline for project managers as they prepare their budgets. Detailed project budgets are aggregated into functional unit budgets and, finally, into an organizational budget that top management reviews and, if necessary, modifies. Based on the approved budget, functional units and project managers modify their respective budgets. The process may undergo several iterations until convergence takes place at the strategic, tactical, and operational levels.

This process is based on input from all levels of management and usually produces better coordination between the different budgets (functional versus project and long-range versus short- and midrange). Major disadvantages center on the relatively long duration needed for agreement and the excessive use of management time.

The process of adjusting a project budget to the framework of the organizational budget is based on the internal relationship among schedule, resources, and cost. This relationship can be exploited in several ways, as explained next.

11.4 TECHNIQUES FOR MANAGING THE BUDGET

The project budget represents scheduled expenditures and scheduled revenue as a function of time. The simplest approach to budgeting is to estimate the expected costs and income associated with each activity, task, and milestone. Based on the project schedule, these costs are assigned specific dates and a budget is generated; however, it may be only a partial budget because some of the indirect costs are often not included at the preliminary stage. Typical indirect costs are those for management, facility operations, and quality control and are not always related to specific activities. Adding them results in a more realistic estimate. The product of this effort can serve as the basis for developing a detailed, comprehensive financial plan for each project. The development of project budgets based on schedule and resource considerations is the first step in an iterative approach. The next step is to integrate the individual project budgets into an acceptable organizational budget.

11.4.1 Slack Management

One approach to integrating individual project budgets is to change activity timing and the associated expenditure or income, an approach known as slack management. Noncritical activities that have free slack are usually the first candidates for this type of rescheduling. Activities with total slack are the next choices, and the final choices are critical activities that can be delayed only at the cost of delays in project completion time. Rescheduling activities makes the integration of single-project budgets into an acceptable organizational budget easier.

To illustrate the relationship between a project's cash flow and its schedule, let us return to the example project. The length of the critical path in the project is 22 weeks.

TABLE 11.3   Project Activity Durations and Costs

Activity	Duration (weeks)	Cost ($1,000)
A	5	1.5
B	3	3.0
C	8	3.3
D	7	4.2
E	7	5.7
F	4	6.1
G	5	7.2
		31.0

Critical activities are A, C, F and G, whereas activities B, E and D have either free or total slack that can be used for budget planning. Table 11.3 depicts the costs and durations of the project's activities.

An early-start schedule results in relatively high expenditures in the project's earlier stages, whereas a late-start schedule results in relatively high expenditures in the later stages. Table 11.4 presents the project's cash flow for the early-start schedule assuming,

TABLE 11.4   Cash Flow of an Early Start Schedule

	Activity							Weekly	Cumulative
Week	A	B	C	D	E	F	G	cost, $	cost, $
1	300	1000			814.3			2,114	2,114
2	300	1000			814.3			2,114	4,229
3	300	1000			814.3			2,114	6,343
4	300				814.3			1,114	7,457
5	300				814.3			1,114	8,571
6			412.5	600	814.3			1,827	10,398
7			412.5	600	814.3			827	12,225
8			412.5	600				1,013	13,238
9			412.5	600				1,013	14,250
10			412.5	600				1,013	15,263
11			412.5	600				1,013	16,275
12			412.5	600				1,013	17,288
13			412.5					412	17,700
14						1,525		1,525	19,225
15						1,525		1,525	20,750
16						1,525		1,525	22,275
17						1,525		1,525	23,800
18							1,440	1,440	25,240
19							1,440	1,440	26,680
20							1,440	1,440	28,120
21							1,440	1,440	29,560
22							1,440	1,440	31,000
Total	1,500	3,000	3,300	4,200	5,700	6,100	7,200	31,000	

TABLE 11.5   Cash Flow of the Late Start Schedule

				Activity					Weekly cost, $	Cumulative cost, $
Week	A	B	C	D	E	F	G			
1	300								300	300
2	300								300	600
3	300	1000							1,300	1,900
4	300	1000							1,300	3,200
5	300	1000							1,300	4,500
6			412.5						412	4,913
7			412.5	600	814.3				1,827	6,739
8			412.5	600	814.3				1,827	8,566
9			412.5	600	814.3				1,827	10,393
10			412.5	600	814.3				1,827	12,220
11			412.5	600	814.3				1,827	14,046
12			412.5	600	814.3				1,827	15,873
13			412.5	600	814.3				1,827	17,700
14						1,525			1,525	19,225
15						1,525			1,525	20,750
16						1,525			1,525	22,275
17						1,525			1,525	23,800
18							1,440		1,440	25,240
19							1,440		1,440	26,680
20							1,440		1,440	28,120
21							1,440		1,440	29,560
22							1,440		1,440	31,000
Total	1,500	3,000	3,300	4,200	5,700	6,100	7,200		31,000	

for budgeting purposes, that the cost of each activity is evenly distributed throughout its duration. Table 11.5 enumerates the cash flow of the project for the late-start case.

Figure 11.1 depicts the cash flows for the early- and late-start schedules; Fig. 11.2 depicts their cumulative cash flows. From Fig. 11.2, we see that if the strategic long-range organizational budget allocates only $4,913 to the project for weeks 1 through 5, then during this period, only a late-start schedule is feasible. Also, increasing the project's budget over $10,398 for the first 5 weeks makes an early-start schedule feasible. Any budget in-between will force a delay of noncritical activities.

The choice between an early- and a late-start schedule affects the risk level associated with the project's on-time completion. Using a late-start schedule means that all of the activities are started as late as possible without any slack to buffer against uncertainty, increasing the probability of delays. Therefore, the budgeting process should resolve the conflict between a project budget that supports the organizational budgeting requirements versus the higher risk of a schedule overrun.

Projects with large numbers of activities tend to have a large choice of schedules with associated budgets. For example, in Fig. 11.2, any schedule that falls between the early- and late-start budget lines would be feasible from the point of view of meeting the critical milestones on time.

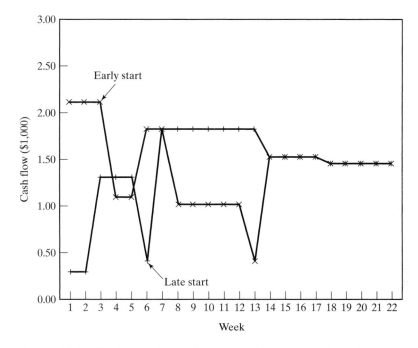

Figure 11.1 Cash flow for early-start and late-start schedules.

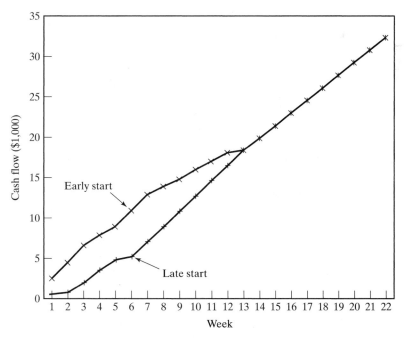

Figure 11.2 Cumulative cash flow for early-start and late-star schedules.

11.4.2 Crashing

In addition to using slack management as part of the budgeting process, another option may be available: change the mode and duration of an activity by changing the technologies used to perform it and add or delete the necessary resources. So far we have assumed that each activity is performed in the most economical way, which, in Chapter 10, was defined as the normal mode. That is, the combination of resources assigned to each activity was selected to minimize the cost of completing it. However, in many cases, it is possible to reduce an activity's duration by spending more money. This implies that tradeoffs exist between the minimum cost–longest duration (normal time–normal cost) option at one extreme and any other option that reduces an activity's duration at a higher cost.

This is the essence of the original version of the critical path method (CPM), which places equal emphasis on time and cost. The emphasis is achieved by constructing a time–cost curve for each activity, such as the one shown in Fig. 11.3. This curve plots the relationship between the direct cost for the activity and its resulting duration. In its simplest form, the plot is typically based on two points: the *normal* point and the *crash* point. The former gives the cost and time involved when the activity is performed in the normal way without extra resources, such as overtime, special materials, or improved equipment that could speed things up. By contrast, the crash point gives the time and cost when the activity is fully expedited; that is, no cost is spared to reduce its duration as much as possible. As an approximation, it is then assumed that all intermediate time–cost tradeoffs are possible and that they lie on the line segment between these two points (see the line segment in Fig. 11.3). Thus, the only estimates needed are the cost and time for normal and crash points.

Consider, for example, a manual painting operation that requires 4 days at $400 per day. With a special compressed airflow system, however, two workers can complete the job in 2 days for $1,000 per day. Thus, the activity can be performed in 4 days for

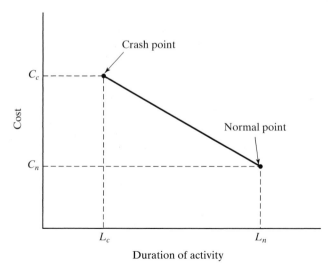

Figure 11.3   Typical time–cost tradeoff curve.

$400 \times 4 = \$1,600$ or in 2 days for $\$1,000 \times 2 = \$2,000$. The normal duration is associated with the lowest-cost option for the activity. This value is used in a CPM analysis and in the preparation of the initial budget.

More formally, the normal duration of an activity is the duration that minimizes the direct cost. In some instances, a schedule that is based on normal durations may produce high indirect costs, for example, when a project due date is given and a penalty is charged for completion after the due date. Even when the due date can initially be met by a normal schedule, uncertainty during the project execution may cause schedule overruns. The resultant penalties must be traded off with the cost of shortening the duration of some activities to minimize (or avoid completely) these late charges.

A similar situation occurs when a fixed overhead is charged for a project's duration. Rent for facilities would be such an example. In this case, management might consider shortening some activities to reduce the project's duration and hence save on indirect costs.

Crashing is the procedure whereby an activity's duration is shortened by adding resources and paying extra direct costs. A crashed program includes activities performed more quickly than they normally would be as a result of the allocation of additional resources. To plan a crashed program, management must decide which activities to crash and by how much. To illustrate this point, consider the crashing costs and durations list in Table 11.6 for the example project.

In Table 11.6, the normal duration and the normal cost of each activity are those used in the basic schedule. Each activity can be crashed at least once. Five of the activities (A, C, D, F, G) can be crashed twice, as the table shows.

It is possible to construct the relationship between the project's duration and its direct cost, starting with an all-normal schedule in which each activity is performed at its lowest direct cost and at a normal duration. To reduce the project's length, the critical path must be shortened. Thus, at each step, the critical paths are examined and the activity that is least expensive to crash is selected for crashing on each critical path. These activities are crashed, and the process continues with the new critical paths being examined. In case the activities are not crashed in the same amount of time, it is possible to use the cost of crashing per period as a measure of attractiveness to select candidates.

TABLE 11.6   Duration and Cost for Normal and Crashed Activities

	Normal		Crashing activity the first time		Crashing activity a second time	
Activity	Cost	Duration (weeks)	Additional cost	Duration (weeks)	Additional cost	Duration (weeks)
A	$1,500	5	$2,000	4	$1,000	3
B	$3,000	3	$2,000	2	—	—
C	$3,300	8	$2,000	7	$1,000	6
D	$4,200	7	$2,000	6	$2,000	5
E	$5,700	7	$1,000	6	—	—
F	$6,100	4	$1,000	3	$2,000	2
G	$7,200	5	$1,000	4	$1,000	3

To illustrate this heuristic process, consider the data in Table 11.6. The project's normal duration is 22 weeks, and the critical activities are A, C, F, G. Reducing the project's length requires crashing one critical activity. At this stage, the cost of crashing each critical activity is as follows:

Activity	Cost to crash
A	$2,000
C	$2,000
F	$1,000
G	$1,000

Activities F and G are the least expensive to crash. In particular, the cost of activity F crashed from 4 to 3 weeks is $7,100, as illustrated in Table 11.7. The first column in the table represents the project with a normal duration (22 weeks). The second column represents the project after crashing F from 4 to 3 weeks; the project's duration is now 21 weeks, and the crashed activity (F) is marked by an asterisk (*). The crashing procedure can continue until a 14-week span is obtained. At this point, two critical paths emerge: A-C-F-G, which lasts 14 weeks and contains no activities that can be crashed further; and B-D-F-G, which also lasts 14 weeks but contains two activities, B and D, that can be crashed for $2,000 and $3,000, respectively. Because the length of sequence A-C-F-G cannot be reduced, the project's minimum duration is 14 weeks. Table 11.7 summarizes the results.

Budgeting decisions are easier when the time–cost relationship for a project is known. The following example analyzes the tradeoff between direct and indirect costs. Suppose that a fixed overhead of $500 per week is charged for a project's duration. Furthermore, assume that the project is due in 18 weeks and that a penalty of $1,000 per week is imposed starting the 19th week. The budget problem in this case translates into a tradeoff between the cost of crashing and the overhead plus penalty. Table 11.8 summarizes these cost components, accompanied by the project's total costs as a function of its length. As we see, the minimum cost occurs at a project length of 19 weeks; that is, it is more economical to pay a $1,000 penalty and $500 in overhead for the 19th week than to crash activity F for $2,000.

The total project cost may not be the only criterion for budget planning. If, for example, customer satisfaction depends on project completion within 18 weeks, then the $500 savings should be evaluated against the customer goodwill that might be lost. Budgeting decisions should be based on this consideration.

Figure 11.4 graphically depicts the different cost components and the total cost of the project as a function of its duration. The crashing problem can be modeled as either a linear or a mixed-integer linear program, depending on whether a continuous tradeoff exists between an activity's duration and cost (as assumed in Fig. 11.3), or whether only certain combinations are possible. The formulation presented below reflects the latter

TABLE 11.7 Crashing the Project (Cost in $1,000, Duration in Weeks)

Activity	22 weeks Cost	22 weeks Dur	21 weeks Cost	21 weeks Dur	20 weeks Cost	20 weeks Dur	19 weeks Cost	19 weeks Dur	18 weeks Cost	18 weeks Dur	17 weeks Cost	17 weeks Dur	16 weeks Cost	16 weeks Dur	15 weeks Cost	15 weeks Dur	14 weeks Cost	14 weeks Dur
A	1.5	5	1.5	5	1.5	5	1.5	5	1.5	5	3.5*	4	4.5*	3	4.5	3	4.5	3
B	3.0	3	3.0	3	3.0	3	3.0	3	3.0	3	3.0	3	3.0	3	3.0	3	3.0	3
C	3.3	8	3.3	8	3.3	8	3.3	8	3.3	8	3.3	8	3.3	8	5.3*	7	5.3	6
D	4.2	7	4.2	7	4.2	7	4.2	7	4.2	7	4.2	7	4.2	7	4.2	7	6.2*	6
E	5.7	7	5.7	7	5.7	7	5.7	7	5.7	7	5.7	7	5.7	7	5.7	7	5.7	7
F	6.1	4	7.1*	3	7.1	3	7.1	3	9.1*	2	9.1	2	9.1	2	9.1	2	9.1	2
G	7.2	5	7.2	5	8.2*	3	9.2*	3	9.2	3	9.2	3	9.2	3	9.2	3	9.2	3
Total cost of activities	31		32		33		34		36		38		39		41		44	

* Crashed activity

TABLE 11.8   Project Costs as a Function of its Duration

Project length (weeks)	Direct cost of activities	Late completion penalty	Overhead cost	Total project cost
22	$31,000	$4,000	$11,000	$46,000
21	$32,000	$3,000	$10,500	$45,500
20	$33,000	$2,000	$10,000	$45,000
19	$34,000	$1,000	$9,500	$44,500
18	$36,000	0	$9,000	$45,000
17	$38,000	0	$8,500	$46,500
16	$39,000	0	$8,000	$47,000
15	$41,000	0	$7,500	$48,500
14	$44,000	0	$7,000	$51,000

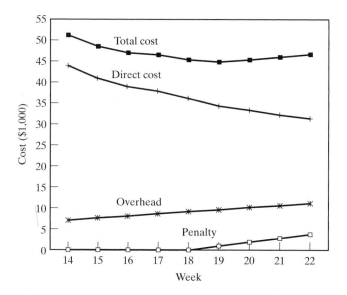

Figure 11.4   Example project cost as a function of its duration.

case, whereby only a finite number of time–cost combinations are available for each activity. Assuming an activities-on-arrow (AOA) network, the following notation is used:

A = set of activities

i = index for events on the AOA network model; $i \in N = \{1, \ldots, n\}$, where $i = 1$ is the unique "start" event that has no predecessors and $i = n$ is the unique "finish" event that has no successors

(i, j) = project activity that starts at event i and ends at event j; $(i, j) \in A$

k = index for a particular time–cost combination

$K(ij)$ = index set of possible time–cost combinations for activity (i, j)

L_{ijk} = duration of activity (i, j) when it is performed at time–cost combination k

C_{ijk} = direct cost of activity (i, j) if performed at time–cost combination k

C_o = overhead cost per period of time

Decision Variables

t_i = time event i takes place

y_{ijk} = (binary) equal to 1 if time–cost combination $k \in K(ij)$ is selected for activity (i, j); 0 otherwise

The problem of minimizing total cost is

$$\text{Minimize} \quad C_o t_n + \sum_{(i,j) \in A} \sum_{k \in K(ij)} C_{ijk} y_{ijk} \tag{11.1a}$$

$$\text{subject to} \quad t_j - t_i \geq \sum_{k \in K(ij)} L_{ijk} y_{ijk}, \qquad \text{for all } (i, j) \in A \tag{11.1b}$$

$$\sum_{k \in K(ij)} y_{ijk} = 1, \qquad \text{for all } (i, j) \in A \tag{11.1c}$$

$$t_1 = 0, \quad t_i \geq 0, \quad y_{ijk} = 0 \text{ or } 1, \quad \text{for all } i, j, k \tag{11.1d}$$

The objective function (11.1a) represents the project's total cost, which is composed of a direct and an indirect component. The first set of constraints (11.1b) maintains the precedence relations in the network; the second set (11.1c) ensures that each activity is performed at one of its time–cost combinations. Constraint (11.1d) defines the variables.

As an example of the model, consider the following project:

Activity (i, j)	Time–cost combination 1		Time–cost combination 2	
	Time (weeks)	Cost	Time (weeks)	Cost
(1, 2)	5	$100	3	$150
(1, 3)	4	$70	3	$100
(2, 4)	4	$200	3	$300
(3, 4)	6	$500	3	$900

The effect of the overhead cost per period (C_o) on the optimal schedule can be analyzed by solving (11.1) for the example and varying the value of C_o. The specific model for this example follows:

$$\text{Minimize} \quad C_o t_4 + 100 y_{121} + 150 y_{122} + 70 y_{131} + 100 y_{132} + 200 y_{241}$$
$$+ 300 y_{242} + 500 y_{341} + 900 y_{342}$$

subject to $\quad t_2 - t_1 \geq 5y_{121} + 3y_{122}$

$$t_3 - t_1 \geq 4y_{131} + 3y_{132}$$

$$t_4 - t_2 \geq 4y_{241} + 3y_{242}$$

$$t_4 - t_3 \geq 6y_{341} + 3y_{342}$$

$$y_{121} + y_{122} = 1$$

$$y_{131} + y_{132} = 1$$

$$y_{241} + y_{242} = 1$$

$$y_{341} + y_{342} = 1$$

$$t_1 = 0, \quad t_i \geq 0, \quad i = 2,\ldots,4$$

$$y_{ijk} = 0 \text{ or } 1 \text{ for } (i,j) \in A = \{(1,2),(1,3),(2,4),(3,4)\}, k = 1,2$$

Solving the model for different values of the overhead cost, C_o, gives the solutions presented in Table 11.9. The tradeoff between the overhead cost and the cost of crashing activities is clear from these results. It is not justified to crash any activity whose overhead cost is below \$20 per period. The first activity to be crashed is $(1,3)$, and it is the only one for a wide range of C_o values. Only when the overhead per period is between \$180 and \$190 is it justified to crash all four activities.

TABLE 11.9 Parametric Solution to Time–Cost Tradeoff Example (Cost in \$, Duration in Weeks)

Overhead cost, C_o	Activity (1,2) Cost	Activity (1,2) Duration	Activity (1,3) Cost	Activity (1,3) Duration	Activity (2,4) Cost	Activity (2,4) Duration	Activity (3,4) Cost	Activity (3,4) Duration	Project Cost	Project Duration
10	100	5	70	4	200	4	500	6	970	10
20	100	5	70	4	200	4	500	6	1,070	10
30	100	5	100	3	200	4	500	6	1,170	9
40	100	5	100	3	200	4	500	6	1,260	9
50	100	5	100	3	200	4	500	6	1,350	9
60	100	5	100	3	200	4	500	6	1,440	9
70	100	5	100	3	200	4	500	6	1,530	9
80	100	5	100	3	200	4	500	6	1,620	9
90	100	5	100	3	200	4	500	6	1,710	9
100	100	5	100	3	200	4	500	6	1,800	9
110	100	5	100	3	200	4	500	6	1,890	9
120	100	5	100	3	200	4	500	6	1,980	9
130	100	5	100	3	200	4	500	6	2,070	9
140	100	5	100	3	200	4	500	6	2,160	9
150	100	5	100	3	200	4	500	6	2,250	9
160	100	5	100	3	200	4	500	6	2,340	9
170	100	5	100	3	200	4	500	6	2,430	9
180	100	5	100	3	200	4	500	6	2,520	9
190	150	3	100	3	300	3	900	3	2,590	6
200	150	3	100	3	300	3	900	3	2,650	6

Budgeting decisions are influenced by external factors such as the time value of money. If the minimum acceptable rate of return is high, then the NPV of the project may become an important criterion in budgeting. The reference list at the end of the chapter contains several papers dealing with this subject. The intuitive approach to project budgeting under the NPV criterion is to delay activities that require a capital outlay and to start, as early as possible, activities that generate cash. Because some activities lead to customer payment (i.e., cash generation) but require a capital outlay, a tradeoff analysis is required to schedule these activities in the best possible way from the perspective of the budget.

11.4.3 PERT/Cost

Program evaluation and review technique (PERT)/cost is a cost accounting technique for achieving realistic cost estimates associated with activities and for providing an information system that allows good control of interim outlays. The federal government, which originally published the technique, uses it regularly for controlling cost overruns in government contracts. The need for an accounting system that is conceptually consistent with project management becomes evident when one considers that traditional accounting systems group costs not by activities but by organizational areas, flows of materials, and time periods. PERT/cost provides a means for structuring costs that is consistent with project management models.

With respect to planning and scheduling, PERT/cost generates cumulative and average expenditures on a period-by-period basis for alternative schedules. This feature is useful in deciding when activities should be started between their earliest and latest starting dates. In addition, the information system for PERT/cost provides reports that allow project managers to control costs and evaluate performance with respect to the schedule. For example, suppose that at some point in time, the actual cost for an activity is 80% of its budgeted cost. One might think that cost is under control; however, the activity may be only 50% complete. To overcome this problem, the federal government requires its contractors to adhere to *cost/schedule control systems criteria* throughout a project. These criteria are discussed in Chapter 12.

11.5 PRESENTING THE BUDGET

The project budget is a communications channel that must serve both project-related and organizational planning and control needs. Two dimensions are used to measure the quality of a project's budget: its ability (1) to advance organizational goals within the imposed constraints and (2) to communicate the proposed plan to the project team and organization and sometimes to subcontractors and the client.

The budget is easier to understand and use if it is presented clearly and concisely. Consider the following recommendations when preparing and presenting a project's budget:

1. Incorporate a schedule indicating the time that expenditures and revenues are expected to be realized.
2. Present the budget in quantitative, measurable units such as dollars or person-hours. If you use different units in the same budget, then clearly define the conversion between units.

3. Make an effort to define milestones that correspond to the achievement of measurable goals. Typical milestones for research and development projects are system design review, preliminary design review, critical design review, and the passing of prototype performance tests. In contractor/client projects, the achievement of such milestones can serve as the basis for client payments. It is important to budget milestones according to the costs of activities that lead up to them. In the example project (see Fig. 9.23), if event 3 is defined as a milestone that represents the completion of activities A and B, then its budget is based on the costs of activities A and B ($4,500). Assuming an early-start schedule, these activities are scheduled to terminate 5 weeks after the project initiation. Assuming a $2,500 overhead (or $500 per week), the total payment of this milestone is likely to be above $4,500 and close to $7,000.

4. Use the budget as a baseline for progress monitoring and control. If a weekly progress report is required, then plan the budget at the weekly level. However, if weekly progress reports are issued but the budget is prepared on a monthly basis, then a meaningful comparison between planned progress and actual progress is possible only once every four progress reports. Similarly, break down the budget to enable a direct comparison with the progress reports. The cost breakdown used in preparing the budget should be the same as the breakdown used to collect and analyze data for both the project and the organizational control systems.

5. The budget should translate short-range objectives into work orders, purchasing orders, and so on. This links the design and development phases to the production phase through the budgeting and work authorization processes.

6. Break down the budget by the organizational units responsible for its execution and the work content assigned to such units. For example, Table 11.10 itemizes the activities by assigned departments of the example project.

7. Whenever you use a specific standard in budgeting, reference it. For example, suppose that activity C is welding the pressure tank of a submarine and is budgeted at $3,300. This figure might have been derived from the company standard, which says that it costs $300 per inch to perform a weld. The estimated welding length is 11 inches. Such information should be referenced in the budget. By referencing the standard used, you can later trace any deviations in actual cost to the

TABLE 11.10   Breakdown of the Budget by Organizational Units

Activity	Department 1	Department 2
A		$1,500
B		$3,000
C	$3,300	
D	$4,200	
E		$5,700
F	$6,100	
G	$7,200	
Department total	$20,800	$10,200

deviation's source (i.e., the cost per inch or the length of the welding) and, if necessary, update the standard.

8. Include five components in the short-term (operational) budget:

   a. *WPs of discrete effort.* Each WP defines the organizational element responsible for a task and the task's WBS element. Identifying the WP this way allows you to present the budget along WBS and OBS lines. Such an identification also serves as a baseline for a control system that is capable of tracing the sources of deviations between planned and actual progress, as explained in Chapter 12.

   b. *Level of effort.* This category, which includes the cost of efforts related to more than one WP, occurs as the activities progress over time.

   c. *Apportioned effort.* This category includes the cost of efforts based on a factor of a discrete effort (WP) as exemplified by such activities as inspection and quality control.

   d. *Cost of material.* These costs include the WBS element for which it will be used and the OBS element that will use it.

   e. Other costs. Costs such as those associated with subcontracting must be included.

9. Budget planners should try to define most of the project's effort in discrete terms as part of the WPs. These packages present units of work at levels at which the work is performed and at which the effort is assignable to a single organizational element.

10. Budget overhead costs for each organizational element with a clear definition of the procedures used for allocating these costs. One option is to include a management reserve in the long- and midrange budgets as a buffer against uncertainty. The level of management reserve depends on the amount of uncertainty involved in estimating the actual cost, timing, and technological maturity of the effort required. This reserve should be factored into the budget, once again in discrete terms, as work progresses and information becomes available.

11. Define a target budget at completion as the total budget costs plus management reserve and undistributed monies.

Following this list of recommendations will make it easier to prepare and use the budget. Much can be gained by presenting a financial plan quantitatively in terms that relate the required effort to cost, timing, responsible organizational elements, and project components. Nevertheless, each organization has its own guidelines for budget preparation and presentation, so the recommendations above should be used advisedly to supplement such guidelines in areas where they are unclear or incomplete.

11.6 PROJECT EXECUTION: CONSUMING THE BUDGET

During the project's production phase, three processes occur simultaneously:

1. The short-range budget is translated into work and purchasing authorizations. This process generates work orders, purchase orders, and contracts with suppliers and subcontractors. It requires a feedback system that facilitates a comparison

between actual progress and the original plans and compares the actual cost of the effort performed with the budgeted cost. The exact structure of a feedback system used for project control depends on the project's structure and the organization's needs. This is explained in Chapter 12.

2. The tactical (midrange) budget is translated into a short-range budget through a rolling horizon mechanism. Cost estimates and schedules are accumulated into cost accounts as well as into apportioned effort and level of effort. This is a multistage process because the tactical budget for each period contains several short-range (operational) budget periods. Developing a new, realistic short-range budget requires detailed planning involving the integration of original project plans with reports on actual progress. The short-range budget should detail the midrange budget and, in case of cost or schedule deviations, present a detailed plan for corrective action. Thus, development of the operational budget is based on knowledge regarding the planned execution of activities and the project's actual status.

3. The long-range budget is gradually converted into the midrange budget. This process involves the distribution of accumulated funds, the allocation of management reserves to specific WPs, and the handling of engineering changes. Such changes are frequent in long projects. During the project execution phase, new market requirements (stakeholders needs) or new technological developments may call for modifications in the project's technological aspects. The configuration management system handles all of these change requests. This system keeps track of change requests and the steps followed that lead to approval or rejection. An approved technological change may have both cost and schedule consequences. Thus, the process of translating long-range budgets into midrange budgets should address all approved technological changes and their impact on the project.

Management reserves, designed to buffer uncertainty, should be consumed as soon as the results of tests and studies are available. Such results provide the basis for developing a detailed project plan that translates management reserve budgets into WPs, thus reducing the level of uncertainty. For the project manager, budgeting is not static but an ongoing process. Long-term plans are translated into detailed short-term budgets, and short-term budgets are translated into work orders, purchase orders, and contracts with subcontractors and suppliers.

11.7 IMPORTANT POINTS IN THE BUDGETING PROCESS

The budgeting process provides an interface between organizational goals as perceived by top management and the project managers' actions to achieve those goals. The techniques for budget preparation link the project's schedule, required resources, and NPV. The outcome provides an action framework for each organizational element. This framework integrates the budgets of the individual functional units and projects, as well as those of routine, ongoing activities into the total organizational budget.

Each project's budget is important in transforming goals into both plans and actions while providing guidelines for integration across the OBS and WBS. Management uses the budget as a communications channel to inform organizational elements of resource allocation decisions and the level of performance that is expected of them over time. This channel should be designed with rapid response in mind so that approved changes and deviations from the plan can be communicated quickly. The clearer the budget presentation, the easier it is for management at all levels to win over resistant elements in the organization. Thus, not only is the quality of the budget important but also the planning that goes into its presentation.

TEAM PROJECT

Thermal Transfer Plant

Your proposed schedule has been reviewed by the contract department at TMS and has been given tentative approval. However, the vice president of finance has requested a detailed budget for the project of designing and manufacturing the rotary combustor. The budget should tie the OBS and the WBS to the project's activities. Use the following format:

Week	Direct cost			Indirect cost		
	Labor	Material	Other	Labor	Material	Other
1						
2						
.						
.						
.						

For each line item in the budget, identify its OBS and WBS relationship, and specify the *expected* cost and corresponding variance. Along with the budget, discuss the effect of an early-start schedule and a late-start schedule on cash flow, and explain why the selected schedule is the best from the cash flow point of view. (Is it?)

DISCUSSION QUESTIONS

1. Develop a budgeting procedure for a university. Explain the role of each management level together with its input and output.
2. Develop a budgeting procedure for a contractor who works on small housing projects.
3. Develop a budget for the project "getting an undergraduate degree." Explain your assumptions and your analysis.
4. Assume that you are in charge of developing your state's department of transportation budget. Write specific instructions for project managers in your department to facilitate a bottom-up budgeting process.
5. What kind of logic is used in the budgeting process of the federal government?
6. Give an example of a project in which a late-start schedule is used because of budgeting and cash flow considerations.

7. Give a detailed example of an activity that can be performed in several modes. Describe each mode, the technology required, and the associated cost.

8. Develop a flowchart for a computerized project budgeting program. Explain the input and output of each element and the data processing required.

9. Identify two projects for which the top-down budgeting approach would be most appropriate. What advantages does it provide?

10. Assume that you have crashed a project as much as possible but that the length of the critical path is still not acceptable. What other options are available?

11. Most computer codes that have been developed to solve the crashing problem assume a linear relationship between the time and the cost for an activity. This leads to a linear program. What does this assumption say in terms of resource allocation, and when might it be acceptable?

12. When a project leader tries to perform slack management, what difficulties might he or she encounter?

13. Read the article by Herroelen and Leus (2001) on the merits and pitfalls of critical chain scheduling listed in the Bibliography section of Chapter 10. Explain the relationship between the critical chain and the critical path and the relationship between the critical chain and resource allocation.

14. Discuss the pros and cons of the critical chain and explain under what conditions it might be a good approach to scheduling resources.

EXERCISES

11.1 Develop a budget for the project described in Table 11.11 assuming that the cost of each activity is linearly distributed over its duration.

  a. Assume an early-start schedule.

  b. Assume a late-start schedule.

  c. Assume that a "leveled budget" is desired (i.e., the same daily cost is desired for each day of the project).

TABLE 11.11

Activity	Duration (days)	Immediate predecessors	Cost
A	3	–	$3,000
B	4	–	$2,000
C	3	–	$6,000
D	2	C	$2,000
E	1	B	$1,000
F	5	A	$10,000
G	2	B	$4,000
H	3	B	$9,000
I	11	C	$11,000
J	3	D, E	$3,000
K	1	F, G	$1,000
L	4	K	$2,000
M	4	J, H	$8,000

11.2 Using the data in Exercise 11.1, assume that the activities can be crashed as shown in Table 11.12:

TABLE 11.12

Activity	Normal time	Crash time	Cost of crashing per day
A	3	2	$1,000
B	4	2	$500
C	3	2	$500
D	2	1	$1,000
E	1	1	—
F	5	4	$500
G	2	1	$1,500
H	3	2	$1,000
I	11	8	$1,500
J	3	1	$1,000
K	1	1	—
L	4	3	$1,000
M	4	4	—

Develop the functional relationship between the direct cost of this project and its duration.

11.3 Using the data in Exercise 11.2, assume that the overhead for the project is given by

$$\text{Overhead} = \$2,000 + \alpha \times \$1,000 \text{ per day}$$

What is the project duration that minimizes its total cost if:

a. $\alpha = 1$?

b. $\alpha = 3$?

11.4 Assume that a continuous time–cost tradeoff exists for each activity, as shown in Fig. 11.3. Write out the corresponding linear program for minimizing the total project cost, defining all notation used. What constraint would you add to ensure that the project is completed within T time periods?

11.5 For the project data given in Table 11.13, assuming an overhead of $350 per period, find the minimum cost schedule. What are the critical activities? How much total slack and free slack exist for the noncritical activities? Find the cost of the early-start and late-start schedules. Re-solve the problem with a deadline of 9 weeks using the linear program developed in Exercise 11.4.

11.6 Given the data shown in Table 11.14 for the direct costs of the normal and crash durations, find the different minimum cost schedules between the normal and crash points for the project defined in Exercise 9.16.

11.7 Consider the time–cost estimates for the product development project in Exercise 9.19 as given in Table 11.15. Indirect costs are made up of two components: a fixed cost of $5,000 and a variable cost of $1,000 per week of elapsed time. Also, for each week that the project exceeds 17 weeks, an opportunity cost of $2,000 per week is assessed.

a. Construct a table that enumerates the critical path and corresponding *direct cost* and *duration* for each possible funding strategy. The first two entries should be the "normal"

TABLE 11.13

Activity	Immediate predecessors	Normal Duration	Normal Cost	Crash Duration	Crash Cost
A	—	4	$100	2	$300
B	—	3	$200	1	$200
C	A, B	2	$50	1	$100
D	A, B	3	$100	2	$300
E	A	4	$150	1	$400
F	C, D	4	$250	1	$100
G	D, E	2	$300	1	$200
H	F, G	3	$200	2	$100

TABLE 11.14

Activity (i,j)	Normal Duration	Normal Cost	Crash Duration	Crash Cost
Project (a)				
(1, 2)	5	$100	2	$200
(1, 4)	2	$50	1	$80
(1, 5)	2	$150	1	$180
(2, 3)	7	$200	5	$250
(2, 5)	5	$20	2	$40
(2, 6)	4	$20	2	$40
(3, 4)	3	$60	1	$80
(3, 6)	10	$30	6	$60
(4, 6)	5	$10	2	$20
(4, 7)	9	$70	5	$90
(5, 6)	4	$100	1	$130
(5, 7)	3	$140	1	$160
(6, 7)	3	$200	1	$240
Project (b)				
(1, 2)	4	$100	1	$400
(1, 3)	8	$400	5	$640
(1, 4)	9	$120	6	$180
(1, 6)	3	$20	1	$60
(2, 3)	5	$60	3	$100
(2, 5)	9	$210	7	$270
(3, 4)	12	$400	8	$800
(3, 7)	14	$120	12	$140
(4, 5)	15	$500	10	$750
(4, 7)	10	$200	6	$220
(5, 6)	11	$160	8	$240
(5, 7)	8	$70	5	$110
(6, 7)	10	$100	2	$180

TABLE 11.15

Activity	Time estimates (weeks)		Direct cost estimates ($1,000)	
	Normal	Crash	Normal	Crash
A	3	1.0	3.5	10.0
B	1	0.5	1.2	2.0
C	5	3.0	9.0	18.0
D	1	0.7	1.0	2.0
E	6	3.0	20.0	50.0
F	1	0.5	2.2	3.0
G	2	1.0	4.0	9.0
H	8	6.0	100.0	150.0

and "all crash" strategies. Then either crash or compress (1 week at a time) all activities on the critical path, and calculate the corresponding direct cost and duration for the resulting strategies. Use the data in the table to construct a bar graph of completion time versus total cost (direct + indirect + opportunity).

b. Construct the Gantt chart for the minimum total cost schedule.

c. Construct a two-part schedule of direct costs (of the type illustrated in Figs. 9.10 and 9.11) based on the time schedule in part (b). Of the two, which schedule yields the lowest peak cost? Also, on the bases of variance, which of the two levels costs the most?

11.8 Develop a mathematical programming formulation for the problem of minimizing the total cost of completing the project discussed in Exercise 11.7. Use a commercial optimization package to find the solution.

11.9 Planmatics is undertaking a modernization program. The set of activities in Table 11.16 has been defined for refurbishing one of its wave soldering machines. The AOA network is given in Fig. 11.5.

a. Find the critical path, total slacks, and free slacks.

b. Find the probability of completion within 45 days.

TABLE 11.16

Activity	$\hat{d}_{ij}$ (days)	$\hat{s}_{ij}$ (days)	Crash date Maximum possible compression (days)	Crash date Expediting cost per day ($)
A	6	2	0	—
B	2	0	1	50
C	12	3	2	80
D	8	1	2	175
E	7	2	1	100
F	16	4	0	—
G	23	2	1	100
H	25	5	3	300
I	4	1	1	1,000

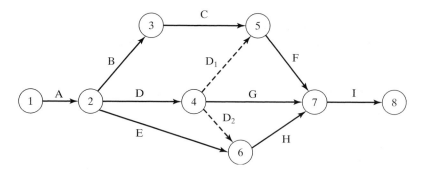

Figure 11.5　AOA network for Exercise 11.9.

   c. Find the minimum cost increase to reduce the expected project duration by 1 day.
   d. Find the minimum cost increase to reduce the expected project duration by 2 days.
   e. Find the minimum project duration and the expected cost increase.

11.10　Consider the project information given in Table 11.17.

TABLE 11.17

Activity	Immediate predecessors	Expected time (weeks)	Normal cost ($)	Expediting cost per week ($/week)	Minimum time (weeks)
A	—	3	3,000	1,500	2
B	—	6	7,200	1,000	4
C	A	2	2,000	2,000	1
D	A	7	7,000	2,000	3
E	C, B	1	4,000	—	1
F	B	3	3,000	1,500	2

   a. Calculate the project cost based just on the costs of the activities.
   b. Generate the weekly and cumulative cash flow charts, once for an early-start schedule and once for a late-start schedule.
   c. Discuss the implications of the charts generated in part (b).

11.11　For the project described in Exercise 11.10:

   a. Generate the time–cost chart.
   b. What is the shortest completion time for the project, and what bottleneck activities prevent further time reduction?

11.12　A managerial fee of $1,400 per week is to be paid as long as the project in Exercise 11.10 has not been completed.

   a. Calculate the optimal project duration.
   b. You have been offered a bonus of $5,000 if you complete the project within 8 weeks. Will you make it? Explain.

11.13 Each activity in the project described in Exercise 11.10 has a duration variance of 1 week. For example, the expected time for activity A is 3 weeks, with a variance of 1 week. Assuming that the normal cost of each activity is to be used, discuss the possible impact of the activity variance on the project cash flow.

11.14 You have signed a contract to complete the project described in Exercise 11.10 within 10 weeks. The weekly managerial fee is $2,000.

    a. Generate the schedule that will delay expenses to the last possible moment and indicate its associated cash flow.

    b. Generate the cash flow requirement resulting from the objective to increase the probability that the project will be completed on schedule.

11.15 Find a schedule for Exercise 10.3 that minimizes the cost of the project assuming that resource I costs $10/hour, resource II costs $15/hour, and there is an overhead of $150/day for the project.

11.16 Assuming that the weekly labor cost per employee is $1,200 and that the fringe benefit rate is 25%, determine the cumulative cash flow requirement for the project described in Exercise 10.5.

    a. For an early-start schedule.

    b. For a late-start schedule.

    c. What if the allocated budget is below the late-start cash flow line?

    d. What if the allocated budget is above the early-start cash flow line?

BIBLIOGRAPHY

Budgeting Process

Bard, J. F., "Coordination of a Multidivisional Firm through Two Levels of Management," *Omega,* Vol. 11, No. 5, pp. 457–465, 1983.

Fields, M. A., "Effect of the Learning Curve on the Capital Budgeting Process," *Managerial Finance*, Vol. 17, No. 2-3, pp. 29–41, 1991.

Meyers, R. T. (Editor), *Handbook of Government Budgeting*, John Wiley & Sons, New York, 1998.

Pearson, N. D., *Risk Budgeting: Portfolio Problem Solving with Value-at-Risk*, John Wiley & Sons, New York, 2002.

Rasmussen, N. H. and C. J. Eichorn, *Budgeting: Technology, Trends, Software Selection, and Implementation*, John Wiley & Sons, New York, 2000.

Smith, R. W. and T. D. Lynch, *Public Budgeting in America*, Fifth Edition, Prentice Hall, Upper Saddle River, NJ, 2004.

Tavares, L. V., "Stochastic Planning and Control of Program Budgeting: The Model Macao," in A. Coelho and L. V. Tavares (Editors), *OR Models on Microcomputers,*" Elsevier Science Publishers, North Holland, Amsterdam, 1986.

Time–Cost Tradeoff Models

Elmaghraby, S. E., "The Determination of Optimum Activity Duration in Project Scheduling," *Journal of Industrial Engineering,* Vol. 19, No. 1, pp. 48–51, 1968.

Elmaghraby, S. E. and S. Arisawa, "Optimal Time-Cost Trade-offs in GERT Networks," *Management Science,* Vol. 18, No. 11, pp. 589–599, 1972.

Falk, J. E. and J. L. Horowitz, "Critical Path Problems with Concave Cost-Time Curves," *Management Science,* Vol. 19, No. 4, pp. 446–455, 1974.

Goyal, S. K., "A Note on a Simple CPM Time-Cost Tradeoff Algorithm," *Management Science,* Vol. 21, No. 6, pp. 718–722, 1975.

Lamberson, L. R. and R. R. Hocking, "Optimum Time Compression in Project Scheduling," *Management Science,* Vol. 16, No. 10, pp. B597–B606, 1970.

Cash Flow and Net Present Value Models

Elmaghraby, S. E. and W. S. Herroelen, "The Scheduling of Activities to Minimize the Net Present Value of Projects," *European Journal of Operational Research,* Vol. 49, No. 11, pp. 35–49, 1990.

Etgar, R. and A. Shtub, "Scheduling Project Activities to Maximize the Net Present Value—The Case of Linear Time-Dependent Cash Flows," *International Journal of Production Research,* Vol. 37, No. 2, pp. 329–339, 1999.

Etgar, R., A. Shtub and L. J. LeBlanc, "Scheduling Projects to Maximize Net Present Value—The Case of Time-Dependent, Contingent Cash Flows," *European Journal of Operational Research,* Vol. 96, No. 1, pp. 90–96, 1996.

Herroelen, W. S. and P. Van Dommelen, "Project Network Models with Discounted Cash Flows: A Guided Tour through Recent Developments," *European Journal of Operational Research,* Vol. 100, Issue 1, pp. 97–121, 1997.

Herroelen, W. S. and E. Gallens, "Computational Experience with an Optimal Procedure for the Scheduling of Activities to Maximize the Net Present Value of Projects," *European Journal of Operational Research,* Vol. 65, pp. 274–277, 1993.

Kazaz, B. and C. Sepil, "Project Scheduling with Discounted Cash Flows and Progress Payments," *Journal of Operational Research Society,* Vol. 47, pp. 1262–1272, 1996.

Kogan, K. and A. Shtub, "Scheduling Projects with Variable-Intensity Activities: The Case of Dynamic Earliness and Tardiness Costs," *European Journal of Operational Research,* Vol. 118, No. 1, pp. 65–80, 1998.

Shtub, A., "The Trade-off Between the Net Present Cost of a Project and the Probability to Complete It on Schedule," *Journal of Operations Management,* Vol. 6, No. 4, pp. 461–470, 1987.

Shtub, A. and R. Etgar, "A Branch and Bound Algorithm for Scheduling Projects to Maximize Net Present Value: The Case of Time-Dependent, Contingent Cash Flows," *International Journal of Production Research,* Vol. 35, No. 12, pp. 3367–3378, 1997.

Smith-Daniels, D. E. and N. J. Aquilano, "Using a Late-Start Resource-Constrained Project Schedule to Improve Project Net Present Value," *Decision Sciences,* Vol. 18, pp. 617–630, 1987.

Smith-Daniels, D. E. and V. L. Smith-Daniels, "Maximizing the Net Present Value of a Project Subject to Materials and Capital Constraints," *Journal of Operations Management,* Vol. 7, No. 1-2, pp. 33–45, 1987.

Vanhoucke, M., E. Demeulemeester and W. Herroelen, "On Maximizing the Net Present Value of a Project Under Renewable Resource Constraints," *Management Science,* Vol. 47, No. 8, pp. 1113–1121, 2001.

Yang, K. K., F. B. Talbot and J. H. Patterson, "Scheduling a Project to Maximize Its Net Present Value: An Integer Programming Approach," *European Journal of Operational Research,* Vol. 64, pp. 188–198, 1992.

Chapter 12

Project Control

12.1 INTRODUCTION

Planning is a fundamental component of project management. A detailed plan that covers the technological, budgetary, scheduling, organizational, and risk-related aspects is essential to facilitate coordination among the participants. Those with major roles and influence most often include the various support departments, such as marketing and sales, outside contractors, and the technical disciplines.

Unfortunately, even the best of plans cannot guarantee success. Uncertainty and changing environmental conditions are bound to intervene in unforeseen ways, sometimes positively, sometimes negatively. Plans are based on assessments of needs and the estimation of such factors as activity durations, resource availability, labor efficiency, and cost, each of which may be subject to a high degree of variability. Furthermore, needs and goals are dynamic, changing over time. New technologies developed during the life cycle of the project, a rethinking of corporate strategy, the replacement of key personnel, and new market or legal circumstances all may conspire to make the original plans obsolete. Thus, it is essential to monitor actual progress and to update the original plans as the need arises. This requirement is more evident in complex, technically advanced projects in which the likelihood of technological, environmental, and economic changes occurring during the projects' lifetimes is greatest.

The design and implementation of a project control system is therefore an important part of the project management effort. The basis of any control system is a statement of the project goals and their relative importance. For each such goal, one or more performance measures are needed. For example, a common goal is to keep the project on schedule. Appropriate performance measures can be based on the actual start or finish times of critical activities, the completion of milestones, or the timing of acceptance tests. The selection of a performance measure depends on the corresponding goal and the level of management to which actual values of the performance measure will be reported. Thus, a low-level manager who is responsible for a specific set of activities needs detailed information on those activities. The project manager is interested in monitoring the actual completion time of critical activities, whereas upper management might be interested in information on the completion time of major milestones.

Once performance measures are selected, the information required to report the actual value of each performance measure must be defined. For example, the completion of a milestone may be reported at the successful completion of an acceptance test and the issuance of an appropriate report by quality control. The same milestone may be reported as completed only after the customer payment, based on the completion of that milestone, has been made. The selection and use of performance criteria require the collection of specific data, which may not be trivial. An effort to use data that are available from existing reporting systems is always justified. This reduces the cost of data collection and minimizes the problem of conflicting data in the project control system and other management information systems.

The data collected are used as a basis for estimating the current value of the performance measures and to forecast their future values on the basis of past performance. Estimates of current values are the basis of "real-time" control. This type of control is achieved by comparing the actual value of a performance measure with its planned value. Control limits are set to assess the severity of deviations. Deviations that are larger than a predetermined value are used to trigger corrective action. This type of control is based on the philosophy of management by exception, whereby actual deviations from plans alert management to a particular problem that needs attention.

A second mode of control is trend control, which is based on forecasts of future performance measures. Actual values of the performance measures are extrapolated into the future in an effort to detect deviations before they occur. Forecasts of future deviations trigger preventive actions designed to minimize future problems. This mode of trend control is important because information on present values of performance measures may not reveal irregularities, but data trends over the last few control periods may indicate a high likelihood of future problems.

The designer of a project control system therefore should address the following questions:

1. What performance measures should be selected?
2. What data should be used to estimate the current value of each performance measure?
3. How should raw data be collected, from which sources, and in what frequency?
4. How should the data be analyzed to detect current and future deviations?
5. How should the results of the analysis be reported, in what format, to whom, and how often?

The answers to these questions underlie the design of the control system's data collection, data processing, information distribution, and response processes. Management should exercise project control throughout the project life cycle. The information provided by the control system is essential for the ongoing decision making aimed at keeping the project on track.

Several measurements can be taken in support of project control. These can be classified into four categories: schedule, cost, resources, and performance. Table 12.1 elaborates on each with an eye toward understanding the difficulties that may arise.

TABLE 12.1   Measurements for Project Control

Measurement	Category affected
Delay in starting critical tasks	Schedule
Delay in finishing critical tasks	Schedule
Noncritical tasks becoming critical	Schedule
Milestones missed	Schedule
Due date changes	Schedule
Price changes	Cost
Cost overruns	Cost
Insufficient cash flow	Cost
High overhead rates	Cost
Long supply lead time for required material	Resources, schedule
Low utilization of resources	Resources, cost
Resources availability problems	Resources, schedule, cost
Changes in labor cost	Resources, cost
Changes in scope of project	Performance, cost, schedule, resources
Lack of technical information	Performance, cost, schedule
Failure in tests	Performance, cost, schedule
Delays in approvals of configuration changes	Performance, schedule
Errors in records (inventories, etc.)	Performance, cost, schedule

Some of the measurements in the table are commonly used by industrial and service organizations to manage their routine functions, such as inventory tracking, accounting/auditing, quality control, production scheduling, and data processing. There are issues, however, that are unique to the project environment that informs a need for special control systems to handle the one-time, nonrepetitive effort that is typical of projects.

Control systems are part of an organization's management information system (MIS). Each organization tends to develop or adopt an MIS that fits its needs, its structure, and the environment in which it operates. Organizations that fund research and development projects and say, because of technological uncertainties, agree to pay the actual cost of the project plus a predetermined contractor fee (cost plus fixed fee contract) face the problem of controlling the activities of different contractors each of whom may be using a different control system. Major organizations such as the U.S. Department of Defense (DOD), the U.S. Department of Energy (DOE), and the National Aeronautics and Space Administration (NASA) have developed guidelines or requirements that their contractors must incorporate into their respective control systems. The common approach is to let contractors choose the MIS and control system that best suit their needs, subject to a set of criteria called *cost/schedule control systems criteria* (C/SCSC). Rules are given for the following five aspects of the project: (1) organization, (2) planning and budgeting, (3) accounting, (4) analysis, and (5) revisions and access to data. Appendix 12B lists the criteria used by the DOE. Similar criteria are used by the DOD and NASA.

In this chapter, we concentrate on techniques specifically developed for cost and schedule control. We also discuss methods used for quality control and the control of technological changes; that is, configuration management.

12.2 COMMON FORMS OF PROJECT CONTROL

Project control can be exercised through formal or informal mechanisms. Small projects that are performed by small teams that are located in the same place under a single organizational unit may not need a formal control system. This is frequently the case when members of the team are highly motivated and communicate well with each other. Examples of such projects can be found in schools, in social clubs, and among members of small communities that perform short-range, technically simple projects.

The decision to introduce a formal control system and the selection of a specific system should be based largely on two aspects of the project: (1) the risk involved and (2) the cost of the control system and its expected benefits. High-risk situations in which the probability of undesired outcomes is significant as a result of the environmental conditions, the complexity of the project, or other factors and when the cost associated with such undesired outcomes is high justify the investment in a formal, well-designed control system.

The selection of a control system depends on many factors, such as the characteristics of the project structures [organizational breakdown structure (OBS) and work breakdown structure (WBS)], the technological nature of the project, the schedule, the budget, and the personality of the members of the project team. Control systems can be very simple, taking the form of weekly team meetings to discuss current status, or can be very sophisticated, comprising a battery of hardware, software, and personnel. The cost of control should never exceed the expected benefits (i.e., savings) as a result of the control system.

Schedule control in its simplest form is based on a comparison between the planned schedule, as depicted by a Gantt chart or the results of a critical path analysis, and actual performance. Data on actual progress are collected periodically (every week, every month, etc.) or continuously (as soon as an activity is completed or a milestone is achieved) and are used as input to the control system. By comparing the initial schedule (the baseline) with the current updated schedule, deviations are detected. These deviations are used to trigger corrective action, such as reallocation of resources to expedite late activities.

Simple cost control is achieved by comparing the actual cost of project activities to the planned budget. Although most organizations have some form of cost monitoring system and cost control system, it might be difficult to get the data required for project cost control from these systems. For example, the direct labor and material cost of specific project activities may not be available because the department in which those activities are performed does not keep records for each activity separately. Actual cost may be accumulated by department or by work orders. To facilitate cost control by project activities or WBS elements, a special cost control system is required. Once the information on actual costs of project activities is available, cost overruns can be detected, trends can be analyzed, and management's attention can be brought to bear when current or future costs are considered out of control.

An important assumption that is usually made when trying to identify deviations from the original plan is linearity over all relevant dimensions. This means that the amount of resources allocated to an activity per period is constant over its duration and that output is proportional to input; i.e., there is no learning. For example, if activity A is expected to cost \$3,600 and is scheduled over a 6-week period, then the budget is

$600/wk. Also, if 2 man-weeks produce a certain level of output, then 4 man-weeks will produce twice that level. Unless there are indications to the contrary, one should proceed with the analysis based on the linearity assumption.

The idea of cost and schedule control that is based on a simple comparison between planned and actual performance is illustrated next, using the example project introduced in Section 9.4. Suppose that a weekly report detailing cost and schedule performance is issued. Referring to the example, three activities (A, B and E) are scheduled to start the first week of the project, assuming an early-start schedule. The duration and cost of these activities are summarized in Table 12.2. Actual performance for the first month of the project (weeks 1 through 4) is summarized in Table 12.3. On the basis of the information in these tables, the following observations can be made:

- *Week 1.* All three activities started on schedule. Assuming for simplicity that the budget of each activity is linear in time, the weekly budget of activity A is $1,500/5 = $300, as shown in Table 12.2. Similarly, activity B is budgeted at $3,000/3 = $1000 per week, and activity E at approximately $5,700/7 = $814 per week. The budget for the first week therefore is $300 + $1,000 + $814 = $2,114. According the plan, the amount that should have been spent on activity A is $300, so activity A shows a cost overrun of $200 ($500 − $300); activities B and E are exactly on target.

- *Week 2.* All three activities are in process, as scheduled. Activity A has a cumulative cost overrun of $400 ($1,000 − 2 × $300), whereas the overrun for week 2 is $200 ($500 − $300). The actual cumulative cost of activity B is as planned, and the actual cumulative cost of activity E for the period is $128 below the planned budget ($1,500 − 2 × $814 = $128).

- *Week 3.* Activity B is late because it was scheduled to be completed by the end of week 3. Activities A and E are in process as scheduled. The cumulative actual cost of activity A is $1,300, whereas its planned cost for the 3 weeks was only 3 × $300 = $900, the difference of $1,300 − $900 = $400 is the same as in week 2. The actual cost of activity B is only $2,500 compared with a budget of $3,000, whereas the actual cost of E is $2,500 compared with a budget of 3 × $814 = $2,442.

- *Week 4.* Activity A is completed 1 week earlier than planned, activity B is completed 1 week late, and the total cost of both activities is exactly as planned. Activity E is in process, and its total cost of $2,900 is below the budget of $3,256 (4 × $814).

TABLE 12.2   Duration and Cost for Activities Performed in Month 1

Activity	Duration (weeks)	Cost	Cost per week
A	5	$1,500	$300
B	3	$3,000	$1,000
E	7	$5,700	$814

TABLE 12.3   Actual Performances in Month 1

	Week 1		Week 2		Week 3		Week 4	
Activity	Activity status	Actual cost	Activity status	Actual cost	Activity status	Actual cost	Activity status	Actual cost
A	Started	$500	In process	$1,000	In process	$1,300	Completed	$1,500
B	Started	$1,000	In process	$2,000	In process	$2,500	Completed	$3,000
E	Started	$814	In process	$1,500	In process	$2,500	In process	$2,900

Analysis.   Depending on when the information on actual activity start and end times becomes available, schedule delays may not be detected in a timely manner. For example, activity B was not completed on time (week 3), but only at the end of week 3 did this become known.

When not related to actual work progress, the information on actual cost is not a sufficient measure for cost control. For example, the cost overrun associated with activity A was due to the fact that it was ahead of schedule (completed in 4 weeks instead of 5). This situation could not be observed from the cost and schedule information above.

In addition to cost and schedule control, performance control with respect to the technical aspects of the project is the third aspect common to all control systems. Simple control of performance can be achieved by using the organization's quality control and quality assurance system. Reports issued by these systems provide information on the level of performance achieved. A major problem with performance control stems from the one-time nature of projects. Engineering changes throughout the project life cycle make quality control a difficult task, primarily because it is not possible to use past data as a basis for statistical process control. In addition, quality control is dependent on the availability of an updated project configuration, something that is difficult to achieve in a timely manner. To monitor and control engineering changes, a configuration management system is needed.

Although "stand-alone" independent control systems for cost, schedule, and performance are common, these three dimensions are not entirely independent in most projects. To integrate the three control systems, project review meetings should be held frequently. In such meetings, representatives from the various groups and organizations that are participating in the project discuss progress and decide on necessary corrective action. Review meetings can be scheduled periodically, upon a request as a result of an exceptional event, or when a predetermined milestone is reached. Typical examples are the *preliminary design review* and the *critical design review*, which are major milestones in the project design phase.

Milestone-related review meetings are typically scheduled to demonstrate and analyze major subsystems and prototypes. The integrative nature of a project review meeting in which progress is assessed and problems are aired is the essential advantage of this form of control. However, the need to bring together experts from different functional areas (and sometimes from different organizations) for such meetings makes this form of control expensive and difficult to organize. There is a need for a project control system that integrates information on cost, schedule, and performance to help management monitor and control projects performed by several organizational units. The basic building blocks of such a system is taken up next.

12.3 INTEGRATING THE OBS AND WBS WITH COST AND SCHEDULE CONTROL

As discussed earlier, the project control system is designed to give management the assurance that the project is proceeding according to plan. Its major function is to monitor progress, detect deviations between the original plan and current conditions and trends that may have a negative impact on the successful completion of the project, and initiate correcting actions. Control limits are established for the important parameters, and any deviations outside these limits are flagged. Corrective action is taken when the deviations are considered significant. A major problem in project control is the lack of standards deriving from past performance. The ad hoc nature of projects motivates the adoption of control limits that are based on intuition and risk analysis rather than on historical data, as is the case in statistical process control.

The idea of control limits is depicted in Fig. 12.1. In Fig. 12.1a, the cumulative budget for activity A in the example project is plotted along with actual cost as a function of time for weeks 1 through 4. The control limits for actual cost are set at $\pm 10\%$ of the cumulative budget. The need for an upper control limit is obvious, as the prevention of budget overruns is a common goal for projects. Actual expenditures below budget are also monitored because they might signal a delay in performing some activities [this lower control limit is important for the detection of delays in noncritical activities that are not monitored by critical path method (CPM)-based schedule control systems].

In Fig. 12.1b, the weekly budget for activity A in the example project is plotted as a function of time for weeks 1 through 4. Again the control limits for actual cost are set at $\pm 10\%$ of the weekly budget. By monitoring the variance between actual cost and planned cost, corrective actions may be taken whenever this variance is considered too high.

A similar report for several activities or for the entire project can be constructed. Each report should be designed according to the needs of the management level for which it is produced. By introducing the cost variance and the control limits, automatic detection of problematic deviations is made possible. On the basis of predetermined control limits, management can be supplied with the cost variance of activities whose periodic or cumulative variance exceeds the acceptable range and therefore may require attention.

A major measure for the effectiveness of a project control system is its average response time; that is, the average time between the occurrence of a deviation outside the control limits and its detection. Another important performance measure is traceability—the ability of the control system to identify the source of the problem causing the deviations. It is important that the relationship between the source of the problem and the affected project components be established and the responsible organizational units notified. The time when the problem occurred should also be recorded as a third dimension of this measure.

An appropriate data structure is required to achieve traceability. This structure must relate plans and corresponding progress reports to the relevant time periods, to

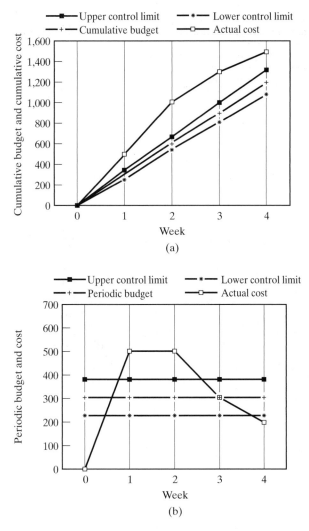

Figure 12.1   Control limits and actual cost for
activity A, weeks 1 through 4.

the appropriate segments of the project work content, and to the organizational units
that are responsible for these segments. Two hierarchical structures are commonly used
in an integrated manner to facilitate traceability: (1) the OBS and (2) the WBS.

12.3.1 Hierarchical Structures

As discussed in Chapter 7, the OBS is a model of the project's organizational structure.
In this model, each entity that is responsible for one or more project tasks is represented.
At the lowest level of the OBS, the operational units that are engaged in the execution
of activities are present. Higher levels represent various management layers such as

foremen and department managers, up to the vice president of operations and the chief executive officer. Along with the OBS, authority and responsibility have to be clearly defined, as well as the policies and procedures promulgated for reporting and authorizing work. The OBS defines the communication lines used for reporting progress (from the bottom up) and for issuing work orders and technical instructions (from the top down). An OBS for the example project is illustrated in Fig. 12.2. Work packages (WPs), or activities, are assigned to organizational units as follows:

Organizational unit	Activities performed
Department 1	C, D, F, G
Department 2	A, B, E

The OBS is integrated with the WBS, which is typically a product-oriented hierarchy composed of hardware, software, services, and tasks required to complete the project. The WBS organizes, defines, and displays the product to be produced as well as the work to be accomplished in the project. At the lowest level of the WBS, specific WPs, or tasks, are listed. These tasks are integrated through the higher levels into subsystems, into systems, and at the top level into the whole project. A simplified WBS that consists of three elements is illustrated in Fig. 12.3. The upper level in the figure represents the entire project, whereas the lowest level comprises the three major elements of the WBS. Assuming that this is the WBS of the example project, the following relationships exist between the project activities and the WBS elements:

WBS element	Activities related to WBS element
Element I	A, C, D
Element II	B, F
Element III	E, G

The same principles apply to larger projects. For example, the upper three levels of a WBS for an electronic system are presented in Appendix 12A (based on MIL-STD-881A).

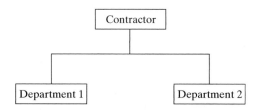

Figure 12.2   OBS for example project.

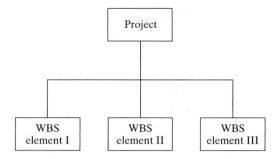

Figure 12.3   Simple WBS.

By integrating the OBS and the WBS, each activity in the project is linked to both structures at their lowest levels, as illustrated in Fig. 12.4. From the figure, it is clear that department 1 performs activities C and D, required for element I in the WBS. As defined by the linear responsibility chart (see Section 7.5), there should be one responsible organizational unit for each WP. The cost associated with each WP is accumulated and controlled by the corresponding *cost account*. WPs and cost accounts form the

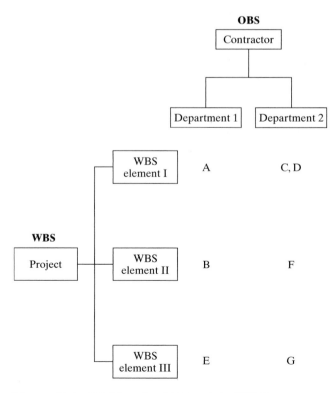

Figure 12.4   Linking the OBS and the WBS.

basic building blocks of a project control system that supports traceability in both the OBS and WBS dimensions.

Design of the control system is initiated during the conceptual design phase of the project as goals and performance measures are defined. Later, the OBS and WBS are developed together with the activities to be performed, related costs, durations, and precedence relations. By the end of the planning phase, the detailed OBS, WBS, schedule, and budget serve as the baseline for the control system.

During project implementation, at the end of each control period, comparisons are made between the work content completed and the work content scheduled for that period. This comparison focuses on the ability of the organization to complete the project within schedule. An effort is made to detect overruns and, if present, to reduce them to a minimum by adjusting the original plan. Simultaneously, at the end of each control period, a comparison between the budgeted cost for that period and the actual costs is performed. Both exercises are done on a regular basis for the most recent period and on a cumulative basis for the time elapsed since the start of the project.

Based on the original schedule for the example project, activity A should be completed 5 weeks after the start date, activity B after 3 weeks, and activity E after 7 weeks. Figure 12.5 presents a Gantt chart for the original plan. A summary report of actual progress after 4 weeks, together with the planned and actual costs, is presented in Table 12.4. The Gantt chart in Fig. 12.5 illustrates the early-start schedule for activities A, B and E. The summary report in Table 12.4 indicates actual progress measured by work content performed, actual cost as reported by the accounting system, and the original budget for these activities.

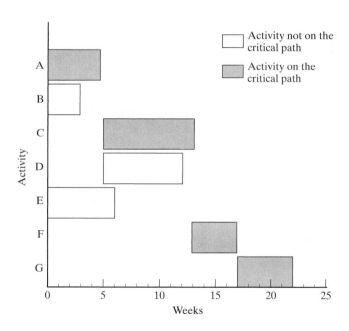

Figure 12.5   Gantt chart for an early start.

TABLE 12.4   Summary Report for Weeks 1–4

Activity	Actual cost	Budgeted cost	Work performed as % of work content
A	$1,500	$300 × 4 = $1,200	100
B	$3,000	$3,000	100
E	$2,900	$814 × 4 = $3,256	$\frac{2}{7} = 28.6$
Total	$7,400	$7,456	

Actual progress made can be estimated by several methods. In many instances, it is a simple matter of measuring output. For example, assuming that activity E involves assembling 70 platforms for a batch of telecommunication systems and that by the end of the fourth week only 20 have been finished, then 2/7, or 28.6%, of the work content has been accomplished. Here the estimate of actual work completed is unbiased and exact. In other cases, it may be more subjective, based on the opinion or observation of an expert such as a foreman, an engineer, the client representative, or the quality control group. A rough estimate can be used when the duration of activities is about the same as the length of the control period. In this case, an activity can be assumed 50% completed when it starts and 100% completed at its finish. This estimate is easy to compute and eliminates the need for a subjective measure.

Continuing with the example, a simple analysis of the costs for the first month does not identify any problems because actual costs ($7,400) are a bit less than budgeted costs ($7,456). Furthermore, a critical path analysis that is based on actual progress reveals that the free slack of activity E (6 weeks) is shortened by 2 weeks as a result of delays but that activity E is still not on the critical path. Nevertheless, none of the analytic techniques discussed thus far is capable of detecting the deviations between the project plan and actual progress. More detail is needed to assess the situation accurately. In particular, an exhaustive cost/schedule control analysis that integrates cost data with information on actual progress reveals that the project is not only behind schedule but also over budget. This is because the actual progress on activity E in 4 weeks is equal to the work content planned for just the first 2 weeks. Thus, activity E is subject to a 50% delay. Furthermore, the budgeted cost of 2/7 of E is only 2 × $814 = $1,628, whereas its actual cost is $2,900 for the first 4 weeks.

This example illustrates the close relationship among cost, schedule, and work content, and the need for an integrative measure that ties all three components together in the control system.

12.3.2 Earned Value Approach

The *earned value* (EV) concept integrates cost, schedule, and work performed by ascribing monetary values to each. In EV-based control systems, only three variables are used as the basic building blocks. Each is discussed below.

1. *Budgeted cost of work scheduled* (BCWS), or *planned value* (PV), is defined as the value (in monetary units) of the work scheduled to be accomplished in a given period of time (a single control period, or an ordered sequence beginning with the first period). The BCWS values of activities A, B, and E in the example project for the first month are as follows:

Activity	BCWS
A	4 × 300 = $1,200
B	$3,000
E	4 × 814 = $3,256
Total	$7,456

Thus, the work content scheduled to be accomplished during the first 4 weeks of the project is budgeted at $7,456.

   2. *Actual cost of work performed* (ACWP), or *actual cost,* is defined as the cost actually incurred and recorded in accomplishing the work performed within the control period. In the example, these costs are

Activity	ACWP
A	$1,500
B	$3,000
E	$2,900
Total	$7,400

As can be seen, a total of $7,400 was spent during the first 4 weeks to accomplish the work performed.

   3. *Budgeted cost of work performed* (BCWP), or EV, is defined as the monetary value of the work actually accomplished within the control period. In the example, 100% of activity A is accomplished. Therefore, its BCWP is equal to the total budget of activity A, which is $1,500. Similarly, for activity B, BCWP = $3,000. However, for activity E, the work performed is only 2/7 of the activity's estimated work content. Therefore, its

BCWP = $5,700 × $\dfrac{2}{7}$ = $1,628. The BCWP values are summarized as follows:

Activity	BCWP
A	$1,500
B	$3,000
E	$1,628
Total	$6,128

In those circumstances in which it is not possible to estimate accurately the percentage of work that was completed, the stage approach can be applied. This approach is based on the assumption that each life-cycle stage of a WP represents a specific percentage of the total value of the WP. Of course, the percentages will differ from one type of WP to another, depending on their type of business. In the analysis, the EV of a WP is a function of its life-cycle stage. The completion of each stage is considered a milestone. As an example, consider the following stages:

Stage	Stage value	Cumulative value (%)
End of planning	15	15
End of execution	45	60
End of testing	20	80
First submission	10	90
Final submission	10	100

If a certain stage has been completed but the next stage has not yet been started, then the EV equals the value stated. If, for example, the execution stage has been completed and the WP is waiting for the testing stage, then the current EV is 60% of the original budget. If testing is under way, then it is assumed that half (50%) has been completed. Therefore, given that the value of testing is 20%, half of 20% is 10%, so the cumulative EV of the WP is 70%. If the total PV of the WP was $10,000, then the present EV is BCWP $= 10,000 \times 0.7 = \$7,000$.

The three measures BCWS, ACWP, and BCWP are the basis of the control analysis by which deviations in time, schedule, and especially cost are detected. In particular, we are concerned with the following.

1. *Schedule deviations.* The difference between the BCWP and the BCWS indicates (in monetary units) the deviation between the work content performed and the work content scheduled for the control period. If the absolute value of the difference is very small, then in terms of work content, the proper volume of work was completed. A positive difference indicates that the project is ahead of schedule, and a negative difference implies that the project is late with regard to work volume. Defining the *schedule variance* (SV) as the difference between BCWP and BCWS, we get

Activity	BCWP − BCWS = SV	
A	$\$1,500 - \$1,200 =$	$300
B	$\$3,000 - \$3,000 =$	$0
E	$\$1,628 - \$3,256 =$	−$1,628
	Cumulative variance =	−$1,328

On the basis of the SV values, we conclude that for activity A, the work performed is worth $300 more than what was planned for the control period; in activity B, the work performed is exactly equal to what was planned; and in activity E, the work performed is worth $1,628 less than what was planned for the period.

The cumulative variance is an indication in terms of work content performed that the project is already late 4 weeks after its start. This measure, together with a simple CPM analysis, provides the means for tracking critical activities and for detecting overall trends in schedule performance. Although the delay in noncritical activities may not cause immediate project delays, the fact that these activities are not performed on schedule means that the resources required to perform them will be needed in a later period. This shift in resource requirements may cause a problem if the load on resources exceeds the available capacity.

The schedule delays detected by the EV analysis should be monitored closely. When the delay extends beyond the control level, analysis of resource requirements should be initiated to test whether, as a result of resource limits, the entire project may be delayed. By combining CPM analysis to detect delays in critical activities with EV analysis, the two major sources of schedule delays are monitored (delays in critical activities and delays caused by resource shortages).

2. *Cost deviations.* Deviations in cost are calculated on the basis of the work content actually performed during the control period. Therefore, the *cost variance* (CV) is defined as the difference between the BCWP and the ACWP. A positive CV indicates a lower actual cost than budgeted for the work performed during the control period, whereas a negative CV indicates a cost overrun. The CV of activities A, B, and E is presented next for the first 4 weeks of the example project:

Activity	BCWP − ACWP = CV		
A	$1,500 − $1,500 =		$0
B	$3,000 − $3,000 =		$0
E	$1,628 − $2,900 =		−$1,272
	Cumulative variance =		−$1,272

Activities A and B are exactly on budget; the actual cost of performing these activities is equal to the budgeted cost for the accomplished work content. Activity E, however, shows a cost overrun of $1,272 because the work performed on this activity was budgeted at $1,628, whereas the actual cost turned out to be $2,900.

The SV and the CV are absolute measures indicating deviations between planned performance and actual progress, in monetary units. Based on these measures, however, it is difficult to judge the relative schedule or cost deviation. A relative measure is important because a $1,000 cost overrun of an activity that was originally budgeted for $500 is clearly more troublesome than the same overrun on an activity that was originally budgeted for $50,000. A *schedule index* (SI) and a *cost index* (CI) are designed to be proportional measures of schedule and cost performance, respectively.

The SI is defined as the ratio BCWP/BCWS. Thus, an SI value equal to 1 indicates that the associated activity is on schedule. Values larger than 1 suggest that the activity is ahead of schedule, and values smaller than 1 indicate a schedule overrun.

The CI is defined as the ratio BCWP/ACWP, implying that when CI equals 1, the activity is on budget. CI values larger than 1 indicate better-than-planned cost performance, and values smaller than 1 indicate cost overruns. CI may be considered a cost effectiveness index because it specifies the value of work obtained from each dollar spent. For example, CI = 1.05 means that for every dollar spent, $1.05 was obtained.

Following are CI and SI values for the example project after 4 weeks:

Activity	$\dfrac{BCWP}{BCWS} = SI$	$\dfrac{BCWP}{ACWP} = CI$
A	$\dfrac{\$1{,}500}{\$1{,}200} = 1.25$	$\dfrac{\$1{,}500}{\$1{,}500} = 1$
B	$\dfrac{\$3{,}000}{\$3{,}000} = 1$	$\dfrac{\$3{,}000}{\$3{,}000} = 1$
E	$\dfrac{\$1{,}628}{\$3{,}256} = 0.5$	$\dfrac{\$1{,}628}{\$2{,}900} = 0.56$

These values indicate that during the control period, 25% more work was performed for activity A than planned (SI = 1.25) but at the exact cost budgeted for that work content (CI = 1). For activity B, the planned work content was performed at the planned cost, and for activity E, only half of the planned work content was performed (SI = 0.5). The cost effectiveness of performing that work content was only 56% (CI = 0.56).

The SI and the CI can be calculated for a single activity, for a group of activities, or for the whole project. This is done by accumulating the values of BCWS, BCWP, and ACWP for the appropriate activities and calculating the values of SI and CI on the basis of these totals. For our example, the project SI after 4 weeks is

$$SI = \frac{\$1{,}500 + \$3{,}000 + \$1{,}628}{\$1{,}200 + \$3{,}000 + \$3{,}256} = 0.82$$

and the CI is

$$CI = \frac{\$1{,}500 + \$3{,}000 + \$1{,}628}{\$1{,}500 + \$3{,}000 + \$2{,}900} = 0.83$$

The above ratios can be interpreted as follows. For scheduling, on average, only 82% of the scheduled work was completed, which suggests that the project may be late. The amount of delay is not clear because the duration of the project is dictated by the critical path and not by the average work content already completed. If a late-start strategy is being used, however, then there is a one-to-one relationship between the SI and delay in project completion. For cost, the index value of 83% means that for every dollar spent, the value of the work completed, on average, was just $0.83. In other words, we can expect a cost overrun for the project.

The EV analysis can be performed on a periodic or on a cumulative basis. Table 12.5 summarizes the three values (BCWS, BCWP, and ACWP) for activities A, B, and E for weeks 1 through 4. This information can also be presented graphically for each activity

TABLE 12.5   The Values of BCWS, BCWP, and ACWP for Weeks 1–4

	Week 1			Week 2			Week 3			Week 4		
Activity	BCWS	BCWP	ACWP	BCWS	BCWP	ACWP	BCWS	BCWP	ACWP	BCWS	BCWP	ACWP
A	$300	$500	$500	$300	$500	$500	$300	$300	$300	$300	$200	$200
B	$1,000	$1,000	$1,000	$1,000	$1,000	$1,000	$1,000	$500	$500	$0	$500	$500
E	$814	$300	$814	$814	$400	$686	$814	$500	$1,000	$814	$428	$400
Total	$2,114	$1,800	$2,314	$2,114	$1,900	$2,186	$2,114	$1,300	$1,800	$1,114	$1,128	$1,100

or for the entire project. Figure 12.6 depicts the cumulative values of BCWS, BCWP, and ACWP for each activity, and Fig. 12.7 presents these values for the entire project.

Depending on the activity, Fig. 12.6 illustrates three different situations:

1. *Activity A.* The EV (BCWP) and the actual cost (ACWP) are the same, and both are above BCWS. This implies that activity A is performed at cost and ahead of schedule.

2. *Activity B.* BCWP and ACWP are the same. During weeks 1 and 2, they are equal to BCWP (i.e., activity B is on budget and on schedule). In week 3, BCWP and ACWP are below BCWS, indicating a delay that causes activity B to finish in week 4 instead of week 3.

3. *Activity E.* The value of BCWP is consistently below BCWS and ACWP. There-fore, activity E is late and experiences a budget overrun.

Figure 12.7 illustrates the project cost and schedule situation. BCWP is below BCWS and ACWP; thus, the entire project is late and over budget. The SI and the CI of the project for the first 4 weeks are summarized in Table 12.6.

An alternative view of the data in Fig. 12.7 is presented in Figs. 12.8 and 12.9, in which the values of SI and CI are plotted as a function of time. Both SI and CI are below 1, which means that the project is late and suffers from budget overruns. Fur-thermore, there is no clear trend of improvement in SI and CI.

To integrate schedule and cost information, the values of SI and CI are plotted to-gether in Fig. 12.10. Each point on the graph corresponds to a control period. By observ-ing the time associated with each point, it is possible to see the trend in the CI and SI.

In project management, the goal is to maintain values of CI and SI that are greater than or equal to 1, which would place them in the upper right quadrant of Fig. 12.10. This

TABLE 12.6   Values of SI and CI for Weeks 1–4

Week	BCWS	BCWP	ACWP	$CI = \dfrac{BCWP}{ACWP}$	$SI = \dfrac{BCWP}{BCWS}$
1	$2,114	$1,800	$2,314	0.78	0.85
2	$4,228	$3,700	$4,500	0.82	0.88
3	$6,342	$5,000	$6,300	0.79	0.79
4	$7,456	$6,128	$7,400	0.83	0.82

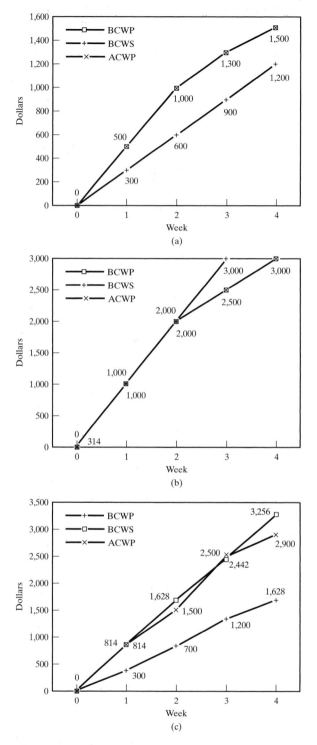

Figure 12.6 EV analysis: (a) activity A;
(b) activity B; (c) activity E.

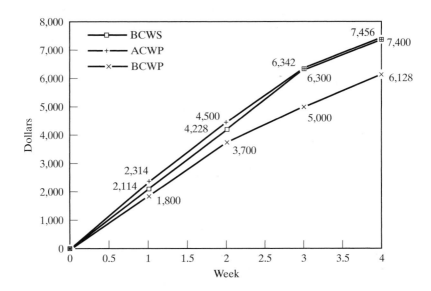

Figure 12.7   EV analysis for the project.

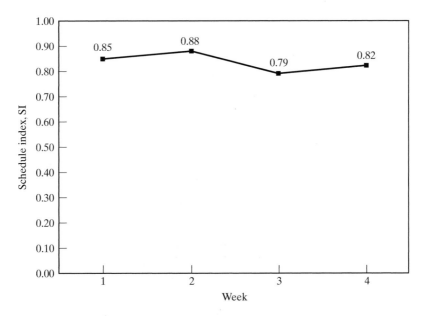

Figure 12.8   SI for the project.

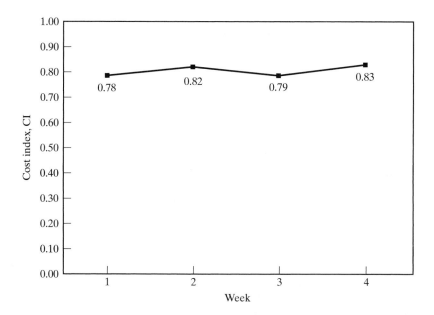

Figure 12.9 CI for the project.

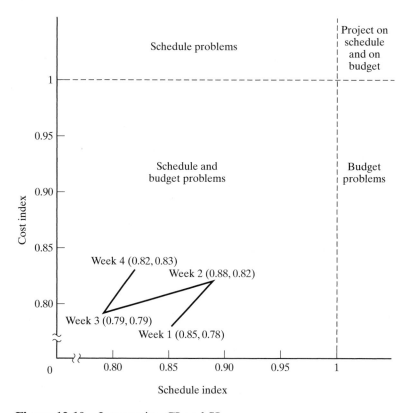

Figure 12.10 Integrating CI and SI.

is not the case here. Nevertheless, we see in Fig. 12.10 that in week 4, both CI and SI show improvement over week 3. This is after a similar improvement in week 2, which was followed by poor performance in week 3.

12.4 REPORTING PROGRESS

The values of BCWP and ACWP for each activity are the building blocks in a progress report. The OBS-WBS matrix that relates each activity to a bottom-level OBS unit and to a bottom-level WBS element facilitates analysis at any OBS level, WBS level, or combination of the two. For example, from Fig. 12.4, we see that activities A, B and E are performed by department 2. None of the activities assigned to department 1 is scheduled for the first month. Thus, the OBS-based progress report given in Table 12.7 for the first month shows no activity for department 1 and a summary of activities A, B and E for department 2.

Based on the data in Table 12.7, it is clear that department 1 was not scheduled to work on the project during the first month and indeed did not perform any activities. Department 2 was scheduled to perform work content budgeted at $7,456 but completed only $6,128 worth of work, whereas the actual cost for the period was $7,400. One therefore can conclude that department 2 ran into trouble performing its work content, precipitating a budget overrun of $1,328 during the first month. This amount is considered "sunk cost" because it cannot be retrieved.

The WBS report for the example project is contained in Table 12.8. The similarity in structure between this report and the OBS report stems from the fact that both are based on the same data—the project plan and the same three measures: BCWS, BCWP, and ACWP. The WBS report reveals that element III should be monitored carefully because it is experiencing both a schedule delay and a budget overrun.

The reports in Tables 12.6 and 12.7 can be produced for each control period or on a cumulative basis from the start of the project. Many computer packages that support EV calculations provide this information. The totals in Tables 12.6 and 12.7 are identical. This is because both represent the total project performance for the first 4 weeks. The accumulation of information from lower-level OBS or WBS elements to the project level (or any other higher level) is called *roll-up* and can be applied to both the OBS and the WBS because of their hierarchical nature. At each level of the OBS or the WBS, the values of ACWP, BCWS, and BCWP associated with each organizational unit or WBS element are calculated as the sum of the corresponding values of the organizational units or WBS elements under it. Using the roll-up mechanism, it is possible to

TABLE 12.7   Cumulative Cost and Schedule Control Report by OBS Element (Weeks 1–4)

Organizational unit	BCWS	BCWP	ACWP	SV	CV	SI	CI
Department 1	0	0	0	0	0	–	–
Department 2	$7,456	$6,128	$7,400	−$1,328	−$1,272	0.82	0.83
Total project	$7,456	$6,128	$7,400	−$1,328	−$1,272	0.82	0.83

TABLE 12.8   Cost and Schedule Control Report by WBS Element

WBS element	BCWS	BCWP	ACWP	SV	CV	SI	CI
I	$1,200	$1,500	$1,500	$300	0	1.25	1
II	$3,000	$3,000	$3,000	0	0	1	1
III	$3,256	$1,628	$2,900	−$1,628	−$1,272	0.5	0.56
	$7,456	$6,128	$7,400	−$1,328	−$1,272	0.82	0.83

generate reports at different OBS and WBS levels according to management needs. On the basis of the cumulative values of BCWS, BCWP, and ACWP, the CV and SV can be calculated. Thus, the integration of the two hierarchical structures (OBS and WBS) with the EV concept provides the foundation for an information system that supports cost and schedule control at each managerial level.

12.5 UPDATING COST AND SCHEDULE ESTIMATES

When data that reflect the current status of tasks and actual costs are collected, it is only logical to update previous estimates of the project's completion time and budget requirements. Estimates tend to improve as actual progress is made. This is due to the completion of activities for which actual duration and cost become known, as well as to better information on workforce productivity and the availability and cost of resources. Bear in mind that the original estimates are usually based on historical records of similar projects and may be problematic. When new data become available, a new critical path analysis in which the actual duration of past activities and updated estimates for the duration of future activities are incorporated should be performed.

New estimates derived from current information on past performance are the basis of trend analysis. If, for example, a recent estimate indicates that the expected total cost of the project is (much) higher than the original budget, then a management decision may be needed. The revised estimate may cause a change in specification if expected total cost should not exceed the budget, a change in schedule aimed at replanning future cash flow according to available budgets, or, in the extreme, abandonment of the project. Other options may also exist. The task of the control system is to focus management's attention on potential problems as soon as the likelihood of such problems, based on trend analysis and updated estimates, is deemed high.

To reestimate the cost of the project, acceptable accounting procedures must be defined together with the necessary data elements. The following notation is used for this purpose:

BAC   *Budget at completion*: total budget of the project activities, based on the original project plan

= sum of BCWS values over lower-level OBS elements, or

= sum of BCWS values over lower-level WBS elements

WR   *Work remaining*: budgeted cost of the work not yet accomplished by the end of the reporting period; $WR = BAC − BCWP$

ETC   *Estimate to complete*: updated estimate of the cost of the WR
EAC   *Estimate at completion*: updated estimate of the total project cost; EAC = ACWP + ETC

Because the value of ACWP is known, only a revised estimate of ETC is required to update the EAC estimate.

Estimating EAC: Original Estimate Approach.   This approach is based on the assumption that the original estimate of the cost of WR is valid and therefore only the original estimate of the work that was already performed should be replaced by the actual cost of that work content.

EAC = ACWP + ETC, and because

ETC = BAC − BCWP, we get

EAC = ACWP + (BAC − BCWP) = BAC − (BCWP − ACWP) = BAC − CV

Thus, in the revised budget, the EAC is equal to the original BAC adjusted by the CV.

Estimating EAC: Revised Estimate Approach.   The updated estimate of WR is based on the assumption that the relative deviation in the cost of the work completed is a good estimate for the relative deviation of the cost of WR.

The relative deviation of cost of work completed is defined as follows:

$$\frac{\text{ACWP}}{\text{BCWP}} = \frac{1}{\text{CI}}$$

Assuming the same deviation factor for WR, we get

$$\text{ETC} = \text{WR} \times \frac{1}{\text{CI}} = (\text{BAC} - \text{BCWP}) \times \frac{1}{\text{CI}}$$

Therefore, we can write

$$\text{EAC} = \text{ACWP} + (\text{BAC} - \text{BCWP}) \times \frac{1}{\text{CI}} = \text{ACWP} + \frac{\text{BAC}}{\text{CI}} - \frac{\text{BCWP}}{\text{CI}}$$

Substituting

$$\text{ACWP} = \frac{\text{BCWP}}{\text{CI}}$$

we get

$$\text{EAC} = \frac{\text{BAC}}{\text{CI}} = \text{BAC} \times \frac{\text{ACWP}}{\text{BCWP}}$$

The two estimation procedures can be applied at each OBS level, at each WBS level, or at the total project level. For the example project with BAC = $31,000 (see Table 11.3), the report after 1 month shows the following results:

BCWS = $7,456	CV = −$1,272	CI = 0.83
BCWP = $6,128	SV = −$1,328	SI = 0.82
ACWP = $7,400		

Thus, revised costs using (1) the original estimate approach and (2) the revised estimate approach are

1. EAC = ACWP + BAC − ACWP = BAC − CV
= $31,000 − (−$1,272) = $32,272

2. $\text{EAC} = \text{BAC} \times \dfrac{1}{\text{CI}} = \$31,000 \times \dfrac{1}{0.83} = \$37,349$

The difference between the two values stems from the fact that in the first approach, we assume that past cost performance is not a predictor of future performance and that the original plan is a better one, whereas in the second, we assume that the past deviations are a good predictor of the cost deviations in the WR.

The two estimating procedures are not the only alternatives available. One may also use a combination of the two: for some activities to assume approach 1 and for others to assume approach 2 for forecasting. Other techniques, such as those based on time-series or regression analysis, may be used as well. The important point is to be consistent and use the same estimation procedure for the entire project throughout its life cycle.

The selection of an estimation procedure is a management decision that should be made in the conceptual design phase of the project. Consistency in predicting total costs results in the ability to show at each control period the current cost status together with the trend of cost predictions from the start of the project. Such consistency enables comparisons of performance between OBS and WBS elements at different time periods, as well as the monitoring of cost trends that foreshadow future problems.

Rather than continually monitor performance, threshold values may be used to trigger management-by-exception activities. For example, by specifying threshold values of 5% and 10% for CI and SI, respectively, any negative deviation from the original plan (100%) for either one of these values would be reported to upper management along with a plan for corrective action. The specific threshold values and the procedures for reporting and reacting to deviations are organization dependent and must be worked out on an individual basis. The more important measure is CI because it is a strong indicator of ongoing budgetary requirements. In contrast, SI does not provide the same level of information about delays and hence is not as strong an indicator. Delays are determined by the critical path, whereas SI is determined from all delays regardless of whether the corresponding activities are critical.

12.6 TECHNOLOGICAL CONTROL: QUALITY AND CONFIGURATION

Cost and schedule control are important management responsibilities. Technological control is required to detect any deviations from technical specifications and standards that may change during the life cycle of the project. To achieve a satisfactory level of performance, an integrated quality control and quality assurance program with well-established procedures must be designed and implemented.

The concept of total quality control is relevant for the success of a project. On the basis of this concept, quality becomes the focal point of any organizational unit (OBS element) that is performing work on any element of the project (WBS element) at any point in the project life cycle. In the early stages, systems engineers evaluate various design alternatives based on performance, quality, and reliability measures, as well as cost and schedule. It is well known among these engineers that the bitter taste of a low-quality, unreliable product lingers long after the sweet taste of low cost and fast delivery.

The alternative selected in the initial stages of a project is designated the "baseline" for purposes of configuration management and control. Recall that configuration management (CM) is a system designed to ensure that the product delivered at the end of the project is built according to the specifications laid out in the baseline and all approved subsequent engineering change requests (ECRs). The components, procedures, and logic of the CM system are discussed in Chapter 8.

The next component—configuration control—is integrated with quality control by a mechanism called *configuration test and audit*. This component of the CM system is designed to guarantee that the quality control activity is based on the most recent configuration composed of the baseline design and all approved ECRs. The integration of CM with cost and schedule control is done at the *change control board* (CCB). The CCB is the focal point of configuration control, as explained in Chapter 8. Members of the CCB are representatives of the project and the functional areas that might be affected by proposed design changes. At the CCB, ECRs are evaluated on the basis of their impact on cost, in schedule, and performance. By linking all four control systems together, deviations in cost, schedule, quality, or design can be detected and addressed in a timely manner.

The four basic control systems—cost, schedule, quality, and configuration—operate throughout the project life cycle within the framework of the OBS-WBS matrix. Together they are used to detect deviations, to identify their organizational source and their effect on various elements of the WBS, and to assist in developing solutions to problems caused by such deviations.

In the previous sections, we presented a generic approach to project control. We now focus on several specific techniques that are applicable under limited but prevalent circumstances.

12.7 LINE OF BALANCE

Project management techniques discussed so far are designed for the one-time effort in which a specific, unique set of goals related to a single project have to be met. There are, however, projects that involve more than one product unit. Examples might include the construction of multiple power plants at the same site or an order to build a fleet of identical submarines at a shipyard. In the latter case, it is possible to view each boat as a project (although no longer unique) or to define the total order as a single project with repetitive activities. Because such projects are not uncommon, a special technique called the *line of balance* (LOB) has been developed to support their management and control.

The LOB technique is based on control points or milestones in the production process of the product. These control points are related to critical activities and resources that are identified during the planning cycle. A typical control point is the successful completion (including test and inspection) of an activity on the critical path. The elapsed time between consecutive control points is estimated, and a milestone schedule for a single product unit is developed.

The master production schedule (MPS) in such projects specifies the planned delivery time of each product unit based on the contractual agreement with the client. As the project starts, control is exercised by comparing the number of units that pass each control point with the number that should have passed that point according to the MPS. Any deviations trigger a detailed analysis aimed at identifying the cause of the deviation and the appropriate corrective action.

To illustrate the LOB approach, consider a manufacturer of communication systems. Each system is tailor-made for the customer who may place one or several identical orders. Suppose that a customer orders a total of 110 systems in a specific configuration. It is estimated that 6 weeks is required to complete one unit. Four milestones are selected as control points (see Table 12.9):

a. End of rack installation: 2 weeks after the start of work on a system
b. End of subsystems (modules) installation: 3 weeks after the start of work on a system
c. End of subsystems integration: 5 weeks after the start of work on a system
d. End of acceptance tests and delivery: 6 weeks after the start of work on a system

The MPS specifies delivery dates for the 110 systems in accordance with the data in Table 12.10. On the basis of the MPS and the list of control points (or milestones), it is possible to forecast the number of systems expected to pass through each milestone at the end of each week. For example, the number of systems expected to pass each milestone by the end of the fifth week is as follows:

- The 20 systems scheduled for delivery on week 10 should be 5 weeks from delivery. Because it takes 6 weeks to complete a system, these systems should be 1 week in process not having passed any milestone yet.

TABLE 12.9   Schedule of Milestones or Control Points

Control point	Description	Week after start of unit production	Lead time to delivery (weeks)
A	Rack installation	2	$6 - 2 = 4$
B	Subsystems installation	3	$6 - 3 = 3$
C	Subsystems integration	5	$6 - 5 = 1$
D	Acceptance test	6	$6 - 6 = 0$

TABLE 12.10   Delivery Schedule for the 110 Systems

Delivery date as of week	Systems scheduled for delivery	Cumulative number of systems
6	30	30
7	20	50
8	10	60
9	30	90
10	20	110

- The 30 systems scheduled for delivery on week 9 should be 4 weeks from delivery or 2 weeks into the process and should have completed milestone A only.
- The 10 systems scheduled for delivery on week 8 should be 3 weeks from delivery or 3 weeks into the process and should have completed milestones A and B.
- The 20 systems scheduled for delivery on week 7 should be 2 weeks from delivery or 4 weeks into the process and should have finished milestones A and B.
- The 30 systems scheduled for delivery on week 6 should be 1 week from delivery or 5 weeks into the process and should have finished milestones A, B and C.

These results are summarized in Table 12.11. Thus 90 systems should have completed milestone A, 60 milestone B, and 30 milestone C. Figure 12.11 displays this information graphically.

It is possible to use a graphical procedure to control a repetitive project by combining the milestone information with the MPS. To construct the control chart, first plot the cumulative number of systems versus time to depict the MPS. On this graph, start at the current control period (week 5), and for each milestone, add its corresponding lead time. For milestone A, the lead time is 4 weeks. Adding 4 weeks to the current control period (week 5), we get 9 weeks. The cumulative number of units corresponding to 9 weeks on the MPS is 90 units, as illustrated in Fig. 12.12.

TABLE 12.11   Scheduled Milestones at the End of Week 5

Deliveries scheduled on week	Number of systems	Time to delivery (weeks)	Number of systems scheduled to finish at milestone:			
			A	B	C	D
5	—	—	—	—	—	—
6	30	1	30	30	30	—
7	20	2	20	20	—	—
8	10	3	10	10	—	—
9	30	4	30	—	—	—
10	20	5	—	—	—	—
		Total =	90	60	30	0

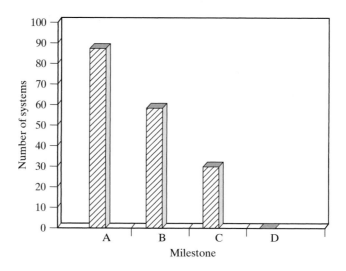

Figure 12.11 Planned number of systems to finish each milestone after 5 weeks.

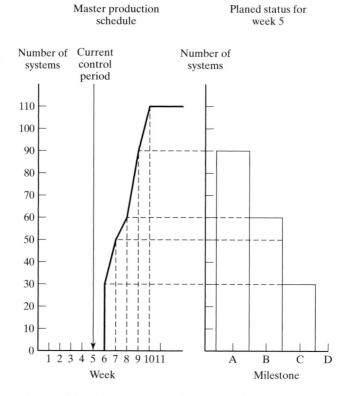

Figure 12.12 Constructing the planned status from the MPS.

Thus, the expected number of systems to complete milestone A is 90 systems. In a similar way, the expected number of systems can be constructed for each milestone.

The LOB displays the work that should be accomplished to ensure delivery according to the MPS. Suppose that after 5 weeks, 80 systems completed milestone A, 60 completed milestone B, 40 completed milestone C, and 20 systems completed milestone D. The deviations between the plan (LOB) and actual achievement are as follows:

Milestone	LOB	Actual	Deviation
A	90	80	-10
B	60	60	0
C	30	40	-10
D	0	20	20

Thus, milestones A and C are late with respect to the MPS. At A, 10 systems late corresponds to a $\frac{10}{90} \times 100\% = 11\%$ delay. Milestone B is exactly on schedule, whereas at C and D, actual performance is ahead of schedule.

A detailed analysis of the activities performed before milestone A should be initiated. In case an increase in the workforce is required to catch up with the MPS, the necessary resources may be obtained from some of the activities that precede milestones C and D, which are ahead of schedule.

A graphical display of the LOB and the actual performance gives a clear indication of the project's status. Figure 12.13 depicts the situation for week 5 in the example.

Figure 12.13   LOB and actual performance.

12.8 OVERHEAD CONTROL

Project execution costs can be divided into the following categories:

- Direct costs resulting from expenses tied explicitly to the performance of WPs, which have a tangible deliverable at the end of their execution
- Direct overhead costs (DOH) resulting from infrastructure expenses required for all stages of the project
- Organizational overhead resulting from the overall support that the project obtains from other organizational units

Summing all categories gives the total cost for completing a project. From a control point of view, it is common to differentiate between the first two categories and the third, because the project manager has some control over the two categories of direct costs, whereas general overhead is "spread" by the company's accounting system over all company activities. In the previous sections, we discussed control mechanisms for direct costs. To complete the picture, we now introduce control mechanisms for DOH.

The estimation of the DOH budget typically proceeds from the assumption that infrastructure support for the project will remain constant during execution. Therefore, a fixed amount of DOH dollars will be required per unit time until the project is completed. Examples of infrastructure activities include project management, quality assurance, and data processing. DOH is also called the *level of effort* because certain levels of resources are required per unit time. The performance associated with those efforts is difficult to quantify because no specific deliverables accompany the resources used other than the project as a whole.

A common method of estimating the amount of resources required for infrastructure support is based on a designated percentage of the direct costs associated with the direct costs of the WPs. The actual percentage is somewhat arbitrary and depends on company policy, judgment, and experience. A typical range might be from 10% to 25%, depending on the nature of the project and its duration. For example, standard projects, such as introducing an "off-the-shelf" software package for salary administration, will require less DOH compared with designing and building a package from scratch.

Project managers often believe incorrectly that in matrix organizations that outsource their WPs, a project's rate of progress does not affect the total cost, especially when the contractual vehicle is based on a fixed fee. What they fail to take into account is the continued need for infrastructure support throughout a project's life cycle. This need explains the high correlation between cost overruns and late completions in such organizations. Without a project control system that evaluates the effectiveness of the resources used for infrastructure support, the total cost of a project may increase significantly without early detection.

Example 12-1

To illustrate the above points, consider a project whose direct costs are estimated to be $4 million. Using historical data on similar projects, coupled with the fact that many technological risks exist, it was decided to add 25% for DOH; i.e., DOH = $0.25 \times \$4M = \$1M$. This means that the total direct budget is $\$4M + \$1M = \$5M$. To simplify, let us assume that there are no organizational overhead costs that need to be included.

Suppose that the customer for the project has agreed to pay \$5.75M upon completion. In percentage terms, the expected profit is ($5.75M − \$5M)/\$5M × 100% = 15%. If the planned execution period is 20 months, then the DOH budget is \$50,000 per month.

Before we continue with the analysis, let us describe what actually happened. First, a 12-month delay was experienced as a result of critical resource shortages, so the project was not completed until 32 months after it began. During the execution, the project manager was under the illusion that there were no lost overruns because the EV analyses, which were performed on each WP periodically, never showed any significant deviations. Second, the appropriateness of the DOH estimates was never verified.

As a result of the delay, an additional \$600,000 (= \$50,000 × 12) was required to cover infrastructure costs, thus dropping the profit to \$750,000 − \$600,000 = \$150,000. That is, the actual profit was 3% rather than the planned 15%.

Let us now demonstrate the use and effectiveness of two EV approaches to control: (1) the classical method and (2) the adjusted method. To begin, let us assume that the status of the project after the 5 months of activity is as follows:

Actual cost of WPs to date:	ACWP = \$650,000
Value of work scheduled to be completed:	BCWS = \$1,000,000
EV of completed work:	BCWP = \$625,000
Overhead cost of infrastructure to date:	DOH = \$250,000

Assuming a linear effort over time, BCWS was calculated by multiplying the total direct cost by the portion of work that was scheduled to be completed within the 5-month period. That is, BCWP = \$4M × (5/20) = \$1M. Similarly, the planned DOH budget for the first 5 months was calculated based on proportional outlays; i.e., DOH = 5 × \$50,000 = \$250,000. Actual DOH expenditures were as originally planned for the first 5 months.

Using the classical analysis approach.   The first step is to calculate the CI, which enables us to determine whether the project is on budget. For this purpose, we use the actual costs and the EVs of the work completed thus far. The actual cost for both the execution of the WPs and the DOH is

$$ACWP + DOH = \$650,000 + \$250,000 = \$900,000$$

The EV of work completed should consider the work performed and the value of the infrastructure work. The first component is calculated in the manner demonstrated in the previous sections. In calculating the value of the work associated with DOH, the assumption made in the classical approach is that the value of the work performed equals the actual cost, in this case \$250,000. Therefore, the total EV is

$$EV = \$625,000 + \$250,000 = \$875,000$$

and the CI is

$$CI = \$875,000/\$900,000 = 0.972$$

This value, which is just below 1, indicates that the budget overrun after 5 months of activity is not very significant, at least in percentage terms. On the basis of the above calculation, the revised budget for the project is

$$\$5,000,000/0.972 = \$5,144,000$$

which means that an additional $144,000 is required at this time to complete all work. Of course, as the project progresses, this estimate might change.

Using the adjusted approach.   In this method, the EV of the DOH expenses are adjusted to reflect actual progress rather than proportional progress. If all of the WPs that are scheduled to be completed during the control period have been completed, then the DOH EV of work is equal to the DOH budget planned for that period. In the analysis, the SI is used to calculate the extent of work progress realized. Recall that SI measures the portion of work completed compared with the portion planned to be completed during the control period. In this case,

$$SI = BCWP/BCWS = \$625,000/\$1,000,000 = 0.625$$

Therefore, the DOH EV is

$$BCWP \times SI = \$250,000 \times 0.625 = \$156,000$$

Using these data, the adjusted value of the CI is

$$CI = (\$625,000 + \$156,000)/(\$650,000 + \$250,000) = 0.868$$

giving a revised total budget of

$$\$5,000,000/0.868 = \$5,760,000$$

Thus, the forecasted budget overrun is now $760,000 rather than $144,000, as calculated by the classical method. The difference is due to a combination of additional execution and especially overhead expenses that are expected to result during the remainder of the project.
    Calculating the cost efficiency index for just the infrastructure support (DOH) during the first 5 months using the adjusted approach, we obtain

$$CI(DOH) = BCWP/ACWP = \$156,000/\$250,000 = 0.625$$

This value is identical to the SI because the $250,000 actually spent on DOH is equal to the amount originally budgeted for the first 5 months. A value of 0.625 for CI(DOH) indicates clearly that the infrastructure resources were not used effectively during this time.   ■

The project manager should continually verify that DOH expenses are in line with the work performed on the WPs during the control period. When progress is less than planned, DOH should be reduced accordingly. Of course, it will not always be possible to achieve a linear reduction because overhead is not necessarily proportional to effort. For example, assume that three machine tools were leased for the purpose of building prototypes. Now, if a change is approved to redesign a subcomponent, then the rate of progress may be slowed considerably. Depending on the leasing arrangements, it may not be possible to reduce the DOH; however, the project manager should at least consider terminating the lease on one of the machine tools and reducing the number of prototypes to compensate for delays and expected cost overruns.

TEAM PROJECT
Thermal Transfer Plant

With the approval of the rotary combustor project, a detailed plan for project control is required. In developing the plan, your team should address the following issues:

1. Which aspects of the project should be monitored (e.g., cost, schedule)?
2. Where will the data come from?
3. What is the original source of data?
4. How often should data be collected?
5. How should the data be processed? (Distinguish between trend analysis and identification of exceptions.)
6. What kind of reports will be issued? Who should get the reports? How often?
7. What kind of ad hoc questions should the control system support?

Be specific as possible. Present a flow diagram for data processing and a format of each report that you suggest. Be careful not to produce too many reports or to collect data that will not be used later. Explain and justify your approach to the control of the project.

DISCUSSION QUESTIONS

1. Describe the control systems used in one organization with which you are familiar.
2. Referring to Question 1, explain how the control system that you identified deals with uncertainty.
3. Give an example of an organization that does not use any control systems. Is this justified?
4. Suppose that you have decided to build a new house. Explain what kind of project control you will consider and why.
5. Why is it important to integrate cost and schedule control? Give an example for which separate cost and schedule control systems may not function properly.
6. Explain how you would measure the EV of the following activities:
   a. Writing a term paper
   b. Building a nuclear power plant
   c. Designing a new car
   d. Developing a new training program
7. Is there a need for "technological control" in developing a new insurance policy? Explain.
8. Explain what the responsibilities of "quality control" are in a project associated with making a Hollywood-style movie. How would these responsibilities differ if the movie were a documentary on, say, the search to identify the human genome?
9. Is there a need for a control system in projects performed by nonprofit organizations? Explain and give examples.

10. Explain the advantages and disadvantages of the line-of-balance technique as opposed to using several program evaluation and review technique networks.

11. How would you build total quality management principles into a project control system?

12. Why will a delay in the completion of a project probably cause a budget overrun?

EXERCISES

12.1 The National Institutes of Health support research and development of new treatments for AIDS (acquired immune deficiency syndrome). Develop a project control system by which the agency will be able to control projects that it supports.

    a. What are the objectives of the control system?
    b. What are the performance measures?
    c. What data are required?
    d. How should raw data be collected?
    e. How should the data be analyzed?
    f. How should the results be reported, and how often?

12.2 Consider the project plan defined in Table 12.12.

TABLE 12.12

Activity	Scheduled start day	Scheduled finish day	Cost/day
A	1	3	$1,000
B	1	5	$5,000
C	3	7	$3,000
D	5	15	$1,000
E	7	22	$2,000
F	7	25	$4,000

A cost schedule control system produces weekly reports. The reports for weeks 1, 2, and 3 (assume 5 working days each week) are shown Table 12.13.

    a. Write a weekly progress report for each activity based on the above information.
    b. Comment on the level of control that can be achieved based on the given information.

TABLE 12.13

Activity	Week 1 Status	Week 1 Cost	Week 2 Status	Week 2 Cost	Week 3 Status	Week 3 Cost
A	In process	$1,500	Finished	$3,000	Finished	$3,000
B	In process	$25,000	Finished	$30,000	Finished	$30,000
C	In process	$7,000	Finished	$10,000	Finished	$10,000
D	Not started	0	In process	$5,000	In process	$7,000
E	Not started	0	Not started	0	In process	$10,000
F	Not started	0	In process	$10,000	In process	$20,000

12.3 In Exercise 12.2, an estimate of the "percent complete" for each activity each week is reported in Table 12.14. Redo parts (a) and (b).

TABLE 12.14

Activity	Percent complete		
	Week 1	Week 2	Week 3
A	50	100	100
B	30	100	100
C	10	100	100
D	0	20	60
E	0	0	25
F	0	30	40

12.4 An activity on the critical path of a project was scheduled to be completed within 12 weeks, with a budget of $8,000. During a performance review, which took place 7 weeks after the activity was initiated, it was found that 50% of the work had already been completed and that the actual cost was $4,500.

   a. Calculate the EV of the activity.
   b. Calculate the CI and SI for the activity.
   c. Calculate the expected BAC using the original estimate approach.
   d. Calculate the expected BAC using the revised estimate approach.
   e. Compare and discuss the results obtained in parts (c) and (d).

12.5 The performance of a project was evaluated 10 weeks after its start. Table 12.15 gives the relevant information.

   a. On the same Gantt chart, show the project plan and the project progress, and discuss the two.
   b. Calculate the SI for each organizational unit U1 and U2 and for the project as a whole. Discuss.

TABLE 12.15

Activity	Immediate predecessors	Normal time	Budget	Organization unit	Percent complete	Money spent
A	–	4	$90	U1	100	$110
B	A	2	$35	U2	100	$20
C	A	6	$75	U2	40	$40
D	B	3	$60	U1	80	$90
E	C	10	$80	U1	0	0
F	–	2	$40	U2	100	$40
G	F	5	$55	U1	50	$30
H	F	7	$80	U2	100	$60
I	D, E, G	1	$40	U2	0	0
J	H	10	$100	U1	0	0

    c. Repeat part (b) for the CI.

    d. On the basis of past performance, update the expected completion time and budget. State your assumptions.

12.6 For the project described in Exercise 12.5, calculate and chart the following values: BCWS, BCWP, and ACWP. Assume linearity of cost versus time. State any additional assumptions that you believe are needed.

12.7 Big State University has decided to start a new program for executives called "Management of Technology." Your task is to design the control system for this project. Discuss the following issues:

    a. The performance measure that should be used.

    b. Ways to collect the relevant data for evaluating the current situation.

    c. How should raw data be selected for evaluating the project?

    d. How should the data be analyzed?

    e. How should the results be reported?

12.8 In designing the new program outlined in Exercise 12.7, identify the WPs and the organizational units that will be responsible for their implementation.

12.9 Explain CM and control within the curriculum of your school. Give three examples that demonstrate a good configuration control process and three that identify poor CM.

BIBLIOGRAPHY

Burke, R., *Project Management: Planning and Control Techniques*, Fourth Edition, Halsted Press, New York, 2003.

Fleming, Q. and J. Koppelman, *Earned Value Project Management*, Second Edition, Project Management Institute, Newtown Square, PA, 2000.

Globerson, S. and J. Riggs, "Multi-Performance Measures for Better Operational Control," *International Journal of Production Research*, Vol. 27, No. 1, pp. 187–194, 1989.

Globerson, S. and A. Shtub, "Effective Measurement of Project Progress," Proceedings of the Project Management Institute Conference, New Orleans, pp. 381–387, October 1995.

Kogan, K., T. Raz and R. Elitzur, "Optimal Control in Project Management: Analytically Solvable Cases," *IIE Transactions on Design & Manufacturing*, Vol. 34, No. 1, pp. 63–75, 2002.

Pinto, J. and J. Trailer (Editors), *Essentials of Project Control*, Project Management Institute, Newtown Square, PA, 1999.

Pryor, S., "Project Control: Part 1: Planning and Budgeting," *Management Accounting*, Vol. 66, No. 5, pp. 16–17, 1988.

Pryor, S., "Project Control: Part 2: Measuring, Analyzing and Reporting," *Management Accounting*, Vol. 66, No. 6, pp. 18–19, 1988.

Raz, T. and E. Erdal, "Optimal Timing of Project Control Points," *European Journal of Operational Research*, Vol. 127, No. 2, pp. 252–261, 2000.

Shenhar, A., D. Dvir, O. Levy and A. Maltz, "Project Success—A Multidimensional, Strategic Concept," *Long Range Planning*, Vol. 34, pp. 699–725, 2001.

Shenhar, A., A. Tishler, D. Dvir, S. Lipovetski and T. Lechler, "Refining the Search for Project Success Factors: A Multidimensional Typological Approach," *R&D Management*, Vol. 32, No. 2, pp. 111–124, 2002.

Shtub, A., "Evaluation of Two Schedule Control Techniques for the Development and Implementation of New Technologies: A Simulation Study," *R&D Management*, Vol. 22, No. 1, pp. 81–87, 1992.

U.S. Department of Defense, *Performance Measurement for Selected Acquisitions*, DOD 7000.2, Washington, DC, June 1977.

U.S. Department of Defense, *Cost/Schedule Control Systems Criteria Joint Implementation Guide*, Washington, DC, Several publication numbers issued by various DOD agencies since October 1976.

U.S. Department of Energy, *Cost/Schedule Control Systems Criteria for Contract Performance Measurement*, DOE/2250.1A, Office of Project and Facilities Management, Washington, DC, September 1982.

U.S. Department of Energy, *Cost/Schedule Control Systems Criteria for Contract Performance Measurement: Work Breakdown Structure Guide*, Office of Project and Facilities Management, Washington, DC, 1981.

Zwikael, O., S. Globerson and T. Raz, "Evaluation of Models for Forecasting the Final Cost of a Project," *Project Management Journal*, Vol. 31, No. 1, pp. 53–57, 2000.

Appendix 12A

Example of a Work Breakdown Structure

The WBS is an important building block of the project management system. Organizations that are frequently engaged in engineering projects have developed guidelines for designing the WBS. The following is a summary WBS for an electronic system. This is one of several WBSs presented in MIL-STD-881-A, "Work Breakdown Structures for Defense Material Items" April 25, 1975.

Level 1	Level 2	Level 3
Electronic system	Prime mission equipment	Integration and assembly
		Sensors
		Communications
		Automatic data processing equipment
		Computer programs
		Data displays
		Auxiliary equipment
	Training	Equipment
		Services
		Facilities
	Peculiar support equipment	Organizational/intermediate (including equipment common to depot)
		Depot (only)
	Systems test and evaluation	Development test and evaluation
		Operational test and evaluation
		Mockups
		Test and evaluation support
		Test facilities
	System/program management	Systems engineering
		Project management
	Data	Technical publications
		Engineering data
		Management data
		Support data
		Data depository
	Operational/site activation	Contractor technical
		Support
		Site/construction
		Site/ship/vehicle
		Conversion
		System assembly
		Installation and checkout on site
	Common support equipment	Organizational/intermediate (including equipment common to depot)
		Depot (only)
	Industrial facilities	Construction/conversion/expansion
		Equipment acquisition or modernization
		Maintenance
	Initial spares and initial repair parts	(Specify by allowance list, grouping, or hardware element)

Department of Energy Cost/Schedule Control Systems Criteria

1. General

a. The management control systems used by the contractor in planning and controlling the performance of the contract shall meet the criteria set forth in paragraph 2 below. Nothing in these criteria is intended to affect the basis on which costs are reimbursed and progress payments are made, and nothing herein will be construed as requiring the use of any single system, or specific method of management control or evaluation of performance. The contractor's systems need not be changed, provided they satisfy the criteria.

b. An element in the evaluation of proposals will be proposer's systems for planning and controlling contract performance. The proposer will fully describe the system to be used. The prospective contractor's cost and schedule control system proposal will be evaluated to determine whether it meets the criteria. The prospective contractor will agree to operate compliant systems throughout the period of contract performance if awarded the contract. DOE will rely on the contractor's compliant systems and, therefore, will not impose separate management control systems.

2. The Criteria

The contractor's management control systems will include policies, procedures, and methods that are designed to ensure that they will accomplish the following:

a. Organization

1. Define all authorized work and related resources to meet the requirements of the contract, using the framework of the contract WBS.

2. Identify the internal organizational elements and the major subcontractors responsible for accomplishing the authorized work.

3. Provide for integration of the contractor's planning, scheduling, budgeting, estimating, work authorization, and cost accumulation systems with each other, the contract WBS, and the OBS.

4. Identify the managerial positions responsible for controlling overhead (indirect costs).

5. Provide for integration of the contract WBS with the contractor's functional organizational structure in a manner that permits cost and schedule performance measurement for contractor WBS and organizational elements.

b. Planning and budgeting

1. Schedule the authorized work in a manner that describes the sequence of work and identifies the significant task interdependencies required to meet the development, production, construction, installation, and delivery requirements of the contract.

2. Identify physical products, milestones, technical performance goals, or other indicators that will be used to measure output.

3. Establish and maintain a time-phased budget baseline at the cost account level against which contract performance can be measured. Initial budgets established for this purpose will be based on the negotiated target cost. Any other account used for performance measurement purposes must be formally recognized by both the contractor and the government.

4. Establish budgets for all authorized work with separate identification of cost elements (labor, material, etc.).

5. To the extent the authorized work can be identified in discrete, short-span WPs, establish budgets for this work in terms of dollars, hours, and other measurable units. When the entire cost account cannot be subdivided into detailed WPs, identify the long-term effort in larger planning packages for budget and scheduling purposes.

6. Provide that the sum of all WP budgets, plus planning package budgets within a cost account equals the cost account budget.

7. Identify relationships of budgets or standards in underlying work authorization systems to budgets for WPs.

8. Identify and control level-of-effort activity by time-phased budgets established for this purpose. Only that effort which cannot be identified as discrete, short-span WPs or as apportioned effort will be classed as level of effort.

9. Establish overhead budgets for the total costs of each significant organizational component whose expenses will become indirect costs. Reflect in the contract budgets at the appropriate level the amounts in overhead pools that will be allocated to the contract as indirect costs.

10. Identify management reserve and undistributed budget.

11. Provide that the contract target cost plus estimated cost of authorized but unpriced work is reconciled with the sum of all internal contract budgets and management reserve.

c. Accounting

1. Record direct costs on an applied or other acceptable basis in a formal system that is controlled by the general books of account.

2. Summarize direct costs from cost accounts into the WBS without allocation of a single cost account to two or more WBS elements.

3. Summarize direct costs from the cost accounts into the contractor's functional organizational elements without allocation of a single cost account to two or more organizational elements.

4. Record all indirect costs that will be allocated to the contract.

5. Identify the bases for allocating the cost of apportioned effort.

6. Identify unit costs, equivalent unit costs, or lot costs as applicable.

7. The contractor's material accounting system shall provide for:

   a. Accurate cost accumulation and assignment of costs to cost accounts in a manner consistent with the budgets, using recognized, acceptable costing techniques.

   b. Determination of price variances by comparing planned versus actual commitments.

   c. Cost performance measurement at the point in time most suitable for the category of material involved but no earlier than the time of actual receipt of material.

   d. Determination of CVs attributable to the excess usage of material.

   e. Determination of unit or lot costs when applicable.

   f. Full accountability for all material purchased for the contract, including the residual inventory.

d. Analysis

1. Identify at the cost account level on a monthly basis using data from or reconcilable with the accounting and budgeting systems:

   a. BCWS and BCWP.

   b. BCWP and applied (actual when appropriate) direct costs for the same work.

    c. EACs and BACs.

    d. Variances resulting from the above comparisons classified in terms of labor, material, or other appropriate elements together with the reasons for significant variances, including technical problems.

2. Identify on a monthly basis, in the detail needed by management for effective control, budgeted indirect costs, actual indirect costs, and variances along with the reasons.

3. Summarize the data elements and associated variances listed in paragraph 2d(1) and (2) above through the contractor organization and contract WBS to the reporting level specified in the contract.

4. Identify significant differences on a monthly basis between planned and actual schedule accomplishment together with the reasons.

5. Identify managerial actions taken as a result of paragraph 2d(1) through (4) above.

6. Based on performance to date and on estimates of future conditions, develop revised estimates of cost at completion for WBS elements identified in the contract and compare these with the contract budget base and the latest statement of funds requirements reported to the government.

e. Revisions and access to data

1. Incorporate contractual changes in a timely manner recording the effects of such changes in budgets and schedules. In the directed effort before negotiation of a change, base such revisions on the amount estimated and budgeted to the functional organizations.

2. Reconcile original budgets for those elements of the WBS identified as priced line items in the contract and for those elements at the lowest level of the project summary WBS, with current performance measurement budgets in terms of changes to the authorized work and internal replanning in the detail needed by management for effective control.

3. Prohibit retroactive changes to records that pertain to work performed and that will change previously reported amounts for direct costs, indirect costs, or budgets, except for correction of errors and routine accounting adjustments.

4. Prevent revisions to the contract budget base except for government-directed changes to contractual effort.

5. Document, internally, changes to the performance measurement baseline, and on a timely basis, notify the government project management through prescribed procedures.

6. Provide the contracting officer and his or her duly authorized representatives access to all of the foregoing information and supporting documents.

Chapter 13

Research and Development Projects

13.1 INTRODUCTION

Over the past decade, 40% of the Fortune 500 have dropped off this select list, victims of complacency, poor financial management, and a failure to keep pace with the competition. It should come as no surprise that today's organizations, especially the behemoths, are not designed for innovation. They are the by-products of a more orderly and regulated environment. Courting change, acting opportunistically, and shifting direction at a moment's notice were not, until recently, required for survival, never mind excellence. Not only were such traits not required, but to have emphasized them would have detracted from performance! Doing yesterday's job just a little better—at most—was the prescription for success. Indeed, this is the saga of the post-World War II U.S. automobile industry, steel industry, chemical industry, and even the first two decades of the computer industry.

In the field of high technology, the key to staying competitive is product innovation supported by a strong commitment to research and development (R&D). But how to do this? One school of thought says that we have to be much faster at developing new products. Proponents provide airtight schemes for reducing production cycle times and filling market niches as they appear. The complexity of these schemes is often stunning, but who could argue? As Peters (1990) said, "It's a complex world." New approaches are required to slash product development cycles by at least an order of magnitude in many industries. However, the rigidity of several of the most popular approaches with their "one size fits all" character leaves something to be desired.

The alternative to airtight formulas, some say, is a "ten-man band of lunatics cast adrift." Although this idea, realized in what are sometimes called "skunkworks," has worked well for Lockheed in its development of high-altitude reconnaissance aircraft and for Data General when it developed the Eagle line of super minicomputers (Kidder 1981), there is a wealth of evidence suggesting that the significant breakthroughs of the 1990s, as exemplified by the products and services of Nokia, Yahoo!, Nintendo, eBay, and Cisco, will not come from orderly plans alone or the right company at the right time. Formulas are questionable, and 10-man bands alone are not up to the innovation task. These forms of isolated incubation rarely produce continuous results because they operate too far outside the existing organization. Most established businesses are convergent thinking and survive on order, measurement, and predictability. In contrast, innovation most often arises from divergent thinking environments that thrive on disorder, imagination, and ambiguity. What is needed to foster new ideas is a strategic plan with R&D prominently featured.

Companies vary in the degree of sophistication with which they accomplish planning. Gluck et al. (1980) presented a four-stage evolutionary model for carrying out this task:

- Stage I companies have the basic financial planning system in which everything is reduced to a financial problem and the value standard is to meet the budget.
- Stage II companies extend basic financial planning by means of long-range forecasts.
- In stage III companies, planners try to understand the market phenomena that are forcing change, look for opportunities that may lead to a more attractive portfolio, and devise alternative strategies for top management consideration.
- In stage IV companies, management is involved in strategic planning that stimulates entrepreneurial thinking and promotes all-around commitment to the corporate plan.

This type of classification offers an easy way to segregate and evaluate where companies are in the planning process. Top management should give deliberate thought to the degree of sophistication that they have reached and how R&D fits into the overall plan. In general, planning is a two-pronged effort. The first prong centers on the development of the strategic plan that defines and communicates longer-term business directions; the second involves the development of an operating plan that specifically identifies tasks or projects to be undertaken in pursuit of corporate goals. At this point, a distinction needs to be drawn between traditional capital budgeting and R&D planning. R&D, along with new product development, is a low-probability game, no matter how much you plan, survey, consult with customers, or align yourself with the competition. There are literally thousands of variables that must be juggled at once. There are variables that deal with *technology* (design, engineering, manufacturability, quality, serviceability, operatability), variables that deal with *distribution* (who, through which channels, level of interest in the product, when), and there are variables that deal with *customer use* (the lag time between development of a new product and its routine adoption, even when dramatic and unmistakable benefits are evident from the outset, often runs decades—and almost always occurs via a convoluted, totally unpredictable path); not to mention variables that involve *competitors* (big, small, domestic, foreign) and new entries into the marketplace.

In the remainder of this chapter, we present some of the unique aspects of the R&D project. In so doing, we reflect and extend many of the ideas discussed previously. To be successful, it is necessary for an organization to instill a project orientation everywhere. To be speedy, to practice innovation on every product and process, and to develop new and scintillating products quickly require that all functional boundaries between design, engineering, manufacturing, operations, purchasing, sales, marketing, and distribution be destroyed—not broken down or softened, but destroyed. A second guideline is for virtually every person in the company to spend a fair amount of his or her day on project teams with people from other functions. The essence of perpetual quality improvement, service improvement, rapid product development, and increased operational efficiency is getting people from multiple, warring factions working together on output-oriented activities that generally go unmanaged in traditional "vertical" organizations.

13.2 RISK FACTORS

The crucial elements of risk for a venture based on advanced technology, which are probably the elements unique to this type of business, occur up front during the development and introduction phases of the technology. Bower (1970) put it succinctly: "The most important and expensive decisions must be made well before the last word is heard from technology." There are some ideas, now well documented, that will help an enterprise reduce the risks of undertaking an R&D project or bringing a new product to market. Even so, these are still broad concepts that apply equally to all types of organizations and do not really get to the heart of the issues that high-tech businesses face. The following series of steps provides a useful guide for executives who attempt to construct a risk profile:

1. Be aware of the problem; recognize that risk is a factor that needs to be built into each life cycle stage.
2. Formalize the process of identifying the potential sources of risk and judging the extent to which these apply in particular business situations.
3. Provide an assessment of probabilities so that sensible financial appraisals can take place.
4. Formulate a business plan that takes account of risk.

Most executives regard risk as a way of life. Having accepted this proposition in step 1, they plough ahead using a "you can't get anywhere without taking risks" type of approach. This means that subsequent steps are not dealt with in the best manner. As a consequence, intellectual rigor and quantitative analysis are often replaced with hunches and judgments. In the following subsections, we discuss many of the issues that can have a substantial impact on R&D projects, particularly as they relate to new product development.

13.2.1 Technical Success Versus Commercial Success

New technology may provide a product that does not prove acceptable as a substitute for existing technology. Although the product may deliver benefits beyond what is currently available, its benefit-to-cost ratio may be too low to justify adoption. This does not mean that all potential customers will stay home—there are always some innovators who are willing to try anything. It simply means that initial market penetration is likely to be slow and greater investment may be required to convert technical success into commercial success.

A good example of this existed in the welding field several years ago when automated welding systems were becoming more widely available but had not yet gained significant penetration (Meldrum and Millman 1991). Some customers were forced into using them for safety or manufacturing reasons. Others adopted them because their customers were placing quality demands that could be met only by automated systems. For the vast majority, though, welding was and is a "black art" or, at best, a low-profile activity within their companies. A similar example is found in large-area displays for public information systems where electromechanical devices and LEDs (light-emitting diodes) have proved to be acceptable technologically for this application and have doggedly resisted replacement by liquid crystal alternatives.

The continued embrace of familiar techniques is a situation that has long been recognized by those doing research in diffusion of innovation theory (Rogers 1976), but for marketers of advanced technology, it is a special problem. Their task is to judge just how fast and how far their product will be received as an acceptable substitute by the various sectors of the market. This will depend on how well existing technology solves the customers' problems and how far the extra benefits supplied by the new technology are perceived to offer competitive advantages.

13.2.2 Changing Expectations

Many high-tech products are designed and developed against a customer specification, but specifications are prone to change during the development cycle, causing costs and schedules to deviate measurably from the original plan. Government-linked contracts have attracted media attention—none more so in Great Britain than GEC-Marconi's efforts to win the Nimrod contract with the U.K. Ministry of Defence. Although there were numerous problems surrounding this project, the performance requirements of the ministry shifted continually over its life, thwarting GEC's ability to come up with a suitable product on time.

Turning again to the example of automated welding systems, a similar story can be found. One prospective customer who manufactured components for the automobile industry returned to the developer four times to request a redesign of the system. The problem was that each time a new specification appeared, the customer realized a little better the potential of the product and other areas where the system might have an application. Unwilling to lose the development opportunity, unable to charge for quotation services, and desperate for customers, the supplier found himself involved in a significant amount of redesign work, for little reward in the long run. The customer eventually went back to a system close to the original specification, being unable to afford the more complex system that had taken his fancy.

13.2.3 Technology Leapfrogging

Substitute technologies or new generations of products that are based on existing technologies may appear just as a company is pushing its existing range of products into the marketplace. This is a particular problem in the high-tech field, where rapid innovation can turn obsolete overnight the products that you have spent so much time developing. As a consequence, sustained investment is necessary to stay in the race.

Engines for wide-bodied passenger aircraft provide a useful illustration: The first generation of engines such as the Pratt & Whitney JT9, Rolls-Royce RB211, and General Electric CF6 represented high-risk "discontinuous" product innovation of the make-or-break variety. Indeed, without U.K. government intervention after placing the Lockheed Tri-Star contract, Rolls-Royce would not have survived. Later generations of these large turbo-fan engines have been based on incremental innovation, typically offering higher thrust ratings, improved fuel consumption, lower noise levels, and so on. Similar patterns of discontinuous innovation and subsequent leapfrogging via incremental innovation are to be found in other industries. Witness the vying for leadership by Intel and Motorola in microprocessors, by Kodak and Fuji in photographic products, and by IBM and Dell in computer servers.

An example may again be drawn from the electronic information display market where the cathode ray tube is still the most widely used medium but is recognized as having a number of disadvantages. All companies in the business have therefore invested in the development of alternative technologies that provide a flat-screen or panel replacement. The competing technologies include LEDs, liquid crystal, vacuum fluorescent, electroluminescent, plasma, gas discharge, and incandescent displays. Each technology has associated with it a number of well-known and not-so-well-known names. For several of them, the risk that the substitute technology will substantially reduce the potential market for their product will become a reality.

13.2.4 Standards

Both the existence and the nonexistence of performance and quality standards for technology-based ventures can be a challenge in marketing innovative products. If formal standards do not exist, then customers have nothing against which to evaluate their potential purchase. This has the effect of making the product difficult to sell because it will be a higher-risk purchase and the process of writing specifications will take a lot longer. Conversely, in the absence of formal standards, informal or *de facto* standards that can lead to a mismatch between the proposed technology and the requirements of the customer base may appear.

Airship Industries, a U.K. company that has led efforts to reintroduce airships as a mode of transport and surveillance, provides a classic example of the risk associated with the nonexistence of standards. In their efforts to establish airships as a credible mode of transport, they believed that it would be essential to obtain U.K. Civil Aviation Authority certification, which would have worldwide acceptability. Their problem was that no standards existed, and certification, in any event, proved very hard to come by. As the commercial manager of the company noted, the first production model flew in 1981 but did not gain U.K. certification until 1984. Full U.S. Federal Aviation Administration certification was granted in 1989.

Another example of informal standards or industry-established norms preventing a technology from becoming a profitable commercial venture is the experience of JVC during their early attempts to establish a position in the video recorder market. The first commercial videotape recorder (VTR) was marketed in 1955 by the U.S. firm

Ampex for use in film and television productions (Nayak and Ketteringham 1993). The first Japanese version of the Ampex system arrived in 1958. JVC, later to become the world leader in home video with the VHS system, produced their version of a similar VTR in 1959. This was a better and simpler product, but it failed commercially, as their machine was incompatible with the standards then established, which were derived from the Ampex and Sony technology. Although this provided an important lesson for JVC that proved useful in the now famous battle for home video standards, the failure nearly resulted in JVC's premature withdrawal from this market (Rosenbloom and Cusumano 1987).

A related example centers on the development of standards for high-definition television (HDTV). Since the early 1980s, a battle has been raging between the U.S. Federal Communications Commission and its Japanese and European counterparts. The contentious issues revolve around picture format and compatibility with existing systems. There is still no uniform agreement. As a result, the introduction of HDTV into the United States was delayed by at least 5 years, giving the Japanese electronics industry a breathing space for perfecting the technology, virtually guaranteeing its dominance of the market.

Formal standards can exhibit their ambiguous effects in other ways. Where standards do exist, they provide the supplier and the customer with a reference against which to manufacture and evaluate. However, they often vary among industries and countries, making it difficult for a competitive company to expand its sphere of operation. Instances in which formal standards have created problems for entry and expansion in export markets are not hard to find. For example, a company that sells connectors for optical fiber cabling in the telecommunications market, having developed a good business in the United Kingdom based on British Telecom standards, found it hard to sell in Germany, where DIN standards operate. To gain approval, the company sought a collaborative arrangement with another connector company but ended up supplying them components only, thereby deriving reduced added value from this market.

13.2.5 Cost and Time Overruns

Some products cannot be produced to the specification originally envisaged without running into substantial cost or time overruns. Although the research, design, and development work may have progressed to a satisfactory stage and the market may supply commercial potential, it is sometimes the case that the production technology or component availability necessary to commercialize the product is inadequate. This is a problem that occurs mainly in the earlier stages of new product development and prototype testing. The situation is exemplified by a manufacturer of lithium batteries who had to recall substantial numbers of its initial product because the casing technology used was not secure enough for this dangerous chemical. Another example, uncovered by Meldrum and Millman, relates to a large U.K. multinational that announced a product to the press and then found that the thin-film coating technology that they had assumed would meet the requirements of their product was not up to the task, thereby delaying entry into the market.

In some instances, it has been argued that in the context of two primary risk factors, cost and time, cost overruns will have less impact than time. As noted by John

Doyle, former vice president of Hewlett-Packard, "If we over-spend by 50% on our engineering budget but deliver on time, it impacts 10% on revenue. If we are late, it can impact up to 30% on revenues."

Post-launch problems in manufacturing still occur, although these are more likely to be associated with supply difficulties and are not unique to high-tech enterprises. For example, a small electronics manufacturer had experienced a problem in obtaining the correct type of wound component and ended up frantically winding its own in a back room. Another, more public example is the recent purchase by Amstrad of a stake in Micron Technology to ensure long-term supplies of 256K memory chips, which they were having trouble sourcing.

13.2.6 Lack of Infrastructure

Another area of risk is concerned with support technology that is not adequate to make a proposed product a worthwhile investment. Often this means a product concept awaiting an "enabling" technology.

After almost two decades of promoting the "factory of the future" and the "paperless office," these concepts are only now approaching reality. Molins System 24, for example, is generally regarded as the forerunner of modern flexible manufacturing systems. Although several were installed in the late 1960s and 1970s, the concept was ahead of its time. Computing power and software development were inadequate, and the step was too great for users to take. Islands of automation rather than fully integrated systems were the result; the situation was similar with office automation. There will always be a market for stand-alone equipment, but extensive displacement of manual/paper-based tasks has little chance of acceptance without electronic integration. It is only with the growing provision of sophisticated communications technology and workstations such as multiplexing, networking products, and protocols that real market opportunities arise.

A similar problem was noted by Meldrum and Millman regarding a new optical storage medium, which is an inexpensive plastic film that stores vast amounts of optical information and can be formed into a sheet, disk, tape, or cylinder. One tape of 500 meters can store 1 terabyte (1 billion bytes) of information, but full commercialization and the opportunities that this technology can address are not yet realizable. The development of suitable hardware systems and some further advances in laser technology are still required before the potential market achieves any real size.

The enumeration of potential sources of risk described above covers most of those likely to be faced by high-tech organizations. As with any business problem, the first steps on the long trail to commercialization are recognizing the existence of the problem and identifying its parameters. Only if the range of potential threats is identified successfully can management hope to develop strategies to deal with them. Similarly, the identification of potential risk is the first step in risk analysis that will produce a clear picture of the risk profile for decisions on investment policy and R&D portfolio management.

13.3 MANAGING TECHNOLOGY

The meaning of technology is straightforward: knowing how to do something well. A more elaborate definition would be the ability to create a reproducible way to generate improved products, processes, and services. In fact, a modern manufacturing business must have a substantial portfolio of individual technologies. The management of technology should ensure that the firm maintains command of the technologies relevant to its purposes and that these technologies support the firm's business strategy and shareholder value.

Technology management for strategic advantage is difficult and often frustrating. As Erikson et al. (1990) pointed out, the central issue is the need to reconcile risk and the unpredictability of discovery with the desire to fit technical programs into orderly management of the business. The traditional approach to managing technology has been largely intuitive. R&D is treated as an overhead item, with budgets set in relation to some business measure (e.g., sales) and at a level deemed reasonable by industry practice. Budgets may be projected several years ahead but are usually set annually. Within this budget framework, decisions about areas of concentration and project continuations may be left largely to R&D management. There is no assurance that the R&D organization, left to its own devices, will pursue programs related to corporate strategy, either in focus or in degree of innovation and risk.

In response to this unsatisfactory situation, many firms have become somewhat more sophisticated. Managers outside the technology area participate in suggesting or reviewing projects, but the connection to company strategy is still casual or haphazard. Some firms subject R&D programs to a rigorous financial justification process based on net present value. Arguing that R&D projects are investments—as in a sense they are—corporate management seeks justification based on rate of return or payout. It is difficult, though, to predict financial returns for an R&D project, especially if it is focused on achieving a significant innovation. As a consequence, new activities may be limited to conservative, incremental projects; the results will be more predictable but will have marginal strategic impact.

Clearly, then, there is a need for a measured, sophisticated approach to R&D management. Interest in a better approach has been stimulated by various developments (Erikson et al. 1990, Jain and Triandis 1996, Roussel et al. 1990). First, many corporate leaders have moved beyond the financially driven planning characteristic of the 1970s and 1980s. Second, the success of entrepreneurial, high-technology companies has excited interest in the potential of technology to build company value. Third, firms have seen that industry leaders give high priority to technology management. Fourth, quality and manufacturing capability are now considered strategic business weapons. Together these developments have helped to create a desire to manage technology in a way that is congruent with business strategy.

The first step in the strategic management of technology is to answer the following question: For our firm, what mix of products and markets will best sustain and enhance our cash flow? The next step is to test how well the firm's technologies support the ideal product and market mix. The third step is to focus technology investments so that they better support the firm's strategy.

It is often useful to examine a firm's technologies in light of two questions:

1. What is the significance of the technologies in the firm's portfolio, as measured by their competitive impact and maturity?

2. In each product area or business, how strong is the firm's technological competitive position?

13.3.1 Classification of Technologies

In general, it is possible to identify three broad classes of technologies in a typical firm's technological portfolio:

1. *Base technologies.* These are technologies that a firm must master to be an effective competitor in its chosen product-market mix. They are necessary—but not sufficient—to achieve competitive advantage. These technologies are widely known and readily available. Electronic ignition systems for automobiles is an example.

   The trick for R&D management here is to invest enough—but only enough—effort to maintain competence. The danger is that inertia will sustain programs in these base technologies longer and at greater scale than they deserve, perhaps because these are the traditional areas where the R&D organizations feel at home. The U.S. auto industry in the 1960s and 1970s, for example, invested too heavily in familiar areas of product technology rather than in new, less comfortable areas where opportunities to develop new process technology existed.

2. *Key technologies.* These technologies provide competitive advantage. They may permit the producer to embed differentiating features or functions in the product or to attain greater efficiencies in the production process. An example is food-packaging technology that enables the purchaser to use microwave cooking.

   The primary focus of industrial R&D is on extending and applying the key technologies at the firm's disposal; they should be given the highest priority when contemplating investment opportunities. Unwilling to invest in key process technologies in the 1950s and 1960s, the U.S. steel industry paid the price in the 1970s; foreign competitors, whose entry into the U.S. market had been encouraged by consumer goods manufacturers, far outstripped their domestic counterparts in productivity.

3. *Pacing technologies.* These technologies could become tomorrow's key technologies. Not every participant in an industry can afford to invest in pacing technologies; this is typically what differentiates the leaders (who do) from the followers (who do not). The critical issue in technology management is balancing support of key technologies to sustain current competitive position and support of pacing technologies to create future vitality. Commitments to pacing technologies or potential breakthroughs are hard to justify in conventional, return-on-investment terms. Indeed, these commitments can be thought of more accurately as buying options on opportunity. Relatively modest commitments—and thus modest downside risk—can give the potential for large upside reward. Realizing that potential depends on still-unresolved technical and market contingencies. If the option is not pursued, then the potential does not exist. Smith, Kline & French supported pursuit of receptor modeling in the 1960s, a pacing technology in the pharmaceutical industry at that time. This work led ultimately to the development of TAGAMET and the establishment of the company as an industrial leader.

An effective R&D program must include some investment to build a core of competence in pacing technologies and some effort to gain intelligence from sources such as customers, universities, and scientific literature to help identify and evaluate these technologies. At the same time, disciplined judgments about commitments to pacing technologies are necessary; enthusiastic overspending on advanced technology can undercut essential support of key technologies.

13.3.2 Exploiting Mature Technologies

Technologies mature, just as industries and product lines do. The younger the technology, the greater the potential for further development, but the less certain the benefits. However, a mature technology can often be a key technology. Many Japanese firms use mature technologies as a major competitive weapon. The Sony Walkman, for example, was a wildly successful new product that was based on comparatively mature technologies. The Walkman fortuitously combined Sony's work on the miniaturization of its tape recorder line and its work on lightweight headphones. Company engineers were trying to make a miniature stereo tape player-recorder, but they could not fit the recording mechanism into the target package size. A senior officer realized that combining headphones with a nonrecording tape "player" would eliminate the need for speakers, reduce battery requirements, and result in a small stereo tape player with outstanding sound (Nayak and Ketteringham 1993).

Sometimes a mature technology becomes a key technology when it is applied in a new context. Empire Pencil gained a major cost and quality advantage by using mature plastic extrusion technology as the basis of a new way to manufacture lead pencils. Conventional lead pencil manufacturing requires the use of fine-grained, high-quality wood, such as cedar, and a good deal of hand labor for assembly. Materials are becoming more expensive, and damage to the graphite core during the assembly process causes quality problems. A development team was confronted with this question: How can we improve quality and cut costs? The team realized that wood powder in a plastic binder could simulate the fine-grained wood. From there it was a straightforward step to produce pencil stock in a continuous extrusion process, with wood powder and a core of graphite powder in a plastic binder.

Other mature technologies may be protected (e.g., by patents or proprietary treatment) and thus give their owners a key competitive advantage. A Japanese grinding machine manufacturer successfully diversified into the manufacture of integrated-circuit wafer equipment. A critical factor in its success was its proprietary mature machine technology. Examples such as this may tempt a firm in a mature line of business to diversify into new products and markets where its proprietary but mature technology could have a key competitive impact, but this strategy is risky. The better alternative is to look, as Empire Pencil did, for new technology to invigorate a mature or aging product line.

A business or product line whose key technologies are mature faces a serious threat of being blindsided by a competitor who uses new key technologies. This is what Xerox did to the established copier manufacturers and what word processing did to the typewriter industry.

As an industry or product sector matures, the key technologies often become *manufacturing process* technologies rather than product feature technologies. This is the case in many mature industries, including chemicals, machine tools, consumer appliances, and food products.

13.3.3 Relationship between Technology and Projects

Defining projects by type provides useful information on the role of existing technology in their development and how resources should be allocated. Wheelwright and Clark (1992) suggested a two-dimensional qualitative scale for classifying projects: (1) the degree of change in the product and (2) the degree of change in the underlying manufacturing process. The greater the change along either dimension, the more resources that are needed. They also identified five project types. The first three—derivative, breakthrough, and platform—are associated with the marketplace; the remaining two—research and development—precede commercialization.

Each of these five project types requires a unique combination of development resources and management styles. Understanding how the categories differ helps managers predict the distribution of resources accurately and allows for better planning and sequencing of projects over time. A brief description of the first three categories follows.

Derivative projects range from less expensive versions of existing products to add-ons or enhancements to established production processes. For example, Kodak's wide-angle, single-use 35-mm camera, the Stretch, was derived from the no-frills Fun Saver introduced in 1990. Designing the Stretch was primarily a matter of modifying the lens.

Development work on derivative projects typically falls into three categories: incremental product changes, say, new packaging or a new feature, with little or no manufacturing process change; incremental process changes, such as a lower-cost assembly technique, improved reliability, or a minor change in materials used, with little or no product change; and incremental changes on both dimensions. Because design changes are usually minor, incremental projects are more clearly bounded and require substantially fewer resources than do the other categories. Because derivative projects are completed in a few months, ongoing management involvement is minimal.

Breakthrough projects are at the other end of the development spectrum because they involve significant changes to existing products and processes. Successful breakthrough projects establish core products and processes that differ fundamentally from previous generations. Like compact disks and superconducting ceramics, they create an entirely new product area that can define a new market.

Breakthrough products often incorporate revolutionary technologies or materials and hence usually require revolutionary manufacturing processes. Management should give development teams considerable latitude in designing new processes, rather than force them to work with outdated or marginally efficient equipment, operating techniques, or supplier networks.

Platform projects are the middle of the development spectrum and thus are harder to define. They entail more product or process changes than do derivatives, but they do not introduce the untried technologies or materials that are found in breakthrough products. Honda's 1990 Accord line is an example of a new platform in the auto industry. Computer-integrated manufacturing techniques were successfully exploited to improve assembly operations, but no fundamentally new technologies were introduced. In the computer market, Sun's Fire B1600 Blade is a workstation platform; in consumer products, Proctor & Gamble's Liquid Tide is the platform for a full line of Tide brand products.

Well-planned and well-executed platform products typically offer fundamental improvements in cost, quality, and performance over preceding generations. They introduce improvements across a range of dimensions: speed, functionality, size, and weight. (Derivatives, conversely, usually introduce changes along only one or two dimensions.) Platforms also represent a significantly better system solution for the customer. Because of the extent of changes involved, successful platforms require considerable up-front planning and the participation of marketing, manufacturing, and senior management, as well as engineering.

Companies target new platforms to meet the needs of a core group of customers but design them for easy modification into derivatives through the addition, subtraction, or removal of features. Well-designed platforms also provide a smooth migration path between generations so that neither the customer nor the distribution channel is disrupted. Consider Intel's family of Pentium microprocessors. This family was aimed at a core customer group—the high-end desktop/workstation user—but variations addressed the needs of most other users. Moreover, software compatibility with predecessors such as the Celeron permitted existing customers to make the transition to the Pentium family with minimal effort. Over the life of this platform, Intel will introduce a host of derivative products, each offering some variation on speed, cost, and performance and each able to leverage the process and product innovations of the original platform.

Platforms offer considerable competitive leverage and the potential to increase market penetration, yet many companies underinvest in them systematically. The reasons vary, but the most common is that management lacks an awareness of the strategic value of platforms and fails to conceive projects that exploit their capabilities.

13.4 STRATEGIC R&D PLANNING

All corporate departments, operating divisions, and companies must develop plans. In each division, R&D, engineering, manufacturing, marketing, sales, and the various support groups should participate to produce the division's strategic plan. The purpose of this plan is to define how each unit will carry out relevant corporate goals. The relationship between corporate planning with R&D planning is shown in Fig. 13.1.

It may seem obvious that R&D portfolios should be aligned with corporate goals, but too often R&D groups are not given support and guidelines by top management. Successful planning depends on a dialogue between top management and the R&D leader regarding mission, goals, strategies, and means of implementation. These are important aspects of participative R&D management.

13.4.1 Role of R&D Manager

An R&D manager fulfills corporate strategy by planning for change throughout the planning exercise. He or she must include uncertainties of innovation (probabilities of technical and market success) and uncertainties of the environment (effects of public policy, consumer mood, actions by the competition) in his or her deliberations. The manager must recognize technology push (the brilliant idea seeking a market) and market pull (a market need seeking a product) and what the general corporate climate or attitude is on projects that are based on either.

If you are a manager of an operational R&D group, you must recognize the needs of the parent business unit; if you are in a central R&D group, then you must recognize

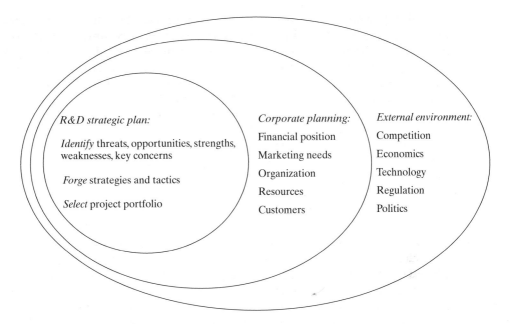

Figure 13.1   Relationship between corporate and R&D planning.

the needs of the corporation as a whole. In either case, you must have the means and the ability to monitor technology and to forecast change. A key requirement is to keep your eyes on horizons well beyond current technology. Also, you must recognize where and who the entrepreneurs and project champions are in your company.

Finally, top management must understand the sources and effects of uncertainty, be receptive to innovation, and be the stimulus for strategic planning and the agitator for an innovative environment. If they are not, then strategic technical planning will never evoke empathy and the group will flounder and fail.

13.4.2 Planning Team

The head of the R&D group in a business unit (a *unit* may be a section, department, division, combinations of these, or a company) and the managers of the various R&D areas in the group should be the planning team members. How deeply the team draws its members from the organization depends on company size, commonality of interests among business units, and questions such as, "What is a reasonable team size?" Ideally, senior professionals, managers of various functions, and planners in the business unit will assist.

Research Managers Form the Planning Team.   To simplify the discussion, consider a corporate R&D planning group. In this example the vice president of R&D is the team leader, with other members being managers of the group's various R&D areas. Managers of relevant operations will assist or be asked for assistance. Corporate officers and staff from selected functions may be asked to review critical points in the developing plan.

If you are the head of R&D and thereby the team leader, then you cannot delegate the thought processes required for the planning process and the derivation of results. You can, of course, use every fact-finding function available, but the team does the actual manipulation of inputs and produces the output results. This may seem like a lot of work, but once accomplished, you will know more about your operation than ever before and be equipped to manage your assigned functions.

Good Managers Do Not Delegate the Planning Process.   When the planning team is assembled, the leader should remind members of the unit's mission (also called *charter* or *definition* of business) and the mission of the R&D group. If the team is in an operations unit, then the mission statement emphasizes upgrades and means to advance market share of present products; if the team is in central R&D, then emphasis is on new products, new technologies, and new opportunities. These mission statements are important because they define the business and give its scope in clear, concise language. Two typical mission statements would be

- Division X designs, manufactures, and sells sensors and monitoring equipment to meet the severe environments within the mining industry. The mission of the R&D group is to enhance the performance of current products and to discover and develop new products that will aid in maintaining and advancing market leadership of the division. In so doing, the R&D group will provide technical surveillance over current and emerging relevant technologies, monitor competitors' products and services, maintain and advance market share through upgrades and extensions to the product line, and develop selected new products within the scope of the business.
- Company Y designs, manufactures, and sells hardware and services to energy producers. The mission of the R&D group is to discover and develop products that will give the company commanding leadership in its selected business areas. In so doing, the corporate R&D group will provide surveillance over current and emerging relevant technologies, conceive and develop new products to meet future change, and provide problem-solving research and services to operations as needed.

Such mission statements focus the team on the issues that are important to the business of its parent unit. The team leader presents to the team the needs of top management and discusses specifically the goals that management wants R&D to meet. (These needs should reflect, in part, the inputs from R&D.) The goals of top management may be cast as general statements, such as

- Look at area X over the next few months and see if you can conceive an advanced method.
- Create a new generation of products in the near future from emerging technology A.

  Alternatively, the goals may be

- Provide division Y with an upgraded product Z using your materials technology, and let's see where you are in 6 months.
- Reduce materials costs of product B this year.

The planning team reviews any goals previously set by the R&D group to determine their compatibility with current goals. The team identifies what can be done within available resources, which employee and equipment resources are needed, and so on. Goals are reviewed, refined, and revised at the end of the planning phase. (A *goal* is usually defined as something to be accomplished within a specified period.) Finally, the team discusses how to accomplish the six stages of planning enumerated in Table 13.1 and sets out tasks and schedules. The team leader also discusses the methods to be used in fulfilling the assigned tasks.

TABLE 13.1   Stages of the Strategic Technical Planning Process

1. Information-gathering stage

   - Determine status of the business unit
   - Ascertain needs of operations
   - Determine status of competition
   - Conduct technical planning studies
   - Consider key concerns and issues

2. Consolidation stage

   - Derive scenarios of possible futures
   - List needs, opportunities, threats, and impacts
   - List key concerns and issues
   - List strengths and weaknesses

3. Strategy-formulation stage

   - Analyze and evaluate lists of needs against lists of key concerns and issues
   - Evaluate maturity of present technologies and possible use of new technologies
   - Match lists with strengths and weaknesses
   - Develop preliminary alternative strategies
   - Develop candidate tactics
   - Evaluate and suggest priority of strategies

4. Selection stage

   - Select one set of strategies, or
   - Look again at some new technologies and then decide

5. Implementation stage

   - Consider project candidates (tactics) in depth
   - Test tactics against best and worst scenarios
   - Consider funding limitations
   - Suggest priorities of specific projects
   - Describe the group's R&D areas
   - Set goals
   - Draft strategic and operational plans

6. Review stage

   - Submit plans for review
   - Adjust plans as necessary

Planning Is a Multistage Process.   The strategic technical planning task required of the team can be facilitated by use of the six planning stages. In the first stage, the team collects information. In the second stage, the team consolidates (categorizes, digests, and assimilates) this information into various lists. These lists are used in the succeeding stages of planning, so their comprehensiveness is critical to the overall effort. The next three stages are progressive refinements of the current findings.

13.5 PARALLEL FUNDING: DEALING WITH UNCERTAINTY

A primary role of the R&D project manager is to narrow the range of technological choices that the organization faces without sacrificing market or performance goals. Because of the inherent uncertainty at each stage of project development, it is not uncommon to identify and explore several alternatives to facilitate selection of the most promising candidates. During the development of the Airborne Warning and Control System by the U.S. Air Force, for example, both Hughes and Westinghouse were awarded multimillion-dollar contracts to design and build prototype radars for the Boeing aircraft. Considering the extent of the technological unknowns, the Air Force believed that the additional money spent in a runoff competition was justified given the rigorous technical requirements and tight timetables surrounding the program. This approach has become standard for virtually all U.S. government agencies, whether the system involved is an unmanned combat air vehicle or a multiline optical character reader.

The use of parallel strategies is one means by which experienced managers cope with the uncertain nature of the R&D environment (Abernathy and Rosenbloom 1969). Such an approach has the threefold advantage of avoiding the difficulty of trying to predetermine which ideas or technologies will succeed, hedging against the risk of outright failure, and building a broader technological base. The decision to fund more than one alternative at each juncture, though, must be tempered by the potential tradeoffs between increased probability of success and increased cost, as well as the behavioral issues associated with parallel choice (Balthasar et al. 1978). When a particular alternative evidences clear superiority, however, a sequential strategy may be called for wherein other candidates are pursued only if the preferred candidate fails to meet expectations.

A stream of technical choices, made by project managers, group leaders, and their clients, determines the cost of an R&D project and the value of its outcome. Choices between competing approaches to the solution of technical problems must be made in the face of substantial uncertainty in situations in which time and resources are limited.

By a "parallel strategy," we mean the simultaneous pursuit of two or more distinct approaches to a single objective, when successful completion of any one would satisfy the stated requirements. Nevertheless, the sequential strategy, that is, commitment to the best evident approach, is most common in practice. In a majority of situations, the benefits of a parallel strategy may seem obscure, whereas its additional costs are quite real.

13.5.1 Categorizing Strategies

In principle, the logic of the decision to use a parallel strategy is the same in all circumstances. The manager's task is one of sequential choice under uncertainty. Any complex development project must be undertaken in steps or stages, the later stages depending on the results of the earlier ones. It is therefore a problem in sequential decision making, as discussed in Section 5.7. At each stage, it is possible to make use of economic calculus in comparing the costs and gains from various alternative ways of proceeding. The costs in this case are those of the next stage of development, not the costs of procuring and operating the full system.

In practice, however, there is a significant difference between the calculus of sequential decision making in planning a program and in reducing a solution to practice. Thus, one can generalize more advantageously about the structure of the decision problem by distinguishing two broad categories for the use of parallel strategies (Abernathy and Rosenbloom 1969). In the first category, called a *parallel synthesis strategy*, the uncertainty is broad, the cost of information is relatively low, and there may be only a limited commitment to further work. In the contrasting case, the *parallel engineering strategy*, the bounds of uncertainty are more definite, the information cost is relatively high, and there is a strong commitment to satisfy developmental objectives.

The parallel synthesis strategy is most often found in the first phase of a program. At that point, substantial uncertainty exists concerning the types of needs that the developmental product is to satisfy, the potential of each alternative to satisfy those needs, and the probable cost of each alternative. Information that can reduce those uncertainties can be obtained by means of analytical studies, special tests, and limited development of the several prototypes. This sort of activity frequently serves to synthesize an approach to the larger problem and defines many of the outcome characteristics. A parallel synthesis strategy typically is a means of gaining information and maintaining options so that the best path may be selected for subsequent development.

In the synthesis phase, definition of the program is incomplete. Attempting to map a "decision tree" that specifies a sequence of possible acts and consequences would be misguided. At that stage, the manager may still be ignorant of factors that will prove to be the most significant sources of later uncertainty. For example, Admiral Rickover said in reference to the nuclear submarine program, "In the beginning of naval development, neither the technical problems nor their solutions were well understood. Many of the problems were not even known." The various approaches to development are seldom independent, and a new approach may be synthesized from elements of those initially defined. In general, the history of R&D projects shows that initial judgments of cost, performance, and value are highly inaccurate.

The situation in which a parallel engineering strategy might be appropriate has a different economic structure and offers a different decision problem. It occurs in a later stage of the development process, when a great deal of information has already been acquired and there is little chance that the total program will be abandoned. In fact, one of the principal uncertainties of the earlier formative stages of the program— the gross worth and cost of the development—can now be estimated more accurately. With knowledge of the potential value of success, the consequences of failure or delay can also be made explicit.

With the parallel engineering strategy, in contrast to the synthesis strategy, the decision maker usually is committed to bring the development project to successful completion. If he or she chooses only the preferred alternative and it does not prove acceptable, then the decision maker must seek a new solution. This implies time delays and higher costs, however, because the development will continue at its high expenditure rate until a solution is found. Thus, the basic cost structure of engineering development work influences the characteristics of a parallel engineering strategy. Additional costs stem from loss of reputation, penalty charges, and out-of-pocket and opportunity costs that result from not having the product available when it is needed or can be sold. Studies have shown that the cost of late completion is often the major component of the cost of following a single, unsuccessful approach. In the contrasting case of the synthesis strategy, the consequences are somewhat different. An incorrect choice may mean that the program is discontinued, because the benefits that would be offered by a different alternative may never be demonstrated.

13.5.2 Analytic Framework

For complex situations in which many technological alternatives exist, an analytic methodology can be helpful in selecting among those project tasks whose outcomes can be described only in probabilistic terms. What makes the underlying problem exceptionally difficult is that both systemic and statistical dependencies are likely to exist among these tasks. Typical dependencies include an overlap in resource use, technical interrelationships among task outcomes, and externalities for which the value contributions or joint performance of several tasks may be nonadditive.

To address the combination of uncertain outcomes and task dependencies, analysts have relied on Monte Carlo–based simulation models such as SIMRAND developed by the Jet Propulsion Laboratory (Miles 1984) and Q-GERT developed by Pritsker (1979). In a similar vein, Bard (1985) formulated the decision problem as a probabilistic network and used a heuristic embodying simulation within a dynamic program as a solution methodology. In particular, he divided the R&D project into a number of different parts or stages, such that it was possible to complete each stage by undertaking one or more competing tasks. The corresponding problem can be represented diagrammatically as a directed network that comprises sets of parallel arcs linked in series. An example of such a network is depicted in Fig. 13.2, in which each arc represents a specific task whose outcome is characterized by an empirical probability distribution or random variable. Typical outcomes or performance measures might be eventual unit production costs, mean time to failure, or technical probability of success. In the model, Bard assumed that each task is defined by an algebraic expression that consists of one or more input (random) variables. As a consequence, outcome distributions are difficult to obtain in closed form, hence the need for simulation.

The full methodology was demonstrated by a three-stage project that centered on the development of a flat-plate photovoltaic solar module. The three stages consisted of silicon purification, cell production, and module fabrication. In the first two stages, three tasks were considered, one each at two different funding levels; in the third stage, two tasks were considered, each at a single funding level. The results provided the necessary guidance for the project manager to initiate full-scale development.

13.5.3 Q-GERT

The most heralded use of the program evaluation and review technique (PERT) and the critical path method (CPM) network techniques since their inception has consistently

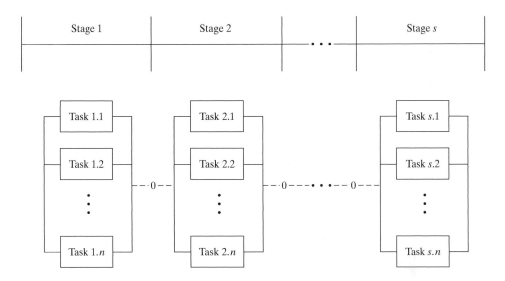

Figure 13.2 Network representation of parallel funding problem.

been in R&D planning and control. These techniques, however, are somewhat limited in that they are unable to reflect many of the real complexities associated with R&D projects. Many situations, such as multiple branching (e.g., the success or failure of a task), probabilistic branching, and repeating activities via feedback loops, that are frequently part of the R&D process cannot be modeled in a PERT/CPM network. These limitations gave rise to the graphical evaluation and review technique (GERT), a simulation methodology designed to accommodate the interdependencies and uncertain nature of project tasks (Moore and Clayton 1976).

An additional aspect of R&D management that occasions even greater complexity and difficulty is the scheduling and planning of several projects when more than one research team is involved. This problem has also been explored with GERT, and promising results have been reported for applications of modest scope. Nevertheless, a limiting factor in GERT is that as the number of R&D teams and projects increases, the accompanying network becomes impossible to construct and decipher, thus defeating the value of the methodology. In response, Q-GERT was developed to provide even greater potential for planning and scheduling in a multiteam, multiproject environment.

Q-GERT is an extension of the GERT modeling procedure and, as such, contains most of the capabilities and features of the latter, including probabilistic branching, network looping, multiple sink nodes, multiple node realizations, and multiple probability distributions. Q-GERT derives its name from the special queue nodes that it has available for modeling situations in which queues build up before service activities. However, Q-GERT contains other unique and innovative features for handling specific and complex networks that are particularly applicable in R&D planning. The most outstanding of these features is the ability to assign unique network attributes such as activity time and node branching probabilities to each individual project and then process each project through a single generalized network.

In addition to the relative advantages that Q-GERT offers with respect to other simulation and network techniques, Taylor and Moore (1980) attested to its ease of use. The methodology requires only that the R&D projects under consideration be diagrammed in network form and then converted into a standard input format for the Q-GERT simulation package. To demonstrate the power of the approach, Taylor and Moore presented two case studies that centered on an R&D subsidiary of a large textile manufacturer in the southeastern United States.

13.6 MANAGING THE R&D PORTFOLIO

R&D is an investment that must compete for corporate support with other investment opportunities, such as plant modernization, advertising, and market expansion. Program and laboratory directors must continually defend the value of their research to top management as well as decide what mix of projects is best for the firm. Project managers must determine whether their projects are on schedule and whether expected payoffs outweigh costs.

As part of their normal functions, upper management periodically reviews research programs, projects, and staff to assess progress and determine the contribution that each is making to the corporation's goals. The R&D management and review process, shown in Fig. 13.3, is nearly identical to that discussed in Chapter 5 for more conventional projects. The information gathered from the four basic reviews identified can be used to justify research expenditures, assist in budget and program planning, and provide a means of evaluating individual performance. The consequences of continuing to fund an R&D project when failure is imminent go beyond the actual dollars lost. The additional waste in human and material resources may have far-reaching effects: marginal projects may fail to receive the extra boost needed to move them beyond a critical stage, apparently healthy projects may begin to deteriorate when additional resources are not forthcoming, and promising new projects may have to be deferred as the competition moves ahead.

These points are underscored by Liberatore (1987), who attributed the importance of the R&D project management decision to two factors. First, R&D spending represents a sizable investment for many firms and may have a significant impact on their current and future financial position as well as on their ability to compete technologically. Second, projects often entail companywide commitments that translate into large opportunity costs if managed improperly.

Most projects do not begin until an in-depth assessment of their probability of success is made and the outcome seems favorable. As the project evolves, uncertainties that jeopardize completion may develop. In some instances, the market for the end product may change, falling below acceptable levels and calling into question overall profitability. Alternatively, technological problems that become either too expensive or too difficult to solve may arise. This is most critical during the early stages of development, when quality and cost decisions are made and research directions are forged.

Although there has been much work in project selection and resource allocation (e.g., see Martino 1995, Schmidt and Freeland 1992), the examination of decisions involved in project termination is a more recent phenomenon (Balachandra 1984, Balachandra and Raelin 1980). To help isolate the causal factors, Baker et al.

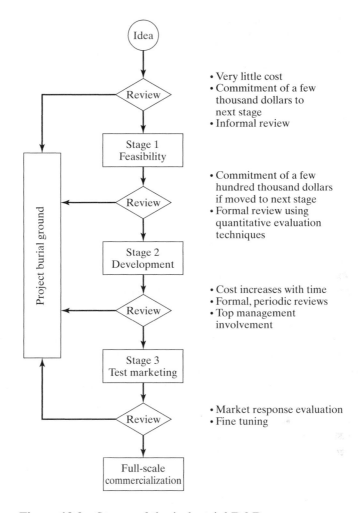

Figure 13.3   Stages of the industrial R&D process.

(1986) analyzed 211 R&D projects that were carried out between 1975 and 1982 by 21 companies and found that a positive answer to the following four questions is a likely sign of success:

- Has a relevant business need, problem, or opportunity been identified?
- Has an appropriate scientific need, problem, or opportunity been identified?
- Can the project results be transferred effectively to the internal user?
- How well can the internal user produce, market, distribute, and sell the resulting product or process?

Conversely, they found that a project has less of a chance to succeed if R&D personnel are unsure about its commercial potential, if the match between its technical and commercial aspects is vague, or if the level of uncertainty on how the results are to be brought to the marketplace is high.

Much of this work corroborated the earlier findings of Balachandra (1984), who identified a set of 14 key variables shown to be highly correlated with project failure. The implied conclusion was that by evaluating changes in these variables periodically, the R&D manager would be better able to make the crucial decisions related to project initiation and termination.

In light of this research, Bard et al. (1988) developed a decision support tool to be used by the R&D manager to help update his or her portfolio at review time. In the remainder of this chapter, we highlight their methodology and the ideas surrounding its implementation. Appendix 13A presents the results of a case study that centered on a small computer firm that specializes in peripheral equipment. Specific issues related to terminating a project once the decision has been made are detailed in Chapter 15.

13.6.1 Evaluating an Ongoing Project

To be useful to managers, quantitative methods must provide reliable results and fit within the existing decision-making framework. At a minimum, models should include those variables that managers believe are most important and for which they can provide hard data or firm opinions. As mentioned, Balachandra (1984) identified two groups of factors that strongly influence project outcomes. His work was based on a discriminant analysis of 114 R&D projects gleaned from 41 firms spanning heavy manufacturing, oil and gas, electromechanics and instrumentation, utilities, chemicals, and electronics. Table 13.2 summarizes the characteristics of the database. Each group is discussed below.

Critical Factors.   The successful completion of an ongoing R&D project is closely linked to a number of critical factors. If it is determined that any one of the following has deteriorated significantly since the last review, then immediate termination is implied.

1. Government regulations
2. Raw material availability
3. Market conditions
4. Probability of technical success

TABLE 13.2   Characteristics of Database for Determining Critical Factors

Item	Range
Number of employees	50–2000
Sales	$50M–$2B
R&D budget	$1M–$50M
Number of employees in R&D	10–50
Number of R&D projects	1–50
Project duration (years)	0.5–8

The first three, termed "exogenous critical factors," are generally outside the control of the firm. The fourth is assumed to be a function of the resources allocated to the project.

As an example of a negative change in government regulations (1), recall that the development of many diet foods based on saccharine had to be discontinued when the U.S. Food and Drug Administration affirmed their cancer-causing properties. With regard to raw material availability (2), we note that shortages are likely to have a damaging effect on market potential. In the 1970s, many Mexican pharmaceuticals had to discontinue research into the development of synthetic hormones from the barbasco root when the export market abruptly changed and the price of the plant soared.

Similarly, markets (3) may suddenly vanish as consumer tastes change or when substitutes seem to offer more immediate benefits. A good example of this was Polaroid's attempt to introduce instant movies (Polarvision). Unfortunately, the onslaught from videocassette recorders was too great to contend with, and the product met a quick demise. The last critical factor is the probability of technical success (4)—a measure that is extremely difficult to assess (Rubenstein and Schroder 1977). In any event, if it is perceived to fall below some acceptable level, then dependent projects must be set aside until the necessary technology materializes. In the early 1970s, a number of computer firms had to shelve various bubble memory projects because CMOS chips did not become available on schedule. Today, however, many products that use this memory device have found a niche as a result of belated technological advances. If none of these critical factors has deteriorated significantly since the last review, then the project would then be evaluated with respect to the key variables described below.

Key Variables.   Variables in the second group are more volatile than those is in the first but are not as strongly critical. A significant deterioration in a minority of them may not measurably affect outcomes. Thus project termination is implied only when a substantial majority have declined since the last review.

The key variables can be broadly categorized as environment related, project related, and organization related. Each subgroup is outlined below. An in-depth discussion is given by Balachandra (1984).

I.   Environment-related variables

    1. Positive chance event

    2. Product-life-cycle stage

These two variables are outside the control of the organization but are very much influenced by the environment. A positive chance event (1) might be associated with the introduction of a complementary product into the marketplace that would enhance the desirability of a product currently in R&D. The development of 40+ megabyte tape backup units was abetted significantly when large-capacity hard drives were included on personal computers as standard features.

When a product is in the initial stages of its life cycle (2), the probability of false starts is greatest. Unfortunately, this is largely a function of the technological environment and is beyond the control of the R&D team. If a product quickly moves out of its infancy stage into its growth stage, then R&D projects that pertain to the product are more likely to be successful.

II. Project-related variables

    3. Pressure on project leader

    4. R&D manager is project champion

    5. Probability of commercial success

    6. Support of top management

    7. Project personnel commitment

    8. Smoothness of technological route

    9. End user market

    10. Project champion appearing toward end

The eight variables in this subgroup are directly related to the project. A fraction of these depend on the subjective perceptions of the team managers and personnel. Specifically, it was found that positive pressure and feedback (3) from top management, as evidenced by the enthusiasm that they show toward the project team, smoothes the route to completion. If a project champion emerges (10), then this can also strongly influence the chances for success. Without such a person, most desirably in the form of the R&D manager (4), organizational as well as technical barriers may become very difficult to overcome. The time when the project champion emerges also seems to make a difference.

The probability of commercial success (5) is the single most important variable in the group. To assess this measure, a solid knowledge of the market and the costs associated with production and distribution are required. As the project evolves, these factors become clearer to management. A product whose costs will be higher because of unanticipated technical and production problems is a serious candidate for termination. The probability of commercial success should increase or at least remain the same from one review period to the next.

The support of top management (6) and the commitment of project workers (7) are also highly correlated with success. The latter may decrease if problems such as poor leadership or snags in technology are perceived but not acknowledged.

The smoothness of the technological route (8), as viewed by the project leader and evidenced by delays in meeting deadlines, is another important variable. So is a limit on the number of end users (9). An increase in possible applications for a new product during its development may dilute the effort, resulting in delays and indecision. This, in turn, may lead to complicated redesign and subversion of the original goals.

III. Organization-related variables

    11. Company profitability

    12. Anticipated competition

    13. Presence of internal competition

    14. Number of projects in R&D portfolio

Each of the four variables in this subgroup is affected by conditions throughout the firm. In particular, it seems that the more profitable a company (11), the greater the chances of completing the project. This may be attributed to better managerial controls and better screening of new product ideas. If a product has no competition in the market

(12), however, then it is likely that the R&D team will take a more relaxed attitude toward its mission. This is a prelude to failure. Conversely, if the competition is known to be working on a similar project, then both pressure and motivation intensify.

In many cases, emergence of internal competition (13) for common resources can act as a catalyst. The existence of multiple demands for technicians and equipment enhances the motivation of the project team. Nevertheless, as the size of the portfolio grows (14), there is a greater chance of individual failures as a result of less management oversight and a proportional reduction in funding.

Monitoring Scheme.   During the review process, if significant shortcomings in any of the four critical factors (regulations, raw materials, markets, and technology) are observed, then the project is marked as a good candidate for scrapping. (Further investigation may be required before a final decision is made.) If no serious problems are found, then the project is reviewed for negative changes in the key variables. A project score is computed by adding one point for each variable that has not deteriorated since the last review. A total of nine or more points indicates a high probability of success. Projects with scores between six and eight are deemed to be on the verge of failing and hence require an immediate and detailed evaluation. A score of six or less indicates a high probability of failure.

At any stage in the evaluation process, it may be possible to save a marginally failing project by allocating additional resources to alter (5), (7), and (13) or by influencing the qualitatively controllable variables (3), (8), (9), and (14). For example, if the technological route is problematic or pressure on the project leader has declined, then a commitment on the part of management may be all that is needed to bring a project score up to the desired level. A model that addresses this situation and takes into account the competition for resources among ongoing projects is developed in the next section. Because of the qualitative nature of most of the factors, an interactive approach is prescribed. This facilitates a timely assessment of the portfolio by allowing for on-line updates of performance data and the immediate disposition of marginal projects.

13.6.2 Analytic Methodology

At the beginning of a review period, each project is evaluated individually and collectively in accordance with the monitoring scheme outlined above. The first stage of this two-stage process involves the critical factors. If one or more of these are strongly negative, then the project is terminated and its remaining resources are redistributed. Next, the 14 key variables are evaluated. If the resulting score for a specific project equals or exceeds the threshold, T, then it remains in the portfolio; if not, then a judgment is made to determine whether the score can be raised to the desired level by altering one or more of the controllable factors. If this is not possible, then the project is terminated and its resources are reallocated.

These ideas are formalized in a three-step procedure using the following notation:

i = index for projects
j = index for key variables
n = number of projects in the active portfolio

$\hat{n}$ = total number of projects in the portfolio and on the candidate list

n_{max} = maximum number of projects to be included in the portfolio

B = total budget

B_i = current budget for project i

b_i = maximum funding allowable for project i

p_i = probability of technical success for project i

P_i = threshold value of p_i

$f_{ij}(t)$ = value of key variable j for project i during review period t

a_{ij} = dependent zero-one scoring variable, indicating whether key variable j for project i is at an acceptable level

T = threshold value for project score

Step 1

a. Screen each project separately with respect to the three exogenous critical factors; terminate those with strong negative indicators.

b. Screen remaining projects in portfolio with respect to probability of technical success using threshold P_i; terminate those that cannot be improved sufficiently within budgetary guidelines.

Step 2

a. Compute total score a_i for project i as follows. Let

$$a_{ij} = \begin{cases} 1, & \text{if } f_{ij}(t) - f_{ij}(t-1) \geq 0 \\ 0, & \text{otherwise} \end{cases} \qquad \text{for all } i \text{ and } j$$

$$a_i = \sum_{j=1}^{14} a_{ij}, \qquad i = 1, \ldots, n$$

b. Compare the score obtained with threshold value T, and define a zero-one indicator variable $\hat{a}_i$ as follows:

$$\hat{a}_i = \begin{cases} 1, & \text{if } a_i \geq T \\ 0, & \text{otherwise} \end{cases} \qquad i = 1, \ldots, n$$

c. Determine the disposition of project i. If $\hat{a}_i = 1$, then place project in portfolio; if not, then evaluate the feasibility of increasing $\hat{a}_i$ from zero to one by increasing those a_{ij}'s associated with the controllable key variables currently at zero. Terminate if not possible; otherwise, indicate whether additional effort will raise the score. Include the project in the portfolio if the response is positive.

Step 3

Compute the amount of free resources, R, where

$$R = B - \sum_{i=1}^{n} B_i \hat{a}_i$$

These three steps constitute the updating and qualitative evaluation of the current portfolio at the beginning of review period t. Some projects will be canceled outright; others will be further scrutinized by the decision maker to determine whether their condition can be improved.

To operationalize steps 1 and 2 in a manner that promotes consistency across projects and managers, two procedures are recommended. The first is to provide benchmarks for the interviewees in terms of background and reference data. With respect to market conditions, for example, the benchmark associated with a negative change might be determined by comparing sales figures for similar products over the last two quarters. The second procedure is aimed at building a consensus by soliciting responses from both the project leader and a subset of team members. Discrepancies can be fed back for reconsideration.

Model Formulation.   At this point, we need to allocate the remaining funds, R, to the active projects, including those on the candidate list. A decision model is formulated for this purpose using the following additional notation:

V_i = present value of returns attributed to project i

y_i = additional amount of resources allocated to project i

x_i = total amount of resources allocated to project i

u_i = zero-one decision variable for continuing project i

$\hat{u}_i$ = zero-one decision variable for selecting project i from set of candidate projects to be in the portfolio

A project that is performing well at the beginning of a review period will not necessarily have its funding continued. Although normally this is not the case, it may be determined that the resources currently allocated to that project should be reduced and the difference reallocated to projects whose payoffs are potentially higher. Under such circumstance, termination will occur if the probability of technical success, p_i, drops below its threshold, P_i. In general, p_i is assumed to be a function of the total budget, x_i, assigned to project i $(x_i = y_i + B_i)$ and will be defined by one of the relationships shown in Fig. 13.4. Now, if the probability of commercial success is denoted by f_{i5} (for simplicity, the dependence of the critical factors on t will be dropped from the notation), we solve the following problem:

$$\text{Maximize} \ \sum_{i=1}^{n} V_i p_i(x_i) f_{i5} u_i + \sum_{i=n+1}^{\hat{n}} V_i p_i(x_i) f_{i5} \hat{u}_i \tag{13.1a}$$

$$\text{subject to} \ \sum_{i=1}^{n} y_i u_i + \sum_{i=n+1}^{\hat{n}} x_i \hat{u}_i \leq R \tag{13.1b}$$

$$x_i = y_i + B_i \leq b_i, \quad i = 1, \ldots, n \tag{13.1c}$$

$$x_i \leq b_i, \quad\quad\quad i = n + 1, \ldots, \hat{n} \tag{13.1d}$$

$$\sum_{i=1}^{n} u_i + \sum_{i=n+1}^{\hat{n}} \hat{u}_i \leq n_{\max} \tag{13.1e}$$

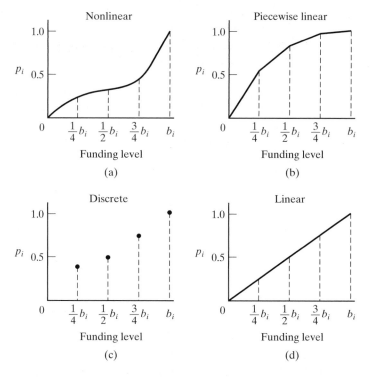

Figure 13.4   Relationships between probability of technical success and funding: (a) nonlinear; (b) piecewise linear; (c) discrete; (d) linear.

$$\sum_{j=1}^{14} a_{ij} \geq T u_i, \qquad i = 1, \dots, n \tag{13.1f}$$

$$p_i(x_i) \geq P_i u_i, \qquad i = 1, \dots, n \tag{13.1g}$$

$$p_i(x_i) \geq P \hat{u}_i, \qquad i = n + 1, \dots, \hat{n} \tag{13.1h}$$

$$x_i \geq 0,\ y_i \geq - B_i, \quad u_i \in \{0, 1\},\ \hat{u}_i \in \{0, 1\}, \quad \text{for all } i \tag{13.1i}$$

The objective function (13.1a) represents the expected return from the portfolio for both active and candidate projects. Constraint (13.1b) restricts the funding in period t to the remaining budget R. Constraints (13.1c) and (13.1d) place a limit on the amount allocated to a given project, whereas (13.1e) controls the maximum number of projects in the portfolio. The remaining structural constraints (13.1f) through (13.1h) ensure that if a project is selected, then its key variable score is at least equal the threshold value $T (= 9)$, and its probability of technical success is at an acceptable level. This formulation permits resources to be removed from an active project as long as $p_i(x_i)$ does not fall below P_i.

Implicit in the construction of problem (13.1) is the assumption that additional resources allocated to project i will affect p_i as well as the three other quantitatively controllable key variables (5), (7), and (13). The functional relationships between x_i and these key variables must be worked out on an individual basis. For example, the probability of technical success might be increased by the acquisition of better or more advanced laboratory equipment, whereas increasing worker commitment might be accomplished through the installation of a minicomputer to facilitate the project's data processing. The formulation above does not treat the key variables (5), (7), and (13) explicitly.

Implementation.   Problem (13.1) is a mixed nonlinear integer program whose degree of difficulty depends in part on the functional forms chosen to represent p_i. In the implementation, Bard et al. (1988) used the discrete model in Fig. 13.4, so the problem reduces to a pure nonlinear integer program whose terms are at most quadratic in the decision variables $\mathbf{x}$, $\mathbf{u}$, and $\hat{\mathbf{u}}$. Such problems may be converted to integer linear programs by adding one variable and two constraints for each quadratic term (see Bard 1986). Because most R&D portfolios usually contain fewer than 30 projects, this type of transformation will yield a problem whose dimensions are well within the reach of current codes. If any of the other three models in Fig. 13.4 are used, then different techniques may be required.

To put the problem into a more manageable form, let us redefine the decision variables x_i such that x_{ik} equals 1 if project i is funded at level k, and 0 otherwise. Also, let p_{ik} be the probability of technical success associated with allocation b_{ik} and K_i be the number of permissible funding levels for project i. This leads to the following pure zero-one linear formulation:

$$\text{Maximize} \quad \sum_{i=1}^{N} V_i f_{i5}\left(\sum_{k=1}^{K_i} p_{ik} x_{ik} \right) \tag{13.2a}$$

$$\text{subject to} \quad \sum_{i=1}^{N} \sum_{k=1}^{K_i} b_{ik} x_{ik} \leq B \tag{13.2b}$$

$$\sum_{k=1}^{K_i} b_{ik} x_{ik} \leq b_i, \qquad\qquad i = 1, \ldots, N \tag{13.2c}$$

$$\sum_{i=1}^{N} u_i \leq n_{\max} \tag{13.2d}$$

$$\sum_{k=1}^{K_i} p_{ik} x_{ik} - P_i u_i \geq 0, \qquad i = 1, \ldots, N \tag{13.2e}$$

$$\sum_{k=1}^{K_i} x_{ik} \leq u_i, \qquad\qquad i = 1, \ldots, N \tag{13.2e}$$

$$x_{ik} \in \{0, 1\}, \quad u_i \in \{0, 1\}, \quad \text{for all } i \text{ and } k \tag{13.2f}$$

where $N = \hat{n}$. Problem (13.2) assumes that if the score of project i is not at least at the threshold, T, then $u_i = 0$. This eliminates the need for constraint (13.1g). Also, the vector $\mathbf{u}$ has been redefined to include $\hat{\mathbf{u}}$.

In solving problems such as (13.2), it is important for the analyst to be able to enter data in a simple format and to be able to change parameters easily while investigating various scenarios. Here, the complete methodology was embodied in three separate modules: (1) a front-end, menu-driven routine for input and control; (2) a model generator for data formatting; and (3) a zero-one integer program solver. Use of the methodology, along with the computations, is demonstrated in Appendix 13A.

TEAM PROJECT

Thermal Transfer Plant

Your team was invited to the CEO's office at TMS. At the meeting, the CEO told you how impressed he was by the prototype rotary combustor project and expressed his confidence in your team leading the new waste management and recycling division. He expects this division to master the leading technology in waste disposal. To begin, you are asked to search the literature and to propose related high-tech R&D projects. The CEO would like you to present your proposal for the most appropriate such project at the next TMS board meeting.

It is clear that a detailed proposal addressing all aspects of the R&D project will be supported by the CEO. You are also aware of the once-in-a-lifetime opportunity for recognition and advancement that has been presented to you.

Prepare a proposal for the new R&D project explaining the following:

- Why the project is the most appropriate for TMS
- What technology will be used
- The nature of the expected risks
- The proposed schedule and budget
- The approach you will take to maximize the probability that the project will succeed

DISCUSSION QUESTIONS

1. What characteristics distinguish R&D project management from conventional project management? What additional skills does an R&D project manager need?
2. Identify a few breakthrough technologies and the products that they spawned.
3. Pick a major U.S. industry, such as automobiles or computers, and discuss the lapses in technology and innovation on the domestic front that permitted foreign competitors to get a foothold and, in some cases, a dominant share of the market. Who or what do you think was to blame for this situation?
4. In the mid-1980s, General Motors undertook a $5 billion program to introduce robotics and computer-integrated manufacturing techniques into many of its assembly plants. The results were disappointing, to say the least. Enormous technical problems dogged the program from the beginning, and the ultimate gains in productivity were decidedly modest. What do you think went wrong? Why? From the long-term perspective, was the automation program a good idea?

5. Give a few examples for which commercial success did not follow technical success with regard to new product introduction. What were the reasons for market failure?

6. Can you think of any example for which lack of standards retarded the introduction of a new product or technology? Give some details.

7. Pick an industry and identify its base, key, and pacing technologies.

8. What are the differences between a strategic technical plan and an operational plan for an R&D project?

9. As the head of an R&D group that is contemplating the development of a notebook computer with a built-in fax machine, who would you like to have on your strategic planning team? Why?

10. Consider a new technology, such as superconductivity or magnetic levitation, and identify several (parallel) ways of realizing it on a commercial rather than a laboratory scale.

11. Identify a new technology for which you believe that parallel development is not warranted. Explain your choice.

12. Why has simulation modeling, which is a descriptive technique, been preferred to mathematical programming, which is a prescriptive technique, for analyzing and providing help in the management of R&D projects?

13. Which of the critical factors and key variables described in Section 13.6 do you think would apply to conventional projects?

14. What are some of the shortcomings of the mathematical programming model presented in Section 13.6.2 to manage an R&D portfolio? Can you suggest ways of correcting or accommodating them?

15. What data are needed to run the mathematical programming model (13.2)? How would you go about collecting these data?

EXERCISES

13.1 Identify a new product that is based on an innovation in technology, and draw up a strategic technical plan for its development. Be sure to discuss the risk factors at each stage, and indicate how you would deal with each.

13.2 Assume that you are in charge of a round-trip mission to Mars. The goal is to spend 3 months on the planet's surface performing experiments and collecting data that will be used to help set up a future colony. Construct a strategic plan for this mission.

13.3 The transonic airplane, now on the drawing board, is intended to be a commercial transport operating between continents at supersonic speeds. It will fly a ballistic trajectory and be able to reach Japan from the United States in only a few hours. Identify the base, key, and pacing technologies for this vehicle. Discuss the economic, political, social, and technical issues surrounding its development.

13.4 Select an industry such as semiconductors or consumer electronics, and go through the six stages of the strategic technical planning process listed in Table 13.1.

13.5 Consider the problem of trying to decide which tasks to fund in parallel to achieve a given technical objective. For example, the objective might be to develop a low-cost rechargeable battery to power an electric vehicle. The funding options might be the various types of battery technologies available (see Bard and Feinberg 1989). What are the decision variables and functional relationships associated with the problem? What data are required? Be specific with respect to probability functions and any other relationships that might exist.

13.6 Construct a mathematical programming model for the parallel funding problem discussed in Exercise 13.5 and Section 13.5.

13.7 Choose a new technology, describe its major features, and explain how you would apply the total quality management principles discussed in Chapter 8 to an R&D project aimed at commercialization. What is different about total quality management applied to an R&D project versus a conventional project?

13.8 For each of the 14 key variables presented in Section 13.6.1, identify the internal and external data sources that can be used to ascertain their status.

13.9 *Computer Assignment.* Write an interactive computer program implementing the three-step procedure discussed in Section 13.6.2 for screening projects and computing project scores.

13.10 Using a commercial integer programming package, solve model (13.2a)–(13.2f) initialized with the case study data presented in Appendix 13A.

BIBLIOGRAPHY

Project Selection

Bard, J. F., "A Multiobjective Methodology for Selecting Subsystem Automation Options," *Management Science*, Vol. 32, No. 12, pp. 1628–1641, 1986.

Bard, J. F., "Using Multicriteria Methods in the Early Stages of New Product Development," *Journal of the Operational Research Society*, Vol. 41, No. 8, pp. 755–766, 1990.

Bard, J. F., R. Balachandra and P. E. Kaufmann, "An Interactive Approach to R&D Project Selection and Termination," *IEEE Transactions on Engineering Management*, Vol. EM-35, No. 3, pp. 139–146, 1988.

Bard, J. F. and A. Feinberg, "A Two-Phase Approach to Technology Selection and System Design," *IEEE Transactions on Engineering Management*, Vol. EM-36, No. 1, pp. 28–36, 1989.

Bu-Bushait, K. A., "The Application of Project Management Techniques to Construction and Research and Development," *Project Management Journal*, Vol. 20, No. 2, pp. 17–21, 1988.

Liberatore, M. J., "An Extension of the Analytic Hierarchy Process for Industrial R&D Project Selection and Resource Allocation," *IEEE Transactions on Engineering Management*, Vol. EM-34, No. 1, pp. 12–18, 1987.

Martino, J. P., *R&D Project Selection*, John Wiley & Sons, New York, 1995.

Schmidt, R. L. and J. R. Freeland, "Recent Progress in Modeling R&D Project-Selection Processes," *IEEE Transactions on Engineering Management*, Vol. 39, No. 2, pp. 189–200, 1992.

Souder, W. E. and T. Mandakovic, "R&D Project Selection Models," *Research Management*, Vol. 29, No. 4, pp. 36–42, 1986.

Watts, K. M. and J. C. Higgins, "The Use of Advanced Management Techniques in R&D," *Omega*, Vol. 15, No. 1, pp. 221–229, 1987.

Resource Allocation and Parallel Funding

Abernathy, W. J. and R. S. Rosenbloom, "Parallel Strategies in Development Projects," *Management Science*, Vol. 15, No. 10, pp. B486–B505, 1969.

Balthasar, H. U., R. A. Boschi and M. M. Menle, "Calling the Shots in R&D," *Harvard Business Review*, pp. 151–160, May–June 1978.

Bard, J. F., "Parallel Funding of R&D Tasks with Probabilistic Outcomes," *Management Science*, Vol. 31, No. 7, pp. 814–828, 1985.

Bower, J. L., *Managing the Resource Allocation Process*, Harvard University Press, Boston, 1970.

Miles, R. F., Jr., "The SIMRAND Methodology: SIMulation of Research ANd Development Projects," *Large Scale Systems*, Vol. 7, pp. 59–67, 1984.

Moore, L. J. and E. R. Clayton, *GERT Modeling and Simulation: Fundamentals and Applications*, Petrocelli-Charter, New York, 1976.

Pritsker, A. A. B., *Modeling and Analysis Using Q-GERT Networks*, Second Edition, John Wiley & Sons, New York, 1979.

Taylor, B. W., III and L. J. Moore, "R&D Project Planning with *Q*-GERT Network Modeling and Simulation," *Management Science*, Vol. 26, No. 1, pp. 44–59, 1980.

Wallin, C. C. and J. J. Gilman, "Determining the Optimum Level for R&D Spending," *Research Management*, Vol. 29, No. 5, pp. 19–24, 1986.

New Product Development

Balachandra, R., "Critical Signals for Making the Go/No Go Decisions in New Product Development," *Journal of Product Innovation Management*, Vol. 2, pp. 92–100, 1984.

Balachandra, R., *Early Warning Signals for R&D Projects*, Lexington Books, D.C. Heath, Lexington, MA, 1989.

Balachandra, R. and J. H. Friar, "Managing New Product Development Processes the Right Way, *Information Knowledge Systems Management*, Vol. 1, pp. 33–43, 1999.

Chapman, C. and S. Ward, *Managing Project Risk and Uncertainty: A Constructively Simple Approach to Decision Making*, John Wiley & Sons, New York, 2002.

Davis, C. R., "Calculated Risk: A Framework for Evaluating Product Development," *MIT Sloan Management Review*, Vol. 43, No. 4, pp. 71–77, 2002.

Kidder, T., *The Soul of a New Machine*, Little Brown, Boston, 1981.

Nayak, P. R. and J. M. Ketteringham, *Breakthroughs! How Leadership and Drive Created Commercial Innovations That Sweep the World*, Second Edition, Pfeiffer, New York, 1993.

Peters, T. "Get Innovative or Get Dead, Part One," *California Management Review*, Vol. 33, No. 1, pp. 9–26, 1990.

Rogers, E. M., "New Product Adoption and Diffusion," *Journal of Consumer Research*, Vol. 2, No. 4, pp. 290–301, 1976.

Rosenbloom, R. S. and M. A. Cusumano, "Technology Pioneering and Competitive Advantage: The Birth of the VCR Industry," *California Management Review*, Vol. 29, No. 4, 1987.

Souder, W. E., J. D. Sherman and M. K. Badaway, *Managing New Technology Development*, McGraw-Hill, New York, 1993.

Wheelwright, S. C. and K. B. Clark, "Creating Project Plans to Focus Product Development," *Harvard Business Review*, pp. 70–82, March-April 1992.

Critical Factors

Baker, N. R., S. G. Green and A. S. Bean, "Why R&D Projects Succeed or Fail," *Research Management*, Vol. 29, No. 6, pp. 29–34, 1986.

Balachandra, R. and J. A. Raelin, "How to Abandon an R&D Project," *Research Management*, Vol. 18, pp. 24–29, 1980.

Meldrum, M. J. and A. F. Millman, "Ten Risks in Marketing High-Technology Products," *Industrial Marketing Management*, Vol. 20, No. 1, pp. 43–48, 1991.

Pinto, J. K. and D. P. Slevin, "Critical Factors in Successful Project Implementation," *IEEE Transactions on Engineering Management*, Vol. EM-34, No. 1, pp. 22–27, 1987.

Rubenstein, A. H. and H. Schroder, "Managerial Differences in Assessing Probabilities of Technical Success for R&D Projects," *Management Science*, Vol. 24, No. 2, pp. 137–148, 1977.

Schroder, H. H., "The Quality of Subjective Probabilities of Technical Success in R&D," *R&D Management*, Vol. 6, No. 1, 1975.

Strategic Issues

Elton, J. and J. Roe, "Bringing Discipline to Project Management," *Harvard Business Review*, Vol. 76, No. 2, pp. 78–83, 1998.

Erickson, T. J., J. F. Magee, P. A. Roussel and K. N. Saad, "Managing Technology as a Business Strategy," *Sloan Management Review*, Vol. 31, No. 3, pp. 73–77, 1990.

Gluck, F. W., S. P. Kaufman and A. S. Walleck, "Strategic Management for Competitive Advantage," *Harvard Business Review*, Vol. 58, pp. 154–161, July-August 1980.

Hickman, C. and C. Raia, "Incubating Innovation," *Journal of Business Strategy*, Vol. 23, No. 3, pp. 14–18, 2002.

Jain, R. K. and H. C. Triandis, *Management of Research and Development Organizations: Managing the Unmanageable*, John Wiley & Sons, New York, 1996.

Roussel, P. H., K. N. Saad and T. J. Erikson, *Third Generation R&D: Managing the Link to Corporate Strategy*, Harvard Business Press, Boston, 1991.

Portfolio Management Case Study

Portable Solutions is a Texas-based company that has been selling personal computers and peripherals since 1982. In May 1985, it expanded its operations and began to produce its own brand of tape backup units for PCs. Since that time, the company has introduced three different but related products to the market, including a 10-gigabyte self-threading backup system, a 20-gigabyte streaming tape backup system, and a 40-gigabyte streaming tape backup.

To maintain profitability and ensure its survival, Portable Solutions has been exploring two new ventures. The first involves vertical integration of its current line; the second centers on the development of new products to compete in complementary areas. To put these ideas into motion, the company has established an R&D portfolio that includes the following six projects:

1. A signature verification system that has the capacity to store 145,000 signature files on an optical, nonerasable medium and the ability to access each within 3 seconds. The system is intended for use by banks and would replace current methods, which typically rely on microfiche as the storage medium. With respect to performance, optical technology offers far greater speed and reliability than do any of its competitors. In addition, the permanent nature of the files offers built-in security.

2. A signature verification system that has the capacity to store 85,000 files on a hard drive and the ability to access each in 3 seconds or less. This system would incorporate most of the features of (1) but would use magnetic tape as the storage medium. The advantage here is lower development cost, while the disadvantage concerns record security (i.e., information can be altered easily).

3. A portable laser drive with the capacity to store 115 megabytes of information. This system should be fully portable without the hint of compatibility or installation problems. To date, speed and capacity have been limited by mechanical hard-drive

technology. Optical technology, however, now permits storage of vast amounts of data in compact form, free of maintenance, and without the data integrity problems that have plagued magnetic media.

4. A small computer standard interface (SCSI) for existing and future product lines. This interface will be compatible with most mainframes as well as the Apple Macintosh and various workstations. At this time, the company's market is limited to PCs. A SCSI will open up new opportunities throughout the industry.

5. A port extender interface for personal computers. This device permits the addition of peripherals when no extra slots for interface cards are available. It plugs directly into a floppy port, leaving the bus slots available for other applications. The proliferation of add-ons makes this an especially attractive product.

6. A combination 20-gigabyte hard disk/20-gigabyte portable backup system for military applications. This unit must pass stringent military quality and durability standards. The marketing department indicates that the demand for this product is high and that many channels exist for its promotion. Nevertheless, engineering has expressed serious doubts about achieving the required levels of performance within the target cost range.

In the course of marketing, management has recently identified four additional projects as potentially lucrative and is considering several funding alternatives. The new projects include

7. A downloading peripheral that transfers data from a 9-inch mainframe magnetic tape to a 3.5-inch optical cartridge for use with personal computers. At the time of the study, the mainframe standard for information archiving over the past 20 years had been the 9-inch tape. This medium requires constant maintenance to avoid data loss and consumes expensive central processing unit (CPU) time during retrieval. Downloading tapes to optical media not only creates a maintenance-free environment but also permits easy access through personal computers.

8. A smart system that is capable of downloading 9-inch magnetic tapes to 3.5-inch optical cartridges. This system would be self-contained, not needing additional equipment to operate. It would differ from the system described in (7) by the incorporation of a CPU.

9. A record management system that is capable of storing up to 2 terabytes of information in a 12-inch optical cartridge. As envisioned, a microcomputer would serve as processor, and up to 1,000 cartridges could be managed at once using a jukebox principle.

10. An image-scanning device that is capable of tracking pavement conditions on highways and determining when to record a damaged sector. In addition, it must be capable of classifying the damage and deriving a repair schedule that is based on severity of damage and equipment availability. The goal is to develop a system that will reduce highway repair costs by approximately 50%.

As is usually the case, Portable Solutions does not have the resources to fund all of these projects. Model (13.2) presented in Section 13.6 will be used to determine the best allocation of materials and personnel and to decide the level of activity for each project accepted.

Given the demand for resources, management believes that at most seven projects should be undertaken at one time and has imposed a $250,000 ceiling on the R&D budget. Table 13A.1 lists the input data for the 10 projects, and Table 13A.2 specifies the relationships between probability of technical success, p_{ik}, and funding level, b_{ik}. These data were derived from extensive interaction with the firm's four principal officers and represent the consensus that emerged after two iterations of individual and joint discussions.

At the time of the study, five of the first six projects were actively being pursued at a cost of $240,000. The third project was not in the portfolio but was still considered a candidate. Table 13A.3 indicates the individual funding levels along with the total.

In the process of updating the portfolio, all current projects passed the critical factors test at step 1, and all but project 5 passed the key variables test at step 2. Running the model with the four remaining projects, project 3, and the four new ones, led to the selection of six projects, as shown in Table 13A.4. The total budget allocation accompanying this solution is $249,000, and the expected return is $19.56M. The specific funding levels are also shown in Table 13A.4.

The fact that projects 1, 3, and 7 were not chosen does not necessarily mean that they will be discarded but simply that they will be shelved until the next review or until additional funds become available. It is also possible that project 5 could be resurrected at a future time.

Regarding the computations, the solution was obtained in 15.22 minutes on an IBM-PC. This involved solving a 32-variable, zero-one integer program with 11 constraints. With today's technology, problems of this size can be solved in fractions of a second. Of course, the computational effort grows exponentially with the total number of levels and projects, so large problems may still take some time. Note that constraints (13.2c) and (13.2d) can be handled implicitly and that the nine project variables, u_i, can be eliminated by appropriately redefining (13.2d) and (13.2f).

Assessment of Methodology   The above presentation demonstrates the facility with which an R&D manager can update his or her portfolio provided that all of the

TABLE 13A.1   Input Data For R&D Case Study

Project	Probability of commercial success (f_{i5})	Threshold probability (P_i)	Present value of return (V_i)	Maximum budget (B_i)
1	0.75	0.35	$3.7M	$75K
2	0.82	0.40	$8.2M	$105K
3	0.67	0.45	$7.5M	$145K
4	0.92	0.35	$4.1M	$110K
5	0.55	0.30	$5.1M	$90K
6	0.88	0.35	$7.8M	$145K
7	0.68	0.40	$3.5M	$90K
8	0.75	0.35	$9.0M	$100K
9	0.67	0.30	$7.5M	$128K
10	0.94	0.45	$8.6M	$129K

TABLE 13A.2　Relationship Between Probability of Technical Success and Funding Level

Project	Level 1		Level 2		Level 3		Level 4	
	p_{i1}	b_{i1}	p_{i2}	b_{i2}	p_{i3}	b_{i3}	p_{i4}	b_{i4}
1	0.44	$22K	0.56	$34K	0.72	$54K	0.89	$72K
2	0.36	$18K	0.45	$26K	0.57	$47K	0.82	$64K
3	0.40	$25K	0.58	$52K	0.72	$90K	0.95	$130K
4	0.35	$20K	0.50	$38K	0.75	$84K	0.94	$100K
5	0.30	$15K	0.55	$40K	0.70	$60K	0.90	$90K
6	0.25	$25K	0.50	$50K	0.75	$65K	0.98	$120K
7	0.25	$15K	0.56	$40K	0.76	$60K	0.89	$82K
8	0.36	$20K	0.49	$40K	0.62	$81K	0.82	$94K
9	0.25	$25K	0.54	$50K	0.77	$98K	0.95	$125K
10	0.35	$25K	0.50	$48K	0.75	$89K	0.94	$129K

TABLE 13A.3　Funding for Basic Portfolio

Project	Level	Funding
1	2	$34,000
2	4	$64,000
4	1	$20,000
5	3	$60,000
6	3	$62,000
	Total =	$240,000

TABLE 13A.4　Results for Updated Portfolio

Project	Level	Funding
2	2	$26,000
4	1	$20,000
6	3	$65,000
8	2	$40,000
9	2	$50,000
10	2	$48,000
	Total =	$249,000

pertinent data are available and that an accurate assessment of the key variables can be made. Updates can take place at any time but are commonly scheduled around the budgetary cycle. As some projects reach their critical stages, though, it may be desirable to increase the frequency with which the portfolio is reviewed.

　　After testing the methodology with a number of high-tech firms, it was found that most managers were less interested in the final results than in the process itself. The value for them was in systematically stepping through each project and assessing its status. The biggest stumbling block arose in the evaluation of changes in the key variables. The lack of up-to-date information often led to difficulties in making consistent judgments across the portfolio. In some instances, for example, not all managers were aware of a lapse in worker commitment or the critical need for a technological breakthrough.

Nevertheless, the information gathered at the interview sessions was prized as much for the insight that it provided as for the confidence that it instilled in the decision-making process. By isolating the major components of that process, the interactive dynamics enabled the participants to gain a better understanding of the forces at work.

Chapter 14

Computer Support for Project Management

14.1 INTRODUCTION

Project management is the process of achieving multidimensional goals related to on-time delivery, adherence to requirements and cost minimization in a unique environment that is subject to resource availability, cash flow, and technological performance constraints, all in the presence of uncertainty. The tools and techniques that have been developed to assist project managers in their job were introduced earlier. Most of these tools are based on a model that transforms input data into some form of output that facilitates decision making. For example, scheduling by the critical path method (CPM) transforms information about required activities, performance times, and precedence relations into a list of critical activities, available slack for noncritical activities, and an estimate of project completion time. Each tool is designed to handle a specific aspect of the project management process. However, a project manager frequently needs an integrated mechanism to deal with several aspects of a project at once. This has led to the development of software packages, many Web based, that now make it possible for different organizations to interact efficiently by standardizing procedures, reports, and data files.

The new generation of software packages (or information systems) integrates project management with other activities of the organization. For example, enterprise resource planning (ERP) systems can simultaneously manage projects and recurrent activities that share the same information and the same resources (e.g., in a matrix organization). Furthermore, these information systems support the definition, execution, monitoring, and control of project management processes, as discussed in Chapter 2.

Early software packages typically concentrated on a limited set of tools and techniques for scheduling and managing costs. Data input and processing were batch oriented, and only a prespecified set of output reports were available. The introduction of PCs, workstations, and the Web, coupled with rapid advances in software engineering and re-duced processing and computer memory costs, led to the development of integrated software packages that are able to address a multitude of functions simultaneously.

The current trend in the area of software development is toward interactive, fully integrated systems that can handle multiple projects and use the Web for communication. Many of these systems can handle all of the different aspects of project management throughout a project's life cycle, including

- Configuration management
- Scheduling
- Budgeting
- Cost analysis
- Resource management
- Monitoring and control

Potential users face two issues: (1) how to select the most appropriate software package for their needs and (2) how to introduce the chosen package into their organization successfully. In the next section, guidance is offered to those who are charged with the responsibility of resolving the first issue. We use the software package Microsoft Project to illustrate concepts. This is followed by a discussion of the major criteria that accompany a benefit-cost analysis aimed at making the selection. The remainder of the chapter offers insights into smoothing the implementation of project management software.

14.2 USE OF COMPUTERS IN PROJECT MANAGEMENT

Project management requires the deliberate treatment of organizational processes, economic factors, and technological aspects, as well as the implementation of methodologies for planning, scheduling, and control. When choosing a project manager, it is important to consider (among many other things) leadership abilities, verbal communication skills, and motivation level. Today's computers cannot replace a skilled project manager because computers do not possess these attributes. However, they can support a project manager in certain decision-making processes if the problems at hand are well defined and amenable to quantitative or symbolic manipulation. Even if this is only partially the case, the computer's ability to store, retrieve, and process large quantities of data, along with its powerful communication capabilities, can help prepare information for the decision maker. In particular, we rely on software to

- Supply needed information from the database
- Support decisions with appropriate models and data
- Support project monitoring and control
- Support multiple project monitoring and control
- Support communication among stakeholders
- Support project management processes with workflow models
- Support the integration of projects and recurrent activities that share the same resources.

These functions were discussed throughout the book. We now elaborate on several of them in the following subsections.

14.2.1 Supporting the Project Management Process Approach

The software support in this case is integrated in the sense that the processes are connected to each other as the output of one process serves as the input to another process. Using the PMBOK framework as an example, the 39 processes in the 9 knowledge areas form a complete project management methodology. Each process is defined by its required input, the tools and techniques used to manipulate the input data, and the output produced. The software uses a workflow management module to route the required input to the person who is responsible for each process, along with the tools and techniques (models) needed to execute the process. This module monitors the progress of each process and alerts the project manager to delays. The system saves predefined data and process outputs in its database for future use. Lessons learned are transformed into procedural updates, and the tools and technique discussed next are used to support both organizational and individual learning.

14.2.2 Tools and Techniques for Project Management

Some software packages are limited in scope and are mainly a collection of tools and techniques (a model base) supported by a database, a user interface, and a report generator. These systems are essentially a subset of those described in Section 14.2.1 and support the following basic functions:

1. *Scope of work and work breakdown structure (WBS).* The initial step in using most project management software is to define the project's content in the form of a statement of work (SOW) or scope of work and translating it into a WBS. A template for the SOW is a handy tool for organizations that perform similar projects. The development of a WBS is greatly facilitated by computer packages whose input and presentation format reflect the underlying hierarchical structure of the project, that can assign appropriate codes to WBS elements at each level, and that can check for inconsistencies such as disconnected or lower-level WBS elements connected to more than one higher-level element. The division of the project/program into its basic building blocks is easier using a module that automatically assigns WBS codes and checks for inconsistencies as part of the data input process. Figure 14.1 illustrates a WBS diagram that corresponds to the seven tasks of the example project used throughout the book.

2. *Organizational breakdown structure (OBS).* The next step in project management is to allocate the work content among participating organizations; i.e., to develop the project's OBS. This structure depicts the communication lines for reports, work authorization, and so on. A module similar to the one that supports the WBS supports the creation of a clearly defined organizational structure. Integrating the WBS module with the OBS module generates a matrix that assigns each lower-level WBS element to a lower-level OBS element.

The OBS and WBS hierarchies allow for information processing through a roll-up mechanism. This mechanism transfers information from lower- to upper-level elements through the connections defined in the OBS-WBS matrix. The established relationships help to generate reports at several managerial levels. This is also a good

	Task name	WBS
1	- EXAMPLE	**1**
2	- ELEMENT 1	**1.1**
3	A	1.1.1
4	C	1.1.2
5	D	1.1.3
6	- ELEMENT 2	**1.2**
7	B	1.2.1
8	F	1.2.2
9	- ELEMENT 3	**1.3**
10	E	1.3.1
11	G	1.3.2

Figure 14.1   WBS for example project.

starting point for the development of work flow when project management processes are introduced and supported by the software.

One important aid to a project manager is a software package that supports the development, maintenance, and integration of the WBS and OBS. The process subdivides the project's work and allocates it to the participating organizations. This division capability is also important in integrating individual efforts and helping update all groups on their share of the total effort as it relates to the entire project. The WBS and OBS modules not only generate reports at various managerial levels but also keep these reports coherent and synchronous. By using the same OBS-WBS hierarchy throughout a project's life cycle, the plans developed during startup are used to execute, monitor, and control each stage of the project.

Once the organizational structure is defined and each participating organizational unit is assigned tasks or a scope of work within a specified work package (WP), it is possible to break down the project's work content further into activities and to estimate each activity's duration. This breakdown forms the basis for the following steps in the project's planning cycle.

3. *Scheduling*. Defining the time frame or calendar for the project is the first step in scheduling. In the calendar definition phase, the project manager may select a current organizational calendar or develop one that is project specific. The calendar defines working days per week, daily working hours, scheduled holidays and vacations, and so on. One important decision is to select the minimal time unit. Some projects (e.g., the maintenance of electric power plants or airplanes) require a detailed schedule at the level of minutes or hours. For long-term construction projects, a minimum time unit of a day or a week may suffice. Figure 14.2 illustrates a calendar for the example project, which is scheduled to start in the beginning of March 2005. The figure shows only the first 4 weeks because the rest of the calendar is defined similarly.

Based on the calendar and the estimated activity durations, scheduling can begin. In most software packages, this is done by defining precedence relations among activities. The first step is usually to enumerate finish-to-start precedence relations; that is, when an activity can start as a function of its immediate predecessors. The CPM logic is then applied, and the early-start, early-finish, late-start, and late-finish dates are calculated for each activity. These dates are based on the calendar selected, with its predetermined

December	2004	February	2005	January 2005						◄
28 29 30 1 2 3 4		30 31 1 2 3 4 5								
5 6 7 8 9 10 11		6 7 8 9 10 11 12								
12 13 14 15 16 17 18		13 14 15 16 17 18 19								
19 20 21 22 23 24 25		20 21 22 23 24 25 26								
26 27 28 29 30 31 1		27 28 1 2 3 4 5								

Sun	Mon	Tue	Wed	Thu	Fri	Sat
Sun 02 Jan '05	Mon 03 Jan '05	Tue 04 Jan '05	Wed 05 Jan '05	Thu 06 Jan '05	Fri 07 Jan '05	Sat 08 Jan '05
			A, 5 wks			
			B, 3 wks			
Sun 09 Jan '05	Mon 10 Jan '05	Tue 11 Jan '05	Wed 12 Jan '05	Thu 13 Jan '05	Fri 14 Jan '05	Sat 15 Jan '05
			A, 5 wks			
			B, 3 wks			
Sun 16 Jan '05	Mon 17 Jan '05	Tue 18 Jan '05	Wed 19 Jan '05	Thu 20 Jan '05	Fri 21 Jan '05	Sat 22 Jan '05
			A, 5 wks			
		B, 3 wks				
Sun 23 Jan '05	Mon 24 Jan '05	Tue 25 Jan '05	Wed 26 Jan '05	Thu 27 Jan '05	Fri 28 Jan '05	Sat 29 Jan '05
			A, 5 wks			

Figure 14.2   Calendar for the example project.

holidays and vacations. The resulting schedule can be a table of activities with the corresponding dates and slacks, a Gantt chart, or a network model [activity on arrow (AOA), activity on node (AON)]. Some software packages include all three formats, whereas others include only a tabular report or a Gantt chart. Figure 14.3 presents the early-start Gantt chart for the example project with the critical activities in bold; Fig. 14.4 depicts the same information in an AON diagram with the boxes identifying the critical activities in bold. All dates are given in the following format: day/month/year.

The basic schedule developed by the process described above is called an "unconstrained" schedule. The precedence relations among activities are assumed to be the only limiting factors. The next step is to introduce the time constraints imposed on activities or events (project milestones). Time constraints may require an activity to start or end on a given date and may produce an infeasible schedule as a result of conflicts between the critical path's length and the imposed milestones. For example, a conflict occurs if the length of the critical path is 12 months but the contract calls for a delivery date 11 months after kickoff.

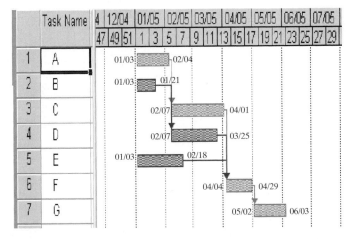

Figure 14.3   Early-start Gantt chart for example project.

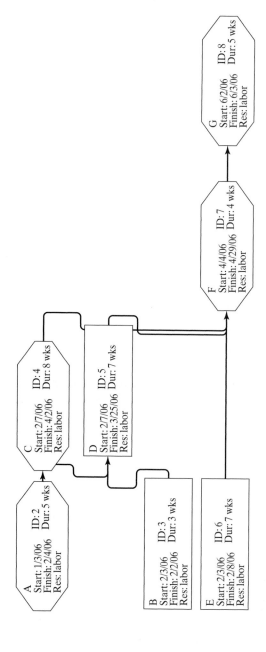

Figure 14.4 AON network for example project.

	Task name	Duration	Free slack	Total slack
1	A	5 wk	0 wk	0 wk
2	B	3 wk	2 wk	3 wk
3	C	8 wk	0 wk	0 wk
4	D	7 wk	1 wk	1 wk
5	E	7 wk	6 wk	6 wk
6	F	4 wk	0 wk	0 wk
7	G	5 wk	0 wk	0 wk

Figure 14.5   Slack report for example project.

In some projects, managers can resolve conflicts by introducing other forms of precedence relations, such as start-to-start and finish-to-finish. Modeling the real situation with these alternatives may alleviate the problem. Some software packages support all types of precedence relations mentioned in Chapter 9, including those with built-in delays or lags. Understanding and controlling precedence relations is crucial in the scheduling process and helps develop a more realistic model. If managers cannot resolve conflicts, then they must modify the project master plan until a feasible schedule is achieved.

In projects for which a major concern is uncertainty, as evidenced by stochastic activity durations, program evaluation and review technique (PERT) logic can be applied to analyze the effects of unanticipated disruptions on overall project length. Most commercial software packages do not handle stochastic activity durations. The few that do usually rely on Monte Carlo simulation, as explained in Chapter 9. Most commercial software packages are limited to calculations of the total slack and free slack of each activity, as depicted in Fig. 14.5. As a rough estimate, it can be assumed that the larger the slack of an activity, the smaller the risk that it will become critical.

4. *Hammocks and subnets.* The scheduling process occurs at the activity level, but it is desirable to be able to generate reports at any of the various OBS or WBS levels. Many software packages that support the OBS and WBS have this capability. In addition, many packages have roll-up mechanisms, such as hammock activities and subnets. A hammock activity replaces a group of activities. This type of aggregation is suitable for high-level reports that do not require a single activity level of detail. The subnet or subnetwork facility is similar to the hammock concept but represents activity groups by two or more "aggregate" activities. Another possibility is to aggregate activities into tasks and tasks into hammock tasks. Figure 14.6 summarizes the schedule of the example project using both aggregated activities for WBS elements and detailed project activities.

Charts that are designed for upper-level management normally present aggregated activities or tasks only; however, any mix of activities, tasks, subnetworks, and hammocks is possible. Figure 14.7 summarizes the schedule of the example project in a tabular format. The schedule reports each activity's duration, early start and finish, and late start and finish.

5. *Resource planning.* In addition to time constraints, a project may be circumscribed by the availability of resources. Thus, the next step in the planning process is to add a resource dimension. The simplest approach is to assign resources to each activity, assuming that the same resource level is used throughout the activity's duration.

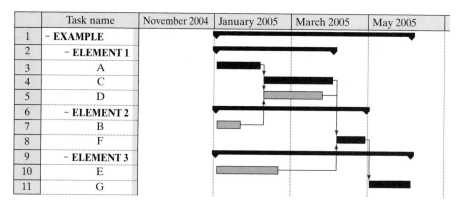

	Task name	November 2004	January 2005	March 2005	May 2005
1	- EXAMPLE				
2	- ELEMENT 1				
3	A				
4	C				
5	D				
6	- ELEMENT 2				
7	B				
8	F				
9	- ELEMENT 3				
10	E				
11	G				

Figure 14.6   Gantt chart with hammock activities for the example project.

	Task name	Duration	Early start	Late start	Early finish	Late finish
1	A	5 wks	Mon 01/03/05	Mon 01/03/05	Fri 02/04/05	Fri 02/04/05
2	B	3 wks	Mon 01/03/05	Mon 01/24/05	Fri 01/21/05	Fri 02/11/05
3	C	8 wks	Mon 02/07/05	Mon 02/07/05	Fri 04/01/05	Fri 04/01/05
4	D	7 wks	Mon 02/07/05	Mon 02/14/05	Fri 03/25/05	Fri 04/01/05
5	E	7 wks	Mon 01/03/05	Mon 02/14/05	Fri 02/18/05	Fri 04/01/05
6	F	4 wks	Mon 04/04/05	Mon 04/04/05	Fri 04/29/05	Fri 04/29/05
7	G	5 wks	Mon 05/02/05	Mon 05/02/05	Fri 06/03/05	Fri 06/03/05

Figure 14.7   Schedule summary report for example project.

Based on the earlier schedule, the required level for each resource type is calculated for each period. This approach helps identify time periods when resource requirements exceed resource availability. Project managers can reschedule activities to avoid resource overload, or, if needed, they can try to acquire more resources.

Some sophisticated software packages allow for the uneven distribution of resource consumption over the activity's duration. When using such a package, a manager should specify each activity's required resource level during every period in which the activity is performed. Figure 14.8a gives the resource profile for the example project, accompanied by a Gantt chart assuming an early-start schedule.

Figure 14.8b gives the resource profile and the Gantt chart for the late-start schedule. As can be seen by examining the two figures, the maximum of the resource profile is moved from the project's early phase in the early-start schedule toward the project's middle phase in the late-start schedule.

Software packages that support scheduling under resource availability constraints offer a large variety of decision support applications. One application is *resource allocation*, which specifies the availability level of each resource type for each calendar period.

Figure 14.8a Resource profile and Gantt chart for example project: early-start schedule.

Figure 14.8b Resource profile and Gantt chart for example project: late-start schedule

If resource requirements exceed resource availability for one or more resource types in a given period, then the resource allocation procedure reschedules activities. Rescheduling may be limited to each activity's slack or be subject to a constraint imposed by a given project termination date. Priorities may be assigned to projects or to activities within projects so that high-priority activities receive scarce resources first.

Some packages allow for several types of resource capacities, such as overtime, second shifts, and subcontracting. The different types of capacities eliminate infeasibilities while allowing for tighter control of resource costs and usage. Moreover, some software packages offer the option of activity preemption. If this option is available, then low-priority activities that are already started may be stopped if higher-priority activities compete for the same resource. When one or more of the higher-priority activities terminate, the preempted activities are resumed.

Another application that is available for resource management is *resource leveling*. Software packages with this option can reschedule activities to achieve a relatively constant use of one or more resources. As explained in Chapter 10, a leveled usage profile tends to decrease resource costs and increase resource use.

Many resource allocation and resource leveling procedures are available. The resource management module of each software package is based on a specific algorithm. Because of the complexity of these scheduling problems, most commercial packages apply a *heuristic*, an algorithmic procedure that seeks a "good" feasible solution but does not guarantee an optimum. As a result, the performance of the resource leveling or resource allocation modules in different software packages will vary with respect to computation times and quality of schedules produced.

6. *Resource management.* The resource management modules of commercial software packages use a variety of approaches to model the relationship between resource availability and a project's schedule. Some packages assume that all resources are renewable; that is, the same resource capacity level is available during each period. This assumption may be correct for a fixed workforce and equipment complement but not for subcontracting or materials, and typically not in a matrix organization. Other packages assume that resources are depleted with use, which is true for materials. Some packages assume that an activity's duration is a function of the resources available to perform the activity (the time-resource tradeoff). Other packages assume that the duration of an activity is fixed. Consequently, when selecting a software package for a specific project, a manager should carefully examine the type of resources that the package can handle as well as the quality of resource leveling and resource allocation procedures.

The OBS-WBS matrix depicts the relationship between resources and functional management. Each resource is assigned to an organizational unit in the OBS and to activities related to WBS elements. This dual resource link provides a trace ability during the project's life cycle. Software packages that include the OBS-WBS matrix may support resource management by keeping track of the resources that each OBS element uses to perform the activities on its assigned WBS components or WPs. Resource use is calculated by recording the actual effort associated with each resource in each period and comparing this effort with the resource's available capacity. Functional management and the project manager commonly use this calculation as a performance measure.

Software packages that support resource management are very helpful during the planning phase, when an important goal is to resolve conflicts. These packages are also helpful in the implementation phase, because uncertainty may cause changes in the original schedule, leading to shifts in priorities. However, managing resources is important for other reasons as well: budgeting and cost management.

The most sophisticated software packages of the ERP type can integrate resource management of projects with the resource management of the rest of the organization that deals with recurrent activities. The advantage of this integrated approach is its early warning mechanism that alerts management to overloaded resources that are needed simultaneously both for projects and for recurrent activities.

7. *Budget preparation.* The WBS, OBS, and schedule form the basis for project budgeting and cost estimation. Direct labor and direct material costs are prepared at the activity level. Indirect costs can be added at any OBS level. Each activity's direct costs should include its assigned resource costs. Therefore, managers should select a software package that can correctly represent these various components.

Some resource costs are based on an hourly rate and calculated as the rate times actual activity hours. Other resources, such as materials, have a per-unit cost, for which the measurement unit might be a kilogram or a cubic meter. Some resources may even have several rates; for example, overtime labor costs might be different from labor costs on regular time or a second shift. Overhead costs are charged against various baselines. Level-of-effort costs, such as those for project management, accrue as a passage of time, whereas apportioned-effort costs are based on a factor of a discrete effort, such as in-spection. The initial project budget should specify other overhead costs, including facility operations and energy. Therefore, a software package's ability to communicate with the databases that store information about rates and actual costs is an important criterion for software selection. Figure 14.9 presents a cost-schedule report for the example project, which includes each activity's total costs along with its scheduled start and finish times.

Contractors who respond to requests for proposals (RFPs) in an effort to win contracts must prepare cost estimates for each RFP. Thus, the ability of a project man-agement software package to support cost estimation may be an important aspect for such contractors. Cost estimates are based on a cost breakdown structure (CBS). (Refer to Chapter 4 for a discussion of cost component classification.) Information on the actual costs of previous projects stored in a user-friendly database is very helpful in preparing cost estimates.

	Task name	Duration	Start	Finish	Cost
1	A	5 wks	Mon 03/01/05	Fri 04/02/05	$1,500.00
2	B	3 wks	Mon 03/01/05	Fri 03/19/05	$2,700.00
3	C	8 wks	Mon 04/05/05	Fri 05/28/05	$3,300.00
4	D	7 wks	Mon 04/05/05	Fri 05/21/05	$4,200.00
5	E	7 wks	Mon 03/01/05	Fri 04/16/05	$5,700.00
6	F	4 wks	Mon 05/31/05	Fri 06/25/05	$6,100.00
7	G	5 wks	Mon 06/28/05	Fri 07/30/05	$7,200.00

Figure 14.9   Cost-schedule report for example project.

Some software packages support a CBS and life-cycle cost (LCC) analyses. The need for these functions becomes obvious when a client requires them in a contract or RFP. In some cases, the contractor may want to use LCC analysis for his own benefit. By consistently updating the CBS for each project, historical cost data are accumulated and bid preparation for future projects is more accurate and less time consuming.

In addition to budgeting, managers may need to forecast and manage the cash flow. Tying milestones and activities to cash flows makes it possible to schedule a project to achieve a desired cash flow or to schedule several projects simultaneously under a variety of cash flow constraints. The schedule affects a project's budget and in many projects is subject to a host of monetary restrictions. The relationship between costs and schedule can be analyzed by time-cost models, whereby each activity's duration is assumed to be a function of the activity's costs. Recall that *crashing* is the term used to describe time-cost trade-offs. Not all commercial packages support this function, though, so managers with such needs should purchase a package that permits crashing or accommodates user-written subroutines.

ERP-type systems support organizational cash flow management combining the cash flow of projects with the cash flow of ongoing activities. This allows the chief financial officer of the organization to plan, monitor cash flows, and better control the cash position of the entire organization.

8. *Configuration management.* In engineering projects, the technological aspects should be coordinated with the project management support system. The need to select a configuration baseline; to evaluate proposed engineering changes and their performance, cost, and schedule impacts; and to keep track of the current configuration translates into handling and controlling large data sets and transactions. Although software packages for configuration management are available on the market, most do not support the other facets of project management. Thus, when selecting a software package, a project manager should consider the interaction between that package and the configuration management system and define the required interfaces.

A new generation of software packages are called *product data management systems* (PDMSs). These systems combine configuration management with workflow management and database management. The database is used to keep records of parts and related files. The PDMS then facilitates the design process, providing the security, file storage, revision control, classification, notification, and application integration.

9. *Sensitivity analysis and project monitoring.* Once a plan is established, the project manager should examine its sensitivity to changing conditions. Uncertainty plays a major role in most projects. Examples of sources of uncertainty are activity duration estimates, resource availability and costs, and lead time for material deliveries. The basic project planning models do not consider these aspects of uncertainty, so performing a sensitivity analysis in the form of "what if" questions is recommended. This allows the team to study the project's plan under various conditions. The results may signal a need to develop a risk management plan and a contingency plan, especially when a major failure is possible. A software package's ability to perform a "what if" analysis and to store several plans for the same project is therefore essential when significant levels of uncertainty are present.

An acceptable project plan (1) outlines how the schedule, costs, and resource use fit within the imposed constraints and (2) allocates the work in a feasible manner. The

	Task name	Duration	Early start	Baseline start	Early finish	Baseline finish
1	A	5 wks	Mon 01/03/05	Thu 01/01/04	Fri 02/04/05	Wed 02/04/04
2	B	3 wks	Mon 01/03/05	Thu 01/01/04	Fri 01/21/05	Wed 02/25/04
3	C	8 wks	Mon 02/07/05	Thu 02/05/04	Fri 04/01/05	Wed 03/31/04
4	D	7 wks	Mon 02/07/05	Thu 02/26/04	Fri 03/25/05	Wed 04/14/04
5	E	7 wks	Mon 01/03/05	Thu 02/26/04	Fri 02/18/05	Wed 04/14/04
6	F	4 wks	Mon 04/04/05	Thu 04/15/04	Fri 04/29/05	Wed 05/12/04
7	G	5 wks	Mon 05/02/05	Thu 05/13/04	Fri 06/03/05	Wed 06/16/04

Figure 14.10   Detailed schedule for labor.

project is ready to begin when a feasible plan, accepted by the project stakeholders, is constructed and approved.

During the execution phase, the process of issuing work orders and managing resources can be automated with the help of a computer. A schedule for each resource that includes all of its assigned tasks and activities and their planned start and finish dates is a valuable tool. Figure 14.10 presents a schedule for the example project.

To monitor progress, it is essential to keep track of all activity start and end times. In some cases, estimates of the percentage of work completed for ongoing activities are also provided to the software package. Accompanying this information are accumulated data on resource use and expenditures. The analysis can take many different forms. Progress reports in the form of a Gantt chart, with completed activities marked, are very popular. Also common are tabular reports that indicate, from the project's start, actual progress versus planned progress for each task or activity during the current period or on a cumulative basis. Whereas periodic reports are useful in exception identification, the cumulative reports are important for trend analysis. Figure 14.11 depicts a progress report based on a Gantt chart, each task's status and original schedule. Figure 14.12 displays a resource-oriented progress report. For comparison, each task's actual start, actual finish, status, and actual hours are reported, along with scheduled finish times. This type of report is helpful in monitoring resource use.

Figure 14.11   Gantt chart–based progress report.

	Task name	Actual start	Actual finish	0% Complete	Actual work	Finish
1	− **EXAMPLE**	**Mon 01/03/05**	**NA**	**3%**	**44 hrs**	**Fri 06/03/05**
2	− **ELEMENT 1**	**Mon 01/03/05**	**NA**	**2%**	**13 hrs**	**Fri 04/01/05**
3	A	Mon 01/03/05	NA	7%	13 hrs	Fri 02/04/05
4	C	NA	NA	0%	0 hrs	Fri 04/01/05
5	D	NA	NA	0%	0 hrs	Fri 03/25/05
6	− **ELEMENT 2**	**Mon 01/03/05**	**NA**	**11%**	**31 hrs**	**Fri 04/29/05**
7	B	Mon 01/03/05	NA	26%	31 hrs	Fri 01/21/05
8	F	NA	NA	0%	0 hrs	Fri 04/29/05
9	− **ELEMENT 3**	**NA**	**NA**	**0%**	**0 hrs**	**Fri 06/03/05**
10	E	NA	NA	0%	0 hrs	Fri 02/18/05
11	G	NA	NA	0%	0 hrs	Fri 06/03/05

Figure 14.12   Progress report for labor.

Information on actual resource use by various OBS elements can serve as a basis for performance or management quality assessments, whereas actual cost information is the basis for project cost performance reevaluations. Although an ability to store information on actual resource use and project costs is important, not all commercial packages can track both sets of data. Some packages can track actual resource use and from these data, estimate actual expenditures. Other packages can track actual costs but not actual resource use. Therefore, selecting a software package for a specific organization or project depends on the availability of other systems to perform these functions.

10. *Project control.* Tracking progress, actual costs, and resource use forms the basis of the project control system. Project control detects the deviations between planned and actual performance and analyzes trends. Deviations are examined to identify the source of a problem and to forecast future trends. On the basis of the results, corrective measures are implemented. The control system compares planned and actual progress in several dimensions, including scope of work, schedule, expenditures, resource use, and technological performance. When a deviation is found in any of these dimensions, the source is investigated to determine its influence on elements of the OBS and WBS.

One major problem with a control system that is based on a simple comparison between planned and actual values is the interaction between different dimensions of a project. For example, under some conditions, the interaction between costs and schedule makes it possible to shorten an activity's duration by increasing its direct costs. Similarly, technological changes may affect a project's costs, schedule, and resource requirements. A partial solution to the interaction problem is the Department of Defense (DOD) approach, summarized in the cost/schedule control systems criteria (C/SCSC). That approach, which is based on the earned value (EV) concept, is discussed in Chapter 12. In the case of a DOD project or a client who requires C/SCSC, one major issue when choosing a software package is compliance with the criteria. Even

	Task Name	Actual Start	% Complete	Actual Work	BCWP	BCWS	ACWP	SV	CV
1	EXAMPLE	Thu 01/01/04	12%	1,100 hrs	$0.00	$0.00	$2,588.05	$0.00	−$2,588.05
2	− ELEMENT 1	Mon 01/03/05	12%	288 hrs	$0.00	$0.00	$720.00	$0.00	−$720.00
3	A	Mon 01/03/05	48%	288 hrs	$720.00	$1,500.00	$720.00	−$780.00	$0.00
4	C	NA	0%	0 hrs	$0.00	$3,300.00	$0.00	−$3,300.00	$0.00
5	D	NA	0%	0 hrs	$0.00	$4,200.00	$0.00	−$4,200.00	$0.00
6	− ELEMENT 2	Mon 01/03/05	23%	642 hrs	$0.00	$0.00	$1,443.00	$0.00	−$1,443.00
7	B	Mon 01/03/05	54%	642 hrs	$1,605.00	$3,000.00	$1,443.00	−$1,395.00	$162.00
8	F	NA	0%	0 hrs	$0.00	$6,100.00	$0.00	−$6,100.00	$0.00
9	− ELEMENT 3	Thu 01/01/04	4%	170 hrs	$0.00	$0.00	$425.05	$0.00	−$425.05
10	E	Mon 01/03/05	7%	170 hrs	$425.06	$5,700.00	$425.05	−$5,274.94	$0.00
11	G	NA	0%	0 hrs	$0.00	$7,200.00	$0.00	−$7,200.00	$0.00

Figure 14.13   Earned value–based progress report.

if compliance is not required, the control system's ability to detect deviations, to trace their source(s), and to forecast future performance from past accomplishments is an important consideration in selecting a project management system. Figure 14.13 presents a report based on EV logic. The budgeted cost of work performed (BCWP), actual cost of work performed (ACWP), and budgeted cost of work scheduled (BCWS) values are enumerated for each task.

Another important aspect of project control is technological change control. This activity involves evaluating changes and deciding whether to accept them. A software package that supports configuration management activities is a useful tool in engineering project management.

11. *Software supporting multiproject management.* The allocation of resources among competing projects in the same organization, the management of multiple project cash flows, and the sharing of information and data among different projects performed at different locations are very important for project-oriented organizations. Special models such as the critical chain can support the management of several projects, whereas buffer management is an important component of monitoring and control.

12. *Internet access to the software.* The widespread use of the Internet makes it an attractive communication link for project participants who have special information requirements. For example, stakeholders who travel frequently and need access to the current project data from different locations find Internet access invaluable. In a similar way, subcontractors and suppliers in different cities or countries can share information and communicate via the Web. As a result, some project management software packages are Web based. A common arrangement is for the using organization to purchase a license to use the software, which is installed on the vendor's server, rather than purchase it outright. The vendor allocates database and model base resources to the users and provides them with all information needed. This way, the users do not have to deal with purchasing, installing, maintaining, and updating the software; they simply enjoy the latest version. Multinational organizations find the Internet extremely useful because it provides a common database for projects that are performed all over the globe.

13. *Software life-cycle support.* A computer software package's ability to support decision making throughout a project's life cycle is an important factor in the software selection process. Analyzing a package's decision-making capabilities involves answering the following questions:

- What does the package do?
- How does the package do it?
- What costs are involved in purchasing, using, and maintaining the package?

Related issues are the time and effort required to learn the software, the human–machine interface, available logistics support for users, and hardware requirements.

The human–machine interface is a crucial factor that affects implementation costs and user acceptance. Team members who are unfamiliar with a package will be more accepting if it can be learned quickly. User friendliness and easy learning are achieved with descriptive menus, on-line help screens, error-tolerant commands, and windows with pointing devices. A package that can access data from existing databases and can communicate with other management information systems is easier to introduce because some of the input formatting is already familiar.

14. *Report generation.* Report capabilities are another important aspect to consider. Some packages contain only a standard set of tabular reports that summarize the results of the CPM analysis and, if applicable, resource allocation, resource leveling, and budgeting data. The problem with standard reports is that they may not use the organization's terminology and, therefore, may not be able to provide a specific answer to a specific question without additional work. Furthermore, it may not even be possible to derive the answer by scanning the output files.

Packages that are equipped with report generators are much more flexible and can produce reports for a given activity, for a given WBS or OBS element, and for a specific WBS or OBS level. Some generators produce reports that integrate information from the project management system with information from spreadsheets and word processors.

A user should also consider a package's ability to design and produce graphical reports. Various types of charts and diagrams can summarize large amounts of data, including trends and correlations between different aspects of the project, on a single graph. Some packages contain a standard set of graphical reports, whereas more advanced packages allow the user to produce them from any data set in the project management system.

15. *Vendor support.* Apart from a software package's functions, the vendor's logistic support is an important factor that affects the success of the implementation effort. A software package requires logistic support throughout its life cycle. In the early stages, importing data, integrating with existing databases and software, and teaching the package are crucial. Vendors can provide numerous training options, including in-house training, training at the vendor's facility, remote learning through the Internet, tutorial programs, and manuals. A vendor can offer assistance in the early implementation stages, such as help with installation, data entry, and initial processing. Users may need additional assistance during the operational phase, because they may discover bugs or request tailoring for special needs. Finally, if the software is to be integrated with existing or new information systems, then the vendor's services will be needed to establish interface protocols and communication links.

16. *Hardware requirements.* Another issue to consider in the selection process is hardware requirements. Hardware costs, especially for personal computers, have decreased radically in recent years. Software that can use larger amounts of random access memory (RAM) will run more quickly and so might be better than less-expensive packages that perform numerous disk access operations to reduce RAM use. A software package's ability to support a variety of existing input/output devices is also important, as well as its ability to work in a network.

Software that is available through the Web—installed on the vendor's server—offers a relatively inexpensive means of managing a project. This type of application can use existing PCs and input/output devices, so little if any new investment is needed.

Well-designed and actively supported software packages can make routine tasks, such as data collection, data processing, and data retrieval, easier for a project manager. However, successful implementation ultimately depends on how well the package fits the organization's needs. The following section lists helpful criteria for selecting the most appropriate software package for a specific application.

14.3 CRITERIA FOR SOFTWARE SELECTION

Most organizations purchase project management software as an addition to existing information systems. When a new system is introduced, such as an ERP system, it is important to make sure that it functions smoothly with the project management software. Integration of the two allows the organization to manage its resources simultaneously, assigning them to projects or to ongoing operations with the same system.

An organization that purchases stand-alone project management software is unlikely to find commercial packages that provide 100% of the support that it needs to manage its projects. Even if such a package is found, its cost may be prohibitive. Therefore, managers must systematically evaluate and select the most appropriate package. In so doing, three sets of criteria should be considered:

- Operational criteria related to the software's capabilities and performance.
- Information systems' evaluation criteria applicable to any type of software package, not just project management software. These criteria are related to hardware requirements, software integrity, quality, and so on.
- LCC criteria.

The first set of criteria is based on the package's intended use and includes questions about the different functions, such as scheduling, budgeting, and control. The second set is important in the selection of any management information system and addresses questions related to the software's ability to function properly under different organizational and operational conditions. The third set is concerned with the cost of purchasing, installing, maintaining, and using a software package throughout its life cycle.

Although the specific criteria in each set depend on the package's intended applications and on the organization's software needs, evaluators can develop a "generic" list of criteria. Such lists frequently appear in articles that evaluate and compare software packages, a sampling of which is included in the reference section at the end of the chapter.

The level of sophistication of the various packages varies considerably. The evaluation and selection criteria should reflect the level of support needed. The set of functions that are available defines the scope of the package. Unsophisticated users would be interested primarily in packages at the lowest level, mainly supporting the planning phase, which includes scheduling and budgeting. Most packages can also handle resources to some degree. In addition, they often are capable of producing a prespecified set of reports. Recall that a progress report is generated by replanning the project on the basis of updated data. A comparison between the updated and the original plan forms the basis for project control.

Software packages at the next level support all of the functions performed by low-level packages as well as resource leveling, resource allocation, and project control. The corresponding modules identify cost and schedule variances and predict the budget at completion. Flexible report generators are also available at this level. These generators facilitate data presentation by permitting the user to select the most appropriate output formats. Many of these packages can integrate easily with popular tools such as Excel or word processing tools to provide additional data processing and reporting capabilities.

Packages at the high end support process management by workflow logic as well as OBSs and WBSs for multiple projects. They can handle several projects that are competing for the same resources and can assign resources to projects that are based on predetermined priority rules. At this level, software packages allow users to write their own applications using a high-level programming language. Thus, the packages can include applications such as configuration management and inventory and material management. Some of these packages have a graphical report generator and a relational database so that they can retrieve any data set to which the software has access and print it out using the report generator. This enables users to construct special reports to specific needs.

The following criteria, suggested by articles, books, and the authors' experience, have proved useful for selecting project management software packages. An appropriate subset can be adopted for each situation.

- Operational criteria

  Multiproject management
  > Functionality for all phases of the project management process
  > Summarization capability for all projects in the organization
  > Strategic decision support

  Process management logic
  > Process flowcharting
  > Ability to launch supporting software and reference material
  > Help customized to guide the user through the corporate methodology

  Scheduling activities
  > Number of activities per project
  > Number of projects that can be analyzed simultaneously

Types of precedence relations supported

Modeling of delays or lags within the precedence relations

Possible time units (hours, days, weeks)

Number of calendars that can be defined and saved

Critical path analysis

Computation of free and total slacks

External constraints on activity start and end dates

Support of milestones

External constraints on milestones

Support of hammock activities

Support of subnetworks

Network presentations as AOA

Network presentations as AON

Network drawings on screen, on a plotter, on a printer

Zooming capability on network drawings

Presentation of Gantt charts

Interactive editing of Gantt charts and of network drawings

Handling of stochastic activity duration: PERT or simulation analysis

Activity duration presented as a function of resource availability

Time–cost analysis

Automatic check of network logic for loops, disconnected activities

"What if" analysis

Critical chain analysis

Budgeting, cost estimation, and cash flow

Support of several currencies

Handling of inflation rates

Connection between cost and activities, resources, milestones, organizations, WBS elements

Communication with existing cost accumulation, cost control, and cost estimation systems

Identification of direct versus indirect cost

Identification of cost categories, such as labor and material

Planning and budgeting the cost of materials and inventories

Support of CBS

Support of statistical analysis of cost estimating relationships

Development of budgets and cash flows for a given schedule

Scheduling subject to budget constraints

Scheduling to minimize direct and indirect costs (PERT/cost)

Support of LCC models and analysis

"What if" analysis

Resources

    Number of different resources per activity

    Number of different resources per project

    Number of different resources for multiple projects

    Handling of renewable resources (labor)

    Handling of depleting resources (material)

    Resource leveling

    Resource allocation

    Planning with alternative resources (e.g., subcontracting)

    Preemption of activities

    Definition of resource availability by dates, hours, organization

    Allocation of resources among competing projects

    Variable rate of resources (e.g., regular time versus overtime)

    Variable usage of resources during the execution of an activity

    "What if" analysis

Project structure

    Definition of OBS: number of levels

    Logical checks on completeness of OBS

    Definition of WBS: number of levels

    Logical checks on completeness of WBS

    Integration of the OBS and WBS to form WPs

    Drawing of OBS and WBS on screen, plotter, printer

    Definition of communication lines and work authorization responsibility

    Coding system for OBS-WBS matrix

    Roll-up mechanism in OBS-WBS matrix for cost analysis

    Limited access to data by passwords assigned to OBS units

    Definition of a linear responsibility chart

    Operation in a computer network

Configuration management

    Definition of configuration items

    Coding system for configuration items

    Definition of baselines

    Handling engineering change requests

    Support of configuration identification

    Support of configuration change control

    Support of configuration status accounting

    Support of configuration review and audits

Project control

> Number of project baseline plans that can be handled and stored
>
> Ability to define cost accounts and WPs
>
> Ability to construct the BCWS at all WBS and OBS levels
>
> Ability to accumulate, store, and retrieve the BCWP (or EV) at all WBS and OBS levels
>
> Ability to accumulate, store, and retrieve the ACWP at all WBS and OBS levels
>
> Ability to calculate cost and schedule variances and indices at all WBS and OBS levels for each period and on a cumulative basis
>
> Ability to forecast the estimated budget at completion based on actual progress (estimated by the EV) and actual cost
>
> Ability to compare actual progress with different baselines
>
> Ability to signal cost and schedule deviations larger than predetermined thresholds
>
> Ability to analyze trends in cost and schedule performances
>
> Compliance with C/SCSC
>
> Ability to control use of material and actual cost of material used
>
> Ability to control use of resources and actual cost of these resources
>
> Buffer management integrated with critical chain

Reporting

> Standard reports available
>
> Report generator
>
> Graphical reports
>
> Integration with word processor
>
> Output to plotters

- General system characteristics criteria

> Friendliness: time to learn, help facilities, use of a menu, windows
>
> Documentation: operations, maintenance, installation
>
> Security: data input, output, editing
>
> Integrity of database
>
> Communication with other information systems
>
> Hardware requirements
>
> Support available from vendor
>
> User base: recommendations of current users

- LCC-related criteria

> Purchase cost (per unit, quantity discounts)
>
> Cost of hardware, facilities, and so on

Estimated cost of operation and maintenance

Expected service life

Cost of updating and new versions

Estimated value at phaseout time

The list above is generic and should be modified according to the specific needs of the project or organization. Appendix 14A presents an example of a criteria set developed by the Project Management Institute (PMI). In the next section, we demonstrate how a comprehensive list of criteria can be used to guide the software selection process.

14.4 SOFTWARE SELECTION PROCESS

Effective project management is a direct function of the tools that are available to support decision making at all levels of detail. An adequate software package facilitates the project manager's job by integrating different aspects of the project and simplifying routine data processing tasks. A software package that does not serve the project team's needs is of little value and may even prove to be a burden. Therefore, those who are responsible for choosing the software should approach their task advisedly.

The selection process begins by identifying data processing needs. This involves addressing the following questions:

- How many projects will be managed in parallel?
- What is the expected size of each project?
- How many different resources are needed?
- How many organizations will participate in each project?

The second step is to analyze the type of management decisions that the software package will support. Should the package support integrated resource and cash management across many projects or the whole organization? Should the package support configuration management? Should it support budgeting and cost estimates? Do existing systems already perform these functions satisfactorily?

Third, a criteria list should be constructed. This list is used, along with one of the selection/evaluation methodologies described in Chapters 5 and 6, to select and identify the most appropriate package. Because the evaluation techniques are subjective (relative importance or scores are subjectively assigned to each criterion), the selection decision should not be based on this analysis alone, neither should a final decision be made at this point in the process.

In fact, now is the time to analyze data from past projects and perhaps to construct one or more test projects with attributes that reflect the current environment. The test projects can be simulated by "planning" them with the help of the software. Information on "actual" performance is added, and reports are generated to support project "control." Because the simulation can be performed quickly, a 10-year project, for example, can be studied in 1 to 2 days and the results analyzed immediately. Allowing future system users to participate in the simulation helps them to better understand the

TABLE 14.1   Relative Weights Used in the Scoring Model

Criteria set	Weight
Activities and scheduling	20
Budgeting, cost estimation, and cash flow	15
Resources	15
Project structure	0
Configuration management	10
Project control	10
Reporting	10
General system characteristics	10
	100

software package and to identify and adjust for various package weaknesses. In any case, the package should be approved only for a trial period and only after all intended users are satisfied with the simulated results.

We recommend trying out the package for a short period to test its suitability for the organization and upcoming projects. The selection team can then decide whether to adopt the package or to investigate another based on the experience over the trial period.

To demonstrate the software package selection process using a scoring model, consider an organization that wishes to compare two project management software packages, A and B, using the generic criteria list presented above. Table 14.1 contains the relative weights assigned to each criteria type (set). Criteria related to software costs are not included, because a cost-effectiveness measure will be used as part of the selection process.

Next, a scale is developed for each criteria set that assigns a weight to each member of the set. The sum of the weights associated with each criterion in a set is 100. In the evaluation, each criterion is given a score between 0 and 10. This number is translated into points by multiplying it by the corresponding weight. Once the points are tallied for each criteria set and normalized by dividing them by 100, the total score for the package is calculated. This is done by forming the weighted sum using the weights in Table 14.1; the maximum package score is 100. The input data and the calculations for each package are summarized in Table 14.2.

The cost data for the two options is contained in Table 14.3 and the results of the analysis are presented in Table 14.4. The latter shows that package B is better than package A in the total score but ranks lower in scheduling, budgeting, and project structure. Package B's purchase cost is $6,000 higher than package A's and requires $300 more per year to update. Based on these results, management must now weigh B's higher cost against its superior performance and select the package that is more appropriate for the organization. Computing an "effectiveness/cost" ratio indicates that package A, with a score of 1.34 points per $1,000, is somewhat better than B, whose score is 1.29.

TABLE 14.2   Calculations for the Operational Criteria

Operational criteria	Weight	Package A score/points	Package B score/points
Activities and Scheduling			
Total weight: 20			
Number of activities per project	5	8/40	6/30
Number of projects that can be analyzed simultaneously	5	7/35	7/35
Types of precedence relations supported	5	8/40	8/40
Modeling of delays or lags within the precedence relations	3	9/27	6/18
Possible time units (hours, days, weeks)	4	4/16	9/36
Number of calendars that can be defined and saved	5	5/25	4/20
Critical path analysis	5	8/40	5/25
Computation of free and total slacks	5	6/30	6/30
External constraints on activity start or end dates	5	2/10	6/30
Support of milestones	3	0/0	5/15
External constraints on milestones	2	0/0	3/6
Support of hammock activities	5	5/25	2/10
Support of subnetworks	1	3/3	5/5
Network presentation as AOA	5	6/30	0/0
Network presentation as AON	5	0/0	3/15
Network drawings on screen, on a plotter, on a printer	5	7/35	3/15
Zooming capability on network drawings	2	6/12	4/8
Presentation of Gantt charts	5	8/40	5/25
Interactive editing of Gantt charts, network drawings	2	6/12	4/8
Handling of stochastic activity duration PERT or simulation analysis	3	0/0	0/0
Activity duration presented as a function of resource availability	5	5/25	3/15
Time–cost analysis	5	7/35	6/30
Automatic check of network logic for loops, disconnected activities	5	10/50	5/25
"What if" analysis	5	7/35	5/25
Total	100	$\dfrac{565}{100} = 5.65$	$\dfrac{466}{100} = 4.66$

TABLE 14.2   (Continued)

Operational criteria	Weight	Package A score/points	Package B score/points
Budgeting, Cost Estimation, and Cash Flow			
Total weight: 15			
Support of several currencies	7	3/21	5/35
Handling of inflation rates	5	5/25	0/0
Connection between cost and activities, resources, milestones, organizations, WBS elements	10	7/70	5/50
Communication with the current budgeting and cost control systems	10	8/80	7/70
Identification of direct versus indirect cost	7	6/42	8/56
Identification of cost categories such as labor and material	5	7/35	5/25
Management of the cost of materials and inventories	5	5/25	6/30
Support of CBS	10	8/80	7/70
Support of statistical analysis of cost estimating relationships	5	5/25	0/0
Development of budgets and cash flows for a given schedule	10	8/80	6/60
Scheduling subject to budget constraints	8	6/48	6/48
Scheduling to minimize direct and indirect costs (PERT/cost)	5	5/25	6/30
Support of LCC models and analysis	8	5/40	6/48
"What if" analysis	5	6/30	7/35
Total	100	$\frac{626}{100} = 6.26$	$\frac{522}{100} = 5.22$
Resources			
Total weight: 15			
Number of different resources per activity	10	8/80	9/90
Number of different resources per project	10	6/60	8/80
Number of different resources for multiple projects	10	6/60	9/90
Handling of renewable resources (labor)	5	5/25	6/30
Handling of depleting resources (material)	8	6/48	6/48
Resource leveling	10	7/70	8/80
Resource allocation	10	6/60	6/60

(*Continued on next page*)

TABLE 14.2   (Continued)

Operational criteria	Weight	Package A score/points	Package B score/points
Planning with alternative resources (e.g., subcontracting)	5	3/15	6/30
Preemption of activities	3	0/0	2/6
Definition of resource availability by dates, hours	8	5/40	4/32
Allocation of resources among competing projects	8	6/48	5/40
Variable rate of resources (e.g., regular time versus overtime)	5	6/30	8/40
"What if" analysis	8	5/40	9/72
Total	100	$\frac{576}{100} = 5.76$	$\frac{698}{100} = 6.98$

Project Structure

Total weight: 10

Definition of organizational structures: number of levels	20	8/160	7/140
Definition of WBS: number of levels	20	8/160	6/120
Integration of the OBS and WBS to form WPs	20	9/180	7/140
Definition of communication lines and work authorization responsibility	15	6/90	5/75
Roll-up mechanism in OBS-WBS matrix for cost analysis	15	8/120	6/90
Limited access to data by passwords assigned to OBS units	10	10/100	8/80
Total	100	$\frac{810}{100} = 8.10$	$\frac{645}{100} = 6.45$

Configuration Management

Total weight: 10

Definition of configuration items	10	10/100	10/100
Definition of baselines	10	8/80	10/100
Handling engineering change requests	10	8/80	10/100
Support of configuration identification	15	10/150	10/150
Support of configuration change control	15	6/90	10/150
Support of configuration status accounting	20	7/140	10/200
Support of configuration review and audits	20	7/140	10/200
Total	100	$\frac{780}{100} = 7.8$	$\frac{1,000}{100} = 10.0$

TABLE 14.2   (Continued)

Operational criteria	Weight	Package A score/points	Package B score/points
Project Control			
Total weight: 10			
Number of project baseline plans that can be handled and stored	10	5/50	6/60
Ability to define cost accounts and WPs	10	4/40	10/100
Ability to construct the BCWS at all WBS and OBS levels	10	5/50	7/70
Ability to accumulate, store, and retrieve the BCWP (EV) at all WBS and OBS levels	10	6/60	8/80
Ability to accumulate, store, and retrieve the ACWP at all WBS and OBS levels	10	5/50	9/90
Ability to calculate cost and schedule variances and indices at all WBS and OBS levels for each period and on a cumulative basis	5	6/30	8/40
Ability to forecast the estimated budget to completion on the basis of actual progress: EV and actual cost	7	5/35	10/70
Ability to compare actual progress with different baselines	7	4/28	8/56
Ability to signal cost and schedule deviations larger than predetermined thresholds	7	5/35	6/42
Compliance with C/SCSC	8	6/48	8/64
Ability to control use of material and actual cost of material used	8	9/72	8/64
Ability to control use of resources and actual cost of these resources	8	6/48	8/64
Total	100	$\frac{546}{100} = 5.46$	$\frac{800}{100} = 8.0$
Reporting			
Total weight: 10			
Standard reports available	20	8/160	9/180
Report generator	20	5/100	8/160
Graphical reports	20	3/60	8/160
Integration with word processor	20	5/100	5/100
Output to plotters	20	3/60	8/160
Total	100	$\frac{480}{100} = 4.8$	$\frac{760}{100} = 7.6$

(*Continued on next page*)

TABLE 14.2   (Continued)

Operational criteria	Weight	Package A score/points	Package B score/points
General System Characteristics			
Total weight: 10			
Friendliness: time to learn, help facilities, menus, windows, etc.	20	5/100	7/140
Documentation for operation, maintenance, installation	5	8/120	6/90
Security, data input, output, editing	15	3/45	8/120
Integrity of database	20	5/100	7/140
Communication with other information systems	10	6/60	6/60
Hardware requirements	10	8/80	8/80
Support available from vendor	5	6/30	9/45
User base: recommendations of current users	5	5/25	9/45
Total	100	$\frac{560}{100} = 5.6$	$\frac{720}{100} = 7.2$

TABLE 14.3   Cost Data for Selection Problem

LCC-related criteria	Package A	Package B
Purchase cost (per unit, quantity discounts)	$6,000	$12,000
Cost of hardware, facilities, etc.	$15,000	$15,000
Estimated cost of operation and maintenance	$2,500/yr	$2,500/yr
Expected service life	5 yr	5 yr
Cost of updating and new versions	$500/yr	$800/yr
Estimated value at phaseout time	0	0

14.5 SOFTWARE IMPLEMENTATION

The successful implementation of project management software depends largely on its ability to support the project team's activities. If, for example, the software can produce reports that were prepared manually in the past, then the project team benefits from using the package. However, if top management requests new reports that are based on increased expectations of the software's capabilities, then the extra work required to generate these reports may produce unanticipated slippage in the schedule.

The software evaluation team should include all end users who are expected to be involved in selection and implementation. Clearly, the end users know which functions need support and which priorities should be assigned to each. Incorporating the end users into the decision-making process (criteria list development, assessment of each criterion's weight, and evaluation scale development) will go a long way toward smoothing acceptance of the selected package. In addition, including future users in package testing

TABLE 14.4   Weighted Scores for Criteria Sets and Results

Criteria	Weight	Package A score/points	Package B score/points
Activities and scheduling	20	5.56	4.66
Budgeting, cost estimation, and cash flows	15	6.26	5.22
Resources	15	5.76	6.98
Project structure	10	8.10	6.45
Configuration management	10	7.80	10.00
Project control	10	5.46	8.00
Reporting	10	4.80	7.60
General systems characteristics	10	5.60	7.20
Total points	100	48.40	56.10
Total cost		$36,000	$43,500
Relative cost (with respect to the lowest-cost package)		100%	121%
Effectiveness ratio (points/$1,000)		1.34	1.29

and project simulation allows them to contribute their insights and experiences to the selection process and, later, during implementation. Thus, choosing the software should be a joint effort among information systems experts, analytic support personnel, and all potential system users.

Once the team selects a system, implementation starts with a training program in which future system users learn operational procedures and gain an understanding of each module's basic logic. This training program should precede actual system use to eliminate learning difficulties and unnecessary frustrations. We all have a limited tolerance for failure.

Only trained personnel should use the system, and the vendor or internal system experts should support initial applications because they can solve startup problems quickly. Management should begin implementation by focusing on functions that the users are currently performing and then expand the reach until all desired functions are included. When introducing the system, a manager should avoid assigning additional tasks to the project team. During the initial stages, the system should help users perform routine tasks efficiently. By performing routine tasks and alerting users early to potential problems, the system can free users' time to deal with exceptions and uncertainty. This will increase the chances for acceptance.

After a predetermined time, management should conduct a survey of users' opinions regarding the performance of the software. At this point, final procedures for system assessment, data updating, and data processing should be established. These procedures should support management's need for information while simplifying routine data-handling tasks.

Once again, we recommend a deliberate process that involves potential users in package selection, training, and phased implementation. Management should implement the software in stages to avoid overwhelming users with new and unfamiliar applications. Project management is greatly simplified when appropriate software tools are selected intelligently and introduced into the organization. Nevertheless, the best tools are useless if the project team does not accept them.

14.6 PROJECT MANAGEMENT SOFTWARE VENDORS

The PMI in its publication "Project Management Software Survey" listed some 80 vendors of project management software packages, and many of these vendors have more than one product (PMI 1999). As we have tried to indicate, the selection of the right software package for a specific organization is not a trivial or an inexpensive task. According to the above reference, Linda Williams of Electronic Data Systems Project Management Consulting Division estimated the cost of the selection process at $12,000 to $15,000; however, the use of a well-structured selection process and a good source of information can reduce this cost drastically.

Appendix 14A provides a list of selection criteria developed by the PMI. The weight for each criterion and the score of each software package with respect to each criterion are application specific, however, and should be determined by the team that is responsible for the selection process. For those who desire other sources of information, we note that magazines such as *OR/MS Today*, published by the Institute for Operations Research and the Management Sciences (INFORMS), and *The Industrial Engineer*, published by the Institute of Industrial Engineering (IIE), periodically review software packages and survey vendors.

TEAM PROJECT

Thermal Transfer Plant

The research and development project that you have proposed in Chapter 13, coupled with your experience with the prototype rotary combustor, has made your team the project management experts at TMS. Your success has motivated top management to introduce project management techniques throughout the organization. The information technology (IT) department has made a proposal to develop a project management application on a spreadsheet to support TMS's needs in this area. The department chief argues that because most TMS engineers and managers are familiar with Excel, it would be much easier for them to learn and use an application that is based on this product. In addition, he foresees that full integration with existing databases and software will be achieved more quickly.

Because of your experience and expertise, TMS management has asked you to compare Microsoft Project, the software used by your team, with the proposed Excel application. In so doing, explain which aspects of project management can be supported by a spreadsheet. Discuss the advantages and disadvantages of the IT proposal.

Develop a software selection plan, including appropriate models that can be used to help in the selection process. Analyze Microsoft Project's ability to satisfy the requirements and compare it with a tailor-made spreadsheet program. Write a report and prepare a presentation that will summarize your analysis.

DISCUSSION QUESTIONS

1. For which aspects of project management are computers most useful? Explain.
2. Are there aspects of project management for which computer support cannot be used?

3. Develop a list of criteria for a project management software package to be used in a project management course.

4. Which aspects of project management can be supported by a simple spreadsheet application?

5. Write a description of one application from the list you developed in your answer to Question 4.

6. Which aspects of project management can be supported by a database system?

7. Write a description of one application from the list you developed in your answer to Question 6.

8. You are in charge of the selection and implementation of a new project management software package in your organization. Develop a project plan and explain the details.

9. What risks are associated with the project discussed in Question 8?

10. Prepare a risk management plan for the project discussed in Question 8.

11. What improvements or changes in Microsoft Project would you recommend?

12. To simplify Microsoft Project, which features would you eliminate?

EXERCISES

14.1 Write a report on the software package Microsoft Project or another one with which you are familiar. Identify the advantages and disadvantages of the package as a tool for supporting the study of project management.

14.2 Develop a software selection methodology for the project "Design of a New Space Laboratory for Crystal Manufacture." Use the methodology to assess Microsoft Project's ability to support the management of this project.

14.3 Try to solve several of the exercises in Chapters 9, 10, 11 and 12 using Microsoft Project or some other package. Rewrite your answer to Exercise 14.1 based on your experience with the software.

14.4 Obtain a project management software package with which you are not familiar. For the example project in the book, determine how much time is required to learn its basic functions, including data entry, critical path analysis, and report generation.

14.5 Develop a spreadsheet application for project scheduling that calculates the early start, early finish, late start, late finish, total slack, and free slack for each activity.

14.6 Develop a spreadsheet application for resource management within an OBS-WBS framework. The application should present planned use, cost of resources, actual use and cost, and the deviations for each organizational unit.

14.7 Develop a PERT program on a spreadsheet that is based on the three time estimates for each activity. Your program should be able to calculate the probability of completing the project by a given date.

14.8 You have been asked to choose the project management software to be used as a teaching aid for a project management course.

a. Write the software specifications for such a package.

b. What might be the main differences in the software specifications associated with the following needs?

    1. A software package to be used as a teaching aid in a course

    2. A software package to be used for planning and controlling projects managed by your school

14.9 Develop a benchmark project to be used to evaluate the suitability of software packages as a teaching aid in project management studies.

14.10 Discuss the following comment and develop a numerical example to validate your remarks: "The purchasing price of a project management software package is a negligible issue as long as the price is no more than a few thousand dollars."

14.11 As part of your company's effort to select a project management software package, you have been asked to approach several other companies that presently use such packages.

a. Develop a questionnaire to help collect the relevant information.
b. Fill out two questionnaires, each representing a different software package.
c. Compare the responses of the companies and select the best software of the two.

14.12 Read a recent article evaluating project management software packages. Such articles frequently appear in technical journals and magazines such as *Industrial Engineer, OR/MS Today*, and *PC World*. Discuss the following issues, based on the article:

a. Which features do most of the packages have in common?
b. What new features are starting to emerge?
c. Which seem to be the leading packages, and what are the major reasons for this?
d. Specify some of the more important criteria used in evaluating the packages.
e. Suggest criteria for software evaluation other than those used in the article.

BIBLIOGRAPHY

Allnoch, A., "Choosing the Right Project Management Software for Your Company," *IIE Solutions*, Vol. 29, No. 3, pp. 38–41, 1997.

Coulter, C., "Multiproject Management and Control," *Cost Engineering*, Vol. 32, No. 10, pp. 19–24, 1990.

De Wit, J. and W. S. Herroelen, "An Evaluation of Microcomputer-Based Software Packages for Project Management," *European Journal of Operational Research*, Vol. 49, No. 1, pp. 102–139, 1990.

Fersco-Weiss, H., "High-End Project Managers Make the Plans," *PC Magazine*, Vol. 8, No. 9, pp. 155–195, September 1989.

Fox, T. L. and J. W. Spence, "Tools of the Trade: A Survey of Project Management Tools," *Project Management Journal*, Vol. 29, No. 3, pp. 20–27, 1998.

Hegazy, T. M. and H. El-Zamzamy, "Project Management Software that Meets the Challenge," *Cost Engineering*, Vol. 40, No. 5, pp. 25–33, 1998.

IMA, "Choosing the Best PC-Based Project Management Software," Engineering Management and Administration Report, Institute of Management and Administration, New York, April 1992.

Levine, A. H., "Computers in Project Management," in D. I. Cleland and R. W. King (Editors), *Project Management Handbook*, Van Nostrand Reinhold, New York, pp. 692–735, 1988.

Liberatore, M. J. and B. Pollack-Jackson, "Factors Influencing the Usage and Selection of Project Management Software," *IEEE Transactions on Engineering Management*, Vol. 50, No. 2, pp. 164–173, 2003.

PMI, "Project Management Software Survey," Project Management Institute, Newtown Square, PA, 1999.

Snow, A. P. and M. Keil, "The Challenge of Accurate Software Project Status Reporting: A Two-Stage Model Incorporating Status Errors and Reporting Bias," *IEEE Transactions on Engineering Management*, Vol. 49, No. 4, pp. 491–504, 2002.

Wallace, R. and W. Halverson, "Project Management: A Critical Success Factor or a Management Fad," *Industrial Engineering*, Vol. 24, No. 4, pp. 48–53, 1992.

Walsh, J., "Primavera, Microsoft to Face off on Project Management," *Infoworld*, p. 29, June 2, 1997.

Wheelwright, J. C., "How to Choose the Project Management Microcomputer Software that's Right for You," *Industrial Engineering*, Vol. 18, No. 1, pp. 46–52, 1986.

Winship, S., "High-End Project Manager Buyers Have High Expectations," *PC Week*, Vol. 7, No. 49, pp. 81–82, 1990.

PMI Software Evaluation Checklist

The following checklist was developed by the PMI (1999). Its purpose is to guide the potential user of project management software through the time-consuming process of evaluating the multitude of products on the market. The weights to be assigned to the various criteria are applications dependent.

The criteria are listed according to the software category—there are seven categories. Most software packages on the market fit into more than one category.

14A.1 Category 1: Suites

Software packages that are designed to bring together all information required to manage the project and to provide features such as:

Functionality for all phases of the project management process
Summarization capability for all projects in the enterprise
Strategic decision support
Executive information system type interface

14A.2 Category 2: Process Management

Software packages that are designed to make the corporate methodologies and supporting processes available electronically and to provide features such as:

Process flowcharting
Ability to launch supporting software and reference material
Help customized to guide the user through the corporate methodology
Interfaces to project management software

14A.3 Category 3: Schedule Management

Software packages that are designed to support project or program planning and control and to provide features such as:

Define the sequence of activities
Critical path calculation
Time analysis
Resource leveling
Schedule status
Reports

14A.4 Category 4: Cost Management

Software packages that provide features such as:

Proposal pricing
Budget management
Forecasting including rate escalation
Performance measurement
Variance analysis

14A.5 Category 5: Resource Management

Software packages that are designed to bring together all information required to manage the project and to provide features such as:

Identifying the resource pool
Organizing resources by skill, department, or other meaningful codes
Requesting resources from functional or departmental managers
Demand management based on current projects, future projects, strategic initiatives, and growth
Summary views and reports across multiple projects

14A.6 Category 6: Communications Management

Software packages that are designed to provide features such as:

Electronic to-do lists for resources assigned to the project
Audit trail for changes to time sheets
Interfaces with popular project management software packages to automate updates to the project schedule
Support for billable and nonbillable projects
Interface with financial systems
Customizable views for preparers and approvers

14A.7 Category 7: Risk Management

Software packages that are designed to provide features such as:

Documentation of project risk
Mathematical schedule simulation
Risk mitigation planning

14A.8 General (Common) Criteria

Document management

Version control
Document collaboration

Reporting

Report writer
Report wizard
Publishes as HTML
Number of user-defined fields
Drill-down/roll-up
Import/export
Automatic E-mail notification
Macro recorder/batch capable
Can "canned" reports be modified?
Sort, filter

Architecture

Databases supported
Supports distributed databases
Three-tier client/server
Client operating systems
Server operating systems
Network operating systems
Minimum client configuration
Minimum server configuration
Client runs under Web browser

Open architecture

Supports OLE
Documented object model
Documented application programming
  interface

Simultaneous edit of data file
Does product have a programming
  language?
Are years stored as four-digit numbers?

Online help

Right mouse click
Hover buttons
Interactive help
Help search feature
Web access to product knowledge base

Vendor information

Training
Computer-based training
Training materials available
Customized training materials
Online tutorial
Consulting available from vendor
Site license discounts
Enhancement requests
Modify source code, support through
  upgrades

Global presence

Global offices
Multilingual technical support
Language versions (list)
Audit software quality assurance process?

Security

Configuration access privileges
Passwords expire (forced update)

Electronic approvals

Password protect files

Category-Specific Criteria
14A.9 Category 1: Suites

Integrated components

Timesheets

Methodology/process

Cost

Estimating

Repository

Reporting module

Configuration management

Requirements management

Risk management

Issues management

Action items

Communications management

Document management

Additional components (list them)

Repository (enterprise database)

Multiproject Gantt charts

Multiproject resource utilization

Multiproject resource work graphs

Time period analysis

Trending analysis

Variance analysis

EV reporting

Ad hoc query for reporting

New project estimating

New project definition

Number of projects

Resource management

Capacity analysis

Demand analysis

Unused availability analysis

Maps employees to resource type

Skills and proficiency levels

Standard role definitions as supported
by the organization's methodology

Methodology integration

Product comes with methodologies (list)

Can input corporate methodologies

Suggests routes through methodologies

Captures and re-uses best practices (re-use
successful project plans as new models)

Attach guidelines

Attach reference documents, templates

Customized, context-sensitive guidelines
(help for corporate methodologies)

14A.10 Category 2: Process
Management

Estimating

Top-down

Bottom-up

Generated WBS for use in scheduling tool

List scheduling tools

Role/resource assignment

Work effort estimates by resource

Methodologies

Product comes with methodologies (list)

Can input corporate methodologies

Suggests routes through methodologies

Reference

Attach guidelines

Attach reference documents, templates

Customized, context-sensitive guidelines
(help)

Tasks in schedule linked to methodology
guidelines

Miscellaneous

Navigate methods via hyperlinks

Complexity factor adjustments

What-if analysis
Cost-benefit analysis
Issues management
Action items
Change management
Requirements management
Risk management

14A.11 Category 3: Schedule Management

Time analysis

Full critical path

Relationship types

SS, FS, SF, FF
Allow SS and FF on a set of tasks
Lags on relationships
Calendars on relationships
Mixed durations (minutes, hours, days, weeks, months)
Time-limited schedule calculation
Resource-limited schedule calculation

Query over-allocations by

Skill
Resource type
Department
Other (user defined)

Resource calendars

Individual resource calendars
Variable availability

Scheduling/leveling features

Resource leveling
Resource smoothing

Leveling by date range
"Do not level" flag (bypass project during leveling)
User-defined resource profiles (spread curves)
Team/crew scheduling
Skill scheduling
Number of skills per resource
Alternate resource scheduling
Rolling wave scheduling
Activity splitting
Perishable resources
Consumable resources
Assign role (skill), software replaces with name at specific point in process
Heterogeneous resources
Homogeneous resources
Hierarchical resources
Share resource pool across multiple projects
Number of resources to be included in resource scheduling

Resource costs

Rate escalation
Overtime
Top-down budgeting

Performance analysis/cost reporting

Calculates BCWS
Calculates BCWP
Calculates ACWP
Physical % complete (in addition to schedule % complete)

Reports

30-60-90 day and user-defined report windows
Predecessor/successor report

Updates out-of-sequence report

To-do list (turnaround report)

Number of structures per project

WBS, OBS, CBS

User defined

Maximum number of structures supported

Features

Outline view

Number of tasks

Number of resources

Multiproject

Number of projects scheduled simultaneously

Prioritize projects for scheduling

Dependency trace view

Charting

Early-start versus resource leveled–start Gantt chart

Highlight critical path in charts

Variable timescale Gantt charts

Variable timescale network logic diagrams (time-phased network logic)

Zoned network diagrams

Structure drawings

PERT chart

Maximums

Number of tasks per project

Number of projects per multiproject

Number of layers of projects in program

Number of resources per task

Number of defined resources

Number of calendars per project

14A.12 Category 4: Cost Management

Performance measurement calculation methods

Weighted milestones

Apportioned

50-50

Level of effort

Percentage complete

Units complete

50-50, 0-100, 100-0

User defined

EV calculations

BCWP

BCWS

ACWP

Proposal pricing

Top-down budgeting

Forecasting

Forecasting (what if budget increases by 10%; statistical methods)

Saves simultaneous forecasts

Budget management

Rate build-up

Customize budget elements

Number of WPs in a cost account

Direct costs

Indirect costs

Burden templates for indirect costs

Custom calculations

Multiple estimate-to-complete (ETC) calculations

Foreign currencies supported (list)

Reporting

Aggregate costs over multiple projects
Cumulative reporting
Fiscal calendars
Irregular reporting calendars

Cash flow

Periodic cost profile (cost during a time period)
By resource (summarize costs incurred by use of a resource)
Cash flow reports
Report writer
Report wizard
Publishes as HTML
Number of user-defined fields
Drill-down/roll-up
Import/export
Automatic E-mail notification
Macro recorder/batch capable A67
Can "canned" reports be modified?
Sort, filter

14A.13 Category 5: Resource Management

Scheduling/leveling features

Resource leveling
Resource smoothing
Leveling by date range
"Do not level" flag (bypass project during leveling)
User-defined resource profiles (spread curves)
Team/crew scheduling
Skill scheduling
Number of skills per resource
Alternate resource scheduling
Rolling wave scheduling
Activity splitting
Perishable resources

Consumable resources
Assign role (skill), software assigns role later
Hierarchical resources
Heterogeneous resources
Homogeneous resources

Query over allocations by

Skill
Resource type
Department
User defined

Resource costs

Rate escalation
Overtime
Top-down budgeting
Bottom-up cost summarization
Calculate unit cost

Skills database

Resumes
Search by skill

Portfolio resource analysis

What-if scenarios
Project templates

Miscellaneous

Individual resource calendars
Share resource pool across multiple projects
Electronic resource requestor (send message to functional manager asking for his or her people)

14A.14 Category 6: Communications Management

Communications features

Team "push" communication channels
Threaded discussion
Bulletin board
Newsgroups

Team management

- Creates and delivers action items
- Creates and delivers task lists
- Delegates work requests to team
- Electronic resource requestor (send message to functional manager asking for his or her people)

Document management

- Version control
- Document collaboration
- Online project management methodology
- Online deliverables templates

Features

- Action items
- Risk documentation
- Issues management
- Meeting minutes
- Agendas
- Project templates

Integrates with scheduling tools

- Project templates
- Task status updates
- E-mail enabled
- Workflow management

Graphics add-ons

- Custom graphics
- Gantt charts
- Network logic diagrams
- WBS
- Other structure drawings

Gantt charts

- Text wrapping
- Multiple rows of text per activity
- Zones (horizontal bands labeled based on a field value)
- Multiple milestones
- Highlight critical path in charts
- Variable timescale Gantt charts
- Variable timescale (time-phased network logic)

Network logic drawings

- Zones (horizontal bands labeled based on a field value)
- User-defined node positioning
- Multiple milestones
- Variable timescale

Breakdown structures

- User-defined box styles
- User-defined positioning
- Mixes connecting line styles (dotted, solid, etc.)
- Collapse/expand to any level
- Number of levels supported

Management graphics

- Pie charts
- Trend charts
- Bar charts
- Scatter diagrams

Histograms

- Horizontal bars
- Vertical bars
- 3D effects
- Mountain charts
- Supported data sources (list)

Timesheet features

- Support for project and nonproject time
- Timesheets generated from scheduling software
- Users can add tasks not on schedule

Supports rate escalation

Status reporting by task

Customizable user interface (view/suppress fields)

Number of user-defined fields

Incorporates business rules and data validation criteria

Can user retrieve approved timesheet or adjustments

Can retrieve feature be turned off?

Timecard adjustments recorded in audit trail

ETC in effort

ETC in duration

Remaining duration

Reports

Creates a report identifying changes made to the schedule

Exception reports

Summary reports

Web enablement

Can timesheet be updated through a Web browser?

Which browsers/versions are supported?

Security

Approver security

Alternate approvers

Field level security: lock specific fields

Management validation: approve/reject electronically

Miscellaneous

Runs served (doesn't have to be installed on each client)

Drill-down/roll-up

14A.15 Category 7: Risk Management

Simulations

Monte Carlo simulation?

Custom sample size?

Performs schedule simulation

Performs cost simulation

Performs resource simulation

Analysis

Analyzes schedule risk

Standard deviation and variance

Other statistical coefficients (e.g., mean to complete, confidence interval, median, mode, mean)

Based on project data (e.g., determine overloaded resources, dependencies at risk)

By experiment, comparing runs

Analyze cost risk

Standard deviation and variance

Other statistical coefficients (e.g., mean to complete, % confidence level, median, mode, mean)

Graphical representations

Histograms

Gantt chart

Comprehensive reports (i.e., tabular)

Features

Calculation of expected monetary value (risk event probability $\times$ risk event value)

Track criticality index

Suggest and document mitigation strategies based on knowledge database

Ability to enter assumptions and analysis defaults (e.g., time or resource constraints)

Capability to import and export from/to other standard office automation tools

Risk identification (e.g., checklist)

Identification of "hangers," sources of risk

Tracks historic risk data (to be used as a baseline) to enable comparisons with ongoing changes

Support of probability distribution curves

Uniform, triangular, normal, beta

Maximum and minimum duration

PERT

Input of low, most likely, and high duration

Chapter 15

Project Termination

15.1 INTRODUCTION

Project termination is an important yet often mismanaged phase in a project's life cycle. At some point, management must decide to terminate the project. However, this can be a difficult and agonizing activity, because projects tend to develop a life and constituency of their own. Team members, subcontractors, and other support personnel often become effective advocates for continuing a project long after its useful life has expired. Nevertheless, all projects must end, and it is up to management to ensure that their concluding phase is smooth, timely, and as painless as possible.

The reality is that team members frequently overlook or try to delay termination to the last possible moment. Such delays can have serious consequences because they create unnecessary stress and are costly for both the organization and the project personnel. Therefore, a successful project must include a well-planned and executed termination phase that saves time and money and avoids unnecessary conflict.

Managing project termination revolves around two central questions concerned with "when" and "how" to close down the project. The answer to the first question seems obvious: Terminate the project when its goals are met. Some projects, though, are perforce canceled before this point is reached because of changing market conditions, organizational shakeups, cost overruns, or technical difficulties. However, if a manager is convinced that a project will produce results, then he or she may be predisposed to slant cost and performance data in the most favorable direction. Sometimes when managers realize that a project is in real trouble, rather than accept failure, they may choose to invest more resources. As a general rule, though, premature termination should be considered only when the probability of success is clearly too low to justify further investment in the project.

The PMBOK identifies three major outputs that should be generated during project termination:

1. *Project closure* provides the assurance that the project has met all customer and other stakeholder requirements. The customer must formally accept the project results and deliverables and confirm that the project has been terminated to his or her satisfaction. The project closure documents may include approval of regulations, approval of standards, internal and external test results, and integration and final acceptance test results.

2. *Lessons learned* includes documents that analyze the causes of variances, the reasoning behind corrective action taken, and other inferences and conclusions regarding the project. This information should be documented and stored so that it becomes part of the historical database for both the current project and future projects that might be undertaken by the performing organization. The cumulative record provides a mechanism for understanding the consequences of technological choices and a vehicle for knowledge management.

3. *Project archives* contain a complete set of indexed project records. All information collected during the project life cycle should be saved in files or electronic databases, and any project-specific or programmable historical databases that are relevant to the project should be updated. When projects are performed under contract or when they involve substantial procurement, it is especially important to maintain accurate financial records. The central database for the project archives should be designed to interface with other information systems, such as procurement management, human resources management, and accounting.

How to terminate the project requires a clear set of procedures for reassigning materials, equipment, personnel, and other resources. A project manager with good leadership skills can decrease anxiety levels within the organization and among the outside participants by carefully planning and executing the project's termination.

15.2 WHEN TO TERMINATE A PROJECT

Judging when a project's goals are met is difficult because the degree of success or failure at any given time may not be quantifiable in terms of the performance measures agreed on at the outset. In addition, success tends to increase at a decreasing rate, implying that change is less visible with the passage of time. As an example, the goals associated with the initial stages of a project are often easier to accomplish than those associated with the later stages. Because detecting a partial success or failure is not a simple matter, management tends to delay termination until the outcome is clearer or more information is available. This "wait and see" attitude can be very expensive. Project costs may escalate, and in most failed projects, these costs cannot be recovered. In many cases, the project manager is forced to act subjectively without full confidence in the decision.

Conversely, a project's termination costs may be a stumbling block to what objectively looks like the best course of action. When the initial decision to start a project is made, managers rarely know or even consider what the closing costs and salvage value of the project will be if it is terminated prematurely. New projects are supposed to succeed not fail. It would be psychologically disturbing to think or plan otherwise, so when management is faced with a budget-busting bill for closing out a project prematurely, the decision might be to continue spending money with the hope that the situation will improve despite the evidence to the contrary. At the end of the Cold War, the United States was faced with just such a dilemma. The reality of canceling tens of billions of dollars in defense contracts meant skyrocketing unemployment in the aerospace and shipbuilding industries and huge financial penalties to buy out extant contracts. To cite one example, in the early 1990s, the U.S. Congress decided to go ahead with a $3 billion program to build a prototype of the next-generation nuclear attack submarine to avoid closing down General Dynamic's Electric Boat Division in Groton, Connecticut. Politics and the severe short-term economic effects that the local community would probably have experienced were the determining factors.

Economics and politics alone, though, do not always drive the termination decision. The L1011 Tri-Star program of Lockheed is a prime example. For more than a decade, the aircraft accumulated enormous losses and, in fact, was never really expected to earn a profit, but the program was Lockheed's reentry into commercial aviation and became a symbol that broadened the company's image beyond simply being a defense contractor.

This suggests another difficulty in reaching consensus on the exact termination point of a project; namely, defining the goals. For example, consider a construction project in a residential neighborhood. The project may accomplish its goals as soon as the houses are built, as soon as they are sold and tenants move in, or, possibly, at the point at which the 1-year contractual warranty period expires. The situation may be even more difficult when the project involves new or untested technologies, such as the development of an Earth-orbiting space station. In this example, the design team is likely to make engineering changes throughout the station's construction, assembly, and even operation. Members of the research and development (R&D) team may be assigned to other parts of the organization (National Aeronautics and Space Administration) or may continue as a team involved in related projects and activities. Here, project termination is almost impossible to define. A third scenario involves an engineering team that is designing a new product intended for mass production, such as a DVD recorder. When a prototype is successfully developed, the team may be integrated into the parent company as a division to manufacture, support, and improve the new product.

Meredith and Mantel (2003) proposed three approaches to project termination: extinction, inclusion, and integration.

1. *Termination by extinction* occurs when the project stops because its mission is either a success or a failure. In either case, all substantial project activities cease at the time of assessment. The project team or special project termination team conducts the phaseout. Either team's aim is to reassign resources, close out the books, and write a final project report. This is discussed in Section 15.5.

2. *Termination by inclusion* occurs when the project team is given a new identity in the parent organization. Resources are transferred to the new organizational unit, which is integrated into the parent organization. This type of termination is typical for organizations with a project/product structure.

3. *Termination by integration* occurs when the project's resources, as well as its deliverables, are integrated into the parent organization's various units. This approach is very common in a matrix organization because most people involved in a project are also affiliated with one or more functional units. When the project terminates, team members are reintegrated into their corresponding units.

Many projects may not reach clear success or failure points. Therefore, management should monitor each project vigilantly to look for signs that suggest that the termination point has been reached. Monitoring is facilitated by the project control system, which is operated by the project team as discussed in Chapter 12. In addition, an external organizational unit, not directly involved with the project, should conduct a termination audit to ensure a more objective analysis. The client may also require formal evaluations and audits as each phase ends. These audits should be included as part of the initial project plan.

Financial audits commonly used in organizations concentrate on their financial well-being and economic status. By contrast, the project audit covers a large number of aspects, including

- The project's *current status versus stated goals* as related to schedule, costs, technical performance, risk, human relations, resource use, and information availability
- *Future trends*, that is, forecasts of total project costs, expected completion time, and the likelihood that the project will achieve its stated goals
- *Recommendations* to change the project's plans or to terminate the project if success seems unlikely

When performed conscientiously, an audit report will be more objective than the project control system reports. However, because of auditing costs, these reports are not issued regularly. Termination decisions, then, frequently result from information provided by the control system. If the cumulative information indicates that success is unlikely, then an audit team may be assembled to evaluate the situation more closely. We note here that a decision against initiating the termination phase (i.e., the "do nothing" decision) should be based on a project's satisfactory performances, not on a lack of alarm signals. For assistance in this matter, the project manager must rely on the control system throughout the project life cycle. The information that it provides can trigger an audit to support the termination decision.

Assuming that the control system functions well and that current information is available, management needs a methodology for reaching a termination decision. Project management researchers have developed lists of questions designed to address this issue. Although most studies have focused on R&D projects, the following list is appropriate in the majority of circumstances. The questions may be difficult to answer, requiring a special audit to obtain the necessary information.

- Did the organization's goals change sufficiently so that the original project definition is inconsistent with the current goals?
- Does management still support the project?
- Is the project's budget consistent with the organizational budget?
- Are technological, cost, and schedule risks acceptable?

- Is the project still innovative? Is it possible to achieve the same results with current technology faster and at lower cost without completing the project?
- How is the project team's morale? Can the team finish the project successfully?
- Is the project still profitable and cost-effective?
- Can the project be integrated into the organization's functional units?
- Is the project still current? Do sufficient environmental or technological changes make the project obsolete?
- Are there opportunities to use the project's resources elsewhere that would prove more cost-effective or beneficial?

Based on the answers to these questions, perhaps obtained with the help of the economic analysis and project evaluation/selection techniques discussed in Chapters 3, 5 and 6, management should be able to decide whether it is time to cancel the project. Once a termination decision is made, the question then becomes how to minimize the likely disruption that such action would cause.

As mentioned, management should repeatedly consider whether to continue or to terminate a project throughout its life cycle. In addition, an external group should be asked to provide input to the decision, because the project manager and team members have a vested interest that may compromise their candor. The external analysis should be a part of the project audit effort, which should be designed to yield an objective evaluation of the project's status.

Because project success (or failure) is multidimensional, the evaluation should at least cover the following:

- *Economic evaluation*. Given the costs of all project efforts to date, is project continuation justified?
- *Project costs and schedule evaluations*. Given the current costs, schedule, and control system's trend predictions, should the project be canceled?
- *Management objectives*. Given the organization's current objectives, does the project serve these objectives?
- *Customer relations and reputation*. If premature termination is justified, then how will this affect the organization's reputation and its customer relationships?
- *Contractual and ethical considerations*. Is project termination possible given current client and supplier contracts? Is project termination ethical?

In conjunction with these questions, the auditing process should consider a multitude of quantitative and qualitative factors, such as the following:

Quantitative factors

Probability of commercial success
Anticipated annual growth rate
Capital requirements
Project use
Investment return

Annual costs

Probability of technical success

Amount of time actual project costs equaled budgeted project costs

Qualitative factors

Degree of consumer acceptance of the project's outcome

Probability of government restrictions

Ability to react successfully to competition

Degree of innovation

Degree of linkage with other ongoing projects

Degree of top management support

Degree of R&D management support

Degree of the project leader's commitment

Degree of the project personnel's commitment as perceived by top management, R&D management, and project leaders

Presence of people with sufficient influence to keep the project going

One methodology that supports a project termination decision is the early termination monitoring system (ETMS), designed to generate an overall index of a project's viability (Meredith 1988). By using input from the project's control system, ETMS reports the effects of an early termination on the organization's image, the project team's performance, the marketplace economics, and the penalty costs that will be incurred.

Finally, Table 15.1 enumerates 10 critical reasons identified by Dean (1968) in a study of 36 companies for premature R&D project termination. In conjunction with the lists above, we begin to see why this life-cycle phase is so difficult to manage. The difficulty stems from the many factors involved in the decision to begin phaseout, as well as in the complexity of termination planning and execution.

15.3 PLANNING FOR PROJECT TERMINATION

Like any other phase in the project life cycle, termination planning aims at increasing the project's probability of success. Once management approves cancellation, the following action should be taken:

• Set project termination milestones
• Establish termination phase target costs and budget allocations
• Specify major milestone deliverables
• Define desired organizational structure and workforce after termination

Although each project may have a different set of goals, some activities are required in almost all cases. The following activity termination list covers most aspects of the problem (Archibald 1976):

Project office (PO) and project team (PT) organization

Conduct project closeout meetings

Establish PO and PT releases and reassignments

TABLE 15.1 Major Reasons for Canceling R&D Projects

Factors	Reporting frequency
Technical	
Low probability of achieving technical objectives or commercial results	34
Available R&D skills cannot solve the technical manufacturing problems	11
R&D personnel or funds required for higher-priority projects	10
Economic	
Low investment profit or return	23
Individual product development too costly	18
Market	
Low market potential	16
Change in competitive factors or market needs	10
Other	
Too much time to achieve commercial results	6
Negative effects on other projects or products	3
Patent problems	1

Carry out necessary personnel actions

Prepare a personal performance evaluation for each PT member

Instructions and procedures

Terminate the PO and PT

Closeout all work orders and contracts

Terminate the reporting procedures

Prepare the final report(s)

Complete and dispose of the project file

Financial

Close out the financial documents and records

Audit the final charges and costs

Prepare the final project financial report(s)

Collect the receivables

Project definition

Document the final approved project scope

Prepare the project's final breakdown structure, and enter it into the project file

Plans, budget, and schedules

Document the actual delivery dates of all contractual deliverable end items
Document the actual completion dates of all other contractual obligations
Prepare the project's final and task status reports

Work authorization and control

Close out all work orders and contracts

Project evaluation and control

Ensure the completion of all action assignments
Prepare the final evaluation report(s)
Conduct the final review meeting
Terminate the financial, personnel, and progress reporting procedures

Management and customer reporting

Submit the project's final report to the customer
Submit the project's final report to management

Marketing and contract administration

Compile the final contract documents, including revisions, waivers, and related correspondences
Verify and document compliance with all contractual terms
Compile the required proofs of the shipment and customer acceptance documents
Officially notify the customer of the contract's completion
Initiate and pursue any claims against the customer
Prepare and conduct the defense against the customer's claims
Initiate public relations announcements regarding the contract's completion
Prepare the final contract status report

Extensions—new business

Document the possibilities for project or contract extensions or other related new business
Obtain an extension commitment

Project records control

Complete the project file, and transmit it to the designated manager
Dispose of other project records as required by established procedures

Purchasing and subcontracting (for each purchase order and subcontract)

   Document compliance and completion
   Verify the project's final payment and proper accounting
   Notify the vendor/contractor of the project's completion

Engineering documentation

   Compile and store all engineering documents
   Prepare the final technical report

Site operations

   Close down all site operations
   Dispose of all equipment and materials

On the basis of this list and additional (project specific) activities, management can perform a project scheduling analysis of the termination phase. The results obtained from the analysis form the basis for budgeting and staffing during phaseout. Spirer (1983) suggested a work breakdown structure (WBS), as shown in Fig. 15.1, to identify the problems that are likely to arise in the process.

The project termination phase has a significant emotional impact on the people involved. Four types of groups may be identified: end users, customers, team members and producers, and consultants and maintenance personnel. The following example clarifies the differences among the groups. A company that manufactures elevators is the producer, its customer is the builder, the end users are the tenants who are going to occupy the building, and maintenance personnel are those who maintain the elevator. Each of the four groups is involved and affected differently by project termination. Therefore, it is important to identify the nature of the impact and have a plan for dealing with the misfortunes that arise. Although the contractor is the immediate customer of the elevator manufacturer, the end users and the other interested parties, such as the maintenance crew and the consultants, represent future customers who should be taken into account. The immediate customer may want to terminate the project as soon as possible, even if the unit installed has not been tested sufficiently under normal operating conditions. However, if this unit does not meet the expectations of the end users, then costly rework may be required and the reputation of the elevator company may be damaged.

Below we identify the typical problems that employees who work on a project may face during the termination phase:

- Loss of interest in the project
- Insecurity regarding their prospect to get new jobs
- Insecurity regarding the uncertainty involved in a new project
- Problems in handing the project to the customer

From an emotional point of view, project termination has a separation effect. Each project team member faces the following troublesome questions:

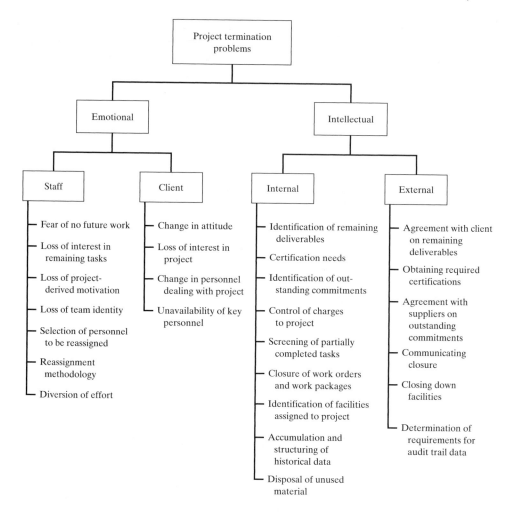

Figure 15.1   WBS for problems that accompany termination.

- What, if any, are my plans after the project?
- What is my future role in the organization?
- What is my next assignment?

The project manager should consider specific answers as well as the best way to communicate these answers to the team members. Furthermore, the project manager may worry about his or her own future after closeout. Planning ahead how to resolve these personal problems and fears will help to reduce high levels of individual anxiety among all team members.

During phaseout, as a result of the natural feelings of uncertainty, project team members may experience low morale, lose their interest in the project, or try to delay its termination. The frequency and intensity of conflicts tend to increase, and even successful projects may leave many members feeling angry, upset, or both. To minimize these effects, management should try to reduce the members' uncertainty levels. Suddenly canceling a project may be disastrous. Team members may find it difficult to terminate the project effectively if they face sudden unexpected changes, requiring them to invest their time and energy developing adaptive strategies. Consequently, management's sensitivity, thoughtful planning, and consideration of members' emotions can reduce the negative effects of cancellation and support a project's successful closing.

15.4 IMPLEMENTING PROJECT TERMINATION

Once management decides to cancel a project and develops a closeout plan, a termination phase leader must be chosen. Project managers are natural candidates, but if they are emotionally unsettled and uncertain about their own futures, then they might not be able to do a reliable job. A second candidate is a professional project termination manager who may be unfamiliar with the project's substance but experienced and well trained in closing down projects efficiently and effectively. The choice depends on the answers to the following questions:

- Did the project achieve its goals?
- Is the project manager assigned to a new project? If yes, then when will the new assignment begin?
- Is the client satisfied?
- Is an experienced project termination manager available?

If the project is completed successfully, the client is satisfied, and the project manager knows his or her next assignment, then the project manager is the best candidate to head up the termination effort. Otherwise, appointing an experienced alternative is a wiser choice because the current project manager may not be motivated to do the job conscientiously.

The termination leader should implement the closeout plan by notifying all project team members of the decision to cancel the project. Communicating with team members and laying out a road map for their futures reduce their uncertainty levels. Once this is accomplished, the next step is to reduce and eventually eliminate the use of all resources while implementing procedures that will facilitate a smooth transition of all personnel to their next assignments.

Throughout project termination planning, implementation, and execution, management should be extremely sensitive to the various aspects of human relations. The need for cooperation in future projects should guide all interactions with current team members, the client, suppliers, and subcontractors. The termination phase is a bridge to future projects. One cornerstone of this bridge is the final report.

15.5 FINAL REPORT

A company that wishes to survive in today's competitive environment should strive for continuous improvement. Because each project has a limited lifetime, improvement should be the goal from one project to the next. To facilitate this goal, one important outcome of the termination phase is the final report, which documents activities at each stage of the project's life cycle. Such a report emphasizes weak points in the planning and implementation phases to improve organizational procedures and practices. The report also explains working procedures that were developed during the project's life cycle and contributed to its success and proposes adopting these procedures in future projects. The report helps management to plan future projects and to train future managers and team members. Thus, the report forms the basis for improving organizational project management practices and developing new and improved working procedures.

To accomplish these objectives, the final report begins by stating the project's mission. Next, it discusses in detail the plans developed to achieve that mission, the tradeoff analyses conducted, and the planning tools used. Finally, the report compares the project's original mission and plans with the actual results and deviations and explains why such deviations occurred.

On the basis of this analysis, the report evaluates the project's specific procedures and tools for planning, monitoring, and control. Details should be furnished on any new procedures and analytical methods developed during the project, and recommendations should be made regarding their adoption if it is believed that they can be implemented successfully by the entire organization. Recommendations on the future uses of or modifications to existing procedures should also be cited. Next, the report evaluates resource use and the performance of vendors and subcontractors, judging specifically whether they should be included in future projects. Finally, the report evaluates and documents the performance of project team members, auxiliary personnel, and functional unit managers.

Developing a standard format for final reports allows an organization to store the information collected in a database, making it accessible for future projects. Many standard formats are designed around one of the following:

- *Standard WBS*, such as the one suggested by MIL-STD-881A. Using a standard WBS allows management to retrieve information on relevant WBS elements in past projects.
- *Standard cost breakdown structure (CBS)*. Storing cost information in a standard CBS allows cost estimators and life-cycle cost analysts easy access to this type of data for future project use.
- *Standard statement of work (SOW)*. Storing work statements in a standard format makes responding to future requests for proposals easier, because similar SOWs from past projects can serve as a basis for new proposals.

A well-structured final report can help an organization improve and learn from its experience. Submitting the report to management is the last step in any well-managed project.

TEAM PROJECT

Thermal Transfer Plant

The rotary combustor was assembled, tested, and successfully delivered to the client organization. TMS management wants to learn from your experience with the project and has requested a final report. This report should be a prototype for future project teams at TMS to use.

Explain in your report the plan for phasing out the rotary combustor project. Present a schedule to execute this task, and list resources required. Comment on the experience that you have gained, the lessons that you have learned, and the mistakes that you have made and how this information can be used to guide others in future projects. Include in your report a chronological review of recommendations regarding project management tools and techniques used throughout the project's life cycle and all of the data that might be helpful in TMS's future development activities.

DISCUSSION QUESTIONS

1. Develop a flow diagram that shows how project termination decisions should be made.

2. Explain the difference between termination by integration and termination by inclusion using an example for each process.

3. In what ways does the termination phase of a project differ from the closedown of a failed company? What are the similarities?

4. How might the input requirements differ for a project control system versus an audit team evaluating the process that accompanied a project termination decision?

5. In what way should the planning of the project termination phase be influenced by personnel considerations?

6. Why do some projects that are clearly "losers" seem to go on forever? Can you identify a few at the national level? State level? Local level?

7. What is the most important information that a final report should contain?

8. Several years ago, the U.S. Congress canceled funding for the development of a battery-powered electric vehicle. Do you think that was a good decision? Can you imagine what the pros and cons were?

9. Assume that you are working for a computer manufacturer as a software engineer and that you are told abruptly that your project will be canceled within 4 weeks. List the questions that you would have for management. After absorbing the shock, what would you do?

10. Identify the closeout costs for a big project, such as the International Space Station after it becomes operational but before it is occupied or a nuclear power plant that is, say, 90% complete.

11. Many people in and out of government have proposed sunset laws for all projects and agencies. That is, after a fixed amount of time, a project or an agency would be closed down unless sufficient justification to continue its activities were offered. Why is such a law needed? What might constitute "sufficient justification"?

12. List the political and sociological reasons that a project might continue to be supported even though it cannot be justified economically. Can you identify such a project in your private life?

EXERCISES

15.1 Develop guidelines for writing a project final report.

15.2 Write a job description for a project termination manager.

15.3 Develop a "generic" project termination plan that is based on the list of activities presented in the chapter. What are the precedence relations among these activities? Develop a linear responsibility chart for the termination phase.

15.4 Develop a CBS for the termination phase, assuming that only activities that are not related to the substance of the project are performed in that phase.

15.5 In the United States, a flagrant example of a program that has outlived its mission is the Rural Electrification Program that was started in the 1930s by the Roosevelt administration. Its original goal was to bring electricity to all rural communities. Today, with its mission long since accomplished, the program, budgeted at $5 billion annually, provides subsidies to such unneedy giants as MCI, Houston Lighting and Power, and Worldcom. The Office of Management and Budget has tried periodically to shut down this program, but has never been able to prevail over its powerful beneficiaries. Nevertheless, anticipating the emergence of more rational heads, you have been asked to write a final termination report for this program. The report should document its beginnings, its successes, and the reasons that it has flourished for so long, as well as the more traditional information associated with termination.

15.6 Identify two projects in which you have been involved recently.

    a. Describe each project briefly.

    b. Suggest criteria that may have been used to identify the start of the termination phase of each project.

    c. Give two examples of activities that were performed poorly during the termination phase of either project, and suggest measures that might have been taken to improve the situation.

15.7 Develop a questionnaire to capture the importance of various activities that should be performed during the termination stage.

    a. Administer the questionnaire to a sample of project managers.

    b. Summarize and analyze the results.

15.8 Identify two projects (local or national) that were terminated prematurely.

    a. Analyze the reasons that each was canceled.

    b. Compare the results of the two cases.

15.9 Discuss the following statement made by a project manager: "We have already spent 70% of the budget required to complete the projects it would be a waste of money to abandon it at this stage."

BIBLIOGRAPHY

Archibald, R. D., *Managing High Technology Program and Projects,* John Wiley & Sons, New York, 1976.

Balachandra, R. and K. Brockhoff, "Are R&D Project Termination Factors Universal?" *Research Technology Management,* Vol. 38, No. 4, pp. 31–37, 1995.

Balachandra, R., K. Brockhoff and A. Pearson, "R&D Project Termination Decisions: Processes, Communication and Personnel Changes," *Journal of Product Innovation Management,*" Vol. 13, No. 3, pp. 245–257, 1996.

Balachandra, R. and J. A. Raelin, "How to Decide When to Abandon a Project," *Research Management,* Vol. 23, No. 4, pp. 24–29, 1980.

Brockhoff, K., "R&D Project Termination Decisions by Discriminant Analysis—An International Comparison," *IEEE Transaction on Engineering Management,* Vol. 41, No. 3, pp. 245–254, 1994.

Cooke-Davis, T., "Project Closeout Management: More than Simply Saying Good-bye and Moving On," in J. Knutson (Editor), *Project Management for Business Professionals*, pp. 200–214, John Wiley & Sons, New York, 2001.

Dean, B. V., *Evaluating, Selecting, and Controlling R&D Projects*, American Management Association, New York, 1968.

Deutch, M. S., "An Exploratory Analysis Relating the Software Management Process to Project Success," *IEEE Transactions on Engineering Management*, Vol. 38, No. 4, pp. 365–375, 1991.

Kumar, V., A. Persuad and U. Kumar, "To Terminate or Not Ongoing R&D Project: A Managerial Dilemma," *IEEE Transaction on Engineering Management*, Vol. 43, No. 3, pp. 273–284, 1996.

Meredith, J. R., "Project Monitoring and Early Termination," *Project Management Journal*, Vol. XIX, No. 5, pp. 31–38, 1988.

Meredith, J. R. and S. J. Mantel, Jr., *Project Management: A Managerial Approach*, Fifth Edition, John Wiley & Sons, New York, 2003.

MIL-STD-881, *A Work Breakdown Structure for Defense Military Items*, U.S. Department of Defense, Washington, DC, 1975.

Pinto, J. K. and S. J. Mantel, Jr., "The Causes of Project Failure," *IEEE Transactions on Engineering Management*, Vol. 37, No. 4, pp. 269–276, 1990.

PMI Standards Committee, *A Guide to the Project Management Body of Knowledge (PMBOK)*, Project Management Institute, Newtown Square, PA, 2000 (http://www.PMI.org).

Pritchard, C., "Project Termination: The Good, the Bad, the Ugly," in D. I. Cleland (Editor), *Field Guide to Project Management*, pp. 377–394, Van Nostrand Reinhold, New York, 1997.

Shafer, S. M. and S. J. Mantel, Jr., "A Decision Support System for the Project Termination Decision," *Project Management Journal*, Vol. XX, pp. 23–28, 1989.

Spirer, H. F., "Phasing Out the Project," in D. I. Cleland and W. R. King (Editors), *Project Management Handbook*, pp. 245–262, Van Nostrand Reinhold, New York, 1983.

Staw, B. M. and J. Ross, "Knowing When to Pull the Plug," *Harvard Business Review*, Vol. 65, No. 2, pp. 68–74, 1987.

Toffel, M. W., "The Growing Strategic Importance of End-of-Life Project Management," *California Management Review*, Vol. 45, No. 3, pp. 102–129, 2003.

Index